Handbook of Hedge Funds

For other titles in the Wiley Finance Series
please see www.wiley.com/finance

3074990

Handbook of Hedge Funds

François-Serge Lhabitant

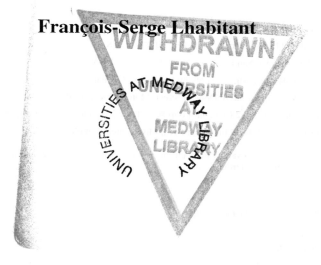
WITHDRAWN FROM UNIVERSITIES AT MEDWAY LIBRARY

John Wiley & Sons, Ltd

all the individuals who helped me with this book, and in particular the invaluable editorial assistance of Ian Hamilton, Rebecca Davies and Claire Breen whose reviews and comments have helped me to clarify and define my thoughts in plain English. I would also like to thank my colleagues at Kedge Capital, at HEC University of Lausanne and at the EDHEC Business School for fruitful discussions on the topic of hedge funds as well as suggestions and comments on earlier versions of the text.

Writing a book and simultaneously holding a challenging job requires the unstinting support of the book's publisher. I wish to thank the staff at John Wiley & Sons for their patience for missed deadlines and enthusiasm in bringing this project to a successful conclusion. Finally, I owe the biggest debt of gratitude to my family, whose forbearance I have tried. Once again, and as usual, this book was written using time that was literally stolen from them.

Naturally, I must stress that the opinions expressed in this book represent solely my viewpoint and may not reflect the opinions or activities of any of the above-mentioned organizations. It also goes without saying that this book should not be taken as an investment recommendation or as a solicitation. In particular, the few hedge funds that are mentioned explicitly in this book were taken as representative examples, but are not positively or negatively recommended in a given portfolio. Anyone interested in investing in hedge funds should first seek professional *and independent* advice. But in the world of hedge funds, independence is both essential and, unfortunately, often elusive.

It is now time for you to start reading and I hope that you will find some pleasure in doing so. Please address any comments or suggestions to me at f@lhabitant.net

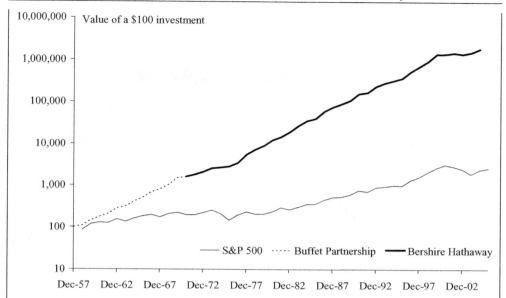

Figure 2.2   Performance of the Buffett Partnership and Berkshire Hathaway vs the S&P 500, 1957–2002

Note: The vertical scale is logarithmic. The S&P 500 numbers are pre-tax whereas the Berkshire numbers are after-tax.

areas such as commodities (his foray into silver in 1997), fixed income arbitrage, many instances of distressed debt through the use of private investment in public equity (PIPE) vehicles, merger arbitrage, relative value arbitrage, and so on. Buffett can thus be seen as a precursor of hedge funds.

The performance of Berkshire Hathaway, with a 21.5% average annual gain from 1965 to 2005, has been stunning. Let us suppose you were alive in 1956 and had $100 to invest. If you had invested it in the Buffett Partnership at its inception and reinvested the cash distribution at its termination in 1969 into shares of Berkshire Hathaway, and supposing nothing else was done, today your investment would be worth a hard-to-believe $2.1 million *after all fees and expenses.*

2.3   THE DARK AGES (1969–1974)

To imitate Jones' investment style and, hopefully, his performance, many new hedge fund managers started selling securities short despite their lack of experience in that activity. Unfortunately, during the bull market of the 1960s (see Figure 2.2), haphazard short selling was time consuming and unprofitable. Simply leveraging long positions and ignoring the short side often yielded much better results. Many funds predictably drifted from long/short equity to long only with leverage, thus departing from the original Jones model. As the saying goes, they were swimming naked, and the prolonged bear market that started in 1969 caught them by surprise.

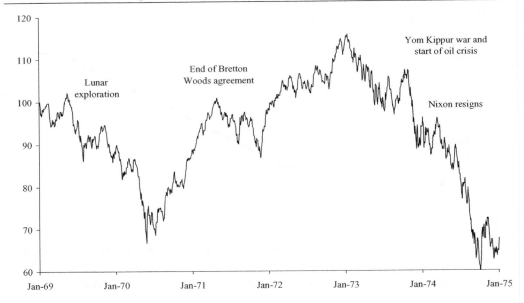

Figure 2.3 Evolution of the US stock market (S&P 500) from 1969 to 1974, scaled to a value of 100 on 1 January 1969

Hedge funds suffered heavy losses in the 1969–1970 bear market but the major bloodletting ensued during the 1973–1974 recession. Both the Dow Jones and the S&P 500 were slashed nearly in half, and even Morgan Guaranty, the largest US pension-fund manager, lost an estimated two-thirds of its clients' money. Trading volume dried up and numerous hedge funds went out of business, whittling down the amount of assets under management. Their managers were grateful to find jobs as bartenders and taxi-drivers. Only the most experienced hedge fund managers survived the bursting of the bubble.[5] Their funds were small and lean, and usually specialized in one strategy; they returned and operated in relative obscurity for several years.

2.4   THE RENAISSANCE (1975–1997)

From 1975 to 1982, markets moved sideways, with pronounced lows in 1978 and 1982, and major peaks in 1976 and 1981 (Figure 2.4). One of the features of that era was that the Dow Jones Industrial Average was never able to climb much over 1000. It is hard to determine precisely the number of hedge funds active at that time due to the lack of marketing and public registration. However, when Sandra Manske formed Tremont Partners in 1984 to track hedge fund performance, she was able to identify only 68 hedge funds. Most of them were limited partnerships with high minimum investment requirements, access thus being restricted to an exclusive club of high net worth individuals informed by word of mouth.[6] They operated in

---

[5] By the fall of 1969, Warren Buffett had liquidated his partnership and returned the money to investors. With the exception of Berkshire, he remained out of stocks until 1974, when he loaded up again on undervalued companies.

[6] An interesting sidelight is that, in 1982, at age 82, Jones amended his partnership agreement, formally becoming a fund of funds investing in a diversified selection of external managers.

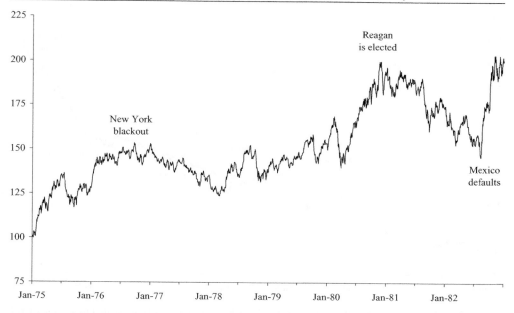

Figure 2.4 Evolution of the US stock market (S&P 500) from 1975 to 1982, scaled to a value of 100 on 1 January 1975

secrecy and did not report to anyone beyond their limited partners. Their growth was fuelled by exceptional performance, some of them earning compounded returns in excess of 30% per annum through both rising and falling markets.

The popularity of hedge funds was revived once again in 1986 by an article in *Institutional Investor,*[7] which described the impressive performance of Julian Robertson's Tiger Fund. The fund had yielded a compound annual return of 43% during the first six years of its existence, net of expenses and incentive fees. In comparison, a large diversified index such as the S&P 500 compounded at only 18.7% for the same period.

Julian Robertson's investment approach was radically different from Jones' original concept. Robertson's initial area of focus was equities and bottom-up stock picking, but he rapidly expanded it to other strategies. In particular, based on macroeconomic analysis, he occasionally took aggressive and purely directional bets with no particular hedging policy – a strategy referred to as "global macro". In addition, Robertson often used financial derivatives such as futures and options, which did not exist when Jones started his fund.

The macroeconomic environment of the late 1980s (US dollar weakening, gold and commodity prices taking off, interest rates rising above the 10% level, bond markets falling and equity markets bullish) was particularly favourable to the global macro strategy. Despite the inherent risks, numerous hedge funds implemented some global macro bets, particularly in the realm of currencies and interest rates. Equity markets were again on the rise and rather supportive of long aggressive positions. But the party ended abruptly on 19 October 1987, a date that subsequently became known as "Black Monday" (Figure 2.5). With a 22.6% drop,

---

[7] See J. Rohrer (1986).

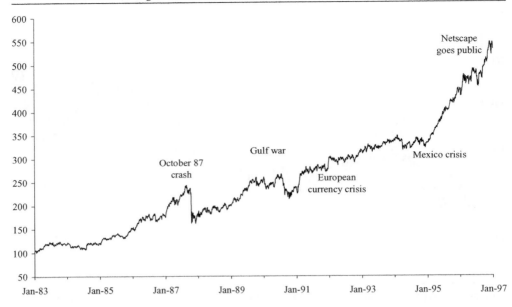

Figure 2.5   Evolution of the US stock market (S&P 500) from 1983 to 1996, scaled to a value of 100 on 1 January 1983

the Dow Jones made the headlines, but other markets suffered similar damage. The NYSE composite plunged by 19.2%, the S&P 500 by 20.5%, and the Wilshire and Value Line indices by 17.9 and 15.1% respectively. Many foreign markets fared even worse, as the selling frenzy carried the day everywhere. Like most other investors, hedge funds were severely hurt by the crash. For example, Julian Robertson's Tiger Fund shrank from $700 million in August 1987 to $300 million at the beginning of 1988. However, unlike the sequence of events in 1929, markets recovered quickly, as did hedge fund managers. At the end of 1987, the S&P 500 was up 5.2%, growth mutual funds were up 1%, and hedge funds as a group returned 14.5%.

By the time Alfred Winslow Jones died in 1989, the market had regained all the ground it had lost in the 1987 crash and the so-called global macro funds were still basking in their golden years. Some of the global macro funds even emerged as major players in financial markets and attracted widespread media attention, notably because of the large profits generated by taking large and aggressive positions, particularly during market crises. George Soros' Quantum Fund, for example, notched up a billion dollar gain in 1992 when he forced the British pound to exit from the European Monetary System. Whether or not Soros and his fund were entirely responsible for the pound's collapse is still a moot question, but the size of the gains raised concern that hedge funds could contribute to financial instability and perturb the efficient operation of markets.

Concerns about the trading and position-taking activities of hedge funds gained momentum in 1994, when the Federal Reserve unexpectedly raised interest rates. Several global macro funds had large long positions funded with margin. They were then forced to deleverage hastily, causing bond prices to fall and thus magnifying the impact of the Federal Reserve's action on the economy. According to the US Congress, several global macro funds had to sell European securities to face their margin calls, thereby transmitting the fall in US securities prices and rise in US interest rates to European markets more powerfully than would otherwise have been the case. Needless to say, hedge funds also suffered from the falling markets, but recovered well in 1995 and 1996.

2.5 THE ASIAN AND RUSSIAN CRISES (1997–1998)

The 1997 Asian crisis had its roots in the collapse of the Mexican financial markets in 1994, which was followed by an aggressive IMF-led and US Treasury-sponsored rescue early in 1995. The success of the rescue established the model whereby the US Treasury and the IMF worked in tandem to ensure financial stability in emerging markets. During the following two years, a speculative bubble gradually developed in Asia, where the emerging markets of Thailand, Indonesia, Korea and Taiwan had come to be seen as economies with unlimited upside potential. Capital flowed rapidly into the region and the bubble developed in real estate and a variety of other investment types. The strain began to show in 1997 as widespread signs of excess capacity emerged.

The financial crisis that erupted in Asia in mid-1997 led to sharp declines in the currencies, stock markets and other asset prices of a number of emerging countries. Hedge funds were blamed once again for their destabilizing actions during the crisis, particularly because of their massive short positions. According to Eichengreen *et al.* (1998) and de Brouwer (2001), hedge funds sold between $7 billion and $15 billion worth of Thai baht in 1997. The Market Dynamics Study Group (MDSG) of the Financial Stability Forum reported that hedge fund positions accounted for at least 50% of the short open positions on the Hang Seng index in the summer of 1998. Last but not least, Rankin (1999) claimed that hedge funds cornered and manipulated the Australian dollar market. All these stories fuelled numerous press reports that vilified hedge fund managers as wild-eyed speculators operating outside government regulations, bound only by the laws and rules of the markets in which they operated.

However, not all hedge funds were successful global macro traders, and we should recall that several funds also suffered heavy losses as a result of unusual market events. For example, David Askin's three hedge funds (Granite Partners, Granite Corp, and Quartz Hedge) lost $420 million in 1994 when the Federal Reserve unexpectedly raised interest rates. Victor Niederhoffer bankrupted his three hedge funds (Global Systems, Friends, and Diversified) by selling short S&P 500 put options prior to the October 1997 plunge of the index. The High Risk Opportunity Hub Fund managed by III Offshore Investors as well as three funds managed by Dana McGinnis (Partner's Focus, Global, and Russian Value) filed for bankruptcy in 1998 after Russia had devalued the rouble and defaulted on rouble-denominated debt. The III Offshore Investors fund lost more than $350 million and McGinnis' funds lost roughly $200 million. Even George Soros' Quantum Fund posted losses of $2 billion after the Russian crisis. But the worst was still to come, with the collapse of Long Term Capital Management (LTCM), which marked an important turning point for hedge funds on several fronts, almost 50 years to the day since the inception of Jones' fund. The reasons for this collapse are examined in detail in Chapter 5, where we discuss leverage and its consequences. In the meantime, here is a brief summary of what happened.

At the beginning of 1998, LTCM was expecting the spread between low-quality and high-quality bond yields to shrink. Overconfidence in their models had encouraged LTCM's partners to excessively leverage their positions – they turned $4 billion equity capital into $100 billion of assets, which were then used as collateral for more than a trillion dollars of notional in over-the-counter derivatives. In theory, LTCM's long and short positions were highly correlated, so that the net risk was supposedly small, and highly liquid. Consequently, reducing the exposure, should things go wrong, should not have been a problem. Unfortunately, LTCM's models turned out to be wrong on both points.

On 17 August 1998, in an attempt to stop the haemorrhaging of its foreign currency reserves, the Russian government devalued the rouble, defaulted on its domestic debt, halted payment on rouble-denominated debt, and unilaterally declared a 90-day moratorium on payments by commercial banks to foreign creditors. Although the Russian debt was a relatively small component of the world financial markets (281 billion roubles, or $13.5 billion), the default fed a panic that swept world markets already wrestling with the consequences of the Asian crisis. In particular, many Russian banks and securities firms exercised the *force majeure* clauses in their derivative contracts and terminated them. Many customers who had been using these contracts to hedge their Russian currency and debt positions were suddenly left with unprotected positions that had lost much of their value. Most investors rushed to quality, thereby transferring their capital from highly risky assets with no liquidity to liquid assets with a low level of risk. The spreads that LTCM had been betting against ballooned. As an illustration, the spread between emerging market debt and North American Treasury bonds increased from 6% in July to 17% in September 1998.

LTCM quickly ran into trouble and lost most of its equity capital. Its remaining $600 million equity capital was totally insufficient to support balance-sheet positions in excess of $100 billion. Had LTCM then been forced to default and sell its remaining assets at fire-sale prices, a cascade of losses for other financial firms could have hugely disrupted markets and wreaked global economic havoc. For the first time, a hedge fund was deemed "too big to

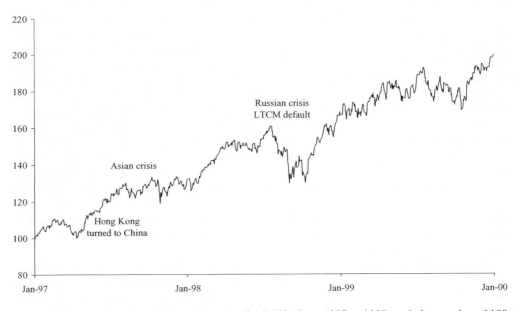

Figure 2.6   Evolution of the US stock market (S&P 500) from 1997 to 1999, scaled to a value of 100 on 1 January 1997

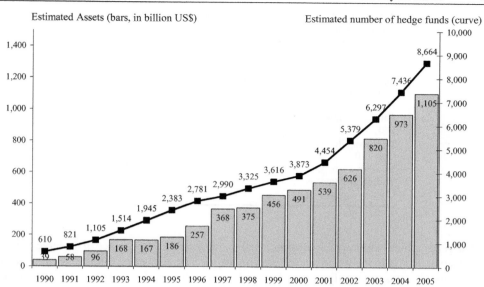

Estimated Assets (bars, in billion US$)   Estimated number of hedge funds (curve)

Figure 2.9 Estimated assets managed by the hedge fund industry (bars) and number of hedge funds (curve), 1990–2005. These statistics are based on the Hedge Fund Research database

longer track records, use multiple managers and decision makers, and rely on improved risk management systems. Not surprisingly, they are the ones often cited in the media, but they are not necessarily representative of the industry if we consider the average fund rather than the average dollar invested.

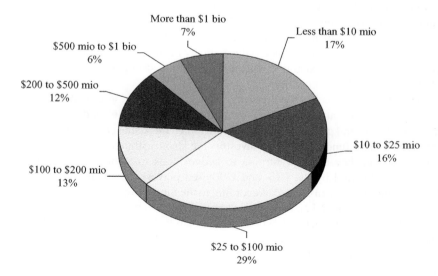

Figure 2.10 Breakdown of hedge funds by size. These statistics are based on the Hedge Fund Research database

Table 2.1   Assets managed by the largest US hedge fund firms in 2006 (1st quarter)

	Assets 2006
Goldman Sachs Asset Management	$21.0 billion
Bridgewater Associates	$20.9 billion
D.E. Shaw	$19.9 billion
Farallon Capital Management	$16.4 billion
ESL	$15.5 billion
Barclays Global	$14.3 billion
Och Ziff	$14.3 billion
Man Investments	$12.7 billion
Tudor Investments	$12.7 billion
Caxton Associates	$12.5 billion

The geographic evolution is also instructive. For many years, the presence of the largest, most liquid stock market in the world combined with the greatest pool of investment talent resulted in the United States dominating the hedge fund scene in terms of assets managed, number of hedge funds and sources of invested capital. But as the US market matured, Europe started to emerge as a valid alternative and gradually became the new focus for hedge fund management companies. Although US managers still control almost three-quarters of the global assets of the hedge fund industry, Europe is now at the leading edge of the industry's growth and appears to be avid in its quest for hedge funds. Since 2000, substantial amounts of capital have moved into European single-manager hedge funds, both new and existing.

According to the EuroHedge database (Figure 2.11), European hedge funds have reached a combined total of over $325 billion in January 2006, i.e. a growth figure of over 25% in 2005 (compared to almost 100% in 2003 and 50% in 2004). Over 330 new European hedge funds were launched during 2005 and amassed assets of approximately $28 billion, while 109 funds disappeared, yielding a total of 1258 hedge funds in activity. Almost two-thirds of European-based hedge funds' assets are managed or advised from the UK, the vast majority from London. London's predominance is due to many factors, including its local expertise, the proximity of potential and existing clients and markets, a strong asset management industry and a favourable regulatory environment.

More recently, the focus has also turned to Asia, where Chinese growth and the Japanese recovery have attracted attention. Asian sentiment towards hedge funds has been mixed in recent years after several government officials attributed the Asian crisis of 1997 to the attacks of large global macro funds. But Asian investors are also frustrated by low yields and volatile stock markets, and they are now turning to hedge funds to stabilize their portfolios. The market remains dwarfed by the UK- and US-based players, but a large number of Asian-based hedge funds have been created. According to the Singapore-based investment consultant Eurekahedge (See Figure 2.12), their assets topped the $100 billion mark at the end of 2005. More importantly, the number of London-based Asian hedge fund start-ups reduced from 45 in 2004 to 21 in 2005, suggesting a growing acceptance of Asia as a domicile. Most of these funds are based in Hong Kong, Singapore, Sydney or Tokyo – although the last-mentioned has a particularly unfavourable tax regime. On average, they are rather young and small, with 70% of them having less than $50 million of assets and 30% having less than $10 million.

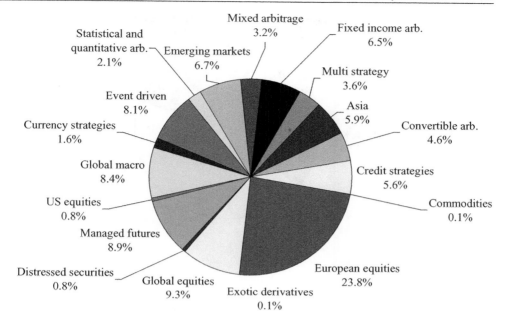

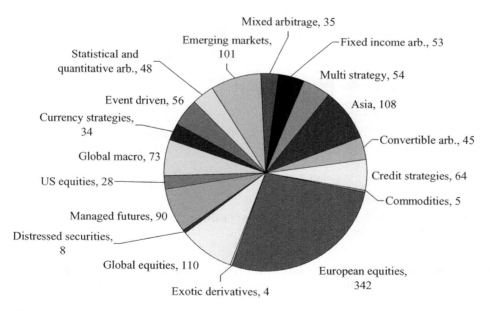

Figure 2.11   The European hedge fund industry in terms of assets (top) and number of funds (bottom). These statistics are based on the Eurekahedge database

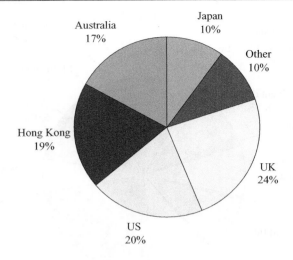

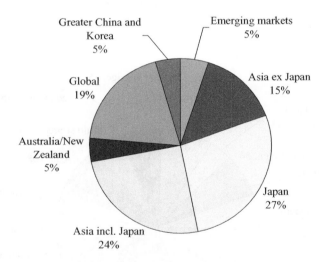

Figure 2.12   The Asian hedge fund industry in terms of fund domiciles (top) and investments (bottom). These statistics are based on the Eurekahedge database

Not surprisingly, an increasing number of US hedge funds have also set up European and Asian offices or concluded alliances, acquisitions, or distribution agreements.

2.8   THE KEY CHARACTERISTICS OF MODERN HEDGE FUNDS

The most surprising fact is that, despite sustained media and regulatory attention, the term "hedge fund" still has no precise legal definition. Even worse, several contradictory definitions exist (see Box 2.3) based on legal structures, investment strategies, superior returns, risk

---

Box 2.3 What is a hedge fund?

Here is a series of definitions of the term "hedge fund":

- "A risky investment pool, generally open only to well-heeled investors, that seeks very high returns by taking very great risks." (Money Central Investor)
- "A hedge fund is a private investment portfolio, usually structured as a limited partnership, open to accredited investors, charging an incentive-based fee, and managed by a general partner with every financial tool imaginable at his disposal." (Sierra Capital Planning Inc.)
- "An aggressively managed portfolio taking positions on speculative opportunities." (Investopedia.com)
- "A multitude of skill-based investment strategies with a broad range of risk and return objectives. A common element is the use of investment and risk management skills to seek positive returns regardless of market direction." (Goldman Sachs & Co.)
- "A loosely regulated private pooled investment vehicle that can invest in both cash and derivative markets on a leveraged basis for the benefit of its investors." (Thomas Schneeweis, University of Massachusetts)

---

taking or hedging, etc. Clearly, disagreement over a standard definition of hedge funds reflects the exponential growth in the number of products in existence. The industry has expanded to include indiscriminately pooled investment funds with strategies departing from long positions in bonds, equities or money markets, or a mix of these. This has led to the misleading situation in which the term 'hedge fund' no longer implies a systematic hedging attitude.

Fortunately, most new hedge funds still share a series of common characteristics that distinguish them easily from more conventional investment funds. Let us now review some of them, bearing in mind that these are just positive indicators of hedge fund activities rather than absolute signals.

Hedge funds are actively managed

There are only two ways to make money in a market. The first way is to take on a systematic risk (called "beta") for which the market rewards you with a risk premium. For instance, asset classes like equities have a higher expected return than cash over time for the simple reason that they are a riskier investment than cash. The same is true for long-duration bonds versus cash, corporate bonds versus treasuries, mortgages versus treasuries, emerging market debt versus developed market debt, etc. The second way is to take on specific risks and expect to be excessively rewarded by some "alpha". However, producing alpha requires some skills, because the alpha of the market is by definition a zero-sum game.

The performance of real hedge funds should normally result from active management decisions combined with the skills of their advisers (the "alpha") rather than from passively holding some asset class and enjoying the free ride of a risk premium (the "beta"). Indeed, there is no need to use hedge funds to gain some passive exposure to an asset class – the investor can do it alone at a much cheaper price. By contrast, hedge funds have a competitive advantage in the active management world – they collect information faster, they benefit from cheaper access to markets, they can afford to hire the best analysts and they enjoy superior trade execution and portfolio structuring.

Hedge fund advisers should therefore seek to add value through active management and skill-based strategies, and reject traditional investment paradigms, such as the efficient market hypothesis[9] or modern portfolio theory.[10] Rather, hedge fund managers believe that markets do not price all assets correctly. They therefore adopt specific strategies to exploit these inefficiencies.

Hedge funds are securitized trading floors

From a functional perspective, hedge funds are also very similar to the trading floors of investment banks. Indeed, several of the hedge fund strategies find their roots in investment banking activities, and the fund managers themselves often have a trading or investment banker background. The emergence of new technologies simply gave talented individuals and investment banking gurus (genuine or fake) the opportunity to start doing for their own account what they had been doing for several years within large institutions.

In addition, following the Asian crisis of 1997, several investment banks became a lot more nervous about proprietary trading – that is, taking risky positions on their own books. Consequently, they farmed out a lot of their proprietary trading activities to hedge funds, and numerous proprietary traders started creating their own hedge fund. Therefore, shrinkage in proprietary trading activities coincided neatly with a welter of hedge fund launches.

Hedge funds have flexible investment policies

To enhance the possibility of outstanding returns, hedge fund managers are usually given broad discretion over the investment styles, asset classes and investment techniques they can use. In particular, they can combine both long and short positions, concentrate rather than diversify investments (sometimes with some risk, see Box 2.4), borrow and leverage their portfolios, invest in illiquid assets, trade derivatives and hold unlisted securities. In the case of adverse markets, a hedge fund manager can try to move into cash, hedge against market declines, or implement short sell in an attempt to earn profits. He can also switch strategies or markets if there are better opportunities. This is in sharp contrast to mutual funds, which tend to have narrowly defined charters, a practice driven by industry and regulatory conventions.

A flexible investment policy is clearly a double-edged sword: it subjects the fund to greater "manager risk" but also allows the manager to adapt to market conditions so that he can pursue profits or control risk. It is, however, important to understand that a hedge fund does not necessarily employ all the permitted tools or pursue simultaneously all the available trading strategies. It merely has them at its disposal, if needed. By contrast, in a bear market, a narrowly focused manager would be compelled to stick to his mandates while his asset class or sector is sinking.

Hedge funds use unusual legal structures

Hedge funds come in a variety of legal forms. However, to avoid the numerous regulations that apply to financial intermediaries and/or to minimize their tax bills (Box 2.5), hedge funds

---

[9] The efficient market hypothesis states that at any given time, security prices fully reflect all publicly available information.

[10] Modern portfolio theory believes in perfect markets and results in the systematic passive indexing of portfolios.

Box 2.4 eNote.com and the dangers of overconcentrated positions

The dangers of overconcentrated positions, illiquid stocks and price manipulation are perfectly illustrated by the eNote case.

eNote.com Inc. was a small Vermont-based firm that developed a television-based internet mail appliance for consumers and businesses that do not need or want to use personal computers. In May 2001, the Securities and Exchange Commission sued Burton G. Friedlander for misrepresenting the performance of his hedge fund, Friedlander International Inc. According to the SEC, Friedlander's hedge fund bought 5 million eNote preferred shares and 2 million warrants for eNote common stock in April 1999. It rapidly became eNote's biggest shareholder and kept increasing its position. In December 2000, it owned warrants for 11.7 million eNote shares, and eNote represented 40% of its portfolio.

Friedlander then started inflating the net asset value of his fund by buying large volumes of eNote shares at prices over their market value. Meanwhile, he continued to solicit new shareholders for his hedge fund, while simultaneously redeeming his personal shares at artificially inflated prices (Figure 2.13).

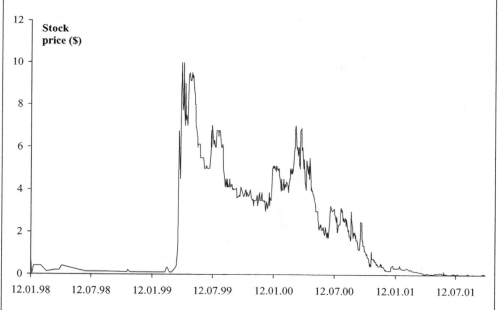

Figure 2.13   Movement of eNote share price, 1998–2001

This process continued for almost one year, until the SEC discovered the case and sued Friedlander.

use legal structures that are unusual in the asset management world. These are often limited partnerships or limited liability companies when targeting US investors, and offshore investment companies established in tax-favourable jurisdictions when operating outside the United States (Figure 2.14).

> **Box 2.5 Offshore funds, but Uncle Sam's courts**
>
> Offshore funds are usually intentionally designed and structured to avoid US taxes and laws. This is necessary to attract offshore investors, and in some instances, even certain tax-exempt US persons. Nonetheless, if something goes awry with the fund, investors and securities regulators seem to be increasingly inclined to bring claims in US courts against the fund and its service providers (most of the time the administrator and auditors). This has the obvious advantage of being able to claim huge damage awards against defendants who have deep pockets.
>
> Defendants often argue that US courts lack subject-matter jurisdiction, because they carry out their functions entirely offshore and they have no US investors, and that forcing litigation on them in the US has the sole aim of saddling them with a heavy burden. But US courts often reject the *forum non conveniens* argument and are increasingly willing to extend their jurisdiction to securities law claims against offshore hedge fund managers and service providers. For instance, the simple fact that an offshore fund traded US securities or that some meetings took place in the US are now considered sufficient for a US court to exercise jurisdiction. The recent extension to offshore funds of the obligation to register as an investment adviser in the US is another example of this trend towards extra-territoriality.

Hedge funds offer limited liquidity

A hallmark of traditional investment funds is the opportunity for daily subscription and redemption. Investors perceive this daily liquidity as an advantage, because they can enter or exit

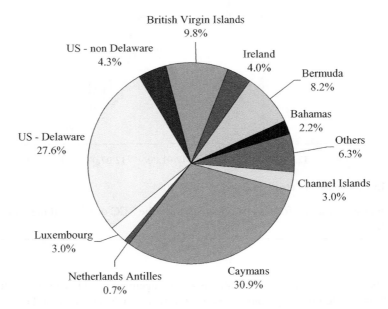

Figure 2.14   Estimated distribution of hedge fund domiciles (country of registration). These statistics are based on the Hedge Fund Research database

a fund whenever they wish. However, they often forget that a high liquidity normally comes at a cost:

- The fund needs to maintain a small cash pool as a liquidity buffer. Whether between the fund and the investor, or purely within the fund, most operations will actually impact this cash pool. For example, an investor purchasing shares in the fund will pay for them using cash that will go into the pool. An investor redeeming his shares in the fund will receive cash from the pool. And selling an asset in the fund will also generate cash for the pool, while purchasing an asset will require cash from the pool. Since the return on cash is usually lower than the expected return on other investments, the existence of the cash pool tends to lower the overall performance of the fund.
- The fund's shareholders are penalized with respect to newcomers or early withdrawers. When subscribing, new shareholders begin to participate in the fund's existing assets as soon as they receive their shares while, in reality, their cash contribution is still not yet invested. Moreover, their cash contribution will result in transaction costs (when the fund invests) to be shared between all shareholders. Similarly, when redeeming their shares, old shareholders are paid on the basis of the market value of the fund's assets, while in reality some of these assets will be sold to ensure the repayment, generating transaction costs to be shared by the remaining shareholders.
- Managers lose focus. Fund managers must also face the hassle of anticipating and dealing with daily subscriptions and redemptions from investors trying to time the markets themselves. They progressively become cash-flow managers rather than asset managers, and focus on shorter-term horizons.
- Some investment opportunities are not compatible with daily liquidity, simply because they are illiquid and hard to sell.

Hedge funds and their managers face the challenge of reconciling their objective of achieving above-average market returns relative to risk with their investors' desire for liquidity through periodic exit routes. The solution chosen by most hedge funds is simply to limit the subscription and redemption possibilities and to insist upon a minimum investment period.

- The **terms of subscription** specify at which dates investors can enter a hedge fund. Subscribing to a closed-end fund is only possible during its initial issuing period, while open-end funds offer new subscription windows on a regular basis (typically quarterly or monthly). Other than during these windows, subscription to an open-end fund is not possible.
- An initial **lock-up period** is mandatory. It is the minimum time an investor is required to keep his money invested in a hedge fund before being allowed to redeem his shares according to the terms of redemption. The usual lock-up period is one year, but longer periods are not uncommon, particularly in reputed funds. For instance, relying on its aura, the famous hedge fund, Long Term Capital Management, required a three-year lock-up from its investors, before it collapsed in 1998.
- The **terms of redemption** specify on what dates and under which conditions investors can redeem their shares. The current market standard seems to be at the end of each quarter, but longer redemption periods are not unusual, particularly in funds investing in rather illiquid markets or securities. However, many funds also have provisions to extend the terms of redemption if necessary, and some charge decreasing penalty fees to dissuade early redemption, or limit the number of shares that can be redeemed on any given redemption date (**gate**) see Box 2.6. Moreover, investors are often required to give **advance notice** of their wish to redeem (typically 30 to 90 days before actual redemption).

Box 2.6 Gate provisions

Hedge fund managers are increasingly using gate provisions, i.e. limits on the maximum percentage of the fund's overall capital that can be withdrawn on a scheduled redemption date. Common limits are 20% in the case of annual redemptions or 10% in the case of more frequent redemptions.

   A gate provision allows the manager to increase exposure to less liquid assets or trades without having the risk of facing a sudden liquidity crisis if a redemption date approaches and several investors want to redeem their shares. The exercise of a gate provision is usually left to the discretion of the board of directors of the fund. In extreme cases, a manager may also suspend the redemption rights (which investors hate) or decide to pay the redemptions in kind (which is not much appreciated either).

Although somewhat cramping from an investor's point of view, these restrictions should have a positive impact on a hedge fund's performance. They benefit all the partners by controlling cash-flow transactions, allowing managers to focus on investing rather than on redeeming assets of investors trying to time the markets themselves. With these guidelines, managers can also focus on relatively long-term horizons, hold illiquid positions (emerging markets, distressed or unlisted securities, etc.) and reduce cash holdings. We should also remember that these terms are much more favourable than the terms of private equity funds where investor liquidity is far more restricted, generally to the point of being tied to the disposal of the underlying investment or another liquidity event such as a public listing.

   Of course, the existence of periodic exit routes for investors requires the hedge fund to periodically (concurrently with the timing of the exit route) strike a net asset value of its portfolio of investments to allow the investors to redeem (or purchase in the case of an entrance) units at the relevant net asset value at the relevant time.

Hedge funds charge performance fees and target absolute returns

While traditional fund managers charge solely a management fee, hedge fund managers impose both a management fee and an incentive fee. *Management fees* (Box 2.7) are usually expressed as a percentage of assets under management and are charged annually or quarterly. They range from 1 to 3% per year, and are essentially intended to meet operating expenses. *Incentive fees* aim at encouraging managers to achieve maximum returns. They typically range from 15 to 25% of the annual realized performance and enable hedge funds to attract the high-end talent necessary to run them.

   To avoid agency problems and excessive risk taking, many funds include a *hurdle rate* and/or a *high-water mark* clause in their offering memorandum. The hurdle rate indicates the minimum economic performance that the fund adviser must achieve in order to be allowed to charge an incentive fee. The high-water mark states that any previous losses must be recouped by new profits before the incentive fee is to be paid. Generally, the high-water mark varies for each investor and is based on the maximum value of the investor's interest in the partnership since his initial investment in the fund. This protects investors from paying an incentive fee while they are just recovering from previous losses.

Box 2.7 RAM Capital changes its fees

Ritchie Capital Management is a global alternative asset management firm. It is considered to have some of the most innovative terms in the hedge fund business – although most investors might disagree with them. Its multi-strategy fund, RAM Capital, had approximately $300 million invested in the Ritchie Energy Fund in 2005, and the rest of its capital in global macro, arbitrage, long–short equity and "experimental" strategies. RAM Capital used a series of internal and external managers, and their expenses were simply passed through to investors in the fund, resulting in a management fee of 7.9% in 2003 and more than 6% in 2004 – on top of the 20% performance fee.

On 29 August 2005, RAM Capital asked its investors to approve a set of changes to its terms. Rather than maintaining the pass-through structure, RAM Capital proposed charging a 1% management fee on equity contributions, plus 2% of all assets in the fund's portfolio, including those bought with leverage. Investors had the choice of (i) accepting the new conditions and being subject to the new terms effective 1 September 2005; (ii) voting for the changes, opting out of the fund and paying an early-redemption fee; or (iii) voting against the changes. However, if the new terms were accepted, investors who voted against the changes would automatically be transferred to a dedicated share class whose first redemption date would be ... 31 August 2008.

In addition to the fee terms, RAM Capital also sought approval to change its liquidity terms (quarterly with 45 days notice, or three-year by with 90 days notice), introduce a gate (10% of the fund size per quarter, with a maximum use for six consecutive quarters), allow the creation of illiquid side-pockets for private equity and reinsurance investments, change its Cayman Islands legal counsel, and change its name to Ritchie Multi-Strategy Global. Note that the auditor of the fund would remain the same – it had been changed the year before.

Several hedge funds also include a ***proportional adjustment clause*** in their offering memorandum. This clause states that if the fund manager loses money and some investors consequently withdraw their assets, the fund manager is allowed to reduce proportionally the amount of loss he has to recover by the percentage of the assets that were removed. As an illustration, a fund manager who lost $20 out of $100 would have to recover the same $20 before charging performance fees. But if investors withdraw $40 out of the remaining $80 (that is, 50% of the remaining assets), the loss carried forward would be reduced to $10 (that is, 50% of the loss).

Some funds have even gone one step further by introducing a ***clawback clause*** and a ***loss recovery account***. The clawback clause stipulates that a portion of the incentive fee will be retained every year in a clawback account, usually until the account reaches a certain percentage of the assets. If future performance turns out to be negative, the clawback account is then debited to the client's credit at the incentive fee rate. As an illustration, this allows a client paying a 20% incentive fee to recover 20% of his losses in a losing year by recovering portions of former incentive fees. If the negative relative performance exceeds the clawback account, then a loss recovery account will be established. Future incentive fees will be credited to this account, and no incentive fee will be earned by the manager until the loss recovery account has been reduced to zero.

Box 2.8 Jeff Vinik and Julian Robertson

Two interesting examples of the potential side-effects of performance fees are provided by the legendary hedge fund managers, Jeffrey Vinik and Julian Roberston. After four years running Vinik Asset Management, Jeffrey Vinik announced in October 2000 that he was quitting the industry to spend more time with his family. In those four years, the assets of his fund had soared from $800 million to $4.2 billion, for a gross return of 645.8%. This red-hot track record on Wall Street had allowed Jeffrey Vinik, Mike Gordon and Mark Hostetter, the three partners in the fund, to collect about $1.7 billion of performance fees.

   More recently, Julian Robertson, one of the most successful stock pickers on Wall Street for more than two decades, announced that he was closing his Tiger Management LLC hedge fund group. In 18 months, the assets under management had dwindled by $16 billion to $6 billion. The firm did not generate enough cash to pay its employees, essentially because it was unable to collect fees. Given the -4% performance in 1998, -19% in 1999 and -13% at the beginning of 2000, Robertson would have needed to earn 48% before he could again charge his clients fees!

All these mechanisms explain why hedge fund managers pursue an ***absolute return target,*** meaning that their goal is to be profitable regardless of the stock or bond market environment – their payroll depends directly on performance (Box 2.8). This differs significantly from traditional investment vehicles, which do compare their performance relative to standard market benchmarks and mostly care about the amount of assets they manage. However, it should be noted that incentive fees and high-water marks might also have adverse gambling effects on managers' behaviour. For instance, a manager who has achieved a good performance at the beginning of a given year may be tempted to lock in and secure his incentive fee by avoiding any risk taking until the fee is paid. Conversely, a manager with a high-water mark who has recorded a relatively poor performance has nothing to lose and may take on much more risk in an attempt to recover,[11] or possibly close his fund to start a new one. Fortunately, reputation costs should mitigate these effects.[12]

Note that several hedge fund managers in the US are using *deferred incentive compensation* for their offshore funds. Simply stated, prior to the start of the fiscal year, they elect to defer for up to 10 years payment of all or any portion of the management fee or performance fee earned with respect to that subsequent fiscal year. The deferred fees remain in the hedge fund's account and will appreciate or depreciate on the basis of the fund's subsequent performance. Technically, the deferred fees will be reflected on the hedge fund's books as a liability and will reduce the fund's net asset value. Any appreciation will be expensed as additional fees and any depreciation will be treated as a reduction of fees. Upon expiry of the deferral period, dissolution of the fund, or termination of the investment adviser agreement by the fund, all deferred performance (and management) fees are payable. On the termination of the investment adviser agreement, fees elected to be deferred will remain in the hedge fund until the end of the

---

[11] See, for instance, Brown *et al.* (1999).
[12] See, for instance, Fung and Hsieh (1997).

deferral period or the dissolution of the fund, whichever is the earlier. This permits a deferred taxation, if the managers do not have the ability to accelerate the payment.[13]

Hedge fund managers are partners, not employees

A hedge fund manager generally shares both upside and downside risks with investors because he has a significant personal stake in his fund. Combined with the incentive fee, his stake is supposed to closely align his interests with those of his investors, and encourage managers to seek substantial total returns while prudently controlling risks.

However, contrary to common belief, the personal wealth commitment is not necessarily a good indicator of motivation and can even produce undesirable side-effects. At the beginning of his career, for example, the fund manager has little to lose. He may be tempted to increase risk, knowing that in case of disaster, he can go back to being a traditional asset manager and recover quickly. At the other extreme, a successful fund manager at the end of his career will have so large a commitment in the fund that he will refrain from taking risks, even though these are well remunerated.

Hedge funds have limited transparency

Transparency is a controversial issue in the hedge fund community. First, let us recall that "transparency" is derived from the Latin words *trans* and *parere*, which translate into "to show oneself". In the world of fund managers, this can be understood as the ability to see what is behind the net asset value.

A feature of hedge funds has traditionally been their lack of transparency, which can easily be explained by two factors. First, the particular legal structure and the offshore registration of hedge funds preclude them from publicly disclosing performance information, detailed asset allocations or earnings. This could be considered by regulators as a public marketing activity, which is prohibited. Second, revealing specific positions about individual holdings or strategies could be precarious, both for the fund and for its investors. For instance, a fund beginning to accumulate shares with a view to achieving a strategic position in a company would not want to announce publicly what it is doing until it has finished accumulating the position. Nor would a fund short in an illiquid market disclose its holdings, fearing a short squeeze. As an illustration, Lowenstein noted that when Long Term Capital Management's problems became known to its Wall Street competitors, the latter began to take trading positions to exploit the difficulties faced by the struggling hedge fund. In that particular case, disclosure of specific positions clearly had a very damaging impact.

Therefore, hedge funds consider transparency as a double-edged sword. They prefer to remain rather discrete and sometimes opaque, at least when compared to mutual funds and when talking to non-investors. This has helped to perpetuate the mystery and uneasiness surrounding the hedge fund industry. However, the situation is gradually changing. Investors

---

[13] Note that in 2005, the new Section 409A of the Internal Revenue Code came into application. Although it does not repeal the basic principles underlying the typical hedge fund fees deferral programme, it now requires certain deferred amounts to be included in current income and therefore subject to current tax. It also imposes a penalty equal to 20% of the compensation required to be included in gross income, unless certain technical requirements are satisfied. This has significantly curtailed the existing benefits for US-based fund managers. UK-based managers were also able to create similar tax characteristics through the use of Employee Benefit Trusts, but their use has now been severely restricted.

constantly request more information, and a minimum level of transparency for effective due diligence is now usually provided. Fund managers are also less reluctant to disclose aggregate data and risk data rather than detailed position data.

Hedge fund strategies are not scalable

Unlike the case of traditional investment management, size is not a factor of success in the hedge fund industry. The reason is that hedge fund strategies crucially depend on manager skills and available investment opportunities – two factors that are not scalable. Therefore, hedge funds have a limited ability to absorb large sums of money, and a manager may prefer to close his fund to new subscriptions once it has reached a target size. This allows managers to maintain a higher performance, and therefore to obtain higher performance fees. And if they really see opportunities, they still have the possibility of increasing their leverage. The recent demise of Julian Robertson's Tiger Fund, the liquidation of Jeff Vinik's fund, and the capitulation of George Soros' Quantum Fund are anecdotal evidence that smaller is usually better in single strategy funds. However, as we shall see, size may be an advantage in multi-strategy funds which actively deploy capital as market opportunities arise.

Hedge funds target specific investors

While mutual funds typically target retail investors, high net worth individuals (HNWIs) were historically the primary investors in hedge funds, as they sought to generate reasonable returns while protecting their capital.[14] This is due to several factors, among which are:

- The legal limits on the number of partners if the fund is structured as a limited partnership. A small number of partners implies a large minimum capital investment per investor, frequently above $1 million, to ensure that the fund has a sufficient amount of capital to enable it to operate properly.
- The relative complexity of hedge fund strategies and the lack of understanding of such strategies among smaller investors, on average.
- Other regulatory reasons requiring that only "sophisticated" investors may gain access to hedge funds.

In March 2004, Merrill Lynch and Cap Gemini Ernst & Young reported that, as at December 2003, 73% of HNWIs in the US held hedge fund investments. And according to US-based consultant Hennessee, they control approximately 44% of hedge fund assets. However, the landscape is gradually changing, with institutional investors increasing their allocations to hedge funds, as they seek alternative investments with low correlations to traditional portfolios of cash, bonds and stocks (Figure 2.15).

Affluent private individuals are also becoming increasingly interested in hedge funds, particularly because of the introduction of lower minimum fund requirements by funds of hedge funds and the creation of structured products such as capital guaranteed notes. This "affluent"

---

[14] The term "HNWIs" usually encompasses individuals with more than $1 million in net worth, as well as family offices and trust departments of private banks. Ready to commit for the long run, willing to bear high risks in exchange for high return prospects and having a sufficient level of net worth to invest sizeable amounts directly in a fund as partners, HNWIs are ideal targets for hedge funds. Their numbers have soared in recent years owing to the sudden creation of new wealth in successful initial public offerings, creation and sale of businesses, mergers and acquisitions, and the expansion of stock option plans as incentive compensation.

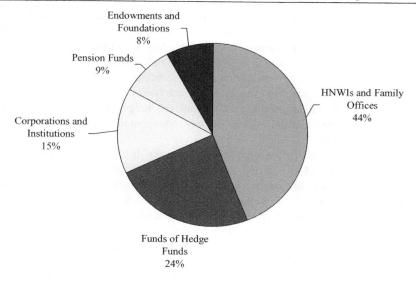

Figure 2.15 Estimated sources of capital for US hedge funds at the end of 2005

group typically comprises individuals with net worth ranging between $500 000 and $1 million (Table 2.2).

2.9 THE FUTURE

Today, the major source of future growth for hedge funds clearly seems to be institutional investors, i.e. pension and benefit plans, endowments and foundations, insurance companies and corporations. Entangled in their bureaucratic investment decision-making processes and restricted by their strict fiduciary responsibilities and the "prudent man" rule, institutional investors have long been under-represented in the hedge fund market. Initially, only the most adventurous institutions allocated small amounts of capital to hedge funds, with the goal of

Table 2.2 Categories of private investors in hedge fund

Category	Investable assets	Major distribution channels
Ultra-high net worth individuals	More than $25 million	Private banks, trust companies, family offices, financial advisers
High net worth individuals	$1 million to $50 million	Private banks, trust companies, brokerage firms, attorneys, financial advisers
Affluent investors	$500 000 to $1 million	Commercial banks, mutual fund companies, brokerage firms, attorneys, insurers, financial advisers, funds of funds
Retail investors	Less than $500 000	Funds of funds

diversifying their sources of returns and reducing portfolio risk. But the wake-up call came in 2000 with the decision of the California Public Employees Retirement System (Calpers) to commit $11 billion in alternative investments, including $1 billion of direct investments in hedge funds. This was a major stamp of approval, which convinced several pension funds, endowments and foundations to dip their toes into the hedge fund waters. This constituted a radical departure from their traditional approach, which had been heavily centred on bonds and light on anything remotely associated with risk. However, hedge funds and their absolute return approach also brought in a compelling new money management paradigm, which fiduciaries felt compelled to embrace.

The search for quality hedge fund capacity is not easy. It took Calpers almost four years to fully allocate its initial $1 billion hedge fund commitment. Interestingly, rather than being secretive, Calpers widely publicized both its investment process and the list of specifications for the type of hedge fund it was looking for. This established a pattern that several other institutional investors emulated, therefore accelerating institutional participation in the hedge fund arena. US institutions are clearly well ahead in this process but European institutions are also increasingly attracted to hedge funds. However, several issues are still open, such as (i) the lack of transparency, (ii) the lack of regulation and risk control and (iii) the high level of fees. The answers to these and the increasing use of consultants for alternative investment manager selection will undoubtedly determine the shape of the hedge fund industry in the years ahead.

3

Legal Environment

On average, the life span of a regulation is one-fifth as long as a chimpanzee's, one-tenth as long as a human's, and four times as long as the officials who created it.

In the past, the need for regulation and supervision of financial intermediaries dealing with the general public was rarely challenged. The regulators' objective was threefold: (i) to protect small investors and depositors from abuse and default through licensing, registration, minimum disclosure requirements and increased transparency; (ii) to reduce systemic risks and ensure soundness and integrity of the financial system by imposing capital adequacy and margin requirements; and (iii) to ensure that customers were provided with quality service at competitive prices.

The regulatory situation of hedge funds, compared to that of traditional financial intermediaries such as banks, mutual funds, brokerage houses or insurance companies, has always been equivocal. On one hand, hedge funds operate in regulated markets, utilize the infrastructure of regulated financial centres and deal with regulated financial institutions (e.g. brokers and banks) to implement their investment strategies. They are therefore in a sense indirectly regulated. On the other hand, hedge funds tend to structure themselves in such a way as to avoid direct regulation oversight and escape the registration or licensing requirements generally applicable to investment companies. They want to operate with maximum flexibility, which is precisely what regulators do not want traditional retail funds to do.

Initially, hedge funds were therefore criticized, but tolerated. They were occupying only a small corner of the market, and their high minimum investment was an insurmountable hurdle to retail investors. Only sophisticated and affluent investors could afford them, and these investors were supposedly capable of protecting their own interests – and after all, who cares if a few millionaires lose some money? In addition, hedge funds were often registered in offshore jurisdictions and regulators had no extraterritorial powers to control them. Therefore, regulatory approaches to hedge funds tended to favour enhanced market discipline and private risk management in lieu of affirmative but hardly applicable regulatory duties.

However, this situation changed in the late 1990s and early 2000s. In the wake of the rescue of Long Term Capital Management (LTCM), several politicians argued that hedge funds were shadowy investment vehicles that escaped regulation by exploiting loopholes in the securities laws in order to freewheel in the equivalent of a Wild West financial frontier. According to them, strict regulation of hedge fund activities was urgently needed to bring the cowboys of capitalism back under control. Also, as a result of the 2000–2002 bear market, there was a widespread move into retail[1] distribution of hedge funds or hedge fund related products.

Various proposals were examined by international financial authorities and regulators. After extensive discussions, the consensus was that direct regulation of hedge fund activities would not achieve the desired aims. There were three reasons for this. First, the blurring of lines

---

[1] The term "retail" refers here to investors other than those normally referred to as "professional", "qualified" or "sophisticated".

between institutions with different primary regulators and supervisors (e.g. banks, asset management firms, mutual funds and hedge funds) could result in similar activities being treated inconsistently, which would create incentives for "regulatory arbitrage" and thwart the initial intent of regulation. Second, excessive direct regulation or tax barriers against hedge funds could push them towards offshore centres, where they would be completely uncontrollable. Third, there were some concerns that SEC oversight of the hedge fund industry could create a "moral hazard" by persuading investors that their due diligence had already been done for them. Therefore, regulators' opinions went in favour of requiring more transparency about the size and risk of hedge fund portfolios, since most of the desired effects could probably be obtained by relying on disclosure rather than regulation. This opinion was supported by some of the leading hedge fund managers – Caxton, Kingdon Capital Management, Moore Capital Management, Soros Fund Management and Tudor Investment – who made a proposal for self-regulation and circulated a set of recommended risk management guidelines in a sponsored report.[2]

In the early 2000s, the hedge fund industry's expansion became driven by the quest for protection against falling equity markets. As disenchantment with traditional methods of investment management increased, long-established hedge fund investors such as wealthy individuals, family offices and endowment funds were joined by pension funds, insurance companies, and affluent investors. With gathering momentum, retail investors also embraced hedge funds to varying degrees. This expansion into retail markets heightened regulators' concerns about several aspects of hedge fund products, including the applicability of securities law exemptions used, the marketing practices of both hedge funds and dealers, the potential conflicts of interest, the high levels of fees and charges (some of which were not transparent), the ability of hedge fund managers to meet the expectations raised by their marketing, and the lack of disclosure of hedge fund operations and financial affairs. In addition, many regulators were increasingly uncomfortable with the prospect of having a hugely influential trillion dollar industry falling outside their scope. Several countries therefore started implementing rules and practices to deal with hedge funds and to establish a sensible balance between opening retail markets and appropriate policing. Several regulatory environments were also altered to allow the establishment of onshore hedge funds and their distribution to retail investors, as well as the sale of certain offshore hedge funds.

Regulatory environments and industry solutions are intrinsically interdependent and it is necessary to analyse both, in order to understand the business landscape. In this chapter, we therefore provide a snapshot of some of the major regulatory environments as well as the solutions adopted by the hedge fund industry to deal with them, both within and outside the US. Indeed, as we shall see, most of the complexities of hedge fund structures result from the desire to benefit from regulatory exemptions and/or to cater to the needs of specific taxable or non-taxable investors.

At this stage, it is worth stressing that this chapter is intended to serve as a general guide only. It is not a comprehensive manual on the regulation of investment companies, investment company service providers or related entities. It is not intended to provide formal or binding legal advice, and in no case should it be relied upon instead of the actual securities laws and the advice of legal counsel.

---

[2] See Various (2000).

3.1   THE SITUATION IN THE US

The US economy is primarily founded upon the market discipline dogma. Consequently, the government should intervene only as a remedy when market forces fail to properly address certain disruptions. However, the stock market crash of 1929 and its ensuing depression also established the firm conviction that unregulated financial markets could lead to rampant speculation, eventual market bubbles, and ruin for unprotected investors. The result was the imposition of strict federal regulation to control the access of investors to investment vehicles and constrain financial institutions with regard to the types of investment activities they could undertake.

Today, three sets of federal regulators oversee financial institutions dealing with the public. The Securities and Exchange Commission (SEC) is concerned with public issues or trades of securities. The Commodity Futures Trading Commission (CFTC) monitors futures and commodities. Finally, the Federal Reserve, the Office of the Comptroller of the Currency and the Office of Thrift Supervision are in charge of banks. Hedge funds based in the US or primarily operating in the US are essentially concerned with the SEC and, to a lesser extent, with the CFTC.

The SEC is a quasi-judicial government agency whose primary mission is to protect investors, maintain the integrity of the securities markets, and guarantee all investors equal access to certain basic facts about investments. The SEC derives its regulatory powers from a series of Acts, among which are:

- The Securities Act (1933), which regulates the issue of securities to the public, as well as the necessary information disclosure.
- The Securities Exchange Act (1934), which regulates brokerage firms, transfer agents and clearing agencies as well as the nation's securities self-regulatory organizations, including stock exchanges.
- The Investment Company Act (1940), which regulates the organization of companies that engage primarily in investing, reinvesting or trading in "securities", and whose own securities are offered to the investing public.
- The Investment Advisers Act (1940), which regulates firms or individual practitioners remunerated for advising others about securities investments.

While all these Acts set rules that seem to work well for traditional investment funds, they are often incompatible with hedge fund operations and policies, such as selling short, using derivatives and charging performance fees. US hedge funds must therefore use some of the well-established exemptions and loopholes that are built into the securities law regime to operate outside its scope. So far, hedge funds have been successful in this hide-and-seek activity, simply because their investors were wealthy individuals – the federal securities laws presume that such investors can protect their own interests without SEC intervention.

3.1.1   The Securities Act (1933)

The Securities Act of 1933 regulates the issuance and sale of securities to the general public. Its primary objectives are to ensure that all investors receive all necessary information concerning securities being offered for public sale, and to prohibit deceit, misrepresentation and fraud in the sale of securities.

To attain these objectives, Section 5 of the Securities Act requires registration with the SEC of all securities being offered for public sale. Registration forms must contain specific information such as a description of the registrant's properties and business, a description of the significant provisions of the security to be offered for sale and its relationship to the registrant's other capital securities, information about the management of the registrant company as well as its financial statements (balance sheets, budget and other items) certified by independent public accountants. Immediately after registration, all these elements become public so that investors can make an informed and realistic evaluation of the worth of the securities they want to buy. Note however that the fact that a security is registered does not imply approval of the issue by the SEC, or that the SEC has found the registration disclosures to be accurate. It simply indicates that the issuer has provided the set of necessary information to register its securities with the SEC.

For purposes of the Securities Act, the offering of an interest in a hedge fund is considered as a public offering of securities, even if the fund is structured as a limited partnership (LP) or as a limited liability company (LLC). Consequently, hedge funds should either register their securities with the SEC, or qualify for an exemption from registration. In practice, most hedge funds avoid the expensive and time-consuming registration process and its associated disclosure requirements by structuring their offering as a "private placement", which is exempt from registration. The federal private placement exemption arises under Section 4(2) of the Securities Act, which allows the SEC to exempt from registration certain offerings of securities that do not involve a public offering.

Regulation D

Regulation D provides a safe haven for private placement offerings. Of particular interest to hedge funds is Rule 506, which specifies the requirements that offerings must meet in order to be exempted.[3] In summary, the offering must be restricted to and personally directed to *accredited investors* (Box 3.1), in unlimited number, and up to 35 other purchasers. All non-accredited investors, either alone or with a purchaser representative, must be sophisticated, i.e. they must have sufficient knowledge and experience in financial and business matters to make them capable of evaluating the merits and risks of the prospective investment. This implies that offerings cannot be publicized by general soliciting or advertising, whether in the form of advertisements, newspaper articles, general mailings, broadcasts or the like, or seminars or meetings whose attendees have been invited by general soliciting or advertising. A good criterion to determine whether this rule was effectively respected is the existence of a substantive pre-existing relationship between the potential investors and the general partner of the fund, or any person acting on the general partner's behalf.

If offers and sales of securities are made solely to accredited investors, there is no need to prepare a comprehensive private placement memorandum. But if one or more sales of securities are made to investors who are not accredited, a *detailed private placement memorandum* must be prepared and distributed to all prospective investors in the offering, including the accredited ones. Since the preparation and distribution of such a memorandum requires extensive legal work and is a time-consuming and expensive undertaking, most hedge funds restrict their focus to accredited investors.

---

[3] Note that Rules 504 and 505 are similar to Rule 506, but they set ceilings on the size of the offerings, based on the aggregate amounts raised by the issuer over a set period of time (i.e. less than $1 million and less than $5 million in any 12-month period, respectively). This explains why they are rarely used by hedge funds to be exempted from registration.

Box 3.1 What is an accredited investor?

Rule 501 of Regulation D defines the term "accredited investor" as follows:

1. A bank, insurance company, registered investment company, business development company, or small business investment company.
2. An employee benefit plan, within the meaning of the Employee Retirement Income Security Act (ERISA), if a bank, insurance company, or registered investment adviser makes the investment decisions, or if the plan has total assets in excess of $5 million.
3. A charitable organization, corporation, or partnership with assets exceeding $5 million.
4. A director, executive officer or general partner of the company selling the securities.
5. A business in which all the equity owners are accredited investors.
6. A natural person who has individual net worth, or joint net worth with the person's spouse, that exceeds $1 million at the time of the purchase.
7. A natural person with income exceeding $200 000 in each of the two most recent years or joint income with a spouse exceeding $300 000 for those years and a reasonable expectation of the same income level in the current year.
8. A trust with assets in excess of $5 million, if not formed purposely to acquire the securities offered.

In all cases, the issuer must file a *Form D* with the SEC no later than 15 calendar days after the first sale of securities. Form D essentially notifies the SEC that the fund used the Regulation D programme and provides very basic information on the issuing company and the offering.

Note that it is the responsibility of fund managers to be aware of the financial status and sophistication of their investors, and to verify whether or not they are accredited. The verification is usually made using a standardized questionnaire, in which prospective purchasers are required to state that they are accredited investors. Hedge fund managers can then use good faith in determining whether a potential subscriber can effectively be considered as accredited. They have no obligation to verify the accuracy of the financial data supplied through financial statements or other means, unless there are reasons to believe it is inaccurate.[4]

Hedge funds relying on Rule 506 to be exempted must also exercise reasonable care to ensure that their investors are acquiring the securities for themselves and are not investing with a view to distributing their interests in the fund to the general public. Most of the time, hedge funds will simply prohibit a transfer of the interests without the written consent of the general partner.

Regulation S

Alternatively, US hedge funds targeting non-US investors may use *Regulation S* to claim exemption from registration. Regulation S was adopted by the SEC in 1990 in order to clarify the effect of the registration provisions of Section 5 of the Securities Act on offshore transactions.

---

[4] Note that, owing to the internet and the financial press, information about privately offered securities is far more available than Regulation D was intended to require. Recently, SEC commissioners and staffers clearly indicated that they were considering loosening the restrictions on how privately offered securities could be sold, but requiring fund managers to conduct stricter due diligence on the accredited status of their clients.

This regulation is now the US securities law framework which governs the offshore offering and sale of securities which are not registered under the Securities Act.

The General Statement of Regulation S recognizes the primacy of the laws of the jurisdiction in which particular securities markets are located and explicitly excludes "offers and sales that occur outside the US" from the reach of the Securities Act's registration requirements. In practice, a transaction is deemed to have occurred outside the US when both the offer and the sale occurred outside the US.

In addition to the General Statement, Regulation S provides two havens. If any one is satisfied, it is not necessary to register the offer and sale of the relevant securities under the Securities Act. The first haven ("Issuer Safe Harbour") applies to issuers, distributors, their respective affiliates and any person acting on behalf of any of these parties. The second ("Resale Safe Harbour") applies to resales by all persons other than parties eligible to utilize the issuer safe harbour. Two general conditions must be met before offers, sales or resales of securities may be made in reliance upon either of the two safe harbours.

- The offer or sale must be made in an *offshore transaction*. To meet this requirement, no offer may be made to a US person and either (i) the buyer must be outside the US at the time the buy order is originated, or (ii) for purposes of the Issuer Safe Harbour, the transaction must be executed in, on or through a physical trading floor of an established foreign securities exchange located outside the US, or, for purposes of the Resale Safe Harbour, the sale must be made in, on or through the facilities of an offshore securities market designated by the SEC (which is not always a stock exchange) and neither the seller nor any person acting on his behalf must know that the transaction has been prearranged with a buyer in the US.
- No directed selling or reselling efforts may be made in the US during a *distribution compliance period* (DCP) in connection with an offer or sale of securities made in reliance upon a safe harbour. The Issuer Safe Harbour establishes three categories of securities offerings and applies a set of procedural safeguards to each category to ensure that any securities offered or sold in reliance thereon will come to rest offshore. The length of the compliance period varies depending on the category – see Table 3.1.

In short, Regulation S securities are exempted from the requirement of registration in the US, but they can only be held by non-US residents and citizens and cannot be sold in the US for a certain time after their date of issue. No hedging transactions with respect to Regulation S securities may be conducted unless in compliance with US securities laws. Note that in 1998, the SEC had to amend Regulation S to curb abuses by corporations which were using it to make indirect distributions into the US while bypassing the registration requirements.[5]

Note also that Regulation D and Regulation S affect only the application of the registration provisions of the Securities Act. They do not affect the application of other provisions of the federal securities laws, including the anti-fraud provisions. The reach of the anti-fraud provisions has been construed more broadly, so that they may be violated when either significant conduct occurs within the US or conduct, although occurring outside the US, has a significant effect within the US or on the interests of US investors.

---

[5] For instance, the GFL Ultra Fund, a British Virgin Islands corporation, engaged in the following strategy for more than a year: it purchased securities issued overseas at significant discounts from the US market price pursuant to Regulation S and hedged these purchases through short sales in the US. After the 40-day Regulation S restricted period, the fund unwound its short positions by covering them with the Regulation S shares. Clearly, this was an abuse of Regulation S to offer securities in the US before the end of a restricted period.

Table 3.1 The three categories of securities defined by the Issuer Safe Harbour

Cat.	Type of securities	Requirements
1	• Securities issued by a foreign issuer[a] with no substantial US market interest.[b] • Securities offered and sold in an "overseas directed offering."[c] • Securities backed by full faith and credit of a foreign government. • Securities offered or sold pursuant to an employee benefit plan established under non-US law.	(1) Offering effected as an "offshore transaction". (2) No "directed selling efforts".
2	Securities not eligible for Category 1 and that are: • Equity securities of foreign 1934 Act reporting companies; or • Debt securities of (i) US and foreign 1934 Act reporting companies, and (ii) foreign non-reporting companies.	(1) All Category 1 requirements. (2) "Offering restrictions"[d] apply. (3) No offers or sales to (or for the account of) any US person (other than a distributor) during 40-day DCP.
3	Securities not eligible for Category 1 or Category 2, that is: • Equity securities of US Exchange Act (1934) reporting companies; and • Debt and equity securities of US non-reporting companies.	**Debt offerings:** (1) All Category 1 and Category 2 requirements. (2) Temporary global security representing the securities, which is not exchangeable for the securities until end of 40-day DCP. **Equity offerings:** (1) All Category 1 and Category 2 requirements. (2) One-year DCP. (3) Purchaser certifies that he is not (and is not buying for account of) a US person. (4) Purchaser agrees to resell the securities only pursuant to registration under the Securities Act or an exemption therefrom. (5) US issuers must legend securities. (6) Issuer is required (by contract or charter document provisions) to refuse to register any transfer that violates Regulation S.

[a] An issuer is not a foreign issuer if more than 50% of its outstanding voting securities are held of record by persons with a US address and any of the following factors is present: (i) the majority of executive officers or directors of the issuer are US citizens or residents, (ii) more than 50% of the issuer's assets are located in the US or (iii) the issuer's business is administered principally in the US.

[b] For equity securities, "substantial US market interest" exists if (i) US securities markets and inter-dealer quotation systems in the aggregate constituted the largest market for such class of securities, or (ii) 20% or more of all trading in such class of securities took place in, on or through the facilities of securities exchanges and inter-dealer quotation systems in the US, and less than 55% of such trading took place in, on or through the facilities of securities markets of a single foreign country. For debt securities, "substantial US market interest" exists if (i) the debt securities are held of record by 300 or more US persons, (ii) $1billion or more aggregate principal amount of its debt securities are held of record by US persons, and (iii) 20% or more of the outstanding principal amount of the debt securities are held by US persons.

[c] That is, (i) an offering of securities by a foreign issuer directed into a single country other than the US to residents of that country, in accordance with local law and practices, or (ii) offerings by US issuers of certain types of non-convertible debt securities that are denominated in a non-US currency in a single country overseas.

[d] "Offering restrictions" consist of (i) the written agreement of each "distributor" (the underwriter, dealer or other person who by contractual arrangement participates in the distribution of the securities) that, during the applicable DCP, it will not offer or sell the securities in the US except pursuant to registration under the Securities Act or an exemption there from, or engage in hedging transactions with regard to the securities except in compliance with the Securities Act and (ii) the inclusion in all offering materials (except press releases) of a legend stating that the securities have not been registered under the Securities Act and may not be offered or sold in the US or to US persons without registration or pursuant to an exemption.

3.1.2   Securities Exchange Act (1934)

The Securities Exchange Act aims at providing governance of securities transactions on the secondary market (after issue) and regulating exchanges and broker–dealers in order to protect the investing public. The Securities Exchange Act created the SEC and assigned it broad regulatory and oversight powers on securities markets, self-regulatory organizations including stock exchanges, and the conduct of personnel such as brokers, dealers, and investment advisers involved in security trading. All companies listed on stock exchanges must follow the requirements set forth in the Securities Exchange Act. Its primary requirements include the registration of securities (Form S-1), but also periodic reporting requirements (Section 13), proxy requirements (Section 14) and insider reporting and short swing profit provisions (Section 16).

Hedge funds may be affected by the Securities Exchange Act in two ways.

- Hedge funds may be considered as dealers rather than traders. Section 3(a)(5) of the Securities Exchange Act generally defines a dealer as "a person that is engaged in the business of buying and selling securities for its own account". By contrast, a trader is "a person that buys and sells securities, either individually or in a trustee capacity, but not as part of a regular business". The distinction is subtle, but crucial, because dealers need to register while traders are normally exempted. To avoid registration under the Securities Exchange Act, hedge funds must trade solely on their own account and refrain from executing trades directly for clients. In particular, the fund's adviser as well as any of the fund's employees must not receive any transaction-related compensation when buying or selling securities from or to US investors, since this would qualify them as dealers, therefore requiring registration. Moreover, a trader should not be posting simultaneously both a bid and an ask price for a particular security in an inter-dealer quotation system.
- Hedge funds may have more than 500 investors. Section 12(g) of the Securities Exchange Act requires that any issuer having 500 holders of record of a class of equity security and assets in excess of $10 million at the end of its most recently ended fiscal year register its equity security under the Securities Exchange Act. To avoid registration, hedge funds should therefore always have less than 500 investors.

Note that all hedge funds, like any other large institutional managers, are subject to disclosure if they hold large public equity positions. In particular, Sections 13(d) and 13(g) of the Securities Exchange Act require the reporting of information with respect to long positions relevant to corporate control and its transfer (i.e. more than 5% of a class of equity security registered pursuant to Section 12 of the Securities Exchange Act). In addition, Section 13(f) requires hedge fund managers who exercise investment discretion over $100 million or more of equity securities registered under Section 12 to disclose their long positions on a quarterly basis. This information is available to the general public. However, this disclosure does not necessarily provide significant insight into any particular hedge fund's portfolios or strategies because (i) it is aggregated, (ii) the short positions are not disclosed, and (iii) it is delayed and the portfolio may have changed in the meantime.

The soft dollar practice

The Securities Exchange Act also regulates the way hedge fund advisers pay for the services provided by their brokers, and in particular the "hard dollar" (the adviser pays with his own funds) versus the "soft dollar" payments (the payment is subsidized by investors).

In the US, prior to 1975, brokerage commission rates were fixed at artificially high levels by the rules of various securities exchanges. The only way for brokers to compete and attract new clients was by offering them additional "free" services, such as access to in-house and third party research. In 1975, the Congress abolished fixed brokerage commission rates and introduced negotiated rates, but some brokers continued to provide research in exchange for higher commissions. Since then, with the emergence of prime brokers and the increase in competition, the popularity of soft dollar accounts has grown substantially. In a typical soft dollar arrangement, a hedge fund agrees to place a designated dollar value of trading commission business with a broker. In consideration for this promise, the broker provides the fund adviser with credits usually set as a percentage of the promised commissions. The adviser may use these credits to buy any third-party service (e.g. third party research, price and news delivery systems, portfolio management tools), and the broker pays the bill by cancelling the appropriate number of credits from the fund's soft dollar account.

Soft dollars are particularly attractive for new hedge funds that need to focus their limited resources on asset gathering. However, the potential agency problems with soft dollars are numerous. First, the adviser may use the services he obtained through the soft dollar arrangement for purposes unrelated to the management of the accounts effectively paying for the brokerage service.[6] Second, a soft dollar agreement may conflict with a client's interest, e.g. a best execution policy by using the broker with the lowest commission rate, and therefore violates the investment adviser's fiduciary duty to his clients. As an illustration, Conrad, Johnson and Wahal (1998) found that soft dollar trades added approximately 17% to the cost of a representative transaction. Third, the costs and benefits of soft dollar trades and research should be allocated among all the accounts and strategies run by the investment adviser, which is not an easy task. There are inherent flaws with almost any way the allocations can be made, and being fair often requires the patience of Job, the fortitude of Hercules and the cunning of Inspector Columbo.

Soft dollars are obviously a potential source of conflicts of interest. Nevertheless, Section 28(e) of the Securities Exchange Act provides a haven for investment managers using client commissions to pay for research and brokerage if three conditions are met:

- The expense must be associated with eligible brokerage[7] or research[8] products or services.
- The expense must provide lawful and appropriate assistance to the manager in the performance of his investment decision-making responsibilities.
- The investment manager must make a good faith determination that the commission paid is reasonable in relation to the goods and services provided by the broker.

To avoid abuses, the SEC has also provided some guidelines regarding the definition of *research*. Expenses related to travel, entertainment, office equipment, office furniture and business supplies, telephone lines, rent, accounting fees and software, website design, email software, internet services, legal fees, personnel management, marketing, utilities, membership dues, professional licensing fees and software to assist with administrative functions such as managing back-office functions, operating systems and word processing are no longer covered

---

[6] There have been several cases of misappropriation of soft dollars from clients in the US – the SEC has for instance settled charges against Republic New-York Securities Corporation, a New York broker-dealer firm and Sweeney Capital Management Inc., a San Francisco investment adviser.

[7] Brokerage includes all products and services that the manager uses, from communicating with a broker to execute an order through the point at which the funds or securities are delivered to the fund's account.

[8] Research includes advice, analyses and reports that reflect the expression of reasoning or knowledge, as well as access to databases, quantitative analytical software and research seminars.

Box 3.2 What is an investment company?

Section 3(a)(1)(A) of the Investment Company Act defines an investment company as any issuer which is or holds itself out as being engaged primarily, or proposes to engage primarily, in the business of investing, reinvesting or trading in securities.

Section 3(a)(1)(C) of the Investment Company Act defines an investment company as an issuer that is engaged or proposes to engage in the business of investing, reinvesting, owning, holding or trading in securities, and owns or proposes to acquire investment securities having a value exceeding 40% of the value of its total assets (exclusive of government securities and cash items) on an unconsolidated basis.

---

by the safe harbour. Expenses for mixed-use items (items with research and non-research uses) need to be allocated between their safe harbour and non-safe harbour uses, and that allocation needs to be documented.

3.1.3 Investment Company Act

Enforced by the SEC, the Investment Company Act regulates the organization of companies that engage primarily in investing, reinvesting and trading in securities, and whose own securities are offered to the general public (Box 3.2). Its main goals are to protect the general public and prevent abuses by regulating (i) the registration of investment companies; (ii) transactions between an investment company and its affiliate, e.g. the investment adviser to the investment company; (iii) purchases and sales of investment company shares, and (iv) the responsibilities of the investment company's directors or trustees.

In theory, any investment pool that meets the definition of an investment company should register under the Investment Company Act and abide by its regulations. Being registered implies several restrictions on the types of investments that one may hold as well as on the investment strategy, in particular relative to the ability to leverage positions,[9] use derivatives, engage in short selling,[10] purchase less liquid securities or run a concentrated portfolio.[11] It also imposes a considerable amount of disclosure on the content of portfolios. Not surprisingly, hedge funds, which would normally fall under the definition of an investment company, often attempt to qualify for non-registration by using the exceptions of Sections 3(c)(1) and 3(c)(7).

Section 3(c)(1) excludes from the definition of investment company any issuer whose outstanding securities (other than short-term paper) are owned by not more than 100 US beneficial owners. In addition, the issuer should not publicly offer its securities, which is fine if the hedge fund relies on the safe harbour available under Regulation D.

Note that counting to 100 is not as straightforward as it might seem. Initially, if an entity comprising several investors had control over 10% or more of the outstanding voting securities of a fund, then the fund had to look through the investing entity and count each of its investors. Since the introduction of the National Securities Market Improvement Act of 1996, a company can own more than 10% of a hedge fund's securities and still be considered one beneficial

---

[9] Section 18(f)(1) of the Investment Company Act generally allows open-end investment companies to leverage themselves only by borrowing from a bank, and provided that the borrowing is subject to 300% asset coverage.

[10] Registered investment companies are required to disclose their short-selling activity in their financial statements that accompany their annual and semi-annual reports.

[11] Section 13(a)(3) of the Investment Company Act requires registered investment companies to obtain the consent of their shareholders before deviating from their fundamental policies, including to concentrate a portfolio in certain industries.

Box 3.3   What is a qualified purchaser?

There are four categories of qualified purchasers (also referred to as "super-accredited" investors):

- Individuals (including holders of joint or community property) owning investments[12] of at least $5 million.
- Family-owned businesses owning not less than $5 million in investments.
- Trusts not formed for the specific purpose of acquiring the securities offered, whose trustees or equivalent decision makers, and whose settlers or other asset contributors, are all qualified purchasers.
- Any person (acting for his own account or for other qualified purchasers) who has discretion over $25 million in investments.

---

owner of the fund, as long as the value of that company's securities in the fund is less than 10% of the company's total assets. Note also that an offshore hedge fund that relies on Section 3(c)(1) may exclude non-US investors when determining whether it is in compliance with the 100-investor limitation.

One may think that hedge fund managers could attempt to circumvent the 100-investor limitation simply by opening as many US funds as needed and running them in parallel. But, under the current rules, if a manager runs more than one hedge fund, their investment strategies should not be similar; otherwise, regulators consider the series of funds as being essentially the same entity for the 100-investor count and therefore require their manager to register.

Section 3(c)(7) excludes from the definition of investment company any issuer whose outstanding securities are owned exclusively by persons who, at the time of acquisition of such securities, are *qualified purchasers* (Box 3.3). In addition, the issuer should not publicly offer its securities – which is fine if the hedge fund relies on the safe harbour available under Regulation D.

A fund relying on Section 3(c)(7) could theoretically have an unlimited number of qualified purchasers; in practice, however, most funds are subject to a 499 investors limit in order to avoid the registration and reporting requirements of the Securities Exchange Act.

Note that:

- Section 3(c)(7) does not have a "look-through" provision in the event that a registered investment company or a private investment company owns 10% or more of the fund's outstanding voting securities. A Section 3(c)(7) fund is only required to look through any company (investment company or otherwise) that invests in its shares to determine whether that company's investors are qualified purchasers if the company was "formed for the purpose" of investing in the Section 3(c)(7) fund.
- Rule 2a51-3 under the Investment Company Act provides that any company may be deemed to be a qualified purchaser if each beneficial owner of the company's securities is a qualified purchaser. The staff of the Division of Investment Management takes the position that a hedge fund that is incorporated offshore but relies on Section 3(c)(7) to offer its securities privately in the United States is not subject to the qualified purchaser requirements with respect to its investors who are non-US residents.

---

[12] Rule 2a51-1 under the Investment Company Act defines the term "investments" for purposes of Section 2(a)(51), and details how the value of a qualified purchaser's investments should be calculated.

- There are also alternative ways for some investment pools to avoid the qualification of an investment company. For instance, pools that do not invest in securities (e.g. commodity pools) are not investment companies and therefore are not subject to the Investment Company Act.

3.1.4 Investment Advisers Act (1940)

The Investment Advisers Act was promulgated to regulate the actions of investment advisers. With certain exceptions, this Act requires that firms or sole practitioners compensated for advising others about securities investments must register with the SEC and conform to a myriad of regulations designed to protect investors. These include extensive record-keeping requirements and restrictions on performance-based fees (Box 3.4).

For a long time, only a few hedge fund advisers were registered as investment advisers with the SEC, primarily because their US institutional clients made it a prerequisite to investing. But the majority of hedge fund advisers were not registered. Instead, they took advantage of the so-called "private adviser exemption" under Section 203(b)(3) of the Investment Advisers Act. Under this Section, an investment adviser was not required to register with the SEC if (i) it had fewer than 15 "clients" during the preceding 12 months, (ii) it did not hold itself out generally to the public as an investment adviser and (iii) it was not an adviser to any SEC registered investment company. The opening lay in Rule 203(b)(3)-1, which provided guidance in relation to the definition of a "client". It stated that an investment adviser could count a legal organization as a single client as long as the investment advice provided was based on the objectives of the legal organization rather than the individual investment objectives of any owner of the legal organization. Consequently, a hedge fund manager could manage up to 14 hedge funds, regardless of the number of hedge fund investors, without triggering the obligation to register with the SEC as an investment adviser under the Investment Advisers Act.

Over the years, it became clear that the prior safe harbour had become inconsistent with the apparent purpose of Section 203(b)(3) to exempt a category of advisers whose activities were not sufficiently large or national in scope to justify federal regulation. In particular, the SEC was concerned that the objectives of the Act might be substantially undermined if an adviser with more than 15 clients could evade its registration obligation through the simple expedient of having those clients invest in a limited partnership or similar fund vehicle. This concern was strengthened by the fact that the growth of non-registered hedge funds had been accompanied by an increase in the enforcement actions involving registered hedge fund advisers. Between 1999 and 2004, the SEC instituted 46 enforcement actions against hedge fund advisers for having defrauded investors or using a hedge fund to defraud others. The SEC therefore wanted to close the loophole, but without imposing burdens on the legitimate investment activities of hedge funds.

Following a heated debate on 14 July 2004, the SEC approved a new Rule 203(b)(3)-2 under the Investment Advisers Act to close that loophole. This rule fundamentally changed

---

Box 3.4   What is an investment adviser?

Section 202(a)(11) of the Investment Advisers Act generally defines an investment adviser as "any person who, for compensation, engages in the business of advising others, either directly or through publications or writings, as to the value of securities or as to the advisability of investing in, purchasing, or selling securities, or who, for compensation and as part of a regular business, issues or promulgates analyses or reports concerning securities."

Box 3.5   What is a private fund?

A private fund is defined as any company, including trusts and partnerships:

- that would be subject to regulation under the Investment Company Act of 1940 but uses the exception provided in either Section 3(c)(1) or Section 3(c)(7) of the Investment Company Act;
- that permits investors to redeem interests in the fund within two years of purchasing them (except for extraordinary redemptions or redemptions of interests acquired through reinvested capital gains or income); and interests which are being or have been offered based on the investment advisory skills, ability or expertise of the investment adviser.

---

the method by which clients are counted. It stipulates that, when eligibility for registration exemption is being determined, advisers to *private funds* (Box 3.5) that manage more than $30 million are requested to look through the fund and count each person who invests in it as a client. In addition, an adviser to a private fund in which a registered investment company or another private fund invests should look through these entities and count their investors as its own clients. Needless to say, under the new rule, most hedge fund advisers had to register by the 1 February 2006 deadline.

Note that the new registration requirement also applies if an investment adviser was already registered as such with a state securities authority or as a commodity trading adviser or commodity pool operator with the CFTC. An investment adviser with less than $25 million in gross assets under management (without reducing the amount by any borrowings) is not eligible to register with the SEC, but remains subject to state investment adviser regulation if applicable in the relevant state. An adviser with at least $25 million but less than $30 million under management may register but it is not a requirement.

An important point concerning the new regulation is that advisers in non-US jurisdictions may also need to register. They are also required to look through the funds they manage and count their investors, regardless of whether those funds are located in a US or non-US jurisdiction. If they qualify for registration, non-US advisers are then subject to jurisdiction in the US as well as to periodic examination by the SEC. However, the SEC has limited the application of the new rule to offshore advisers in the following ways:

- For purposes of counting clients, non-US advisers only have to count US residents that invested in their funds or were otherwise advisory clients starting 1 February 2006. Advisers doing business in the US, in contrast, must count all of their investors regardless of their place of residence.
- US residency is determined at the time of investment or transfer of investment, regardless of any subsequent relocation of the investor. The decision is based on (i) in the case of individuals, their residence, (ii) in the case of corporations and other business entities, their principal office and place of business and (iii) in the case of discretionary or non-discretionary accounts managed by another investment adviser, the location of the person for whose benefit the account is held.
- For the purpose of the Investment Advisers Act, non-US advisers can treat an offshore private fund as a single client, rather than having to look through to count its investors.

The new rules provide an exemption from the definition of "private fund" for those funds regulated in a non-US country that are making public offerings in that country, as well as

---

Box 3.6 Two year lock-ups

On 8 December 2005, in response to a request by the American Bar Association Subcommittee on Private Investment Entities, the SEC released interpretive guidance to clarify the two-year lock-up rule. Simply stated, investors must maintain their investment in a hedge fund for two *full* years.

The rule applies equally to US and non-US investors, as well as to the personnel and principals of the adviser. The only accepted exceptions are:

- A transfer between classes of a multi-class fund, if the two classes share the same underlying portfolio and provide the same redemption rights (i.e. above two years).
- Redemptions due to "extraordinary" events, for example, when it becomes impractical or illegal for an investor to continue to hold the interest, when redemption is necessary to avoid materially adverse tax, regulatory or ERISA consequences, when an investor dies or becomes disabled, when an entity owner ceases to operate bona fide, and when key personnel of the adviser die or become disabled. Note that a significant withdrawal of an investment by its adviser or its principals is not considered an extraordinary event.
- The redemption of incentive fees and accrued performance compensation by the adviser. Fees earned by a manager are deemed part of compensation and are not subject to the two-year lock-up.

An adviser may not, however, use side letters to circumvent the two-year lock-up; the SEC has stated that a hedge fund whose documents require a two-year lock-up but that enters into side letters with some investors allowing them to redeem within two years will be treated as a "private fund" and will therefore need to register.

---

for US-based funds that impose on their investors an initial lock-up in excess of two years (Box 3.6). This two-year exemption was initially intended to exempt private equity funds, venture capital funds and similar funds having a medium to long-term investment horizon.

What does SEC registration entail?

Although all advisers, whether or not required to be registered with the SEC, are subject to the Investment Advisers Act's anti-fraud and anti-manipulation provisions, advisers subject to SEC registration are required to comply with many additional requirements and rules.

In order to register, an investment adviser must file a *Form ADV* which contains two parts.

- Part I contains information regarding the firm, the firm's business practices, the persons who own and control it (directly or indirectly), and the person who provides investment advice on the firm's behalf, as well as the minimum investment commitment, current value of assets and other information about each private fund that an investment adviser or its related person manages. It also reports disciplinary events involving the firm or persons affiliated with the firm. Part IA must be filed electronically with the SEC, using the Investment Advisers Registration Depository (IARD).[13] The filing cost is based on the firm's assets under management, with a maximum of $1100 initial set-up fee and $550 annual update fee for firms with more than $100 million of assets. Part IB consists of additional information

---

[13] See http://www.sec.gov/divisions/investment/iard.shtml.

required by various state securities authorities. It must be completed by firms if they are registering with one or more state securities authorities.

- Part II is known as the brochure. It must be provided to all clients and updated as often as necessary. It contains information about the advisory services offered by the firm, the fees being charged, the way securities are analysed, and the discretion the adviser has over clients' investments, as well as general background information about the adviser and a description of his potential conflicts of interest.

Once an investment adviser has registered with the SEC by filing Form ADV, he must comply with all the requirements of the Investment Advisers Act. In particular:

- Registered investment advisers must have a *written compliance manual* in place and implement all its provisions.[14] The compliance manual should be reviewed annually and include at least policies for portfolio management processes (including trade allocation among clients and consistency of portfolios with clients' investment objectives, disclosures by the adviser and applicable regulatory restriction), proxy voting policies and procedures, trading practices (including the use of soft dollars, personal securities trading allowance and best execution), record keeping, marketing activities, disaster recovery and valuation.
- Registered investment advisers must designate a competent and knowledgeable *Chief Compliance Officer (CCO)* to oversee their compliance programme and keep abreast of new developments in hedge fund regulation. For smaller advisers, the SEC has stated that they may designate a business person as the chief compliance officer if that person is qualified – which requires at least undergoing compliance and securities law training.
- Registered investment advisers must adopt a *Code of Ethics* to address issues such as conflicts of interest, personal securities reporting, pre-approval of certain transactions and reporting of violations of the code of ethics.
- Registered investment advisers must *maintain books and records* for almost everything they do regarding the management of clients' money for a period of five years. This includes:
  - Accounting records: cash receipts and disbursement journals, cheque books, bank statements, cancelled cheques, invoices, profit and loss statements, balance sheets and trial balances.
  - Advisory records: trade tickets, written communications (including trade confirmation, internal and external emails and instant messages) and due diligence research.
  - Personal trading records: duplicate accounts statements and confirms of all personal trades of all of the adviser's personnel.
  - Other records: marketing and advertising materials, limited trading powers of attorney, written agreements, Form ADVs, solicitor's acknowledgements, trading blotters, securities cross references and proxy voting records.
  - Emails sent and received in an electronically searchable format.

Not only do these records have to be saved in a secure location, they also have to be readily retrievable and promptly produced to the SEC staff upon request. Electronic filing is accepted as long as a backup copy exists. Most documents must be maintained for two years in the adviser's office. Some documents must be retained for longer, even after the time the hedge fund goes out of business.

---

[14] Several UK hedge fund advisers who now will have to operate under the dual registration FSA/SEC had to fit the two regulatory regimes into one single manual. This is really an achievement, as the two regulators are sometimes incompatible, the FSA being principles-based and the SEC rules-based.

- Rule 204-2 (the "Recordkeeping Rule") states that registered investment advisers should have sufficient documentation to allow a complete recalculation of performance, e.g. the original records showing what was purchased, what was sold, etc. Note that this only applies to periods after 10 February 2006 for newly registered advisers. Existing hedge funds that were required to register as a result of the new rule may still include their past performance in their presentations, even if they have not previously retained all of the records required to support it.
- Registered investment advisers must maintain each hedge fund's assets (and the assets of the adviser's other clients) with a qualified custodian and notify the fund's investors where those assets are held. Unless the hedge fund distributes annual financial statements audited in accordance with the Generally Accepted Accounting Principles (GAAP) within 180 days of the end of the fund's fiscal year, an SEC registered adviser must also arrange for the fund's account statements to be sent rapidly to the fund's investors.

In addition, registered investment advisers face restrictions on performance fees. For example, under Rule 205-3 of the Investment Advisers Act, registered advisers may only charge performance fees to qualified clients that have net worth of at least $1.5 million or have at least $750 000 of assets under management with them. Advisers to 3(c)(1) funds must therefore either develop procedures to ensure that all *new* investors are qualified clients or create a separate class of interests that is not charged a performance fee. Consequently, all accredited investors under Regulation D of the Securities Act who are not qualified clients under the Investment Advisers Act will be kept from investing in hedge funds since hedge fund managers will not choose to forgo the 20% carry they typically charge. However, note that the SEC has amended Rule 205-3 (the "Performance Fee Rule") to add a grandfather provision that will allow hedge fund advisers to charge a performance fee to investors in 3(c)(1) funds who are not qualified clients, as long as the person was an existing investor as of 10 February 2005.

Last but not least, registered investment advisers are subject to periodic on-site examinations by the SEC, which can occur as frequently as every two years and last from one week to several months. The SEC inspection staff may also conduct more frequent sweep examinations that focus on a few specific issues, as well as "for cause" examinations. If deficiencies are identified, the SEC sends a deficiency letter noting violations or control weaknesses uncovered during the examination within 90 days after its on-site visit. The hedge fund manager must take corrective action within 30 days of receiving the SEC's letter. Historically, approximately 90% of all SEC examinations resulted in a deficiency letter.

Not surprisingly, lots of criticisms were aimed at the new hedge fund regulation. Some said that it would drive hedge funds offshore, and that the cost of compliance would erect entry barriers and keep new funds from launching.[15] Others were afraid that the new regulation might deter hedge fund managers from undertaking new and innovative investment strategies, leading to less efficient, less liquid and less stable financial markets. A few voices suggested that registration would not add to the SEC's ability to combat hedge fund frauds.[16] As the SEC's own report stated, "both registered and unregistered investment advisers have engaged in fraud". (See Box 3.7.)

---

[15] The SEC estimates filing fees of approximately $1000 in the first year and approximately $500 subsequently. In addition, the SEC estimates average initial compliance costs of $20 000 in professional fees and $25 000 in internal costs including staff time.

[16] Out of the 46 enforcement actions instituted by the SEC against hedge funds from 1999 to 2004, eight cases involved hedge fund advisers who were already registered, and five cases involved advisers that would be required to register under the new rule. The remaining cases were related to managers that were still too small to register, broker dealers (which are already regulated) or cases that would have occurred anyway. Most frauds involved valuation problems, and only perfectly timed inspections would have improved the SEC's detection of the frauds at issue.

Box 3.7 Springer Asset Management and the Apollo Fund

From 2000 to 2002, Keith Springer and his investment firm, Springer Investment Management, misrepresented the performance of the Apollo Fund they managed by overvaluing a privately – held internet security called Citi411.com, which constituted 70% of the fund's holdings. Based in Davis, California, Citi411 was an internet portal company seeking to provide online city guides for second tier cities, predominantly college towns. Citi411's only employee was its majority owner, a 20-year-old college student. Springer's fund was Citi411's first outside investor.

Notwithstanding the dramatic decline in the price of publicly traded internet stocks during the early 2000s, the Apollo Fund continued to value the fund's Citi411.com shares at the price it had paid for them. The fund even increased its valuation from $1 to $5.50 a share in late 2000, without disclosing the change to investors. This allowed the fund to provide misleading assurances of its performance to investors, although the rest of its publicly traded investments declined in value. None the less, the valuation was clearly inflated, as other individuals (including Springer himself) bought additional shares at an average price of approximately $2.83 per share. However, Keith Springer was the fund's sole full-time employee and had full control on its valuation.

From late 2000 until October 2002, the Apollo Fund did not adjust the pricing of its Citi411 holdings, and continued to report its performance based on the $5.50 per share stock valuation. Citi411 purported to derive the $5.50 stock price from the company's projected price/earnings ratio – although Citi411 had no actual earnings at the time; it was failing to meet its business objectives and had not added the requisite investors needed to fund its business plan. Later on, the SEC reported that Citi411 had erroneously calculated the P/E ratio used for its financial projections by using revenue, rather than earnings, resulting in a substantially embellished financial picture.

In its June 2002 statement, the Apollo Fund stated that "Citi411 continues to show relatively strong performance in its business and the share price has once again held steady, largely because it is a privately held company and not subject to the emotional roller coaster that all other publicly traded stocks are."

The SEC examined the Apollo Fund in October 2002, and requested the Citi411 position to be written down to half its value. In addition, the SEC found that Springer had failed to update his Form ADV to mention a prior disciplinary matter. In 1999, when Keith Springer was employed as a registered representative of a broker–dealer, he made improper post-execution trade-asset allocations at the expense of his clients. The New York Stock Exchange censured him and barred him from membership and from employment or association in any capacity with any member or member organization for four years – a decision subsequently upheld by the SEC. While the Form ADV disclosed the violation and initially properly reported that it was under appeal, Springer failed to update the form when his appeal failed.

As often happens in the US, the case was resolved by an agreement. Springer Investment Management and Keith Springer agreed to cease and desist from wrongful actions, to be censured and to pay a $50 000 fine. In settling, neither admitted nor denied the allegations against them. The fund also agreed to distribute the administrative order to clients and potential clients for one year, and to retain an independent consultant to review its pricing of non-public equity securities and its Form ADV filings for one year.

Box 3.8   So, where does that leave us today?

As of 31 March 2006, just over 10 000 advisers were registered with the SEC.

- Of these 10 000 advisers, approximately 2400 (24%) were hedge fund advisers.
- Of these 2400 registered hedge fund advisers, 1 149 (46%) registered with the SEC after adoption of the new rule (most did so by the 1 February 2006 compliance date; 170 did so after 1 February but before 31 March 2006).
- The vast majority of registered hedge fund advisers are based in the US (over 2100, or 88% of the 2400 total). In contrast, 165 hedge fund advisers based in the UK (7% of the 2400) are registered with the SEC.
- Since 1 February 2006, the Commission's Office of Compliance Inspections and Examinations has started 375 examinations of advisers and funds. Of these, 88 (or 23.4%) came from hedge fund advisers.

A number of members of Congress publicly opposed the rule, and Alan Greenspan himself declared in a testimony before the Senate: "I grant you that registering advisers in and of itself is not a problem. The question is: What is the purpose of that unless you are going to go further? And therefore I feel uncomfortable about that issue." The Managed Funds Association and a number of hedge fund attorneys have also lobbied against the registration (Box 3.8). Many of the largest hedge funds have shown little interest in registration and have announced that they would take advantage of the two-year lock-up provision or have stopped taking new money to avoid the reach of regulators.[17] Last but not least, many people have questioned whether the SEC, which is woefully underfinanced and understaffed, would have the resources to provide the necessary oversight of the hedge fund industry. The question is especially relevant because all the qualified resources – including numerous ones of the SEC – were willing to join hedge funds, most of the time as Chief Compliance Officers, to prepare their registration process. Nevertheless, the new registration rule was only voted by a slim 3–2 majority, over strong dissent from two SEC commissioners, Glassman and Atkins, who insisted that their dissenting opinion be included in the proposing release.

The whole issue of investment adviser registration was seriously challenged in a court case brought by petitioners Philip Goldstein, Kimball & Winthrop, and Opportunity Partners L.P. against the SEC (see Box 3.9). The SEC lost the case, did not appeal the ruling and, as of 7 August 2006, the Court decision to vacate the registration rule became final.

In a statement, the SEC Chairman Christopher Cox indicated that the SEC "concluded that, since the appellate court's decision was based on multiple grounds and was unanimous, further appeal would be futile and would simply delay and distract from our goal of advancing investor protection." Many hedge fund professionals generally cheered the prospect of apparent liberation from SEC oversight, but quickly realised that the court ruling represents only a pause in increasing regulation, not a retreat. Christopher Cox announced that the SEC might soon seek to regulate hedge funds in new ways, with separate anti-fraud mechanisms or by increasing the minimum asset and income requirements for individuals who invest in hedge funds, possibly by amending the definition of "accredited investor". It also plans to issue guidance encouraging

---

[17] *The Wall Street Journal* named SAC Capital Management LLC, Kingdon Capital Management LLC, Citadel Investment Group PLC, Eton Park Capital Management LLP; Lone Pine Capital and Greenlight Capital as firms that are opting out of SEC investment adviser registration.

Box 3.9   Goldstein versus the SEC – David versus Goliath

Philip Goldstein is a shareholder activist who runs the small Bulldog Investors hedge fund. Goldstein called the registration rule "overreaching" and said it would lead to SEC "fishing expeditions" that displace valuable time from managing money to "filling out forms and checklists." His view was that the SEC exceeded its regulatory authority, as a ruling forcing hedge funds to register with regulators should have come from Congress – not from the regulators themselves. In addition, Goldstein challenged the SEC's constitutional rights, since it should have a statutory basis to adopt rules. Last but not least, Goldstein challenged the look-through rule by arguing that the SEC incorrectly equated the term "client" with "investor".

To the general surprise, the Court rejected the SEC's arguments and vacated the new SEC rule that effectively required most hedge fund managers to register as investment advisers under the Investment Advisers Act (the "Hedge Fund Rule"). In particular, the Court stated that even though the term "client" does not have a statutory definition, this does not automatically render the meaning of the word ambiguous. Because the hedge fund adviser does not directly advise the fund's investors ("the adviser does not tell the investor how to spend his money; the investor made that decision when he invested in the fund"), it follows that the entity controlling the fund is not an investment adviser to the investors and thus each investor cannot be a "client" of the fund adviser. Therefore, the Court concluded that the SEC's interpretation of the word "client" in the look-through rule "comes close to violating the plain language of the statute" and "at best it is counterintuitive to characterize the investors in a hedge fund as the 'clients' of the adviser."

---

voluntary registration and providing incentives for advisers to remain registered. As of this writing, no proposed new or amended rules have been issued, and the specifics of any new or amended rules are unclear.

3.1.5   Blue-sky laws

In addition to the federal laws discussed above, each US state has its own statutes and regulations that supplement the federal laws and govern the offer and sale of securities into or from such states or to residents of such states. These laws are nicknamed 'blue-sky laws' after the preamble to an early Wisconsin law designed to prevent companies from selling pieces of the blue sky to unsuspecting investors. In theory, compliance with a state's blue-sky laws needs to be determined before any offer is made into or from the state or to a resident of such a state. Fortunately, in 1956, a Uniform Securities Act was adopted in about 40 states to bring some consistency to state securities regulation, and to integrate that system as far as possible into the federal securities laws.

3.1.6   National Securities Markets Improvement Act (1996)

On 11 October 1996, President Clinton signed the National Securities Markets Improvement Act (NSMIA), which has been modestly described by its sponsors as the "first major overhaul of securities law in 60 years". The NSMIA was essentially an attempt to update and amend previous security acts and create one uniform code that companies and regulators could follow. It provides several crucial amendments to the above-mentioned Acts and liberalizes a number of rules affecting investment companies that are exempt from registration with the SEC.

In particular, the Act:

- Impacts a fund's ability to sell interests to more than 99 investors by adding a new Section 3(c)(7) to the Investment Company Act, which excludes from the definition of "investment company" any issuer whose securities are privately offered and owned solely by qualified purchasers. It also allows Section 3(c)(1) funds to convert into Section 3(c)(7) funds and be covered by the expanded exemptions, provided that existing beneficial owners are given an opportunity to redeem.
- Includes a "grandfather" clause, which enables non-qualified beneficial owners of Section 3(c)(1) funds that convert to Section 3(c)(7) funds to continue to participate in the fund and even increase their investments.
- Pre-empts the blue-sky registration for federally registered investment advisers offering and selling fund interests to "qualified purchasers".
- Simplifies the "look-through" provisions. Previously, if certain types of entities such as endowments and foundations owned more than 10% of the fund's assets, the "look-through" rule would count them as multiple investors. Under the new law, they are counted as one single investor.
- Changes the requirements to comply with state blue-sky laws regarding registration as an investment adviser.
- Enhances a registered adviser's ability to charge performance-based fees.

By removing some arbitrary and burdensome limits and recognizing that some smart investors do not need these protections, the National Securities Markets Improvement Act has significantly reshaped the landscape of the hedge fund industry. In particular, it has effectively increased the number of hedge funds and investors that would be exempt from government regulation.

3.1.7   Employee Retirement Income Security Act (1974)

The Employee Retirement Income Security Act (ERISA) is a federal law that establishes legal guidelines for private pension and employee benefit plans. Its aim is to protect the interests of employees and their beneficiaries (such as spouses and children) who are enrolled in pension plans. In particular, ERISA requires participants to receive disclosure and reporting and establishes the obligations and responsibilities of the "fiduciaries" that administer the plans.

Hedge funds may be affected by ERISA rules and standards if more than 25% of the capital in any class of their equity comes from ERISA investors. In practice, most hedge funds simply keep investments from ERISA plans below the 25% limit to avoid falling under its associated requirements.

3.1.8   Other regulations

Hedge funds and hedge fund managers, both registered and unregistered, are subject to the extensive anti-fraud provisions of the Securities Act (Section 17), the Securities Exchange Act (Section 10 and Rule 10b-5) and the Investment Advisers Act. The anti-fraud provisions apply to any offer, sale or purchase of securities, or any advisory service of such offer, sale or purchase.

Furthermore, hedge funds must not engage in activities that are considered detrimental to market integrity, such as market manipulation and insider trading.

Following the 11 September tragedy, the Uniting and Strengthening America by Providing Appropriate Tools Required to Intercept and Obstruct Terrorism Act of 2001 (USA PATRIOT Act) was signed into law on 26 October 2001. To prevent terrorist funds being laundered, this Act requires all financial institutions, including hedge funds, to establish an anti-money-laundering programme by 24 April 2002. Section 352 of the USA PATRIOT Act also imposes minimum internal policies, procedures and controls, a compliance officer, an ongoing employee training programme, and an independent audit function.

3.1.9   The Commodity Futures Trading Commission

The Commodity Futures Trading Commission (CFTC) is a federal regulatory body established by the Commodity Exchange Act in 1974. It has exclusive jurisdiction over all US commodity futures trading, futures exchanges, futures commission merchants and their agents, floor brokers, floor traders, commodity trading advisers, commodity pool operators, leverage transaction merchants and associated persons of any of the foregoing. It also supervises a self-regulatory organization called the National Futures Association (NFA).

Although there are some notable exceptions, any hedge fund investing in or trading one or more futures or options contracts on a regulated commodity exchange, or soliciting US funds to engage in the purchase and sale of commodity interests, is considered as a commodity pool (CP). The fund manager is considered as a commodity pool operator (CPO), the fund adviser – or more generally, anyone advising on US commodity futures or options on futures – is considered as a commodity trading adviser (CTA).

The Commodity Exchange Act subjects CPOs and CTAs, but not the commodity pools themselves, to registration with the CFTC and compliance with a series of core principles, and also to compliance with the rules of the NFA. These principles are essentially centred on disclosure, ethics training, accounting, reporting and record keeping, and are particularly problematic for hedge funds. As an illustration, let us consider the offering document requirements.

The CFTC mandates that all prospective investors must receive an offering document before a commodity pool may accept subscriptions. This document, which must be approved by the NFA, should contain information on a series of topics such as:

- The various types of securities that will be traded and the investment policies that will be followed by the commodity pool, including any material restriction.
- A detail of all the expenses of the commodity pool, including an expense ratio that includes all trading commissions.
- A tabular presentation of the hypothetical amount of income the commodity pool would have to generate over 12 months in order to offset all expenses allocable or chargeable to the investor and enable the investor to recoup his initial investment upon withdrawal.

The problem is that this type of information is usually not found in the offering memorandum of hedge funds that do not trade exclusively commodity interests. In addition to the offering document, a commodity pool should also provide all its investors with a quarterly account statement, and provide all its investors and the CFTC with annual audited statements within 90 days of the end of the fund's fiscal year. All performance presentations should be in accordance with CFTC rules. This implies calculating performance net of all fees, expenses and performance allocations, and disclosing statistics such as monthly returns, the largest monthly drawdown and the worst "peak to valley" drawdown for the most recent five full years[18] as well as the year to date. Any use of simulated data should be clearly disclosed and accompanied with meaningful disclaimers.

The situation is even worse for a commodity pool investing in other commodity pools, particularly when they start to concentrate their investments. Regulators refer to a commodity pool holding more than 10% of the assets of another commodity pool as a "major investee pool". In such a case, the owning pool operator should report information on all its major investee pools, such as their past returns, volatility, leverage and the strategies they utilized, as well as a five-year business background of their managers. Any significant change in the asset allocation (such as a commodity pool going below or above this 10% threshold) should also be immediately disclosed and amended in a new offering document. The commodity pool operator should also report performance of its major investee pools in accordance with the above-mentioned CFTC principles.

It is amazing to observe that most of these stringent disclosure requirements have a blind spot. They only concern positions on US commodity futures and options exchanges, but not positions in the over-the-counter (OTC) derivatives market. This was particularly striking in the debacle of Long Term Capital Management, which was registered as a commodity pool operator and reported all its positions on US futures exchanges daily to the CFTC. But neither the CFTC nor the US futures exchanges had information on its positions on the OTC derivative markets where most of LTCM's risks were concentrated.

Nevertheless, it is natural that most fund operators and advisers prefer to avoid the complexity of compliance with CFTC registration and rules, as well as the burden of undergoing periodic examinations by NFA examiners. In theory, there are a few exemptions available. Let us quote the major criteria:

- The fund has less than $200 000 in capital and fewer than 15 participants.
- Fund access is restricted to family members.
- The general partner manages only one fund, does not receive any compensation for that, and is not subject to CFTC registration by virtue of its other activities.
- The fund is already regulated by another US domestic federal agency. This is the case for registered investment companies, regulated insurance companies, banks, trust companies and other ERISA fiduciaries.
- The fund avoids any transactions in US-regulated commodity futures and options and uses surrogate instruments, such as over-the-counter instruments or equity index options (which are not regulated by the CFTC).
- The fund limits its security offers to "qualified eligible persons" (QEP). The QEP rule (Rule 4.7) is much more complex than the accredited investor rule applicable to a Regulation D private placement, particularly for non-natural persons and funds of funds.
- The fund is primarily engaged in security transactions. It infrequently uses futures and options on futures, and limits the amount of margins and premiums invested in commodity futures to 10% of the current fair market value of its assets.

To sum up, let us say that qualified eligible persons include: (a) registered commodities and securities professionals; (b) those considered as accredited investors under the 1933 Act who also have an investment portfolio of at least $2 million or $200 000 on deposit as commodities

---

[18] If a fund has less than three years of existence, its partner should then disclose the performance of any other pool he operated during the corresponding five-year period, if any.

margin; (c) attorneys, accountants, auditors and other financial service providers similarly engaged whose activities and degree of sophistication would merit their being treated as qualified eligible participants; and (d) non-US persons.

While significant profits can be made in trading commodity futures and options, these should be weighed against the additional operating expenses, compliance duties and legal risks inherent in these transactions. Given that even a small investment in futures or commodity options could result in significant administrative compliance obligations, most hedge fund managers avoid commodity markets, or maintain their commodity investments below 10% of the market value of their fund.

3.2   THE SITUATION IN EUROPE

As we have just seen, the US regulators have adopted a sort of Coasean approach. Rather than imposing mandatory "one-size-fits-all" requirements on hedge funds, they have set default rules, but allow sophisticated investors and hedge fund managers the flexibility to opt out and set up negotiated contracts. This flexibility provides an important safety valve against the risk of overregulation. In contrast, it seems that European regulators prefer to adopt strict operating rules or even simply prohibit hedge funds without conceding any alternative, only to observe finally in dismay that both hedge fund managers and their investors . . . have migrated to more favourable and accommodating locations.

3.2.1   The UCITS directives and mutual fund regulation

Since the European Economic Community was established in 1957, one of the fundamental principles underlying the process of European integration was the creation of a single internal market, in which four fundamental freedoms – the free movement of goods, people, services and capital – would be assured. By the early 1980s, this objective had been partly achieved in specific domains, but was still an aspiration for financial markets and services. In particular, the mutual fund situation was clearly unsatisfactory. As each state in Europe had maintained its own system of financial regulation and supervision, European mutual funds had to grapple with a multiplicity of legal systems,[19] regulators, supervisors and tax codes, several official languages, domestic investment laws and country-specific distribution rules, as well as less tangible, difficult to define, yet very real cultural barriers. Cross-border distribution was complex, burdensome and costly, and therefore almost non-existent. Consequently, most European mutual funds were created, managed, administered[20] and distributed almost exclusively on a national scale. This resulted in an excessive fragmentation of the mutual fund industry and in higher costs, which were ultimately passed on to European investors through higher fees and lower yields on their savings.[21] By contrast, US mutual funds had only one regulator, one tax code, one language and a single legal framework; they enjoyed multi-channel distribution and fund supermarkets, and the larger average fund size allowed for significant economies of scale.

In December 1985, the European Community approved the Directive 85/611/EEC on "the

---

[19] Some EU countries, such as France, Italy and Germany, have legal systems based on the Napoleonic Code, while other countries' legal systems are based on common law.

[20] Some member States required fund administration to be located in the fund's domicile. Therefore, a fund group with funds domiciled in several member States was not able to centralize its administrative operations.

[21] As foreseen in the Cecchini Report, the price Europe has been paying for not having a single European financial market has also been slower economic growth, stagnation and a massive increase in structural unemployment.

coordination of legislative, regulatory and administrative provisions relating to Undertakings for Collective Investment in Transferable Securities" or UCITS – a complicated way of saying "funds". The primary goal of UCITS was to create a single passport for the marketing and distribution of mutual funds across the 15 member countries. Under UCITS, the home country was responsible for regulating funds, while rules regarding disclosure and selling practices were a host country matter. The Directive also provided that member States should have introduced the relevant national laws, regulations or provisions pursuant to the aims of the Directive no later than 1 October 1989, with the exception of Greece and Portugal.[22]

Despite its praiseworthy intentions, the UCITS directive was only a qualified success:

- The range of UCITS funds was restricted to those investing in "transferable securities", i.e. basically shares and bonds. Rules preventing the holding of cash and money market instruments other than as ancillary liquid assets effectively prevented the creation of UCITS money market funds or UCITS funds of funds.
- In theory, once a fund had been licensed as a UCITS in a member State, approval by regulators in any other member State was merely a formality. In practice, the UCITS directive was interpreted and implemented differently in member States. This opened the door to abuse and delays in several States that wanted to prevent an influx of foreign funds competing for market share with their domestic funds. For instance, in Italy, registering a non-Italian UCITS fund for sale could take up to six months, much more than the 60-day waiting period set forth in the Directive.
- The marketing rules were left to individual member States, which led to varied, costly and changing requirements. For instance in Spain, authorities systematically required an official translation of the latest prospectus.
- Several countries had implemented indirect protectionist rules against foreign managers. For example, the German pension product known as the *Altersvorsorge Sondervermögen* or the similar French *Plan d'épargne en actions* were restricted to domestic funds.

As a result, UCITS funds created in one country were predominantly sold to individuals living just round the corner. As reported by Moody's Investor Services in August 2000, only 30% of the then 12 000 registered UCITS were sold truly cross-border, and most of them came from Luxembourg and Dublin, which had evolved as offshore centres within the EU. Dublin tended to be a domicile for rather complex funds targeting institutional and sophisticated investors, e.g. hedge funds or complex fixed-income funds, while Luxembourg was generally a domicile for simple products (see Table 3.2).

A UCITS-II regulation was drafted in the early 1990s, with the goal of successfully harmonizing laws throughout Europe and allowing the creation of money market funds, funds of funds, derivative funds and tracker funds as UCITS. But the Council of Ministers could not reach a common position and UCITS-II was subsequently abandoned as being too ambitious. The European Commission published a new proposal in July 1998, which was drafted in two parts: a product proposal and a service provider proposal. These proposals were finally adopted in December 2001 as two directives, and are now generally referred to as UCITS III.

- The Management Directive seeks to give fund management companies a European passport to operate throughout the EU. Once a management company is authorized in its home State, that authorization extends to all member States, subject to compliance with host State

---

[22] For these two countries, the date for implementation of the directive was 1 April 1992.

Table 3.2   Net assets of the European investment fund industry (end-2005, data from the European Fund and Asset Management Association)

Country	UCITS (billion euros)	%	Non-UCITS (billion euros)	%	Total (billion euros)	%
Austria	107.96	2.1	0.05	3.5	156.70	2.4
Belgium	107.18	2.1	0.01	0.4	112.94	1.7
Czech Republic	4.73	0.1	0.00	0.0	4.73	0.1
Denmark	63.74	1.2	0.04	3.1	106.43	1.6
Finland	38.50	0.7	0.01	0.4	44.67	0.7
France	1,155.10	22.3	0.12	8.3	1,270.60	19.4
Germany	262.37	5.1	0.70	50.4	965.54	14.7
Greece	27.94	0.5	0.00	0.0	28.30	0.4
Hungary	5.47	0.1	0.00	0.1	7.08	0.1
Ireland	463.04	9.0	0.12	8.6	583.28	8.9
Italy	381.89	7.4	0.03	2.0	410.08	6.2
Liechtenstein	12.78	0.2	0.00	0.0	13.22	0.2
Luxembourg	1,386.61	26.8	0.14	9.9	1,525.21	23.2
Netherlands	79.98	1.5	0.02	1.1	95.77	1.5
Norway	34.01	0.7	0.00	0.0	34.01	0.5
Poland	15.02	0.3	0.00	0.1	15.88	0.2
Portugal	26.21	0.5	0.01	0.7	36.45	0.6
Slovakia	2.71	0.1	0.00	0.0	2.74	0.0
Spain	268.60	5.2	0.01	0.5	275.07	4.2
Sweden	103.79	2.0	0.00	0.1	105.59	1.6
Switzerland	100.78	1.9	0.02	1.1	116.71	1.8
Turkey	18.44	0.4	0.00	0.1	20.20	0.3
UK	502.92	9.7	0.13	9.4	634.65	9.7
All funds	5,169.76	100.0	1.40	100.0	6,565.83	100.0

notifications – not authorizations. The Management Directive also introduces the concept of a simplified prospectus, which is intended to provide more accessible and comprehensive information in a simplified format to potential investors.

• The Product Directive allows funds to invest in a wider range of financial instruments. Under this directive, it is possible to establish money market funds, derivatives funds, index-tracking funds and funds of funds as UCITS.

The success of UCITS III will now depend on the way each member State implements the directives, but also on the awaited updates from the European Commission. So far, the situation looks very much ... European. For example, short-selling is prohibited in the Directive but a recommendation issued in 2004 confirms that funds may use cash-settled derivatives to obtain the same economic effect. The Directive requires fund management groups to submit the details of their risk management process to their local regulators, but it is still unclear exactly what a minimum "risk management process" should look like.

The way to UCITS III therefore seems long and winding. By October 2005, only 20% of the many fund management groups in the UK market had converted to UCITS III, while they all *must* convert to UCITS III status by February 2007 if they want to have a European passport to operate and market freely within the EU.

3.2.2   The case of European hedge funds

The situation of hedge funds in Europe has, in a sense, paralleled the evolution of mutual funds. Initially, in an attempt to protect individual investors from outright risk, most European regulators imposed specific guidelines on the use of individual investment instruments by onshore asset managers and limited their short-selling activities as well as the distribution of their products. As a consequence, most European managers went offshore, with the exception of two countries, the United Kingdom and Switzerland, which had relatively accommodative regulations. Elsewhere, European onshore hedge funds were a rare species, and distribution was directed mainly through offshore markets or using insurance policy wrappers or structured products to circumvent regulation.

As both the demand for, and the supply of, hedge fund products increased, most European regulators finally embraced the principles of hedge fund investing as a plausible form of investment management. They progressively loosened laws on hedge funds and funds of hedge funds, eased requirements, and allowed mainstream investors to buy into hedge funds. As a result, onshore hedge funds have started to emerge, and onshore distribution has shifted its focus away from the traditional offshore domain inhabited by high net worth individuals towards onshore markets and into the path of mass affluent private investors.

Naturally, national regulators have adopted differing approaches, and the variety of regulatory regimes has created a fragmented marketplace. Consequently, both hedge fund managers and distributors must understand the complexities of the local environment and actively address issues such as cultural differences, attitudes to savings, taxation laws and/or disparities in national legislation on consumer protection. The European Union has not yet adopted a common marketing passport for hedge funds similar to the UCITS, but it is certainly being considered. The Committee on Economic and Monetary Affairs has drafted a report on the future of hedge funds and derivatives. Surprisingly, this report concluded that hedge funds contribute to the efficiency and self-balancing of financial markets. It recommended the creation of a "sophisticated alternative investment vehicle" (SAIV) and suggested a new appropriate regulatory regime for this type of vehicle. Even more surprisingly, the European Parliament welcomed the report as helpful guidance for the European Commission.

In May 2004, the Asset Management Expert Group delivered another report, which recommended that the European Commission review the EU regulatory framework to allow hedge funds to be allowed on an EU-wide basis, subject to appropriate safeguards. It also concluded that a flexible principle-based approach would offer the best prospect of designing an appropriate SAIV framework, and suggested adapting the current UCITS legislation as a reference, and harmonizing the private placement rules.

Although such a unified system would be a boon to industry participants and investors alike, the author's view is that we need to remain prudent, and even sceptical. Given the difficulties encountered with simple mutual funds, we should not expect much in the near future from a European unified regulation. In the meantime, hedge funds and funds of hedge funds still need to cope with local regulations. They can either register domestically as non-UCITS,[23] or register offshore and try to enter the domestic market using private placements – if possible. The following sections provide an overview of the situation in selected countries, namely,

---

[23] The "non-UCITS" part of the European investment fund market is regulated in accordance with specific national requirements. It is dominated by five types of products: the German "Spezialfonds" reserved for institutional investors, the British closed-ended investment trusts, the property funds, the French open-ended employee saving funds and more recently "other" Luxembourg non-UCITS funds.

> ### Box 3.10   The European Union Savings Directive – a myopic policy
>
> The European Union Savings Directive (EUSD) came into effect on 1 July 2005, the main purpose being to allow tax authorities to share information about savings income payments made to individuals. Under the EUSD, a paying agent making an interest payment to a beneficial owner resident in the EU must gather and report certain basic information (e.g. the beneficial owner's identity and residence, the account number, and the total amount paid) to a relevant authority in his home State, which will then transmit the information to the taxing authority in the beneficial owner's home State. This is known as "automatic exchange of information" – a polite term for forced denunciation.
>
> In practice, however, the EUSD had a very limited effect on non-European hedge funds, as long as their paying agent was not based in an EU country. As an illustration, consider the case of the Cayman Islands, which initially obtained a ruling from the European Court of First Instance to the effect that the UK government had no constitutional authority to impose the EUSD on anyone other than itself. But to general surprise, the Cayman Islands subsequently radically changed direction and entered into negotiations with the UK Treasury to introduce the EUSD to all funds licensed by the Cayman Islands Mutual Funds Law. The reason for this is that 75% of the regulated mutual funds in the Cayman Islands are exempted from the licensing requirements – being registered as a mutual fund with the Cayman Islands Monetary Authority and requiring minimum investments in excess of $50 000 are sufficient conditions for the exemption. They are therefore not concerned by the EUSD.
>
> Perhaps the greatest irony in the EUSD is that it may unintentionally prompt the exact reverse dynamic to that which occurred in 1962 in New York. There the US legislators in their wisdom decided to introduce a withholding tax on interest payments made by domestic issuers. The net effect of that act of fiscal bombast was to establish, almost overnight, what subsequently became known as the London Eurobond market. Since the EUSD only bites when the paying agent is in the EU or indeed in any jurisdiction where the EUSD applies, the obvious strategy is to locate the paying agent outside the EU, say for example … in New York.

Germany, France, Italy, Ireland, Switzerland and Spain, in order to illustrate the different paths taken by European countries to regulate hedge funds.[24] Some have been successful, some were clearly completely wrong, and some are only at the beginning of their learning process. Financial directives are presented in Boxes 3.10 and 3.11.

3.2.3   Germany

For a long time, virtually no alternative investments were offered to German investors, essentially for regulatory and tax reasons. On the demand side, private pension funds and insurance companies were subject to the German Insurance Supervisory Act, which prohibited investment in funds that did not fulfil minimum liquidity and risk diversification requirements. Hedge

---

[24] For other countries, we highly recommend the series of documents issued by PriceWaterhouseCoopers under the generic name "The regulation and distribution of hedge funds in Europe: changes and challenges", as well as the country documents provided by AIMA on its website (www.aima.org).

Box 3.11   The Markets in Financial Instruments Directive (MiFID)

The implementation date for the new MiFID has been deferred until October 2007 in order to allow for an extended consultation period. However, the information available at present suggests that there will be a number of changes that could affect hedge fund managers and hedge fund adviser firms. In particular:

- The range of investment activities that will require authorization in all EU States is to be increased to include investment advice. Currently, investment advice is not regulated in some countries, and there are still various definitions of what constitutes "advice".
- MiFID is to introduce three classes of customers, and specific rules of conduct for each class. These classes are: (i) eligible counterparties, such as investment firms, credit institutions, insurance companies, UCITs, pension funds and other financial institutions authorized or regulated in a EU member State; (ii) professional customers, who have the experience, knowledge and expertise to make their own investment decisions and assess relevant risks; and (iii) retail customers, who comprise all the others.
- MiFID is to introduce common EU-wide conduct of business standards for MiFID firms in areas such as compliance, risk management, conflict of interest, customer agreements and periodic reporting.

---

funds were therefore regarded as non-eligible investments for German institutional investors. On the supply side, creating an onshore hedge fund in Germany was extremely difficult. Two investment vehicles were theoretically available, the German investment fund and the German corporation. However, by law, the former structure could invest only in listed securities, could not take short positions, and was unable to use leverage – three requirements that are often incompatible with hedge fund activities. The latter structure allowed for more flexibility in terms of investments, but was viewed as conducting a business in Germany. Consequently, its profits were taxed twice, once at the corporate level and later when distributed at the investor level, which made it highly inefficient.

The situation of offshore (non-German) hedge funds was hardly enviable. First, their promotion among German investors was restricted to private placements, where the promoter had an existing investment advisory relationship with each prospective investor and used the format of one-to-one presentations to meet with investors. Second, the taxation of offshore funds at the investor level was subject to the German Foreign Investment Act, which distinguished three categories of funds:

- White funds, which were listed on a German stock exchange or had a licence for public offering. These enjoyed the same taxation status as the German funds but their activities were strictly regulated. In practice, therefore, their status was only applicable to a few non-leveraged long/short equity funds and certain low-risk event-driven strategies.
- Grey funds, which were not listed on a German stock exchange and did not have a licence for public offering, but had mandated a German tax representative, and were taxable on all their income for both institutional and private investors. Very few funds fell into this category.
- Black funds, which encompassed all other offshore hedge funds, i.e. most of the industry. These were heavily penalized: 90% of their annual net asset value variation (when positive) or 10% of their absolute net asset value at the year end (if higher) was deemed to be a taxable capital gain.

This particularly unattractive regulatory and tax framework was set up purposely by regulators in order to deter investments in offshore hedge funds. This explains the scarcity of alternative products offered in Germany until the end of the 1990s. The only exceptions were managed futures funds, which could be set up and distributed more easily if they were packaged with a capital guarantee at maturity. Several successful managed futures products were launched at this time and sold mainly to private investors through direct marketing. A noteworthy example is Man Investment Products, which raised €400 million and became one of the largest commodity trading advisers world wide.

The situation of hedge funds started to change as a result of the bull equity market at the end of the 1990s. The quest for diversification suddenly became a hot topic among German investors, naturally arousing interest in alternative investments. The relative difficulty of accessing traditional forms of hedge funds forced German financial intermediaries to be creative in their response to a growing demand from their clients. They turned to financial engineering and came up with a good way of bypassing regulations and making hedge funds palatable to institutional and even retail investors. For institutional investors, index-linked bonds with a capital guarantee became the most favoured structure. For private investors, index-linked bonds without any capital guarantee (also called index certificates) were preferable, because they were tax free after a one-year holding period. In both cases, the underlying asset of the structure was essentially a fund of hedge funds pompously renamed "hedge fund index".

As might be expected, the market became literally submerged with a flood of such structures. The Landesbank Baden-Wuerttemberg started with a conservative guaranteed hedge fund product in early 1999, shortly followed by Commerzbank with its Comas series, and Vereins und Westbank with its Prince product. But the major surprise came in September 2000, when Deutsche Bank announced that its new product, Xavex HedgeSelect Certificate™ (Box 3.12), had attracted around 1.8 billion euros in four weeks from retail and institutional investors. Moreover, Deutsche Bank found a way of getting Xavex HedgeSelect registered in Germany, Belgium, the Netherlands, Luxembourg and Switzerland. The argument used to register it was purely technical: Xavex HedgeSelect was not a fund but used certificates. Certificates give all the economic rights of ownership without actually giving ownership – owners of certificates cannot vote. Therefore, certificates should not be subject to the same restrictions as funds. Needless to say, the argument was technically correct, but hard to swallow from a regulator's perspective.

In January and March 2003, respectively, the German regulator (BaFin) issued two consultative questionnaires to institutions and hedge fund managers with a view to regulating properly direct hedge fund investments. On 1 January 2004, the new Investment Act and the new Investment Tax Act were enacted as major parts of the new German Investment Modernization Act. The latter Act aims at promoting Germany as an investment fund market, halting the exodus of investment funds to other European countries and implementing the amendments of the UCITS III Directive. The Investment Act replaces the Investment Companies Act dealing with domestic investment funds and investment companies and the Foreign Investment Act dealing with foreign investment funds. The Investment Tax Act harmonizes the taxation of domestic and foreign funds. For the first time, these two Acts create the prerequisites for the establishment and direct distribution of hedge funds within the German investment market.

Under the new Investment Act, a German domestic hedge fund can now be set up by means of two different legal entities. First, a hedge fund may be established as an investment stock corporation which can be open-ended with variable capital. This structure is completely new for Germany. Second, a separate hedge fund can be established by a financial investment management company, in which case the fund's assets are either part of the financial management

---

Box 3.12   The Xavex HedgeSelect Certificate™

Deutsche Bank issued the Xavex HedgeSelect Certificate™ on 29 September 2000. The new product was structured as an eight-year index certificate, member of the Xavex product family. It aimed at giving investors full participation in the upside and downside performance of the HedgeSelect Index™, that is, a performance objective of 12 to 15% annual growth with neither a maximum nor a minimum redemption amount, and a risk as close as possible to the risk level of bonds (as represented by the J.P. Morgan Global Government Bond Index). Actively managed by Deutsche Asset Management on a continuous basis according to a "Judgement with Quantitative Discipline" approach, the HedgeSelect Index™ reflected the performance of a diversified portfolio of 15 to 50 hedge funds, plus a cash balance.

With respect to other products available in Germany, the HedgeSelect Certificate™ had several innovative features. First, the minimum investment was relatively small (€10 000, with a €1000 increment), which allowed all types of investors to subscribe. Second, the certificates were denominated in euros – the US dollar exchange rate risk was hedged by rolling over one-month currency forwards. Third, the certificates enjoyed a favourable tax treatment in Germany. For instance, capital gains were tax free for private investors if the certificate was held for more than one year.

To enhance liquidity, Deutsche Bank offered a two-tiered market-making feature. On the one hand, the certificates were listed on the Frankfurt Stock Exchange, allowing immediate trading with a bid–ask spread of 5% around the estimated net asset value. On the other hand, investors could redeem their shares at the official net asset value at the end of each month with a 35-day notice. In practice, this translated into at least 85 days between the exit notice and the cash settlement, as the final net asset value was usually only available 45 days after the end of the corresponding month and five additional days were needed for the settlement. In terms of fees, the certificates charged an origination fee of 2% (included in the offer price), plus a flat fee of 0.27% every month, but no performance fee. The underlying hedge funds only charged their usual fees, with no entry or exit fees.

---

company's property (fiduciary relationship with the investors) or are co-owned by the investors. Funds in the second category are governed by sections 112–120 of the Investment Act under the official title "Investment Funds with Additional Risks".

The new Investment Act makes a clear distinction between single manager hedge funds and funds of hedge funds. Single manager hedge funds are allowed to use short selling, leverage and derivatives. While adhering to the principle of risk diversification, they are not restricted in terms of strategy or with regard to their selection of assets – except for unlisted private equity assets, which must remain below 30% of the funds' assets, and a prohibition to invest in real estate or real estate companies. Single manager hedge funds are required to use depositary banks which meet minimum quality standards. Their liquidity must be at least quarterly, with a notice period that should not exceed 40 calendar days. Lastly, their distribution is restricted to private placements, i.e. access is only possible for institutional investors and high net worth individuals.

Funds of hedge funds are funds that invest in other single hedge funds. They are not subject to a minimum investment but they are subject to several restrictions. In particular, they can only invest in hedge funds established under the German Investment Act or in foreign investment funds with an equivalent investment policy.[25] Funds of hedge funds cannot use leverage or short selling and are prohibited from investing more than 49% of their assets in bank credits or money market instruments. They may not invest more than 20% of their assets in a single target fund, nor invest in more than two target funds of the same issuer or fund manager – this is in order to ensure sufficient risk diversification. They may use currency futures and option contracts, but only for hedging purposes. In addition, to prevent cascade effects, a German fund of hedge funds may not invest in target funds which invest in target funds themselves again.[26]

The managers of funds of hedge funds must ensure that they possess all information necessary to make their investment decisions (statutory minimum requirements). They must continuously monitor their underlying hedge funds to make sure that they comply with their stated investment policies and strategies, and regularly receive risk ratios. All this information must be submitted to BaFin upon request. Furthermore, the persons responsible for investment decisions must have adequate experience of hedge fund investing and comparable foreign investments.

Funds of hedge funds may be publicly distributed in Germany if they allow redemptions on a quarterly basis with at most a 100-calendar day notice. However, investors must receive a detailed sales prospectus informing them of the features and risks of the fund, as well as the following mandatory warning in bold print: "Warning by the Federal Minister of Finance: investors in this investment fund must be prepared and able to sustain losses of the capital invested up to a total loss."

The situation regarding distribution of foreign hedge funds is also clarified in the new Investment Act. The public distribution of foreign single manager hedge funds is prohibited, but their private placement remains allowed if their investment policy is subject to requirements comparable to those for German single hedge funds. The public distribution of foreign funds of hedge funds is allowed once they have registered for public distribution. The registration process imposes a series of requirements: (i) the fund of funds and its management company must be located in jurisdictions which provide for effective public supervision of financial services; (ii) the respective supervisory authorities have to be, in the assessment of the German Financial Services Supervisory Authority, willing to cooperate to a satisfactory extent[27]; (iii) the fund of funds has to appoint a domestic representative and at least one paying agent in Germany; (iv) the fund of funds must be approved by the German Financial Services Supervisory Authority; (v) all the documents required for the approval must be delivered together with a translation into German; (vi) at least 51% of the investment must be in single hedge funds; (vii) there is a maximum of 49% liquidity; (viii) foreign exchange financial instruments may be used only for hedging currency risks; (ix) short sales and leverage are not permitted at the fund of funds level; and (x) minimum diversification requirements need to be observed. However, unlike for German funds of hedge funds, the following rules also apply: (xi) short-term borrowings up to a limit of 10% of the fund are generally possible; and (xii) the role of the custodian bank of the fund of hedge funds may be performed by a comparable institution,

---

[25] In particular, the investment policy must be comparable for investment in private equity and commodities. The assets of these foreign funds must be deposited in a custodian bank or a comparable facility, and their respective jurisdiction must cooperate with the Financial Action Task Force (FATF) in combating money laundering in accordance with applicable international agreements.

[26] Many offshore hedge funds use, for instance, money market funds to invest their cash. This is prohibited by the German law.

[27] The registration of funds from "exotic" jurisdictions, such as the British Virgin Islands, the Bahamas and the Cayman Islands, is not possible because the regulatory authorities of these countries are not willing to cooperate enough with the BaFin.

in particular a prime broker. Additional requirements apply to the detailed sales prospectus, the content of which must correspond to the sales prospectus for German funds of hedge funds.

The new Investment Tax Act also introduces several changes. In particular, the tax consequences for domestic and foreign investment funds have now largely been equalized. In theory, this is of advantage to foreign funds, but it also imposes more stringent requirements on these funds. The Act now distinguishes between transparent (previously white) and non-transparent (previously black) funds – there is no longer a middle ground (previously grey) in Germany for tax treatment. Investors holding assets through a transparent fund have the most enjoyable status. For private investors, capital gains are taxable at the investor's individual tax rate if the fund shares are redeemed within a year; any redemption or disposal after this period is entirely tax exempt. For corporate investors, capital gains are subject to trade tax and corporation tax, except for that portion of the capital gain consisting of income. In contrast, investors in non-transparent funds are subject to taxation on a lump-sum basis. They are taxable on all actual distributions plus 70% of the appreciation in the value of the share during the calendar year, as well as a minimum of 6% of the last redemption price of the calendar year, irrespective of whether the fund's NAV increased or decreased during the year in question. Although this tax treatment is more lenient than the previous quasi-penal approach to black funds, it still prevents the distribution of non-transparent funds in Germany.

In order to qualify for the transparent tax regime and enjoy the benefits, a fund must comply with detailed reporting and income calculation requirements, and its auditor or tax adviser must certify that the fund's German tax figures and investor information have been collected under the tax law governing German funds. In addition, foreign funds must publish on a daily basis accumulated retained earnings[28] together with the redemption price. Foreign funds must provide the Federal Tax Office, on request, with proof of correctness of their published distributions, deemed distributions and accumulated retained earnings within three months. In practice, this implies that a foreign fund cannot use a foreign regulatory or tax accounting system, including the GAAP, in order to determine the figures relevant to German investors.[29] In addition, the tax certificate triggers *de facto* an unofficial German tax audit since the entity confirming the tax data, according to German tax law (Box 3.13), is liable for incorrect figures up to a maximum amount of €1 million per certificate (i.e. per share class).

In the case of a fund of funds, not only must the fund of funds comply with the same duties regarding detailed reporting and income calculation requirements, but also *each* underlying hedge fund must do the same – including the publication of its tax information in the *Electronic Federal Gazette* – in order to generate an acceptable tax treatment for its German investors. Where a fund of hedge funds invests in target funds that do not comply with these requirements, the earnings of those target funds that are attributable to the fund of funds are taxed on a lump-sum basis in accordance with the rules for non-transparent funds.

The new Investment Act officially aimed at creating a liberal regulatory framework for the establishment of onshore hedge funds and the distribution of funds of hedge funds in the German capital market. However, as one could expect, it was only a qualified success.

---

[28] The accumulated retained earnings are the sum of the (positive) deemed distributions since 1994.

[29] For example, the accounting information must be calculated on the basis of a cash-oriented accounting scheme. The relevant definitions of dividend, interest, capital gains, securities lending, repos, bonds and derivatives, etc. are based upon the specific German tax concept. The computation of investment income must differentiate between various income sources, because they generate either fully taxable, semi-tax exempt or tax-free investment income. Dividends must be accounted for on the first ex-dividend day and interest must be determined under the accrual method.

Box 3.13   When hedging becomes costly

In Germany, investors and fund managers should tread carefully in using derivatives as part of an investment strategy. In the past, equity gains or losses were tax-free in domestic funds, whereas derivatives used for hedging purposes were fully taxable. Many corporations ended up in a situation where, in a plunging equity market, their funds hedged the equity positions only to find that they had non-deductible losses on the equity side and taxable gains from the derivatives side. The new Investment Tax Act seems to have solved the issue for equities as long as the corresponding gains remain accumulated within the fund. However, the issue is still open when the underlying asset is interest or fixed income. A manager hedging fixed income positions via derivatives is therefore likely to face the same problems.

The strict limitation with respect to the avoidance of cascade effects combined with the complicated tax regime and administrative hurdles prevented the growth of a real onshore German hedge fund industry. According to the German regulator BaFin, only 18 single manager funds and 10 funds of funds based in the country were approved, and a further 10 foreign funds of funds have approval for public distribution. In total, German-based hedge funds are thought to have only around €2 billion of assets, while the initial forecasts cited €40 billion to €100 billion. Nevertheless, some providers have attempted to position themselves in the market. For instance, Lupus Alpha, a small firm based in Frankfurt, was the first manager to win approval for a German onshore hedge fund, followed by DWS's inaugural currency hedge fund. And Citigroup applied to BaFin to launch a platform for hedge funds within the master KAG investment structure, which would allow foreign hedge funds to access the German market using Citigroup's legal and administrative services. But without a friendlier environment, it may take a while for the nascent German hedge fund industry to reach anything like its full potential.

The status of offshore hedge funds and funds of hedge funds is not much better, as most of them do not comply with the tax reporting requirements of the new Investment Tax Act and are not willing to take on the additional burden of meeting them in the near future. Consequently, they are considered as non-transparent funds from a tax perspective. For investors, the fastest way to identify tax-compliant funds is in fact to use managed accounts. To meet this expected demand, several managed account platforms have implemented measures in order to ensure that their clients' reporting would be German tax-compliant. But, as discussed in Chapter 4, managed accounts are not a panacea. Not all hedge fund managers – particularly not the best ones – are willing to operate managed accounts, and several illiquid strategies are not suitable for inclusion in a managed account platform that requires a high level of liquidity. So German investors still widely use structured products to access offshore hedge funds.

3.2.4   France

As a result of several years of fiscal privileges granted to life insurance products as well as pay-as-you-go State-funded pension schemes, France is currently in a unique situation within Europe. Simply stated, French investors greatly lack an equity culture – most of them assimilate long-term investing in equities to gambling at casinos, and leverage or speculation to criminal activities. It is therefore not surprising that for many years, hedge funds were banned from the country. French regulators allowed the use of alternative management techniques in the context of segregated account mandates or synthetic products, but they were strictly forbidden in French collective investment schemes. In particular, whatever its structure, no French fund could, in practice, benefit from prime brokerage services.

The result has simply been, as usual in finance, a massive brain drain towards more accommodating countries. Although a large number of non-US hedge funds were run in practice by French organizations, they were officially registered in and managed from offshore locations. In particular, London and Geneva became the favourite destinations of French hedge fund managers wishing to enjoy lower tax rates and more flexibility. Traditionally, mathematics was the key to the French educational system and French always excelled in quantitative investment strategies, but it was accepted wisdom that talented French hedge fund managers were easier to find in London rather than in Paris.

Unfortunately, the perception of French authorities was also that offshore (read: out of France) investing was almost synonymous with tax evasion. They were not able to oppose the brain drain, although they attempted to, but they could easily prevent distribution and canvassing. French regulators therefore retaliated by subjecting any act of solicitation from a non-UCITS fund to prior authorization by both the Ministry of Finance and the *Commission des opérations de bourse*. Of course, advertising, mailing a prospectus or an offering memorandum, meeting with or calling potential investors as well as organizing presentations were considered as an act of solicitation, whether these activities were carried out from within France or from abroad. The same rule applied when marketing to banks or sophisticated investors. Predictably, the prior authorization was never granted. Moreover, any document used to provide information to French clients was required to be in the French language, creating an important entry barrier for foreign hedge funds and fund of hedge funds groups. In addition, it was not permitted to offer non-UCITS foreign investment funds in France, and violators faced the prospect of jail – the guillotine was not far off.[30]

Since individual freedom cannot be totally constrained in a democracy, individual investors could still approach hedge funds on a wholly unsolicited basis. Disappointed by the stock market's poor performance and worried by the almost bankrupt status of State-funded pension schemes, both institutional and individual investors became more and more interested in alternative products. Initially, a large number of dynamic money market funds were introduced, and they rapidly gained popularity. Most of them invested the majority of their assets in traditional money market instruments, and the rest (5 to 10%) in hedge fund strategies to obtain a higher performance. Later, bond-plus types of products were also launched around low-volatility hedge fund strategies (fixed income arbitrage, convertible arbitrage, etc.), as well as capital-protected notes built around hedge fund portfolios. French banks, which had shunned hedge funds after a string of failures, gradually started lining up their offerings once again, hypocritically waiting for "unsolicited requests".

French regulators attempted to control this flow by creating a series of adapted investment structures. The FCMIT (*Fonds commun d'investissement sur les marchés à terme*) was specifically designed for managed futures funds, as well as to support the MATIF – the French futures and options exchange. And the simplified procedure OPCVM[31] (*OPCVM à procédure*

---

[30] Note that the concept of a private placement exemption exists in France, but its benefits are limited in practice by restrictions on the canvassing of securities.

[31] OPCVM is the French term for UCITS.

allégée) was a special category of fund reserved for institutional investors and high net worth individuals. Unlike the case of standard funds, no prior approval was required to set up a simplified procedure OPCVM, although the AMF (*Autorité des marchés financiers*) had to be notified subsequently.

However, despite their hedge fund flavours, these two structures were not sufficient to allow French funds to establish themselves as a real alternative to offshore funds. Despite the regulation, the strong "unsolicited" demand pushed offshore hedge fund assets to over $12 billion, and France became the second largest and fastest growing market in Europe's burgeoning hedge fund industry. Concerned by this trend and wishing to restore its credibility, the AMF organized numerous consultations in 2003 and 2004 with representatives of the French asset management industry. The goal was to draft a decent regulated framework for hedge funds while also protecting the public. As a result, new regulations were adopted in November 2004. They amended the existing rules, and introduced a series of new investment structures, namely OPCVM Aria (*à règles d'investissement allégées*, which means "with lighter investment rules") and contractual funds.

The OPCVM Aria category is divided into simple Aria, Aria EL (leveraged funds) and Aria FA (funds of alternative funds).

- The simple Aria is similar to a regular fund, except that it is able to derogate from some risk diversification and concentration rules. Its eligible financial instruments include listed shares, OPCVMs, French debt securitization funds (*fonds communs de créances*), liquid assets (on an ancillary basis), medium-term notes, bonds and bank deposits meeting specific criteria. A leverage of up to 2 is accepted (100% of the fund's assets off the balance sheet), and the fund must offer at least a monthly net asset value.
- The leveraged Aria (*OPCVM Aria avec effet de levier*) is similar to a regular fund, except that it may use a prime broker and leverage its assets by up to 400% with no restrictions on counterparty risk. It is also able to derogate from some risk diversification and concentration rules. A leverage of up to 4 is accepted (300% of the fund's assets off the balance sheet), and the fund must offer at least a monthly net asset value.
- A fund of alternative funds Aria (*OPCVM Aria de fonds alternatifs*) can invest in other hedge funds, called "target funds". These funds of funds must follow the "5/10/40" rule, i.e. maximum of 10% in one holding, and the sum of 5% or plus holding being limited to 40%. In practice, this rule implies a minimum of 16 target funds, with a maximum of four target funds each representing 10% of the fund's assets and 12 target funds representing 5% of the fund's assets.

By July 2005, the AMF completed the regulation by specifying a list of 13 criteria governing eligible underlying hedge funds (including non-French funds) for a fund of alternative funds Aria – see Box 3.14.

One of the most revolutionary aspects of the new regulation is the definition of a new framework for stock borrowing. Prior to the new regulation, the fund custodian had to be a French bank and was responsible for the assets held by the fund. This responsibility could not be delegated. As a consequence, prime brokers were not allowed to reuse stocks held in a fund's portfolio in exchange for stocks borrowed by the funds, which restricted the borrowing of securities on a large scale. With the new Aria regulation, the delegation of responsibility of the custodian to an AMF-approved prime broker on the control of the fund's assets is now possible, if it is specifically disclosed in the fund's prospectus.

Box 3.14 The 13 criteria

On the basis of article L.411-34 of the AMF General Regulations, target hedge funds that wish to become a component of an Aria fund must comply with the following criteria at all times:

1. The target hedge fund shares must be freely transferable, by registration on the register of shareholders or by delivery, via a custodian.
2. Shareholders of the same share class or category should have equal rights to the capital or assets of the target hedge fund.[32]
3. The target hedge fund must have the legal capacity to have its own rights and obligations arising from the existence of its own assets and liabilities.
4. The custody of the target hedge fund assets must be held by a company which is separate from the management company, regulated for such purpose and clearly identified in the fund's prospectus.
5. The target hedge fund's assets must be segregated from the custodian's own assets or those of the custodian's delegates.
6. The target hedge fund's assets may be reused only by the custodian or its delegates, or by any other person having a right over the target hedge fund.
7. The entity managing or advising the target hedge fund must be registered with and under the regulatory supervision of a relevant regulatory authority.
8. Independent auditors must audit and certify the financial statements of the target hedge fund on an annual basis.
9. Risk of loss for any investor in the target hedge fund must be limited to the amount of his investment.
10. There must be a prospectus for the target hedge fund which describes its statutory and management rules.
11. Investors must receive information on the evolution of the portfolio and the financial results of the target hedge fund on at least a quarterly basis.
12. The net asset value per share (or estimated net asset value) must be made available, on at least a monthly basis, to all investors of the target hedge fund.
13. The target hedge fund may not be established in a country whose legislation is recognized as being insufficient or whose practices are not considered to conform to anti-money laundering and anti-terrorist financing regulations, as decided by international cooperative bodies which coordinate anti-money laundering and anti-terrorist financing activities.

Note that initially, Decree no. 89-623 added the requirement that target funds should be listed. This severely constrained the breadth of the investment universe and often resulted in sub-optimal portfolios. As a result, the listing requirement was abolished. However, a target fund listed for instance on the Irish Stock Exchange would automatically comply with eight of the above-mentioned requirements. This facilitates the screening of target funds as investments for an Aria.

---

[32] The fact that different shareholders may pay different management fees or support different transaction costs or have different subscription and redemption rights is acceptable, as long as these differences do not affect the relevant shareholders' rights to the fund's capital or assets.

Finally, the AMF also approved the equalization method for Aria funds, which was previously not possible as all shareholders in French funds had to be treated equally.[33]

In addition, the AMF introduced the category of contractual funds (*OPCVM contractuels*) which are permitted to establish their own investment rules by means of internal regulations or bylaws, free of AMF restrictions on the type of assets they may hold, including shares in foreign investment funds. Contractual funds are very close to a dedicated investment mandate, except that they have a fund structure. They can have quarterly net asset value calculations, up to three-month notice periods for redemptions and a potential lock-up period of up to two years. They must also impose a minimum investment of €250 000.

French managers performing direct alternative management or multi-management activities are also targeted by the new regulation. They must present a draft of *general activity* with the characteristics of their new funds, and *specified activity* programmes have to be submitted for approval of the fund of funds Aria, leveraged Aria and contractual funds. This essential document, which must be approved by the AMF, should demonstrate the manager's relevant expertise and experience to manage alternative investments. It should also evidence that the manager has sufficient resources, infrastructure, experience and skills to select and monitor hedge fund investments, assess their risk and performance, and establish commercialization arrangements. French managers must also submit a specific marketing programme to the regulatory authorities for approval. This marketing programme should include the type of client targeted (private wealth, institutional, etc.), and the distribution channels and means used to approach potential subscribers, as well as the salespeople's training on alternative investment in general and on the product being approved.

The new French regulation is indeed a breath of fresh air for the French hedge fund industry, but we have to realize that it is extremely restrictive for offshore funds. In particular, the requirements for the underlying hedge funds in the case of a fund of funds Aria are only met by 10% of the hedge funds world wide, which means that 90% of the available offshore hedge funds do not qualify for a French fund of funds. In practice, only the contractual funds are well suited for hedge funds in strategies such as global macro or fixed income arbitrage, or for investing in hedge funds that do not fulfil the criteria required by the AMF. As a consequence, structured products should continue to be the simplest way to access offshore hedge funds for French investors. Nevertheless, as of 31 December 2005, the AMF had registered 142 funds of funds Aria representing €16.3 billion of assets, as well as 26 contractual funds for a total of €2.7 billion.

From a tax perspective, French investors are much better placed than those in Germany (see Table 3.3). A French individual is taxed at his personal income tax rate on income received from a distribution by an offshore fund and will pay capital gains tax on disposal of his interest. In addition, if a French investor holds at least 10% of the voting or controlling rights of the fund and the fund is domiciled in a "favourable" tax jurisdiction, he will be taxed on the fund's income proportionate to his interest, with a minimum lump-sum payment based on net assets, should the fund not be based in a jurisdiction with a reciprocal tax treaty. Institutions are taxed when the fund distributes and are also subject to the 10% rule.

---

[33] As we shall see in chapter 18, the equalization method is a process used to ensure that all shareholders pay the adequate amount of performance fees. It may involve different treatment for shareholders that would enter a hedge fund at different point in time.

Table 3.3 Summary of the French rules for hedge funds

	Need AMF's agreement	Controlled by AMF	Qualified investors	Other investors Low minimum[a]	Other investors High minimum	General activity program	Specific activity program	Minimum subscriptions/ redemptions	Maximum notice period
OPCVM (UCITS)	Yes	Yes		No restriction			No	Twice in a month; daily if the size is above €150 mio.	
FCIMT	Yes	Yes		0	€10 000	Yes	No	Daily	
OPCVM Aria Fund of funds Aria	Yes	Yes	No restriction	0 if guaranteed; €10 000 otherwise			Yes		35 days (10 days if daily NAV)
OPCVM Aria Simple Aria	Yes	Yes		€10 000	€125 000		No	Monthly	
OPCVM Aria Leveraged Aria	Yes	Yes		€10 000	€125 000		Yes		
Contractual funds	No	Yes		€30 000	€250 000		Yes	Quarterly	3 months, 3-year lock-up is acceptable
Offshore hedge funds	No	No							

[a] These investors must have a minimum wealth of €1 million, or must give evidence of at least one year's experience with the strategy of the fund considered. Note that qualified investors, foreign investors, banks, or large corporations at least two of the following criteria – more than €20 million of total balance sheet, more than €40 million of earnings, or more than €2 million of capital – do not have a minimum investment required.

3.2.5 Italy

Italy is another latecomer to alternative investments. Indeed, the constant changes of government[34] and the resulting regulatory changes have helped to create and maintain uncertainty among sophisticated investors. This resulted in money flowing out of the country, particularly to Lugano, an exquisite Italian-speaking money-management centre in Switzerland close to the border. This is not surprising when one considers, for instance, that Italian residents were allowed to buy offshore hedge funds, but were taxed on their gains at their marginal tax rate (that is, in excess of 45%), whereas Switzerland has no taxes on capital gains and benefited – at that time – from strict banking secrecy. But the supreme affront came in January 1999, when Milan-based UniCredito Italiano, the first Italian bank to launch a hedge fund, decided to set up its operations in Ireland. The Bank of Italy could no longer ignore the hedge fund issue and decided to establish a new legal framework allowing hedge funds to be set up onshore.

According to this new law, any group wishing to establish onshore hedge funds in Italy needs (i) to be authorized by the Bank of Italy; (ii) to set up a special investment management entity (*societá di gestione del risparmio, SGR*) with the exclusive object of forming or managing one or more hedge funds; and (iii) to request approval of each individual hedge fund, on a case-by-case basis. In practice, two types of funds are available, the *fondi di reservati* for professional investors and the *fondi di speculativi*. Both types of fund enjoy broad investment discretion[35] but they may only be distributed through private placements to, at most, 200 Italian investors, each with a minimum investment of €500 000.[36] Lastly, the approved hedge funds are subject to a 12.5% withholding tax on their NAV increase, as are ordinary mutual funds.

Offshore hedge funds may only be distributed in Italy if a series of stringent conditions are met:

- The fund manager must be compatible with the Italian SGR fund structure.
- The fund must be regulated by an authority that applies controls comparable to the Italian authorities.
- The country of the fund's domicile must have cooperation agreements with the Italian authorities.
- The fund must be distributed also in its country of domicile – many offshore funds are prohibited from local distribution in their registration country.
- The fund must appoint a local correspondent bank as paying agent and local authorized distribution intermediaries.

Note that structured products (such as guaranteed notes or unit-linked products on hedge funds) are permitted, subject to satisfactory transparency and liquidity and a guarantee of the initial capital by a bank or an investment firm authorized to deal in financial instruments for its own account.

The Italian alternative investment industry has since grown, but at a much slower pace than some had expected. Several firms (*Kairos Partners, Ersel Asset Management* or *Banca Intermobiliare di Investimenti e Gestione*) have been authorized to start Italy-based funds of hedge funds. *Kairos Partners* was the first to launch, with a series of four funds. Despite its

---

[34] Prodi's is the 60th government that Italy has had since World War II!

[35] Note that the *fondi di reservati* cannot implement long/short strategies because of the prudent investment rules for institutional investors, but they can invest in units of other hedge funds.

[36] Initially, the limit was 100 investors and €1 million. Further relaxations – possibly, to reduce the minimum subscription to €250 000 and increase the number of participants to 300 – have been proposed.

temporary monopoly, the amount of capital initially committed by Italian investors was still very low ($86 million in total). The major reason was probably that the market was not mature enough. Most potential Italian investors were still in the process of moving from domestic bonds and equities to international investments and were not yet familiar with hedge funds. Several pension funds did not like the idea of using consultants and still heeded fees more than performance. In addition, most hedge fund managers complained about the lack of effective prime brokerage services on the peninsula, as well as the legal difficulties when using a long position as collateral against a borrowed stock.[37] In this context, the creation of a true Italian hedge fund (rather than a fund of funds) was still a nightmare.

Nevertheless, Italian investors still have a keen appetite for performance coupled with a strong aversion to risk. There is therefore an ongoing debate about the benefits that hedge funds could bring to private and institutional portfolios, as well as numerous signals that the market share of hedge funds should increase significantly in the coming years. There are three reasons. First, the size of the Italian pension fund market is still very small compared to the size of the mutual funds, which are mostly controlled and distributed by banks and their asset management subsidiaries, but it should increase rapidly.[38] These new actors are mainly investing in bonds and equities, but are likely to increase their allocation to hedge funds in the future. Second, although it is not yet possible to register foreign hedge funds or funds of funds, there might be an opening for these products in the near future through the emergence of capital guaranteed notes and other structured products, as was the case in Germany. Third, the Milan Stock Exchange is considering changes designed to ease share trading. These include (i) allowing trades of just one share at a time, and (ii) allowing shareholders of companies traded on the Nuevo Mercato (the local version of the Nasdaq) to lend part of their stock, even if they are bound by an agreement not to sell their holding. This could strengthen the Italian hedge fund market in the coming years.

3.2.6 Switzerland

Switzerland is still the world's premier wealth management centre, despite the emergence and growth of an increasing number of both onshore and offshore centres. It would therefore be surprising if the Swiss were not involved in some way or another in hedge funds. The fact of the matter is that Switzerland is a very important consumer of hedge funds, but not necessarily a place to manage them. The Swiss are comfortable with hedge funds because several Swiss private banks have been putting their wealthy clients' money – and sometimes their own capital – into funds such as Haussmann Holdings and Quantum for more than two decades. Several insurance companies and pension funds have started to invest in hedge funds, though only a few of them have so far admitted to doing so. However, very few hedge funds have chosen Switzerland as a place of domicile.

The regulatory framework governing Swiss investment funds depends on their chosen organizational structure. Investment companies are regulated by a specific section of the Swiss Code of Obligations, while multiple investors' contracts and investment funds are subject to the Law on Investment Funds and are regulated and audited by the Swiss Federal Banking Commission.

---

[37] Due to an incompatibility between Italy's Civil Code and common law (and English law in general), the right of the prime broker to hold guarantees if a hedge fund busts is not clearly established. Clarification would require a change in the Civil Code, implying a lengthy parliamentary process.

[38] The law allowing the creation of complementary pension funds only came into force in 1999.

There was initially a strong tendency to structure hedge funds and funds of hedge funds as closed-end investment companies, mostly to avoid the stricter rules of the Law on Investment Funds. This gave rise to entities such as Creinvest AG (Bank Julius Baer), Castle Alternative Investment AG (LGT), Altin AG (Banque Syz & Co.), and Alpine Select AG (Citibank), to mention a few. These investment companies were listed on the Swiss stock exchange, and were therefore considered as Swiss stocks – which attracted a lot of interest from domestic and foreign investors, particularly those who could not access hedge funds otherwise. However, the Swiss stock exchange reacted in 1997 by introducing additional rules for the listing and necessary disclosure of such investment companies and later created a special segment for the trading of their shares, closing the regulatory gap.[39]

The amended Swiss Investment Funds Act of 1994 distinguishes three types of fund: real estate funds, securities funds and the so-called "other funds", the last-mentioned category being split into "other funds" and "other funds with special risks". Hedge funds are considered by the Federal Banking Commission to be "other funds with special risks", because of the few restrictions they place on their investment strategies and the sort of financial instruments they can use. Consequently, the creation of a Swiss hedge fund is subject to (i) meeting the requirements of the law for such funds and (ii) successfully passing the Federal Banking Commission's extensive due diligence process.

This due diligence is aimed at verifying that the fund managers, as well as their representatives and agents (i.e. administrators, custodians, trustees and auditors), have sufficient know-how, training and experience in dealing with hedge funds, as well as a suitable internal organization to control the particular risks attached to hedge funds. In addition, the legal basis of the management contracts and the content of the prospectus are carefully examined. In particular, the fund's prospectus must explicitly disclose and explain the particular risks faced by investors. A warning clause must specify the fund's name and declare that the particular hedge fund is a fund with special risks and may thus (i) be engaged in alternative investment strategies, (ii) use alternative investment instruments and (iii) have, if applicable, an alternative structure (e.g. fund of funds, feeder fund). In addition, the warning clause has to explicitly mention that the investor might face the possibility of incurring considerable losses.

Once authorized by the Federal Banking Commission, hedge funds can freely advertise in Switzerland. They are not required to impose minimum investment requirements or a maximum number of investors. They face only a few investment restrictions, such as no investments in closed-end funds that are not listed on an exchange or on a regulated market, and no investments in managed accounts. The funds have no limitations with respect to markets, products, asset classes, concentration of positions, leverage, etc., as long as this is declared in the fund's prospectus.

Although the law was amended in 1994, it was only in 1997 that the general public had access to hedge fund investments for the first time, when the Federal Banking Commission first approved two domestic and three foreign hedge funds for public sale and marketing in Switzerland. These were AHL Alpha plc, AHL Diversified plc, Leu Prima Global Fund, Sinclair Global Macro Fund, and Von Graffenried Olympia Multi-Manager Arbitrage Fund. The market has since boomed, and Switzerland has become one of the leading European centres for hedge fund investors. Private banks in particular have been key actors investing in hedge funds and introducing hedge funds into their clients' recommended asset allocations.

---

[39] For more information, please refer to the Swiss stock exchange's *Règlement complémentaire de cotation des sociétés d'investissement*,

The Swiss authorities have adopted a more pragmatic attitude to non-authorized offshore funds? than their European counterparts. Officially, non-authorized offshore funds are not allowed to advertise publicly in Switzerland. The notion of "advertising" includes printed or electronic media, unsolicited mails, offering circulars, fact sheets sent to the customers of a bank or other financial intermediary, press conferences, phone marketing, cold calling, road shows, sponsored fund reports and visiting of potential investors. However, there is no advertising if customers subscribe to units of investment funds on their own initiative, or if they request information regarding investment funds on an unsolicited basis. In practice, advertising becomes "public" if it is addressed to more than 20 potential investors during a business year, regardless of the way in which these persons are contacted or whether these investors have invested in the fund. Therefore, any solicitation, regardless of its form, that is targeted at more than 20 persons is deemed to be public solicitation and therefore requires the registration of the offering fund according to Swiss law. An important amendment to this is the Institutional Investors' Exemption, which allows non-registered offshore hedge funds to be offered and sold in Switzerland to institutional investors with a professional treasury, such as banks, insurance companies and pension funds. However, this exemption is legally and theoretically not applicable to high net worth individuals or to independent asset managers. Well, let us say it is seldom applied in practice and the number of "unsolicited requests" is surprisingly high.

However, this situation is likely to change, as the proposed new Federal Law for Collective Investment Schemes is expected to replace the existing regulation in 2007. This new law adapts the existing law to the new UCITS III directive and strengthens the competitiveness of Switzerland as a location to register collective investment schemes. Among the proposed changes that could impact hedge funds are the creation of a qualified investor status,[40] the introduction of a simplified prospectus, new legal forms for funds (including limited partnerships and companies with variable capital), the introduction of a dual approval concept (product and managers/promoters), the recognition of prime brokers to replace domestic custodian banks, and the elimination of the required written contract for the sale of non-traditional funds. Last, but not least, the fund classification "other funds with special risk" should be replaced by "other funds for alternative investments" – another sign of changing attitudes.

3.2.7 Ireland

Over the last 15 years, Ireland has emerged with the approval of the European Community as a leading European jurisdiction for the registration of offshore investment funds, including hedge funds. It has now an investor base that represents many times the size of its domestic investor base. We will therefore look at Ireland in a different way, that is, as a potential regulated jurisdiction to register a European hedge fund.

Ireland's financial sector is based primarily in the International Financial Services Centre (IFSC) in Dublin's central Custom House Docks area. Its principal regulator is the Irish Financial Services Regulatory Authority (IFSRA). Since 1 May 2003, it has been responsible for the supervision of all financial service firms in Ireland. It constitutes part of the Central Bank and Financial Services Authority of Ireland (formerly the Central Bank of Ireland) but carries out its functions in an independent manner.

---

[40] To be considered a qualified individual investor and be able to invest in foreign unregistered funds, two conditions must be fulfilled: (i) the bank or security dealer must have a written advisory agreement with the investor for an unlimited period of time, and (ii) the investor must provide proof of ownership of 5 million Swiss francs of assets. Note that banks, securities dealers and other institutional investors are considered as qualified.

The original legislation that is relevant to hedge funds can be found in Sections 126 and 127 of the 1995 Finance Act. These sections allow for a wide range of fund structures. Broadly speaking, these can be categorized as undertakings for collective investment in transferable securities (UCITS) and non-UCITS. Irish UCITS funds are extremely popular with traditional asset managers. They can be constituted as unit trusts, variable capital or fixed capital companies. Once authorized, they may sell their units/shares in any European Union member State without the need for further domestic authorization. However, UCITS funds are not allowed to sell short, use leverage or concentrate their investments, which make them unsuitable for hedge fund activities. Non-UCITS funds can be constituted as unit trusts, variable capital or fixed capital companies as well as limited partnerships. Because they are not subject to the constraints of an EU directive, the IFSRA has more flexibility in its regulation and may allow them to use a much wider and more flexible range of investment and borrowing strategies than the UCITS.

Non-UCITS funds can be divided into four subcategories:

- Retail schemes have no minimum subscription requirements, but are extremely regulated in terms of investments.
- Qualifying investor funds (QIF) have a minimum subscription requirement of €250 000 per investor and can only be marketed to "qualified investors". Qualified investors are defined as natural persons with a minimum net worth requirement of €1 250 000, entities owning or investing on a discretionary basis at least €25 000 000, or the beneficial owners of which are qualifying investors in their own right. Qualified investors must self-certify that they meet these minimum criteria and that they are aware of the risks involved in the proposed investment. The qualifying investor fund structure is an ideal one for hedge funds because there are no investment restrictions and no limits on leverage.
- Professional investor funds (PIF) have a minimum subscription requirement of €125 000 per investor or its equivalent in another currency. They face some investment restrictions, such as a maximum two-to-one leverage and a maximum of 20% of their assets invested in unlisted securities or a single issuer.
- Collective investor schemes were introduced by the Finance Act 1995 and are specifically designed for "collective investors" (life assurance companies, pension funds, etc.). They are tax exempt and cannot be sold publicly, and if they are set up as an investment company, can be non-designated, meaning that there are no minimum subscription requirements and no investment or borrowing restrictions.

The PIF and QIF are the preferred structures for establishing a hedge fund in Ireland. The IFSRA has issued a series of notices to specify the minimum requirements, e.g. the information to be provided in the prospectus, and the appointment of a trustee/custodian and a prime broker. The latter must have a minimum credit rating of A1/P1 and hold a regulated broker status granted by a recognized regulatory authority. The maximum leverage is 140% for the PIF and is unlimited for the QIF, but the extent of the potential exposure should be disclosed in the prospectus. The counterparties of the fund must have a minimum rating of A2/P2; counterparty risk should be lower than 20% for the PIF and is unlimited for the QIF.

Ireland was also one of the first EU jurisdictions to open its doors to hedge fund style investments at the retail end of the spectrum. On 29 December 2002, the IFSRA authorized retail funds of hedge funds, and in June 2004 the minimum investment requirement was abolished. These funds can invest in unregulated schemes, subject to a maximum of 20% of their assets per underlying scheme. Note that a fund of hedge funds may also be established as a PIF or QIF and invest up to 100% of its net assets in unregulated hedge funds, subject to

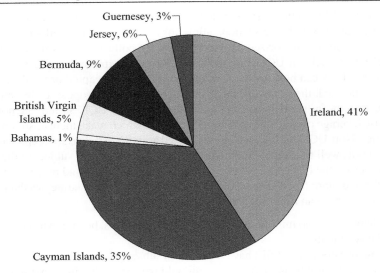

Guernesey, 3%

Jersey, 6%

Bermuda, 9%

British Virgin
Islands, 5%

Bahamas, 1%

Ireland, 41%

Cayman Islands, 35%

Figure 3.1   Domicile of funds listed on the Irish Stock Exchange

a maximum of 40% in any one such unregulated fund. All Irish investment funds which are available to the public are exempt from tax on their income and gains irrespective of where their investors are resident.

Another interesting characteristic of Ireland is the Irish Stock Exchange (Figure 3.1). Created in 1989 as part of the development of the funds industry in the IFSC, it allows for the listing of both Irish and non-Irish funds. It is therefore widely regarded as a leading location for listing offshore investment funds and hedge funds. Such a listing usually does not provide a large secondary liquidity in the fund's securities, but it may help meet specific investors' regulatory and technical requirements (e.g. pension funds that can invest only in listed products).

3.2.8   Spain

Spain is the latest European country to adopt new regulations for alternative investments, as the new Collective Investment Institution (Institución de inversión colectiva, or IIC) regulations were approved by the Ministry of Finance on 4 November 2005. Two structures are available – the IIC de Inversión Libre (hedge funds) and the IIC de IIC de Inversión Libre (funds of hedge funds). Both are regulated and supervised by the Spanish regulatory watchdog, the National Securities Market Commission (CNMV), from which the management companies intending to manage such funds have to receive prior authorizations.

There is no restriction for hedge funds on any kind of underlying assets, but they must follow the general principles of liquidity, diversification and transparency and submit a monthly statistical and operational information statement to the CNMV. Indebtedness of up to five times the value of the hedge fund assets is possible. Distribution should only target qualified investors, with a minimum investment of €50 000. Foreign open-ended funds may be marketed if they are expressly authorized, comply with criteria applying to Spanish funds, and are managed by an OECD-domiciled entity and supervised accordingly.

Funds of hedge funds must have at least 60% of their assets in Spanish incorporated hedge funds or other similar foreign funds domiciled in OECD countries. Diversification rules must be followed (e.g. a maximum of 10% per underlying fund), and redemption notices are limited to 15 days. Funds of hedge funds may be freely marketed.

The future restrictions on the minimum standards for alternative investment fund managers will be defined soon by the CNMV. It is therefore too early to say if the Spanish case will be successful, and there are still open issues – for instance, the tax treatment for investors in non-Spanish non-UCITS hedge funds remains highly unfavourable. Nevertheless, all hedge fund and fund of funds distributors are already fighting to get a slice of the pie and its associated fees.

3.3   THE SITUATION IN ASIA

Given that most of the hedge fund industry is located in countries within Europe and North America, the Asian investor was for a long time, geographically, far from where the action was. Nevertheless, interest in hedge funds has surged in Asia since 2003, and the competition between Singapore and Hong Kong to become the second most important Asian financial centre after Japan is intense. Both have recently adjusted their regulatory systems to encourage the development of onshore hedge funds.

So far, Singapore seems to have taken the lead, thanks to the relative regulatory ease with which hedge fund managers can set up and operate in Singapore, when compared to some other regional locations. This is further sweetened by some tax exemptions and incentives offered by the Singapore government to investment managers and advisers that set up in the country.

In Hong Kong, the alternative fund management industry has also experienced significant growth, in terms of both number of funds and assets under management. According to EurekaHedge, the number of alternative funds grew from 22 in the year 2000 to 81 by the end of 2004 and 113 in 2005. The assets stood at HK$ 3,821 billion in the year 2000 versus almost HK$ 9,014 billion at the end of 2004 and HK$ 11,202 billion in 2005. This growth is likely to continue, as the Securities and Futures Commission (SFC) has appointed a board to consider authorizing the distribution of hedge funds to the general public, and the Revenues Bill passed by the Legislative Council on 1 March 2006 exempts offshore hedge funds from profits tax.

3.4   INTERNET AND THE GLOBAL VILLAGE

The internet is obviously a great medium of communication. It is global, borderless, instantaneous, convenient, and efficient. Used properly, it offers issuers the ability to provide information, conduct capital-raising activities and reach potential investors quickly and in a cost-effective manner. Many regulators have accepted the internet as an effective media to distribute information to investors. As an illustration, let us consider the situation in the United States. In its release number 33-7233 (6 October 1995), the Securities and Exchange Commission stated its position very clearly:

> The Commission appreciates the promise of electronic distribution of information in enhancing investors' ability to access, research, and analyze information, and in the provision of information by issuers and others. The Commission believes that, given the numerous benefits of electronic distribution of information and the fact that in many respects it may be more useful to investors than paper, its use should not be disfavoured. Given the numerous benefits of electronic media, the Commission encourages further technological research, development and application. The Commission believes that the use of electronic media should be at least an equal alternative to the use of paper-based media. Accordingly, issuer or third party information that can be delivered in paper under the federal securities laws may be delivered in electronic format.

Good news? Not really. What was good news for most of the money management industry heralded the demise of hedge funds' presence on the internet. An internet website is accessible to millions of people, a significant number of whom could be potential investors. And this is strengthened by the existence of search engines and hyperlinks from other sites. Therefore, a homepage describing a hedge fund or its past performance, or indicating that it is accepting new investors could be construed as conducting a "general solicitation or general advertising". This presents a significant obstacle for issuers attempting to rely on the commonly used exemptions from the registration requirements of the federal securities laws. Consequently, hedge funds need to be extremely cautious when using the internet.

Fortunately, in 1998, the SEC issued an instructive report entitled "Use of Internet Websites to Offer Securities, Solicit Securities Transaction or Advertise Investment Opportunities Offshore". It clearly presents its opinion as to the general application of US securities laws to the internet activities of offshore funds, issuers and other market participants. It also establishes a clear distinction between the active electronic targeting of US investors and the passive use of the internet to disseminate information to selected authorized investors. Three cases need to be distinguished:

- In the case of domestic offerings, hedge funds must be privately placed and cannot engage in public solicitation, including on the internet. In particular, the SEC determined that spamming (i.e. sending out mass emails), providing offering materials for a hedge fund on a website or offering links to this material constituted a general advertisement or solicitation. Internet usage is therefore limited to providing fund-specific information to qualified investors. In order to fulfil this requirement, most hedge funds have implemented password-protected sites, whose access is only granted after the operator of the site has confirmed that the investor is properly qualified. Most funds also request a 30-day waiting period between granting access to their website and accepting an investment from a given investor.
- In the case of offshore offerings, the corresponding hedge funds are off limits to most US investors. Nevertheless, the SEC is also aware that the global nature of the internet means that the websites of offshore funds are still accessible to US investors, and has issued a policy statement[41] on the matter. This set of guidelines states that offshore funds must "implement measures that are reasonably designed" to guard against sales to US investors through electronic media. Such measures must include, but are not limited to, prominent meaningful disclaimers indicating the non-US nature of the offering,[42] and obtaining proofs of non-US residency, e.g. checking mailing address, telephone number, or area code before sale, refusing cheques drawn on US banks, etc.
- Finally, funds concurrently conducting a security offering offshore and a private placement in the US must take reasonable steps (meaningful disclaimers, passwords, etc.) and exercise extra care to safeguard against a US investor accessing documents originally targeted at offshore investors. In addition, the hedge fund should not allow a US person accessing the offshore website to participate in the US private placement, even if otherwise an accredited investor.

An interesting situation is that of a hedge fund posting information about itself on the internet through a database operated by a third party information provider. The SEC addressed this

---

[41] See "Statement of the Commission Regarding Use of Internet Web Sites to Offer Securities, Solicit Securities Transactions, or Advertise Investment Services Offshore" (Release Nos. 33-7516, 34-39779, IA-1710, IC-23071 of 23 March 1998).

[42] It should be noted that the standard disclaimer "the offer is not being made in any jurisdiction in which the offer would or could be illegal" is not considered as meaningful.

Box 3.15   The Greedy website

It was once said that any criminal who fails to exploit the internet to promote a scam should be sued for malpractice. Indeed, the internet offers inexpensive and anonymous access to millions of potential victims. And these victims will even sometimes look for a scam. Not surprisingly, with the popularity of the internet, unscrupulous individuals have sought to take advantage of emerging technologies to defraud the public, and this includes fake hedge fund managers.

On 13 February 2003, the SEC decided to make investors aware of their vulnerability and illustrate how easy it is to be taken in by false statements. The Commission staff developed a website advertising a simulated hedge fund called Guaranteed Returns Diversified, Inc. ("GRDI" or "greedy", for short). GRDI presented itself as "the world's leading operator of hedge funds", with $17 billion of capital, 68 offices world wide, 18 years of existence and 17 successful hedge funds. The (fake) historical track record claimed an overall 39.5% annual return, including 21% per year over the 2000–2002 bear market. By avoiding the "disclosure and filing requirements" imposed by the SEC and using "offshore tax havens" to store its monies, GRDI also claimed to be positioned to generate "a 22% return during the first quarter after launch" and "no less than 32%" afterwards. The offering web page ended with the words, "Remember that past performance is not indicative of future results. However, GRDI's track record has been outstanding over the past 18 years and we see no reason why those returns would not continue in the future." Between 13 February 2003 and 22 May 2003, the GRDI web site received over 80 000 hits and submissions for application . . .

---

situation in two no-action letters sent in 1997 and 1998 to Lamp Technologies. This company was primarily engaged in the business of data processing, software development, and the creation and maintenance of internet websites. It had the intention of offering non-US registered hedge funds the possibility of posting descriptive and performance-related information on a common website. All these funds would be paying Lamp Technologies a fixed fee for the posting service, independent of the number of sales and/or performance of the manager. Before starting operations, Lamp Technologies requested the SEC's opinion.

In its letters, the SEC confirmed that internet posting of hedge funds' private information on a third party website was allowed. This would not be considered as a general solicitation nor constitute a public offering of securities if certain procedures were followed: (i) any fund information on the site was password protected; (ii) potential subscribers to the site were pre-screened to determine if they would qualify to invest; (iii) the screening questionnaire and any invitation to complete the questionnaire were generic and did not mention any particular fund; and (iv) subscribers would be required to wait during a cooling-off period of 30 days after receiving their password before investing in any fund listed on the site (other than those for which the subscriber was being solicited or in which the subscriber had invested or was actively considering investing).

Finally, we should also mention that persons trading commodities, but who are not registered with the CFTC as commodity pool operators or commodity-trading advisers, may only use websites containing contact information. The posting of other material (e.g. performance data, biographies) will be considered as solicitation, therefore necessitating the establishment of specific disclosure documents in accordance with the CFTC rules.

Box 3.16   The ICE Team

California was one of the first US states to recognize the threat to investors from unscrupulous dealers intent on defrauding consumers using the internet. In 1998, it established the Internet Compliance and Enforcement Team (ICE Team) to administer a comprehensive programme of legal analysis, surveillance, investigation, training and prosecution. The ICE Team obtains leads from a number of sources, which include surveillance, undercover operations, junk emails, public complaints, and referrals from other law enforcement agencies. It also searches the internet for illegal solicitations, such as web-based bulletin boards, chat rooms, and Usenet newsgroups.

Since the Department's first internet securities enforcement sweep, the ICE Team has assisted in enforcement actions against hundreds of companies and individuals engaged in the illegal and fraudulent offering of investments and financial services, unlicensed investment adviser and broker dealer activity, and market manipulation.

As the internet transcends national boundaries, there is also increased scrutiny and enforcement by foreign jurisdictions, so hedge funds should also be cautious when posting information that may be accessible to foreign investors (Box 3.16). For instance, in Germany, the regulatory authority (BAKred) considers an offshore site written in the German language and providing information about a hedge fund to be a public offer to German citizens, and that, therefore, the fund should be regulated and taxed by the German authorities. A similar regulation exists in the UK as concerns websites accessible to British investors. In the UK, the Financial Services Authority issued a Guidance Release in February 1998. This Release clearly states the need to include disclaimers and warnings on a website, indicating that the site is addressed only to persons who can lawfully receive investment services, an approach similar to that of the SEC.

4
Operational and Organizational Structures

Did we overspend our budget, or did it fall short of our expenditure?

Regular personal problem

From a functional perspective, hedge funds are very similar to traditional investment companies. Both are separate collective investment schemes that issue shares to investors and manage pools of securities on their behalf. The primary differences are to be found on the organizational and legal sides. Mutual funds tend to be simple onshore organizations, while hedge funds need to be set up using complex onshore and offshore structures.

Ten years ago, a stand-alone hedge fund manager could open shop in relative obscurity with minimal cost and little or no infrastructure. He could operate with no internal or external control, and still have investors flocking to invest. This is less and less the case. Regulators have turned the spotlight on to the hedge fund industry and hedge fund investors are doing more and more organizational and structural due diligence. Hedge fund managers can no longer hope to operate purely as traders and outsource everything. They need to care about the quality of their organization, and so do their investors. In this chapter, our goal is therefore to "open the black box" and start looking at the different components that form the operational engine of a hedge fund.

4.1 LEGAL STRUCTURES FOR STAND-ALONE FUNDS

In essence a stand-alone hedge fund – or more generally an alternative investment fund – is an unregulated pool of capital contributed by a variety of sophisticated investors. The legal structure of this pool largely depends on who its investors will be and where the fund will be registered. For example, an onshore private investment vehicle formed for the benefit of US residents will be organized completely differently from an offshore investment vehicle formed for the benefit of non-US residents.

In this chapter, we will discuss the different structures available within and outside the US to create a stand-alone hedge fund. To keep things simple, we will denote by "onshore" anything that is located in the US and "offshore" anything outside the US.

4.1.1 In the United States ("onshore")

In the United States, the principal forms of business organization are sole proprietorships, partnerships (general or limited), corporations (C or S types), and limited liability companies. However, most of these forms are not suitable for establishing a hedge fund. Sole proprietorships have no separate legal identity. General partnerships' partners must assume unlimited liability. C-type corporations are separately taxable entities, i.e. their profits are taxed when realized at the corporation level and later when they are distributed as dividends at the investor level. Lastly, S-type corporations are restricted to no more than 75 shareholders and cannot have non-US residents as shareholders.

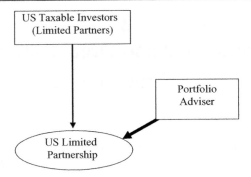

Figure 4.1   A typical limited partnership structure

We are therefore left with two possible pooling vehicles that could serve the particular needs of hedge funds, namely the limited partnership and the limited liability company. Both are separate legal entities that are created by a state filing. Both offer the same limited liability protection – the owners are typically not personally responsible for the debts and liabilities of the business. Both are pass-through entities, i.e. no tax is payable at the fund level and the tax attributes of the various investments are passed through directly to the investors. However, there are a few differences between them.

- A limited partnership has one or more *general partners* and raises money from investors who become *limited partners*. The general partners are responsible for running the fund and can be held personally responsible for any debts the partnership incurs.[1] Limited partners, in contrast, have no responsibility for making investment or management decisions and they are not liable for the partnership debts. The most they can lose is their investment – though with a hedge fund that is often a substantial amount.
- A limited liability company is a business entity with some characteristics that resemble a corporation and other characteristics that resemble a partnership. It consists of property and a single type of owner, who is called a *member*. Members are the equivalent of shareholders of a corporation or limited partners of a limited partnership in that they own an economic interest in the limited liability company. Unlike limited partners, some members (called manager members) can be officers of the limited liability company and can manage and control it. However, none of the members, including the manager members, is liable for the debts and obligations of the company.

The limited partnership (Figure 4.1) has historically been the preferred structure in the US for domestic funds, because it can easily accommodate investors subject to US income taxation (pass through) and avoid the problems linked to a public offering of securities (limited number of partners). The partnership structure also gives fund managers (general partners) the ability to take performance fees as a profit allocation rather than as fee income, which reduces the investors' adjusted gross income (AGI). This can be an advantage because itemized deductions on the investors' individual returns are limited at higher levels of AGI.

---

[1] In practice, general partners often take the form of a corporation or limited liability company in order to limit their liability. Note that in the US, the principals cannot limit their liability from the application of the anti-fraud provisions of the federal securities laws.

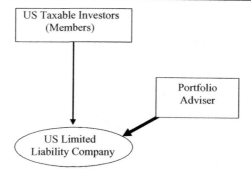

Figure 4.2   A typical limited liability company structure

However, limited liability companies (Figure 4.2) have recently emerged in several states as a viable alternative.[2] Delaware in particular has become the home of numerous hedge funds structured as limited liability companies because of its pro-business attitude, sophisticated filing system and knowledgeable employees, which makes the formation process relatively painless. In addition, Delaware generally allows more flexibility in the structure and operation of a business entity than other states (e.g. greater ability for the shareholders to act by written consent instead of via a shareholder meeting, and more permissible types of shareholder voting agreements).

Note that non-US investors in a US-based hedge fund are subject to withholding tax on any distributions, which makes US registration unattractive. Locating the fund in an offshore tax haven eliminates the problem of withholding tax on distributions for non-US investors.

4.1.2   Outside the United States ("offshore")

Hedge funds domiciled outside the United States are generally structured as offshore open-ended companies. The majority of them are registered in sunny jurisdictions such as the Cayman Islands, British Virgin Islands, Bahamas, Netherlands Antilles or Bermuda for funds investing in North and South America. Alternatively, Ireland (Dublin) may be used for funds targeting Europe and willing to be registered there, while Mauritius, Hong Kong and Singapore are the favourite offshore centres for Far East investing. The advantages offered by these jurisdictions are obvious. They offer well-thought-through legislation, an easy registration process, a reasonable level of confidentiality, limited reporting responsibilities, and last but not least, a benign level of taxes. By contrast, when offshore funds come into contact with the United States, they and their promoters encounter one of the most highly regulated investment management jurisdictions and complex tax codes in the world (Figure 4.3).

The choice of a particular place of incorporation is extremely important for a hedge fund. Several requirements will usually dictate the final choice, including:

• The tax-free or tax-favourable nature of the jurisdiction (profits, capital gains, distributions, withholding taxes, deferring of incentive fees, etc.). Most offshore hedge funds operate tax free as long as no nationals from the jurisdiction of organization are investors and local

---

[2] Note that a few US states still consider the limited liability company as a separate taxable entity.

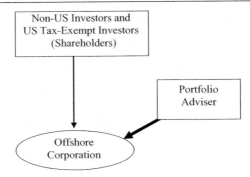

Figure 4.3   A typical offshore corporation structure

operations are limited primarily to administrative operations. Therefore, the tax characteristics of the underlying income no longer pass through directly to the shareholders (as in the limited partnership) but the income is not truncated.

- The public image of the country, since this will directly affect the fund. In particular, the Financial Action Task Force of the OECD has identified a series of jurisdictions that are non-cooperative with respect to fighting money laundering. Most hedge funds will attempt to avoid countries mentioned on this list to protect their image.
- The availability of competent local service providers, such as banks, lawyers, accountants, administrators and staff.
- The various types of investment vehicles available.
- The operating costs. Some countries have developed a comprehensive scheme for the organization and administration of investment funds. This provides additional security to potential investors, but increases the costs of establishing and maintaining a fund there.
- The convenience of the location in terms of travel time, time-zone difference, language, etc. In particular, the time difference with European offshore jurisdictions can create important administrative difficulties for US managers.
- The local regulations regarding confidentiality and secrecy, money laundering, restrictions on investment policy, etc. In particular, most non-US investors do not want any information about them reported to the US tax authorities.
- The targeted investments and their location.
- The targeted investors and their countries' regulations.

In practice, most offshore funds maintain their custody and administration in the offshore country, while the hedge fund adviser is located elsewhere, e.g. in the United States or Europe.

Offshore hedge funds generally attract the investment of non-US residents, who prefer to retain their anonymity and avoid paying Uncle Sam taxes. They might not, however, escape the scrutiny of their home tax jurisdiction, and this might result in a prohibitive level of taxation. German tax authorities, for instance, consider any increase in the value of the fund as being dividend income and tax it as such.

Offshore hedge funds also attract the assets of US tax-exempt entities, such as pension funds, charitable trusts, foundations and endowments. The reason is that US tax-exempt investors are subject to taxation in respect of unrelated business taxable income (UBTI) if they invest in domestic limited partnership hedge funds – see Box 4-1.

Box 4.1 Unrelated business taxable income (UBTI)

Under US income tax laws, most tax-exempt organizations engaging in an investment strategy that involves borrowing money are liable to tax on unrelated business taxable income, notwithstanding their tax-exempt status. In practice, UBTI includes any income earned from investments that are financed with indebtedness. Yet, the entire strategy of a hedge fund revolves around using leverage, which allows it to increase gains for the shareholders. For that reason, tax-exempt investors, bodies or individuals would generally prefer to invest in a corporation – including an offshore one – rather than in a domestic partnership. As a result, fund sponsors usually organize separate offshore hedge funds for US tax-exempt investors. This is the simplest way for tax-exempt entities to legally avoid paying US taxes.

However, offshore hedge funds are usually not attractive to other traditional US investors primarily for tax reasons. Indeed, prior to 1986, US individuals could invest in an offshore corporation and avoid paying tax on any income from the investment until they disposed of it. This situation changed in 1986 with the application of the so-called passive foreign investment company (PFIC) rules. These rules were primarily designed to dissuade US investors from deferring recognition of the income earned in a passive investment vehicle. According to them, the income earned by an investor in a PFIC may be taxed in one of three different ways:

- *Qualified electing fund*: the US investor elects on his income tax return to pay tax on a current basis on the ordinary income and net capital gains from the offshore corporation, almost as if the corporation was a limited partnership.[3] However, this requires that the offshore fund issue to each US investor an annual statement detailing the investor's share of ordinary earnings and net capital gains generated by the fund during the year. Not all hedge funds are in a position to calculate and supply such information. In addition, the offshore fund must agree to allow the investor and the US Internal Revenue Service (IRS) to inspect its records so that the income can be verified. Most offshore funds object to this requirement, which may jeopardize the confidentiality of the other investors.
- *Excess distribution*: US investors are taxed on a PFIC investment when they receive a distribution in the form of a dividend or when they receive cash from the redemption or sale of shares. To balance the implicit deferral, there is an interest charge to be paid in addition to the tax liability.
- *Mark to market*: if the PFIC fund is traded on an exchange, the investor can make a mark-to-market election on his income tax return. Unrealized gain is treated as ordinary income and unrealized loss is treated as an ordinary loss.

The choice between the three taxation approaches is at the discretion of the taxpayer. However, in practice, the first option is not always possible if the fund manager cannot comply with the associated requirements, the second option is extremely complex, and the third option requires a fund listing, which is not always available. Consequently, most US investors choose to stay away from offshore hedge funds. Last but not least, offshore entities are always surrounded by an aura of suspicion by the IRS.

---

[3] Tax losses do not pass through the PFIC investors.

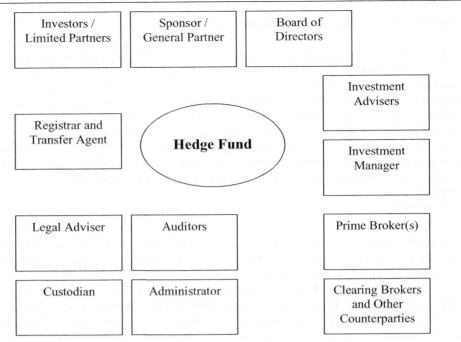

Figure 4.4 The typical hedge fund network

4.2   A NETWORK OF SERVICE PROVIDERS

Contrary to mutual funds, which tend to be large integrated monolithic structures with a large number of staff, a typical hedge fund business is small, at least at the outset (Figure 4.4). Most hedge funds operate through various external service providers to which certain functions are delegated. This allows a small number of personnel to easily access a wide skill base. In return, the service providers receive a specified fee from the fund pursuant to various agreements.

The use of specialized external service providers has often resulted in a better quality of service at a lower cost than doing everything in house. This explains why quality hedge funds tend to have better operational environments than traditional investment managers.[4] In addition, since hedge funds are loosely regulated, spreading responsibilities minimizes the risk of collusion between parties to perpetrate a fraud. Most hedge funds recognize these benefits and, before starting operations, they establish relationships with all the necessary industry service providers. Of course, the danger is that a network of service providers is only as strong as its weakest link, and vulnerability arises in the coordination of activities between the various service providers. It is therefore imperative to ensure that they work in harmony and that they all perform the tasks they were initially expected to perform. Let us now focus on the various roles of each player.

---

[4] For instance, the 1999 Global Investor/Latchly Management survey of UK *traditional* investment management firms highlighted the poor support of in-house back-office for core operational functions, even in the larger firms. This problem should not occur in a hedge fund, as an inefficient service provider would be promptly dismissed.

4.2.1 The sponsor and the investors

The sponsor is usually the creator of the hedge fund. Most sponsors are entrepreneurs in nature – they are former traders, stock analysts or portfolio managers who left investment banks, investment management firms and other large financial institutions to establish their own firm. They were lured by the potential earnings but also by the idea of owning their own company and leaving the burden of a traditional institution behind them. If the hedge fund is structured as a company, the sponsor typically receives founder shares. If the fund is a limited partnership, the sponsor (or an entity that he controls) is usually its general partner. In either case, the sponsor controls the management of the fund apart from a limited number of major decisions, and he receives an allocation of income from the fund based on performance – typically, 20% of the realized and unrealized appreciation of the fund each year over the high-water mark.

Investors contribute capital and receive some form of ownership – in companies, they hold shares and in limited partnerships they are the limited partners and have a capital account. Most of the time, the sponsor will also be an investor and contribute his own capital.

4.2.2 The board of directors

Most offshore hedge funds have a board of directors to oversee the way the fund operates and to ensure that corporate policies are followed. A board of directors normally contains both interested and independent directors. Interested directors are typically employees of the fund's investment adviser. Independent directors, in contrast, should not have any significant relationship with the fund's adviser, which allows them to provide an independent check. They are usually prominent individuals with diverse backgrounds in business, government or academia, often with distinguished careers and experience.

In theory, the board of directors has a long list of duties:

- To review and approve the investment advisers' contracts and fees, the selection of independent auditors and attorneys, and the appointment of the fund's transfer agent, custodian, etc.
- To regularly verify whether the selected service providers have the relevant expertise to work with the fund's particular strategy. For instance, administrators must have the skills and resources to value all the fund's assets and not allow fund managers to overwrite valuations of certain instruments; custodians must understand the legal aspect of ascertaining ownership of the instruments they hold; lawyers must understand the strategy and the underlying investments in order to recommend the disclosures and risk factors that are appropriate in the offering documents, etc.
- To ensure compliance with the fund's prospectus and the fair treatment of all investors.
- To oversee matters where the interests of the fund and its shareholders differ from the interests of its investment adviser or its portfolio manager.
- To ensure that risk management guidelines are adhered to.
- To review the manager's risk management system and check that it is relevant to the chosen investment strategy.
- To review the operations of the fund manager himself and in particular issues such as cross-selling between funds, allocation of trades, and personal dealings.

In practice, however, it is questionable whether boards of directors have a sufficient understanding of the nature of the investment strategies utilized by hedge funds; their judgements about investment strategy will therefore be of limited value. In addition, if ownership of a hedge fund is concentrated in the hands of a limited number of sophisticated shareholders, the role of the independent directors remains unclear. What criteria would they use that did not involve substituting their judgement of risk for that of the investors they represent?

4.2.3   The investment adviser

The fund adviser is often the linchpin of a hedge fund. Most of the time closely related to the sponsor, his role is to establish the hedge fund, organize it and run it. The activity of the hedge fund adviser usually starts by overseeing the preparation of the legal and subscription agreement, as well as the applicable limited partnership or limited liability company agreement and the arrangements with external service providers. The adviser is also often in charge of marketing and distributing the fund's shares to investors, as well as providing periodic reports to investors about the fund's performance.

Having a separate entity to function as the fund adviser offers several advantages. First, it allows the distribution of equity interests in the investment adviser entity to retain, motivate, and compensate key personnel. Second, in many cases, the incentive compensation is paid directly to the investment adviser rather than to the sponsor. The incentive compensation can take the form of a performance fee, in which case it is an item of expense that is paid by the hedge fund. Alternatively, if the investment adviser is, or is intended to become, a partner (e.g., an investor) in the hedge fund, the incentive compensation can also take the form of a performance allocation. The latter is a special allocation to the investment adviser's capital account of net investment income, realized capital gains, and unrealized capital appreciation that would otherwise be allocated to investors.

The size and organization of hedge fund advisers varies greatly. It can range from one individual with multiple hats and few formal procedures to large organizations with sophisticated systems and numerous employees. However, in the US since February 2006, almost all hedge fund advisers have been subject to many of the same requirements as mutual fund advisers – see Chapter 3. This includes in particular registration with the SEC, the designation of a chief compliance officer, the implementation of policies to prevent the misuse of non-public customer information and ensure that the votes of client securities are used in the best interests of the client, and the implementation of a code of ethics. In addition, the SEC is allowed to inspect all registered hedge fund advisers at any time and may deny the registration of anyone convicted of a felony or having a disciplinary record.

4.2.4   The investment manager or management company

The investment manager's primary responsibility is to manage the portfolio of the fund from an operational perspective and implement the recommendations of the investment adviser. The investment manager normally covers his operating expenses by an asset-based fee.

In the case of an onshore fund, the investment manager is usually structured as a company that belongs to or is affiliated to the fund sponsor. This limits the sponsor's responsibility and is often more efficient from a tax perspective. In the case of offshore funds, a single entity may act as both sponsor and investment manager.

4.2.5 The brokers

Unless a hedge fund has direct access to the market, it needs to place its orders with brokers. The traditional solution was to use the services of an executing/clearing broker, which compiled the best bids and offers, executed trades, and provided full reconciliation as well as limited administrative services. These brokers were typically rewarded explicitly by a fee for custodial and trade processing services, and competition was only about best execution, basic clearing services and consolidated reporting statements. This was possible because there were very few firms that catered to hedge funds in this capacity and consequently there was little pressure on providers to improve their services. However, over the years, the increased importance of hedge funds combined with their demand for additional services beyond simple trade execution convinced a large number of investment banks to enter the market and develop their prime brokerage activities.

Today, prime brokers should be seen as full service providers across the core functions of execution and operations. Among the key services that they can offer are:

- *Clearing the trades*: Prime brokers clear trades, which are executed with their own broker–dealer, or if desired by the fund, which are executed with other brokers. When a fund designates a prime broker, it instructs all its executing brokers to settle its trades with a single firm. Then, when there is a trade, both the hedge fund and its executing brokers report the trade to the prime broker. The latter settles the trade, custodies the securities or reports to the designated custodian if the details match, or resolves the case with the fund and the executing broker in the case of a mismatch. Trade allocation, confirmation and settlement are consolidated with the prime broker, allowing hedge funds to maintain a small operations staff but still execute complex and high-volume trades.

- *Acting as global custodian:* A key item of information for a hedge fund is the consolidated reporting of trades, positions and performance. It is therefore common to see prime brokers acting as global custodian for hedge funds.

- *Margin financing:* Most hedge funds use leverage to implement their investment strategy, but commercial banks are usually unwilling to take credit exposure directly to all but the largest hedge funds. Since prime brokers are able to take and monitor full asset collateral on their loans, they can intermediate and provide the leverage that hedge funds require, typically through revolving lines of credit, loans, or repurchase transactions. This streamlines the credit and documentation process, given that the hedge fund is subject to only one internal credit review and executes one master trading agreement and credit support annex with the prime broker, rather than many agreements with multiple credit providers.

- *Securities lending:* The ability of a hedge fund to take short positions is a key part of its trading strategy and it is the securities lending desk at the prime broker that mainly facilitates this process. Prime brokers maintain a securities-lending network, comprising banks, large institutional holders and other broker–dealers, and act again as intermediaries – most institutional securities lenders would not accept the credit risk of dealing directly with hedge funds whereas they are more than happy to take exposure to the prime broker. Although some pure custodians do offer limited securities lending and financing to hedge funds, this is on a very small scale compared to the operations of prime brokers operating out of broker–dealers.

- *Risk reporting:* As collateralized lenders (see below), prime brokers need to have robust risk monitoring systems in place to protect them. It is therefore relatively easy for them to provide customized periodic reports at no extra cost to their clients. These reports may concern the pricing of securities, or the risk of the portfolio (value at risk, liquidity, etc.), or may even allow fund advisers to provide investors with some limited transparency information.

- *Research:* Prime brokers can provide access not only to their own research but also to third party research, which might complement hedge funds' own research and lead to additional trades.
- *Collateral management:* To cover their exposure in the borrowing and securities lending obligations incurred by the hedge fund and ensure their rights of legal recourse in the event of default by the fund, prime brokers usually request some collateral. This collateral may take the form of either a full transfer of some assets or a conventional mortgage or charge over the hedge funds assets. Most prime brokers offer cross-margining facilities, i.e. the positions that need collateral are grouped and margined together. Such an approach, where offsets and hedges are taken into account, allows for the most efficient use of capital and optimizes the collateral management process.[5]
- *Capital introduction:* Brokers are entitled to distribute private hedge fund information to their own customers (i.e. potential hedge fund investors), even though the hedge fund itself has no pre-existing relationship with the brokers' customers. Prime brokers regularly arrange for hedge fund managers to speak at various conferences they arrange, where high net worth clients of the prime brokers are likely to be in attendance.[6]
- *Valuation:* Some brokers may also function as a source of pricing for certain types of securities.

It is essential to understand that the prime brokerage relationship still allows hedge funds to maintain relationships and execute trades with multiple brokers (Box 4.2), and yet provides them with a centralized source of information and leverage. In fact, a prime broker transaction occurs when a trade is executed by one party (the executing broker) on behalf of a hedge fund which directs that the trade be forwarded to another party (the prime broker) for clearance and settlement. The hedge fund then faces its prime broker as counterparty – the prime broker mirrors the transaction with the executing broker as counterparty, effectively intermediating between the two. The hedge fund obtains the economic benefit of the transaction, as intended, while the prime broker assumes the credit risk of the executing broker.

Overall, the move to prime brokers was a paradigm shift that was both significant and beneficial for the hedge fund industry. Most of the time, it resulted in simplified operational procedures, better service and lower costs. Today, prime brokers provide a wide range of essential services to the hedge fund universe, and many hedge funds would be unable to carry out their investment strategies efficiently without them. However, this is also a win-win strategy. With the development of this business model, prime brokerage-derived revenues have burgeoned. Anecdotal evidence suggests that prime brokerage now accounts for more than half of the equities division revenue of several leading investment banks. Big bonuses should follow . . .

---

[5] In the particular case of a prime broker acting simultaneously as a custodian, there exists a potential conflict of interest if the fund defaults. Should the broker put the emphasis on holding the assets as collateral or rather as a safe custody function? This should be clarified initially.

[6] It is likely that in the future, prime brokers will undertake more due diligence when promoting hedge funds via capital introduction conferences. The NASD has recently stated that if a prime broker offers capital introduction services for a hedge fund, this could be considered as a recommendation, depending upon its content, context and presentation, even when it does not explicitly suggest a purchase, sale, or exchange of securities. Consequently, prime brokers must ensure that the recommendation is suitable for the particular client notwithstanding the fact that the client is a qualified investor. Suitability means that the prime broker must have (i) a reasonable basis for believing that the hedge fund is suitable for any investor ("reasonable-basis suitability") and (ii) must determine that its recommendation to invest in a hedge fund is suitable for the particular investor ("customer-specific suitability"). The first condition implies that the prime broker has done a due diligence on the hedge fund, and the second that the broker knows the potential investor sufficiently well to recommend that investment.

Box 4.2   Trade execution

When (1) a hedge fund executes a trade with executing brokers, (2) those brokers inform the prime broker and "give up" the trade. (3) The fund manager provides all trade information to the prime broker. (4) The prime broker reconciles the positions between the fund and the brokers, consolidates all securities and reports back to the fund manager (Figure 4.5).

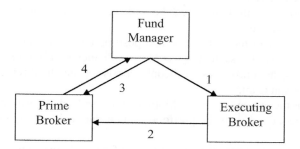

Figure 4.5   Trade execution with a prime broker – the simplified view

In reality, the detailed execution of a trade via a prime broker is far more complex than it first appears. As an illustration, let us review the various steps of a prime broker transaction on a US stock executed with Morgan Stanley (Figure 4.6).

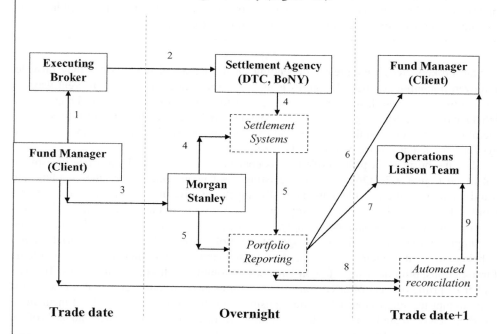

Figure 4.6   Details of a trade using Morgan Stanley as prime broker

(1) The fund manager places his order with an executing broker.
(2) The executing broker submits the trade to a settlement agency.

(3) The fund manager communicates the executed trade to Morgan Stanley Prime Brokerage, which processes the trade into its system.

(4) The processed trade is submitted to the settlements system to set up a delivery vs payment (DVP) or receipt vs payment (RVP) instruction to the settlement agent (e.g. a depository trust account (DTC), or Bank of New York) vs the executing broker. The DTC does an automated overnight match of instructions and sends back data of matched and unmatched trades.

(5) The processed trade information and the settlements system information are submitted to the portfolio system.

(6) The portfolio system feeds the trade and position data to the client – the client may have a direct feed to the system or use Morgan Stanley portfolio reports.

(7) The portfolio system produces hard-copy reports for the client representative and the operations liaison team.

(8) The client has the option of sending Morgan Stanley a feed of position and cash balance data to be reconciled with the portfolio system data using Morgan Stanley internal software.

(9) The reconciliation software produces reports of breaks between the client and Morgan Stanley's prime brokerage portfolio data.

For international trades, the process is similar, but the prime broker settlement system sends instructions to the international depositories and agent banks. International trades executed in a currency other than the local currency have a simultaneous transfer of cash and securities. For offshore accounts, the prime broker can also provide automated links to offshore administrators for communicating portfolio information.

Prime brokers' fees vary greatly depending on the nature of the services they provide. Moreover, obtaining comparable figures is usually hard. There are several different ways in which prime brokerage firms can be remunerated for services rendered, e.g. directly via a global fee or indirectly using spreads, ticket charges, stock loans or credit interest. In addition, several prime brokers bundle their fees and use soft dollars, so that the exact amount a fund pays for a particular service can be an elusive figure.

Today, the business of prime brokerage is concentrated in the hands of a few investment banks (see Figure 4.7). Owing to their existing asset management, securities lending and custody activities, these banks have natural competitive advantages and are able to offer a complete front-to-back suite of technology products. However, as the prime brokerage business has grown it has also become increasingly competitive and has moved from a demand-driven to a supply-driven state. A few years ago, prime brokers were able to impose strict criteria for being accepted as their client, such as minimum capital requirements, minimum volume of transactions, minimum size of debit balances or volume of shorting transactions. Today, a number of prime brokers offer capital introduction as an additional service at no extra cost in an attempt to obtain more hedge fund business, or even serve as hedge fund incubators, providing newly created funds with the technology, infrastructure, office space and back-office services that they need to grow.

Several prime brokers have attempted to lock hedge fund managers into exclusive relationships by offering them value-added services such as exclusive research, tax-compliance reporting, online communication, and trade date versus settlement date reconciliation. But the desire to reduce counterparty risk, to preserve some privacy for their proprietary trades and

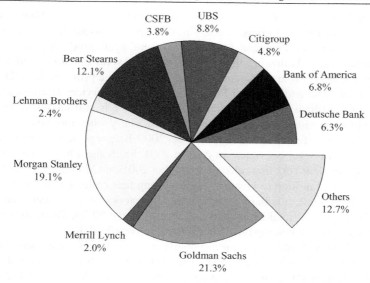

Figure 4.7   Top ten prime brokers as of March 2006 based on the number of hedge funds as clients (data from the CogentHedge database)

to clear and settle trades in multiple time zones has gradually persuaded the largest funds to use several prime brokers simultaneously. This reduces the potential consequences of a major prime broker failure but it also increases the complexity of the administrator's task, since he must ensure that he has all the feeds necessary to produce a daily profit and loss or position statement. If the administrator fails in this task, or even worse, there is no administrator, the consequences may be dramatic (see Box 4.3).

Box 4.3 The cases of Michael Berger's Manhattan Fund and David Mobley's Maricopa family of funds

In 1996, Michael Berger, a 29-year-old Austrian, started a hedge fund called The Manhattan Investment Fund Ltd. Following a strategy based on the overvaluation of the market, specifically the internet sector, Berger engaged in short selling. He immediately started to suffer losses but kept reporting large positive gains to his investors. This allowed him to raise over $350 million of capital over a period of three years, while most short sellers were displaying negative performance figures.

The reality came to light at the beginning of the year 2000: The Manhattan Investment Fund had lost more than $300 million, but Berger had failed to disclose these losses. His tricks were quite simple. The fund administrator used to calculate the fund's net asset value on the basis of daily statements sent by Bear Stearns that summarized the securities held by Bear Stearns on the fund's account. From September 1996, Michael Berger had started producing fictitious statements from Financial Asset Management, supposedly another broker to the fund, and sent them to Bear Stearns. The latter used both statements to compute the net asset value, overstating the true value of the fund. As an illustration, the reported net market value for August 1999 was $427 million, whereas the true value was less than $28 million.

The fund's auditor naturally requested information from Financial Asset Management. The latter forwarded the request to Berger, who simply responded to the auditors as if the information was coming from Financial Asset Management, again producing fictitious reports and overstating assets. Following the fund's collapse, several investors filed a lawsuit at the SEC against Berger (the fund manager), Bear Stearns (the prime broker), Deloitte and Touche Bermuda (the auditors) and Fund Administration Services (Bermuda), an Ernst and Young LLP affiliate (the administrator). The outcome is still unknown, but the case resulted in closer monitoring by administrators, particularly when more than one broker is alleged to be holding a fund's assets. In November 2000, Berger pleaded guilty to one charge of fraud, but he was never convicted. In August 2001, he changed his plea to "not guilty". A federal judge in New York first ruled on 9 October 2001 that Manhattan Investment Fund had to pay back $20 million to investors, representing fees collected. Since the fund only has about $240,000 left, it is hard to believe that investors will ever receive anything. As a matter of comparison, total legal costs are already above $9.5 million. Berger failed to appear at his sentencing hearing on 1 March 2002, in New York City.

The case of David Mobley is even more striking. In 1993, he announced that he had created a "black-box" timing tool to predict market movements and he started a group of hedge funds (Maricopa Investment Fund, Ltd, Maricopa Index Hedge Fund, Ltd, Maricopa Financial Corporation, Ensign Trading Corporation, etc.). Until the end of 1999, he regularly provided statements to his investors showing stunning gains of above 50% per year without any losing year. However, his performance was not audited, officially because it would be too easy to copy his proprietary trading system. The reality was that during these seven years, David Mobley used most of his clients' money to fund his lavish lifestyle and to actively invest in many of his own businesses as well as in local charities. All Mobley's close relatives held the fund's top positions, including his older brother William (President) and his 25-year-old son David Jr (Vice-President and Head Trader). Furthermore, it was revealed later that David Mobley had a grand-theft indictment, had been convicted of passing bad cheques, had made false representations on his application to the National Futures Association and had also previously declared personal bankruptcy.

The establishment of a prime brokerage arrangement requires specific legal documentation that sets forth the rights and responsibilities of the client, the prime broker, and any executing dealers. This document usually includes:

- A *prime brokerage agreement*, in which the prime broker agrees that the hedge fund may enter into transactions with dealers approved by the prime broker, and that the prime broker, rather than the hedge fund, will become the party to these transactions. Lastly, the agreement describes the procedure by which the prime broker will be notified of the transaction and specifies a list of allowable products and the applicable limits in terms of amounts.
- A *give-up agreement* between the prime broker and the executing dealer, in which the executing dealer agrees to give up its trades, on a principal basis, to the prime broker for trade processing, subject to compliance with specified terms. As such, the prime broker becomes the credit and accounting consolidation vehicle, managing the customer's settlements, confirmations, record keeping and other administrative tasks. A give-up agreement is normally executed as a master ISDA agreement, supplemented by a give-up agreement notice for each prime-broker client that will execute trades with the applicable executing dealer. The give-up

agreement notice clearly identifies the client (in our case: the hedge fund) and specifies the allowable products, tenors and specific limits that apply to the trades that the prime broker must accept for that client. This allows an executing broker to verify for a given trade and a given hedge fund whether the prime broker is obliged to accept the give-up of the transaction. If a trade falls outside the limits specified in the give-up agreement, the prime broker can still be contacted for explicit approval, but he may decline the execution.

- A *compensation agreement* between the hedge fund and the executing broker. This agreement provides for the compensation of losses, costs or expenses incurred in the close-out of a position in the event that the give-up of a transaction is not accepted by the prime broker. In practice, the risk of a prime broker rejecting a trade is minimal, but it is always preferable to provide for such risk and its consequences in advance, rather than after the event.

Needless to say, a prime broker must always maintain a complete separation between its prime brokerage operation and its proprietary trading desks, if any. This separation should also include technology, research and operations departments. Prime brokers are also required to give equal treatment to their clients' transactions, whether executed with their own trading desk or with other brokers.

4.2.6   The fund administrator

Historically, as long as the hedge fund industry operated on a fairly modest scale, the role of the hedge fund administrator was rather limited. Most onshore hedge funds were internally administered and only offshore hedge funds outsourced their valuation to external offshore administrators, primarily to avoid US taxation.[7] Most of these offshore administrators were small boutiques often seen but not heard, and they played a very limited role for hedge fund managers.

As the hedge fund industry developed and the product offerings expanded, hedge fund managers had to cope with more and more challenges such as a changing regulatory landscape, the increased demand from investors for additional services and more frequent reports, and the request for full independent pricing and net asset value (NAV) calculation. The role of fund administrator therefore started to strengthen and the small boutiques metamorphosed into a number of highly professional businesses, operating with the help of highly advanced technological systems.[8] Today, the primary role of a hedge fund administrator is to provide back-office support by taking responsibility for the operations, administrative, accounting and valuation services, and the investors interface, thereby allowing the fund manager to concentrate on his trades. However, the level and scope of work involved varies substantially, depending on the type of hedge funds covered, their sophistication, and the activities already covered by the prime broker.

The NAV calculation is of paramount importance for a hedge fund and its investors, since its result will be used as the basis for all subscriptions, redemptions, and performance calculations. The first step in calculating the NAV is normally to download the daily trade activity of the fund manager from his custodian and/or prime broker(s). Then, the corresponding portfolio listing is matched to corporate action data supplied by various vendors to accrue dividends, coupons, etc. Automatic reconciliation matches the portfolio to the trades fed from the manager and to the holdings indicated by prime brokers.

---

[7] Prior to 1998, an offshore fund using a US-based administrator would be considered as having its principal office within the US, and therefore would be deemed taxable in the United States.

[8] The dwindling number of administrators may suggest that they are gradually disappearing. The fact is that several acquisitions took place over the past three years, thus reshaping the industry. Examples are Bisys/Hemisphere, Citigroup/Forum, HSBC/Bank of Bermuda, Mellon/DPM, J.P. Morgan/Tranault, Northern Trust/IFMI (Barings) and State Street/IFS, to name but a few.

The next step in the NAV calculation is to price all the positions. For non-concentrated investments in liquid securities, fair and impartial valuations are fairly easy to achieve, as recent transaction prices as well as marketable bids and offers are readily available from major data feeds (Bloomberg, Reuters, IDC, etc.). But for many other less-liquid, restricted or more complex investments favoured by some types of hedge funds, this is not necessarily the case. Transactional prices may not be available, or securities may be difficult to value without use of mathematical models. In such cases, the administrator must have a clear procedure to determine a fair value for these securities independently from the portfolio manager. This procedure should normally be outlined in detail in the offering document or in a separate document, which must be properly approved by the fund's board of directors.

In extreme market circumstances, when valuation becomes *really* problematic and the fund's board of directors may have to suspend dealing. For instance, during the 1998 Russian crisis, some previously liquid Russian securities traded at US$ 11 bid/US$ 23 ask. If the valuation formula for a particular hedge fund had stated that the NAV should be calculated on the basis of the mid-price, then investors would have been able to indirectly buy and sell at $17. The problem is that anyone buying or selling at the NAV would be diluting the remaining investors. The simplest solution in such a case is to suspend dealing in the fund's shares until markets stabilize and become liquid.

The importance of having the fund valuation performed independently from those charged with managing the fund cannot be overemphasized (see Box 4.4). In particular, a person who performs, checks or approves net asset values should never receive incentives or inducements based directly on the performance of the investment being valued, and should not report to managers who do. People such as traders or portfolio managers should never perform final valuations, or communicate prices to the administrator – except in very exceptional, fully disclosed and auditor-approved circumstances. This separation of duties and independence in mark-to-market has long been a fundamental principle of control in financial institutions, but it is still inconsistently applied in the hedge fund industry. Not surprisingly, failures to separate duties and lack of independence have often been important factors in recent valuation-related hedge fund failures.

Box 4.4 Beware of valuation problems

A study by the financial services consultancy and technology provider Capco offers some grist to the proponents of minimizing operational risk. The study investigated 100 hedge fund failures over the last 20 years and found that half of them were caused by operational problems rather than poor investment decisions. Valuation problems were an obvious concern in a large number of cases (35%), and they were generally caused by one of the following three factors (Figure 4.8):

- Fraud/misrepresentation, such as a deliberate attempt to inflate the value of a fund, either to hide unrealized losses, to be able to report stronger performance, or to cover up broader theft and fraud. Examples of such cases include the failure of the Manhattan Investment Fund and Lipper Convertible Arbitrage.
- Mistakes or adjustments, either for illiquid securities, or for large blocks where any attempt to sell would move the market. Significant variations were observed depending on which "correct" price was being used – i.e. the bid, offer or mid-point – especially when it came to instruments where bid/offer spreads were sizeable.

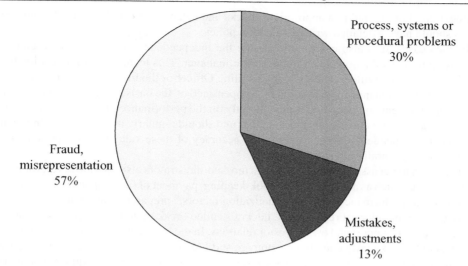

Figure 4.8 Causes of valuation issues implicated in hedge fund failures, according to the consulting firm Capco

- Process, systems or procedural problems, particularly for over-the-counter (OTC) instruments that cannot be handled by automated processing systems. Faults included incorrect pricing, but also positions being incorrectly captured on the fund's books and records.

As mentioned in the Capco report, "the devil is in the details", namely the procedures for obtaining prices from independent third parties on a regular basis and verifying the capability of these third parties to provide accurate prices. In cases of hedge fund failures due to valuation issues, Capco found that fraud and misrepresentation was the cause in 57% of cases, followed by process, procedural or systems problems (30%) and mistakes or adjustments (13%).

According to Capco, some strategies are obviously more sensitive to valuation problems than others. Let us mention in particular convertible arbitrage (limited liquidity, complex option clauses), mortgages, mortgage-backed securities and asset-backed securities (limited liquidity, high dispersion of market marker quotes), credit default swaps, OTC derivatives, bank debt, loans and distressed debt (illiquid and difficult to model), emerging markets (liquidity issues), and highly concentrated positions, and positions that make up a large proportion of a single issue (high market impact).

Note that there still exist a series of hedge funds that perform their valuations internally rather than externally. The reasons vary from a lack of confidence in external administrators to fear of the loss of a certain amount of control, or a focus on securities that are extremely difficult to value – in some cases, the hedge fund *is* the market. Our view is that this approach is definitely not acceptable for smaller boutique funds, where generally the organization is not large enough to allow appropriate segregation of duties and an appropriate level of checks and balances. It might be acceptable in the case of large organizations, provided there is sufficient segregation of duties and that appropriate checks and balances are in place. In addition, these funds should have a detailed written valuation policy.

In such cases, it is also essential to ensure the independence of the financial/accounting team running the valuations from the portfolio manager. This team should report directly to the Chief Financial Officer or the Chief Operating Officer of the fund management company, but not to the fund manager, and should be compensated on the basis of the overall profitability of the management company rather than directly on the performance of any of the investment vehicles managed by the firm. In addition, the fund should regularly use an external third party such as an independent auditor to verify the accuracy of these valuations – a periodicity of once a year is generally not sufficient.

In addition to net asset value calculations, most administrators also provide several administrative services, such as accounting and book-keeping, payment of fund expenses, including the calculation of performance fees and equalization factors,[9] preparation and mailing of reports to existing shareholders at regular time intervals called break periods,[10] help with tax assessment, basic legal support and even investor relations. In the US, hedge fund administrators may also ensure blue-sky laws compliance, prepare and file tax returns, including the realized and unrealized capital gains, and sometimes send some of the standard reports required by the SEC.

Administrators may also act as an independent body to ensure that the rules defined in the prospectus and other documents are respected, and that laws and regulations are followed. This includes activities such as paying the funds' filing fees on time, making sure that accounts are filed, and verifying that stock exchange rules and, more generally, international rules are followed, etc.[11] Lastly, administrators also provide hedge funds with several important documents, e.g. a full set of financial statements, including a statement of assets and liabilities, a statement of operations, a statement of changes in net assets and a portfolio. This is often backed up by portfolio analysis and other statistics of interest to the fund adviser, such as value-at-risk calculations. In the author's opinion, the administrator may supply such data but should not participate in the fund's risk management function. The reason is that this latter task is judgemental and should therefore be performed by another independent party. Nevertheless, in times of crisis, the administrator should remain proactive in the interests of shareholders.

Naturally, a fund administrator charges fees for his services. Depending on the complexity of the fund and the number of tasks performed, the administrator's fees may be as little as a few thousand dollars a year or go up to as much as 0.5% of the net assets per annum. However, to know the true amount it is important to dig deeper than the announced figure because some fees may be hidden or not immediately disclosed.[12] Needless to say, most of the administrator's services are common to all hedge funds, and substantial economies of scale can be gained by centralizing these functions and using cutting-edge technology and experienced personnel.

It should be noted that some offshore jurisdictions explicitly require the use of an independent administrator operating within their borders. These administrators are usually subject to specific licensing, auditing and record-keeping requirements as well. They are subject to anti-money laundering provisions, which set forth client identification and record-keeping requirements

---

[9] The subject of equalization factors is covered in Chapter 18.

[10] Break periods typically coincide with redemption and subscription dates, departures or admittance of new partners, etc. Any action that affects the hedge fund's capital is likely to result in a break period and in the administrative costs of valuing the entire portfolio. Note that reducing the number of break periods to reduce administrative costs is not really effective, since a valuation must obviously be done each time a contribution or redemption is made.

[11] The new EU Savings Directive, for instance, requires administrators to analyse the character (i.e. original capital, capital gain or interest/dividend income) of any monies distributed to or redeemed by an EU resident investor in a fund and, if applicable, report the numbers to the investor's local tax office.

[12] As an illustration, some administrators may charge a few additional basis points for the set-up of the account, for US tax preparation services, or even for custody services . . . which are sometimes already adequately performed by the prime broker.

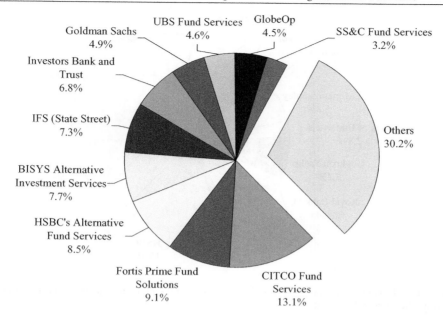

Figure 4.9 Top ten administrators as of November 2005 based on the assets under administration (data from the Hedge Fund Manager/Advent Software Hedge Fund Administrator 5th bi-annual survey)

in addition to obligations to report to the relevant authority in that jurisdiction any suspicious activity with respect to the funds they administer (see Figure 4.9).

4.2.7 The custodian/trustee

The primary duties of the custodian (referred to as "trustee" in the case of a unit trust) relate to the requirement to take into custody the assets of the investment fund on behalf of the fund. After all, what is a fund's extraordinary performance if the assets are not properly recorded in the fund's name? For simple stocks and bonds, this is not a problem, but for more complex financial instruments, the legal document certifying ownership may take a different shape and form and this could cause a risk to a hedge fund if the legality of ownership is not properly ascertained at the right time.

In addition, the custodian is in charge of providing payment when securities are bought and receiving payment when securities are sold, as well as monitoring corporate actions such as dividend payments and proxy-related information. Most of the time, the fund's assets consist of cash and securities that the custodian does not possess but maintains on an accounting system through a central depository. Lastly, the custodian is also responsible for providing periodic reports on the transactions within the account, and ensuring that the operations of the fund are conducted in accordance with its constitutive documentation and the relevant regulations.

The custodial fee can be a fixed fee or a percentage of net asset value, but when a prime broker acts as *de facto* custodian, he may also charge on a transactional basis (see Figure 4.10).

4.2.8 The legal counsel(s)

Legal counsels (Figure 4.11) assist the hedge fund with any tax code and/or legal matters, and ensure compliance with domestic investment regulations as well as with regulations of

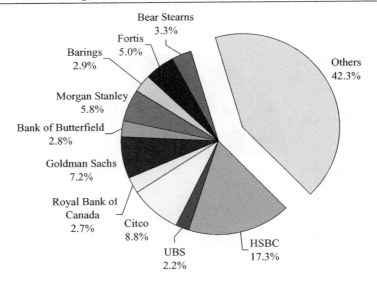

Figure 4.10   Top ten custodians as of March 2006 based on the number of hedge funds under custody (data from the CogentHedge database)

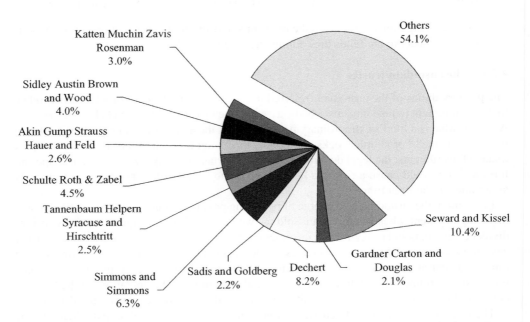

Figure 4.11   Top ten legal counsels as of March 2006 based on the number of hedge funds as clients (data from the CogentHedge database)

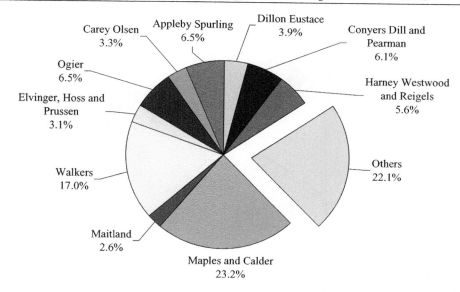

Figure 4.12   Top ten offshore counsels as of March 2006 based on the number of hedge funds as clients (data from the CogentHedge database)

countries where the fund is domiciled or distributed. They usually prepare the key hedge fund documents, e.g. the private placement memorandum, the offering documentation, and the partnership and subscription agreement, as well as all necessary questionnaires (access-accredited investors, qualified purchasers and new issues, etc.). They are also involved in specific transactions and may address tax issues. A hedge fund should appoint a legal counsel in appropriate jurisdictions, including where the hedge fund is domiciled and where the hedge fund manager is located and operates (Figure 4.12).

4.2.9   The auditors

The auditors' role is to ensure that the hedge fund is in compliance with accounting practices and any applicable laws, and to verify its financial statements (Figure 4.13). The audit usually takes place annually, in conformity with the relevant legislation under which the hedge fund is established, regulatory requirements or the constitutive documents of the fund. The auditors report and the financial statements are then sent to investors.

Investors tend to forget that, although the work of auditors is essential, the latter do not normally review fund valuations in detail, unless explicitly requested to do so – for example, in the case of funds that do self-valuations. In a recent survey by PricewaterhouseCoopers entitled "Global Hedge Fund – Valuation and Risk Management Survey", more than 25% of respondents stated that they rely on the auditors for an independent review and verification of the portfolio valuation. In reality, any testing of the portfolio valuation is usually restricted to only one specific date (the balance-sheet date on which reporting is made) and/or sample tested. Other hedge fund reports, e.g. weekly estimated net asset values, monthly statements and quarterly reports, usually remain unaudited.

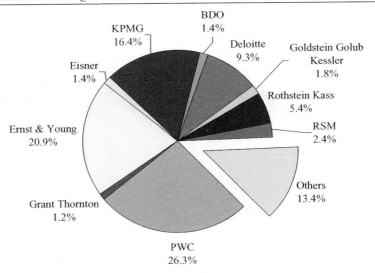

Figure 4.13 Top ten auditors as of March 2006 based on the number of hedge funds as clients (data from the CogentHedge database)

4.2.10   The registrar and transfer agent

The registrar and transfer agent retains and updates a register of shareholders of the hedge fund. He also processes and takes necessary action for subscriptions and withdrawals of shares in the fund as well as for the payment of any dividends and distributions, if any. The registrar and transfer agent also checks the anti-money laundering documentation, and ensures that funds are collected, matched to their application and paid over to the fund or back to the investor.

When a fund has no dedicated registrar and transfer agent, the administrator usually performs the function.

4.2.11   The distributors

Some hedge funds handle their distribution internally, that is, without a separate distributor. Their investors purchase shares in the fund directly from the fund or its registrar and transfer agent. However, in some cases, shares are distributed through a sales force, which may either be affiliated to the fund or independent, e.g. employees of independent broker–dealer firms, financial planners, bank representatives, and insurance agents. This sales force will contact potential clients directly in jurisdictions where this is legally possible, or assist clients willing to invest in the fund on an "unsolicited basis". In both cases, investors pay for the marketing and distribution of fund shares through a front-end load charge that usually varies from 2 to 5% of the amount invested and is deducted from the net proceeds.[13]

The use of commission-based external sales forces in the US calls for great wariness. Someone who introduces investors to the fund as a finder, does not need to be registered as a

---

[13] Note that dealing directly with the registrar and transfer agent does not necessarily reduce this fee. In some cases, it may even increase the fee, since some banks refund a portion of their distribution commission to their clients when subscribing to third-party hedge funds.

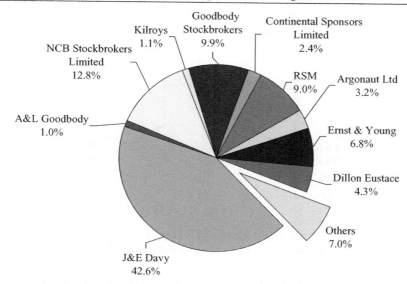

Figure 4.14   Top ten listing sponsors as of March 2006 based on the number of hedge funds as clients (data from the CogentHedge database)

broker–dealer. However, a finder implies a one-time situation involving a one-time payment. If the introduction of clients becomes a regular event, the distributor must be registered as a broker–dealer in the corresponding state or with the NASD.[14] Otherwise, the introduction is not valid, which means the private placement is not valid either. If the fund loses money, the investor who was sold his shares by a non-registered entity could sue the fund and ask for his full investment back on the basis that the offer was not valid. In addition, the state could sue the fund for violation of broker–dealer rules.

4.2.12   The listing sponsor

Many institutional investors are restricted or prohibited from investing in unlisted securities or securities which are not listed on a recognized or regulated stock exchange. A listing on a recognized and regulated exchange can therefore provide a valuable marketing tool for hedge fund and fund of hedge funds promoters. Several exchanges dedicated to hedge funds have been established, notably the Irish Stock Exchange, the Channel Island Stock Exchange and the Bermuda Stock Exchange. Most of the time, these exchanges offer no real liquidity or trading opportunities, but they facilitate the marketing of the shares/units to specific categories of investors.

Each hedge fund that wishes to list on the exchange is usually required to appoint an approved listing sponsor (Figure 4.14), which is registered at the exchange. The listing sponsor provides the fund with fair and impartial advice and guidance as to the application of the listing rules It is also responsible for ensuring the fund's suitability for listing prior to submission of an application, and for dealing with the exchange on all matters in relation to the application for

---

[14] Registration as an investment adviser is not sufficient, because there is no sale of advice.

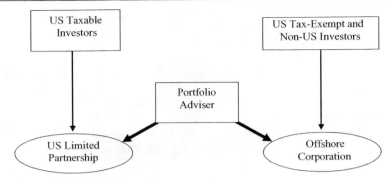

Figure 4.15   A typical side-by-side structure

listing. When a fund has been granted a listing on the exchange, the listing sponsor usually continues to act as the primary contact for the fund with the exchange.

4.3   SPECIFIC INVESTMENT STRUCTURES

It is often the case that hedge fund advisers need to deal simultaneously with US and non-US investors, or to provide particular conditions to specific investors (more transparency, better liquidity terms, etc.). Fortunately, there exists a series of well-established solutions to these requirements.

4.3.1   Mirror funds

In mirror funds, also called "side-by-side structures" (Figure 4.15) or "clone funds", two separate funds are created with identical or substantially similar investment policies, a common investment adviser, a common portfolio manager and a common custodian/administrator. The portfolio composition of the two funds is all but identical, although tax considerations and some differences of investment opportunities may cause portfolio and performance differences.[15] The cloning process essentially consists of facilitating bunched trades among the cloned funds and rebalancing cloned funds that have experienced different cash flows.

Mirror funds represent an effective solution to the problems inherent in reconciling inconsistent regulatory regimes, because each cloned portfolio maintains its distinct legal character and can implement individualized investment parameters. Take, for instance, the case of a hedge fund investing in US securities. The adviser could establish an onshore limited partnership or an onshore limited liability company for US investors, and a separate offshore company for non-US investors. This offshore entity allows offshore investors to remain outside the US tax and regulatory regime while allowing them to invest in the strategy pursued by the investment adviser. The investment adviser usually has an investment management agreement with the offshore fund under which the adviser's fees are paid – this permits the investment adviser to elect tax-advantaged fee deferrals from the offshore entity.

Mirror funds are very convenient for dealing with tax planning and tax-sensitive investments. As each type of investor has its own structure, no conflict of interests arises. However, the

---

[15] For instance, offshore investors will not hold US real estate in their portfolio, while US investors will.

potential conflicts of interest are usually found in the trade allocation – at the end of each day, the trades made by the investment adviser must be allocated between the domestic fund and the offshore fund. In addition, side-by-side structures do not provide for economies of scale in terms of account aggregation.

4.3.2   Master/feeder structures

Rather than running separate portfolios in parallel, some investment advisers prefer to aggregate their investments in one master fund. In such a case, the master/feeder structure is an efficient alternative.[16] Simply stated, a master/feeder is a two-tiered investment structure in which investors invest their capital in a "feeder" fund, which in turn invests in a "master" fund managed by the same investment adviser (see Box 4.5). The master fund has substantially the same investment objectives and policies as its feeders and will conduct all the investment activities. Each feeder shares in the profits and losses of the master fund according to its contributed capital. The flow of funds is of course reversed when an investor redeems his

---

Box 4.5 Master fund tax allocation

Master-feeder accounting is anything but simple. As an illustration, consider the example of a master fund with two feeders. Initially, the offshore feeder invests $1 million in the master, while the onshore feeder invests nothing. The first month, the master earns $50 000 of unrealized gain, which goes entirely to the offshore feeder. Then, the onshore feeder invests $1 050 000 and becomes a 50% owner of the master. The second month, performance is nil, and the securities are sold at the end of the month. Each feeder fund will receive $25 000, i.e. 50% of the $50 000 realized gain. For tax purposes, though, that is not appropriate, as the onshore feeder did not participate in any of the unrealized gain from the first month. Although taxes do not apply to the shareholders in the offshore feeder, this is significant for the partners in the onshore feeder, who are more acutely aware of tax issues.

   To avoid the problem, it is necessary to track each feeder's historical participation in the master in order to determine how much taxable realized gain it should receive from the master. A possible approach is the "aggregate allocation" or "book-tax differential" method, which works as follows. New partners acquire a percentage of the entire partnership and not a percentage of each individual asset, and the administrator maintains a "memorandum account" to track each partner's share of realized and unrealized gains and losses in the partnership.[17] Moreover, a similar calculation must be performed at the onshore feeder level to fairly distribute taxable income based on each investor's historic participation.

   Note that it is relatively simple to determine how to allocate gains and losses to the feeders invested in a master fund when all investors participate in the gains and losses on a pro-rata basis. However, the situation gets more complicated when some investors are restricted to participating in some securities such as new issues, as we will see later in this chapter.

---

[16] A master/feeder structure is sometimes called a "fund for funds" – not to be confused with a "fund of funds". In a fund of funds, the portfolio manager invests in funds that he/she does not manage, while in a master/feeder environment, the feeder fund and the master fund are managed by the same investment adviser.

[17] See Advent Software (2002) for examples.

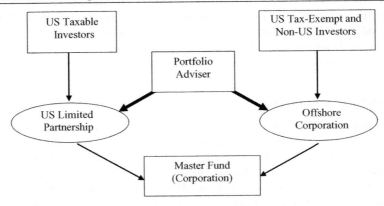

Figure 4.16   A typical master/feeder structure

shares: the master fund makes a distribution to the feeder, which in turn pays back the investor. Thus, the feeder fund is where investing starts, but the master fund is the entity where most of the trading activity occurs (see Figure 4.16).

There are several advantages to using a master/feeder construction:

- Each feeder fund can have its separate identity, regulator, management, fee structure, investment minimum and/or distribution channel.
- Several categories of investors can participate in the same investment strategy. As an illustration, fund sponsors may find it desirable, for tax or any other reasons, to establish separate investment vehicles for US investors and for foreign investors. Rather than establishing two separate investment vehicles (as is the case with the side-by-side structure), the sponsor may establish an offshore master fund with a domestic feeder for US investors and an offshore feeder for non-US investors.
- Master/feeders remove the administrative burden of splitting trades or using average prices to allocate securities between several funds. In the master/feeder structure, all transactions are centralized in one place.
- Master/feeders increase the critical mass of assets. This allows for a reduction in the number of transactions and reduces the trading costs. It also increases the collateral available for leveraged transactions, therefore yielding better terms for both feeders.
- Incentive fees can be taken either as a profit allocation from the master fund, or at the feeder level. In the latter case, they can be structured as a profit allocation from the domestic partnership and as a straight fee from the offshore corporation. This allows the fund adviser to defer recognition of the income and thus the payment of the tax liability associated with the performance fees earned.

On the negative side, the following should be considered:

- Master/feeder constructions can result in a conflict of interests between the tax-planning needs of taxable US investors and the lack of such needs on the part of both non-US and tax-exempt US investors. This conflict may relate to the realization of capital gains or losses, or the payment of withholding taxes – see Box 4.5. It may also relate to US dividend tax rules, as US taxable investors generally prefer their stocks not be loaned so they can potentially earn qualified dividend income (QDI), whereas non-US and tax-exempt investors, who do not qualify to earn QDI, prefer their stocks be loaned to generate additional income.

- Offshore investors and their feeders often have more favourable redemption terms than their onshore counterparts. When facing adverse market conditions, offshore investors may decide to redeem their shares, forcing the fund to realize losses and affecting the continuing onshore investors, who do not have the option to redeem.
- Due to the duplication of entities, master/feeder funds entail additional fees in terms of operations and organization. This will be negligible for large funds, but may significantly affect small start-up funds.
- When an offshore feeder feeds into a master fund, the offshore administrator may have to rely on the valuation of the master fund to produce the NAV of the feeder, but has no access to the master fund's underlying data. This may result in a serious problem if the valuation of the master fund is provided by the manager.

An essential question is: Where should the master fund be located? Two common types of hedge fund structures exist – the US master-feeder and the offshore master-feeder. The tax implications differ for each depending on the type of investor.

- In offshore master-feeders, the master fund is located offshore and is typically structured as a corporation under local law. The master fund can remain offshore and eliminate the potential risk of being classified as a US investment company and the necessity of blue-sky compliance, or it can choose to "check the box" and elect to be taxed as a partnership for US tax purposes. In the latter case, the onshore feeder will receive "pass-through" treatment for its share of the master fund's profit and losses.
- In onshore master-feeders, the master fund is located onshore (Figure 4.17). This allows US investors to invest directly in the master fund without having to set up another feeder.

In both cases, US source dividends earned by non-US investors in the feeder are subject to a 30% US withholding tax.

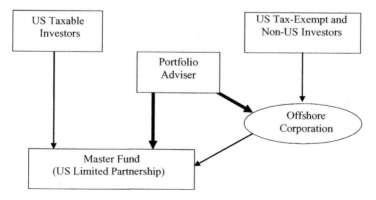

Figure 4.17   A typical onshore master/feeder structure

4.3.3   Managed accounts

Some hedge fund advisers offer managed accounts rather than fund shares to some of their clients, typically for accounts larger than $100 million. Simply stated, a managed account can be seen as a segregated investment account in which the investor has direct ownership of the individual securities in the account.

From an operational perspective, a managed account simply takes the form of an account opened by the client at a prime brokerage house or at a bank. The fund adviser receives a mandate to manage the account by giving orders to purchase and sell securities on behalf of the client, as if he was managing his own fund. However, this mandate can be withdrawn without notice, and the assets are held in the name of the client in a segregated account. The advantages for the investor are full transparency and high liquidity, since he receives daily reports from the prime broker about his position and can easily close his position within a few days. In addition, since it is run independently, a managed account can be tailored to his unique circumstances and objectives, including tax considerations, risk versus return requirements, and other financial goals.

Several financial intermediaries have taken the managed account concept one step further by creating managed account platforms (Figure 4.18). For a fee or a retrocession, these platforms offer the full range of middle- and back-office services as well as independent valuation and risk monitoring to fund managers that want to offer their clients managed accounts. In this case, the fund manager is simply employed as an investment adviser, an agent, of the managed account platform under the terms and conditions of an investment advisory agreement. He can still run his own hedge fund independently of the managed account platform.

Marketers often cite managed accounts as the panacea when it comes to hedge fund investing and investor protection. However, the truth is that managed accounts also suffer from serious limitations. In particular, the monitoring of security level positions remains a challenge in itself, which is absolutely not resolved by managed accounts. The transparency offered by the managed account may be at the security level, but it is completely useless if the investor or

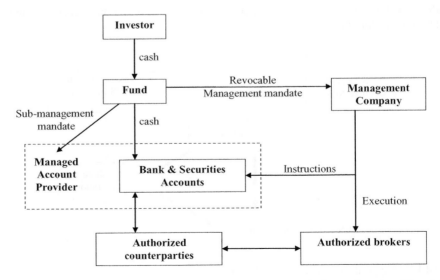

Figure 4.18   Organization model of an advanced managed account platform – based on Giraud (2005)

the managed account platform does not have sufficient resources to analyse risk exposures on a daily basis, verify the pricing of all securities, check the risk limits, etc. And just looking at the numbers is generally not sufficient. For instance, the Beacon Hill Fund, which collapsed in 2002, was offering managed accounts. The average leverage Beacon Hill historically employed was eight times but the most that they could use was set at 15 times. So when Beacon Hill's leverage rose towards 15 times prior to collapsing, no alarm bells started ringing at any managed account platform as this was still within the maximum permitted. Indeed, managed account owners generally require a deep infrastructure to support the ongoing legal, operational, administration, risk management and daily oversight of the account – but not many platforms actually have all these elements.

In our experience, another key limitation is that the best hedge fund managers are in so much demand that they do not offer investors the facility of a separate managed account.[18] Indeed, managers agreeing to – not to say, needing to – offer managed accounts tend to be:

- New hedge fund managers who are having difficulties raising assets by themselves and hope to grow by agreeing to do a managed account.
- Established managers who have gone through a period of poor performance, or a poor environment for their strategy leading to poor performance, or faced redemptions, and therefore are looking for new capital.
- Managers with weak or immature operational infrastructures in their main fund. Investors often believe that the security and protection of a managed account will be sufficient to negate or reduce operational risks while they will help the manager on his learning curve to improve this part of his business. Needless to say, this belief is illusory. If a manager's infrastructure is not up to standard in his own fund, it is not going to be sufficient to meet the demands of running the additional burden of a separate managed account.
- Managers that the investor does not trust sufficiently to invest in his fund. Here again, investors somehow believe that having a managed account will protect them from the risk of fraud or other operational risks. It is again our view that if you do not trust the manager or have any reservations about his integrity or infrastructure, then you should not invest with him, whatever the investment vehicle. Hoping to turn lead into gold by using managed accounts is a pipe dream.

Last, but not least, managed accounts often depend on the institution behind the managed account platform and its trading capabilities. Divergences in execution and restrictions in terms of trading instruments or markets may result in important discrepancies between the managed account and the original fund, particularly when considering less liquid instruments or OTC derivatives. Moreover, in thinly traded markets, the fund manager will be doing the trade on his own fund, but will have to wait for approval to allow the trade to be done on the managed account . . . possibly until after the prices have moved.

Nevertheless, despite these disadvantages, managed accounts have taken off in recent years for a number of reasons, including (i) the greater demand by institutional investors for transparency, (ii) the growing use of structured products leading to increased liquidity requirements and (iii) the increasing appetite for investable hedge fund indices, which are largely based on managed account platforms. Indeed, managed accounts are the only practical solution for

---

[18] A review of the blue chip managers shows they either have never offered a managed account facility or no longer offer it. As an illustration, Caxton terminated all his separate accounts in the mid-1990s, and Tudor and Moore stopped offering such a facility in the late 1980s and very early 1990s when they set up their own offshore and onshore funds.

investors wishing to invest in hedge funds but requiring extreme liquidity conditions, e.g. weekly or daily. But they should carefully assess the real costs and benefits of their decisions before taking the plunge.

4.3.4   Umbrella funds

Invented more than 20 years ago in Europe, the concept of an umbrella structure has become popular among some hedge fund managers. Umbrella funds are simply a collection of sub-funds with a common or central administration and brand. Each sub-fund has a separate investment policy and a separate portfolio of assets, and is run by a team of portfolio managers and analysts (Figure 4.19). A net asset value is calculated separately for each sub-fund, and shareholders are entitled only to the assets and earnings of the sub-fund in which they have invested.

Umbrella funds are tax-efficient, since investors can usually transfer shares from one sub-fund to another without creating a capital gain, which would be taxable. Should investment objectives and needs change over time, investors in an umbrella fund can usually also switch between the sub-funds available, incurring reduced or minimal charges. They also provide fund managers with greater market proximity and quicker reaction to customer requests, as well as cost-effective sales within a standardized marketing concept.

The danger of umbrella funds is that under some regulations (for instance the British Virgin Islands), the rights of creditors against one of the sub-funds would apply to all the assets of the fund vehicle, implying a potential risk of cross-liability for other sub-funds' shareholders. One common way of limiting this risk is for each sub-fund to trade exclusively through a separate trading subsidiary in order to ring-fence any liabilities.

As an alternative, several countries have implemented a *protected cell company (PCC)* regulation, which allows for segregation of assets and liabilities between sub-funds of an umbrella structure. Technically, there is only one legal entity, but the assets of each sub-portfolio are, as a matter of law, ring-fenced and are thus not available to creditors of other portfolios. In Delaware, where most US limited partnerships are formed, similar legislation is in place.

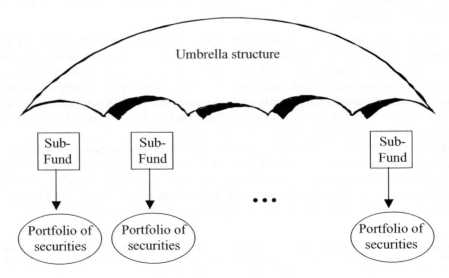

Figure 4.19   A typical umbrella fund structure

4.3.5   Multi-class/multi-series funds

Some hedge funds have a single portfolio of investments but issue different classes of shares to investors. This typically allows, for instance, distribution and accumulation shares to be offered simultaneously, or different expense charges to be applied, depending on the investor type, the amount invested and/or the redemption policy.

Another reason justifying the use of multiple shares concerns the fund's participation in the "new issues" market. A new issue refers to the securities of a public US offering that trade at a premium to their offered price immediately after public trading has started. According to the US National Association of Securities Dealers, certain categories of investors are barred from participating in new issues. Hedge funds have therefore the choice of (i) staying away from new issues, (ii) refusing restricted investors, or (iii) establishing a specific profit allocation procedure (e.g. separate brokerage accounts and independent verification) to isolate returns from new issues and deny participation in new issue profits to restricted investors. The last-mentioned choice is relatively easy to implement with multiple shares, although the accounting may be quite complicated if multiple shares are combined with a master/feeder structure – see Box 4.6.

Box 4.6 New issues and feeders

When there is a new issue and a non-new issue class in a master/feeder structure, there exist essentially two methods of allocating the profits and losses from new issues to the feeders: the "pro rata" method and the "look through" method (Figure 4.20). In the former, the new issue profit or loss is simply divided based on the feeder's ownership of the master. In the latter, the administrator peers into the attributes of each participant's capital to see whether he is new-issue-eligible or not, and then comes up with the exact ratio.

Consider the following example. Feeders 1 and 2 each invested $200 in the master fund. Using the pro rata method, since each feeder invested $200, they would each receive 50% of the new profit or loss from the master. Using the look-through method and drilling down into the attributes of each partner's ability to participate in new issues, the onshore new issue partner would get 60% or $150 while the offshore new issue partner would receive 40% or $100.

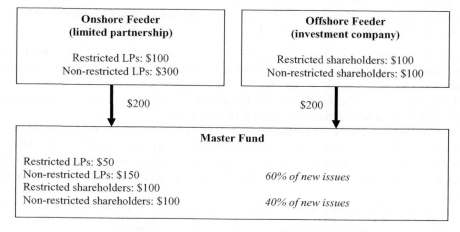

Figure 4.20   New issues participation and feeders – the "look-though" method

4.3.6   Side pockets

In recent years, many hedge funds have started combining illiquid – or what are sometimes referred to as "special" or "designated" – investments in the same pool as traditional hedge fund assets, which are by their nature marketable. If the designated investment is held in the general portfolio and some but not all investors redeem, the remaining investors will hold a disproportionately large interest in the illiquid and perhaps non-marketable investments owned by the fund. This creates a serious liquidity threat, but also a valuation issue. Since designated investments are by their very nature difficult to accurately price until their realization or the occurrence of a liquidity event such as a public offering or take-over, their presence in the general portfolio may distort the net asset value (NAV) of the fund. If the distortion is on the high side, this will benefit investors redeeming before the distortion is determined to the detriment of those redeeming later. If the distortion is on the low side, the opposite but equally unfair result occurs. And related to valuation is the question of the manager's fees that are typically based on a percentage of NAV and a performance incentive over a hurdle or high-water mark. In extreme cases, the distortion in NAV arising from mixing liquid and illiquid assets may be so significant as to cause the NAV to be suspended because of the uncertainty in valuation.

Several hedge funds have resolved these issues by creating mini-funds within the hedge fund – often referred to as "side pockets". A side pocket is in essence similar to a single-asset private equity fund. When the fund acquires a designated investment, a portion of every investor's holding in the general portfolio at the relevant time is redeemed and exchanged for a portion of the newly issued class of shares representing this designated investment. Investors then have two classes of shares, the original ones (in lesser amount) and a side pocket (just created). Investors continue to keep the same redemption rights in relation to the liquid portion of the general portfolio, but they must hold the side pocket until the designated investment is liquidated, which may take several years. Then, the proceeds of the liquidation are either paid to the investor or reinvested by way of subscription into the general portfolio shares. Of course, investors that subscribe fund shares after the creation of the side pocket will not be affected by its existence. Side pockets, however, technically remain a part of the same fund and are included in its NAV, so their valuations must be calculated at least monthly to comply with generally accepted accounting principles.[19]

Owing to their illiquidity, side pockets must be structured properly to align the interests of investors and the fund adviser. In particular:

- It should be clearly specified when the fund adviser can decide that an investment will be structured as a side pocket. Otherwise, there may be a temptation to sideline a non-producing asset in order to maximize the performance fee on better performing investments.
- Management fees should typically be charged on side-pocket assets based on their cost, although some advisers mark-to-market for this purpose.
- Incentive fees should be charged only on realized proceeds, i.e. at the liquidation of the side pocket.[20] Note that this may result in conflicting situations if not properly understood by investors. For instance, a poorly performing side pocket may flatten the fund's NAV, but the adviser will still receive a performance fee based on the positive returns from the

---

[19] The valuation of side-pocket assets may be done using a third-party valuation firm or calculated in house by the fund manager. In either case, the fund administrator should request documents supporting the valuations. Typically, side-pocket assets are left at cost until their estimated fair market values change significantly and in a way that can be documented.

[20] Unlike a private equity fund, side-pocket losses do not result in the clawback of fees.

larger liquid portion. However, if the more liquid portion of the fund has a negative performance while the side pockets do well and bring the fund's NAV into positive territory, the adviser will not receive any performance fee – at least until the side-pocket investment is realized.

- The funds' constitutional documents and offering document should clearly disclose limitations on the overall level of investments which may be allocated to side pockets (typically a percentage of the overall assets) and which may require ongoing disclosure of allocation and realization events as they occur. It is normally the role of administrators to monitor the agreed upon side-pocket limit to make sure it is not exceeded.

When properly used, a side pocket is a useful tool, which adds flexibility to traditional hedge fund structures. The side pocket's ability to segregate illiquid and liquid investments for accounting purposes allows hedge funds to take advantage of investment opportunities that would otherwise cause valuation and liquidity issues. Side pockets can create a potential private equity type vehicle of reasonable size within a hedge fund. In a sense, they even provide more flexibility than a private equity fund, because they have no fixed maturity and therefore no requirement to liquidate at a certain date.

4.3.7   Structured products

When there are legal, tax, currency or regulatory barriers to investing directly in a hedge fund, it is usually possible to create a structured product that miraculously accommodates the investor's needs and provides similar economic benefits. Structured products are discussed at length in Chapter 26, but the key structures that are used to create them are as follows.

In most cases, a structured product involves the creation of a special purpose vehicle (SPV) – see Figure 4.21. This SPV acquires the hedge fund shares or becomes a limited partner in the hedge fund and issues a back-to-back structured product that investors can buy. In the simplest case, this structured product may take the form of a zero-coupon note whose principal is linked to the performance of the hedge fund. The final investors are then note holders rather than direct shareholders or limited partners in the hedge fund. In more complex cases, the structured product may be engineered to provide capital guarantees, leverage, specific coupons, etc.

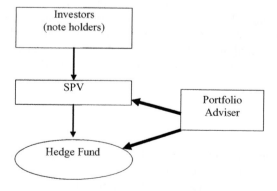

Figure 4.21   A typical structured product on a hedge fund, involving a special purpose vehicle

4.4   DISCLOSURE AND DOCUMENTS

Hedge fund advisers typically provide information on their fund in a limited series of documents. Rather than being widely distributed, these documents are restricted to serious prospective investors.

4.4.1   Private placement memorandum (PPM)

As a matter of practice, the private offering memorandum or private placement memorandum (PPM) is one of the principal vehicles by which hedge funds are introduced to potential investors. It is an overview document designed to provide a summary of the key elements needed to make an investment decision. The information disclosed in a PPM varies from one adviser to another, but it is often general in scope and includes a considerable amount of surplus verbiage. The reason is that this document serves many purposes, including legal ones.

The cover page of the PPM usually contains the name of the issuer, a summary description of the securities to be sold, a date and a handwritten number inscribed to help record the destination of each PPM. In addition, the first page often includes some self-serving exculpatory language relative to the limited and private nature of the offering and the confidentiality of the associated information.

There is no standard but the main sections of a PPM typically include: (i) an executive summary; (ii) the firm and fund investment philosophy and objectives; (iii) the biographies of key investment professionals and members of the board of directors; (iv) a summary of the terms and conditions, including the fees and expenses; (v) the investment track record and prior fund performance; (vi) legal and tax matters; (vii) inherent investment risks and potential conflicts of interest to investors, which serve as a notice of *caveat emptor*; (viii) accounting and reporting standards; and (ix) information concerning the use of affiliated services providers.

4.4.2   Memorandum and articles of association

The memorandum and articles of association of a hedge fund together act as its constitution. The memorandum is the charter of the company *vis-à-vis* the outside world, in particular the parties with whom the company will transact business, either directly or indirectly. The articles (sometimes called "by-laws") set out the regulations for a company's internal management and ordinarily govern, among other things, quorums for ordinary and extraordinary meetings of shareholders, quorums for meetings of the board of directors, voting rights of shareholders and directors, various procedural rules for the conduct of such meetings, election of directors, the binding signatory power of the company, the frequency of subscriptions and redemptions, and the valuation procedures.

4.4.3   ADV form

The ADV form is simply a form filed with the SEC by registered investment advisers. The form contains information about assets under management, types of fee arrangements, types of investments, other business activities, adviser backgrounds (including a 10-year disciplinary history) and a firm balance sheet – see Chapter 3.

4.4.4 Limited partnership agreements

Investors in hedge funds structured as limited partnerships enter into a specific limited partnership agreement. These agreements specify the respective rights and responsibilities of the limited partners and the general partner, who is usually the investment adviser. For example, these documents frequently list any restrictions on the percentage of an investor's assets in the hedge fund that a hedge fund will repurchase at any one time.

4.4.5 Side letters

Over the past few years, the hedge fund industry has witnessed a significant increase in the use of side letters, particularly among early-stage and institutional investors. For the record, a side letter is essentially a document that gives an investor contractually binding assurances from either the hedge fund or its investment manager that modify the rights and entitlements of that investor. Most commonly and in their purest form, side letters are used to cut side deals outside the constitutional or contractual arrangements of the hedge fund with specific investors, sometimes to the detriment of other investors.

Common terms in side letters include:

- *Different fees*: Investors love to negotiate reduced incentive and management fees on their investment. Typically, these fees are specified by a side letter between the investor and the investment manager whereby the manager agrees to rebate to the investor a part of the fee it receives from the fund. Note that nothing in these side letters is unfair – some investors end up paying more in fees than others, but all investors pay the fees they agreed to at the time of their investment.
- *Secured capacity:* A hedge fund's capacity depends upon the resources of its manager and the strategy it employs. An investor may require from the manager access to a predetermined amount of a fund's future capacity in excess of his previous investment.
- *Preferred liquidity terms*: Side letters often require a fund to provide notice of important events such as the resignation, death or other termination of a principal of the investment manager, a large number of redemptions, a redemption by a principal of the investment manager, a significant fall in the net asset value per share; or an investigation by a regulator of the fund or of the investment manager. Special redemption rights for the beneficiary of the side letter usually accompany such notification provisions. In practice, the principle of preferred liquidity terms is highly questionable. If a crisis occurs, certain shareholders will have advance notice and will be able to redeem their shares sooner than other shareholders. The early redeemers will take whatever cash and liquid assets are available, and leave the remaining shareholders holding the baby. The remaining shareholders will actually be worse off than if the shareholders with the side letters had never invested in the fund. The directors of the fund have to be extremely cautious before agreeing to such terms for fear of being held personally responsible for any loss suffered by an investor who did not have the benefit of such a side letter.
- *Key man clause:* In the event that a hedge fund manager is principally owned or controlled by a few key persons, the fund's success will depend primarily on their skill and acumen. A typical key man provision provides that if the key man dies, becomes legally incapacitated or ceases to be involved in the management of the hedge fund for more than a certain number of consecutive days, the manager will notify the investors who may then immediately redeem their investment.

- *Transparency:* some investors may require additional information or specific reporting regarding the fund's portfolio.
- *Grandfathering:* Grandfathered investors are ensured that, if there is an adverse change in the terms of the offer of shares set out in the subscription agreement or the private placement memorandum for new investors (e.g. an increase in the management fee), this change will not apply to their existing and future investments.
- *Payment of redemption proceeds*: Side letters often include a term stating that redemption proceeds shall be paid all in cash rather than in securities-in-kind, and within a certain period of time, which is usually sooner than the time period set out in the private placement memorandum.
- *Most favoured nation:* As the use of side letters has become more common, investors have sought to protect themselves from less favourable terms or conditions than those provided to other investors. An investor having the most favoured nation status is ensured that no other current or future investor will be offered more favourable terms for investing unless the same terms are offered to him.

As the use of side letters by hedge fund investors appears to be increasingly common, several questions and concerns arise:

- Do any terms of the side letter result in a breach of fiduciary obligation by the hedge fund's general partner, managing member or board of directors? If the answer is positive, then the side letter might be non-enforceable, as fiduciaries to a hedge fund owe an identical obligation to each investor. In such a case, it is preferable to create a separate class of shares for any investor who requests specific terms or conditions. Otherwise, the directors of the fund may be in breach of their fiduciary duties and may be personally liable for the losses of these other investors, if any.
- How can the adherence to numerous side letters be monitored, and in particular, how can one avoid conflicting side letters? If a hedge fund is subject to the terms of several different side letters, it is essential to ensure not only that the terms of individual side letters are tracked, but also that no conflict arises.
- Do the fund's offering documents disclose that certain investors have received preferential terms?
- Does the systematic demand for the same type of side letter indicate that the hedge fund's offering documents are "biased"? Whenever possible, the manager should attempt to address investors' genuine concerns in an organized and comprehensive manner, e.g. by building common side-letter items into the corporate documents.

Some regard side letters as "ticking time bombs". However, side letters are also useful, particularly for investors who have specific needs or reporting requirements that may not be covered by a hedge fund's offering documents. In order to avoid any detonation, hedge fund directors and investment managers should therefore simply ensure that their side letters are not unfairly advantageous to some or prejudicial to others.

5
Understanding the Tools Used
by Hedge Funds

Give me a lever long enough and a place to stand and I will move the world

Archimedes

Before going into detail about the various hedge fund strategies, we believe that it is useful to introduce the basic tools used by hedge funds to implement their trades, namely, buying, selling, short selling, buying on margin, using derivatives and leveraging. Several of these tools are not used in the traditional investment world, which explains why people often have trouble understanding them, or perceive them to be extremely complicated and/or purely speculative. In this chapter, we will therefore cover the basic mechanics and rationale of each of these tools and provide a good understanding of the subject-matter.

5.1 BUYING AND SELLING USING A CASH ACCOUNT

The key to successful investing – buy low and sell high – is one of the oldest pieces of investment advice on record. It sounds so simple that one could hardly argue with it. In terms of operations, the strategy involves two basic transactions, *buying long* and *selling* at a later date, hopefully at a higher price. Its profit simply equals the difference between the sale price and the purchase price.

Buying long is the most common strategy, at least from an individual investor's perspective. A hedge fund buying long has some cash and simply exchanges it for the security that it wants to hold. In a sense, the transaction can be represented as a swap (see Figure 5.1). Once the transaction has been concluded, the hedge fund has no further commitment. It fully owns the security and enjoys all its benefits (dividends, coupons, voting rights, etc.).

Selling is simply the opposite of buying long. A hedge fund wanting to sell a security that it no longer wishes to hold exchanges it for cash (see Figure 5.2). Once the transaction has been concluded, the hedge fund has no further commitment. It fully owns the cash, and can use it for any purpose.

Buying long and selling are called *cash transactions*, because they do not involve any loan and do not require any collateral. All the flows take place at the same time, and do not involve any future commitment. By contrast, other transactions are based on some form of lending and therefore require the posting of collateral and repayment of the loan. In this case, a securities company – typically a brokerage firm – will lend some securities or some cash to the hedge fund and will hold other assets in the fund's account as collateral for the loan. The collateral in this case is termed *margin* and can be made up of cash, securities or other financial assets.

The two major transactions requiring collateral are *buying on margin* and *selling short*. Both are usually confusing for neophyte investors. While conventional security transactions involve only two parties, the buyer and the seller, margin transactions involve a third party, the security

Figure 5.1   Flows resulting from a long buy operation

Figure 5.2   Flows resulting from a sell operation

lender. This is because both buying on margin and selling short imply borrowing an asset. When buying on margin, the hedge fund borrows some cash; when selling short, the hedge fund borrows a security. In the following, we attempt to clarify the differences between these two strategies by looking at the detailed flows they generate.

5.2   BUYING ON MARGIN

5.2.1   Mechanics

Simply stated, a hedge fund buying on margin has no cash, but would like to buy a security that it expects to appreciate in the future. It therefore borrows some money from a broker and exchanges it for the security. Naturally, the broker will ask for some kind of collateral to secure the loan (see Figure 5.3).

Later, once the hedge fund has enough cash and no longer needs the loan, it will pay it back with interest, and receive back its collateral. The cash may come from the sale of the security that was bought on margin, or from any other source (see Figure 5.4).

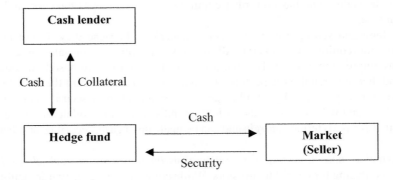

Figure 5.3   Flows resulting from initiating a buy on margin transaction

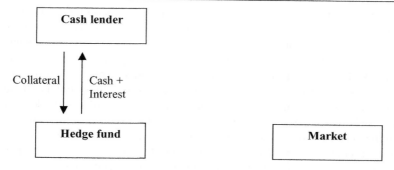

Figure 5.4   Flows resulting from closing a buy on margin transaction

There are several reasons for a hedge fund to buy on margin. First, buying on margin is an efficient way of borrowing against the securities already held in a portfolio, using them as collateral. The proceeds of such a loan can be used for both investing and non-investing needs. The interest rate charged is usually lower than in bank loans, and the repayment terms are much more flexible. Second, buying on margin increases the buying power and allows a greater amount of securities to be purchased per dollar of capital (i.e. leverage). Indeed, a fund manager buying on margin does not need to fully pay for his purchase – he just needs to post some collateral. With little cash or even no cash, it is therefore possible for him to take a position and enjoy its rise in price without really paying for it.

Brokerage firms also find several advantages in margin trading. They make money on both the margin accounts (from the interest they charge on the loans) and the trading (from the higher commissions they receive, due to the larger transaction sizes that leverage allows). Since margin loans are always secured by collateral, the default risk of a borrower is relatively limited. Indeed, the only risk is that the collateral plus the securities held in the margin account decline in value to a point where they are worth less than the loan balance itself. This raises two new questions. First, which type of collateral should be accepted? Second, how can one prevent the value of the collateral from dropping below the balance of the loan? To answer these questions and to prevent the excessive use of credit to purchase securities, most regulatory bodies and exchanges have enacted rules that govern margin trading. Whatever the country, these rules should cover three dimensions: minimum margins, initial margins and maintenance margins.

To open a margin account with a broker and before any trade takes place, an investor must deposit a *minimum margin*. This rule primarily targets small investors; it is not really relevant to hedge funds, because the corresponding amount is small. For instance, in the United States, the National Association of Securities Dealers (NASD) and the New York Stock Exchange (NYSE) now impose a minimum of $25 000 in cash or fully paid securities in order to open a margin account.[1] Of course, amounts differ in other countries and markets.

The *initial margin* requirement represents the minimum amount of funds an investor must put up to purchase securities on credit. For example, with a 50% initial margin requirement,

---

[1] Note that this amount used to be only $2000 in the early days of electronic trading.

the maximum amount of credit an investor can obtain from his broker to purchase stocks is 50% of the stocks' value. An investor willing to buy one share of common stock valued at $100 per share must do so with at least $50 of his own funds or additional collateral.

In the US, the Federal Reserve sets the initial margin requirement as part of its monetary policy. Since 1934, it has changed 23 times, and even at one time reached a full 100% payment. The current rate, set in 1974, is 50%. As a matter of comparison, the initial margin requirement in the 1920s was usually around 10%. It resulted in high levels of margin debt and unstable stock prices, and created perfect conditions for the stock market crash in 1929.

The *maintenance margin* represents the minimum amount of funds an investor must have on his margin account to maintain an open position. It is expressed as a fixed percentage of the total market value of the securities held on margin. For instance, in the US, the NASD and the NYSE impose a minimum 25% maintenance margin requirement on their customers.

The positions purchased on margin are marked-to-market each day, which results in their regular revaluation. The gains, or losses, associated with the daily price changes are applied to the margin account. If the value of the margin account falls below the maintenance margin, the hedge fund receives a *margin call*. This is basically a request to deposit additional collateral. The fund manager can respond either by selling a part of his open position to reduce his exposure, or by depositing additional cash and/or new securities, until the maintenance margin requirement is met. The cash transferred due to a margin call is referred to as the *variation margin*.

Of course, security lenders prefer having a collateral made of stable assets, such as cash or T-bonds, while hedge funds prefer using risky securities (including the shares they purchased on margin) to secure their loans.[2] Most of the time, security lenders use a *haircut table*, which defines those securities that are accepted as collateral and the rule to determine their marginable value (usually a percentage of the market value). The riskier the asset considered, the more severe the haircut – for instance, cash and T-bills are usually taken at 100% of their value, while a diversified portfolio of stocks may only be accepted at 50 to 70% of its value.

Regulators may change the minimum margin rules whenever market conditions justify it. Brokerage houses must follow these rules, but they may freely apply more stringent requirements to their clients if they want to. In practice, most brokers officially request higher margins than the minima set by regulators and exchanges, but they may further differentiate their margin requirements and haircut tables by individual stocks and by the trading behaviour and credibility of their customers.

5.2.2 Buying on margin: an example

Let us now illustrate the mechanisms of buying on margin. Consider the case of a hedge fund buying on margin 10 000 shares at $10 each. Its broker applies the 50% initial margin and the 25% maintenance margin requirements.

The current market value of the purchase is $100 000. In accordance with the 50% initial margin requirement, the hedge fund would need to deposit collateral or safe securities worth $50 000 into its margin account. The broker would lend the remaining $50 000 and execute

---

[2] In the US a few securities cannot be used as collateral, e.g. penny stocks (stocks trading below $5), initial public offerings (not marginable for 30 days), mutual funds held for less than 30 days, securities held in a retirement account, and securities held in a custodial account.

the purchase transaction. The hedge fund account would then appear as follows:

Assets		Liabilities	
Long stocks	100 000	Debit balance	50 000
		Equity	50 000

The debit balance consists of the amount due to the broker, plus interest on this loan amount, while equity is defined as the difference between the current market value of the long stocks and the debit balance. The fund's equity covers exactly 50% of the market value of the stocks held long. The basic accounting equation is:

$$Equity = Assets - Liabilities$$

For margin investing, this equation changes slightly to:

$$Equity = Market\ value\ of\ long\ stocks - Debit\ balance$$

The equity will therefore change as the current market value of the long stocks rises and falls and as interest is added to the debit balance. For the sake of simplicity, let us ignore interest and focus on stock price movements.

If the stock price goes up, say to $12, the value of the assets will increase to $120 000. On the liability side, the corresponding gain would be credited to the fund's equity. The fund's equity would then cover 58.33% (70 000/120 000) of the market value of the stocks held long. The hedge fund account would appear as:

Assets		Liabilities	
Long stocks	120 000	Debit balance	50 000
		Equity	70 000

If the stock price goes down, say to $8, the value of the assets will decrease to $80 000. On the liability side, the corresponding loss would be attributed to the fund's equity, which would fall to $30 000. The fund's equity would then cover 37.5% (30 000/80 000) of the market value of the stocks held long, which is still acceptable since it is above the minimum maintenance margin. The hedge fund account would appear as follows:

Assets		Liabilities	
Long stocks	80 000	Debit balance	50 000
		Equity	30 000

To trigger a margin call, the value of the hedge fund's equity needs to equal 25% (the maintenance margin) of the value of open positions. The corresponding threshold stock price can be calculated as:

$$Equity = (Long\ stock\ value - Debit\ balance) = 0.25 \times Long\ stock\ value$$

That is:

$$(10\,000 \times Stock\ price - 50\,000) = 0.25 \times 10\,000 \times Stock\ price$$

Solving yields a stock price equal to $6.6667. If the stock price reaches this threshold value, the hedge fund account will appear as follows:

Assets		Liabilities	
Long stocks	66 667	Debit balance	50 000
		Equity	16 667

The fund's equity then covers exactly 25% (16 667/66 667) of the market value of the stocks held long. Any additional drop in the stock price would further reduce the equity value, leading to insufficient coverage of the position. The broker would have to issue a margin call – a request to increase the amount of equity.

As an illustration, let us say that the stock price falls to $6 per share. The hedge fund account appears as follows:

Assets		Liabilities	
Long stocks	60 000	Debit balance	50 000
		Equity	10 000

If the fund decides to respond by depositing an additional amount of $5000 in its margin account, the cash deposit will be applied against the debit balance. The new account status will look like this:

Assets		Liabilities	
Long stocks	60 000	Debit balance	45 000
		Equity	15 000

The equity finances exactly 25% of the long stock position. However, any subsequent decrease in the stock price will prompt a new margin call from the broker. It would therefore be safer for the fund manager to deposit an amount larger than $5000, or to liquidate some shares to reduce its exposure.

Note that if the hedge fund manager ignores the margin call or is not reachable, the broker is entitled to protect his interests without prior notice and bring the equity coverage into an acceptable range by selling a portion of the long stock position. The fund manager has no right to control such liquidation decisions. For instance, in the case of a diversified portfolio, the broker can freely decide which securities among the ones collateralized will be sold. The fund will be held responsible for any losses incurred during this process.

5.3   SHORT SELLING AND SECURITIES LENDING

Short selling – selling something that you do not own yet – is neither very complex nor entirely simple. Nevertheless, it is a concept that many investors have trouble understanding and its practice is among the most controversial activities on financial markets. Since it benefits from falling prices, short selling is regularly criticized, particularly during times of crisis or following major price declines. The general idea seems to be that short selling is malevolent, morally wrong, and even against the word of God (Proverbs 24:17: "Do not rejoice when your enemy falls, and do not let your heart be glad when he stumbles."). However, as we will see in this section, reality is not that sombre, and short sellers also provide markets with important

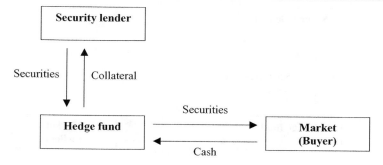

Figure 5.5   Flows resulting from initiating a short sale transaction

benefits. Moreover, short selling is now a key tool used by hedge funds, but it is also a long-standing market practice for other market participants such as market makers, broker–dealers and investment banks. In order to understand market reactions, it is therefore necessary to understand how short sellers operate.

5.3.1   Mechanics of short selling

Although short selling is commonly considered as one transaction, it really consists of a series of basic operations.

- The hedge fund sells a given number of securities that it does not yet own.[3] The buyer of the securities is not aware that this is a short sale, but the short seller needs to make arrangements to cover his delivery obligations before they fall due. Note that in some instances short sellers make no delivery arrangements, either before or following the normal settlement date, and let the open position run as long as market rules allow or until the market or settlement system takes action to close the position out (Figure 5.5).
- The hedge fund borrows the same number of securities from a security lender and contracts to retransfer an equivalent number of the same securities at some point in the future to the lender. The security lender receives a daily fee from the hedge fund, which is a function of supply and demand for the borrowed securities. In addition, the hedge fund has to put up collateral to provide the lender with a perfected security interest until the securities are returned. This collateral can be either in cash or other acceptable securities, to at least the value of the securities borrowed.
- The hedge fund delivers the securities to the buyer with full legal ownership, including voting rights. The sale proceeds are credited on the hedge fund account.
- At some later date, the hedge fund will repurchase the same number of securities from the market.
- The purchased securities will be returned to the lender. The short position is then closed (see Figure 5.6).

---

[3] In some cases, the hedge fund may have already borrowed the necessary securities before selling them short.

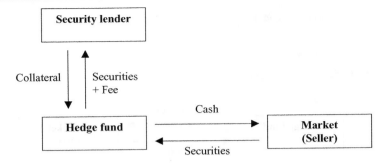

Figure 5.6   Flows resulting from closing a short sale transaction

To introduce some terminology, as soon as the stock has already been borrowed or is known to be available at the time of sale, the transaction is commonly called a *covered short*. If the seller does not *yet* own the stock he is selling and has made no provision to borrow or otherwise provide for delivery of stock to the purchaser by the settlement date, the transaction is referred to as a *naked short*. If shares are not found by the time the transaction must be settled, there is a *failure to deliver* shares to the buyer.

Note that a huge increase in naked short selling could create a virtually unlimited quantity of shares, even to the point that a normal market based on supply and demand could be seriously distorted. One of the arguments frequently used against naked short selling is that brokers and dealers accommodate stock price manipulation by permitting naked short sales to occur when there is no possibility of actually delivering shares to the buyers. However, naked short sales are not always associated with an attempt to manipulate prices. In fact, they can even sometimes protect investors from price manipulation. For instance, market makers such as intermediaries on the NYSE or the Nasdaq may choose to sell short if there is a sudden but temporary series of buy orders on a stock with no real fundamental justification. Their short sale will avoid an unjustified run-up in the stock's price and stabilize the market.

During a short sale operation, the securities lender has in essence turned his security position into cash while still retaining the economic benefits of ownership. This implies that there are in fact two positions to consider when analysing a short sale: a "real" position occupied by the buyer of the security sold short, and a "phantom" position held by the entity lending the security to the hedge fund. As a consequence of the phantom position, the hedge fund is responsible for any corporate action with respect to the stock lender. For instance:

- If the corporation whose shares are held short pays a dividend, the hedge fund must pay the amount of the dividend to the stock lender.
- If the corporation whose shares are held short splits two-for-one, the hedge fund owes the lender twice as many shares.
- If the corporation whose shares are held short spins off, the hedge fund is short two securities: the original security and the spin-off security.
- If the corporation whose shares are held short makes a rights offering, the hedge fund must go into the marketplace and deliver the rights to the stock lender.

Technically, short selling does not require any initial investment – it just requires finding a security lender and having enough collateral. Nevertheless, short selling involves important risks:

- A *market risk*. Short sellers must buy back an equivalent number of the same securities that were sold. They are therefore exposed to the risk of the price of shorted securities rising rather than falling.
- A *recall risk*. Borrowed securities may be recalled at any time by the lender. If the short seller is unable to find an alternative lender, he will be forced to close his position and repurchase the securities in the open market at any price. This is called a short squeeze, or a market corner (see Box 5.1).
- A *liquidity risk*. With less liquid securities, the market may dry out and the sort seller may be unable to find securities to buy, making it difficult for him to close out his positions.

Box 5.1 Examples of early short squeezes

The oldest short squeezes in the US date from the 19th century and involved well-known industry barons, in particular Cornelius Vanderbilt and Daniel Drew.[4] For instance, the first Harlem Corner (Figure 5.7) occurred in 1863, when Vanderbilt bought stock in the Harlem Railway Company at around $8 to $9 a share and the New York City Council passed an ordinance allowing him to build a streetcar system the length of Broadway. The stock rallied to $75, but Daniel Drew conspired with members of the Council to sell the stock short, repeal the ordinance, and thus force the price down. Vanderbilt secretly bought the entire stock of the company, and forced short sellers to settle at $179 per share after the repeal of the ordinance.

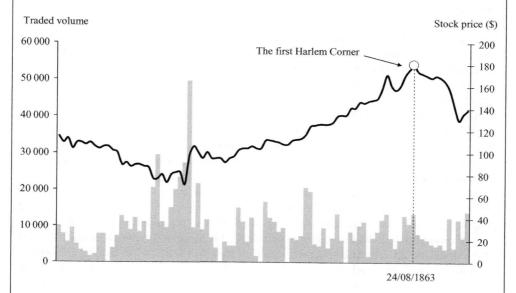

Figure 5.7   Stock price (black curve, right hand scale) and volume chart (grey shade, left hand scale) of the first Harlem Corner

---

[4] See for instance Allen and Gale (1992) or Chancellor (2000).

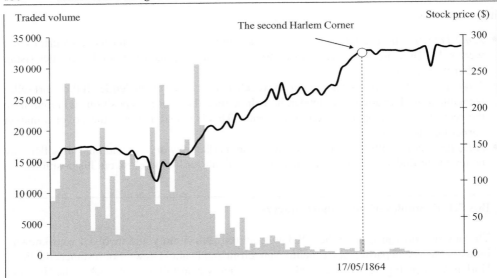

Figure 5.8 Stock price (black curve, right-hand scale) and volume chart (grey shade, left-hand scale) of the second Harlem Corner

Vanderbilt then decided to get authorization for his Harlem Railway extension directly from the New York State Legislature. Hoping for revenge, Drew conspired with the unwary state legislators, spread news about the likely passing of the legislation, pushed up the price of the Harlem Railway, then proceeded to sell the stock short, defeated the bill and forced the price down. The stock price dropped from $150 to $100 in two days. Vanderbilt bought more shares than were actually in existence and forced short sellers – including Drew – to settle at $285. This was the second Harlem Corner (Figure 5.8).

However, Vanderbilt was not always successful when fighting Drew. For instance, in March 1868, Vanderbilt was doing battle over the Erie Railroad Corporation – he was buying the shares while Daniel Drew and Jay Gould were short-sellers. At some point, Vanderbilt had bought more shares than were in existence, and thought he had won the battle. But Drew was a director of the company and surprised Vanderbilt by converting a large hidden issue of convertible bonds into common stocks and flooding the market with these new shares. This allowed him to cover his shorts and avoid the short squeeze.

Another famous example of a short squeeze occurred in spring 1901, as J.P. Morgan and a group of investors led by Edward Harriman fought for control of Northern Pacific Railroad (Figure 5.9). Harriman started by acquiring $40 million of the common stock, running just a few thousand shares short of gaining control, but J.P. Morgan went out to acquire the rest of the stock and his purchase sent prices soaring from $114 to $147 in five days. Noticing the unusual and unjustified increase in the stock price, a group of short sellers built a large short position. However, on 9 May, they realized that they could no longer cover their shorts and the price jumped from $170 to $1000 during the day. The volume traded was 3 336 000 for the day, a record not broken until 1925. Morgan and Harriman agreed to settle with the short sellers at $150 the next day.

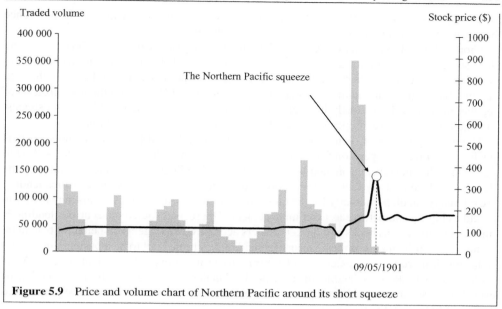

Figure 5.9   Price and volume chart of Northern Pacific around its short squeeze

The cost and difficulty of short selling is determined by supply and demand in the securities lending market. Generally, it is relatively easy to borrow most large cap stocks in established markets at a cost varying from 25 to 75 basis points per year. It is much harder to borrow securities that have low institutional ownership or that are in high demand for borrowing – typically the stocks many people believe to be overpriced. The cost may then increase dramatically, and the recall risk may be high. This leads to an interesting paradox: the securities lending market works well, except when everybody wants to use it to sell short, in which case it works very badly.[5] This paradox explains why most hedge fund managers do not want to disclose their short positions – the cost of borrowing securities rises when other investors are also trying to short.[6] A key indicator to monitor is therefore the *short interest*, i.e. how many shares have already been sold short. Last but not least, secrecy might be preferred if the short seller wants to avoid being sued or harassed by the firm he is currently shorting.

If we ignore all lending and execution costs, it should be clear that a hedge fund engaged in a short position will make money only if the repurchase price is lower than the original sale price; the hedge fund will incur a loss if the repurchase price is higher than the sale price. Consequently, the most obvious reason to short is to profit from an overpriced security or market. More sophisticated hedge fund strategies may also use short selling as a hedge for

---

[5] A good illustration of this phenomenon is the internet bubble period. D'Avolio (2002) studied data on loan supply, loan fees, and recalls from a large lending intermediary from April 2000 through September 2001. Although most stocks could be borrowed to sell short for a cost of no more than 20 basis points per year, about 9% of the stocks (called the "specials") had loan fees in excess of 100 basis points per year, and the most difficult stocks to borrow had loan fees in excess of 25% per year. D'Avolio also found the unconditional probability of recall to be about 1% for a particular day, 2% over a month and 18% over the entire 18-month period. The median time to reborrow the stock from another lender was nine days.

[6] The question of short sale and short position disclosure has been raised by regulators several times in the past. In the US, the Subcommittee on Commerce, Consumer and Monetary Affairs of the House Committee on Government Affairs held hearings on the market role of short selling and introduced a bill in 1990 that proposed requiring the public reporting of material short positions. The US Congress did not take any action on the bill.

other long positions with offsetting risk, or as a way to speculate on spreads, i.e. the difference between two securities, as we shall see in Part II of this book.

Short selling relies heavily on securities lending, i.e. the practice of security holders making their securities available for a small fee to sellers in the market, on condition that equivalent securities be returned to them at a future date. Securities lending existed in the US in the 19th century, but it only really gained momentum in the 1970s and 1980s with the liberalization of regulations that had previously hampered the practice. Today, available official data suggest that the US market size of open securities loan positions is close to $3 trillion.

The primary source of securities lending remains portfolios of beneficial owners, such as institutional investors, pension funds and insurance companies. These investors are willing to generate additional revenue on their long-term strategic holdings and they are motivated by the desire to reduce custody fees for their portfolios. Although the returns on securities lending are relatively small, particularly for the most liquid securities, a few basis points may matter in a field as highly competitive as asset management. The second source of securities lending is financial firms such as banks and broker–dealers acting as either agents on behalf of beneficial owners, or as principal. For them, securities lending has turned out to be a business in its own right, much more than an extension of a firm's basic inventory management process. Most broker contracts allow the lending of securities held in their margin accounts, and several firms even borrow securities in advance, with the expectation that others will shortly be prepared to pay more to borrow them (Box 5.2).

Box 5.2 Shorting and short squeezes

Before April 1932, US brokers could and did lend the shares of their clients without requiring their secure written authorization. The New York Stock Exchange announced the end of this practice on 18 February 1932, but most brokers were slow to request the necessary authorizations. This led to several memorable squeezes, in which share lenders were able to extract substantial concessions from borrowers. For instance, on 31 March 1931, US Steel (Figure 5.10) – generally the most actively traded issue on the NYSE and easy to borrow for shorting purposes – was loaned at a premium of $1/2\%$ per day, i.e. an annualized cost of more than 180% per year to maintain a short position. These high premiums did not last for long, as brokers suddenly woke up and more shares became available for lending.

Regulation SHO

In the US, Regulation SHO was adopted by the SEC and came into effect on 3 January 2005. Its goal is to control the potentially manipulative effects of abusive naked short selling and extended fails-to-deliver of outstanding short positions. Among other things, Regulation SHO:

- Prohibits a broker–dealer from executing a short sale order for his own account or the account of another person, unless the broker–dealer: (i) has borrowed or entered into an arrangement to borrow the security; (ii) has reasonable grounds to believe that the security can be borrowed so that it can be delivered on the date delivery is due; and (iii) has documented compliance with this provision.

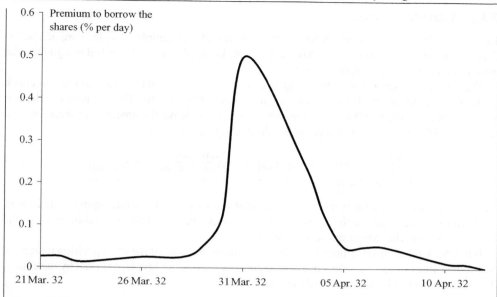

Figure 5.10   Evolution of the daily premium needed to borrow US Steel shares

- Mandates all clearing brokers to close out any fail-to-deliver in "threshold securities" by purchasing securities of like kind and quantity 10 days after the normal settlement date.[7]

The rules include exemptions for market makers engaged in bona fide market-making activities, and for certain transactions between brokers. Prior to this rule, it was common to see some funds giving a vague indication to their broker, and therefore selling a share that neither they nor their broker possessed. It was usually not a problem, because if the fund or the broker bought back the missing stock the next day, the fund would be "flat" by the time it was to be delivered anyway. However, in some cases, the stock was hard to locate and borrow, and this would lead to a fail-to-deliver situation.

Is the situation much better with the SHO rules? Not necessarily. Complaints are regularly heard that some brokers evade the requirements by passing fail-to-deliver positions from one to another. What is more, Regulation SHO has unintentionally created opportunities for short squeezes. The threshold securities list obviously identifies stocks where short sellers (i) are active and (ii) did not find the necessary securities. Certain traders have reportedly made large purchases of stocks listed as threshold securities, driving their price up, and putting pressure on short sellers as their positions lose money and their prime brokers issue margin calls. If the short sellers cannot meet these margin calls, they must close out their positions by purchasing the shares, driving the price still higher.

---

[7] Rule 203(c)(6) defines "threshold securities" as publicly traded securities where (1) for five consecutive settlement days, aggregate fails-to-deliver at a registered clearing agency are 10 000 shares or more; (2) the volume of fails in a security is equal to at least 0.5% of the reported total shares outstanding in the security; and (3) the security is included on a daily list published by an exchange identifying securities that exceed specified fail-to-deliver levels.

5.3.2   A detailed example

Let us now illustrate the mechanisms of selling short with an example. Take the case of a hedge fund selling short 10 000 shares at $10 each. Its broker applies the 50% initial margin and the 30% maintenance margin requirements.

The current market value of the short sale is $100 000. First, the hedge fund has to check with its broker to ensure that the shares are available for borrowing. Then, it needs to deposit safe securities worth $50 000 into its margin account, and leave the proceeds of the short sale as collateral.[8] The hedge fund account would then appear as follows:

Assets		Liabilities	
Cash	100 000	Short position	100 000
T-bills (collateral)	50 000	Equity	50 000

The short position represents the market value of the short stocks, while equity is defined as the current market value of the assets minus the current market value of the short stocks. The cash comes from the sale of the shorted stocks.

If the stock price climbs from $10 to $11, the (absolute) value of the short position increases. Since the value of the assets does not change, the corresponding loss is absorbed by the equity. The new hedge fund account would then appear as:

Assets		Liabilities	
Cash	100 000	Short position	110 000
T-bills	50 000	Equity	40 000

Now, the new equity amount represents 36.36% (40 000/110 000) of the value of the short position, which is still above the 30% maintenance margin. Note that the equity is computed as a percentage of the short position, because this is what changes when market prices change.

One may wonder which stock price will create the first margin call. With a 30% maintenance margin, we have:

$$\text{assets} - \text{market value of short position} = 0.30 \times \text{market value of short position}$$

That is:

$$\$150\,000 - (10\,000 \times \text{Stock price}) = 0.30 \times 10\,000 \times \text{Stock price}$$

Solving for the stock price and rounding yields $11.54. Assume that the stock price climbs suddenly to $12 per share. The hedge fund account then appears as follows:

Assets		Liabilities	
Cash	100 000	Short position	120 000
T-bills	50 000	Equity	30 000

The equity value now represents 25% (30 000/120 000) of the short position – less than the required 30% maintenance margin. The broker will therefore issue a margin call. The fund manager must respond by depositing an additional amount of $6000 in the fund's margin account. The cash deposit will be added to the cash amount held on the assets side and to the

---

[8] In the US, Regulation T requires that 150% of the value of the position at the time the short is created be held in a margin account. This 150% is made up of the full value of the short (100%), plus an additional margin requirement of 50% of the value of the position. A less conservative broker could allow the fund to purchase other risky securities later on with the short sale proceeds.

equity on the liabilities side. The new account status will be as follows:

Assets		Liabilities	
Cash	106 000	Short position	120 000
T-bills	50 000	Equity	36 000

The equity now represents exactly 30% (36 000/120 000) of the short stock position. However, any subsequent increase in the stock price will prompt a new margin call from the broker. It would therefore be safer for the fund manager to deposit an amount larger than $6000. Alternatively, the fund manager may also use some of the cash to buy back some shares and return them to the lender, thereby reducing his short position. Note that if a hedge fund ignores the margin call, its broker may use the cash to buy back and close the short stock position, or to bring the equity coverage into an acceptable range. The hedge fund will be held responsible for any losses incurred during this process.

Once again, prime brokers have a key role to play in the short-selling process. Large prime brokers are more likely to have access to hard-to-borrow securities. In addition, they can often offer some sort of cross-margining facilities, i.e. positions held by the hedge fund in various instruments which all require collateralization are grouped and margined together, taking into account offsetting risks and hedges. Such an approach allows for the most efficient use of a hedge fund's capital and optimizes the collateral management process.

5.3.3   Restrictions on short selling

Despite its potential attractiveness, short selling is not widely practised. In fact, it is amazing to observe how our current financial system and its constellation of laws, regulations, institutional norms, variations in practice and fine print are obviously set up to encourage individuals to buy stocks, but not to sell them short.

Since short selling increases the supply of long sale orders in the market, which in turn increases the potential for both disorderly and manipulative trading, the common conjecture seems to be that short sale restrictions can reduce the severity of price declines. Consequently, many regulators have imposed a series of specific short sale constraints that mechanically impede short selling, or at least restrict it to some market participants and/or some liquid securities. These constraints vary from one market to another (see Figure 5.11), but some examples are:

- In Sweden, traders can go short without having borrowed the shares in advance, while individual investors must borrow the shares before they go short.
- In Greece, prior to 2001, short selling was only available to the members of the Athens Derivatives Exchange.
- In Brazil, a short seller must have a domestic legal representative.
- In Hong Kong, until 1996, short sales were only allowed for specific securities designated by Hong Kong Exchanges and Clearing Ltd.
- In Taiwan, foreign and institutional investors are prohibited from shorting, and individuals can only short with special authorization from the Ministry of Finance.
- In Chile, short selling and securities lending are allowed, but they are rarely used because lending is considered an immediate, taxable sale at the highest price of the stock on the day it is lent.
- In Turkey, stock lending is treated as a normal transaction and as such is liable to capital gains tax.

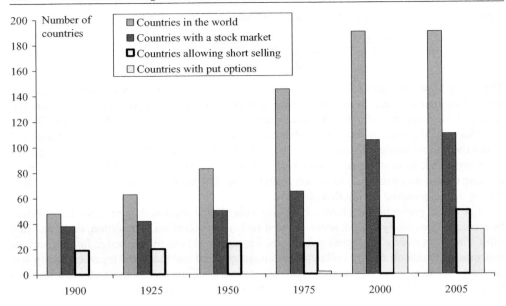

Figure 5.11   Evolution of the number of countries allowing short selling

In addition, several exchanges require short sales to be executed only in a *plus tick* or more commonly in a *zero-plus tick* situation (Table 5.1). A plus tick (also known as an *up-tick*) rule means that the short sale can only take place at a price higher than the last previous transaction in that security. A zero-plus tick rule requires the short sale to take place at a price that can be the same as the immediately preceding transaction but higher than the last transaction in that security at a different price.[9] Both rules are intended to prevent the short selling of a stock that is already declining in price in order to avoid sending stock prices into a free fall. Not surprisingly, no exchange has yet prohibited buying at a price above the last traded price, even though one could argue that it pushes stock prices up.

In some countries, the crusade against short selling has been even more strident. In 1995, for example, the Malaysian Finance Ministry proposed mandatory caning as the punishment for short sellers, and declared that the beating would be "light, similar to the punishment carried out on juveniles" – see Jayasankaran (1995).

These extreme views that regulators seem to have about short selling appear to derive, at least in part, from the relative opacity that surrounds short sales and securities lending. Since securities lending is a private agreement, it is extremely difficult to distinguish a normal sale from a short sale. In addition, a few financial intermediaries (e.g. prime brokers) have information on short positions and stock borrowing figures, while most market participants do not, leaving those with the information in a privileged position. Several jurisdictions and markets have therefore decided to improve the transparency of short selling by publishing

---

[9] The tick condition that a security is trading in at any given time is indicated on quotation terminals by a "+" or a "−" next to the symbol. On the consolidated ticker tape, a "+" symbol next to the price indicates a plus tick or zero-plus tick from previous trades. Note that, in practice, the strict up-tick rule is hard to apply. Short sellers must never be second in line at a given price, as that would cause the short sale to execute on a zero tick, which is prohibited. Similarly, short sales cannot be easily broken up and executed in multiple pieces, as each transaction sent to the tape would have to take place on an up-tick.

Table 5.1   Summary of short selling practice in various countries

Country	Short selling permitted?	Short selling practised?	Short selling details and restrictions	Tick rule
Albania	No	No		
Argentina	Yes	No	Only allowed for 16 stocks and cannot last more than 360 days in a row. Securities lending is rare and occurs only between brokers	
Australia	Yes	Yes	Liquid securities only, and maximum 10% of the capital issued may be sold short. Not allowed during takeovers. Disclosure is required	Yes
Austria	Yes	Yes		
Belgium	Yes	No	No organized market for securities lending	
Brazil	Yes	Yes	Disclosure on securities lending	
Bulgaria	No	No	Short selling is prohibited	
Canada	Yes	Yes	Disclosure is required	Yes
Chile	Yes	No	Not market practice for tax reasons and cannot last more than 360 days in a row	Yes
China	No	No	Short selling is not permitted	
Colombia	No	No	Securities lending is not permitted	
Czech Republic	Yes	Yes	Possible but the securities must be bought or borrowed in the market before the settlement	
Denmark	Yes	Yes		
Ecuador	Yes	No	Not market practice for tax reasons	
Egypt	No	No	Short selling is not permitted	
Estonia	No	No	Short selling is not permitted	
Finland	Yes	No	The transfer tax laws place a serious burden on the activity	
France	Yes	Yes		
Germany	Yes	Yes		
Greece	Yes	Yes	Short selling has recently been introduced as part of the ADEX securities lending programme	Yes
Hong Kong	Yes	Yes	Liquid securities and underlying securities of a derivative or an approved exchange-traded fund. Extensive disclosure	Yes
Hungary	No	No	Short selling is not recognized market practice	
India	No	No	Not allowed for foreign investors, but local investors (i.e. retail investors and broker/dealers on proprietary books) are permitted to short sell in the market	
Indonesia	Yes	No		
Ireland	Yes	No	Securities lending is limited	
Israel	Yes	No	Short selling in the market is permitted only under certain conditions and circumstances	
Italy	Yes	Yes		
Japan	Yes	Yes	Disclosure is required	Yes
Jordan	No	No		
Lithuania	No	No		
Luxembourg	Yes	Yes		
Malaysia	No	No	Short selling and securities lending were suspended during the Asian crisis of 1997	
Mexico	Yes	Yes	Liquid equities only, with restrictions for foreign investors. Disclosure required	Yes

(Continued)

Table 5.1   Summary of short selling practice in various countries (*Continued*)

Country	Short selling permitted?	Short selling practised?	Short selling details and restrictions	Tick rule
Morocco	No	No		
Netherlands	Yes	No	Although permitted, short selling is rarely practised. Disclosure required	
New Zealand	Yes	No	Not market practice for tax reasons	
Norway	Yes	Yes	Reporting required	
Pakistan	No	No	Short selling is not allowed	
Peru	Yes	No	Reporting required	
Philippines	Yes	No	Rules are not clearly defined	
Poland	Yes	No	Although permitted, short selling is rarely practised	
Portugal	No	No		
Russia	Yes	No	Short selling is not a recognized market practice	
Singapore	Yes	No	No restriction, but the exchange may declare a security ineligible for short selling if speculative activity is excessive	
Slovakia	No	No		
South Africa	Yes	Yes		
South Korea	Yes	No	Prohibited to insiders and available only for designated securities. Naked short sales are not permitted	Yes
Spain	Yes	No	Reporting required	
Sri Lanka	No	No	Short selling is prohibited	
Sweden	Yes	Yes	Disclosure required	
Switzerland	Yes	Yes		
Taiwan	No	No		
Thailand	Yes	No	Short selling is allowed only for securities listed in the SET 50 index. Disclosure required	
Turkey	Yes	No	Short selling is allowed only for securities listed in the ISE-100 Index. Disclosure required	
United Kingdom	Yes	Yes		
United States	Yes	Yes	Short selling is permitted	Yes
Venezuela	No	No		
Zimbabwe	No	No		

Source: *International Encyclopaedia of the Stock Market*, *Handbook of World Stock*, Derivative and Commodity Exchanges, and various foreign nationals linked to the finance industry.

aggregated data on short sales. For instance, in April 2003, Hong Kong introduced a disclosure requirement for short economic interests with a view to improving the transparency of the economic interests of substantial shareholders in a company. The major benefit is that investors can then see the extent of aggregate short selling in any particular security and draw their own conclusions from that information. Of course, there must be a limit to the disclosure level as well as to the public transparency, because knowledge of individual market participants' and market makers' open short positions could jeopardize their trading strategies and expose them to increased risk of being caught in a short squeeze. Hence, information is usually aggregated per security and published on an anonymous basis. So far, we are not aware of any exchange

Table 5.2   Example of a few short-selling disclosure regimes

Country	Information required	Frequency	Collector/Publisher
Australia	Aggregate net short position per security	Daily	Exchange
Canada	20 largest short positions	Daily	Exchange
Hong Kong	Short sales per security	Twice daily	Exchange
Japan	Balance of margin transaction per "daily publicized stock"	Daily	Exchange
	Lending balances for "standardized margin transactions"	Daily	Margin lenders
	Balance of margin transaction per issue	Weekly	Exchange + JSDA
	Total balance of margin transactions	Weekly	Exchange + JSDA
	Trading values of short selling	Monthly	Exchange + JSDA
United States	Aggregate short position per security	Monthly	Self Regulated Organizations (e.g. AMEX, NYSE, NASD)

publishing real-time information. The most frequent disclosure is twice daily, in Hong Kong (see Table 5.2 and Figure 5.12 in Box 5.3).

Note that another approach to disclosure adopted in several jurisdictions, including Spain, Sweden and Brazil, is to publish securities lending figures rather than short sales. In some countries these figures may provide a reasonably precise proxy for short-selling activity. In others, they are less useful because stock lending is also used for other activities, e.g. receiving dividends by parties to whom they offer some particular advantage (exercising voting rights, etc).

5.3.4   Potential benefits of short selling

Despite all the arguments advanced by its opponents, short selling brings with it numerous benefits which should not be overlooked. In particular:

- Short selling contributes positively to market efficiency by conveying into the market negative information about securities, facilitating price discovery and reducing the likelihood of overpricing of securities and irrational exuberance. This is borne out by Lamont and Thaler (2003) and Ofek and Richardson (2003), who furnish empirical evidence that the restricted availability of shares for borrowing inhibited short selling and contributed significantly to the recent dot-com bubble.
- Short selling constitutes the first line of defence against financial frauds and even unjustified bubbles. Rumours, false press or internet releases, and unexpected purchases may all cause a run-up in stock prices, which may be followed by a sudden collapse, as the manipulators sell their shares to the unwary. Without short sellers as a counterweight, the magnitude and duration of such fraudulent surges are likely to be much greater.
- Short selling facilitates dealer liquidity provision, particularly where that service guarantees liquidity on a continuous basis. For instance, by going short, a market maker or dealer can meet a customer buy order when he does not hold the relevant securities in inventory, thus facilitating liquidity and continuous trading.
- Short selling facilitates the implementation of several arbitrage strategies, which keep related prices properly aligned (statistical arbitrage, pairs trades, etc.).

Box 5.3 The pulse of the market: short interest

The monthly or daily short interest in a market is not necessarily representative of the intra-day shorting activity. As an illustration, Diether, Lee and Werner (2005) studied the first six months of 2005 and found a tremendous amount of short-term trading strategies involving short sales. According to their study, short sales represent on average 27% of Nasdaq share volume while the monthly short-interest for the same period was only about 3.1% of shares outstanding. Most of the short-term short-sale strategies cannot be explained by the activities of equity and options market makers, which are exempt from short-sale rules. Short selling by exempt traders represented only 7.8% of reported share volume, leaving the remaining 18.9% unexplained.

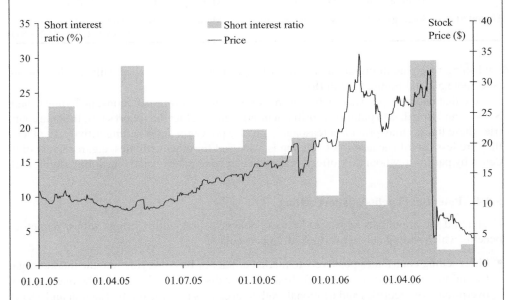

Figure 5.12 Evolution of the short interest ratio for the Escala Group stock. The short interest ratio is the ratio of the number of shares sold short over the average daily trading volume

Unlike investment banks and financial intermediaries, short sellers have no conflict of interests because they have no ties with the companies they are targeting (see Box 5.4). Their research is independent, and sometimes visionary. In 1989, for example, the House Committee on Government Operations (Commerce, Consumer and Monetary Affairs Subcommittee) held hearings about the alleged evils of short selling, featuring testimony from three supposedly victimized firms. Later, the SEC charged the presidents of two of these three firms with fraud, and their stock prices collapsed.

5.3.5 Alternatives to securities lending: repos and buys/sell backs

As we have seen, short selling requires an efficient market of securities lending. In practice, when borrowing securities is difficult, there are several alternative ways of obtaining exactly

Box 5.4 When Osama bin Laden sells short

Following the 11 September 2001 attacks in the US, David Ruder, chairman of the SEC from 1987 to 1989, raised the question of whether terrorists may have profited from their attacks by short selling stocks. Indeed, there had been a sharp increase in short selling of the stocks of American (+20%) and United Airlines (+40%) during the month before 11 September. The trading activity far outpaced the rise in short selling for all stocks on the New York Stock Exchange – or other major airline stocks as a group (+11%) on the Big Board, according to a computer analysis released by the New York Stock Exchange. After 11 September, Chicago Board Options Exchange data showed 1575 put options purchased in United Airlines' parent company five days before the attacks, whereas, on an average day, only 390 such put options are purchased. Investors also bought 2258 put options in American Airlines' parent company, compared with 220 on a typical day, and insurance and other stocks also experienced an upswing in short sales.

Federal securities and law enforcement investigators immediately started looking at unusual trading activities in the stocks of AMR Corp. and UAL Corp., the parent companies of American and United, as well as a number of other securities in the days leading up to the terrorist attacks. Their general conclusion was that there were a number of legitimate reasons for the increase in short selling that had nothing to do with terrorism. For instance, the airline industry was in serious financial trouble even prior to the attacks, as business and consumer travel demand slacked off in a weakening economy. Both AMR and UAL had posted huge second-quarter losses in July and said they could be in the red for the rest of the year. Moreover, short selling on the exchange had continued to increase month after month.

It is interesting to note that a similar claim was made in 2005 in the UK following the London transit system attacks, as it appeared that some had profited by short selling the British pound in the 10 days leading up to the attacks. At that time, the pound had fallen by about 6% (approximately 1.82 to 1.72) against the dollar for no apparent reason. The fall did not go unnoticed by investigators, who wondered whether the terrorist masterminds had decided to make some money out of their action or whether other investors with inside information about possible attacks had taken advantage of that knowledge. Despite vigorous efforts to find out who was behind the short selling, hopes are slim that the culprits will be found.

the same economic outcomes, although the legal form and accounting and tax treatment may differ. Let us mention two of them.

Sale and repurchase agreements (repos)

These are a good substitute for direct securities lending, and they form the bulk of bond lending transactions. In a repo transaction, one counterparty (called the "seller") agrees to sell securities to another (called the "buyer") for a fixed amount of cash, and simultaneously undertakes to repurchase the same security at a future date and at a fixed price. In a sense, the seller acts as a security lender – he owns the security, and lends it as collateral to borrow cash. The lending fee is implicitly equal to the difference between the initial selling price and the agreed repurchase price – it is usually translated into an interest rate which is referred to as the repo rate for that security. The buyer acts as a security borrower – he has invested money at the repo rate, but obtained the security as a collateral.[10] Most of the time, the principal of the loan in a repo transaction is less then the full price of the collateral security in order to further protect against any potential losses due to counterparty default. The difference between the price of the collateral security and the loan amount in a repo is referred to as a haircut.

Repos are frequently used by hedge funds to finance their positions and manage their leverage. On the flip side, reverse repos are often used as short-term investments. Note that while repurchase agreements can be negotiated for any term, the majority of repurchase agreements are for overnight terms and the counterparties often choose to renew the repo by renegotiating the repo rate on a daily basis.

Buys/sell backs

These are similar in economic terms to repos, but are structured as two independent transactions, i.e. an immediate sale and a purchase for a future settlement date. In a buy/sell back transaction, the purchaser of the securities receives absolute title to them. In particular, he retains any accrued interest or dividend/coupon payment during the life of the transaction – although from an economic perspective, the repurchase price takes into account these elements. In practice, buys/sell backs apply almost exclusively to bonds.

5.4   DERIVATIVES

Financial derivatives are another useful weapon in the trading panoply of hedge funds, and yet they too are widely criticized. The term "derivatives" refers to a large number of financial contracts in which a payment or delivery depends on the value of an underlying asset, interest rate or index. A derivatives contract therefore *derives its value* from the value of another asset or quantity, hence its name. In this sense, although most investors do not perceive them as such, simple bonds are derivatives because they derive their price from the level of interest rates – who said that all derivatives were risky and speculative?

Financial derivatives are not new. They have been around for years and are an integral part of a market economy. Market historians found evidence of derivatives in ancient India, Israel, Greece and Rome, as well as in medieval Europe and Japan (see Box 5.5). More recently, in 1865, the Chicago Board of Trade organized a large-scale agricultural futures market. However, the real development of derivatives started when the United States and other industrial nations abandoned the Bretton Woods system of fixed currency exchange rates. This resulted in extreme fluctuations in currencies and interest rates, and was followed by an inflationary oil price shock. Both elements created a strong demand for new hedging instruments that would facilitate the transfer of various risks to institutions which, because of their greater financial reserves and/or financial talent, were better able to manage them.

In 1973, the Chicago Board Options Exchange (CBOE) opened for business and started trading options. This was the first time that an exchange itself had acted as counterparty rather than being just the venue where the contracts were negotiated. But trading options without a model was like wandering in the desert without a compass. Fortunately, the same year, Fischer Black, Myron Scholes and Robert C. Merton provided the first reasonable mathematical model

---

[10] Some people call the buyers activity a reverse-repo transaction.

Box 5.5   The first derivatives users

Possibly the most ancient surviving story of two parties entering into a contingent claim contract can be found in the writings of Aristotle, who recounted that Thales, the Greek philosopher from Miletus, used to forecast in the stars the quality of the next season's harvest. He then made option-like agreements with olive-press owners in Chios and Miletus, in which he undertook to pay them some money upfront in exchange for later exclusive access to their olive presses if needed. When the harvest came, all producers suddenly needed these olive presses and paid Thales high prices to use them. In a sense, Thales bought call options on the olive presses to speculate, while the olive-press owners were selling call options in order to secure their annual income. While this story is almost certainly apocryphal, there is no doubting its antiquity. This in itself would tend to indicate that option-like agreements were common in Ancient Greece.

The second well-known instance of derivatives occurred during the tulip mania that swept the Netherlands in the 17th century. Tulips originated in Turkey and were first introduced in Holland in 1593 by a famous botanist, Carolus Clusius. Rare and beautiful, they rapidly became a status symbol. Wealthy aristocrats and merchants vied with one another to buy them. Several hobbyists created intriguing colours by breeding the plants. And speculators actively traded existing and non-existing bulbs. Buyers had to place orders with money upfront for delivery at a later date, which is nothing less than a forward contract. This in turn led to a trade in "tulip futures", where notarized paper orders were traded at the Amsterdam Bourse and the East India Company at higher and higher prices pending delivery of the bulbs themselves. This forced tulip retailers to buy call options and futures to protect themselves against sudden price rises imposed by their suppliers. Finally, growers also bought put options and sold futures contracts in order to make sure they would receive good prices for their bulbs. Around 1636, the tulip speculation reached its peak. Some single tulip bulbs sold for 4600 florins, roughly the price of 460 sheep. In February 1637, tulips crashed. People who thought of themselves as extremely rich were reduced to poverty overnight.

---

for the pricing of options. The methodology that they introduced has since been expanded for use in pricing a wide variety of derivative instruments and contingent claims that have changed the face of finance by creating new ways of analysing, managing and transferring risks.

In the 1980s, the growth of derivatives was further facilitated by the shifting geographic pattern of international savings and investment, and the globalization of financial markets. In particular, the transformation of the United States from a net supplier of funds to a major borrower, and the emergence of Germany and Japan as major lenders, encouraged the development of new, low-cost, risk-managing financial instruments that could be traded in international financial markets in order to reduce the costs and risks associated with international borrowing and lending.

Unfortunately, the tremendous growth of the financial derivatives markets and reports of major losses associated with derivative products have also generated a great deal of confusion about those instruments. Derivatives have often been stigmatized by the media as a new pariah, and have acquired an aura previously associated with deficits and drugs. Our goal here is quite modest, namely, to give a brief introduction to the main types of derivatives contracts. We focus primarily on understanding the way they work rather than on their pricing. Readers interested in knowing more about derivatives and their valuation should refer to Hull (2005).

5.4.1 Terminology

In general, derivatives markets are split into an unregulated *over-the-counter* (OTC) market and a regulated *exchange-traded* sector. Over-the-counter contracts are negotiated between two parties, typically an end-user and an investment bank. Their primary advantage is that they can easily be customized to meet the end-user's specific requirements in terms of size, maturity dates, underlying assets, etc. Unfortunately, this additional flexibility also comes with a series of drawbacks:

- Each OTC contract is drafted with specific terms and conditions, and therefore inherently carries legal risks.[11]
- The selling price may be unfair to the end-user, because it is privately negotiated rather than given by a market where intermediaries compete.
- There is an important counterparty risk, because OTC derivatives are usually not marked-to-market (i.e. there are no margin calls). The consequences of a default may therefore be weighty.
- There is no centralized market and therefore no liquidity. If the end-user wishes to modify or unwind a transaction, he must renegotiate the change with the original dealer, which is not always feasible or efficient.

By contrast, exchange-traded contracts are transacted through a regulated exchange. They are standardized and cannot be specially tailored to specific situations. However, they also have several advantages:

- The exchange or its clearing house acts as the counterparty for each transaction, which ensures sufficient liquidity and reduces default and settlement risks.
- All contracts are marked-to-market on a daily basis by margin requirements and margin calls, so that default risk and its consequences are minimized.
- As a result of the standardized maturities, contract sizes and delivery terms, all contracts are entirely fungible. This means that contracts dependent upon identical terms are totally interchangeable, which allows buyers and sellers to close out a position through a closing transaction in an identical contract.

5.4.2 Basic derivatives contracts

Today, the most common types of derivatives are forwards, futures and options.

- *Forwards* are the original and most basic form of an OTC derivative contract. Simply stated, forwards are agreements to purchase or sell a given quantity of an underlying asset at a fixed price determined at the outset, with delivery or settlement at a specific future date. The settlement can be made by physical delivery or by a net cash payment. Both parties are obliged to perform, and neither party charges a fee. Forwards are not marked-to-market each day, there are no margins required and no interim cash flow occurs.

---

[11] Legal risk may be reduced by using International Swaps and Derivatives Association (ISDA) master agreements that define the general terms and conditions for trading. The actual trades are documented in confirmation sheets, which are then filed as attachments to the master agreement.

- *Futures* are contracts similar to forwards, but they are exchange-traded and standardized as to the quantity, the specific underlying assets or commodities and the time. Only the price and the number of contracts are negotiated in the trading process. Futures are marked-to-market on a daily basis, via postings to the parties' margin accounts maintained at a futures broker and at the clearing house.[12] They are most commonly settled through an offsetting "reversing" trade rather than by delivery of the underlying item or cash settlement.
- *Options* are over-the-counter and exchange-traded contracts that give their purchaser the right, but not the obligation, to buy (call option) or sell (put option) a given quantity of an underlying asset at a specified price (strike price). The right may exist over a time span (American option) or only on a specified date (European option). Since an option is a right and not an obligation, the purchaser of an option has to pay the seller (writer) of the option a fee, referred to as the option premium. The premium will vary depending on several parameters, such as the moneyness of the option (that is, where is the strike price with respect to the underlying asset price), the volatility of the underlying asset, the level of interest rates and the time period over which the option can be exercised. Some options, if exercised, may be settled by a cash payment rather than by delivery of the underlying assets or commodities to which the contract relates.

Of course, there are many variations and combinations of the three contracts described above. For instance, *forward rate agreements* (FRA) are OTC agreements to exchange an amount of money based on a reference interest rate and a reference principal amount, referred to as the notional amount, over a specified period of time. FRAs differ from other forwards in that only an amount based on interest rate differentials, and not the principal, are transferred between parties. Consider, for example, a three-month FRA between a hedge fund and a bank with a $10 million notional principal amount. Then the bank would pay the hedge fund according to the following formula:

$$(\text{Three-month LIBOR rate in three months} - 4\%) \times \$10\,000\,000.$$

If in three months' time, the three-month LIBOR rate is 5%, the bank will pay the fund $100 000. Alternatively, if the three-month LIBOR rate has fallen by 1%, the fund will pay the bank $100 000.

- *Caps* and *floors* are over-the-counter interest rate options. An interest rate cap will compensate the purchaser of the cap if interest rates rise above a predetermined rate (called the strike rate) while an interest rate floor will compensate the purchaser if rates fall below a predetermined rate (also called the strike rate).
- *Swaps* are over-the-counter contracts to exchange cash flows as of a series of specified dates. These cash flows are usually based on an agreed-upon notional amount and agreed-upon fixed and floating interest rates. For instance, in an interest rate swap, one party would agree to pay a fixed rate while the other would pay a floating rate. In a currency swap, the payments would involve two different currencies. In practice, swaps can be synthetically recreated by combining several forward or futures contracts.
- *Total return swaps* are contracts that allow investors to receive all of the cash flow benefits of owning an asset without actually holding the physical asset (Figure 5.13). At trade inception,

---

[12] To reduce default risk, futures exchanges operate a clearing house which acts as a counterparty for all contracts. When an investor takes a position in futures, the clearing house takes the opposite position and agrees to satisfy the terms set forth in the contract. Thanks to the clearing house, the investor need not worry about the financial strength of the party taking the opposite side of the contract.

During the swap:

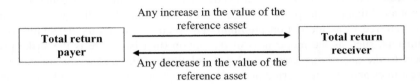

At the maturity of the swap:

Figure 5.13   Mechanics of a total return swap during the swap (top) and at maturity of the swap (bottom)

one party, the total return receiver, agrees to make payments of LIBOR plus a fixed spread to the other party, the total return payer, in return for the coupons paid by some specified asset. At the end of the term of the total return swap, the total return payer pays the difference between the final market price of the asset and the initial price of the asset.

- *Swaptions* are options to enter into swaps.
- *Contracts for difference* (CFDs) are OTC agreements between two parties to exchange in cash the difference between the opening value and the closing value of a given instrument (e.g. a single stock or an index). In a sense, they are similar to futures contracts although they do not have a fixed expiry date or contract size. CFDs are widely used to replicate positions in single shares without the need for ownership of the underlying shares. They only require a deposit of cash collateral rather than the payment of the full value of the underlying position, they are usually exempt from stamp duty and they can be sold short without having to borrow shares – all you need is to find the counterparty willing to buy the CFD. The contracts are subject to a daily financing charge, usually applied at a previously agreed rate above or below LIBOR or other interest rate benchmark. Users pay to finance long positions and receive funding on short positions in lieu of deferring sale proceeds. The use of CFDs has become widespread in the United Kingdom with some commentators suggesting that up to 25% of UK stock market turnover is attributable to CFDs.

5.4.3   Credit derivatives

Credit derivatives emerged in the mid-1990s as bilateral OTC instruments that enable credit risk[13] to be easily transferred from one party to another without transferring ownership of the underlying asset. They enable the credit profile of a particular asset or group of assets to be split up and redistributed into a more concentrated or diluted form that appeals to the various risk appetites of investors. By using them, banks can offer clients as much credit as they need and

---

[13] Credit risk encompasses the consequences of all credit-related events ranging from a spread widening through a ratings downgrade all the way to default.

During the swap:

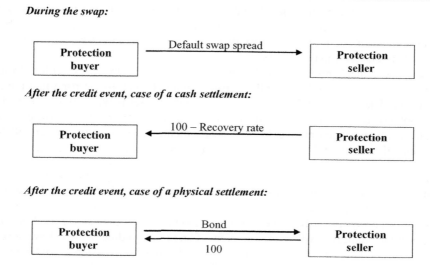

After the credit event, case of a cash settlement:

After the credit event, case of a physical settlement:

Figure 5.14 Mechanics of a credit default swap

simultaneously mitigate the impact of risk concentrations in their portfolio. Industrial firms may hedge the credit risk implicit in their receivables. Investors can gain synthetic exposure to the credit markets without buying bonds or extending loans. And arbitrageurs can arbitrage among credit derivatives and other markets.

Credit derivative products have evolved over time to suit the various needs of buyers and sellers of credit risk, but the most highly utilized credit derivative remains the *credit default swap* (CDS – see Figure 5.14). The CDS is the simplest, most liquid and most efficient way to hedge concentrations of single-name credit risk. In a sense, it is similar to an insurance contract, providing the buyer with protection against the risk of default or significant credit deterioration of an asset issued by a specified issuer.

A credit default swap is an OTC bilateral agreement between a "protection seller" and a "protection buyer". The protection seller promises to compensate the protection buyer against an economic loss in a "reference asset" if a "credit event" occurs. In return, the protection buyer pays a fee, either upfront (for short-dated contracts, the transaction then being called a credit default option) or on a regular basis (for long-dated swaps). In practice, there are several important features that need to be agreed between the counterparties and clearly defined in the contract documentation before a trade can be executed. These include:

- The credit event itself. Typical credit events are a bankruptcy (the issuer becomes insolvent or is unable to pay its debts), a failure to pay (the issuer fails to make interest or principal payments when due), a debt restructuring (the configuration of debt obligations is changed in such a way that the credit holder is unfavourably affected), an obligation acceleration or an obligation default (the debt obligations of the issuer become due before their originally scheduled maturity date), or a repudiation/moratorium (the issuer of the underlying bond rejects its debt, effectively refusing to pay interest and principal). Note that despite ISDA efforts to clarify credit event definitions, CDS default events are not always obvious to the counterparties.

- The reference asset to be considered, and in particular the capital structure seniority of the debt that is covered. This is extremely important, because the reference asset will be used to determine the amount of money lost after the credit event, and therefore the payoff in a cash settled default swap (see below).
- The settlement mechanism. Default swaps can be cash or physically settled. In a cash settlement, the protection buyer will receive an amount equal to the par value minus the price of the defaulted asset. The price of the defaulted asset is typically determined via a dealer poll conducted within 14–30 days of the credit event, the purpose of the delay being to let the recovery value stabilize. In a physical settlement, the protection buyer will deliver the defaulted security to the protection seller in return for its par value in cash.

CDS contracts can efficiently mitigate risks in bond investing by transferring a given risk from one party to another without transferring the underlying bond or other credit asset. Prior to creation of the CDS, there was no vehicle to transfer the risk of a default or other credit event, such as a downgrade, from one investor to another. CDSs can also be used as a way to gain exposure to credit risk with no requirement of an initial funding, which allows leveraged positions. Moreover, a CDS transaction can be entered into where a cash bond of the reference entity of a particular maturity is not available. Further, by entering a CDS as protection buyer, one can easily create a "short" position in the reference credit. With all these attributes, CDSs can be a great tool for diversifying or hedging one's portfolio.

In the early days of the CDS market, pricing of contracts was more an art than a science. Today, however, pricing is more quantitatively based, using parameters such as (i) the default probability of the underlying, established on the basis of credit data, (ii) the floating leg of the swap, i.e. the expected payoff in case of default and (iii) the fixed leg, i.e. the initial swap spread which is valued on the assumption that the protection buyer stops paying after the default takes place. In theory, CDS spreads should be closely related to bond yield spreads, or excess yields to risk-free government bonds. In practice, as we shall see, there may be some tiny differences, and therefore some arbitrage situations.

An *equity default swap* (EDS – see Figure 5.15) is a hybrid of a credit derivative and an equity derivative. As with a CDS, an EDS is a vehicle for one party to provide another party with some protection against a possible event relating to some reference asset. With a CDS, the reference asset is a debt instrument and the protection is provided against a possible default or other credit event. With an EDS, the reference asset is some company's stock and the protection is provided against a dramatic decline in the price of that stock. For example, the EDS might provide protection against a 70% decline in the stock price from its value when the equity default swap was initiated. The event being protected against is called the trigger event or knock-in event.

The EDS has several advantages over the CDS:

- The trigger event – the drop of the stock price below a given level – is easier to define than a credit default, where some corporate events may or may not constitute default.
- The recovery rate is fixed with the EDS, while it must be determined for the CDS.[14]

The EDS is usually quoted as a spread over LIBOR, in basis points per annum. Because an EDS is more likely to be triggered than a CDS, it generally trades at a higher spread. The buyer

---

[14] Note that EDS can also be structured with multiple reference stocks. In this case, the credit event occurs when any first stock in the list defaults (first to default swap), or when the number of defaults in the list reaches a certain number (*n*th to default swap).

During the swap:

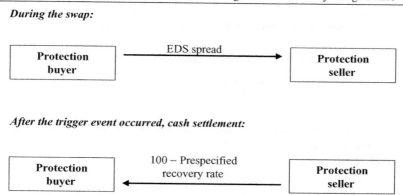

After the trigger event occurred, cash settlement:

Figure 5.15   Mechanics of an equity default swap

of the equity protection pays the protection seller a quarterly premium based on this spread, which is the fixed leg of the swap. If the underlying default event occurs, then the EDS is cash settled, with the buyer paying accrued spread to the protection seller and receiving a fixed amount (100% minus a prespecified recovery rate) on the notional amount of the EDS.

The EDS valuation is therefore based on (i) the level of the trigger event for equity default, (ii) the probability of the equity default, and (iii) the expected recovery rate, which is fixed at the beginning of the contract (Box 5.6). From a pricing perspective, an EDS is similar to a deep out-of-the-money long-dated American digital put. A key difference is that the option premium is paid in a series of instalments that cease when the option is triggered.

5.4.4   Benefits and uses of derivatives

Derivatives would obviously not have become so popular if they did not offer investors attractive opportunities. Let us mention some of them.

- *Risk management (hedging):* It is essential to understand that, unlike *spot transactions*, all *derivatives transactions* are settled in the future and require some sort of uncertainty to take place. The uncertainty might be related to interest rates, exchange rates, the value or volatility of an asset, etc. Derivatives are powerful financial tools that allow market participants to reduce their exposures to uncertainty. Basically, an existing transaction may be hedged by engaging in a derivatives transaction that offsets the potential losses. To an extent, hedging can be seen as a form of insurance, where the insurance premium is equivalent to the price paid for the derivative as well as the lost profit opportunities (in cases where the market movements are favourable). Note that while the concept of hedging is easy to understand, the application is rarely simple. To hedge correctly, one must (1) identify properly one's risk exposure and (2) determine the hedge ratio, i.e. the size of the position to be taken in derivatives in order to reduce the risk exposure by the desired amount.
- *Speculation:* Speculation with derivatives is basically betting on market movements. Whereas hedgers want to eliminate an exposure to movements in the price of an asset, speculators wish to take a position in the market in order to gain from anticipated, but uncertain, price movements.

Box 5.6 Approximations default probabilities

As a first approximation, the EDS spread can be expressed as follows:

$$\text{EDS spread} = \frac{\text{Implied probability of default event} \times (100\% - \text{Recovery rate})}{\text{Number of years}}$$

This approximation ignores the time value of money and the fact that the payments stop after the default event has taken place, but it is relatively accurate for a short-term EDS. Therefore, the equity default probability priced into the EDS is:

$$\text{Implied probability of equity default event} = \frac{\text{EDS spread} \times \text{Number of years}}{100\% - \text{Recovery rate}}$$

The numerator is the amount paid by the protection buyer until the EDS matures, and the denominator is the amount paid by the protection seller if the equity default event occurs.

As an illustration, consider a five-year 30% EDS on Swiss Reinsurance. Say the EDS with an agreed 50% recovery rate trades at 380 basis points p.a. and the company stock price is at 54 euros. This means that an investor would need to pay €380 000 every year to insure €10 million of the Swiss Reinsurance stock for five years. If during these five years the stock drops to or below €16.2 (30% of the initial stock price), the investor will receive €5 million (50% of the value of the original position). In this case, the implied probability of equity default (i.e. a drop of 70% from the current level) assumed by the market is 38% (= 3.80% × 5/(100% − 50%)).

- *Leverage:* The initial amount needed to initiate a derivatives position varies from nil (over-the-counter products) to the initial margin deposit or the premium (exchange-traded contracts). In all cases, this is only a fraction of the cash outlay needed to take a similar position in the underlying asset. For hedgers, this is critical because it allows the hedge to be constructed with less cash resources than would otherwise have been the case. In many situations the hedging strategy would not have been feasible without the high degree of leverage present in derivatives. In the case of speculators, leverage allows a greater capital appreciation per dollar invested. Unfortunately, it also results in steeper losses in situations where the market moves against the speculator.
- *Financial engineering:* Derivatives can also be used to transform existing assets into an endless variety of new assets with a different series of cash flows. For example, through swaps, participants may transform their income or payment flows so that their earnings better match their financial obligations, or vice versa. Using options, the most risky asset can become a capital guaranteed product. In many cases, without derivatives such transformations would not be possible or would be more costly.
- *Arbitrage:* Derivatives are a great tool to facilitate arbitrage, both between and within markets. The simplest form of arbitrage involves buying derivative contracts in one market and selling them simultaneously in another, in order to take advantage of price differences or interest rate disparities. More complex forms of arbitrage are available for those with expert knowledge of derivative markets, and we review some of them in the second part of this book.

Finally, another interesting feature of derivatives is that they are not limited by the market size of an underlying commodity or instrument. In particular, most derivatives positions are closed before maturity and never result in physical delivery of the underlying. In some cases (e.g. weather and inflation derivatives), the underlying asset does not even physically exist. Consequently, the size of any given derivatives market depends on the willingness of counterparties to enter into offsetting transactions to exchange financial risks.

5.5 LEVERAGE

Leverage is cited so often and in connection with so many different types of financial arrangements that it is easily misunderstood. Simply stated, the term "leverage" denotes a situation where the amount of money invested or the economic exposure is higher than the available equity capital.

Leverage can be measured in a number of ways. The traditional measure is the balance sheet leverage, i.e., the ratio of the fund's balance sheet assets to equity. Although it is widely used in the hedge fund world as a risk measure, balance sheet leverage has several weaknesses. In particular, it fails to take into account market, credit and liquidity risks in a portfolio, as well as the use of off-balance sheet products such as derivatives. A better measure is therefore the "economic leverage", which captures the degree of risk taken on by the fund in relation to its ability to bear that risk, i.e. the ratio of potential gains and losses to net worth. Not surprisingly, measuring economic leverage precisely is far from straightforward.

It is important to realize that leverage is not a feature restricted to hedge funds. An investor buying a new home and financing it by a mortgage is in fact doing a leveraged investment. His equity capital is represented by his personal contribution (say 20% of the total amount), while the rest is financed by external funds. In this case, we would say that the leverage ratio is 5 to 1, i.e. $5 invested for any $1 of capital. Similarly, an industrial company issuing debt and using the proceeds to build a new plant is also leveraging its balance sheet.

Nevertheless, leveraging as applied to investing is often considered an aggressive strategy comparable to gambling. The reason is that it magnifies both profits and losses. For instance, say a hedge fund invests $1000 of its equity capital in a stock that rises by 10%. The fund earns $100, that is, a 10% return. By contrast, if the fund had borrowed $10 000 and invested it along with its original $1000, it could have earned $1100, that is, a 110% return, before factoring in the borrowing costs. Now, what if the same stock had dropped by 10%? If the fund had invested only $1000, it would have lost $100, that is, 10%, and its shares would be worth $900. But if the fund had borrowed another $10 000 and invested it in the stock, the total investment of $11 000 would have fallen to $9900. Instead of losing $100, the fund would have lost $1100 plus the borrowing costs, that is, more than its initial equity capital. Clearly, although leverage opens the door to increased income and gain if the market moves on expected lines, it also creates certain risks if the market trend is contrary to expectations.

With hedge funds, leverage can take several forms. It may, for instance, involve explicitly borrowing external funds via a loan, or implicitly borrowing through a margin brokerage account. Last but not least, hedge funds can also use financial instruments (such as repurchase agreements, futures and forward contracts and other derivative products) to establish positions by posting margins rather than the full face value of the position. In all cases, when calculating the real exposure, the amount borrowed should be treated as a negative allocation. It actually becomes a liability of the portfolio as opposed to an asset. For instance, when a hedge fund with $100 capital borrows an additional $25 against its portfolio holdings, it has a $25 liability that must be paid for, but it also has $125 to invest. Of course, the operation only makes sense when the return on investment is higher than the cost of borrowing.

As mentioned already, leveraged investing is often dismissed as gambling. We personally disagree with this assertion. In our opinion, leverage, as long as it stays reasonable, plays a positive role in the financial system. It improves market liquidity, lowers credit costs, and results in a more efficient allocation of resources in the economy. It allows younger people to invest more in equities rather than having to wait until they are older and have sufficient resources to do so. And why, one might ask, is borrowing to buy a new home a perfectly natural thing to do, while funding one's future through an investment loan is apparently another story?

The unpopularity of leverage can be traced back to a few disasters encountered by over-leveraged speculators, most of the time because of pyramidal schemes. Once an investment is financed by leverage, the new asset (e.g. the stock) can be used as collateral for obtaining another loan. The only leverage constraint is therefore the degree to which banks and broker-dealers will finance additional trades and allow leverage on leverage. In a sense, over-collateralization may become an eventual constraint in the same way that a reserve requirement on deposits limits the creation of new money.

The best illustration of over-leveraging is arguably provided by the fund called Long Term Capital Management (LTCM). For several reasons, LTCM's counterparties did not take risks properly into account (see Box 5.7). They granted LTCM huge trading lines in a variety of products, and LTCM took advantage of those lines to achieve its exceptional degree of leverage. When the fund almost went bankrupt in 1998, the whole financial system was at risk, and the Federal Reserve had to step in and organize a rescue.

Box 5.7 Long Term Capital Management (LTCM)

LTCM was indeed a very particular hedge fund. Founded in 1994, it was run by some of the brightest minds world wide. Its 16 partners included John Meriwether, a legendary Wall Street figure who founded the arbitrage group at Salomon Brothers,[15] Nobel Prize winners Myron Scholes and Robert C. Merton, the former Federal Reserve vice-chairman David Mullins, and a group of eggheads who had tamed the business of money management with the most elegant models from academia. This array of talent allowed LTCM to successfully start with a capital of $1.25 billion, the most money ever collected at that time to start a hedge fund. The initial terms were rather tough: $10 million minimum investment, three-year lock-up, 2% management fee and 25% performance fee.

LTCM focused on fixed income arbitrage, i.e. finding inefficiencies in the fixed income markets and taking positions that would become profitable when these perceived inefficiencies were eliminated. In theory, LTCM's positions involved little outright market risk, because a long position in one instrument was always offset by a short position in a similar instrument or its derivative. In a sense, LTCM's success was predicated upon other arbitrageurs finding the same inefficiencies *after* LTCM and exploiting them, which in turn would move the market in the direction of the trades LTCM had placed. Most of the time, these inefficiencies were small in magnitude (a few basis points), so that it was necessary for LTCM to take very large, highly leveraged positions in order to generate worthwhile returns.

---

[15] Although he had to leave Salomon Brothers after its 1991 Treasury bonds trading scandal.

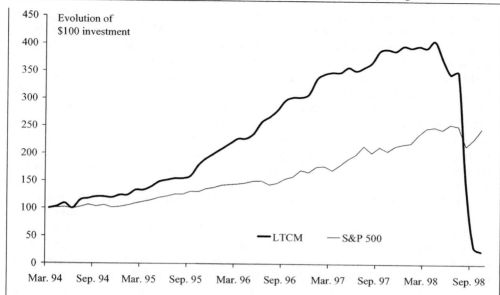

Figure 5.16   Evolution of $1 invested in LTCM and in the S&P 500, 1994–1998

The first years of LTCM were extremely profitable. In 1994-1996, its raw return figures (before fees) were 28%, 59%, and 57% respectively. A dollar invested in LTCM over this time period would have resulted in a net position of approximately $3.50 (Figure 5.16), whereas a dollar invested in the S&P index over that period would have resulted in only $1.60. However, in 1997, the fund showed a dramatic drop-off and only returned 17% versus 31% for the S&P 500. By that stage, the fund's assets had grown to about $120 billion and its capital to about $7.3 billion – a 16 to 1 leverage.

LTCM's partners then analysed the situation and took two decisions. First, they returned $2.7 billion of equity capital to investors, but maintained the size of the fund's positions. This resulted in a significant increase of leverage (25 to 1), and therefore of risk. Second, LTCM branched away from its trademark investment strategies and ventured into new areas where their expertise was less valuable. The new strategies included equity volatility trades (i.e. selling options), equity pairs trading (buying and selling-short equities that were supposed to converge), merger arbitrage, and directional trades on various markets as well as individual stocks.

Most markets were edgy during the first part of 1998, and LTCM did not perform well. Market conditions then started deteriorating in July 1998, when Salomon Smith Barney suddenly decided to liquidate its dollar interest arbitrage positions. LTCM had very similar trades in place and lost 10% over the month. Disaster struck the next month, when the Russian government devalued the rouble and defaulted on its debt.

In early 1998, LTCM had felt that quality liquid investments were overpriced with respect to less liquid or less creditworthy investments. Therefore, it had undertaken many trades in which it was betting that spreads between high-quality and lower-quality investments should narrow. But with the Russian default, the sudden enormous demand for high-quality investments caused these spreads to balloon. Furthermore, the phenomenon was not isolated to one country or region, but affected all markets, cancelling the expected stabilizing effect of being diversified across many markets. The cost for LTCM was $550 million on 21 August alone. To make matters worse, the fund also sustained major losses on its other speculative positions, particularly its five-year equity short options.

By the end of August, LTCM's capital had shrunk to $2.3 billion and its asset base was approximately $107 billion. This implies a leverage ratio over 45 to 1 – a very high ratio by any standards, but especially in such a volatile environment. On 2 September, LTCM's partners faxed a letter to investors acknowledging the fund's problems and seeking to raise further capital to exploit what (quite reasonably) they described as attractive arbitrage opportunities. Not surprisingly, no new capital or assistance was offered, but the fax was posted on the internet and the fund's problems became common knowledge in the market.

Portfolio losses then accelerated across all trades. On 19 September, LTCM's capital was reduced to only $600 million, with an asset base of approximately $80 billion. All LTCM's counterparties had unanswered margin calls and were observing the fund's sinking fortunes with mounting concern. Almost no one could be persuaded to buy, at any reasonable price, an asset that LTCM was known or believed to hold, because of the concern that the markets were about to be saturated by a fire sale of the fund's positions. LTCM's failure was becoming a "self-fulfilling prophecy," in the words of the social theorist and sociologist of science Robert K. Merton, father of the financial theorist and LTCM partner. At this stage, the Federal Reserve felt obliged to intervene. A delegation from the New York Federal Reserve and the US Treasury visited LTCM on Sunday, 20 September, to assess the situation.

As revealed later by the President's Working Group on Financial Markets (1999), the situation was indeed scary. One dollar invested with LTCM in March 1994 was worth about 10 cents in December 1998. LTCM had initially used its capital as collateral to establish bets on about $125 billion in securities, half in long positions and half in short positions. It then used those securities as collateral to enter into off-balance sheet transactions to a total notional amount of more than a trillion dollars. Among these were futures ($500 billion), swaps ($750 billion) and options, as well as other over-the-counter derivatives ($150 billion). In total, the fund had more than 60 000 trades on its books and a leverage of more than 500 to 1. This situation might not have been considered problematic if LTCM had not faced liquidation. Of course, the leverage before the crisis was "only" about 25 to 1. According to LTCM partners, the fund was targeting a 1% return on assets, leveraged 25 times, which would result in a 25% return. This leverage was less than the 34 to 1 leverage common at securities firms and comparable to the 24 to 1 leverage common at money-centre banks. But one could also argue that money-centre banks have much less volatile assets. So big was its portfolio, so leveraged and so intertwined with so many institutions on Wall Street that liquidating the fund would have disrupted most major markets. The Ferrari had suddenly become an Oldsmobile.

At this stage, a group consisting of Warren Buffett's Berkshire Hathaway, along with Goldman Sachs and American International Group, a giant insurance holding company, offered to buy out the existing shareholders for $250 million and inject $3.75 billion into the fund as new capital. The offer was strictly commercial, i.e. buying the fund for less than its value. It would have saved LTCM from failure, but it would have cost the management of LTCM their remaining equity, their jobs, and any future management fees. Convinced that they could get a better offer from the Fed, LTCM's partners rejected Warren Buffet's offer.

On 23 September, a consortium of 14 banks led by the Federal Reserve Bank of New York offered to buy 90% of LTCM for $3.65 billion. The funds from this bail-out, combined with the equity remaining in the fund (which had fallen to $350 million in the meantime), brought the total equity value to approximately $4 billion, and the leverage ratio back to a more comfortable 25 to 1. Existing partners would therefore retain a 10% holding, valued at about $400 million, and existing managers would keep their jobs and rights to management fees – a much better offer than Warren Buffet's.

Needless to say, numerous people questioned the necessity of the Federal Reserve intervention and its future consequences. If the Federal Reserve wants to promote market stability, it should ensure that market participants have strong incentives to promote their own financial health rather than just wait for a bail-out from regulators. On 1 October, defending the Fed's decision to assist LTCM, Alan Greenspan explained:

> The act of unwinding LTCM's portfolio in a forced liquidation would not only have a significant distorting impact on market prices but also in the process could produce large losses, or worse, for a number of creditors and counterparties, and for other market participants who were not directly involved with LTCM . . . Had the failure of LTCM triggered the seizing up of markets, substantial damage could have been inflicted on many market participants . . . and could have potentially impaired the economies of many nations, including our own.

Were the Fed's concerns exaggerated? We will never know. Month after month, the consortium that took over LTCM recovered its money, plus a modest profit, and closed shop. To prevent another collapse, several banks scaled down their proprietary trading desks and imposed higher margin requirements when lending to hedge funds. And hedge funds themselves reduced their use of leverage.

What happened to LTCM partners? It seems that they all ended up . . . somewhere else in the hedge fund industry. In December 1999, John Meriwether started a new relative value hedge fund, called JWM Partners. Also based in Greenwich, Connecticut, it manages more than a billion dollars and pursues bond arbitrage strategies similar to those used by LTCM, but with leverage limited to 20 to 1. Most of Meriwether's partners in LTCM joined JWM Partners, with a few notable exceptions. Robert C. Merton returned to Harvard. Myron Scholes started advising Oak Hill Platinum Partners, a hedge fund owned by Texas billionaire Robert Bass and whose founding principal is Chi Fu Huang, a renowned derivatives modeller and fellow alumnus of LTCM. And James McEntee and Gregory Hawkins joined Caxton Corporation to set up a relative value bond hedge fund. It is definitely a small world!

The primary lesson to be learned from the LTCM debacle is that the combination of tremendous leverage and illiquid markets is similar to a vodka party. It often starts well, but ends up badly. Before the Russian collapse, the level of leverage used by LTCM was comparable to the leverage used by banks and securities firms – see Table 5.3. However, two factors distinguish banks and securities firms from hedge funds: (i) they have more diverse sources of income and of funding and (2) they are subject to government oversight that monitors risk management systems, public disclosure and capital requirements. LTCM, by contrast, had very few sources of income and was completely opaque and largely unregulated.

Fortunately, hedge funds have learned from the disaster and most of them have dramatically reduced their leverage. Moreover, their counterparties (banks, brokers, etc.) are now imposing higher margin requirements when lending to hedge funds and put in place stricter rules to control their exposure. It seems that Wall Street can sometimes learn from its losses.

Table 5.3 Leverage ratios of selected securities firms in 1998, based on the president's Working Group hedge fund report as well as the firm's 1998 annual report

Institution	Leverage ratio (assets to equity capital)
LTCM	28 to 1
Goldman Sachs	34 to 1
Leman Brothers	28 to 1
Merrill Lynch	30 to 1
Morgan Stanley Dean Witter	22 to 1

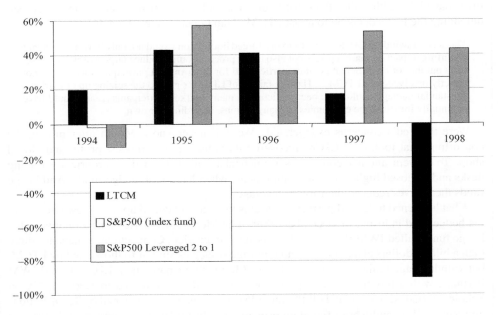

Figure 5.17 Use of leverage: comparing annual returns on three strategies

The second lesson is also related to the use of leverage. Market participants often fail to consider leverage in their comparisons. As an illustration, let us look at the annual return of three investment strategies (Figure 5.17), namely, investing in LTCM, investing in an index fund mimicking the S&P 500, and buying the same index fund on margin using a 2 to 1 leverage. In the last-mentioned case, we assume that interest is paid on debit balances at the rate of 10% p.a.

As can be seen, while LTCM averaged a 29.62% return p.a. between 1994 and 1997, the plain vanilla indexed fund achieved an average return of 20.17% p.a., and the leveraged strategy 28.67% p.a., net of financing costs. If we include the year 1998 (which is obviously unfair), the average return drops to −22.35% p.a. for LTCM, but rises to 21.44% p.a. for the index fund and 31.47% p.a. for the leveraged strategy. Had we taken the risk of leveraging our index fund 50 to 1 as did LTCM, our returns would have been nothing short of spectacular.

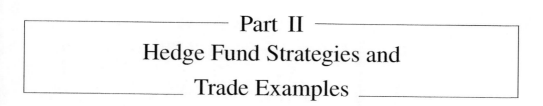

Part II
Hedge Fund Strategies and Trade Examples

6

Introduction

Psychology tends to produce too many subjective answers and no objective theory.

Although the term "hedge funds" is often used generically, it is essential to understand that, in reality, hedge funds no longer form a homogeneous group. As hedge funds have gained size and popularity, they have deviated from the original Alfred W. Jones' model and are now following a plethora of investment strategies with very different risk and return characteristics. Of course, one could argue that their situation is not fundamentally different from the one that prevails with traditional asset classes – equities can be split by industrial sectors, growth and value styles, and cyclical and non-cyclical categories, and bonds can be analysed by durations, credit categories, or industry and geographic categories. Nevertheless, despite the existence of many subcategories, equities and bonds still have some common factors throughout their respective asset class. By contrast, it is usually difficult to identify a common factor for hedge funds beyond the "unregulated" and "privately-offered" attributes. Nevertheless, understanding the common nature as well as the differences between funds that follow the same investment strategy is crucial in order to develop a coherent investment plan.

To analyse hedge funds, consultants, investors and managers alike need to segregate their universe into a range of standardized investment styles. Unfortunately, there is no accepted norm to classify the different hedge fund strategies, and each consultant, investor, manager or hedge fund data provider may design its own classification or decide to adopt an external one. A survey launched by the Alternative Investment Management Association in 2003 evidenced that 50% of the respondents used their own strategy classification, 47% used one or more outside classification systems, while the balance (3%) stated that hedge funds could not be classified. Among the group that used outside classification sources, the primary classifications mentioned were those of CS/Tremont (27%) and Hedge Fund Research (27%), closely followed by MSCI (23%) as well as those of the CISDM, Eurekahedge and Cogent Hedge databases.

In the following, for the sake of simplicity, we have decided to match the classification suggested by CS/Tremont. Note that we do not claim that this classification is better than existing ones. It is just a working tool that is compatible with most existing classifications. Understanding how the universe of strategies is split according to CS/Tremont allows the reader to derive its own classification if he or she wants it.

CS/Tremont distinguishes 10 different strategies. To summarize:

- *Long/short equity* funds invest in equities, and combine long investments with short sales to reduce but not to completely eliminate market exposure.
- *Dedicated short* funds only use short positions. In a sense, they are the mirrors of traditional long-only managers.
- *Equity market neutral* funds seek to exploit pricing inefficiencies between related equity securities while at the same time exactly neutralizing exposure to market risk.

- *Distressed securities funds* focus on debt or equity of companies that are or are expected to be in financial or operational difficulty. This may involve reorganizations, bankruptcies, distressed sales and other corporate restructurings.
- *Merger arbitrage funds* invest in event-driven situations such as mergers or acquisitions, including leveraged buyouts, mergers, or hostile takeovers.
- *Convertible bond arbitrage* funds seek to exploit pricing anomalies between convertible bonds and their underlying equity.
- *Fixed income arbitrage* funds use a wide spectrum of strategies that seek to exploit pricing anomalies within and across global fixed income markets.
- *Emerging market* funds invest in all types of securities in emerging countries, including equities, bonds, and sovereign debt.
- *Global macro* funds tend to make leveraged, directional, opportunistic investments in global currency, equity, bond and commodity markets on a discretionary basis.
- *Managed futures* (commodity trading advisers) trade primarily listed commodity and financial futures contracts on behalf of their clients, mostly on an algorithmic basis.

Each of these strategies will be analysed in a separate chapter, with examples of trades. We invite the reader to understand how these trades work, their rationale as well as the associated risks because we believe that this is actually the best way to get some insight in hedge fund strategies. In addition, we will also illustrate a series of some less popular hedge fund strategies in a dedicated chapter – in a sense, these are the alternative strategies of today's hedge fund managers, and some of them may become the leading strategies of tomorrow.

Figure 6.1 illustrates the breakdown of hedge fund assets by investment strategy, based on the CS/Tremont index in May 2006. This breakdown has significantly changed over the years. In

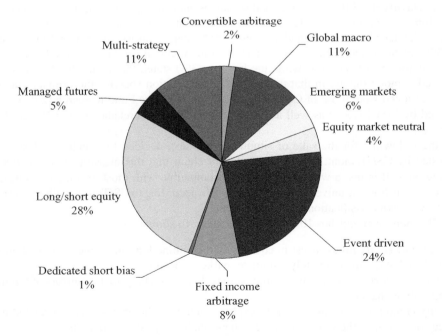

Figure 6.1   Breakdown of hedge fund assets by investment strategy (based on the CS/Tremont index)

the mid-1990s, global macro funds were the Titans of finance and controlled almost two-thirds of hedge fund assets. But this ended in 2000 when two colossi of the industry – George Soros and Julian Robertson ($22 and $20 billion at their respective peaks) – retreated from a game whose rules seemed to have changed. Since, global macro has experienced a significant decline in market share for the profit of long/short equity, which is now the dominant force (28%) of the industry. This is the direct consequence of the long bear market of the early 2000s. Several long-only managers closed their traditional funds to open a new hedge fund in order to be able to sell short . . . and capture performance fees. However, as we will see, long/short equity is an easy strategy to understand, but picking the best managers is a daunting task.

7

Long/Short Equity Strategies

Stock picking is like playing the lottery. It is definitely a game worth winning. But is it a game worth playing?

In the world of hedge funds, the term "equity strategies" is almost synonymous with long/short equity, also known as "equity hedge". As already mentioned, the long/short equity investment approach finds its roots in the original Alfred Winslow Jones model. It consists primarily in combining long and short positions in equities, resulting in portfolios that have reduced market risk.

Long/short equity funds have been around for decades and now represent the biggest segment among non-traditional investments. Most long/short equity managers apply the same fundamental analysis as traditional funds, with the difference that they can – at least in theory – generate profits even in declining markets. However, over the years, the initial strategy has evolved to capture various sources of return and adopt different investment approaches. For instance, sector funds have emerged; some managers have evolved towards more quantitative strategies; others have adopted a more active approach and drifted towards private equity or activist techniques. None of these changes is really revolutionary, but they show that hedge funds are indeed reinventing themselves whenever necessary.

At first glance, because long-only and long/short strategies both use common stocks, one may think that they are closely related. But in reality they are quite different. First, long/short equity investing is not a new asset class, or an extension to the existing equity asset class. Rather, it should be considered as a "new" portfolio construction technique. Second, the mechanics involved in setting up and managing a long/short portfolio are much more complex – many successful long-only managers discover it to their cost when they move to the hedge fund universe. To effectively select and monitor long/short equity funds, investors also need an understanding of these mechanics as well as the unique efficiencies and costs inherent in any long/short strategy.

7.1 THE MECHANICS OF LONG/SHORT EQUITY INVESTING

7.1.1 A single position

Let us first illustrate the mechanics of long/short equity investing by means of a simplified example detailing all the steps in the process. Consider a hedge fund that has a hypothetical initial equity capital of, say, $1000 to invest. Its manager has identified two potential investments: according to him, stock A is undervalued, while stock B is overvalued. The manager therefore wishes to engage in a long/short strategy to profit from both investments. The process can be structured as follows (Figure 7.1):

- *Step 1:* The fund manager deposits the $1000 at a custodial prime broker.
- *Step 2:* The fund manager starts by purchasing $900 worth of stock A that he perceives to be undervalued. He pays for these shares with the fund's equity capital, so that his situation

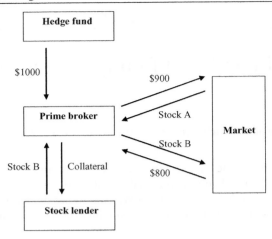

Figure 7.1   Flows in long/short investing

with respect to his broker will be a long position in stock A for $900 and a long cash position of $100. So far, this is very similar to a traditional investment fund's position. Technically, one would say that the hedge fund has no leverage; it has a *net long exposure* of 90% and a *gross exposure* of 90% of its equity capital. To keep things simple, we assume that the newly purchased A shares are custodied by the prime broker.

- *Step 3:* The manager now sells $800 worth of stock B that he perceives to be overvalued. This increases his cash balance by $800. However, since the fund does not own any B shares, this is a short sale. It is therefore necessary to borrow these shares from a third party in order to deliver them to the buyer.
- *Step 4:* The prime broker arranges to borrow $800 worth of the required shares from a stock lending institution such as a large institutional investor. The prime broker freezes some collateral to secure the transaction, say for instance the $800 that the fund just cashed in as well as some of its previously bought A shares. The prime broker also charges the hedge fund a rent of, say, 1% p.a., that is, $8 at the end of the lending period if the short position is maintained for a year.

At this stage, the fund is using leverage. Its assets consist of $900 of stock A (long), $800 of stock B (short), plus $900 in cash that could theoretically be used to purchase other stocks. In total, this represents $2600 of assets, to be compared with the initial $1000 of equity capital. In practice, since cash is not risky, it is excluded from the assets when calculating the leverage. Investors would therefore say the fund has a 90% long exposure, an 80% short exposure, a 170% (= 90 + 80) gross exposure and a 10% (= 90 − 80) net long exposure.

Note that:

- These exposure numbers will change over time, as the value of the long and short positions, as well as the equity capital of the fund, vary.
- The collateral will only secure the current value of the borrowed shares. If the value of the collateral drops or if the shorted stock price increases, the hedge fund will receive at some point a margin call to post more collateral.

- The key element in establishing a long/short position is the ability to sell short – that is, the ability to borrow shares at a reasonable cost. The choice of a good prime broker can be pivotal here, and it may also influence the amount of collateral that the hedge fund needs to supply.

Of course, the various amounts we have used in this simple long/short trade are for illustrative purposes only. In practice, the hedge fund could decide, for instance, to buy $900 of stock A and sell short $900 of stock B, in which case we would have a *dollar neutral* position, with zero net exposure. Alternatively, a more sophisticated hedge fund manager could attempt to create a *beta neutral* position by taking into account the beta of his long and short positions. This is frequently the case with equity market neutral managers.

7.1.2 Sources of return and feasible portfolios

Academic researchers and investment practitioners now recognize that loosening the long-only constraint that applies in traditional asset management is one of the most effective ways of increasing portfolio efficiency, maximizing a manager's investment insights and potentially increasing alpha generation. Traditional long-only equity strategies have only one source of return, that is, the appreciation of the stock purchased. Long/short strategies, in contrast, have four potential sources of return:

- The first source of return is the *spread* in performance between the long and the short positions. Ideally, the stocks on the long side should appreciate in value while the shorted stocks should decrease in value. This is why long/short investing is often referred to as a *double alpha* strategy – the term "alpha" is used here to refer to the outperformance of an investment. In long/short investments, one alpha may come from the long side (the undervalued stock appreciates in value) and the other alpha may come from the short side (the overvalued stock depreciates in value).
- The second source of return is the interest rebate on the proceeds of the short sale that are used as collateral. The lending fee is taken as a haircut (that is, a deduction) on the interest on the proceeds paid to the fund, but this haircut is usually extremely small for most liquid shares.
- The third source of return is the interest paid on the liquidity buffer that remains as a margin deposit to the broker. The interest rate is usually close to the Treasury-bill rate.
- Finally, the last source of return is the spread in dividends between the long and the short position. Stock borrowers need to reimburse stock lenders for dividends paid on borrowed stocks, while they cash in dividends on the long position. Although the difference may be small, it should be taken into consideration when calculating the total return of a position.

It is important to realize that the short position in a long/short investment may serve three purposes:

- It can represent a bet on an overvalued asset that should decrease in value in the near future. As we will see later in this chapter, the strategies used to identify long (undervalued) and short (overvalued) positions vary enormously.
- It can be used just to hedge the market risk of the long position. In such a case, the short position can even be made up of futures contracts, while the long position consists of stocks that are perceived to be undervalued.

- It collects interest on the short amount. A few years ago, the record level of interest rates was obviously an incentive to sell short, as it provided a reasonable buffer against the potential increase in value of the short positions.

A remarkable property of long/short investing is that the manager may be partly wrong in his choice of securities on an absolute basis, but the position may still be profitable even though both the long and the short positions decline or appreciate in absolute terms. Indeed, what matters is that the long position outperforms the short position *on a relative basis*. This explains why long/short funds have the ability to perform well in both bear and bull markets.

Let us turn again to our previous example and assume a one-month holding period. Say the stock A share price increases from $10 to $11 and pays in addition a $1 dividend at the end of the month. This represents a 20% increase in total, i.e. a profit of $20\% \times \$900 = \$180$ on the long position. Say also that the stock B share price increases from $10 to $10.25 and pays in addition a $0.25 dividend at the end of the month. This represents a 5% increase in total, i.e. a loss of $5\% \times \$800 = \$40$ on the short position. If the interest paid on the short proceeds are 6% p.a., this represents a gain of $0.5\% \times \$800 = \$4$ over a month. The unused capital of $100 can also be invested at 6% p.a., which gives $0.5\% \times \$100 = \$0.5$ of interest. Finally, if the fee to borrow the shares is 1% p.a., the cost over one month will be $(1\%/12) \times \$800 = \$0.66$. The total profit and loss of the position can therefore be summarized as follows:

	Rate	Profit/Loss
Variation in A shares (including dividends)	+20%	+ $180.00
Variation in B shares (including dividends)	+5%	− $40.00
Interest on short proceeds	+6% p.a.	+ $4.00
Interest on liquidity buffer	+6% p.a.	+ $0.50
Renting fees	+1% p.a.	− $0.66
Total profit		$143.84

At the end of the month, the hedge fund's profit, based on a $900 long position and an $800 short position, is $143.84. As a proportion of the initial capital, which was only $1000, the total return is therefore 14.38%. Of course, one could object that a long-only portfolio invested equally in shares A and B would have achieved a return of 12.50%, very close to the return of the long/short equity position. So why bother with the additional complexity? Well, this argument misses two important points.

First, in our example, the manager was wrong on the short side: stock B can be considered a winner, with a monthly performance of 5%. If we assume, for instance, that the stock B share price had fallen by 5% over the month, the gain on the long/short position would be as follows:

	Rate	Profit/Loss
Variation in A shares (including dividends)	+20%	+ $180.00
Variation in B shares (including dividends)	−5%	+ **$40.00**
Interest on collateral	+6% p.a.	+ $4.00
Interest on liquidity buffer	+6% p.a.	+ $0.50
Renting fees	+1% p.a.	− $0.66
Total profit		$223.84

The return now looks much more favourable, at 22.38% for the long/short position, versus only 7.5% for the equally weighted long-only portfolio.

Second, the long/short portfolio has a much lower risk than the long-only position. The reason for that is simply the diversification of risks. There is a good chance that securities A and B are somehow positively correlated, so that grouping them in a long-only portfolio will only result in a limited diversification. The long/short portfolio, on the other hand, mixes a long position in stock A and a short position in stock B. Since A and B are positively correlated, the correlation between the long and the short position will be negative. This improves significantly the benefits of diversification. And the phenomenon is further strengthened if securities A and B are highly correlated. Then, the two positions in the long/short portfolio will have a large negative correlation, which will result in higher risk reduction through diversification. This clearly explains why long/short hedge fund managers typically prefer to take positions in highly correlated securities to diversify risk, while long-only managers are rather looking for non-correlated securities.

By way of illustration, let us consider the case of a long/short position in Peugeot versus Renault, the two French car manufacturers. Figure 7.2 shows the movement of both stocks during the year 2001. Peugeot reported a net profit for 2001 of €1.7 billion ($1.5 billion), 29% up on the year before, while Renault reported a 77% decline in operating profits, blaming the economic crises in Argentina and Turkey, two of its key foreign markets. The realized return on the Peugeot stock was 3.2% with a volatility of 33.2%, while the realized return on the Renault stock was −41.7% with a volatility of 38.5%. The correlation between the two stocks was 0.4.

Using modern portfolio theory, we can calculate the set of all feasible portfolios obtained by mixing long positions in Peugeot and Renault. This mini *efficient frontier* is represented in Figure 7.3. Obviously, it is not very attractive. Most of its portfolios exhibit a negative return over the period in question, but this was predictable because of the performance provided by the two stocks.

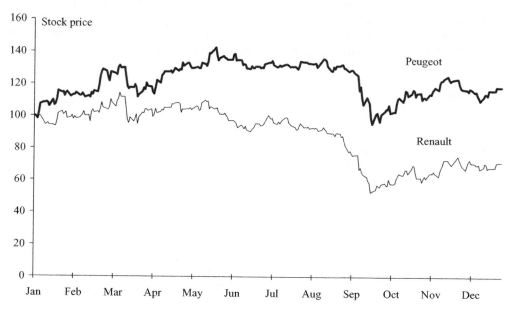

Figure 7.2 Movement of Peugeot and Renault share prices, 2001, scaled to a value of 100 euros on 1 January

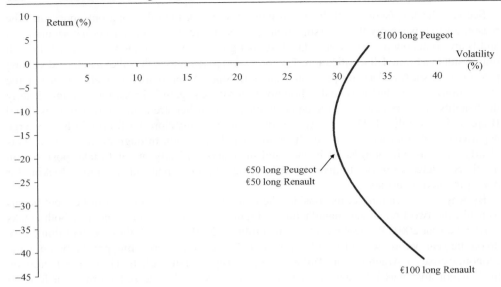

Figure 7.3   The set of all long-only portfolios mixing Peugeot and Renault

Now, what happens if a fund manager decides to mix a long Peugeot position with a *short* Renault position? Let us assume that any cash can be invested at 4.5% p.a. and that borrowing Renault shares costs 0.375% p.a. In a sense, deciding to go short Renault creates a new asset with a positive return (45.825% = 41.7% + 4.5% − 0.375%), a volatility of 38.5% (unchanged) and a negative correlation with the long Peugeot position (−0.4). On a stand-alone basis, this new asset is obviously much more attractive than the original long Renault position. But it looks even better in terms of portfolio construction. The resulting efficient frontier is displayed in Figure 7.4. Clearly, the long/short strategy provides a much better risk/return trade-off, mostly

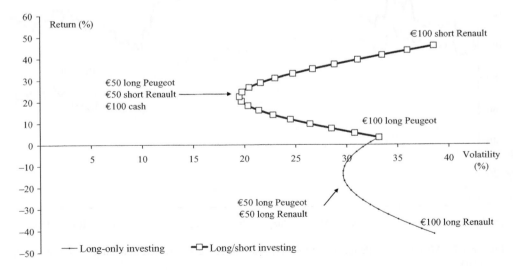

Figure 7.4   The set of portfolios mixing long Peugeot and short Renault positions

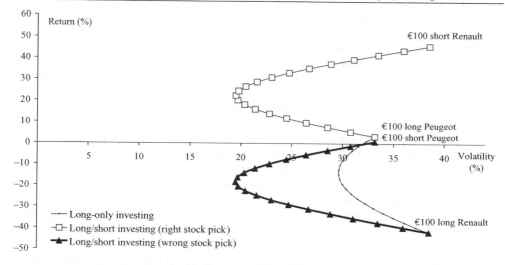

Figure 7.5 The set of portfolios mixing short Peugeot and long Renault positions

because of the negative correlation between the long and the short positions, but also because of the higher return of the short Renault position.

However, we have implicitly assumed that the fund manager had stock-picking skills and used them to identify Renault as a short and Peugeot as a long. What would have happened if the fund manager had made the wrong bet, i.e. had sold short Peugeot and bought Renault? The result is represented in Figure 7.5. In this case, the set of feasible portfolios is much worse than the previous long/short efficient frontier, but it still performs better than the long-only initial frontier most of the time. This dominance, however, depends on the stocks that are being considered. In our example, it exists because of the lack of return difference between the long and the short Peugeot positions. In a sense, being wrong on Peugeot is not really costly. If the Peugeot stock had a much more attractive return, selling it short would penalize dramatically the wrong strategy. Investors therefore need to be mindful that leverage is embedded in long/short structures, and that any investment strategy using leverage can have returns that are more volatile than those in unleveraged portfolios.

To reduce the consequences of a possible wrong stock selection, long/short equity managers diversify their portfolios, both on the long and on the short side. It is therefore common to see portfolios with more than 100 or 200 positions, as well as concentration limits that fix the maximum size that a position could grow to (e.g. 5% of the total portfolio).

7.1.3 Disadvantages of long/short equity investing

At this stage, the reader might be excused for concluding that long/short equity strategies are the panacea of equity investing. However, one should not forget that they also come with some disadvantages:

- *Higher trading costs:* The gross exposure of a long/short equity fund is usually much more than its initial capital, which means that the trading costs expressed as a percentage of the initial capital are usually high. In our previous example, the fund would face trading costs on a $1700 position, plus the borrowing costs for $800 worth of shares. Since higher trading costs are inherent to the strategy, the only way to reduce them is by lowering the fund's exposure – investing only 50% of the initial capital both long and short so that there is no effective leverage and trading costs will be equivalent to a long-only strategy.

- *Higher turnover:* Long/short equity strategies tend to have a higher turnover than buy and hold strategies. The values of both the long and the short portfolio will change over time depending on the performance of the individual securities, and additional trading may be needed to rebalance the portfolio. In addition, large market movements may result in additional trading in order to avoid margin violations or liquidity drawdowns.
- *Delays in execution:* Several stock exchanges only allow short sales on an up tick (i.e. at a price higher than the last traded price) or a zero down tick (i.e., at the same price as the last traded price if that price is higher than the previous price). These two rules may delay the trading of short positions, and the portfolio might have a long bias in the mean time if the long position is already taken.
- *Lag in bull markets:* Although they are invested in equities, long/short equity funds are unable to capture the equity risk premium, particularly during bullish markets where their short positions act as a hedge and reduce their market exposure.
- *Net long bias:* Long/short equity funds tend to have a net long bias, i.e. a higher long exposure than a short exposure. This bias stems from two reasons. First, many newcomers to the long/short equity universe have a long-only background. They are not really comfortable with the idea of being short. Consequently, their long positions tend to dominate in the portfolio. Second, once a long/short equity position has been established, it tends to drift towards a net long exposure. Indeed, the long stock will ideally appreciate in value and increase its weight in the portfolio, while the short stock will ideally decline in value and reduce its weight in the portfolio. Well-balanced long/short equity portfolios therefore evolve naturally towards a long bias as their trades succeed. To counter this trend, managers must regularly reduce the size of their winning long positions and search for new short opportunities.

7.2 INVESTMENT APPROACHES

There are several investment approaches used by long/short equity hedge fund managers to build their portfolios. Below we review only a few of the most popular ones.

7.2.1 The valuation-based approach

A large number of long/short equity managers belong to the school of value investing initiated by the late Benjamin Graham, professor of investments at Columbia Business School and author of *Security Analysis* and *The Intelligent Investor*. Simply stated, they use a disciplined process called *fundamental analysis* (Box 7.1) to determine the long-term intrinsic value of a stock, i.e. what they believe the stock is really worth. They then compare this long-term intrinsic value to what the stock is currently being traded at in the market, and decide whether or not the discrepancy justifies taking a long or a short position. Their goal is to buy ownership positions in companies for less than they are worth, and sell short ownership positions in companies for more than they are worth.

The implicit assumption of long/short equity managers following the valuation approach is that, in the long run, stock prices should be mean reverting and should return towards their intrinsic value. That is, a stock that is trading well above its long-term intrinsic value (i.e. that is overvalued) will eventually decline to that value. If the risk factors are acceptable, it is therefore

---

Box 7.1 Fundamental analysis

To determine a stock's intrinsic value, most fundamental analysts use some sort of discounted cash flow (DCF) analysis. DCF analysis is a two-step process that (i) estimates a company's future cash flows over a specified time period and (ii) discounts these cash flows with a risk-adjusted return rate to determine their present value. The cash flows considered are usually operating cash flows (i.e. cash flows generated by business operations), free cash flows (i.e. cash flows available to shareholders after all other company obligations have been settled) or dividends (which produces the classic dividend-growth model). The result is an absolute stock value or a range of values if a set of different assumptions are used in the process.[1]

Since DCF analysis requires some sort of forecast, which adds an unavoidable element of subjectivity, fundamental analysts often use relative valuation metrics, such as price to earnings, price to book value, and book to market value. These metrics are applied to a carefully selected subset of comparable companies to point at relative over- or under-valuations. However, these models should not be the only component used to select stocks – if all the firms in a particular industry are overpriced, decisions based on relative valuation metrics are likely to result in myopically purchasing overvalued stocks, while a well-crafted DCF model applied with realistic parameters should prevent the purchase of a stock that is cheap only in comparison to its expensive peers.

Lastly, fundamental analysts also use the balance sheet and income statements, as well as more qualitative measures such as the managerial quality, the business model of the company (knowing what the company does and how it makes money), the industry analysis, the competitive strategy and position within the industry, the earnings quality and the operating efficiency.

It should be noted that pricing a security from an absolute value perspective is a notoriously difficult task. It is slightly easier to do relative pricing, i.e. pricing securities against each other.

---

a good candidate to sell short. By contrast, a stock that is trading far below its intrinsic value (i.e. that is undervalued) will presumably migrate back up to its long-term intrinsic value over time. It is therefore a good candidate to buy.

In practice, however, long/short equity managers usually impose a margin of safety on their entry and exit points. They only buy a stock if it is sufficiently undervalued (say it trades at less than 70% of the intrinsic value) and sell short a stock if it is sufficiently overvalued (say it trades at more than 130% of the intrinsic value). As soon as a stock enters the portfolio, it is given a *target exit price* (to take profits) and a *target stop loss price* (to exit from a losing position), as well as an *expected time horizon* to become fairly valued. The stock is then monitored on a daily basis to see how it performs compared to the initial expectations (Figure 7.6).

It is essential to understand that this valuation-driven long/short equity investment approach is in total contradiction with the efficient market hypothesis (EMH), a cornerstone of modern

---

[1] Analysts tend to place too much emphasis on their valuation model because it is the one area where they can achieve a fair degree of precision. However, most of the time, the importance of the valuation model is insignificant compared to the importance of making the correct assumptions.

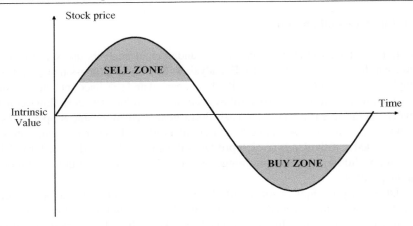

Figure 7.6 Investing according to fundamental analysis and intrinsic value

investment theory, which postulates that markets fully and instantaneously reflect all available information at any given time. If EMH was valid, there would be no value added for hedge fund analysts in doing fundamental research, because the information acquired through it would be useless.

Are markets efficient? The question has fuelled intense debate among academics and financial professionals, and spawned hundreds and thousands of empirical studies attempting to determine whether specific markets are in fact efficient and if so to what degree.[2] Initial tests of market efficiency generally supported the efficient markets view, but the statistical models used for those tests were later shown to be rather weak.[3] Our view with respect to market efficiency is very pragmatic, and relies on a simple paradox. If every investor believed a market was efficient and adopted a passive investment approach, then the market would not be efficient because no one would analyse securities. But if every investor believed a market was not efficient and started analysing securities, then the market would become efficient. Therefore, in reality, markets are neither perfectly efficient nor completely inefficient. All markets are efficient to a certain extent, some more so than others – it depends on how many market participants believe the market is inefficient, do some research, and trade securities in an attempt to outperform the market.

Consider, for example, the small and micro caps market in the US. The lower end of the market counts the higher number of companies, but more than half of them have no bank or broker analyst coverage at all – see Figures 7.7 and 7.8. This is likely to result in inefficiencies, which means numerous investment opportunities for hedge funds. Of course, these investment opportunities are limited in size, and this opens the question of hedge fund capacity. But that is another debate.

---

[2] In fact, the academic literature distinguishes three forms of market efficiency. Under weak-form efficiency, the current price reflects the information contained in all past prices, suggesting that charts and technical analyses that use past prices alone would not be useful in finding undervalued stocks. Under semi-strong-form efficiency, the current price reflects the information contained not only in past prices but all public information (including financial statements and news reports) and no approach that was predicated on using and massaging this information would be useful in finding undervalued stocks. Under strong-form efficiency, the current price reflects all information, public as well as private, and no investor will be able to consistently find undervalued stocks.

[3] See, for instance, Lo and MacKinlay (1988).

Average number
  of analysts

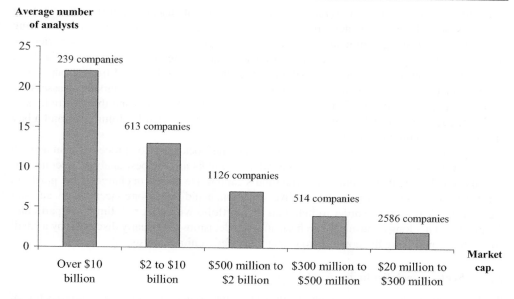

Figure 7.7   Average number of analysts per stock, based on FactSet/Reuters

In a long/short equity fund following the valuation approach, the investment process is usually built around a universe of investable stocks, a portfolio manager and a series of analysts. The universe of investable stocks may be organized by sectors or countries or be global, depending on the size of the fund and number of analysts. It usually excludes illiquid stocks, companies in financial trouble, etc. Each analyst is typically in charge of a small number

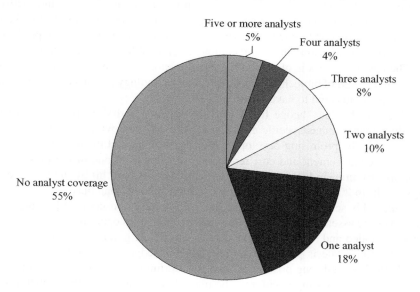

Figure 7.8   Analyst coverage of micro-cap companies (2586 companies with a market cap. of $20 to $300 million), based on FactSet/Reuters

of companies or a sector that he knows thoroughly. Analysts usually split their time among doing research, building financial models and writing reports. Research consists of visiting companies and meeting their management, reading the quarterly and annual reports, reviewing reports produced by investment banks and prime brokers, talking to other analysts and brokers, using contacts outside companies (customers, suppliers, competitors and trade groups), etc. The information gathered in the research process is then fed into financial models to assess the intrinsic value of a company, but also to understand its growth drivers and the sensitivities of its future cash flows. Finally, the analyst's conclusions are recorded for future use, and a buy or sell short recommendation may be issued.

The portfolio manager is usually also involved in the stock selection process, but at a much higher level. His role is primarily to select what he thinks are the best analysts' recommendations and allocate them a portion of the fund's capital. He is also in charge of the portfolio construction, i.e. maintaining sufficient diversification, avoiding sector concentration, and sizing each stock position in order to maintain the portfolio within its risk limits (in particular the gross and net long exposure). Purchase and sale decisions are usually discussed by a small committee comprising the portfolio manager and a few senior analysts.

7.2.2   Sector specialist hedge funds

While several long/short equity funds are global in nature, others specialize in specific sectors of the economy. Their managers usually justify their sector-oriented approach by their particular expertise in the field. Examples of such sector specializations include the following:

- *Life sciences* (e.g. pharmaceutical, biotechnology, medical equipment and healthcare companies). The last 20 years have witnessed an explosion in the understanding of the mechanisms underlying biological processes. Given the favourable demographics, new discoveries in biomedical science will have enormous commercial value. The demand for new and effective treatments is insatiable and shows little price sensitivity. Hedge funds active in life sciences tend to focus on younger and smaller companies for their ability to take the discoveries of fundamental biomedical research and translate them into viable products. They spread the risks by investing in several companies and holding a somewhat diversified portfolio. The key to success is of course the identification of winners and losers, a hard task since about one-half of biotechnology and medical technology products fail in clinical trials. Most of these funds tend to have a long bias.

- *Technology*. Technology hedge funds tend to mix long and short positions in segments where their manager has specific expertise. Spurred by the widening scope of scientific breakthroughs, the promising development of the internet and the benefits accruing from productivity enhancement and cost reductions, this has been one of the most spectacular growth opportunities in history. However, the sector was hard hit by the collapse of technology stocks in 2000, 2001, and 2002, due to its extremely long bias.

- *Real estate*. This sector has evolved gradually from very conservative holdings of stand-alone real estate assets to dynamic investments in companies operating in real estate as well as publicly traded and securitized real estate securities (e.g. real estate investment trusts). Securitized real estate is particularly important for hedge funds, because it allows them to take both short and long positions, i.e. invest during up and down cycles of the market as well as hedging existing positions. The market is still small but the growth potential is large, particularly when one considers the enormous pool of real estate assets suitable for securitization.

- *Energy*. Energy funds fall into two major categories. There are those that invest on both the long and short sides of the energy equity markets, and those that are structured more like commodity pool operators and invest essentially in commodity-related futures. The major investment themes are linked to technological innovation, exploration and development, as well as mergers and acquisitions. Their portfolios tend to be correlated with commodity prices, but remain uncorrelated with stocks.

Several other investment themes are also actively followed, such as entertainment and communications, media, financial institutions, etc. Managers may also use a wide range of primary focus (e.g. large-cap, mid-cap, small-cap, micro-cap, value growth, opportunistic) and investment (e.g. bottom-up, top-down, discretionary, technical) approaches.

In all cases, when analysing the performance of such funds, it is essential to understand the real nature of the short positions. Are they here simply to justify charging hedge fund fees, or are they truly an important contributor to the portfolio performance and/or to the risk reduction? Sector specialist hedge funds may have a dramatically superior performance compared to their long-only peers, but where is it coming from? And how important is the correlation with overall sector returns, since a dramatic drawdown could result if the sector becomes out of fashion.

7.2.3   Quantitative approaches

Most valuation-based portfolio managers, whether global or sectoral, tend to focus primarily on stock selection rather than portfolio construction. They spend a considerable amount of time examining companies' financial statements and investigating their management, products and facilities, but they tend to have a relatively basic approach to portfolio construction. They might use a portfolio management system to slice and dice their portfolio by sector, by country or by market capitalization, but very few of them use quantitative tools such as optimizers or multi-factor models to create "better" portfolios. One of the reasons is that most of them have a fundamental stock analyst background, so they are biased towards bottom-up portfolio construction rather than quantitative risk analysis or top-down portfolio approaches.

Bottom-up portfolio construction, although perfectly valid, has some limits in terms of the number of companies that can be researched; it reduces the breadth of long/short equity portfolios. Quantitative analysis, by contrast, is equipped to deal with a very large number of stocks, and may also add value on the portfolio construction side. It is therefore not surprising to see that some long/short equity funds are run by managers who have adopted a much more rigorous and quantitative approach. Most of them rely on dedicated software and risk models to select their long and short positions, optimize their portfolios, evaluate potential trades, attribute performance to portfolio decisions, and manage portfolio risk.

Since a large number of these quantitative managers are running equity market neutral funds, their strategies will be discussed in detail in Chapter 9.

7.2.4   Equity non-hedge hedge funds

Equity non-hedge hedge funds have, in our view, nothing to do with hedge funds. Run by stock pickers, they are mainly concentrated long-only equity funds that can use leverage to enhance returns. When market conditions really warrant, their managers may implement a hedge in the portfolio, but they do not have to.

Why should we consider them here? On one hand, the answer is purely legal. Since leverage and concentration are not allowed in mutual funds, these investment pools have to structure themselves as hedge funds – even though they do not hedge anything. But, on the other hand, equity non-hedge hedge funds represent an interesting evolution from the traditional long/short equity model. In fact, too many long/short equity managers have no real skills in shorting stocks, but still do it to hedge their risk. The result is that their hedge is extremely costly in terms of performance – most of the time, they should simply hedge by selling index futures. By contrast, equity non-hedge funds focus on what they really know about, that is, running a concentrated portfolio of deeply undervalued stocks. Their approach to managing risk is to buy on the cheap. If they take a short position – I hope you're all sitting down for this – it is because they believe the stock will decline, not just to hedge something else. To sum up, equity non-hedge funds may be an interesting alternative for investors who can deal with their high volatility and trust the skills of their managers.

7.2.5 Activist strategies

Shareholder activism is not a new strategy. Its origins can be traced back 80 years, to the time when Henry Ford decided to cancel a special dividend and spend the money on advancing social objectives. Dissident shareholders contested the decision, and the court ultimately reinstated the dividend, sparking a new paradigm in shareholder activism. Shareholder activism resurfaced in the 1980s, when aggressive corporate raiders launched hostile takeovers of poorly managed companies. And in the 1990s, it found support in institutional investors, with mainstream pension fund managers like CalPERS pushing for the eschewal of staggered boards and poison pills. Today, shareholder activism seems to have convinced several hedge fund managers that they should go one step beyond investment screening and selection, and use their expertise and their fund's influence as a minority shareholder to effect changes in the companies they invest in.

The theory underlying shareholder activism is that finding an undervalued situation is not always sufficient to unlock its associated hidden value. The reason is that companies are managed by directors (who are elected by shareholders) and officers (who are appointed by the directors), some of whom might not care or might not have all the skills and/or vision necessary to maximize shareholder value.[4] As summarized by the corporate raider Carl Icahn, "Many corporate chiefs are not qualified to run their companies. It has been that way for years. But they are not concerned about being ousted for weak performance because there is no accountability." He added, "Often, board members are cronies appointed by the very CEOs they are supposed to be watching. And they use the corporate treasury to keep themselves in power in the rare instances they are challenged in a proxy fight. The result is bloated bureaucracies. US companies could easily cut costs by more than 30% and still operate profitably." In such cases, according to activists, there is no hope in waiting; there is only need for action.

In the US, the modus operandi of an activist hedge fund often starts with a purchase of shares it considers undervalued because of perceived management failures, and the filing of a public Schedule 13D[5] with the SEC. The form, which must contain the buyers' stake and its

---

[4] Not to be overlooked are the interests of these agents, which may not always coincide with the best interests of the owners or the businesses they oversee.

[5] The Schedule 13D form must be filed with the SEC within 10 days of purchase when a person or group of persons acquires beneficial ownership of more than 5% of a class of a company's equity securities registered under Section 12 of the Securities Exchange Act of 1934.

strategic intentions, sends a clear signal to the company and the rest of the market that there is something going on. Usually, just after the filing, the activist fund may also send salty letters to the management and the board to outline a series of initiatives that it expects the company to adopt rapidly. These letters are often made public via press releases to put further pressure on the company and influence other shareholders. Most of the time, the requested initiatives revolve around some of the following themes:

- Sell off assets that are undervalued on the balance sheet.
- Get rid of underperforming management.
- Give cash back to shareholders, either in the shape of dividends or through a stock repurchase programme.
- Push the company to put itself up for sale.
- Assess strategic alternatives such as restructuring plans and cost-cutting initiatives.

In the most extreme cases, if the activist cannot convince the board to effect the changes it has set forth, the matter will be handled in a proxy contest (Box 7.2). Because of their size, hedge funds have a clear advantage over smaller shareholders in proxy battles. They can afford all the associated costs, e.g. printing and mailing proxy statements, which form the basis for voting at annual meetings or engage in a sustained campaign to persuade other shareholders that their suggested changes should be supported.

Box 7.2 Communication, communication!

The SEC recently proposed amendments to federal securities laws to permit parties to deliver proxy material by posting the information on a publicly accessible website and notify stockholders of its availability. If implemented as proposed, the amendments should result in substantial cost savings by reducing the printing and mailing costs associated with delivering hard-copy proxy materials, and provide shareholders with a less costly means of waging a proxy contest. This should lead to more proxy fights.

However, some activist hedge funds have already become experts in using modern means of communication. As an illustration, when William Ackman from the fund Pershing Square Capital Management was trying to force McDonald's to restructure, he broadcast a standing-room-only PowerPoint presentation of his proposals at the Millennium Broadway Hotel in Times Square via internet video and offered a free call-in number. Some 800 shareholders, analysts and reporters attended or tuned in. A week later, McDonald's unveiled a plan to sell 1500 company-owned restaurants, buy back $1 billion of stock in the first quarter, and provide more financial disclosure.

Another expert in written communication is Daniel Loeb, who runs the Third Point fund. His letters to CEOs – as well as to other hedge fund managers – are known for their direct style. Here, for example, is an excerpt from a letter he wrote to Star Gas, an oil and gas utility: "Sadly, your ineptitude is not limited to your failure to communicate with bond and unit holders. A review of your record reveals years of value destruction and strategic blunders which have led us to dub you one of the most dangerous and incompetent executives in America." Three weeks after Star Gas received this letter, its CEO Irik Sevin resigned his post. Two months after that, the CFO resigned as well. In its next quarterly report, in May 2005, the company beat all expectations on revenue and earnings and the stock soared.

Hedge funds do not mind being the public face of discontented investors. They are more outspoken and more willing to take the heat than traditional large shareholders such as mutual funds and institutional investors, who often agree with the requested changes. More recently, activist hedge funds have started focusing on cash-rich companies (Box 7.3). They purchase a significant block of shares and request them to distribute their cash to shareholders. This common goal is nearly always resisted by the companies, who complain that hedge funds are vultures looking for short-term profits and ignoring their long-term strategy. But hedge funds are gaining influence, and many boards end up being forced to listen and carry out their recommendations (Box 7.4).

Box 7.3 Carl Icahn versus Time Warner

The legendary corporate raider Carl Icahn is a regular protagonist in hostile takeovers and proxy fights. He built his reputation after leading the fight to break up RJR Nabisco in the mid-1990s and pocketing some $1.3 billion. From 1996 through May 2004, his stakes in 56 companies produced profits of $2.77 billion for an annual return of 53%, according to *Institutional Investor*.

More recently, Carl Icahn – like many other activist hedge funds – seems to have focused on cash-rich companies. For instance, during the summer 2005, the Icahn Group – composed of Icahn Partners, Icahn Partners Master Fund, certain other affiliates of Carl C. Icahn, Franklin Mutual Advisers, as well as the hedge funds JANA Partners and S.A.C. Capital Advisors – accumulated shares in Time Warner (Figure 7.9), the world's largest media conglomerate. The company was just emerging from its disastrous 2001 merger with America Online (AOL), which precipitated a decline of more than 75% of the company's share value.

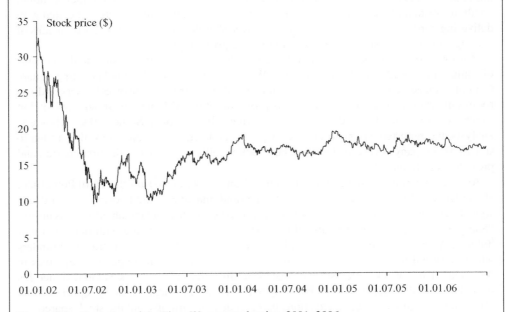

Figure 7.9 Evolution of the Time Warner stock price, 2001–2006

Icahn tried to persuade Chief Executive Richard Parsons to do something to raise the stock price, for instance by spinning off the company's cable TV unit. Richard Parsons listened politely and attentively but no real action was taken. In October, the Icahn Group sent a letter to all Time Warner shareholders suggesting a $20 billion share buyback, a 100% spin-off of Time Warner Cable and the replacement of some or all of Time Warner's board members – 12 of its 15 directors (including the CEO) had been on the board in 2000 and had voted in favour of the AOL merger. It also hired the investment bank Lazard to analyse various strategic alternatives to maximize the value of the company.

In early 2006, Icahn made public the 342-page report that he had commissioned from Lazard. He accused Richard Parsons of underestimating the group's financial capacity, missing market opportunities, failing to cut costs and under-investing in businesses, particularly the AOL internet unit. Icahn called on Time Warner to break its empire up into four separate publicly listed companies – a film and TV company, a publisher, a cable operator and AOL. According to him, this would make each unit more nimble and better equipped to compete in their markets, and could boost Time Warner's stock price by between $5 and $8 a share. Icahn reiterated his request of a $20 stock buyback, and recruited Frank Biondi Jr, the former chief executive of Viacom and Universal Studios, to become the future Time Warner chairman and chief executive if the Icahn Group prevailed in a planned proxy fight for control of the media giant.

Icahn's push met with relatively little reaction on Wall Street, but was highly effective *vis-à-vis* Time Warner. On 18 February 2006, Icahn and Time Warner Inc. reached an agreement. Icahn agreed not to contest the company's slate of directors at its next shareholders meeting, and Time Warner pledged to intensify its cost-cutting and agreed to boost its share repurchase programme from $12.5 billion to $20 billion. After this, Richard Parsons wrote: "We are very pleased to have reached an understanding with Mr Icahn. We appreciate his role as a significant shareholder as well as his constructive recommendations." Icahn replied in a written statement that Time Warner's actions would help to achieve his "long-stated goal of creating value for all shareholders" and that his action had "proved again that shareholder activism can be extremely effective".

Box 7.4 The assault of the London Stock Exchange

Europeans usually love the benefits of capitalism, but they are not yet ready to accept its consequences – particularly when these involve hedge funds.

In December 2004, Deutsche Börse launched a groundbreaking €2 billion bid to take over the London Stock Exchange (LSE). The LSE snubbed the German group's advances, dismissing the €2 billion price tag as too low, but kept negotiating with the Deutsche Börse as well as with Euronext, the pan-European exchange, for a possible deal in the near future. However, several Deutsche Börse shareholders, including two hedge funds – Atticus Capital and The Children's Investment Fund Management (TCI) – expressed severe reservations about the proposed acquisition. Their opinion was that (i) the price was too high, (ii) the deal lacked strategic logic and (iii) Deutsche Boerse would be better off buying back its own shares rather than acquiring the LSE. David Slager, the manager of Atticus Capital, wrote: "The acquisition appears to us to be motivated by empire-building. If they [Deutsche

Börse] were purely motivated by shareholder interests, they would put the acquisition to a vote."

Since German law allows a company to go ahead with a takeover offer without consulting its shareholders, Werner Seifert, the chief executive officer of Deutsche Börse, chose to ignore them – he even refused to take questions from dissident investors at a conference – and appointed a special committee to take the matter forward. The two hedge funds then called for a meeting of the Deutsche Börse's shareholders to vote on the acquisition. Many mainstream long-only asset managers such as Fidelity and Merrill Lynch Asset Management were also fully behind the hedge funds and pressed Deutsche Börse management to change course ... to no avail.

The crux of the matter was primarily a clash of corporate cultures. In Germany, the supervisory board determines a company's strategy, while in the US and the UK, it is the shareholders who wield the greatest influence. But although Deutsche Börse was a German company, its share ownership changed from being 68% German in 2001 (when the company went public) to 65% foreign in 2005 (the majority of whom were British and American institutional investors). It therefore seems that the supervisory board of Deutsche Börse was rather slow in recognizing the radical change in the company's shareholder profile. This is even more surprising in the case of an exchange – which by definition should be extremely sensitive to the needs of international investors.

Given the lack of reaction, the two hedge funds, which together held around 15% of the Deutsche Börse capital, started a campaign for the removal of Deutsche Börse's supervisory board and top executives. Deutsche Börse responded by saying that shareholders had to wait until the annual general meeting before they could vote on such a proposal. This was another blunder, as media reports suggested at the time that as many as 35% of investors in Deutsche Börse were opposed to a takeover of the LSE.

The activist battle was long and bitter. Chris Hohn, the manager of TCI, threatened to seek a special audit analysing "the economic damage to Deutsche Börse and the potential personal liability of all supervisory board members". Atticus' David Slager commented: "We are long-term investors and are experienced in removing management. We are not scared to take this to its conclusion this time." Both hedge fund managers were also frustrated by Breuer's (the Deutsche Börse chairman) refusal to make the planned merger subject to shareholder approval and failure to communicate shareholder dissension over the LSE bid to the supervisory board in a timely and appropriate manner. They therefore raised concerns regarding Breuer's lack of independence and conflict of interest, due to his affiliation with Deutsche Bank as its chairman and Deutsche Bank's role as the financier of a merger with the LSE.

In an attempt to defuse the incendiary atmosphere, Deutsche Börse sought to placate the rebel shareholders, offering to transfer to shareholders "a significant proportion" of the cash reserves it had set aside to finance the takeover. And it also actively sought to give shareholders a greater say in the running of the company. But TCI refused to be appeased and continued to call for the heads of both Breuer and Seifert. As Chris Hohn justly remarked: "Mr Breuer and Mr Seifert have been running the company as if it were theirs. That is rather absurd; we are owners, Mr Seifert is an employee."

As a result, in late March 2005 Deutsche Börse's groundbreaking €2 billion bid for the London Stock Exchange ran aground. Instead the German exchange announced that it would return close to €1.5 billion of cash to shareholders and change the composition of the supervisory and executive boards in order to reflect the new ownership structure of the company. In May 2005, markets witnessed a further surprise, with the announcement of the resignation of the powerful Deutsche Börse CEO Werner Seifert and the even more powerful Deutsche Börse chairman, Rolf Breuer. Their departure was a clear consequence of loss of shareholder confidence, in spite of a broad conceptual consensus on broader strategy.

Werner Seifert later compared the two hedge funds to a plague of locusts in a book entitled *Die Invasion der Heuschrecken* ("The Invasion of the Locusts"). The term "locust" was used again by Frantz Muntefering, the chairman of Germany's ruling Social Democrat Party. Gerhard Schroeder, the German Chancellor, weighed in a few days later and ordered a review of hedge funds "to check whether their philosophy is compatible with our society." Immediately, the German Finance minister, Hans Eichel, raised his voice about the need to outlaw all short-term trading strategies. This was not really a surprise, as he had made similar comments about the undesirability of short selling in the wake of the 11 September events. Maybe he preferred the old German model, whereby shareholder registers were all alike and a cosy coterie of banks controlled the fund-raising pipeline. Unfortunately, German companies have now tapped international capital markets. They may not have meant to attract hedge funds, but now they've got them.

Note that in January 2006, Atticus – whose manager says it now owns a 9.1% stake in Euronext – again cast doubt on a possible merger between the European exchange operator and LSE, saying it would rather "support a friendly merger of equals between Euronext and Deutsche Börse."

Once they have their teeth into a company, the activist hedge funds won't usually let go. Such tenacity, allied with their reputation, makes them formidable infighters and can produce faster results than traditional methods of pressuring managements through shareholder resolutions on the agenda at company annual meetings. In addition, they are so well bankrolled that they do not have to borrow money from others as the 1980s raiders did, and they can afford long-drawn-out fights with management. Companies therefore have to take them seriously, as the balance of power is shifting away from boards. They can not ignore them on the grounds that it is some hedge fund they had never heard of.

Also, many activists suggest eminently sensible ideas. Provided that management can save face, there is scope for the warring parties to arrive at a mutually beneficial outcome.

7.3 HISTORICAL PERFORMANCE

For investors, the historical performance of long/short equity hedge funds has been relatively good. Long/short managers in the aggregate have produced high absolute returns, and they have also outperformed traditional asset classes with far less volatility. Over the January 1994 to December 2005 period, dedicated short hedge funds – as measured by the CS/Tremont Long/Short Equity Index – delivered an average return of 11.9% p.a. with a volatility of 10.72%. By contrast, over the same period, the S&P 500 delivered an average return of 8.6% p.a. with a volatility of 16.0%, and the Citigroup World Government Bond Index (WGBI) delivered an average return of 5.9% p.a. with a volatility of 6.7%.

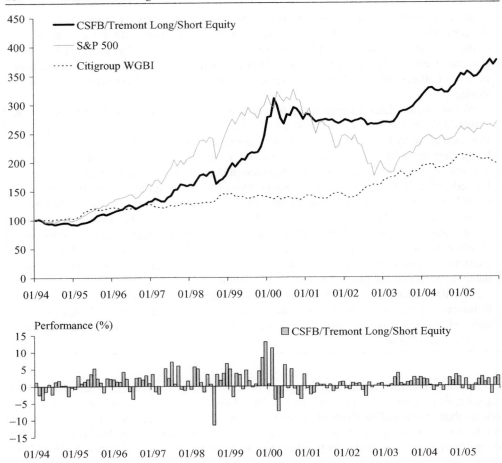

Figure 7.10 Evolution of the CS/Tremont Long/Short Equity Index, 1994–2005

As shown in Figure 7.10 and Table 7.1, equity long/short funds had their best years from 1995 to 1999, when they strongly benefited from the rising equity markets and the higher level of interest rates (which is an important component of the short positions reward). However, they consistently lagged equity markets, except in 1999. When the equity bubble burst in 2000, long/short equity hedge funds were also affected by the bear environment, but much less than equity indices. Their performance was virtually flat during the three years of bear markets. They came back into action in 2003 and have since delivered good absolute returns, although lower than historically.

The monthly returns on the CS/Tremont Long/Short Equity Index (Table 7.2) are not normally distributed, primarily because of an excessive kurtosis (Figure 7.11). This is due to the negative performance in October 1998 (−11.43%), but also to very good months prior to the equity crash (December 1999: +13.01%, and February 2000: +11.14%).

Table 7.1 Performance comparison of the CS/Tremont Long/Short Equity Index, the S&P 500 and the Citigroup World Government Bond Index, 1994–2005

	CS/Tremont Long/Short Equity	S&P 500	Citigroup WGBI
Return (% p.a.)	11.90	8.55	5.87
Volatility (% p.a.)	10.72	16.00	6.74
Skewness	0.23	−0.58	0.37
Kurtosis	3.90	0.61	0.37
Normally distributed?	No	No	Yes
Correlation with strategy		0.59	0.05
Positive months frequency	67%	62%	58%
Best month perf. (%)	13.01	9.67	5.94
Average positive month perf. (%)	2.41	3.44	1.73
Upside participation		74%	254%
Negative months frequency	33%	38%	42%
Worst month perf. (%)	−11.43	−14.58	−4.28
Average negative month perf. (%)	−1.95	−3.53	−1.18
Downside participation		−391%	−373%
Max. Drawdown (%)	−15.05	−46.28	−7.94
Value at Risk (1-month, 99%)	−5.96	−10.24	−3.36

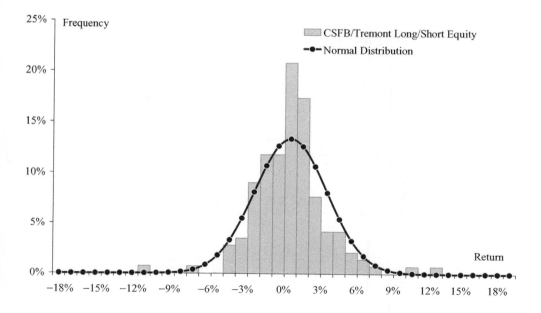

Figure 7.11 Return distribution of the CS/Tremont Long/Short Equity Index, 1994–2005

Table 7.2 Monthly returns of the CS/Tremont Long/Short Equity Index, 1994–2005

	1994	1995	1996	1997	1998	1999	2000	2001	2002	2003	2004	2005
Jan.	1.20	-0.74	1.97	3.49	-0.93	4.97	0.52	-0.58	-0.60	-0.07	2.00	-0.84
Feb.	-2.47	3.04	1.35	-1.58	5.64	-3.14	11.14	-2.42	-0.99	-0.21	1.75	2.03
Mar.	-3.90	0.81	1.21	-2.27	5.03	3.76	-3.98	-1.94	0.91	0.43	0.20	-1.14
Apr.	-1.56	1.36	4.14	0.01	1.14	3.29	-7.46	0.77	0.61	2.44	-1.40	-1.55
May.	0.57	2.03	2.13	5.14	-1.69	-0.82	-3.45	0.40	0.80	3.68	-0.36	0.51
Jun.	-2.31	3.51	-1.53	2.28	3.40	4.65	6.13	0.42	-1.26	0.79	0.66	1.91
Jul.	1.29	5.15	-3.80	7.03	0.61	1.54	-0.63	-0.72	-2.95	0.27	-1.42	2.68
Aug.	1.64	2.26	2.38	0.62	-11.43	-0.27	4.90	0.45	1.01	1.04	0.09	1.12
Sep.	0.25	1.11	2.50	5.91	3.47	0.60	-0.71	-1.57	-0.47	1.21	2.36	2.02
Oct.	0.27	-1.82	1.93	-0.84	1.74	4.39	-2.54	-0.80	0.08	2.46	1.44	-2.29
Nov.	-2.85	2.29	3.07	-1.22	3.74	8.31	-3.80	1.10	0.57	1.70	3.24	2.22
Dec.	-0.35	2.09	0.82	1.55	6.56	13.01	3.42	1.24	0.76	2.40	2.57	2.78
Total	-8.10	23.03	17.14	21.46	17.19	47.22	2.08	-3.67	-1.60	17.30	11.57	9.68
S&P 500	-1.54	34.11	20.26	31.01	26.67	19.53	-10.14	-13.04	-23.37	26.38	8.99	3.00
WGBI	2.34	19.04	3.62	0.23	15.30	-4.27	1.59	-0.99	19.49	14.91	10.35	-6.88

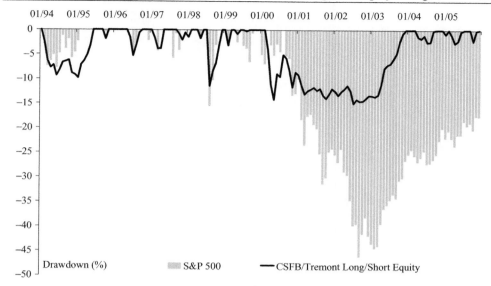

Figure 7.12   Drawdown diagram of the CS/Tremont Long/Short Equity Index compared to the S&P 500, 1994–2005

The analysis of the drawdowns of the CS/Tremont Long/Short Equity Index clearly evidence its superiority compared to the S&P 500 (Figure 7.12). While the drawdowns on the two indices seem to occur over the same periods, the long short equity index resists much better to the downward pressure than its long only cousin. The pattern followed by the 12-month rolling performance of the long short equity index (Figure 7.13) is also much more attractive, except of course when there are exaggerated performance rallies.

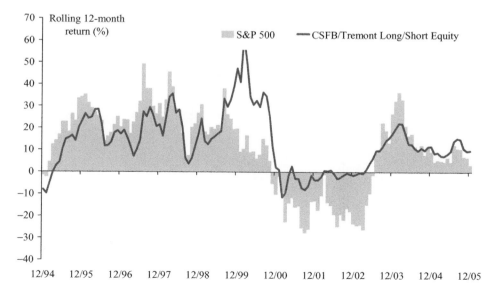

Figure 7.13   Comparison of the 12-month rolling performances of the CS/Tremont Long/Short Equity Index with the S&P 500, 1994–2005

8

Dedicated Short

He that sells what isn't his'n, must buy it back or go to prison.
Attributed to Daniel Drew, a 19th-century speculator

In a sense, dedicated short hedge funds are traditional long-only funds flipped upside down. Their managers follow a radically different approach to investing – they look exclusively for overvalued companies, borrow their shares and sell them short. They then wait for the stock price to decline, so they can buy the shares back at a cheaper price, return them to the lender and pocket the difference. If, contrary to their expectations, the share price increases, the repurchase price will be higher than the initial selling price and they will make a loss.

Dedicated short sellers were once a robust category of hedge funds, but the bull market of the 1990s forced many of them out of business. Despite some revival in 2001 and 2002, hedge funds that exclusively focus on selling short are now rare. Many of them have migrated to the long/short equity space, where they operate with a net short bias. Most of the remaining ones are run by rugged individualists – unconventional men with a reputation for defying convention. They may be regarded as pessimists in an optimistic sort of way, anticipating profit from an imminent market decline that rarely transpires.

8.1 THE PROS AND CONS OF DEDICATED SHORT SELLING

There are several arguments suggesting that dedicated short selling can indeed be a very profitable activity. First of all, in sharp contrast to the crowded world of undervalued companies, the set of short selling opportunities is largely unexploited. In fact, the entire traditional asset management industry seems to be primarily searching for long-term buy and hold opportunities rather than for good short sales. Individual investors are not familiar with the process of short selling, which they perceive as far too risky, and most institutional investors cannot or do not want to sell short. Consequently, brokers and analysts focus on what to buy, not what to sell, and there is virtually no competition to identify overvalued securities. The best proof of this lies in the well known fact that there is almost never an official sell recommendation on Wall Street, no matter how bad a particular company's financial results are or how dismal its business prospects. At best, analysts will write a mildly positive to ambivalent research report. If the outlook for the company is particularly disastrous, there may be a "neutral" or "reduce" recommendation that will leave the average investor in a state of inertia, which means the stock still remains unsold.

One may wonder why such a situation has prevailed for so long. The fact of the matter is that research analysts working in investment banks have a conflict of interests that prevents them from issuing a negative recommendation on a company. If they did so, it would be much harder for them to maintain a good relationship with the company and, going forward, to obtain information from the company's investor relations department. Moreover, a company receiving a strongly negative recommendation from an analyst is likely to be vindictive and avoid using the services of the analyst's bank.[1] And who, by the way, needs the advice and services of an investment bank more than a struggling, downtrodden company?

The consequence of the above is that good news is more widely known and factored into stock prices than bad news. Markets therefore tend to be inefficient with a set of under researched and overpriced securities, thus serving up an ideal free lunch for short sellers. Nevertheless, the life of a dedicated short seller is not always as easy and profitable as it may sound; there are a lot of caveats to be considered.

First, in the long run, stocks tend to appreciate in price and reward investors with a positive *equity risk premium*. The long-only investor buying stocks that he perceives as undervalued can content himself with waiting as long as necessary, provided he has a sufficiently long investment horizon. In the meantime, he will benefit from the equity risk premium and regularly receive dividend payments. But on the short side, the story is quite different. While they wait, short sellers are hit by the natural long-term uptrend of equity markets, and they must pay the dividends on the shorted stocks to their lenders. Moreover, at the request of the stock lenders, they may be forced to buy back the shorted shares at whatever the relevant market price happens to be.

Second, short sellers dealing with small and illiquid companies face the risk of snowball buying, ending up in a *short squeeze*. Simply stated, as prices go up, more and more short sellers will have to buy back shares to close their position. Consequently, the stock price will continue to rise, triggering more covering of losses by short sellers, more buying, and so on. In such a situation, the shorted stock, which was presumably overpriced to begin with, becomes even more overpriced. This clearly shows that short sellers should not just bet on what a stock is really worth, but should also consider what the market will be willing to pay for that stock in the future, which is hard to forecast. Moreover, when establishing short positions, short sellers should always set strict quitting prices (say a 10% loss per investment) and stick to them. If prices reach that limit, short sellers must resist the temptation to hang on, even though the stock is even more overpriced now, and take their losses.

Lastly, it is important to mention that, when implemented on a stand-alone basis, dedicated short selling can be extremely risky, as the downside potential is theoretically unlimited. Indeed, as long as the shorted stock price keeps rising, the short seller keeps losing. And even the worst companies can see their stock rise for a long time before the market becomes rational. Having a diversified portfolio of short sales is obviously an attractive way of reducing the overall risk exposure.

8.2 TYPICAL TARGET COMPANIES AND REACTIONS

Although each short seller tends to have his own way of operating, dedicated short portfolios are typically built up stock by stock, by analysing specific companies and their characteristics. There are several ways of homing in on potential targets. Some of the telltale signs to look for are:

- Companies with weak financials, but a high share price. This includes companies with no profits or – worse yet – little or no earnings, or companies with an excessive amount of leverage on their balance sheet.

---

[1] See, for instance, Michaeli and Womack (1999).

- Companies which regularly change their auditors or regularly delay filing their financial reports with the SEC.
- Companies built around a single product that belongs to a "sexy" category with hard-to-quantify, hard-to-understand performance specifications.
- Companies involved in industries where there is overcapacity, have earnings shortfalls or weak pricing power.
- Companies whose P/E ratios are much higher than can be justified by their growth rates.
- Companies that have been involved in a failed merger. Most of the time, the target company will see its price drop after the merger failure.
- Companies with a potential public image problem.
- Companies that claim to have discovered new reserves of natural resources, such as oil or gold, or have invented new methods of extracting them.
- Companies that issue self-congratulatory press releases all the time.
- Companies where more than 10% of the total market capitalization has been sold short by some market participants.
- Companies with too-clever tickers. Although this may seem a curious indicator, it is true that many companies with "smart" tickers tend to experience problems during their lifetime. One of the best examples is probably Systems of Excellence Inc., which first gained notoriety for its ticker (SEXI), but later turned out to be one of the biggest security frauds of recent years.
- Companies that frequently use Regulation S of the US Securities Laws to issue new shares overseas. Such shares, usually offered at a discount, can be sold back in the US 45 days later, thus resulting in a dilution of existing shareholders.

None of these warning lights is, by itself, conclusive, but they constitute an alert – particularly when more than one of them is flashing. In addition, there is one more signal that is almost unanimously regarded as a good indicator for short selling:

- Companies suing or responding systematically to their short sellers in an attempt to silence them.

Indeed, no legitimate company with a real business should normally be wasting corporate resources, including valuable management time, suing short sellers or even talking to them. If they do so, it is usually a good indicator that something is wrong and that the short sellers have latched on to it.

Short sellers have always been unpopular on Wall Street. Like skeletons at the feast, they seem to oppose rising values, increasing wealth and general prosperity. They predictably tend to have bad relations with their target firms, which do not like the idea of someone shorting their stocks. This is a recurring source of acrimonious conflicts. On the one hand, firms may try to make short selling difficult by implementing specific technical actions, such as special dividend payments or splits requiring the physical presentation of shares and thus creating loan recalls. They can also attempt to hurt short sellers by accusing them of crimes, suing them, hiring private investigators to probe them and/or requesting that regulators investigate their activities. On the other hand, short sellers are often tempted to influence markets by publicly disclosing what they dislike in a company. Although this is desirable, because it strengthens market efficiency, it also has its limits. In some cases, the most unethical traders will attempt to short and distort the market, i.e. take short positions and then use a smear campaign to drive down the target stocks. Such abuses have grown with the advent of the internet and online trading (see Boxes 8.1 and 8.2), but they already existed in the 19th and early 20th centuries – the term "bear raid" was used to point at gangs of speculators teaming up to sell a stock short and cause its price to drop.[2]

Box 8.1 Short sellers and fraud: the case of Solv-Ex

Solv-Ex was founded in July 1980 by engineer John Rendall on the idea of developing a new technology to extract a tarlike substance called bitumen from tar sands. After extraction, the bitumen was to be further refined into crude oil. The company started building a pilot plant and a laboratory to test its new technology, and raised several million dollars through initial public and a series of private offerings.

In early 1995, Solv-Ex claimed that: (i) its plant had developed a solvent-assisted hot water process that produced saleable bitumen from tar sands on a commercial scale; (ii) this bitumen extraction process also yielded industrial minerals of marketable quality and volume; and (iii) Solv-Ex had also successfully tested a revolutionary electrolytic cell capable of producing metallic aluminium. The company had acquired several tar sand leases and claimed to have a resource base of about 4 billion barrels of oil and 1 billion tons of aluminium, thanks to its proprietary technology. Its aggressive message in the financial press was: "You've probably never heard of us. You soon will because our technology will reduce American dependence on Middle East oil."

Not surprisingly, several analysts started recommending Solv-Ex as a strong buy, and the stock price started rising. A Morgan Grenfell recommendation[3] forecast that "Solv-Ex, between now and the year 2008, will be the fastest-growing oil company in the world." At this time, Solv-Ex had essentially over $28 million in cash and $40 million invested in its plant and was supposedly finalizing the latter's construction. Its earnings were forecast to be up to $3 per share, and the stock price reflected investors' confidence in this estimate.

Unfortunately, a group of dedicated short sellers started publicly challenging the company's announcements and heavily shorted the stock. One of them, Manuel Asensio, conducted an extensive examination, including talks to on-the-ground workers and aerial reconnaissance. He concluded that Solv-Ex was a fraud, "perhaps the greatest blizzard of way-over-the-top pumpery I have ever witnessed".

Solv-Ex vehemently denied these allegations and organized a short squeeze. On 5 February 1996, the management of Solv-Ex faxed a letter to its shareholders saying that "to help you control the value of your investment . . . we suggest that you request delivery of the Solv-Ex certificates from your broker as soon as possible". Heeding the suggestion, most shareholders withdrew their shares from the stock lending market, which forced short sellers to buy back Solv-Ex shares to cover their positions.[4] The stock price went from $24.875

---

[2] See, for instance, Bernheim and Schneider (1935), Sobel (1965), and Wycoff (1968).

[3] Charlie Maxwell, managing director of Morgan Grenfell, issued a strong buy recommendation on Solv-Ex on 26 January 1996 in a paper entitled: "Classic Growth Stock of Our Generation." But he forgot to mention that he had previously worked for Solv-Ex president Jack Butler at Mobil Oil, and that he personally owned 100 000 shares of Solv-Ex at the time.

[4] It is interesting to note that over the same period, Rendall himself had secured a loan of $1 million for Solv-Ex by margining his own Solv-Ex holdings.

just before the letter to $35.375 on 21 February 1996 (Figure 8.1). It then traded between the high $20s and mid-$30s until late March 1996, before falling to $7.375 per share following another series of negative reports once again issued by dedicated short sellers.

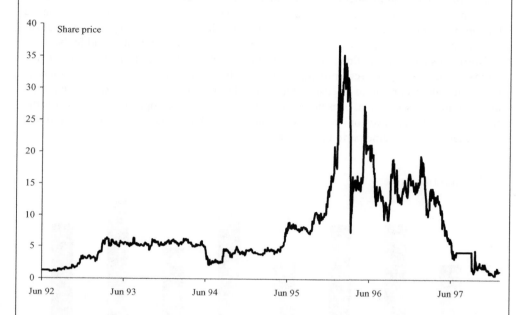

Figure 8.1   Movement of the Solv-Ex share price, 1992–1997

On 12 August 1996, Solv-Ex filed a lawsuit against a group of short sellers whom it charged with revealing certain confidential information and spreading misinformation about the firm. The management of the company even claimed that production of quantities of high-grade bitumen at very low cost had started, and the stock price started rising again. Unfortunately for investors, it turned out that the short sellers were right. Solv-Ex's bitumen extraction process had all along been at the research and development stage. The company's attempts to recover industrial minerals from that process, pursued only on an experimental basis, had failed to yield any commercially viable product. Moreover, Solv-Ex's single test of the electrolytic cell, in 1996, was a failure. Last but not least, the company had largely exceeded the number of shares it was legally allowed to issue.[5]

Solv-Ex was therefore de-listed in July 1997 at $4.25 and entered Chapter 11 bankruptcy. In 2000, a court ruled that the firm had indeed defrauded investors and recklessly violated the anti-fraud and reporting provisions of the securities laws by making material misstatements and omissions – as short sellers had always claimed.

---

[5] Solv-Ex had 30 million shares authorized and 24.3 million shares outstanding, plus a $10 million Reg S convertible outstanding and it was attempting the sale of an additional $11 million convertible Reg S offering.

Box 8.2 A controversial short seller: Manuel Asensio

The most famous and most controversial short seller on Wall Street is likely to be Manuel P. Asensio, the Founder, President, Chairman, Chief Executive Officer and Compliance Officer of Asensio and Company Inc. Depending on whom you are talking to, Asensio will be portrayed as a great investor and whistle-blower, or as an evil exploiter and bully.

During his eight years of dedicated short selling (1996–2003), according to his website, Asensio issued strong sell recommendations on 29 different companies. An investor managing a portfolio according to Asensio's recommendations would have realized a compound annual return of 46.6% p.a. over the entire eight-year period, compared with 8.4% for the S&P 500. And if an investor had sold short the S&P 500, he would have lost 60.8% of his investment over the same period (Figure 8.2).

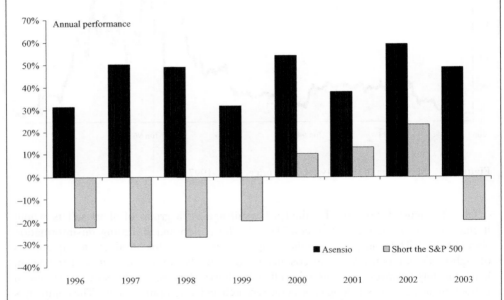

Figure 8.2   Asensio's track record versus selling short the S&P 500

However, Asensio's corrosive style created animosity – he often blasted his targets on his website and referred to companies he shorted as "frauds". For his "advocacy" of short positions, as he calls it, Asensio was sued for "$1 billion in seven states", he proudly says, and spent around $10 million defending himself without losing a monetary judgement. But in November 2000, he was found guilty of "misrepresentation", and the NASD fined him $75 000 for short selling, trade reporting and internet advertising violations.

Despite his impressive track record, Asensio closed his short selling fund on 31 October 2003. For those wishing to know more about him, we can recommend his website (www.asensio.com), which is now a repository for research and public education purposes. Note that Asensio's opponents also have a website (www.asensioexposed.com), which provides a completely different view of Asensio's actions.

8.3   HISTORICAL PERFORMANCE

The historical performance of dedicated short hedge funds has been relatively disappointing. Over the January 1994 to December 2005 period, dedicated short hedge funds – as measured by the CS/Tremont Dedicated Short Bias Index (Figure 8.3) – delivered an average return of −2.0% p.a., with a volatility of 18.6%. By contrast, over the same period, the S&P 500 delivered an average return of 8.6% p.a. (Table 8.1), with a volatility of 16.0%, and the CS/Tremont Hedge Fund Index delivered an average return of 10.7% p.a., with a volatility of 8.1%.

Unsurprisingly, dedicated short hedge funds have delivered their best performance during market crashes (e.g. August 1998: +22.71%) as well as during longer bear market periods (e.g. the years 1994, 2000 and 2002). Their excess kurtosis and positive skewness, which are particularly visible on the return histogram of Figure 8.4, are too important for the return distribution to be considered as normally distributed (Table 8.2).

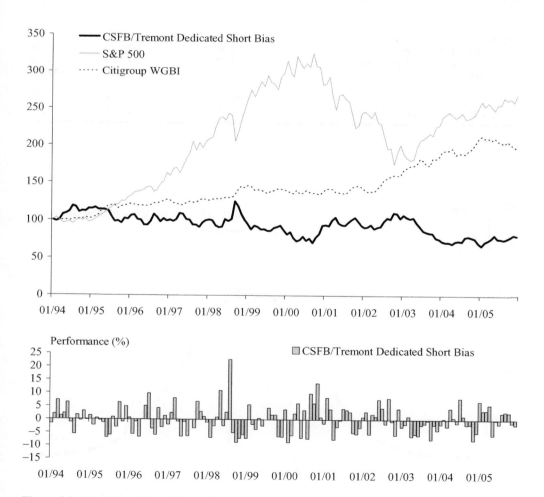

Figure 8.3   Evolution of the CS/Tremont Dedicated Short Index, 1994–2005

Table 8.1 Performance comparison of the CS/Tremont Dedicated Short Index, the S&P 500 and the Citigroup World Government Bond Index, 1994–2005

	CS/Tremont Dedicated Short Bias	S&P 500	Citigroup WGBI
Return (% p.a.)	−2.03	8.55	5.87
Volatility (% p.a.)	18.60	16.00	6.74
Skewness	0.84	−0.58	0.37
Kurtosis	2.08	0.61	0.37
Normally distributed?	No	No	Yes
Correlation with strategy		−0.76	0.00
Positive months frequency	46%	62%	58%
Best month performance (%)	22.71	9.67	5.94
Average positive month performance (%)	4.17	3.44	1.73
Upside participation		−48%	8%
Negative months frequency	54%	38%	42%
Worst month performance (%)	−8.69	−14.58	−4.28
Average negative month performance (%)	−3.62	−3.53	−1.18
Downside participation		−141%	−172%
Max. drawdown (%)	−46.55	−46.28	−7.94
Value at Risk (1-month, 99%)	−8.25	−10.24	−3.36

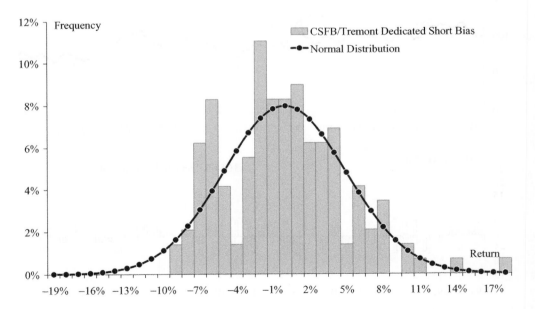

Figure 8.4 Return distribution of the CS/Tremont Dedicated Short Index, 1994–2005

Table 8.2   Monthly returns of the CS/Tremont Dedicated Short Index, 1994–2005

	1994	1995	1996	1997	1998	1999	2000	2001	2002	2003	2004	2005
Jan	−1.60	1.31	0.63	−1.86	−1.05	−7.18	3.74	−1.43	1.02	−2.73	−1.73	6.96
Feb	2.00	−2.24	−5.64	2.50	−6.89	5.59	−8.65	8.27	2.93	−1.73	0.34	3.40
Mar	7.19	0.38	−0.87	8.03	−2.42	−1.77	−5.94	3.97	−5.46	1.23	−2.56	3.46
Apr	1.28	−0.37	−6.64	−0.80	0.86	−3.75	2.29	−7.52	2.05	−6.36	4.23	5.57
May	2.25	−1.25	0.02	−6.50	10.89	0.43	6.14	−2.73	1.19	−5.45	0.76	−5.91
Jun	6.35	−6.91	5.09	−0.84	−2.34	−2.36	−6.99	−0.22	7.63	−6.01	−1.25	−0.21
Jul	−1.18	−5.94	9.83	−6.32	2.72	−0.02	3.59	4.14	4.41	−2.06	8.12	−1.66
Aug	−5.66	0.82	−3.43	−0.07	22.71	4.32	−7.23	3.67	−1.58	−1.44	1.27	2.48
Sep	1.58	−2.93	−5.93	−3.32	−4.98	1.74	9.89	2.91	8.10	−0.42	−1.91	3.00
Oct	−0.41	6.35	4.30	6.75	−8.69	1.85	6.15	−4.97	−0.66	−7.56	−1.78	2.64
Nov	3.03	−0.97	−2.94	2.93	−7.12	−6.48	13.76	−5.44	−5.89	−1.89	−7.71	−1.25
Dec	−0.19	4.94	1.31	1.04	−5.75	−6.60	0.86	−3.03	4.13	−3.98	−4.87	−1.96
Total	14.91	−7.37	−5.48	0.43	−5.99	−14.22	15.77	−3.58	18.15	−32.60	−7.71	16.99
S&P 500	−1.54	34.11	20.26	31.01	26.67	19.53	−10.14	−13.04	−23.37	26.38	8.99	3.00
WGBI	2.34	19.04	3.62	0.23	15.30	−4.27	1.59	−0.99	19.49	14.91	10.35	−6.88

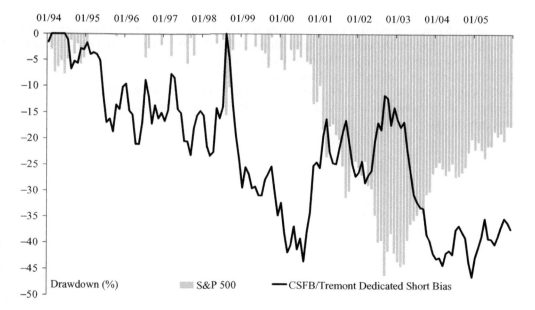

Figure 8.5   Drawdown diagram of the CS/Tremont Dedicated Short Index compared to the S&P 500, 1994–2005

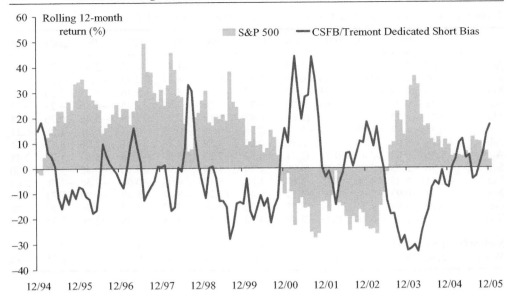

Figure 8.6 Comparison of the 12-month rolling performances of the CS/Tremont Dedicated Short Index with the S&P 500, 1994–2005

Figure 8.5 reveals a massive drawdown that started almost at beginning of the considered period (1994). Even with the bear market of the years 2000–2002, the index did not manage to recover from its previous losses. The magnitude of the maximum drawdown (−46.55%) confirms the absence of hedging of the strategy, and the rolling 12-month return clearly evidences a mirroring effect vis a vis the S&P 500 (Figure 8.6). At this stage, we would be very tempted to say that the dedicated short index offers limited interest, unless one really has a bearish view on equity markets.

9
Equity Market Neutral

An investment process based on a quantitative model is not a black box, but an investment process based on subjective assessments and gut feeling is!

Most long/short equity managers select stocks separately for the long and the short sides of their portfolio. They pay little attention to the relation between their long and their short positions, or more generally, to their portfolio construction process. Consequently, their funds often have a net long or a net short exposure, depending on the set of available opportunities and the manager's outlook for the near term direction of the overall market. In either case, their portfolio performance becomes dependent upon directional market movements. Alfred W. Jones' fund, for instance, had a tilt towards long positions – his shorts were of a generally smaller magnitude than his longs.

The goal of equity market neutral managers is precisely to avoid any net market exposure in their portfolio. Selling and buying are no longer sequential independent activities; they become related and in some cases even concurrent. In addition, long and short positions are regularly balanced to remain market neutral at all times, so that all of the portfolio's return is derived purely from stock selection and no longer from market conditions. This explains why many investors perceive equity market neutral as the quintessential hedge fund strategy. Indeed, when correctly implemented, it offers the promise of true absolute returns (the *alpha*) without having to bear the market sensitivity (the *beta*). But beware! "Market neutral" has become a catch-all marketing term which embeds several different investment approaches with varying degrees of risk and neutrality.

9.1 DEFINITIONS OF MARKET NEUTRALITY

Let us first explain what we intend by "market neutral". As an illustration, consider a plain vanilla long/short equity portfolio with $10 million of initial capital. Say this capital is invested as follows: $9 million long shares and $6 million short shares. The $6 million raised from the short sale are used as collateral and collect interest at the risk-free rate. What should we do to make this portfolio market neutral?

9.1.1 Dollar neutrality

At a first glance, our portfolio has a positive net long market exposure of $3 million ($9 million long minus $6 million short). To be dollar neutral, we need to have equal dollar investments in the long and the short positions, say for instance $9 million long and $9 million short. We therefore need to increase the size of the short position by $3 million. Going forward, we will also need to rebalance our long and our short positions on a regular basis to maintain dollar neutrality. Indeed, if we were right in our stock selection, the long position will appreciate while the short position will shrink in size, pushing the portfolio towards a net long bias.

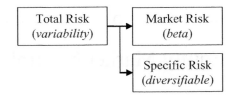

Figure 9.1   Splitting the risk of a stock or a stock portfolio into a market risk component and a specific risk component

Dollar neutrality is extremely appealing because of its simplicity. It has the great benefit of being directly verifiable, as the initial value of the investments is observable, at least to the hedge fund manager. But is it sufficient to make a portfolio market neutral? The answer requires closer examination of some of the unobservable risk characteristics of the long and short parts of our portfolio.

9.1.2   Beta neutrality

A commonly used risk-based definition of market neutrality relies on beta: a portfolio is said to be market neutral if it generates returns that are uncorrelated with the returns on some market index. Since beta is calculated from the correlation coefficient, a zero correlation implies a zero beta.

To create such a beta neutral fund, it is necessary to go back to the basics of Model Portfolio Theory (MPT). According to MPT, the volatility of a stock (or a portfolio of stocks) can be decomposed into a market risk component and a specific risk component. The market risk component depends on the volatility of equity markets as well as on the market risk exposure, which is measured by the beta coefficient.[1] The specific risk component is independent from the market and it normally gets diversified away at the portfolio level (Figure 9.1).

The beta of a portfolio is a weighted average of the betas of its component stocks. Consequently, being dollar neutral does not necessarily guarantee that the portfolio will be insensitive to the market return, i.e. will have a beta equal to zero. It all depends on the beta of the long and the short positions. For instance, if the beta of the long position is 1.4 and the beta of the short position is 0.7, an equal dollar allocation between the two will have a net beta of $0.35 = (50\%) \times (1.4) - (50\%) \times (0.7)$. This positive beta implies that the market risk of our dollar neutral portfolio is not nil and that its correlation to equity markets is actually positive.

To make our portfolio really beta neutral, we need to size the long and short positions adequately. In our example, given the ratio of the two betas (1.4 versus 0.7), we would need to double the size of the short position relative to the long position. That is, for any dollar in the long position, we would need to have two dollars in the short position. In this case, the beta will be exactly zero, which means that the systematic risk of the portfolio has been neutralized. Going forward, if our long position appreciates in value and our short positions decreases in value, we would still need to adjust the size of our positions on a regular basis to avoid the drift towards a positive beta.

At this stage, the reader may wonder why a hedge fund manager might want to have a beta neutral portfolio. The answer is simple: to take risks only where he has skills. Many hedge fund

---

[1] Beta, as commonly defined, represents how sensitive the return of a stock or a portfolio is to the return of the overall market. A beta of 1 means the same sensitivity as the market.

managers prefer to focus on stock selection where they think they have a competitive advantage, rather than on forecasting the returns of the market or of some of its sub-sectors. Consequently, they prefer to run a portfolio of carefully selected stocks but with no net beta exposure, as this makes them completely independent from the behaviour of equity markets (Box 9.1).[2]

Box 9.1 An extension of beta neutrality: mean neutrality and risk neutrality

The notion of beta neutrality, or equivalently, correlation neutrality, needs to be taken with extreme caution. Several hedge fund strategies exhibit returns that are closely linked to some market index, but in a non-linear way. In such a case, the traditional linear correlation coefficient – and therefore the beta – will indicate an absence of *linear* correlation. Investors might conclude that the fund is market neutral or equivalently, that it is independent of the market, while the reality is that the two are closely linked but non-linearly.

As an illustration, consider a fund that would always provide the square of the market return. That is, if the market performance is 5 percent, the fund will return 25 %. If the market performance is −3%, the fund will gain 9%. Such a fund would obviously have a positive correlation with the market when market returns are positive and a negative correlation with the market when market returns are negative. However, the "average" correlation will be zero – this does not mean market neutrality (Figure 9.2).

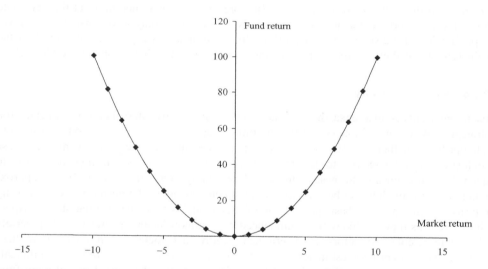

Figure 9.2   Linear correlation cannot measure non-linear relationships

A solution to deal with such non-linear relationships is to extend the definition of neutrality to consider any function of the market returns in the analysis. That is, a hedge fund may be said to be market neutral if it generates returns that are uncorrelated with *any* function –

---

[2] Note, however, that this attitude is going against one of the fundamental MPT results, that is, a portfolio with a zero beta has no market risk and should therefore have a return equal to the risk-free rate. Market neutral hedge fund managers think that they have superior stock selection skills that will allow them to identify overvalued and undervalued securities and therefore, that they will be rewarded for taking on specific risk.

linear or not – of the returns on some given market index.[3] This is often referred to as "mean neutrality", because it implies that the expected return of the hedge fund is unpredictable given the return of the market. This can easily be tested using non-parametric regressions or Taylor series approximations.

For the sake of completeness, we should also mention that some hedge fund investors are also seeking some risk neutrality. That is, they want to avoid having the *risk* of their hedge funds increasing at the same time as the risk of a market index. The term "risk" can be defined in terms of variance, but also in terms of downside risk, value at risk, or even returns in extreme market conditions.

9.1.3   Sector neutrality

Although a portfolio with a zero beta is theoretically market neutral, all practitioners know that it is still exposed to the risk of losing money – for instance, if the long positions are in a sector that suddenly plunges and the short positions are in another sector that goes up. In addition to sector bets, value and growth biases or capitalization exposures may also lead a portfolio to underperformance despite strong returns on the broad market. In 1998, for instance, the extreme difference between the performance of growth and value stocks hindered beta-neutral managers having a value tilt, even though their total long exposure exactly matched their total short exposure.

To avoid that risk, it is necessary to go one step further and balance the long and short positions in the same sector or industry. This preserves the beta neutrality at the aggregate level, but also adds sector neutrality. Similarly, practitioners may also consider the market capitalization of the stocks in their portfolio to ensure that it is capitalization neutral, or the value/growth attributes of their longs and their shorts to ensure that it contains no biases.[4]

9.1.4   Factor neutrality

Factor neutrality is, in a sense, the ultimate and most quantitative step of equity market neutral strategies. Where practitioners had the intuition to use sector or capitalization exposures to attempt to strengthen the neutrality of their portfolios, quantitative portfolio managers use sophisticated *factor models* to determine the precise sources of risks in their portfolios, to quantify their exposures to these sources, and eventually to neutralize them. In first approximation, factor models can be seen as formal statements about the performance of security returns. For instance, the basic premise of a factor model is that since similar stocks display similar returns they are likely to be influenced by common factors. Factor models precisely identify these common factors and determine the individual stocks' return sensitivity to these factors. They also provide estimates of the variances, covariance, and correlation coefficients among common factors, which will be very useful to quantify the overall risk of a portfolio and split it based on its sources.

To create a factor neutral portfolio, it is necessary to have beforehand identified a series of factors that influence the returns of individual stocks. The simplest model is obviously the market model, where only one factor, the market, is common to all stocks and explains their correlation. However, empirical observation and academic research suggest that there are

---

[3] Technically, we could say that the market return does not Granger-cause the fund return in mean.

[4] Note that from a portfolio management perspective, sector or capitalization neutrality is not an exclusive feature of hedge funds. A similar approach exists for long-only manager that need to match the sector or the market capitalization exposures of a given benchmark. In our case, the target exposure of the portfolio is no longer the benchmark's exposure, but it is a zero net exposure for all sectors or market capitalization groups.

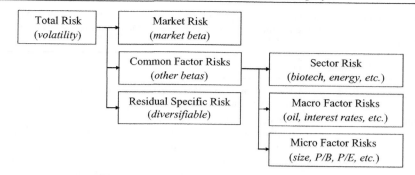

Figure 9.3 Breakdown of an equity portfolio risk

other factors beyond the market influence. Some of these common fluctuations are explained by fundamental characteristics of the portfolio: stocks in the same industry tend to move together, value stocks tend to move together, growth stocks tend to move together, small caps tend to move together, and so on. Some of these common fluctuations are also explained by more general economic factors such as oil price, the level of interest rates, inflation, etc. Since the market risk is obviously not responsible for these common behaviours, specific risk must therefore be the place to investigate.

Multi-factor models simply decompose the "old" specific risk of Figure 9.1 into additional sources of risk, namely common factor risks and residual specific risk (Figure 9.3). Common factor risks represent forces that are not linked to the market risk, but still have a common influence on subgroups of stocks. Examples of such forces include their sector (biotechnology, energy, etc.), but also some macro factor risks (oil prices, the level of interest rates, etc.) as well as some micro factor risks such as the market capitalization of the company, its price to book value (P/B) ratio, its price to earning (P/E) ratio, etc. Residual specific risk then captures a refined source of risk derived from forces that uniquely influence an individual company.

A factor model allows quantitative portfolio managers to statistically construct a portfolio having the highest expected excess return while being neutral to a selected series of underlying factors. How does this work? As an illustration, let us consider the Barra Integrated model for the US stock market. This is a commercial factor model with 55 sector factors (each firm may participate in up to 6 sectors) and 13 common risk factors (variability in markets, success, size, trading activity, growth, earnings/price, book/price, earnings variation, financial leverage, foreign income, labour intensity, dividend yield, and low capitalization). Each month, Barra supplies the evolution of these 68 factors as well as the sensitivities (the betas) of all the US stocks to each of these factors.

The betas of a given portfolio to the respective factors are easily obtained by a weighted average of the component stocks' betas. If some of the portfolio betas are not equal to zero, then the portfolio is not neutral to the corresponding factors. For a long/short equity portfolio to be truly market neutral, the manager must therefore extend his risk controls beyond market risk to include *all* the common factor sources of risk (Table 9.1).

Of course, there is always a limit to market neutrality. As more risk factors are being hedged away, the opportunity set to add value is reduced. Ultimately, if all risk factors are perfectly hedged, the portfolio becomes risk free and should theoretically yield the risk-free rate, minus transaction costs. Market neutrality is therefore a trade-off between eliminating some undesirable risk sources and reducing the set of return generating opportunities. For

Table 9.1 Example of the some of the risk exposures (beta) of a long/short equity fund. Note that each action to make the portfolio market neutral with respect to one factor will influence the exposure to the other factors

Risk factor	Exposure	Commentary
Size	0.25	The portfolio has a large cap bias. To make it market neutral, the manager should sell short some large caps.
Momentum	−0.14	The portfolio has a bias towards shares that have recently performed relatively poorly. To eliminate it, the manager should sell short some past losers, or buy some past winners.
Market	0.11	The portfolio has a small residual market risk. To make it market neutral, the manager should sell some index futures
Growth	0.02	The index has a very small bias towards growth stocks. To eliminate it, the manager should sell short some growth stocks, or buy some value stocks.

skilled quantitative managers, market neutral is a comfortable space to operate into, because it allows them to avoid taking risk in areas where they do not have skills while simultaneously maintaining some risk exposure where they have a competitive advantage.

9.1.5 A double alpha strategy

Market neutral strategies are often termed "double alpha strategies", because they aim to achieve a zero beta exposure to a set of specified risks while harvesting two alphas, or active returns – one from the long position and one from the short position (Figure 9.4). Additional returns are accrued from interest earned on the non-invested cash balance that is maintained for fund liquidity purposes plus an interest rebate earned on the cash proceeds from the short sales that are held as collateral. The final result is often suggested as a substitute for fixed

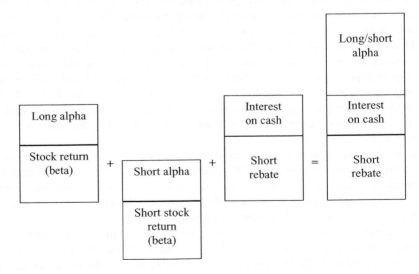

Figure 9.4 The double alpha strategy

income allocations, or even viewed as an enhanced cash equivalent within an investor's asset allocation plan. It will act as such as long as the sum of the two alphas remains positive.

9.2 EXAMPLES OF EQUITY MARKET NEUTRAL STRATEGIES AND TRADES

9.2.1 Pairs trading

Pairs trading is probably the most primitive form of equity market neutral strategy. Its origins can be traced back to the early 1920s, when the legendary trader Jesse Livermore made a fortune in what he called "sister stocks". His investment rules were simple and could be summarized as follows: (i) find stocks whose prices should normally move together; (ii) take a long/short position when their prices diverge sufficiently; and (iii) hold the position until the two stock prices have converged, or a stop loss level has been hit.[5] Today, the heirs of Jesse Livermore are still closely following his traces. Their view is that two securities with similar characteristics that tend to move together and whose relative prices form an equilibrium can only deviate *temporarily* from this equilibrium. Therefore, whenever their spread becomes large enough from a historical/statistical perspective to generate the expectation that it will revert back to the long-term average level, they can profit by establishing a long/short position. In a sense, their strategy is a mean-reverting strategy, which is making a call on the relationship between two securities. Note that although pairs trading does not explicitly require to be market neutral, it is often constrained to be at least dollar neutral by hedge funds that implement it – either each pair is dollar neutral, or there is a systematic hedge overlay at the portfolio level, i.e. sell or buy index futures to neutralize the residual market exposure of the long/short portfolio.

The success of pairs trading depends heavily on the approach chosen to identify potential profitable trading pairs, i.e. model and forecast the time series of the spread between two related stocks. There is a variety of approaches, and the choice of one of them often depends on the background of the fund manager. For instance, the first equity market neutral funds were run by managers with a pure stock-picking background. Not surprisingly, they chose to approach stocks using a fundamental valuation perspective. For instance, they analysed each company in a given sector against all its competitors, and established a long/short position by purchasing the most undervalued company and selling short the most overvalued one. The process was then repeated across sectors, and each position was held until the spread between the associated companies had sufficiently reverted, or a stop loss level had been reached. More recently, numerous statisticians have entered the equity market neutral space. Since their competitive advantage is in time series analysis rather than in fundamental valuation, they often use purely statistical models to identify pairs whose two components deviate sufficiently. Using statistics and being systematic in the application of a model allows them to cover a large investment universe without being exposed to incorrect discretionary judgements, but it also implies that the strategy no longer has the flexibility of incorporating prior economic or financial knowledge in representing the relationship between the two time series.

Most of these models use some sort of *distance function* to measure the co-movements within pairs of securities. The simplest distance between two stocks is the *tracking variance*, which is calculated as the sum of squared differences between the two normalized price series.[6] The position in a pair is initiated when the distance reaches a certain threshold, as determined

---

[5] Note that this investment technique is very close to merger arbitrage, except that it can invest in non-merger related situations.

[6] A typical normalization consists in adjusting the starting price of two price series so that their common initial level is identical.

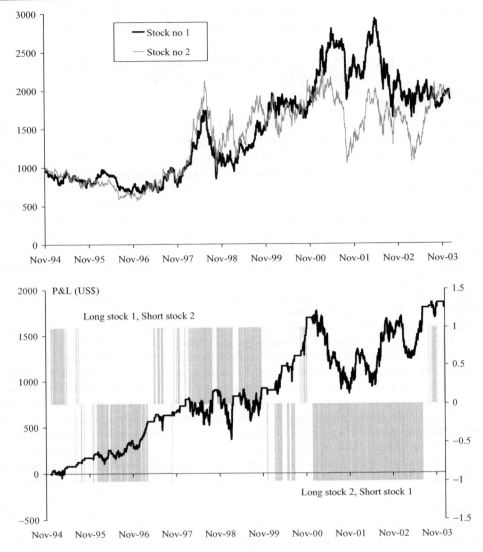

Figure 9.5 An example of pair trading. The upper graph shows the normalized price series of the two stocks, and the bottom graph shows the profit and loss as well as the exposure in the two stocks

during a formation period. For instance, this threshold distance could be two historical standard deviations away from its mean, as estimated during the formation period, or be specified as a certain percentile of the empirical distribution. The pair is closed when the distance reaches another threshold, either with a gain (the mean reversion occurred) or with a loss (a stop loss level was hit).

As an illustration, consider the example of Figure 9.5. The upper graph shows the normalized price series of two related stocks. A normalized price series starts at 1000 and increases or decreases by the stock's gross return compounded daily. Most of the time, the two normalized price series tend to move together. However, the normalized prices of the two stocks differ from each other by more than the trigger value (two historical standard deviations of historical price divergence) on several occasions. On each of these occasions, a position is open, where the most expensive stock is sold and the least expensive is purchased. The bottom graph shows when, and for how long, a position remains open. It also shows the cumulative return to this pairs-trading strategy. Note that there are flat (no profit) periods when the pair's position is not open, but this is usually not a concern at the portfolio level because other pairs will be open during this period.

Of course, more complex distance functions can also be used. Let us mention the *co-integration approach*, which allows for co-integration between the stocks,[7] or the *stochastic spread approach*, in which the evolution of the spread between two stocks is explicitly modelled as a continuous time stochastic process exhibiting some form of mean reversion.[8] This latter approach is extremely convenient for forecasting purposes as well as for calculating information such as the expected holding period and the expected return of each pair. Alternatively, some pairs traders also like to use the *orthogonal regression approach* (Box 9.2) to measure the distance between two stocks.

Box 9.2 Orthogonal regression

Linear regression models try to find the line of best fit through the historical returns of two stocks (R_1, R_2). The usual regression model assumes a causality relationship from R_1 (independent value) to R_2 (dependent value), and finds the line of best fit by minimizing the deviations of R_2 value, or the vertical distances. However, this is not the best way to model a stock pair relationship. When regressing between two stock prices, a more realistic assumption is that the two variables are interdependent and without a known causal direction.

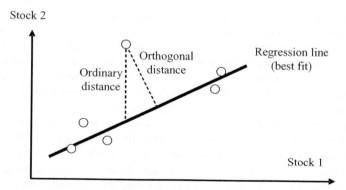

Figure 9.6   Illustration of orthogonal regression

Orthogonal regression (Figure 9.6) treats the two stocks equally. It finds the line that minimizes orthogonal (perpendicular to the line) distances, rather than vertical distances. Technically, it minimizes the sum of the squared R_1 and R_2 deviations, rather than just one variable's deviation.

---

[7] See, for instance, Engle and Granger (1987) and Vidyamurthy (2004).
[8] A typical process is an Ornstein–Uhlenbeck process. See, for instance, Elliott *et al.* (2005).

Data snooping is obviously an important issue when forming such pairs-trading rules. This is why the entry and exit rules for any pair should be based on sensible assumptions, and not just be the result of any back-tests or simulations. Remember that an in-sample optimal trading rule may not remain optimal out-of-sample. Moreover, one of the main risks involved with pairs trading based only on statistical analysis is that a fundamental change in the relationship between the two stocks can get masked and the trader can enter positions when the prices are not expected to revert to historical means. This can happen when, for example, there is a fundamental change in the strategy of one of the companies as a result of which the price level changes permanently.

Surprisingly, the profitability of pairs trading seems now to be well established – see Box 9.3. This goes in complete contradiction with the weakest form of market efficiency, as a relatively simple rule purely based on the behaviour historical prices and their expected mean reversion seems sufficient to make money. More puzzling is the fact that this profitability is not only arising just because of mean reversion – a systematic contrarian strategy, e.g. buying past losers and selling short past winners, should then be highly profitable, but it is not the case, at least not over some considered periods. So far, the most convincing explanation is qualitative: pairs-trading profits would indirectly be related to some sort of "systematic dormant factor" due to the agency costs of professional arbitrage, i.e. the compensation for keeping prices in line. However, the level of that compensation still seems high.

Box 9.3 Is pairs trading profitable?

Surprisingly, although pairs trading has been widely implemented by traders and hedge funds, there is very little academic research which realistically tests its implementation. One exception is Gatev *et al.* (1999), who offer a comprehensive analysis based on the long-term systematic application of a simple distance measure (the tracking variance) which is often used in practice. The three authors begin by defining a one-year observation period, during which they observe normalized stock prices. Each normalized price begins the period with a price equal to 1 and increases or decreases each day by its compounded daily return. At the end of the one-year observation period, they calculate the distance between the daily normalized time series for every pair of stocks. In a market with 500 listed stocks, this entails calculating $124750 (= 500 \times 499/2)$ distances. They then rank their stocks based on their distance and retain the 20 pairs that have the lowest distance.

The trading period immediately follows the observation period and lasts for six months. The prices of the 20 pairs of stocks are again initially normalized to 1. Then, the authors wait until some normalized prices diverge sufficiently, i.e. when the distance between a pair of stocks is larger than two historical standard deviations of historical price divergence – "historical" in this case means measured over the formation period. This triggers a signal to open a position for the pair, i.e. sell the higher priced stock and buy the lower priced stock. The position is held open until the next crossing of the prices, or until the trading period ends – being left with an open position is a risk that finite-horizon arbitrageurs face. Since each pair is effectively a self-financing portfolio, an equal dollar amount is initially allocated to each stock, and the position is marked-to-market on a daily basis.

Over the 1962–1997 period, Gatev *et al.*'s strategy generated an average annualized excess return of more than 12 percent, which exceeds by far any conservative estimate of transaction costs. Andrade *et al.* (2005) repeated their test out of sample using Taiwan data from 1994 to 2002, and also obtain statistically significant performance.

9.2.2   Statistical arbitrage

Statistical arbitrage can be seen as an extension of the pairs-trading approach to relative pricing. The underlying premise in relative pricing is that groups of stocks having similar characteristics should be priced *on* average in the same way. However, due to non-rational, historical or behavioural factors, some discrepancies may be temporarily observed. Rather than looking for a few pairs of securities that diverge from their historical relationship, statistical arbitrageurs slice and dice the whole universe of stocks according to several criteria and look for systematic divergences between groups. Their portfolio will typically consist of a large number of long and short positions chosen simultaneously; for instance, they will buy the 20 percent most undervalued stocks and sell short the 20 percent most overvalued according to some criteria, with the aim of capturing the *average* mispricing between groups.

The criteria selected to slice and dice the universe are the most critical elements in the strategy. In reality, what arbitrageurs are trying to do is use factors that explain well historical equity price movements and also have some sort of predictability. The challenge is to avoid factors with little explanatory power, or factors that just have a temporary impact, and rely only on intuitive and significant factors, whose empirical performance can easily be documented. Examples of such factors are valuation indicators, growth estimates, leverage, dividend yield, earnings revision, momentum, etc. Once a factor is selected, the arbitrageur scores the universe of stocks according to it and goes long the top scorers and short the lowest scorers. The resulting portfolio is factor neutral by construction,[9] and its performance depends on the factor's future ability to separate top from bottom performers. Most of the time, this ability is linked to specific market reactions that can be classified as short-term, medium-term and long-term momentum and reversal patterns. In a momentum pattern, past winners/losers are expected to be future winners/losers, while in a reversal, past losers/winners are expected to be future winners/losers.

Such patterns are well known in empirical finance. For instance, over the short run (3 to 12 months), markets seem to favour momentum.[10] That is, stocks that have performed relatively poorly in the past continue to lag, and stocks that have performed relatively well in the past continue to perform well. This apparent inefficiency can somehow be justified by some momentum in earnings announcements, but it also comes from investor overconfidence and other well-documented behavioural finance biases. In any case, it can easily be exploited by a statistical arbitrage strategy. For instance, an arbitrageur could take again the S&P 500 companies, sort them according to their past three-month performance and create 50 groups of 10 companies. The first group contains the stocks that have realized the highest return (referred to as "winners"), while the last group contains those that have realized the lowest return (referred to as "losers"). The arbitrage portfolio will go long the first group and short the last group. If momentum persists, the arbitrage portfolio will be profitable.

Mean reversion or contrarian trading is, in a sense, the opposite of momentum trading. It is based on the empirical evidence that price reversals tend to take place two or three years after the formation of a momentum portfolio. Some researchers have argued that mean reversion is in fact the long-term consequence of the price momentum effect – investors overreact in the short term, but realize later that they were wrong and prices will therefore adjust. If this is true, then an interesting arbitrage consists in going long past losers and short past winners, where losers and winners are measured over a longer time horizon (say three years).

---

[9] It may easily be constrained further to be dollar neutral or beta neutral.
[10] See for instance Jegadeesh and Titman (1993), Chan *et al.* (1996), Haugen and Baker (1996), Rouwenhorst (1998), or Grundy and Martin (2001).

Another popular trade of statistical arbitrageurs is the value versus growth bias. Growth companies may temporarily outperform value companies, but over the long run (two to five years), value companies display higher average returns.[11] A statistical arbitrageur that would expect this situation to persist in the future and had a sufficient time horizon should immediately attempt to profit by going long value and short growth stocks. For instance, he could take the S&P 500 companies, sort them according to their price/earning (P/E) ratio or their dividend yield and create 50 groups of 10 companies. The first group will contain the stocks that have the highest value attributes, while the last group will contain the stocks that have the highest growth attributes. Our arbitrageur could then go long the first group and short the last group. If value continues outperforming growth over the long run, his portfolio will be profitable.

Of course, these strategies seem relatively simple, but the devil is in the details. The generic idea might be straightforward to understand, but the implementation is not. In particular, each of these trades relies on selection rules that should be carefully calibrated to market data in order to identify the optimal length of the observation period, the optimal number of groups to create and the most efficient way to structure and rebalance the portfolio. Most statistical arbitrageurs spend a lot of time on fine-tuning and back-testing their selection rules. Note that they do not have to limit themselves to using only one rule. As soon as their time horizons are different, momentum and contrarian strategies can actually coexist in a portfolio, very similarly to commodity advisers using several trading rules. Indeed, momentum trading functions very well in trending markets (pro-cyclical strategy) while contrarian trading comes into action when prices revert back to more sustainable levels (anti-cyclical strategy). Mixing them may actually smoothen out the performance of the portfolio. For instance, Figure 9.7 shows the back-test of a strategy that aims at systematically exploiting over-and under reactions in the market by arbitraging short run momentum and a medium run reversal in the S&P 500 stocks. The strategy has worked perfectly from 1986 to 2002.

The next question, of course, is whether it will continue to perform as well in the future.

9.2.3   Very-high-frequency trading

With the increased availability of real time market information and computing power, auto-mated trading has attracted the interest of a growing number of equity market neutral hedge funds in recent years. Automated trading greatly facilitates the arbitrage of multiple markets and timeframes. For instance, our momentum strategy could easily be applied to different markets simultaneously, without running up against human limitations, e.g. clicking the mouse fast enough and managing thousands of trades. It could also capture very short-term opportunities, i.e. momentum that could last a few minutes or even a few seconds. For example, analysing the percentage of trades in the last 15 seconds that have been conducted at the bid and offer and comparing that with current market depth can offer a useful indication of short-term market direction.

However, being successful in very high frequency trading requires four elements: brainpower (to design the trading rules or the learning algorithms), high-frequency historical data (to test the trading rules), computing power (to apply the selected trading rules in real time) and best execution (to limit as much as possible trading costs and slippage). In our opinion, very

---

[11] See for instance Rosenberg, Reid and Lanstein (1985), Fama and French (1992) and Lakonishok, Sheifler and Vishny (1994) in the US, or Chan, Hamao and Lakonishok (1991) in Japan, Brouwer, van der Put and Veld (1996) in Germany, France, the Netherlands and the UK, just to mention a few.

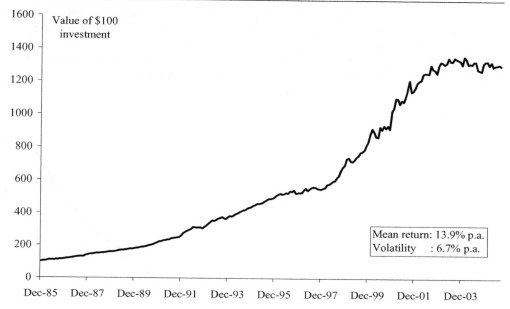

Figure 9.7 The AlphaSwiss Montreal Index describes the out of sample back-test of the Momentum/Reversal-Alpha Model® (MONTREAL) model. The MONTREAL strategy is a quantitative market-neutral US equity strategy developed on the basis of behavioural finance models in 2001 by AlphaSwiss Asset Management, Switzerland. The above track record assumes transaction costs of 0.10%, a borrowing rate of 0.80%, a 0.26% p.a. administration fee, 1.50% p.a. management fee and 20% performance fee with a high water mark

few firms have been successful at combining these four elements. One of them, of course, is Renaissance Technologies – see Box 9.4.

Box 9.4 James Simons and Renaissance Technologies

Renaissance Technologies is one of the few firms that were successful at providing great returns over several years by using only mathematical and statistical models for the design and execution of its investment programme. Renaissance Technologies was founded in 1982 by James H. Simons to focus on the use of mathematical methods. Simons had a long and impressive scientific career, with a PhD in mathematics from the University of California at Berkeley and several years of research in the fields of geometry and topology. He received the American Mathematical Society Veblen Prize in Geometry in 1975 for work that involved a recasting of the subject of area minimizing multidimensional surfaces – a consequence was the settling of two classical questions, the Bernstein Conjecture and the Plateau Problem. Simons also discovered certain measurements, now called the Chern–Simons Invariants, which are now widely used, particularly in theoretical physics. He then became a cryptanalyst at the Institute of Defense Analyses in Princeton, taught mathematics at the Massachusetts Institute of Technology and Harvard University, and was later the chairman of the Mathematics Department at the State University of New York at Stony Brook.

In 1989, Renaissance launched three computer-based funds called the Medallion Fund, the Nova Fund and the Equimetrics Fund. Medallion initially specialized in currencies, futures and commodities, and later on expanded to equities and options. In 1993, Medallion managed $280 million and closed its doors to non-Renaissance employees. In 1997, the Nova Fund was merged into Medallion, followed by Equimetrics in 2002.

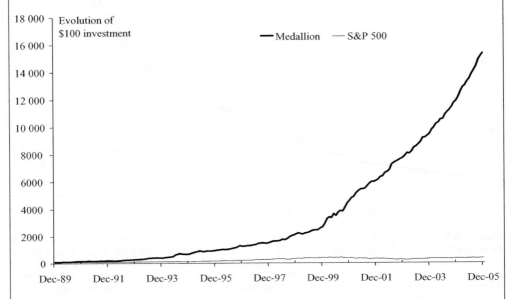

Figure 9.8   Evolution of $100 invested in the Medallion Fund compared to the S&P 500

The track record of Medallion is simply phenomenal (Figure 9.8). Despite the highest management and performance fees in the industry, the fund has returned more than 30% per annum after fees. Capital has been returned to initial non-employee investors on a regular basis to maintain the fund size at $5 billion. In December 2005, the fund finally kicked out the last external investors' money and run only its own capital.

The operational setup of Medallion is as impressive as its performance. For its technical and trading operations, Renaissance Technologies has a 115 000 square foot campus-style building on a company-owned property of 50 acres close to Stony Brook University, as well as backup in Manhattan. The research environment includes a cluster of 1000 processors and five large servers, supported by 150 terabytes of disk space, while the trading environment includes a cluster of 48 processors and 55 Sun machines directly connected to exchanges and brokers. The fund's 39 researchers all have PhD degrees in mathematics or hard sciences – if he wanted to, Simons could launch his own space programme. But they are exclusively focused on short-term prediction, cost modelling, risk modelling, optimization and simulation.

In the fall of 2003, James Simons and his team started working on a new fund, but with a focus on slower frequency trading and equities, with a longer bias than Medallion. Renaissance Institutional Equity Fund was launched on 1 August 2005, with a target size modestly announced at . . . $100 billion. Its $20 million minimum investment commitment gears it to institutions. Its returns: the fund had a slow start and gained only 5% in 2005.

9.2.4   Other strategies

Several other hedge fund strategies are intended to be market neutral to some extent. Let us mention merger arbitrage, which consists of trading pairs of securities related by an expected merger or takeover offer, or convertible arbitrage, which trades a convertible bond and its associated stock. We will review these strategies in their respective chapters.

9.3   HISTORICAL PERFORMANCE

The historical performance of equity market neutral hedge funds has been impressive, particularly on risk-adjusted terms. Over the January 1994 to December 2005 period, equity market neutral hedge funds – as measured by the CS/Tremont Equity Market Neutral Index – delivered an average return of 9.92% p.a., with a volatility of 2.96%. By contrast, over the same period, the S&P 500 delivered an average return of 8.6% p.a., with a volatility of 16.0%, and the CS/Tremont Hedge Fund Index delivered an average return of 10.7% p.a., with a volatility of 8.1% (see Figure 9.9 and Table 9.2).

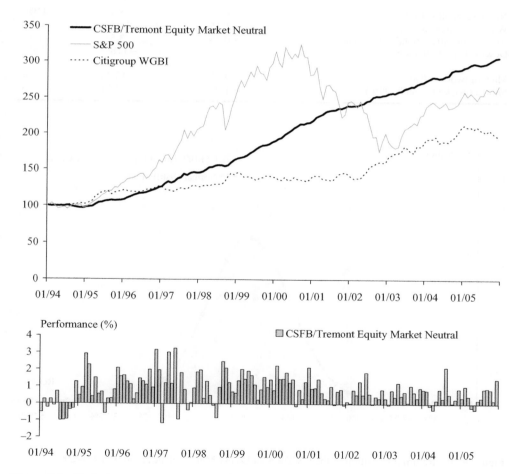

Figure 9.9   Evolution of the CS/Tremont Equity Market Neutral Index, 1994–2005

Table 9.2 Performance comparison of the CS/Tremont Equity Market Neutral Index, the S&P 500 and the Citigroup World Government Bond Index, 1994–2005

	CS/Tremont Equity Market Neutral	S&P 500	Citigroup WGBI
Return (% p.a.)	9.92	8.55	5.87
Volatility (% p.a.)	2.96	16.00	6.74
Skewness	0.34	−0.58	0.37
Kurtosis	0.38	0.61	0.37
Normally distributed?	Yes	No	Yes
Correlation with strategy		0.38	0.09
Positive months frequency	84%	62%	58%
Best month performance (%)	3.26	9.67	5.94
Average positive month performance (%)	1.03	3.44	1.73
Upside participation		55%	159%
Negative months frequency	16%	38%	42%
Worst month performance (%)	−1.15	−14.58	−4.28
Average negative month performance (%)	−0.43	−3.53	−1.18
Downside participation		−118%	−244%
Max. drawdown (%)	−3.55	−46.28	−7.94
Value at Risk (1-month, 99%)	−1.00	−10.24	−3.36

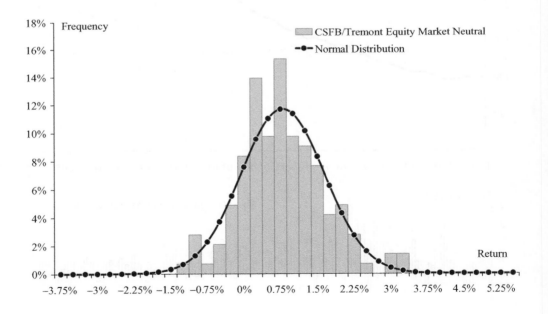

Figure 9.10 Return distribution of the CS/Tremont Equity Market Neutral Index, 1994–2005

Table 9.3   Monthly returns of the CS/Tremont Equity Market Neutral Index, 1994–2005

	1994	1995	1996	1997	1998	1999	2000	2001	2002	2003	2004	2005
Jan	−0.52	0.47	2.10	3.17	0.91	0.69	1.42	2.13	0.12	0.31	0.82	0.35
Feb	0.24	0.94	1.59	1.97	1.85	0.61	0.79	0.89	0.03	−0.06	0.79	1.02
Mar	−0.24	2.92	1.65	−1.15	1.97	1.35	2.24	0.92	0.80	0.79	−0.11	0.43
Apr	0.25	2.27	1.29	1.21	0.29	2.02	1.44	1.44	0.53	0.40	−0.34	−0.22
May	−0.11	0.41	1.14	3.03	1.31	1.44	1.46	0.64	1.29	1.22	0.21	−0.34
Jun	0.70	1.52	0.24	1.18	0.47	1.92	1.82	0.29	0.52	0.46	0.84	0.21
Jul	−1.00	0.55	0.60	3.26	−0.10	1.66	1.23	0.22	1.84	0.68	0.31	0.33
Aug	−0.99	0.68	1.48	−0.92	−0.85	1.11	1.43	1.01	0.57	0.06	2.13	0.86
Sep	−0.94	−0.57	1.32	1.81	0.95	0.22	−0.14	−0.05	−0.03	1.06	0.54	0.90
Oct	−0.37	0.28	1.11	0.81	2.48	0.82	0.81	0.72	0.41	0.67	0.03	0.83
Nov	−0.30	0.29	2.00	−0.38	2.10	1.56	0.28	0.82	0.31	0.33	0.26	0.18
Dec	1.27	0.81	0.95	0.04	1.24	0.96	1.28	−0.08	0.82	0.93	0.86	1.44
Total	−2.02	11.04	16.60	14.82	13.32	15.32	14.98	9.30	7.44	7.06	6.50	6.14
S&P 500	−1.54	34.11	20.26	31.01	26.67	19.53	−10.14	−13.04	−23.37	26.38	8.99	3.00
WGBI	2.34	19.04	3.62	0.23	15.30	−4.27	1.59	−0.99	19.49	14.91	10.35	−6.88

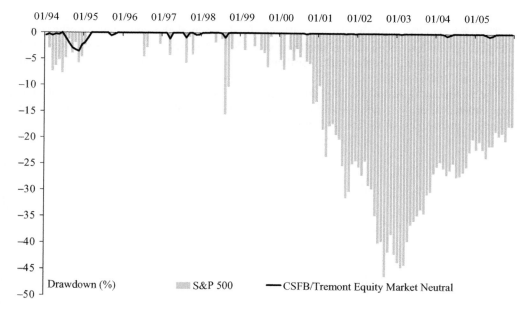

Figure 9.11   Drawdown diagram of the CS/Tremont Equity Market Neutral Index compared to the S&P 500, 1994–2005

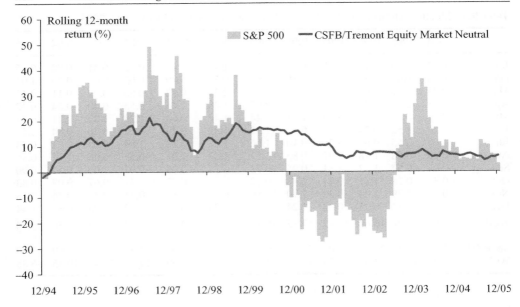

Figure 9.12 Comparison of the 12-month rolling performances of the CS/Tremont Equity Market Neutral Index with the S&P 500, 1994–2005

The track record of equity market neutral hedge funds is remarkably consistent over the years, although returns have been slightly declining since 2001. As a result, the excess skewness and kurtosis are very small, and the return distribution can be approximated by a normal distribution (see Figure 9.10 and Table 9.3).

The maximum drawdown of the strategy is also extremely small (-3.55%) and does not seem related to equity market drawdowns. Lastly, the 12-month rolling return evidences the relative attractiveness of the track record. (see Figures 9.11 and 9.12).

10

Distressed Securities

Debt markets are always sowing the seeds of the next distressed cycle.
The real question is when will it be time to harvest?

Some hedge funds eschew the popular wisdom of investing in blue chips companies. They prefer to focus on investment opportunities from the darkest side of financial markets, namely, the securities of companies in financial distress, default or bankruptcy. The role of these funds is often controversial, particularly for the public. Since they pick the bones of underperforming companies, they have gained the "vulture" sobriquet. Needless to say, the term is quite pejorative. Most people are still philosophically opposed to the idea that some investors may insert themselves into a distressed situation for profit while the firm's original lenders and stockholders are being asked to make material financial sacrifices. Such hostility, however, underestimates the critical role that distressed securities funds may play in the restructuring process. After all, ugly though they may be to look at, vultures also need to be acknowledged for the useful purpose they serve as scavengers.

10.1 DISTRESSED SECURITIES MARKETS

10.1.1 The origins: railways

The origins of investing in distressed securities go back to the 19th century. Following the industrial revolution, an increased volume of goods to be transported had created the need for a faster means of transport. Convinced that railways could generate large benefits, the British Parliament threw out the first Bill for their construction in 1826. Four years later, the first passenger railway was opened between Liverpool and Manchester. It was a great success and investment flowed to the railway industry. In 1846, the Parliament passed no less than 272 acts enabling the laying of new lines. As a consequence, a myriad of private railway building companies sprang miraculously into existence for no reason other than to gratify the speculative instinct of their fellow man. Although their lines did not get any further than the planning stage, their shares were floated successfully. Most of them even soared in value, as the public piled into railway shares and several old companies bought off – on very high terms – rival lines whose plans could threaten their profits. The railway mania had begun.

By November 1845, *The Times* reported that some 1200 railways were planned in the UK, at an estimated cost of more than £500 million – more than the national income. Meanwhile, railway companies had accumulated liabilities amounting to some £600 million. Not surprisingly, the frenzy had to stop at some point. It did in October 1847, when the press discovered that George Hudson, the dominant figure in British railroad industry at that time, had been massaging his financial reports and was in reality paying high dividends out of capital rather than earnings. In a few days, the whole railway sector collapsed. Railway stocks were only worth one-tenth of what they were worth originaly, several banks had to close, and even the Bank of England was caught with only a few million pounds in reserves. Nevertheless, ignoring these alarming signals, a few investors stepped in, purchased railway companies at ridiculously low prices, actively participated in their restructuring and ended up making large profits. They were the first distressed security investors.

Similar situations occurred in the US, although the financing instruments were different. In the US, new railroads were typically launched by small groups of promoters who wanted to maintain control but contribute as little as possible from their personal funds. Consequently, the bulk of railways firms' financing were provided by public sale of bonds, which were underwritten by investment banks and secured with the assets of the railroad. As railroads and trolley companies developed into the dominant corporations, their stock and bond issuances became the centrepiece of a fully mature capital marketplace that included both public and private securities. On several occasions (e.g. 1857, 1873, 1884 and 1893), competition between railway companies and overcapacity within the industry led to a series of failures. Failed railway bonds collapsed, as bondholders realized that individual foreclosures on secured property (i.e. segments of tracks) would result in small recoveries beyond their worth as scrap metal. But on each occasion, organized capital stepped in, bought defaulted debt at discount prices, organized coordinated settlements and restructuring plans to finally sell off with a profit.

Similarly, money flowed into the distressed public utility industry in the 1930s and into distressed real estate in the 1980s. But despite the gains made by the vulture investors on each of these occasions, distressed securities remained unattractive for the majority of investors. In the absence of an effective active secondary market, only specialized investment boutiques dared to introduce them into their portfolios.

10.1.2 From high yield to distressed securities

The foundations of the current US distressed debt market were set in the 1980s with the creation of the junk bond market. In a few years, Drexel Burnham Lambert and its star trader Michael Milken (Box 10.1) transformed a highly illiquid bazaar with only a few specialist buyers into a robust and relatively liquid secondary market for deeply discounted debt. Milken had the issuers, the buyers, the trading capital, the know-how and the historical data – he had boxed the compass. Many institutional investors actually started investing junk bonds because they knew that Milken was acting as a market marker.

Box 10.1 Michael Milken, the "Junk Bond King"

Michael Milken was born in Los Angeles, California, on 4 July 1946. After graduating high school, he attended the University of California at Berkeley as a business major and enrolled in Wharton Business School, specializing in finance, information systems and operational research. Several professors singled him out as the brightest student they had ever taught – no secret there – fellow students reported that Milken studied very hard and late at night. Of particular interest to him was the research of W. Braddock Hickman on bonds with low ratings. He was convinced that the risk of a diversified portfolio of such bonds was excessively compensated by the higher coupon they were paying.

In 1970, Milken went to work for Drexel Firestone in Philadelphia and later in New York. Many thought he would never be successful there, as he was out of place stylistically, socially, religiously and culturally. Nevertheless, against all expectations, Milken stayed at Drexel and specialized in securities that no one else would touch, e.g. high-yield bonds, fallen convertible bonds, preferred stock, and real estate investment trusts. To Milken, some of these securities were clear buying opportunities, because their issuers possessed assets (factories, machines or properties) that were sufficient to cover the associated claims. His extensive research uncovered such values and he made the company a fortune. Occasionally, he was also taking large positions in these securities to provide liquidity to the marketplace, so that institutions would feel comfortable investing there. This generated regular grumblings about the speculative nature of his investment approach and the quality of his investments, but the profits were there. In 1973, Drexel merged with Burnham, and Milken's new salary formula was devised at a base salary and a dollar for every two dollars he made for the firm. This compensation formula never changed afterwards.

In 1978, due to health problems in his family, Milken decided to move his entire team (30 people) to Beverly Hills. He designed a state-of-the-art trading floor, dominated by what became an object of legend, a huge X-shape trading desk where he used to sit to see and hear everything that was going on. His trading system used one of the first computers to calculate yields and cash flows, and contained the trading history of all Drexel customers, i.e. 1700 high-yield securities and 8000 securities in the public bond market. A customized $2 million computer scheme with five times that amount for programming and maintenance gave Milken a detailed knowledge of buyers and sellers as well as a real information advantage over his competitors.

At Drexel, Milken decided to break down the traditional model where investment bankers have to bring in customers and the traders have to trade in those customers' securities. His team progressively expanded from trading junk bonds to underwriting them. Using the trust he had earned from buy side investors, Milken channelled a total of some $93 billion into more than a thousand issuers, including companies such as MCI, CNN, McCaw Cellular, Viacom, TCI, Lorimar, American Motors, Mattel, Warner Communications or Chrysler, as well as other cable, telecom, wireless, publishing and entertainment companies that no other underwriter wanted to touch at that time. Milken was making the market and new issues of junk bonds had to conform to the price and quantity and structure that he influenced by his carefully reading of customer demands. In 1981, he was the first to issue bonds for leveraged buyouts and hostile takeovers. This was again a success. Drexel Burnham Lambert was the most successful Wall Street firm in the 1980s, with profits of $545.5 million in 1986. In 1987, Michael Milken earned a whopping $550 million bonus, a figure that can be compared to the earnings of titans in the 1990s computer industry.

However, by the end of the 1980s, public confidence in leveraged buyouts had waned and criticism of the perceived engine of the takeover movement, the junk bond, had increased. Stock prices were very high by historical standards, but Wall Street kept structuring deals that did not make much sense. Interestingly, Milken repeatedly said in public that it was time to deleverage, time to stop raising money by borrowing and consider other means, but nobody listened to him.

In September 1988, the dream ended abruptly, as Drexel and Milken became the target of a 98-count criminal indictment and a massive civil case filed by the SEC. The charges included insider trading, price manipulation, falsifying records, filing false reports, racketeering, defrauding customers, and stock parking. Drexel pleaded guilty to six felony counts and paid $650 million for alleged insider-trading violations before collapsing for the ties of its managing director Dennis Levine to the merger arbitrageur Ivan F. Boesky. Milken pleaded guilty to six felony counts including securities fraud – the SEC dropped the more serious charges of insider trading and racketeering against his cooperation. He was sentenced to prison for 10 years, barred from the securities business for life, and fined more than $600 million. Milken paid the fine but served only 22 months. After his release, he started working as a strategic business consultant for MC Group, but the SEC charged that this was a violation of his probation. Milken settled with the SEC and paid the government $42 million in fees that he had earned plus interest. Aged 59, Milken is now considered by Forbes as number 133 in the list of the richest Americans, with a net worth of more than $2 billion.

Thanks to Milken, junk bonds became an important alternative source of debt finance over the 1980s for non-investment-grade, small and medium-sized high-tech and innovative firms that used to rely exclusively on bank debt. These "junk firms" became the engine of growth for the US economy. However, a side effect of the junk bond development was that many undeserving companies also managed to gain access to new financing sources and survived rather than disappeared. When Drexel Burnham Lambert collapsed in the early 1990s, junk bond securities were immediately blamed for substantial losses in the portfolios of failing thrifts and banks. Federal regulation forced institutional investors to reduce their junk bond holdings, which led to an excess supply, falling prices and halted new issues. A record number of junk bond issuers became distressed, including large ones such as LTV, Eastern Airlines, Texaco, Continental Airlines, Allied Stores, Federated Department Stores, Greyhound, Pan Am, etc. This time, contrary to the previous crises, institutional investors were among the bondholders and were forced sellers. The cast-off assets again attracted vulture investors who stepped in to acquire defaulted securities at record low prices and restructure their issuers. A highly specialized market emerged and survived throughout the 1990s, despite the decline of default rates.

Default rates spiked again as a result of the economic slowdown that followed March 2000 (Figure 10.1). According to Moody's, the average high-yield bond spread over 10-Year

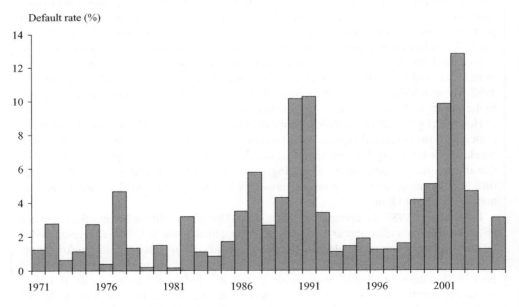

Default rate (%)

Figure 10.1   Evolution of the default rate in the US
Source: Data from the Altman NYU Salomon Center Distress Debt

Table 10.1   The bond rating scales from different agencies

Moody's	S&P/Fitch	Grade	Risk
Aaa	AAA		Highest quality
Aa	AA		High quality
A	A	Investment grade	Strong
Baa	BBB		Medium grade
Ba, B	BB, B		Speculative
Caa/Ca/C	CCC/CC/C	Junk	Highly speculative
C	D		In default

Treasuries rocketed from 746 basis points in June 2000 to a stunning 1029 basis points as of September 2001 – a level comparable to the record high spreads witnessed in 1990 and 1991. A large volume of bankrupt paper hit the market as a result, creating once again many buying opportunities for distressed securities investors.

10.1.3   The distressed securities market today

Today, the real size of the distressed securities market is difficult to measure precisely because of (i) the absence of a universally recognized definition of what distress securities encompass, and (ii) a lack of transparency – while data as to the amount of public debt and equity of distressed companies are readily available, similar information for privately placed debt or bank loans is usually not. Nevertheless, let us try to provide a definition.

Debt instruments are usually characterized in terms of ratings, with reference to Moody's Investor Service or Standard & Poor's. Both agencies have a similar 10-grade scheme ranging from AAA to D.[1] Bonds rated BBB and above are considered investment grade. Bonds rated BBB or below are labelled speculative grade or high-yield. Bonds rated D are in default (Table 10.1).

Distressed debt securities are typically located at the bottom part of the non-investment grade. A widely accepted threshold is that distressed debt includes all debt instruments that offer a yield to maturity which is at least 1000 basis points (10%) above the yield to maturity of a comparable underlying Treasury security – technically, one would say that these debt instruments offer a credit spread larger than 1000 basis points. However, this definition is more indicative than absolute. First, credit spreads vary greatly, and there were periods where they were much lower than the 1000 basis point threshold. Second, there also exist a wide variety of instruments such as bank loans, leases, trade claims and even preferred stocks which are conceptually very close to very junior debt securities. In fact, any instrument used by a company to borrow money and/or finance its operations could eventually become distressed, including common equity – although it is more often than not worthless once the company is distressed.

In the US, a credible source of information on defaulted and distressed securities is the research group led by E. Altman at the New York University Salomon Center. According to its estimations, defaulted and distressed debt represented $585.8 billion of face value at year-end

---

[1] It would be fun to add "E" (for "exterminated") and "F" (for "flushed"), but the two agencies decided to stop at "D".

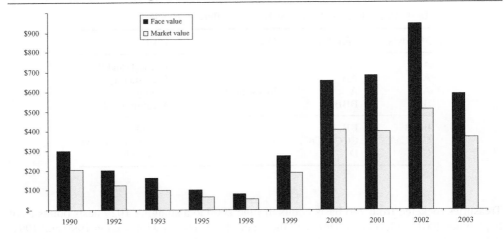

Figure 10.2   Size of Defaulted and Distressed Debt Market (in $ billions)
Source: Data from E. Altman, NYU Salomon Center

2003, split as $244.1 billion public debt and $344.7 billion private debt. This is significantly less than the year-end 2002 figure that culminated at $941.9 billion, but we need to remember that both 2001 and 2002 saw multiple fraud cases and the default of several major US issuers – see Table 10.2.

As expected, the majority of distressed credits originated from issuers with the lowest rating categories, with the 'CCC' category ('CCC+', 'CCC', and 'CCC−') constituting nearly 80% of total speculative-grade distressed credits (Figure 10.3).

Table 10.2   The 20 largest bankruptcy cases in the US

Company name	Bankruptcy date	Total assets pre-bankruptcy (US$ billion)
Worldcom, Inc.	07/2002	$103.9
Enron Corp.	12/2001	$63.4
Conseco, Inc.	12/2002	$61.4
Texaco, Inc.	04/1987	$35.9
Financial Corp. of America	09/1988	$33.9
Refco	10/2005	$33.3
Global Crossing Ltd	01/2002	$30.2
Pacific Gas and Electric Co.	04/2001	$29.8
UAL Corp.	12/2002	$25.2
Delta Airlines	09/2005	$21.8
Adelphia Communications	06/2002	$21.5
MCorp	03/1989	$20.2
Mirant Corp.	07/2003	$19.4
Delphi	10/2005	$16.6
First Executive Corp.	05/1991	$15.2
Gibraltar Financial Corp.	02/1990	$15.0
Kmart Corp.	01/2002	$14.6
FINOVA Group, Inc. (The)	03/2001	$14.1
HomeFed Corp.	10/1992	$13.9
Southeast Banking Corp.	09/1991	$13.4

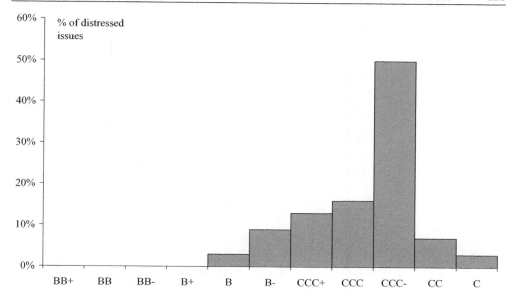

Figure 10.3   Distribution of distressed debt issues by S&P rating

For some investors, this clearly means that high-yield bonds are in a sense the seeds of distressed securities. Monitoring the high-yield market is therefore essential to forecast the future behaviour of distressed securities. Of particular interest is the evolution of the rating transition matrix, which shows the complete possible states a rating can take over a given time horizon – see Table 10.3. The rows of a transition matrix show the beginning of period rating. The columns of a transition matrix show the end of period rating, including default and "WR", which means that the rating was withdrawn. The prime diagonal of a transition matrix shows the percentage of issuers whose ratings did not change over the given time horizon (called the inertial frequency). Consider for instance a company in year 0 in the "Baa1" category. Over a one-year horizon, the corporate had a probability of 6.708% of being upgraded to "A3" and a probability of 7.267% of being downgraded to "Baa2", and so on.

The probability of migration changes not only for every rating category, but also over time and for different sectors. Customized transition matrices may therefore be developed accordingly in order to analyse the migration rates. The analysis may also be extended to longer term horizons in order to analyse cumulative default rates. As an illustration, Table 10.4 shows that a "Baa1" issuer had a probability of 0.166% of having defaulted after one year, but a probability of 2.143% of having defaulted after 10 years, whereas these probabilities were 20.982 and 43.256% for a "Caa" issuer.

The second crucial element to consider when analysing the distressed securities market is the recovery rate, that is, the severity of losses given default. Most of the time, the claimholders in a bankruptcy will only receive some fraction of the value of their original claim, which can range from zero to 100% of par or even higher.[2] The average recovery rate (Table 10.5) allows gauging the severity of these losses at the industry level. Note that the default rate and the

---

[2] Note that while the likelihood of default is roughly the same for various debt obligations of the same obligor, these obligations are readily differentiated by the severity of the loss that may be expected in the event of default.

Table 10.3 Average one-year rating transition matrix, calculated over the 1983–2005 period by Moody's ratings

Initial rating	End of year rating																		
	Aaa	Aa1	Aa2	Aa3	A1	A2	A3	Baa1	Baa2	Baa3	Ba1	Ba2	Ba3	B1	B2	B3	Caa-C	Default	WR
Aaa	89.54	4.91	1.92	0.31	0.26	0.12	0.04	0.00	0.00	0.00	0.02	0.00	0.00	0.00	0.00	0.00	0.00	0.00	2.88
Aa1	2.72	78.03	8.13	6.02	1.04	0.30	0.11	0.11	0.03	0.01	0.04	0.00	0.00	0.00	0.00	0.00	0.00	0.00	3.46
Aa2	0.91	3.42	79.50	7.71	2.67	1.20	0.35	0.09	0.09	0.00	0.00	0.00	0.03	0.02	0.01	0.00	0.00	0.00	4.00
Aa3	0.13	0.51	4.11	79.04	8.28	2.60	0.61	0.20	0.15	0.07	0.01	0.03	0.03	0.02	0.00	0.00	0.00	0.00	4.21
A1	0.06	0.10	0.44	5.70	78.20	7.34	2.73	0.59	0.35	0.10	0.23	0.14	0.06	0.05	0.03	0.01	0.00	0.00	3.87
A2	0.04	0.05	0.28	0.89	5.13	78.03	7.29	2.78	0.89	0.37	0.21	0.10	0.15	0.04	0.05	0.03	0.04	0.00	3.63
A3	0.06	0.09	0.11	0.23	1.82	7.03	74.51	6.35	3.30	1.15	0.49	0.19	0.22	0.12	0.05	0.03	0.03	0.00	4.22
Baa1	0.04	0.04	0.13	0.13	0.28	2.13	6.71	73.33	7.27	3.13	0.94	0.50	0.39	0.51	0.07	0.04	0.12	0.18	4.06
Baa2	0.05	0.10	0.03	0.14	0.22	0.72	3.46	5.81	73.81	6.66	1.70	0.59	0.72	0.58	0.26	0.15	0.23	0.17	4.60
Baa3	0.04	0.01	0.03	0.05	0.17	0.40	0.69	3.21	8.56	70.07	5.57	2.64	1.40	0.68	0.42	0.25	0.63	0.42	4.76
Ba1	0.03	0.00	0.01	0.06	0.23	0.20	0.53	0.77	3.11	9.22	64.46	5.07	4.29	1.37	1.16	0.74	0.38	0.67	7.70
Ba2	0.00	0.00	0.04	0.03	0.04	0.14	0.13	0.43	0.82	2.88	8.78	62.64	7.56	2.57	2.72	1.07	0.74	0.70	8.71
Ba3	0.00	0.02	0.01	0.01	0.03	0.17	0.16	0.23	0.27	0.56	2.93	6.06	64.81	7.08	4.80	2.26	1.03	1.78	7.79
B1	0.02	0.01	0.02	0.01	0.05	0.09	0.07	0.09	0.16	0.23	0.56	2.81	6.19	63.20	9.09	4.03	2.46	2.65	8.26
B2	0.00	0.00	0.01	0.03	0.03	0.02	0.11	0.16	0.10	0.18	0.43	0.72	2.04	7.80	60.51	8.27	6.21	5.43	7.95
B3	0.00	0.01	0.06	0.00	0.01	0.03	0.08	0.09	0.08	0.16	0.11	0.35	0.78	3.26	5.88	58.66	11.23	10.41	8.80
Caa-C	0.00	0.02	0.00	0.02	0.00	0.03	0.00	0.03	0.09	0.11	0.11	0.09	0.40	0.94	1.22	3.31	59.46	14.03	20.14

Source: Data from Moody's

Table 10.4 Average cumulative default rates by Moody's rating, calculated over the 1983–2005 period. *Source*: Data from Moody's

Rating	Year																			
	1	2	3	4	5	6	7	8	9	10	11	12	13	14	15	16	17	18	19	20
Aaa	0.00	0.00	0.00	0.04	0.09	0.14	0.20	0.21	0.21	0.21	0.21	0.21	0.21	0.21	0.21	0.21	0.21	0.21	0.21	0.21
Aa1	0.00	0.00	0.00	0.11	0.17	0.19	0.19	0.19	0.19	0.19	0.19	0.19	0.36	0.58	0.84	0.94	0.94	0.94	0.94	0.94
Aa2	0.00	0.01	0.05	0.12	0.23	0.29	0.35	0.42	0.50	0.59	0.69	0.80	0.85	0.85	0.85	0.97	1.18	1.41	1.68	1.71
Aa3	0.02	0.04	0.08	0.14	0.20	0.26	0.30	0.32	0.33	0.39	0.46	0.65	0.82	0.93	1.04	1.17	1.31	1.48	1.50	1.50
A1	0.00	0.09	0.24	0.34	0.42	0.49	0.55	0.61	0.69	0.79	0.95	1.10	1.29	1.54	1.81	2.12	2.26	2.26	2.26	2.26
A2	0.03	0.08	0.22	0.43	0.61	0.79	1.00	1.21	1.40	1.51	1.55	1.61	1.66	1.73	1.81	1.98	2.36	2.80	3.10	3.17
A3	0.04	0.18	0.36	0.49	0.66	0.86	1.01	1.19	1.33	1.40	1.48	1.48	1.56	1.66	2.00	2.47	2.97	3.58	3.95	4.23
Baa1	0.17	0.45	0.79	1.09	1.37	1.58	1.83	1.95	2.06	2.14	2.23	2.41	2.65	3.06	3.38	3.75	4.17	4.35	4.35	4.35
Baa2	0.16	0.47	0.88	1.51	2.05	2.61	3.12	3.60	4.15	4.89	5.63	6.44	7.05	7.60	8.33	8.77	9.19	9.60	10.06	10.30
Baa3	0.34	0.96	1.67	2.50	3.48	4.42	5.26	6.02	6.55	7.03	7.32	7.54	8.20	8.79	8.91	8.91	8.93	9.26	9.47	9.64
Ba1	0.75	2.00	3.52	5.00	6.42	7.85	8.75	9.55	10.17	10.81	11.52	12.40	12.92	13.31	13.59	14.07	14.87	15.52	16.14	16.34
Ba2	0.78	2.28	4.24	6.24	7.99	9.17	10.39	11.39	12.34	12.94	13.62	14.52	15.34	15.96	16.76	17.38	17.64	17.70	17.78	17.78
Ba3	2.07	5.66	9.76	13.61	16.53	18.97	21.14	22.98	24.42	25.60	26.36	26.86	27.40	28.03	28.31	28.45	28.53	28.57	28.57	28.61
B1	3.22	8.50	13.57	17.64	21.47	24.62	27.29	29.02	30.07	30.83	31.29	31.58	31.79	31.98	32.09	32.16	32.16	32.16	32.16	32.16
B2	5.46	12.07	17.14	21.06	23.81	25.56	26.61	27.28	27.96	28.41	28.64	28.82	28.99	29.25	29.50	29.60	29.68	29.76	29.76	29.76
B3	10.46	18.65	25.25	29.89	33.02	35.38	36.77	37.70	38.17	38.45	38.64	38.87	38.96	38.96	38.96	38.96	38.96	38.99	38.99	38.99
Caa-C	20.98	30.27	36.12	39.50	41.23	42.15	42.59	42.88	43.08	43.26	43.33	43.33	43.33	43.33	43.33	43.33	43.33	43.33	43.33	43.33
Investment grade	0.08	0.23	0.44	0.69	0.93	1.16	1.37	1.55	1.72	1.88	2.04	2.20	2.41	2.63	2.86	3.09	3.34	3.62	3.82	3.92
Speculative grade	5.15	10.11	14.48	17.94	20.63	22.70	24.28	25.43	26.26	26.87	27.30	27.66	27.93	28.19	28.36	28.49	28.59	28.66	28.70	28.72
All corporates	1.74	3.48	5.06	6.37	7.43	8.29	8.97	9.50	9.91	10.26	10.53	10.79	11.03	11.28	11.49	11.67	11.85	12.02	12.13	12.19

Source: Data from Moody's

Table 10.5   Average recovery rates (%) for defaulted corporate debt bonds, calculated over the 2005 year and over the 1982–2005 period

	Issuer-weighted		Value-weighted	
	2005	1982–2005	2005	1982–2005
Bank Loans				
Senior Secured	81.6	70	91.6	64.2
Senior Unsecured	–	57.6	–	46.8
Bonds				
Equipment Trust	–	59.3	–	56.6
Senior Secured	77.9	51.9	76.9	52.6
Senior Unsecured	55.2	36	54.4	34.6
Senior Subordinated	33.6	32.4	37.0	29.2
Subordinated	95.0	31.8	95.0	29.1
Junior Subordinated	–	23.9	–	16.8
All bonds	*55.9*	*35.9*	*54.3*	*33.9*
Preferred Stock	13.8	11.3	7.2	7.3
All debt instruments	54.5	37.7	53.5	35.8

recovery rate seem to be linked by an inverse relationship, i.e. higher default rates correspond on average to lower recovery rates (Figure 10.4).

The losses on distressed securities are a function of both the probability of default as well as the severity of default. Table 10.6 presents historical credit losses for broad rating categories and shows that *on average* Moody's have consistently ranked ordered issuers based on their

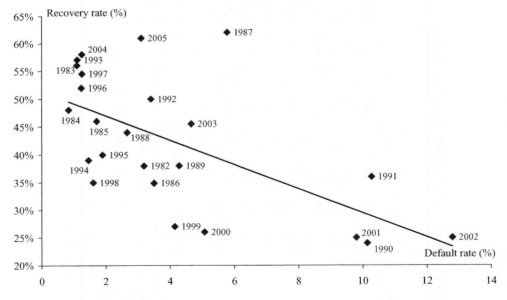

Figure 10.4   Link between default rates and recoveries, 1983–2005
Source: Data from E. Altman, NYU Salomon Center

Table 10.6   Average cumulative credit loss rates (%) by Moody's rating over the 1982 to 2005 period

	Year 1	Year 2	Year 3	Year 4	Year 5
Aaa	0.000	0.000	0.000	0.000	0.004
Aa	0.000	0.001	0.018	0.038	0.080
A	0.007	0.033	0.090	0.159	0.227
Baa	0.108	0.313	0.572	0.902	1.241
Investment grade	0.041	0.111	0.257	0.470	0.766
Ba	0.767	2.173	3.925	5.623	7.042
B	3.605	8.059	12.119	15.590	18.612
Caa-C	14.427	22.966	29.530	34.112	37.701
Speculative grade	3.246	6.709	13.019	18.903	26.965
All corporates	1.078	0.445	2.475	4.358	6.974

Source: Data from Moody's

expected credit loss rates over investment horizons ranging from 1 to 5 years. Of course, one has to remember that hedge funds are not supposed to invest in averages, but rather to identify *specific* distressed securities whose value may be significantly enhanced by an adequate restructuring process. But the magnitude of the opportunity for such profitable distressed securities investments at a given point in time is highly cyclical and variable. Distress debt supply is a function of the amount of unwise financing or excessive leveraging that has been done in the recent past (Box 10.2), the current liquid environment and current economic conditions. And the demand for distressed debt is determined by the amount of capital investors desire to put at work in the sector.

Box 10.2   The case of Europe and Asia

The situation of distressed securities markets in Europe is radically different than the one in the US. One of the reasons is that the European high-yield bond market was virtually non-existent prior to 1997. The market for distressed securities was essentially composed of bank debt, which attracted solely a limited set of specialists. It is only with the emergence of the European Union that the high-yield bond market emerged as a viable alternative to banking finance. Since currency risk had disappeared, investors were forced to develop new strategies based on credit spreads to a much greater extent. This favoured the growth of a full-fledged high-yield market, and, of course, in parallel, resulted in the creation of a distressed high-yield debt secondary market.

Today, the European distressed-securities market still lags far behind the US in terms of both experience and market size. However, the market keeps expanding, supported by strong demand. In the early 2000s, growth was driven primarily by the telecommunication sector, which had huge financing requirements and slipped towards the lower end of the credit-ratings spectrum. More recently, the automotive (parts), retail and airline sectors have been providing most of the opportunities for distressed debt investors. However, there are still major curbs on the growth of a European distressed-securities market:

- European distressed securities are typically issued by holding companies rather than operating companies, which makes it harder to force a default.

- Secured bank lenders often have the right to limit the ability of distressed-securities holders to participate in a restructuring.
- European jurisdictions still have a multitude of bankruptcy legislations, regulators and judicial procedures, compared to a single one in the US.
- In some countries, the transfer of some claims is not possible due to specific aspects of banking supervision (purchasing bank debt requires a banking licence) or bank secrecy and data protection.

Nevertheless, post-communist Europe has become an interesting source of distressed securities. For instance, the Czech Republic has set the pace in post-communist central Europe by auctioning big packages of non-performing loans. The Czech example has been copied by Slovakia and Poland, but investors still experience problems in realizing value, hampered by a cumbersome legal framework that makes enforcing claims and insolvency a long, drawn-out process. Finally, an interesting case is that of Asia, where the opportunity to acquire distressed companies and restructure them has increased significantly, particularly in Japan and Korea.

10.2   DISTRESSED SECURITIES INVESTING

Distressed securities investing can actually encompass many different styles and approaches, but the common strategy usually involves purchasing debt or equity claims on companies experiencing financial, legal or operational difficulties.

10.2.1   Why distressed securities?

At a first glance, distressed securities do not appear to be particularly suitable or attractive investments. First, very few investors like distressed securities. Most institutional investors cannot buy them because their charters, fiduciary responsibility or regulators bar them from buying or holding bonds below investment grade, even if the issuing company is a viable one. Many individual investors are afraid of the potential risk of loss due to the financial distress of the debtor, and most banks do not want to keep them on their balance sheet because they require a large amount of regulatory capital. Second, distressed securities are often highly illiquid. In the best case, trading them will imply very high transaction costs and large bid–ask spreads. In the worst case, they will no longer meet the listing requirements and will become delisted. Third, there is very little information available on distressed securities – analysts' coverage tends to decline significantly as a firm becomes distressed and is almost non-existent for bankrupt firms. This gives a significant advantage to informed professionals over non-specialists.

As a result of what precedes, the market for distressed firms' securities is rather illiquid and has no firm bid–price structure. Most of the order book is concentrated on the sell-side, with traditional investors reluctant to buy. As one could guess, hedge funds love such situations, because they can act as temporary liquidity providers and profit from the market's lack of understanding of the true value of these securities. From the hedge fund perspective, distressed businesses present several opportunities:

- The selling pressure results in attractive discounts. In some cases, some securities even fall in *anticipation* of financial distress when their holders react emotionally to the stigma of current or potential bankruptcy and choose to sell rather than remain invested. In other cases, accounting or window – dressing reasons may provide great opportunities. For instance, many banks and other lenders are managing their assets from a global portfolio perspective as opposed to an account level basis. They are therefore regularly selling non-performing and sub-performing loans in the market at attractive discounts simply to get them off their books around reporting dates.

- Either a restructuring or a cessation of operations may involve the sale of business units at exceptional values. This usually takes time and involves activities close to private equity, but profits will be there at the end.

- In several countries, regulation enables distressed securities purchasers to cherry pick desirable assets while leaving behind over-leveraged balance sheets and undesirable contracts. In all these cases, investment professionals who specialize in researching distressed securities and who understand the true risks and values involved can scoop up these securities or claims at discounted prices, seeing the glow beneath the tarnish.

Valuation expertise in bankruptcy and restructuring proceedings therefore includes not only the technical ability to value a company's assets, but also a thorough understanding of the legal rights and economic incentives of all claimholders.

10.2.2 Legal framework

Bankruptcy laws vary greatly across different countries, but the most advanced legal framework for distressed securities investors seems to be the US Bankruptcy Code. The latter offers essentially two options to a distressed company: reorganizing to recover from crippling debt (Chapter 11), or going out of business, liquidating and distributing the proceeds to creditors (Chapter 7). In the following, we will primarily discuss Chapter 11, as it is the primary framework of concern for hedge funds.

Chapter 11 regulations aim primarily at enabling good firms to reorganize and continue operating while being protected from their creditors. Filing for Chapter 11 suspends all judgements, collection activities, foreclosures, and repossessions of property against the filing firm, at least on the short term. However, it is not a blank card. The filing firm retains possession of its assets, but operates under the close supervision of a bankruptcy court for the benefit of its creditors. A creditor committee is formed to negotiate an acceptable plan of reorganization. The latter must spell out the rights of all investors and what they can expect to receive. For instance, bondholders will generally stop receiving interest and principal payments, but may receive new stock, new bonds, or a combination of stock and bonds in exchange for their old bonds. Stockholders will generally stop receiving dividends, and may be forced to exchange their old shares for a smaller number of new shares in the reorganized company. In some cases, they can even be kicked out of the capital structure. If successful, the reorganization plan will bring the firm back to profitability and out of Chapter 11. Otherwise, the firm will have to liquidate.

In the case of liquidation, the US Bankruptcy Code mandates that claims with higher priority are paid in full before other claims receive anything. The usual order is: first, administrative claims; second, statutory priority claims such as tax claims, rent claims, consumer deposits, and unpaid wages and benefits from before the filing; third, secured creditors' claims; fourth, unsecured creditors' claims; and fifth, equity claims. Analysing the exact priority order as well as the different clauses attached to each claim is therefore essential to understand their real value.

As already mentioned, the US law is a particular case, which has often been described as debtor-friendly. It is oriented towards reorganizing the existing company, i.e. giving the debtor a second chance, and accustomed to deviating from contractual payoff priorities. This is precisely what creates the source of opportunities for hedge funds. By contrast, the traditional bankruptcy procedures in many other developed countries are often described as creditor-friendly. They favour the liquidation of the debtor's assets to pay off creditors in the order of their priority, and leave very little place for a potential restructuring of distressed companies. In the past, this has led to funny situations, where corporations headquartered in countries with weak legal systems but with operations in countries with stronger legal systems, can opt to file for bankruptcy under the strong systems' laws. For instance, Avianca, Colombia's national airline, decided to file for bankruptcy in the US under Chapter 11 in March 2003, because it was unsure whether it would have been able to get protection from their creditors by filing in Colombia.

However, perhaps with an eye to the perceived success of the US system, many countries are now considering instituting a more debtor-friendly US-style reorganization approach into their bankruptcy laws. This trend is encouraged by the World Bank, the International Monetary Fund (IMF) and the European Union, but it will take these new frameworks some time to allow the creation of an active distressed securities market. In the meantime, the US distressed securities market will continue to remain the primary playfield for distressed securities hedge funds.

10.2.3 Valuation

When valuing a distressed firm, it is important to distinguish economic distress and financial distress. In an economically distressed firm, the net present worth of the business as a going concern is less than the total value of its assets were they to be broken up and sold separately. The firm is no longer viable and liquidation is the best option from a financial perspective. Its value depends on the selling price of its assets, which may vary between market value and liquidation value. In financially distressed firms, the business remains economically viable, the assets might be in their highest value use, but the firm is cash-flow insolvent and faces liabilities it is unable to meet, at least as and when they become due. Liquidating and dismantling the assets is still an option, but it would result in a lower value than the true value-generating potential. A better choice for all claimants is to sell the firm's business to some of the company's existing claimants (e.g. distressed hedge funds) and let them restructure.

Whether conducted through formal bankruptcy reorganization or through an out-of-court restructuring or workout, the restructuring process essentially amounts to a re-slicing of the corporate pie. When a financially troubled company is restructured, a new capital structure is created and distributed to claimholders based on the estimated value of their claims *before* the reorganization. Many claimholders will be requested to accept packages of new financial claims in exchange for the claims they currently hold. These packages may imply: (i) the postponement of imminent liabilities into the more distant future; (ii) the conversion of fixed liabilities into fluid ones; (iii) debt write-downs, e.g. all creditors of a particular type agree a pro-rata reduction in the value of their predistress claims; and (iv) in some cases, assets reorganizations. Most of the time, the new capital structure includes some combination of cash, debt and common stock, but it may also include more esoteric instruments such as warrants, payment-in-kind preferred stock and contingent value rights. The valuation of these claims ultimately depends on the valuation of the assets of firm *after* the reorganization.

Valuing a distressed company's assets is a particularly difficult task. Sound answers require an in-depth knowledge of valuation, bankruptcy law and the company's business. In the sophisticated jurisprudence on Chapter 11 of the US Bankruptcy Code, three methods for ascertaining the going concern value of a business have become standard, namely the market comparison approach, the comparable transaction approach and the discounted cash flow (DCF) approach.

- The market comparison approach derives an enterprise value by calculating a financial performance metric (e.g. earnings before interest, taxes, depreciations and amortization, or EBITDA) and applying the average multiple of comparable healthy companies.
- The comparable transaction approach is similar, but derives the enterprise valuation from the prices (enterprise valuations) paid by purchasers in recent acquisitions of comparable companies, if any.
- The DCF calculates the enterprise value based on the present value of a debtor's projected cash flows. It requires projection of the debtor's cash flows for the near-term, typically five years, and discounting them back to present value using a weighted average cost of capital (WACC). The difficulty with DCF is that it requires an explicit modelling of the impact of distress on both expected cash flows and the discount rate. Most of the time, this will be done via scenario analysis.[3]

The practice in the US courts is to use several methods in any given case, with each method acting as a check on the others. However, there is plenty of room for disagreement and discord, starting with the fact that the ability of the existing management to prepare financial plans may be challenged. In addition, one should always keep in mind that (i) the various parties interested in the reorganization proceedings face structural hurdles in determining the company's true value, and (ii) they have a tendency to provide self-serving estimates of that value. In particular, when negotiating a capital restructuring, claimants always have the incentive to overestimate the expected value of their claim and underestimate the value of other claims. For instance, senior bondholders usually have an incentive to undervalue the pre-reorganization company's business, because this will minimize the proportion of the post-reorganization claims given to junior claimholders. On the contrary, junior claimholders – including the old equity holders – will have exactly the opposite incentive and will attempt to inflate the pre-reorganization valuation. As an illustration, consider the case illustrated by Figure 10.5. In a bankrupt company, senior claimholders have a claim of $1000. Both the senior and junior claimholders submit reorganization plans that involve the pro rata conversion of all claims into new equity. The senior claimholders estimate that the company is worth $1500, so that they should get two-thirds of the new equity and the other one-third goes to junior claimholders. But the junior claimholders estimate that the company is worth $3000, so that they should get two-thirds of the new equity and the senior claimholders only one-third.

Now, say the company emerges from bankruptcy and is really worth $2100. If the senior claimholders scenario has been adopted, senior claimholders will capture $400 that should go to the junior claimholders – they obtained a higher ownership percentage of an "unexpectedly" larger company. If the junior claimholders scenario has been adopted, junior claimholders will capture $300 that should go to the senior claimholders – they also obtained a higher ownership percentage of an "unexpectedly" larger company.

---

[3] For instance, there might be a going concern scenario and a distress scenario. For the going concern scenario, you may use the expected growth rates and cash flows estimated under the assumption that the firm will be nursed back to health. Under the distress scenario, you will assume that the firm will be liquidated for its distress sale proceeds. The correct assessment of the probability of each scenario will then be key to the final valuation.

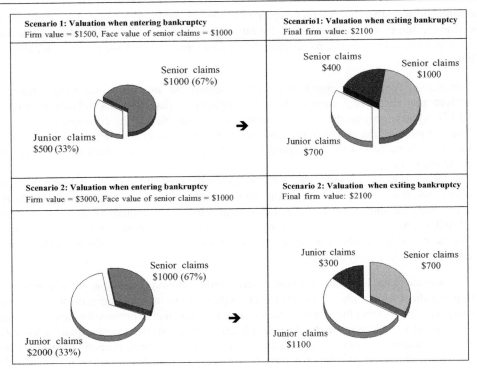

Figure 10.5 The impact of the initial valuation when entering bankruptcy determines the split of the assets when exiting bankruptcy

As a result of such behaviours, the value assigned to the company's assets in bankruptcy reorganizations or out-of-court restructurings is usually the result of intense negotiations. The bargaining power and experience of claimholders such as distressed security hedge funds might obviously give them an advantage in such a process.

10.2.4 Active versus passive

Hedge funds focusing on distressed securities can be divided into two groups based on their investment approach, which can be passive or active. The *passive approach* is characterized by an opportunistic trading or value orientation, in which fund managers do not seek to take control or participate in a restructuring activity. They simply buy stressed and distressed securities that trade below their estimated fair value, wait for them to rise to their fair value and sell them with a profit. The rationale for the appreciation varies and may include elements such as a failure from the market to analyse the complexity of a capital structure, the cyclicality of earnings or an expected attempt from the issuer to repurchase its bonds. These elements are continuously monitored as well as the impact of different outcomes and probabilities to determine an opportune sale or exit point. In some cases, the passive hedge funds are simply waiting for another skilled owner to restructure the company and enhance its value – this is often the case for smaller distressed securities hedge funds.

By contrast, the *active approach* is characterized by the high degree of involvement that hedge fund managers dedicate to the companies they target (Box 10.3). Most of the time, they

---

Box 10.3 The "fulcrum security"

There is often a long list of claims that hedge funds can acquire in order to control the capital structure of a given distressed company, e.g. senior bank debt, senior debt, junior debt, debentures, convertibles, etc. The ideal from a risk/reward perspective is to identify and purchase the "fulcrum security", that is, the senior most impaired debt security in the restructuring process. The fulcrum security normally depends on the amount of debt versus the value of the assets of the debtor. However, with so much senior debt available to and existing at many overleveraged companies, the senior debt very often is the fulcrum creditor class that must be restructured. This type of debt is widely held and regularly traded in normal market conditions, but it is sold at a large discount when there is a bankruptcy because most investors do not want to be involved. The distressed funds that hold this class of debt have therefore the key to many restructurings. Of course, they can also purchase debt higher in the capital structure, but the discount is usually significantly lower.

---

will start by taking control by one of the following means:

- Purchasing sufficient voting shares to gain control of the company and its assets. In practice, this strategy is rarely employed because of the expected dilution due to the reorganization and the fact that equity is junior to debt in the case of a bankruptcy.
- Purchasing a significant position in outstanding debt claims and eventually converting it into voting stock. When done in sufficient quantity and executed properly, this is indeed a win – win situation whereby the hedge fund gets (i) a par recovery in a refinancing or outside purchase or (ii) an equity ownership at a relatively conservative multiple in a distressed equity play.

Note that 'control' does not necessarily require 51% of the voting rights – a blocking position in any of the classes of claims is sufficient to play the role of the spoiler in a reorganization process in hopes of gaining concessions, the so-called "bondmail". For instance, in Chapter 11 reorganizations in the US, each class of claims must approve separately a reorganization plan with a two-thirds majority in value or one-half in number. A creditor owning slightly more than one-third of the value of claims in a *single* class of claims can therefore block the whole process.[4]

Once they control their target, distressed hedge fund managers usually propose a restructuring plan whose goal is to redirect the flow of corporate resources to more highly valued uses, or bargain for a larger share of those resources. As already mentioned, this restructuring plan can focus on the balance sheet when the target is just financially broken, on the assets when it is operationally broken, or on both if necessary. The time horizon is usually longer than with the passive approach and can last up to several years, and the restructuring process is often labour-intensive. Managers utilizing the active approach must therefore selectively limit the focus of their efforts and will tend to have a more concentrated portfolio.

Note that the distinction between the passive and the active approaches to distressed securities is also important for regulatory reasons. Passive distressed securities hedge funds are on the

---

[4] Some distressed managers are well known for their activity, which consists in systematically controlling a sufficient block of bonds to prevent any management-led restructurings, unless they obtain preferential terms for their bonds.

public side of the information wall and can trade all claims – not only loans and trade claims, but also notes, bonds, equities, warrants and options. By contrast, active distressed securities hedge funds usually end up having some direct relationship with issuers and access at some point to private information. This immediately restricts their ability to trade public securities – bank loans are still fine, because they are not considered as public securities, although recent increases in the liquidity of the secondary loan market are rapidly making this distinction less important for all but lawyers.

10.2.5   Risks

The risks of investing in distressed claims are highly firm-specific, and include:

- *Financial risks*, which are primarily linked to the recovery eventually realized by the claims and the period of time it takes to be paid. For any given dollar gain, the shorter the holding period, the greater the annualized rate of return. The obvious risk is that the fund may eventually be stuck with worthless debt, but expenses are also a concern as they can erode returns over time during a protracted reorganization. Because of the importance of the time factor, some investors specialize in companies whose problems are primarily financial rather than operational in nature.
- *Long bias*: Contrarily to other assets, distressed securities are hard to borrow to short sell. Once a company is identified as distressed, all investors want to sell and the time for short selling has generally passed. Borrowing distressed securities is thus generally not feasible or implies paying the lender large fees. In addition, small events or minor news can easily cause sharp rallies, which make short selling a dangerous activity. As a consequence, portfolios are long biased, and the only effective way of reducing risk is by diversification across several unrelated issuers.
- *Title risk* is the risk associated with the legal recognition of ownership of the claims against a firm. For example, a seller may have sold a given claim more than once, creating multiple holders of the claim.
- *Liquidation risk* is the possibility that a reorganization process will fail and that the firm's assets will instead be liquidated. In the US, for instance, a firm's value will generally be higher under Chapter 11 (reorganization) than Chapter 7 (liquidation), so this risk is of particular importance to junior claimholders.
- *Insider trading* is the risk that investors with inside information use it to other investors' detriment. While the SEC governs the activity in publicly traded debt, privately traded claims, however, are exempt and, therefore, pose a greater degree of risk.
- *Tax issues* are an important risk in the reorganization process of a distressed firm, with the two primary issues being the preservation of net operating losses and the cancellation of indebtedness income.
- *The "J" factor*, i.e. the risk associated with the power that judges hold over the reorganization process in some countries. In particular, they determine the voting rights of participants, the suitability of proposed plans and whether an approved plan is acceptable.
- *Liquidity risk*: Once purchased, a distressed position often needs to be held until the end of the restructuring process, which may take several years. Moreover, if the hedge fund holds a controlling position, regulators can prohibit it from selling the position immediately. This often results in the fund applying a very strict redemption policy, with lock-ups often superior to one year.

10.3   EXAMPLES OF DISTRESSED TRADES

10.3.1   Kmart

Kmart is a good example of a long-term illiquid and active transaction in distressed securities. On 22 January 2002, Kmart Corp., the second largest discount retailer in the United States and the seventh largest retailer in the world, filed for Chapter 11 bankruptcy protection (see Figure 10.6). The filing came a day after Fleming Companies Inc., Kmart's biggest food distributor, halted shipments to Kmart after the retailer failed to make its regular weekly payments. The news was somehow expected, as in the weeks prior to the announcement, ratings agencies had downgraded Kmart, its stock plunged and the company had been removed from the S&P 500 index. Nevertheless, with 2114 stores and 275 000 employees, $17 billion in assets and almost $40 billion a year in sales, Kmart was the biggest ever bankruptcy for a US retailer.

The usual retail bankruptcy process model is well established. People usually wait until Christmas to see what happens and then close the worst performing stores. The company then hobbles along until the following Christmas and does the same thing again, closing even more stores. It is usually a slow process that can last for years, while the Boards of Directors and existing managers that put the company into bankruptcy stay in place until the company finally emerges under new ownership pursuant to a plan of reorganization. But in the case of Kmart, two investors stepped in, namely the Third Avenue Value Fund and the very secretive hedge fund ESL Investments. Third Avenue Value Fund was run by Marty Whitman, a well-known vulture investor, and ESL was run by Edward S. Lampert, another alumnus of the arbitrage desk of Goldman Sachs. Both of them identified Kmart as "one of the worst managed companies in its industry", but they were buying.

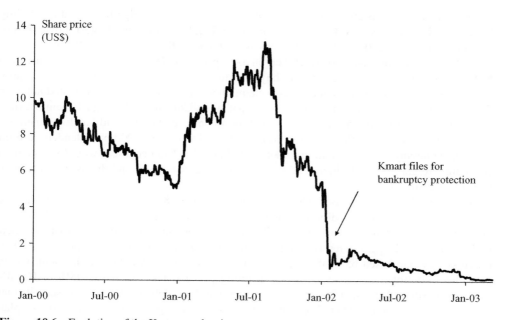

Figure 10.6   Evolution of the Kmart stock price

The Third Avenue Value Fund managed to get onto the creditors committee and started suggesting that Kmart should emerge out of bankruptcy as soon as possible but with little debt. But the idea was highly criticized by many advisers including the press. As later ironically observed by Lampert: "the large annuity aspect for advisers making $10 to $20 million per month made it less urgent for them to make [Kmart] come out of bankruptcy." But ESL and the Third Avenue Value Fund were not the usual creditors. Their power and leverage came from their willingness to put more money into the reorganized company as part of the plan.

Initially Kmart had approximately $1 billion in bank debt, $2.3 billion in bonds, $800 million in preferred stock, some amount of common stock that was worthless and approximately $4 billion of outstanding trade creditors. Edward Lampert purchased $2 billion worth of Kmart creditor claims – it has never been disclosed exactly how much he paid. During its reorganization, Kmart closed 600 stores, cut thousand of jobs and tackle logistical problems and questionable accounting practices. Kmart suppliers were awarded only about 10% of what they are owed, and that amount was paid in stock in the reorganized Kmart.

In May 2003, Kmart emerged from bankruptcy court protection. ESL Investments and the Third Avenue Value Fund converted their claims into approximately 33 million shares of the new common stock, plus a 9% convertible note with a principal amount of $60 million. The holders of Kmart's pre-petition bank debt, other than ESL, received approximately $243 million in cash. Many experts then predicted that Kmart would soon return to bankruptcy – a so-called Chapter 22 situation. They were wrong. In the quarter ended July 2003, Kmart had $1.2 billion in cash, $50 million of mortgage debt and a $2.0 billion three-year line of credit that was not drawn. In 2004, Lampert merged Kmart and Sears in a surprise $11 billion deal that created the US third largest general merchandise retailer.

10.3.2   Failed leveraged buyouts

Leveraged buyout firms are a great source of distressed debt for hedge funds that are willing to go the private equity way. Consider for instance Regal Cinemas, the largest movie theatre operator in the US in 2000, with 3831 screens in 328 theatres. Regal was originally taken private in 1998 in a combined effort of leveraged buyout specialists Hicks, Muse, Tate & Furst and Kohlberg Kravis Roberts & Co. The two buyout firms each put up about $500 million in equity to purchase the firm, but then added massive amounts of bank debt and subordinated notes on the company's balance sheet to finance major expansions. Unfortunately, Regal Cinemas turned out to be unable to support the leverage, as box office receipts fell amid harsh competition from other chains and cable television companies. In December, 2000 bank lenders refused to let the company pay interest to its subordinated bondholders because it would violate loan covenants. Regal's $2.29 billion debt officially became distressed, and the assets were only worth $1.92 billion.

Once Regal became distressed, Hicks Muse and Kohlberg Kravis were limited in what they could do legally and realistically to protect their investment – they were insiders. Distressed debt buyers Philip Anschutz and Oaktree Capital Management were better able to act on their understanding of Regal's enterprise value relative to how debt markets valued the firm. They progressively purchased 65% of Regal's outstanding senior bank debt at a discount, which gave them control over the eventual restructuring process, and purchased 95% of Regal's subordinated debt at less than 25 cents on the dollar. This bank debt was the fulcrum security that was converted into equity when Regal announced its pre-packaged Chapter 11 bankruptcy plan in September 2001. The plan granted Anschutz and Oaktree 100% of the reorganized Regal's common stock, plus payment of accrued and unpaid interest on their loans. Additionally, subordinated note holders received a pro rata share of cash with an aggregate amount of more than $181 million. General unsecured credits with claims of more than $5000 split $75 million in cash payments. Those with less than $5000 in claims received full payment and interest.

When regal exited bankruptcy, it had only $500 million of new bank debt. Anschutz and Oaktree merged Regal with Anschutz's investment in United Artists and sold 22% of the combined entity in a $342 million initial public offering. They still owned 78% of a company that had a market capitalization of $2.8 billion and generated $250 million EBITDA.

10.3.3 Direct lending

In the early 2000s, many hedge funds were flush with cash, but could not find enough attractive high-yield investments. Therefore, their managers started seeking opportunities to finance, or invest in, mid-sized companies that were cash-strapped and needed new capital but did not have the risk credentials mainstream lenders require to provide funding. Most of the time, hedge funds provided "sub-prime" or second-tier financing that a company's cash flow – not equity – secured. These loans were often for shorter time periods and attached to higher-than-market interest rates compared with conventional financing. Alternatively, these loans demanded a chunk of equity in return for their loan, or to buy stock at a discount to the current market price. Frequently, such transactions caused a dilution of the value of the shares held by existing shareholders and created a situation in which the new investors have better claims on a company's assets and income than do existing common shareholders. In exchange, however, the debtors could get relatively fast access to cash with minimal red tape or regulatory approvals. A famous example of such a deal is the battered baker Krispy Kreme Doughnuts. In early 2005, the troubled company shunned banks and obtained $225 million in loans from a group led by Credit Suisse First Boston and the hedge fund Silver Point Capital. It used the loans to pay down $90 million in other debt and provide a cash cushion.

Another famous example is the Omaha-based Level 3 Communications, one of the largest remaining fibre optics network companies. In February 2002, Level 3 was forced to deny that it might be forced to seek Chapter 11 protection as it acknowledged that it might violate a financial covenant with its bondholders later in the year. Nevertheless, in July 2002, it decided to raise $500 million in bonds to help to finance future acquisitions. Among the lenders was Berkshire Hathaway, the group of Warren Buffet. The deal boosted Level 3's cash position by 50% and bolstered its status, but it came at a stiff price. The notes paid 9% annual interest, and the holders could convert them at any time into common stock – a $3.41 conversion price. On the announcement date of the transaction, Level 3's shares leapt 59.5% to $4.61 on the news. Buffett essentially said he would only be willing to buy the stock at $3.41 a share, no matter what price the stock is trading at, and demanded that the company pay him 9% a year for the privilege of holding that right.

Recently, many large buyout firms said they have received offers from hedge funds to meet their financing needs. And some of them accepted the offer. When Texas Pacific Group wanted to refinance its buyout of retailer J. Crew Group Inc. in 2004, Black Canyon Capital LLC, an entity largely funded by Los Angeles-based hedge fund Canyon Capital Advisors, provided a 10-year loan of $275 million.

Clearly, hedge funds have brought liquidity to these debt markets while driving down lending costs for some companies and giving others in a rough patch a chance to breathe. In fact, hedge funds love direct loans, because they help to diversify their investments, have had low default

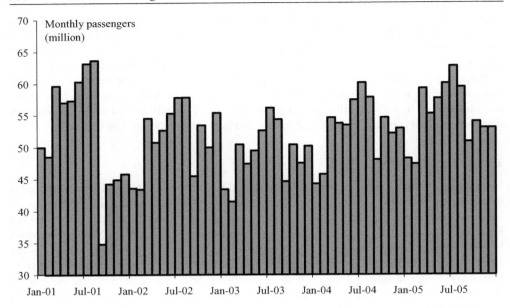

Figure 10.7 Total US airline industry domestic enplanements (in million of passengers)

rates, and offer "double digit" yields. It is therefore not surprising to see that direct lending by hedge funds has grown significantly in a few years. As a side effect, hedge funds are taking a cut of Wall Street's core business of providing financing for takeovers, rescues and bankruptcy-protection proceedings. They also are taking Wall Street's fees and services in arranging and distributing deals out of the equation.

10.3.4   The case of airlines

The air transportation industry has long been a prominent supplier of distressed debt. It has generated 12% of the largest bankruptcies recorded since 1970, and the list of Chapter 22s (twice bankrupt) includes Continental Airlines and US Airways, while the Chapter 33s (three times bankrupt) group include the now defunct Braniff and TWA. This apparent regular weakness results primarily from the high and increasing competition in a high fixed cost industry. Flying a plane between two cities requires an important fixed investment (wages, fuel, depreciation of aircraft, etc.) but only a small variable cost (essentially a sandwich, a diet coke and a napkin.[5]) As long as the fare is higher than the variable cost, it makes sense to carry an additional passenger. This results in a brutally competitive environment, with no guarantee that revenues will cover fixed costs (Figure 10.7). At the extreme, small new companies will price their seats just above their marginal cost to gain market shares. They may not survive for very long, but they will be replaced by other small companies with the same approach. The larger companies therefore have to fight this threat on a continuous basis, particularly on their most profitable segments, and this threatens their survival. And last but not least, unexpected events such as the terrorist attacks of 11 September can result in empty planes for several weeks or even

---

[5] This was in the good old days. Today, you should be happy if a low-cost airline does not charge you extras for travelling with a carry-on luggage . . .

months – many major airlines reported record losses in 2001 and 2002 and several had to file for bankruptcy.

Because of these characteristics, airline stocks tend to have a rather low intrinsic value, but a high volatility and a low average rate of return. Their long term risk-adjusted performance is obviously not attractive, and their chronic operating problems are a real concern for most investors. Nevertheless, they still have shareholders. Most of them are short-term speculators who are primarily interested in the high volatility of the stock and in its potential upward rallies.[6] Their behaviour is, in a sense, comparable to a lottery ticket – most buyers know that they will lose money on average, but each of them expects to be the winner. However, if the company goes bankrupt, many of these short-term gamblers will be willing to sell at any price . . . and hedge funds will wait and buy. More recently, distressed securities hedge funds have also turned to securitized aircraft leases, and what they call the "metal" value rather than the airlines themselves. A good illustration of this approach is provided by the Atlas Air case (Box 10.4).

Box 10.4 Atlas Air

Atlas Air is a cargo airline that operates scheduled freight flights for some of the world's leading airlines, flying to 101 cities in 46 countries. It was founded in April 1992 to specialize in the long-term contract outsourcing of Boeing 747 cargo aircraft. Its subsidiaries Atlas Air, Inc. and Polar Air Cargo Inc. operate the world's largest fleet of Boeing 747 freighter aircraft. In 1995 Atlas Air began trading publicly on the NASDAQ, and in 1997 appeared on the New York Stock Exchange. In 2001, the airline introduced a new programme of leasing and services, based on the ACMI (Aircraft, Crew, Maintenance and Insurance) model. Under this new programme, Atlas Air cargo planes would be available to other airlines for operations such as charter flights.

Atlas Air's business model was sound, but it also implied that it would be the first to leave the sector and the last to return if the aircraft outsourcing activity were to slow down – but in both cases at high prices, which was in theory an advantage. In addition, Atlas Air had to support a serious operational leverage as well as the financial leverage of an airline. To finance its fleet, Atlas Air used enhanced equipment trust certificates (EETC), which are securitized leases secured by collateral. In an EETC transaction, a trust issues series of notes backed by a collateral pool comprising secured aircraft debt or notes issued pursuant to leveraged leases of aircraft. The financial guarantors typically insured the most senior class of such notes, which benefit both from prioritization of collateral cash flows and dedicated liquidity facilities. The aircraft financed via these EETC transactions are used by the sponsoring airline, commonly under a lease or other financing arrangement. In the case of a Chapter 11 bankruptcy, the airline has the right to reject the lease or financing arrangement for aircraft that it no longer needs or that it can obtain on better terms. Such rejection causes the aircraft to be returned for disposition or releasing to new parties, thereby exposing the EETC transaction to market risk on the returned aircraft. The financial guarantors' senior position in EETC structures provides some cushion against market risks on the aircraft, as well as significant control rights on decisions regarding collateral of the EETC trusts.

The post-9/11 environment produced a dramatic excess supply of aircrafts, and capital suddenly fled the sector. Atlas had to file for bankruptcy and started negotiating its

---

[6] The stock of Delta Airlines has several months with a progression higher than 9%, and even one month at 40%.

reorganization plan. A few hedge funds rushed and bought as many EETCs at a serious discount, starting by the most senior tranches and going to the junior ones later. In the case of Atlas, the EETCs were worth $40 million, while the collateral was $120 million worth of 747-400 freighter aircraft of the 1998–2000 vintage, which were ideal for long-haul cargo. The hedge funds participated in the EETC committee, which was primarily made of passive original holders not inclined to play hardball with the company. The hedge fund was, as the market quickly realized, the real value of the EETCs – the senior tranches immediately traded up to par value (+42%). In July 2004, Atlas Air completed its restructuring plan and emerged from Chapter 11 bankruptcy protection. The junior EETC tranches were sold with an 82% profit. Had the bankruptcy been more problematic, the hedge funds would have seized the physical planes. Their view – expressed later in a conference – was that the operation would still have been extremely profitable, but on a longer term basis.

One of the hedge fund managers was actually so convinced by the profitability of these transactions that he went one step further. In March 2004, he partnered with specialists to create a dedicated aircraft leasing platform to capitalize on the opportunity. His company opportunistically purchased debt backed by aircraft collateral during the United Airlines and Delta airlines bankruptcies – most debt buyers ignore the real "metal" value of their paper – as well as planes directly from stressed airlines companies, and leases them to some of the better credits of the airline industry. In March 2006, it now owns approximately $3.5 billion worth of aircraft. Needless to say, it strongly benefited from the airline recovery and its low lease rates (due to the low book value of the aircrafts themselves) protect them from possible new competitors and open the door to numerous growth prospects.

Table 10.7 Performance comparison of the CS/Tremont Event Driven: Distressed Index, the S&P 500 and the Citigroup World Government Bond Index, 1994–2005

	CS/Tremont Event Driven: Distressed	S&P 500	Citigroup WGBI
Return (% p.a.)	13.44	8.55	5.87
Volatility (% p.a.)	6.80	16.00	6.74
Skewness	−2.89	−0.58	0.37
Kurtosis	18.70	0.61	0.37
Normally distributed?	No	No	Yes
Correlation with strategy		0.55	−0.05
Positive months frequency	81%	62%	58%
Best month performance (%)	4.10	9.67	5.94
Average positive month performance (%)	1.68	3.44	1.73
Upside participation		79%	228%
Negative months frequency	19%	38%	42%
Worst month performance (%)	−12.45	−14.58	−4.28
Average negative month performance (%)	−1.42	−3.53	−1.18
Downside participation		−254%	−342%
Max. drawdown (%)	−14.32	−46.28	−7.94
Value at Risk (1-month, 99%)	−4.06	−10.24	−3.36

10.4   HISTORICAL PERFORMANCE

The historical performance of distressed securities hedge funds has been very good, both on absolute return and risk-adjusted terms. Over the January 1994 to December 2005 period, distressed securities hedge funds, as measured by the CS/Tremont Event Driven – Distressed Index, delivered an average return of 13.44% p.a., with a volatility of 6.80%. By contrast, over the same period, the S&P 500 delivered an average return of 8.6% p.a., with a volatility of 16.0%, and the CS/Tremont Hedge Fund Index delivered an average return of 10.7% p.a., with a volatility of 8.1%. However, remember that the risky and illiquid nature of this strategy make such required returns necessary (Table 10.7 and Figure 10.8).

The track record of distressed securities hedge funds evidences large losses in 1998 (LTCM) and during the summer 2002 (default of Adelphia and Worldcom combined with several accounting scandals), as well as a negative skewness and considerable positive kurtosis. Clearly, distressed securities strategies are significantly exposed to corporate event risk and, as a result, their return distribution cannot be approximated by a normal distribution (Table 10.8 and Figure 10.9).

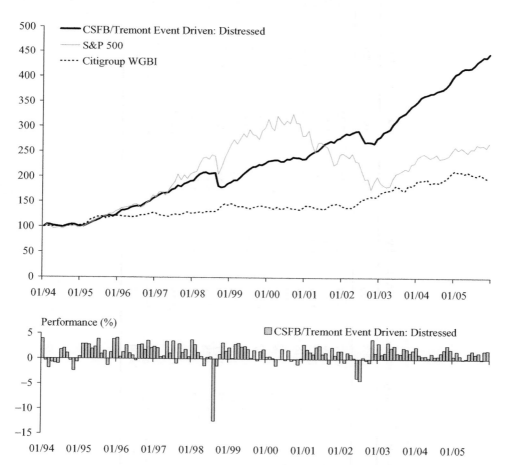

Figure 10.8   Evolution of the CS/Tremont Event Driven: Distressed Index, 1994–2005

Table 10.8 Monthly returns of the CS/Tremont Event Driven: Distressed Index, 1994–2005

	1994	1995	1996	1997	1998	1999	2000	2001	2002	2003	2004	2005
Jan	3.94	0.44	4.10	2.42	3.76	2.22	0.42	2.89	1.58	3.12	2.42	0.55
Feb	−0.34	2.89	0.36	2.16	2.80	0.07	0.49	1.92	−0.63	0.89	0.89	1.55
Mar	−1.83	2.92	1.30	0.38	1.27	2.89	0.15	1.38	1.23	1.19	0.59	0.65
Apr	−0.71	2.78	2.69	0.52	0.51	3.14	−1.32	0.99	0.89	3.27	0.66	−0.06
May	−0.84	1.96	1.09	3.45	−1.41	2.43	0.00	2.42	0.19	2.27	0.26	0.13
Jun	−0.95	2.33	0.67	1.13	0.31	2.49	2.02	2.65	−3.79	2.63	1.06	1.21
Jul	1.80	3.87	−0.33	3.53	0.39	1.96	−0.24	1.00	−4.27	1.14	0.52	1.65
Aug	2.04	0.96	2.74	−0.91	−12.45	0.19	1.77	1.25	0.28	1.02	0.56	1.00
Sep	1.11	1.55	2.84	2.97	−1.43	1.73	−0.31	−0.79	−0.25	2.21	1.23	1.24
Oct	−0.35	−1.31	1.80	1.22	0.89	−0.30	−0.09	2.35	−0.72	1.98	1.86	−0.10
Nov	−2.40	1.28	3.61	1.84	3.17	1.55	−1.06	0.76	3.91	1.21	2.67	1.63
Dec	−0.63	3.89	2.19	0.39	1.55	1.90	0.14	1.62	1.17	1.73	1.92	1.73
Total	0.66	26.13	25.54	20.74	−1.68	22.18	1.94	20.01	−0.69	25.12	15.62	11.74
S&P 500	−1.54	34.11	20.26	31.01	26.67	19.53	−10.14	−13.04	−23.37	26.38	8.99	3.00
WGBI	2.34	19.04	3.62	0.23	15.30	−4.27	1.59	−0.99	19.49	14.91	10.35	−6.88

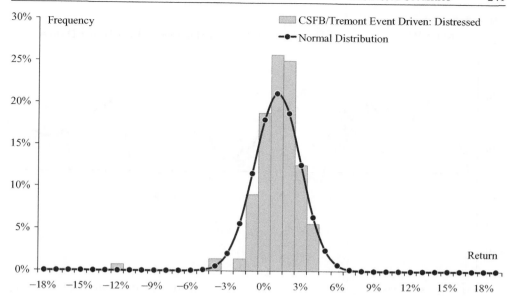

Figure 10.9 Return distribution of the CS/Tremont Event Driven: Distressed Index, 1994–2005

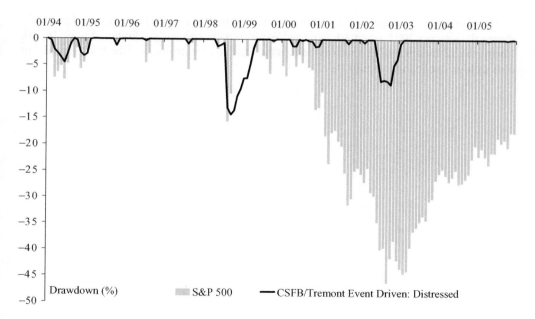

Figure 10.10 Drawdown diagram of the CS/Tremont Event Driven: Distressed Index compared to the S&P 500, 1994–2005

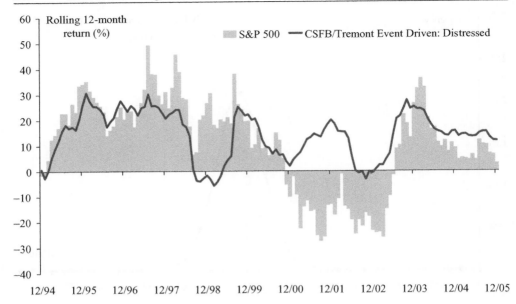

Figure 10.11 Comparison of the 12-month rolling performances of the CS/Tremont Event Driven: Distressed Index with the S&P 500, 1994–2005

The maximum drawdown of the strategy is large/small (−14.32%) and occurred precisely during the summer 2002, when Adelphia and Worldcom unexpectedly defaulted (Figure 10.10). Lastly, the 12-month rolling return evidences the relative attractiveness of the track record, but also its high cyclicality (Figure 10.11).

11
Merger Arbitrage

I don't want hedge fund managers to learn.
At least, not with my money.

Rule no.1

Merger arbitrage, also known as risk arbitrage, is usually recognized as one of the oldest event-driven strategies. Its origins date back to the 1940s, when Gustave Levy officially established the arbitrage desk at Goldman Sachs. Levy's goal was to extract value from the particular price changes of companies involved in corporate control transactions such as mergers and acquisitions. His strategy was relatively simple, but profitable: he invested in merger and acquisition targets after the deals had been announced and pocketed the spread between the market price of the target company following the announcement and the deal price upon closing. This spread was usually narrow and only offered a modest nominal total return. However, since most deals closed in much less than a year's time, Levy was able to translate this modest total return into a much more attractive annualized return figure.

Although merger arbitrage has not evolved much since its origins, the arbitrage desk of Goldman Sachs maintained its reputation and continued to attract talent like a magnet. Among others, its list of alumni includes the former United States Treasury Secretary Robert E. Rubin, as well as his protégés: the star hedge fund managers Daniel Och (Och Ziff), Richard Perry (Perry Partners) and Thomas Steyer (Farallon Capital). But before getting into the details of their strategy, let us first shed some light on the fuel of merger arbitrage, that is, the extraordinary development of mergers and acquisitions in the 20th century.

11.1 MERGERS AND ACQUISITIONS: A HISTORICAL PERSPECTIVE

One of the most conspicuous features of mergers is that they usually come in waves that coincide with increases in share prices and price/earnings ratios. In the US, economists have identified five waves of takeovers, mergers and consolidations. The start date and duration of each of these waves are not specific, although the end dates may be more definite for those that ended in panics, crashes or other financial disasters.

The first merger wave (1895 to 1903) is referred to as "merging for monopoly", because it marked the transition from freely competitive, entrepreneurial capitalism to monopolistic, corporate capitalism. It consisted principally of horizontal mergers, which were supported by the formation of a nationwide market – the emergence of railroads and telegraph making it possible for large companies to produce and distribute their goods on a larger scale. Several dominant firms were created during the first merger wave. Noteworthy among them were Rockefeller's Standard Oil, General Motors, General Electric, AT&T, International Harvester, Du Pont, US Rubber, US Steel, Coca Cola, as well as all the "trusts" that dominated most industries at the beginning of the 20th century. However, the first merger wave petered out with the market panics of 1904 and 1907 and finally ground to a halt with the onset of the First World War.

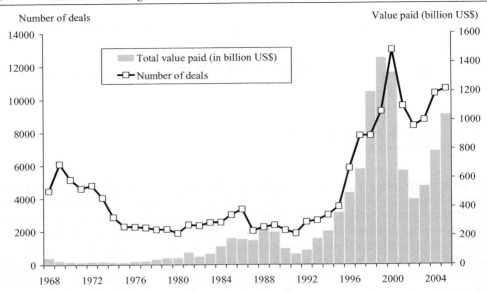

Figure 11.1 Evolution of the M&A activity in the US

The second merger wave (1920 to 1929) is referred to as "merging for oligopoly". It saw further consolidation in the industries that had been involved in the first wave, but there was also a huge increase in vertical integration, particularly in electricity and gas utilities as well as manufacturing firms (e.g. Bethlehem Steel). The second merger wave was brought to an end with the 1929 market crash and the Great Depression.

The third merger wave (1955 to 1973) was fuelled by a bullish stock market and the emergence of new sources of financing (e.g. issues of convertible preferred stocks and debentures). It was also during this wave that several large investment banks followed Goldman Sachs and established their own merger arbitrage desks. The third merger wave resulted in the creation of large conglomerates, essentially through the mergers of companies engaged in non-related activities, examples being IT&T, LTV and Litton. Most of these conglomerates generated power and prestige for their managers, but made no economic sense. Consequently, the third merger wave ended with the oil crisis and a severe decline in the market value of conglomerates ensued (Figure 11.1).

The fourth merger wave took place between 1974 and 1989. It is generally referred to as the "takeover wave", and corresponds to the golden era of merger arbitrage. Buoyed by the accommodating regulatory environment, the low level of interest rates and the easy access to junk bonds, the number of hostile predatory takeovers and leveraged buyouts exploded. Most of these mergers were made in anticipation of gains from three interrelated sources. First, strategic acquisition firms enjoyed synergy gains by expanding their operations in their own industry or business. Second, bidders in financial takeovers produced gains by eliminating the value-destroying effects of excessive diversification, e.g. breaking up inefficient conglomerates and dismembering undervalued companies. Third, bidders purchasing poor performing targets benefited from replacing the existing management, while leaving the target with enough new junk debt to motivate whoever was left.[1]

---

[1] Kaplan (1989) showed that tax savings from leverage explained at least 50% and up to 100% of the takeover premium paid by the bidders for target company stock in leveraged buyouts.

Box 11.1 Ivan Boesky: the world's most (in)famous arbitrageur

Ivan Boesky, on whom Michael Douglas's character of Gordon Gekko was modelled in the Oscar-winning movie "Wall Street", is probably still today the most famous merger arbitrageur. Boesky originally graduated from the Detroit College of Law. When he came to New York, he rapidly went into the merger arbitrage business and started making investments in announced takeover deals, with moderate success. However, in May 1982, Gulf Oil announced the failure of its takeover of Cities Service. Boesky lost $24 million in the deal, which convinced him that he lacked the magic touch. He therefore decided to switch tactics and go in for insider trading.

Illegally obtaining tips about impending mergers through a network of contacts he had set up, Boesky started buying and selling stock *before* the mergers became public knowledge. Among his major sources was the investment banker Martin Siegel of Kidder Peabody. Boesky rapidly accumulated personal gains estimated at more than $200 million and became one of the guru investors on Wall Street. He created the Hudson Fund, the first hedge fund specializing in merger arbitrage, for which Dennis Levine of Drexel Burnham Lambert agreed to raise over $600 million through a junk offering. This resulted in almost $24 million in fees for Levine . . . and a new source of insider tips for Boesky.

Ivan Boesky's activities finally attracted the attention of the Securities and Exchange Commission (SEC), which became suspicious of unusual transactions on stocks prior to public announcements of pending mergers. Convicted of crimes relating to insider trading, Boesky was sentenced to three years in prison, a $50 million fine and $50 million disgorgement. He agreed to cooperate with the SEC in its investigations. This led to several other major court cases and cast a pall over the arbitrage community as well as its supporters. On 13 February 1990, the investment bank Drexel Burnham Lambert filed for bankruptcy and went into liquidation. Its guru, Michael Milken, was indicted by a federal grand jury, much to the distress of junk bond holders who saw him as a buyer of last resort. After plea-bargaining, Milken pleaded guilty to six securities and reporting violations. He paid a $200 million fine and another $400 million in settlements, served about 22 months in prison (from March 1991 to January 1993) and was banned for life from the securities industry.

Surfing on the utter euphoria of leveraged buyouts and boosted by the unprecedented set of opportunities offered by the numerous corporate-control deals, the market reached one of the greatest paroxysms of speculation and usury that the world has ever seen.[2] Legendary figures such as Michael Milken and his Wall Street associates, Ivan Boesky, Dennis Levine and Martin Siegel became the symbols of the decade of greed (see Box 11.1). However, in 1989, the bull market suddenly came to an end when the proposed leveraged buyout of United Airlines fell apart because the management team and employees could not get the $6.5 billion proposed financing. Several leveraged companies declared bankruptcy in late 1989, followed by Drexel Burnham Lambert, the leading investment bank on the junk bond market. The sun thus set on the golden era of merger arbitrage.

The fifth merger wave began in 1993 and is still under way. It is by far the greatest merger wave in history, both in terms of number of deals and their size. Most of its transactions were driven by consolidators and focused on strategic rather than purely financial considerations.

---

[2] For example, the RJR Nabisco leveraged buyout generated senior bank debt of about $15 billion, $5 billion of subordinated debt, and an additional $5 billion of junk bonds that paid interest . . . in other junk bonds.

Merging companies were responding to changing technology, the globalization of the economy, industry upheaval, or deregulation. The relatively restrained anti-trust environment in the US led to once-unthinkable combinations, such as Citibank and Travellers, Chrysler and Daimler Benz, Exxon and Mobil, Boeing and McDonnell Douglas, or AOL and Time Warner. For the first time, international mergers also represented a significant part of the activity, thanks to (i) the adoption in Europe of a true single market with a single currency; (ii) the deregulation and privatization especially of utilities and financial services; (iii) the liberalization of *de jure* or *de facto* restrictions on the foreign ownership of domestic firms, notably in Japan and Korea; and (iv) rising stock market valuations that made the financing of M&A transactions cheaper.

During the fifth wave, thanks to very high market valuations, stock rather than cash became the preferred medium of payment. Of course, the equity bubble which burst in early 2000 took all equity markets down and the economy along with it. The merger market rapidly dried up, and thousands of highly paid stock analysts and investment bankers were tossed out on to the street, their Hermes ties flapping in the wind. But the merger market progressively recovered after 2002, thanks to the combination of a stronger economy, a buoyant stock market, and low interest rates. Remember that Wall Street is now populated with thousands of new private equity boutiques – many of them started up by laid-off bankers. These new players have a lot of cash to spend on target companies and are the most aggressive buyers.

11.2   IMPLEMENTING MERGER ARBITRAGE: BASIC PRINCIPLES

As summarized in the flow chart of Figure 11.2, the investment process of a merger arbitrageur is relatively simple. The starting point is usually the announcement of a merger or a takeover, most of the time just after the close of the market. The acquiring entity makes a tender offer to the current shareholders of the target company, inviting them to sell their shares at a fixed price usually set *above* the last quoted market price. The difference between the offered price and the last quoted market price is called the *arbitrage spread*.

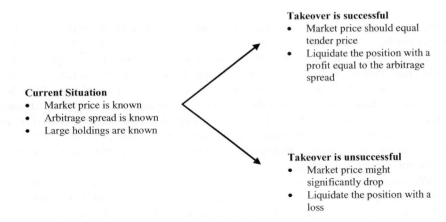

Figure 11.2   A typical takeover process from a merger arbitrageur's perspective

Immediately after the announcement, merger arbitrageurs start gathering as much information as possible about the target and the bidder. This is then analysed. They have essentially two cases to consider: (i) the transaction is successful, the market price of the target shares rises and converges towards the offered price; or (ii) the transaction is not successful, the market price of the target shares diverges from the offered price and may fall dramatically. Each case must be carefully assessed, both in terms of probability of success (subjective and market-implied) and in terms of associated risk (worst case dollar loss). If the risk/return ratio looks favourable, the merger arbitrageur may decide to take a position.

The evolution of the arbitrage spread the next day at the market opening is crucial to understanding the consensus view. Most of the time, the spread tends to be wide at the opening then to shrink before stabilizing at a lower level. Several theories may explain this behaviour. First, the wide opening spread is part of a process of price discovery. The market is not perfectly efficient, and the first minutes of trading represent the time in which the market "finds" the right price for the arbitrage spread. Second, the parties to the transaction often hold conference calls in the morning during the trading day, and the spread movements may simply reflect the dissemination of information in conference calls or SEC filings in a typical deal.

In this environment, institutional holders of the target stock are often concerned that it no longer trades based on fundamentals but rather at a premium based on expectations of the deal outcome. Given their lack of expertise in merger analysis, they would rather monetize a significant portion of the initial merger premium while eliminating exposure to deal risk. Unfortunately, once the deal is announced, they are typically unable to find other institutional buyers for their stocks at merger-premium inflated prices, and they are not allowed to hedge their exposure by selling short the bidder stock. By contrast, merger arbitrageurs are willing to act as a warehouse of merger deal risk, if the associated returns are attractive. They will set up a position that will be profitable if their assessments are correct. The nature of this position varies depending on the type of merger considered, as we shall see.

11.2.1 Arbitraging a cash tender offer

Let us first consider the case of a cash tender offer, i.e. where the acquiring company offers a fixed amount of cash in exchange for each share of the target company (e.g. Box 11.2). As already mentioned, to convince investors to tender their shares, the bid price usually includes a premium with respect to the target's current share price on the market. At a date 30–90 days before the announcement, the premium can be quite large – say 30 to 50% over the market value of the target company. However, by the time of public announcement, the premium has normally shrunk to between 5 and 15%. This shrinkage is obviously due to astute analyst trading in anticipation of the merger as well as inevitable illegal insider trading.

After the announcement and filing of the takeover offer, the market price of the target firm usually moves upward again, but it still does not reach the bid price. The remaining gap between the bid and the market price (the *arbitrage spread*) is usually expressed as the percentage difference between the initial bid price and the target's closing price on the day after the acquisition announcement. This arbitrage spread is precisely what most arbitrageurs are trying to capture – if the transaction is successful, it should converge to zero.

The typical cash tender offer arbitrage trade involves purchasing the target stock on announcement of the takeover and holding it until the end of the offer period. If the bid is successful, the target stock will be sold to the bidder and the full merger arbitrage spread will be captured. Otherwise, the arbitrageur will sell the target stock, perhaps at a loss.

Box 11.2 The cash offer of First Data Corp. on Paymentech Inc.

On 22 March 1999, First Data Corp., an Atlanta-based provider of electronic commerce solutions, announced that it was offering $25.50 in cash for each publicly held share of Paymentech Inc., a company providing full-service electronic payment solutions. The deal was expected to close within four months.

Figure 11.3 shows the movement of the Paymentech share price during 1999. It can be seen that the shares closed at $24 on 22 March, and even went down to $23.25 on 23 March. We can therefore realistically assume that arbitrageurs were able to buy shares at $24 just after the deal announcement. This represents a 6.25% discount with respect to the bid price. The daily trading volume (bottom curve, in thousands of shares) confirms a peak in the trading activity between 22 and 24 March, probably due to risk arbitrage.

On 13 May, First Data received clearance from the Department of Justice for its proposed acquisition, and Paymentech's share price started converging towards $25.50. The deal was successfully closed on 27 July 1999. First Data acquired all of Paymentech's publicly traded shares, and Paymentech became a limited liability company. Paymentech was then merged with Bank One Payment Services, First Data's merchant bank alliance with Bank One Corp. Arbitrageurs that bought shares at $24 were able to sell them at $25.50, i.e. a $1.50 gain (+6.25%) in four months.

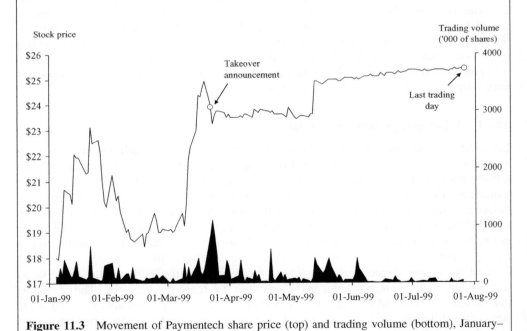

Figure 11.3 Movement of Paymentech share price (top) and trading volume (bottom), January–August 1999

The First Data/Paymentech transaction – see Box 11.2 – was a relatively low-risk deal. In fact, the probability of the deal not going through was extremely limited, because Bank One was already the major shareholder of Paymentech (52.5%) and had a merchant processing alliance with First Data. Bank One therefore supported and even encouraged the transaction. Of course, the merger arbitrage spread was relatively narrow and offered a somewhat modest nominal total return (6.25%, before transaction costs). But this return was achieved over a period of four months, after which the capital was available again for another transaction.

The major risk faced by merger arbitrageurs in a cash tender offer comes from the market risk of their long positions. If equity markets start collapsing in the middle of a deal, their long holdings will fall in value, and the likelihood of their deals being successful is also significantly reduced. To hedge this risk, merger arbitrageurs may sell short equity index futures. This is usually done at the portfolio level rather than transaction by transaction. However, this hedge only offers partial protection, because companies involved in mergers may behave differently from the overall equity market – and in particular lose more money than the market in the case of a deal failure (Box 11.3).

Box 11.3 The cash offer of Nestlé on Ralston Purina

On 16 January 2001, Nestlé S.A., the world's largest food company, and Ralston Purina Company, the premier dry pet food company in North America, announced that they had entered into a merger agreement (Figure 11.4). Under this agreement, Nestlé would acquire all of the outstanding shares of Ralston Purina for US$ 33.50 per share in cash. The transaction had an enterprise value of $10.3 billion ($10 billion equity plus $1.2 billion of net debt, minus $0.9 billion of financial investments) and would be financed by an issue of dollar-denominated debt. The agreement was subject to both regulatory and Ralston Purina shareholders' approval, and the expected completion date was at the latest the end of 2001.

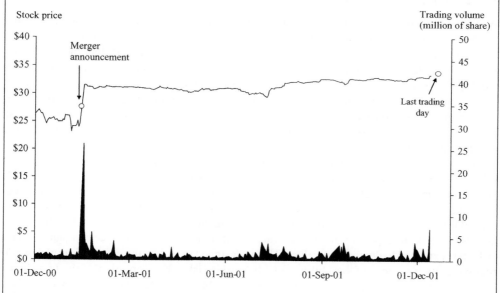

Figure 11.4   Movement of Ralston Purina share price (top) and trading volume (bottom), 2001

The Nestlé offer represented a premium of 34% over the $25 closing price of Ralston Purina on the previous trading day. Ralston Purina shares became the most actively traded on the electronic trading network, Instinet, where investors could get in their trades before the opening bell. At the opening, the shares shot up to $31.50. The post-announcement premium was 6.36% ($2/$31.50). At this stage, arbitrageurs had the opportunity to buy Ralston Purina shares at $31.50 and eventually turn them in for a cash value of $33.50, pocketing the $2 difference (less transaction costs).

The merger went ahead successfully. On 21 May 2001, the shareholders of Ralston Purina Company approved the deal. On 11 December 2001, the Federal Trade Commission announced its proposed consent order, only requesting that several brands of pet food (e.g. "Meow Mix") be divested to meet anti-trust concerns.

Before going any further, it must be stressed that merger arbitrage is fundamentally different from insider trading. Unlike Ivan Boesky, the majority of merger arbitrageurs today only invest in *publicly announced transactions*, once the terms of the deal are known and the initial market reaction has taken place. Merger arbitrageurs provide liquidity to the marketplace and buy typically from those who do not want to bear the risk of waiting to see if a deal will be consummated. In a sense, they leave money on the table and only capture the last coppers of each deal, but this allows them to evaluate more precisely the likelihood of success. Of course, there exist also a few pre-emptive arbitrageurs, who invest in unannounced transactions, i.e. securities subject to rumours or securities that the arbitrageurs think will become involved in arbitrage transactions in the near future. But this approach is not typical of the merger arbitrage industry.

11.2.2   Arbitraging a stock-for-stock offer (fixed exchange rate)

Another simple profitable situation for merger arbitrageurs is the case of stock mergers, where the bidder offers a fixed quantity of its own common stock in exchange for a fixed quantity of target shares, in lieu of cash. This case is slightly more complicated than the cash offer, because the reference price for the target (used to calculate the arbitrage spread) is no longer fixed, but depends on the bidder's stock price. It is no longer sufficient to buy the target stock and have it converted into the bidder's stock. The bidder's stock may fall significantly, so that the converted shares once the merger is completed will be worth less than their initial purchase price. It is therefore necessary to consider the relative evolution of both stocks to establish the arbitrage position.

In a stock-for-stock offer, the spread between the two companies is expected to narrow in relative terms. In a sense, the bidder's stock price is expected to fall *relative* to the target's stock price and the target stock price is expected to rise *relative* to the bidder's stock price. To make money, the arbitrageur must sell short the spread between the two companies. The typical arbitrage strategy therefore consists of buying the target company's stock (which sells at a discount with respect to the offered value) and selling short the bidder company's stock (which is expected to decrease in value). This is designed to isolate the expected spread, while removing other sources of variability, notably market risk. The proportion of the two shares of stock should be the same as the one used in the bidder's offer. Note that since this is a long/short position, the arbitrageur no longer cares about the absolute price variations of the target and bidder shares – he is only interested in their relative evolution (see Box 11.4).

Box 11.4 Microsoft versus Visio

On 15 September 1999, Microsoft Corp. announced that it would acquire Visio Corp., a supplier of enterprise-wide business diagramming and technical drawing software quoted on the Nasdaq. The terms of the acquisition were a fixed share exchange ratio of 0.45 shares of Microsoft for every Visio share. Any fractional shares that resulted from the exchange would be paid in cash based on a Microsoft share average closing price for each of the 20 trading days ending on 31 December 1999. Although the acquisition received the support of Jeremy Jaech, president and chief executive officer of Visio, its completion still required approval both by regulators and by Visio shareholders.

Figure 11.5 shows the movement of the Visio share price from September 1999 to January 2000. On 15 September, Visio shares closed at $39.875 and Microsoft at $92.625. According to the terms of the merger, a Visio share was worth $41.681 – that is, there was a $1.806 merger spread.

Note that a Visio shareholder should have disregarded this spread, since what mattered for him was the price at which Microsoft would trade once the merger had closed and he had received his Microsoft shares. His attention would focus on the absolute variations in the Microsoft share price, hoping that it would increase. A merger arbitrageur, however, would have had a different approach. To capture the spread, he would have bought Visio shares and sold short 0.45 Microsoft shares for any Visio share purchased. His only concern would have been the price difference between his long and his short positions, that is, the narrowing or widening of the spread.

The deal was completed successfully on 10 January 2000, for a total amount of $1.5 billion. Looking at the trading volume once again confirms the unusual activity around the announcement date and just before the exchange of securities.

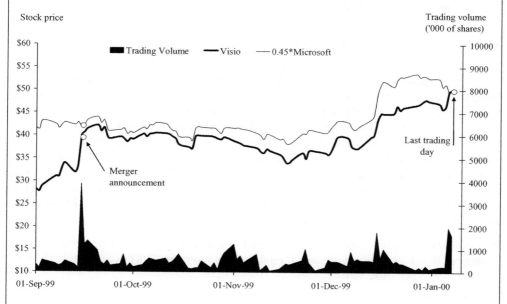

Figure 11.5 Movement of the share prices of Microsoft (top line) and Visio (middle line), and Visio trading volume (bottom), September 1999–January 2000

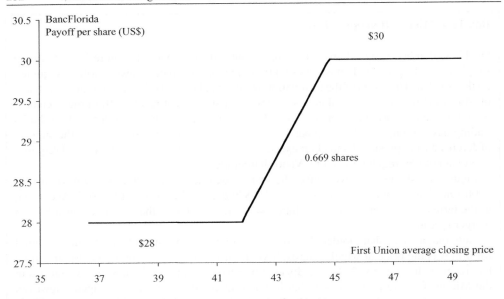

Figure 11.6   The fixed collar offer of First Union and BancFlorida

In stock-for-stock offers, the actions of merger arbitrageurs are not neutral for the share prices of the underlying companies. In particular, the process of selling short the acquiring company's stock may lead to a significant decline in the share prices, particularly when the acquiring company is not very large. Mitchell, Pulvino and Stafford (2004) attributed almost half of the average decline in the acquiring company's stock (normally 1–2% on the day of announcement) to this phenomenon.

11.2.3   Arbitraging more complex offers

In addition to cash offers and plain vanilla stock for stock offers, one can also find *collar offers*, in which the number of shares given to target shareholders depends on the acquirer's stock price during a period of time near the merger closing date. In practice, there are two major types of collar offers, namely fixed collars and floating collars.

A *fixed collar* aims at reducing the threat of overpayment for the bidder or underpayment for the target in a merger deal. In a fixed collar offer, the bidder fixes the exchange ratio between the two shares and defines a price range within which his stock price must remain. If the bidder's stock price moves outside the range, either the target or the bidder has the option to cancel or renegotiate the deal, or there is a cap and a floor on the dollar value of the deal. Consider for instance the example of the merger between First Union and BancFlorida Financial (Figure 11.6). The terms were set as follows:

- BancFlorida's shareholders will receive 0.669 shares of First Union common stock for each share of BancFlorida common stock if First Union's common stock price is between $41.875 and $44.875 per share.[3]

---

[3] To avoid market manipulation, the calculation of First Union's common stock price was based upon the average closing price of First Union common stock for the ten trading days prior to the effective date of the acquisition.

- If First Union's common stock price is below $41.875, BancFlorida's shareholders will receive $28 of First Union common stock for each share of BancFlorida common stock.
- If First Union's common stock price is above $44.875, BancFlorida shareholders will receive $30 of First Union common stock for each share of BancFlorida common stock.

A *floating collar* aims at reducing the threat that the bidder will give away too large a percentage of ownership in the merged firm or that the target will receive too small a percentage. In a floating collar deal, until just before the shareholders vote to approve or reject the merger, the exchange ratio floats within a maximum and minimum level negotiated by the firms in order to yield a constant dollar amount. Once again, if the bidder's stock price moves outside the specified range, either the target or the bidder has the option to cancel or renegotiate the deal. Say for instance the bidder offers not less than one share and not more than two shares of its common stock in exchange for each share of the target's common stock (1:1 to 2:1 ratio). The exact number of shares to be exchanged is determined by dividing a constant dollar amount (the offer price) by the average closing price of the bidder for some number of trading days prior to the shareholder vote. Suppose that the constant dollar amount is $50 and the average bidder's price for 10 days prior to the shareholder vote is $40. In this case, the exchange ratio would be 1.25 to 1 ($50/$40), which is within the prespecified range.

With floating collars, the dollar value of the deal may also be fixed for a given range of the acquirer's stock price, but it varies if the acquirer's price moves beyond the boundaries. For instance, in the merger between BioShield Technologies Inc. and AHT Corp., the terms were as follows:

- AHT shareholders will receive $1.75 worth of BioShield common stock if the average closing trading price of BioShield common stock, as determined in accordance with the merger agreement, is between $6.00 and $18.00 per share.
- AHT shareholders will receive 0.29167 (=$1.75/6) BioShield shares for each AHT share if the BioShield stock price is $6.00 or less and 0.09722 ($1.75/18) BioShield shares if the BioShield stock price is $18.00 or above.

The arbitrage of a collar merger is similar to a stock-for-stock arbitrage. The only difference is that, rather than having a fixed exchange ratio, the exchange ratio fluctuates continuously. Consequently, the arbitrageur must continuously adjust the long and short positions in his portfolio to match the terms of the offer and have the correct hedge in place. These adjustments are similar to the trades that are required when delta-hedging an option – readers who are familiar with option payoff graphs will clearly see them in Figures 11.6 and 11.7.

In a sense, a collar is a portfolio of options on the bidding firm whose time to maturity is equal to the deal duration. The arbitrageur must therefore purchase the target share of stock and sell short Δ shares of the bidding firm to hedge, where Δ is the delta of the equivalent portfolio of options. As an illustration, a fixed collar can be seen as a bullish spread, i.e. a long position in calls with a lower strike price and a short position in calls with a higher strike price on the bidding firm. In our first example, a share of BancFlorida was analogous to 0.669 calls on First Union with a strike price of $41.875 and a short position of 0.669 calls with a strike price of $44.875. The delta of the combined option portfolio was simply 0.669 times the delta of one call option, minus 0.669 times the delta of the put option. Similarly, a floating collar can be seen as a combination of a long position in call options and a short position in put options on the bidding firm. In our second example, a share of AHT Corp. was similar to 0.09722 shares of call options on BioShield Technologies Inc. with a strike price of $18.00 and a short

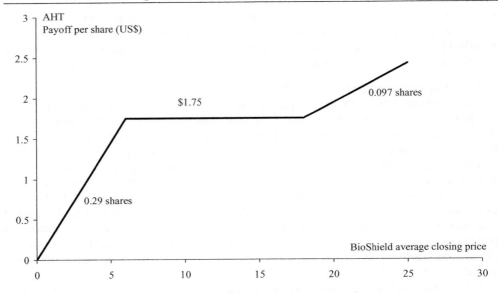

Figure 11.7 The floating collar offer of BioShield Technologies Inc. and AHT Corp.

position of 0.29167 shares of puts with a strike price of $6. The delta of the combined option portfolio was simply 0.09722 times the delta of the call option, minus 0.29167 times the delta of the put option.

More complex collar offers – and in particular the ones where one party retains the right to cancel the deal – can be seen as a barrier exchange option. An exchange option is defined as an option to exchange one asset for another. Since a merger is an agreement to exchange some amount of the bidder's stock for some amount of the target's stock, it can be viewed as an exchange option. The barrier feature allows the cancellation of the option if the bidder's stock price surpasses the upper or lower boundary. From a theoretical point of view, the problem is relatively easy to solve as long as the bidder's stock price does not get close to any of the boundaries of the collar – if it does, the deal may be cancelled or renegotiated and the spread may widen significantly. In practice, however, one must remain attentive to issues such as the liquidity and the bid – ask spreads of the underlying securities, as they can dramatically affect the implementation of the readjustment of the hedge and therefore the profitability of the arbitrage.

Of course, there are also more complicated deal structures involving preferred stocks, warrants, debentures, and other securities concerned in the takeover. There are also takeovers or mergers that result in multiple bids. But most of them can be arbitraged in a way that is similar to the fixed and floating collars.

11.3   THE RISKS INHERENT IN MERGER ARBITRAGE

Simply stated, merger arbitrage is essentially a bet on whether a merger will be successful or not. In such a transaction, the risk does not really relate to the size of the potential profits – since most arbitrageurs only take their positions *after* the announcement of the merger terms, the initial spread is known and corresponds to their maximum gain. The risk is rather in the likelihood of the transaction going through (*transaction risk*) and on its timing (*calendar risk*).

Consider first *transaction risk*. According to Branch and Yang (2003), the median probability of successful consummation of all mergers is 89%, but several exogenous and endogenous factors may affect the likelihood of a given merger. Empirically, the probability of deal success is likely to be correlated with:

- The acquirer's attitude. A hostile attitude leads to use of takeover defence mechanisms which reduce the chances of a successful bid. According to Branch and Yang (2003), a friendly negotiated offer is 20 times more likely to succeed than a hostile tender offer.
- The type of deal. Again according to Branch and Yang (2003), the success rate is slightly higher for flexible stock-for-stock exchanges (93%), and slightly lower for cash and fixed stock-for-stock exchanges (87 and 88%, respectively).
- The takeover premium. The higher the premium offered, the better the chances that the deal will be accepted by the shareholders of the acquired firm.
- The ownership structure of the target company. In particular, if the target company has a lot of merger arbitrageurs as shareholders, the deal is more likely to happen because they will vote in favour of consummation in order to protect their own interests.[4]
- The bidders' toehold – see Betton and Eckbo (2000).
- The target management attitude – see Schwert (2000).
- The lock-up options granted by the target managers – see Burch (2001).
- The presence of potential bidders and arbitrageurs before deals are publicly announced.
- The number of arbitrageurs involved. Arbitrageurs all have long positions in the target company and, in any contested issue, will vote in favour of consummation in order to protect their own interests.[5]
- The presence of anti-trust considerations. For instance, in the US, the parties involved in a merger may be in possession of a preliminary favourable opinion from the Department of Justice prior to announcement, but they still have to obtain the approval of the Federal Trade Commission. The latter approval is often conditioned on the divestment of key holdings of the target company (or the acquiring firm), which may make the merger infeasible.
- The economic conditions. A deteriorating economy is usually unfavourable to mergers.

The *calendar risk* (e.g. Box 11.5) denotes the uncertainty relative to the time that will elapse between the announcement and the consummation of the merger, assuming that the merger does indeed go through. Although this risk is not easily predictable, deals with large premiums at their date of announcement generally involve a long time period between announcement and consummation – see Mitchell and Pulvino (2001). High premiums are often associated with issues of uncertainty about final resolution, and some of these issues are likely to take a long time to resolve.

---

[4] The intuitive explanation for the success of merger arbitrageurs is that they are better informed than the market about the probability of deal success. However, recent theories suggest that arbitrageurs may have a significant impact on the takeover process, regardless of their ability or inability to predict the takeover outcome. For instance, Cornelli and Li (2001) have developed an information-based model in which the information advantage that an arbitrageur possesses arises from his own position rather than from his ability to predict outcomes.

[5] This results in an asymmetry of information in favour of some arbitrageurs, if they know the exact number of shares they control. This also explains why, after a tender offer, the trading volume usually increases dramatically, in large part because of risk arbitrageurs accumulating shares.

Box 11.5 An example of calendar risk

On 7 July 2001, Mars announced its intention to acquire the French pet food specialist Royal Canin. Mars' French subsidiary, Masterfoods Holding, entered into an agreement with BNP Paribas for the acquisition of its 56.4% interest in Royal Canin, offering €145 per share in cash. As required by the French regulation in such a case, Mars extended its offer to the remaining Royal Canin shareholders, and filed its offer with the EU Competition Commission.

Arbitrageurs immediately grasped that, if successful, the transaction would give Mars a share of more than 40% in the dog dry food market, mainly in France and Germany. This could be a potential threat to competition, so the expected timing of the transaction close was estimated to be mid-February 2002. Nevertheless, Mars indicated that it was seeking EU approval within the short Phase I rather than the long Phase II procedure,[6] and therefore started discussing potential disposals with the EU Competition Commission.

Surprisingly, the Commission made an unusual decision after an extended first-stage review: it granted its approval but made it conditional upon agreement on the potential buyers of divested assets. The Commission was in fact concerned that the divested assets could fall into the hands of a big competitor such as Nestlé, and therefore, could hamper competition. Thus, it took Mars another two and a half months to find a buyer acceptable to the Commission, and the deal was finally completed in July 2002.

In order to be successful, merger arbitrageurs must endeavour to be better informed than the average investor in order to evaluate accurately these transaction and calendar risks. Indeed, the consequences of a takeover being delayed, renegotiated or abandoned can have dramatic consequences, which are usually much weightier than the profits that would have been obtained if the deal had succeeded. An illustration is provided by the thwarted merger of General Electric and Honeywell (see Box 11.6), which was the first instance of European authorities vetoing a US-only merger that had already been given clearance by the American Justice Department and 11 other jurisdictions. This rejection represented the culmination of over a decade of growth, development, and changes in European competition policy. It showed that the Europeans were increasingly committed to being major players on the global anti-trust stage.

Box 11.6 A deal that was stymied: General Electric and Honeywell International

On 22 October 2000, General Electric announced its intention to buy Honeywell International in a stock-for-stock transaction valued at $45 billion. The merger was supposed to generate more than $1.5 billion in annual cost savings, and was favourably welcomed by most analysts. Given the size of the two companies, most merger arbitrageurs jumped on the transaction.

The terms of the offer were 1.055 shares of General Electric for each share of Honeywell. The transaction came 10 months after the former Allied Signal had bought Honeywell and assumed the name. Honeywell's shares had since dropped by one-third. Discussions on an offer from United Technologies to acquire Honeywell had just terminated a few days

---

[6] A Phase I review has a timeframe of three weeks, plus a possible three-week extension. A Phase II review is more procedural and requires up to three months, plus an appropriate extension in "extraordinary circumstances".

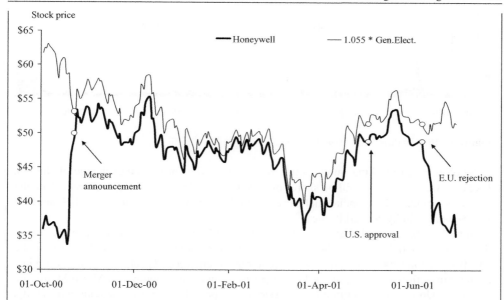

Figure 11.8 Evolution of the arbitrage spread between Honeywell and General Electric

before – General Electric topped the offer by United Technologies, based on the pre-announcement closing prices, by 14.6% (Figure 11.8).

At the beginning of October, Honeywell was trading at $35–$37 a share, with a daily volume of 3 to 4 million shares. On 20 October, two days before the announcement, the share price jumped to $46 with a daily volume of 22 million shares. On 23 October, it reached $49.9375 with a daily volume of 39.3 million shares (Figure 11.9).

In contrast, General Electric was trading at $58–$59 a share at the beginning of October, with a daily volume of 9 to 10 million shares. On 20 October, the share price dropped to $52.25 with a daily volume of 14.6 million shares. On 23 October, it sank to $49.75 with a daily volume of 50.2 million shares (Figure 11.10).

On 2 May 2001, after close scrutiny of the competition effects in the production of jet engines, automation controls and industrial sensors, the US Department of Justice approved the merger. This reinforced the likelihood of the merger, with the result that on 18 May, Honeywell peaked at $53.25 and General Electric at $52.99, that is, an arbitrage spread

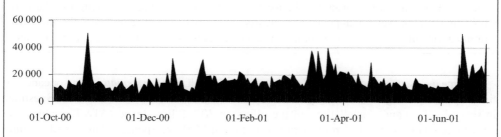

Figure 11.9 Trading volume of General Electric

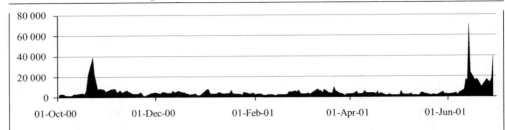

Figure 11.10   Trading volume of Honeywell

of $2.65 per share (taking into account the 1.055 coefficient for the exchange of shares). Investors were short 130 million shares of General Electric, five times more than before the deal was announced. Financial analysts estimated that about $1 billion worth of Honeywell shares were held by risk arbitrageurs.

Initially, arbitrageurs believed this transaction would receive regulatory approval, though there was much debate as to whether the transaction would receive a Phase II review in the EU. In early June 2001, the spread widened as reports emerged of problems in the EU review of the transaction. On 14 June 2001, after several rounds of negotiations, Mario Monti, the European Union's Competition Commissioner, surprised the entire financial community. He announced the Commission's intention to reject the proposed merger between General Electric and Honeywell International, despite the General Electric offer to divest $2.2 billion in assets. The official motive was the European Union's concern that the combined company might use its airplane-leasing units to dominate the market for jet engines and aviation electronics. This was the first time that the European Union had reached a conclusion different to that of the US anti-trust authorities. Honeywell stock sank from $42.26 to $37.10 in a record volume of 71 million shares, while General Electric shares gained $1 at $48.86, also in a record volume of 50 million shares.

The European Union acted to block the transaction on 3 July 2001. While the deal was not officially terminated until 2 October 2001, the consensus view was that the deal was already dead and the firms had already begun trading based on their own fundamental values. The deal's collapse hurt most merger arbitrage funds – given its size, the deal was in almost everyone's portfolio. It created a climate of risk aversion and dampened merger arbitrage activity for several months. It also caused merger spreads to be extremely sensitive to rumours, particularly for transactions with regulatory issues, e.g. GPU/First Energy, Ralston Purina/Nestlé, Quaker Oats/Pepsi Co. Note that since the GE/Honeywell case, several other high profile deals have foundered during their approval process, e.g. Airtours/First Choice, Interbrew/Bass, or the Tesco/Sainsbury/Asda bids for Safeway. All these failed deals went through a Phase I examination followed by a lengthy Phase II investigation, and several appeals. This clearly shows that a full assessment of the anti-trust implications of deals involving competing companies is essential for merger arbitrageurs.

In some cases, unexpected market events may also result in the *systematic* delay or cancellation of pending mergers. For example, the September 2001 terrorist attacks on the US resulted in several delays and cancellations of the offers on AT&T Broadband (AT&T's cable business, targeted by Comcast), Brooks Brothers (a unit of Marks & Spencer), Hughes Electronics (owned by General Motors), Compaq Computer (targeted by Hewlett Packard), Tempus Group (targeted by Havas Advertising) and Telemundo Communications Group, among others. To reduce the impact of such failures, merger arbitrageurs usually hold diversified portfolios and spread their bets over several arbitrage situations at the same time, preferably in different economic sectors and/or countries. This is a wise decision. However, excessive diversification may also impair their performance, because the profitability of the best deals will be diluted. It is therefore important to find the right trade-off between diversifying risk and focusing on the best deals.

The portfolio construction of merger arbitrageurs is usually very basic – the portfolio is essentially a collection of trades that are identified individually and sequentially, and then sized on the basis of each one's expected profitability, likelihood of success or potential downside. By construction, the portfolio is relatively neutral to small variations of the market, but trading around existing positions is common, in order to adjust their size and/or to profit from selective opportunities. Leverage is also sometimes used to magnify performance, but most merger arbitrageurs use it in a very reasonable way. Moreover, merger arbitrageurs usually set up position limits as well as strict stop losses and profit-taking rules for each transaction. Sticking to this discipline is the only way for them to limit the downside risk of their portfolio.

In a few cases, when a deal is expected to break or when the deal spread becomes too tight, merger arbitrageurs may enter into *reverse positions*. Reverse positions are trades that the arbitrageur sets up if he or she believes the transaction will be cancelled or the deal spread will widen due to some development in the transaction. For instance, in the case of a stock-for-stock transaction, the arbitrageur would buy shares of the acquiring company and sell short shares of the target company instead of going long the target company and short the acquiring company (Box 11.7).

From the above case studies, the reader may be tempted to conclude that merger arbitrage is essentially a buy and hold strategy, where the position is established at the announcement and kept until the deal terminates. In reality, most deals are not as smooth as these examples, and there is a lot of activity going on between the companies involved, the regulators and the market. The arbitrage spread varies continuously during this process, as a function of market expectations but also news and rumours. Merger arbitrageurs cautiously monitor its evolution, and may trade to increase or decrease their positions, based on their own assessment of the likelihood of a favourable outcome. In fact, decrypting what regulators are saying or are likely

---

Box 11.7 How to become an involuntary merger arbitrageur: Julian Robertson

When Julian Robertson decided to shut down his Tiger Fund, he announced that he would liquidate most of its holdings and return to investors about 80% of their stakes within two months, mostly in cash and the rest in stocks. The remaining 20% would be paid later on from the sell-off of large stakes in five companies (including US Airways) that had contributed significantly to the fund's poor performance over the preceding year. When UAL, the world's largest airline, announced its intention to take over and merge with US Airways, Julian Robertson found himself in the very comfortable position of a merger arbitrageur, holding an estimated 26% stake in the target company. However, the merger finally fell through when US anti-trust authorities scuttled the deal on the grounds that it would damage competition, and Julian Robertson ended up distributing the fund's 24.8 million shares in US Airways.

to say, but also what the involved companies are doing or are likely to do, is the key to success in this strategy. In some cases, this can lead to extremely confusing situations, where several regulators have conflicting opinions of a merger or a takeover. This will result in a volatile merger arbitrage spread, and will create opportunities to trade, enter into or exit from positions (see Box 11.8).

Box 11.8 Mittal Steel versus Arcelor

Billionaire businessman Lakshmi Narain Mittal has long been looked upon as the "King of Steel". On 26 January 2006, his company, Mittal Steel, the world's largest steelmaker, surprised the markets by announcing an unsolicited €18.6 billion bid for its Luxembourg rival Arcelor. The offer valued each Arcelor share at €28.21, i.e. a 27% premium over the closing price, a 31% premium over the volume-weighted average price in the preceding month, and a 55% premium over the volume-weighted average share price in the preceding 12 months. The offered payment was 25% in cash and 75% in shares.

If successful, this merger would create a giant steel firm with more than 350 000 employees at 61 plants in 27 countries, with revenues in excess of $50 billion. The new group would produce about 10% of the world's steel output. Mittal pledged to create a new European champion, protect European jobs and respect European labour conditions. He announced that the combined entity would be based in Luxembourg, like Arcelor, and would have "ample room for Arcelor's management". However, the deal would have to face scrutiny from the European Commission and other competition authorities, and a few areas might cause anti-trust problems and require divestments – Mittal Steel was the biggest US supplier of high-grade, high-margin auto steel and Arcelor occupied the same position in Europe. Mittal Steel's shares rose 6.4% on the news of the bid, and Arcelor shares rose more than 30%. The market was clearly in favour of the bid. Now, let us examine the reactions generated by Mittal's offer.

Arcelor's Board of Directors rejected the unsolicited proposal, which it considered hostile, and recommended that its shareholders should not tender their shares in response to the proposed offer, if and when submitted. It recalled that Arcelor and Mittal Steel did not share the same strategic vision, business model and values, and expressed its strong concern regarding the potential consequences that Mittal Steel's proposal could have on the group, its shareholders, employees and customers. It therefore mandated the Management Board to explore all possible actions and options that would be in the best interests of all stakeholders. Mittal Steel's bid was also rejected by the Luxembourg government, which was Arcelor's largest shareholder (5.6%). Luxembourg Prime Minister Jean-Claude Juncker said that although the bid offered "opportunities", he did not share Mittal's view that the combined company could form a European industrial champion and was rather concerned about the possible consequences on employment – Arcelor is the largest employer in Luxembourg with 6000 workers. Consequently, he would back Arcelor in its plan to fight the merger. Understandably, his reaction was likely to be more influenced by the threat of losing jobs, tax revenue and votes rather than by a desire to preserve shareholder value.

Other reactions were amazing, including those of certain non-shareholders. France's Finance Minister, Thierry Breton, disparaged Mittal's offer and claimed in the French

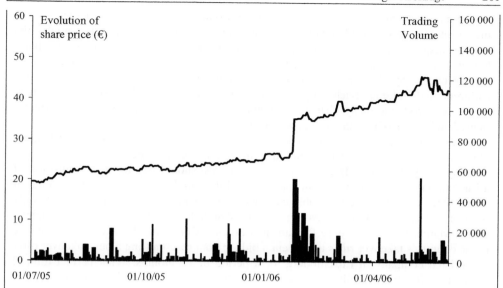

Figure 11.11 Evolution of Areclor share price and trading volume during the Mittal Steel/Arcelor takeover

Parliament that he had never seen such a "badly prepared" takeover attempt. Dominique de Villepin, the French Prime Minister, called publicly for "mobilization" and urged French companies to organize their capital in such a way as to "to resist attacks" – cars were burning in the streets of Paris at that time, which might justify the military allusions. Maybe the French political and business establishment was in favour of free markets, but not in favour of their consequences when corporate control is at stake.[7] Spain's Economy Minister, Pedro Solbes, said that Spain would also oppose the bid, as it had not yet received any concrete information about the deal, about the industrial strategy, about the business plan, or about jobs. India announced that it was in favour of the deal. Belgium took a neutral stance and appointed an investment bank to assess its viability.

The British Trade and Industry Secretary, Alan Johnson, announced his support for the deal, and warned against "advocates of protectionism" and "measures to protect key industries from foreign takeovers where there are no state security issues". In London, a columnist for *The Guardian* spoke of how the bid had unleashed a new wave of "economic patriotism", adding that Mittal and his family were often portrayed as aliens – "the Indians" – rather than as global entrepreneurs. India immediately accused European governments of discrimination and warned that their intervention could derail fragile global trade talks. Asked about the allegations of racism, the French President, Jacques Chirac, said very seriously: "In principle, we have absolutely nothing against a non-European taking over a European company." At this stage, it seemed that Arcelor and its prospective merger were being run by pretty much everybody except its shareholders.

---

[7] It is worth recalling that in 2005, France issued a decree restricting hostile foreign takeovers in 11 so-called "strategic sectors".

The management of Arcelor deployed all the usual tactics to fight the merger, including sweetening its dividend, announcing a rise in profits, negotiating with potential white knights, acquiring Dofasco (a Canadian competitor), and sending several letters to shareholders to convince them that the value it was creating for its shareholders far exceeded the value proposed by Mittal Steel. But this did not convince Société Générale, which joined Citigroup and Goldman Sachs in providing financing for Mittal's bid. Mittal also agreed to sell Dofasco to Germany's ThyssenKrupp if its bid for Arcelor was successful. Arcelor immediately put Dofasco into a special trust to block an eventual sale.

Luxembourg regulators also had a busy spring. On 22 March, the Luxembourg Chamber of Commerce opportunistically proposed . . . amending the merger and acquisition laws so that any company with a free float of less than 25% should pay for any acquisition of a Luxembourg company with cash. Since the Mittal family owns 88% of the capital of Mittal Steel, it would have been obliged to withdraw its first offer and launch a cash-only offer or at least a cash alternative for Arcelor shareholders. But this was not sufficient. On 23 March, the Luxembourg Parliament's Finance Committee backed another change in the country's takeover rules to prevent a bidder from resubmitting a new takeover offer for a listed company in Luxembourg for a period of 12 months. What perfect timing! Fortunately for the credibility of Luxembourg's institutions, the Parliament scrapped the proposed controversial amendments on 6 April 2006.

On 30 March, Luxembourg's Minister of Economy and Foreign Trade, Jeannot Krecke, indicated that as much as 60% of Arcelor's equity had changed hands since the day Mittal Steel announced its bid. Prominent hedge funds were thought to control as much as a quarter of Arcelor's equity. Their collective stake outweighed that of the Luxembourg government (5.6%), the Spanish Aristrain family (3.6%) and the Belgian regional government of Wallonia (2.4%), investors known to be supportive of Arcelor remaining independent.

Mittal Steel then raised its bid from €16.6 billion to €25.8 billion. But on 26 May, Arcelor abruptly announced plans to merge with Russian firm Severstal. According to these new plans, Arcelor would own 68% of the new firm, leaving 32% in the hands of Severstal's owner, billionaire Alexey Mordashov and close friend of Vladimir Putin. More importantly, Arcelor's chairman Joseph Kinsch and chief executive Guy Dolle would continue in their positions. Shares in Arcelor closed 3% lower at €33.05 – the new merger plans were complete nonsense as they handed effective control over to Mordashov by diluting the value of the shares held by Arcelor's stockholders and put a lower price tag on the company than the terms being offered by Mittal.

Not surprisingly, Arcelor received a complaint letter from a group of institutional investors representing almost 30% of its equity. It demanded an extraordinary shareholder meeting to review the conditions of this new offer. But Guy Dolle indicated that Arcelor's board did not need shareholder approval for a share issue that would then pave the way for a tie-up with Severstal. In his view, the new deal was "neither a poison pill, nor a deal breaker". As Richard Wachman wrote in *The Observer*, "the putrid stink of hypocrisy hangs in the air following the disclosure that Arcelor is planning to merge with Severstal".

On 26 June 2006, Arcelor's board finally yielded to a sweetened bid from Mittal Steel, ending a bitter five-month takeover battle. Severstal was in line for a €140 million ($175 million) break-up fee, but reacted furiously, saying it was "very surprised" that Arcelor's board did not invite it to discuss its revised offer or give it the chance to respond (Figure 11.11).

11.4   HISTORICAL PERFORMANCE

Merger arbitrage has always been considered a relatively low-risk hedge fund strategy with steady returns. Indeed, since January 1994, the CS/Tremont Event-Driven/Risk Arbitrage Index (Figure 11.12) has generated an annualized return of 7.7%, with a volatility of 4.3%. In comparison, over the same period, the S&P 500 delivered an average return of 8.6% p.a. with a volatility of 16%, and the Citigroup World Government Bond Index delivered an average return of 5.9% p.a. with a volatility of 6.7% (Table 11.1).

The success of merger arbitrage depends primarily on two factors: (i) the availability of a sufficient volume of mergers and takeovers on the market to permit the construction of a diversified merger arbitrage portfolio; and (ii) a sufficient spread on each successful transaction to compensate for failing transactions. It is therefore not surprising to observe that merger arbitrage yielded its best performance from 1994 to 2000, the boom years of merger deals,

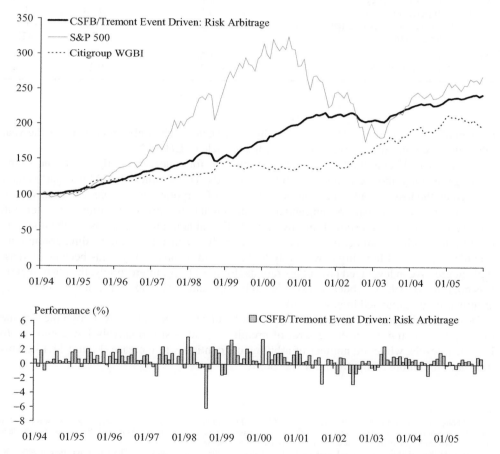

Figure 11.12   Evolution of the CS/Tremont Event Driven: Risk Arbitrage Index, 1994–2005

Table 11.1   Performance comparison of the CS/Tremont Event Driven: Risk Arbitrage Index, the S&P 500 and the Citigroup World Government Bond Index, 1994–2005

	CS/Tremont Event Driven: Risk Arbitrage	S&P 500	Citigruop WGBI
Return (% p.a.)	7.72	8.55	5.87
Volatility (% p.a.)	4.31	16.00	6.74
Skewness	−1.26	−0.58	0.37
Kurtosis	6.50	0.61	0.37
Normally distributed?	No	No	Yes
Correlation with strategy		0.45	−0.02
Positive months frequency	80%	62%	58%
Best month performance (%)	3.81	9.67	5.94
Average positive month performance (%)	1.05	3.44	1.73
Upside participation		39%	108%
Negative months frequency	20%	38%	42%
Worst month performance (%)	−6.15	−14.58	−4.28
Average negative month performance (%)	−1.05	−3.53	−1.18
Downside participation		−165%	−427%
Max. drawdown (%)	−7.60	−46.28	−7.94
Value at Risk (1-month, 99%)	−2.70	−10.24	−3.36

particularly in the media, telecoms and technology sectors. The only exception was the year 1998, in which the strategy was affected by the debacle of LTCM.[8]

The years 2001 and 2002 saw a relatively poor performance, primarily due to the slump in merger activity and the tightness of merger spreads. The summer of 2002 was particularly affected by the loss of confidence following the rash of corporate implosions at Enron, World-Com, Adelphia and Global Crossing and the numerous announcements of earnings restatement. Fortunately, the situation started improving in 2003. Valuation multiples rose high enough to prod hesitant sellers into action, merger volume gradually increased, the lending community provided substantial liquidity at relatively low cost, and private equity firms became increasingly aggressive in leveraged buyout operations (Figure 11.13). Interestingly, the phenomenon was not limited to the US, but also extended to Europe and Asia[9] and a large number of merger arbitrage funds expanded internationally.

However, this return of optimism should not be taken at face value. Although the volume of mergers is rising, the average level of premiums paid is still relatively low compared to historical levels, while the number of arbitrageurs continues to increase (Figure 11.14). This translates into more competition for less profit.

---

[8] Although most market participants were unaware of it, LTCM was running a large merger arbitrage book and was forced to liquidate it in a hurry to reduce its exposure and raise cash. All merger arbitrage funds plunged. Moreover, the subsequent debacle in financial markets also prompted the cancellation of a large number of pending mergers.

[9] At more than $1 trillion in 2005, European merger volume was 49% higher than the $729.5 billion reported in 2004, and Asia–Pacific merger activity hit a record $474.3 billion, a 46% increase from $324.5 billion in 2004.

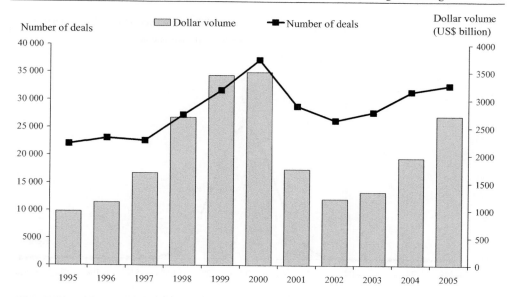

Figure 11.13   The recovery of the merger deal flow, 1995–2005

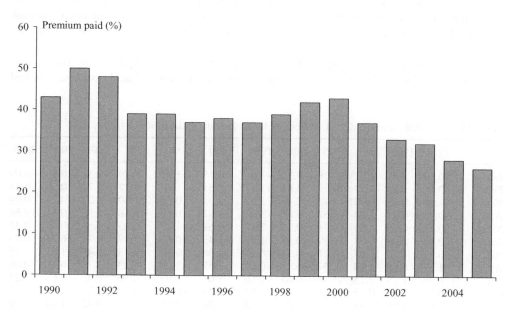

Figure 11.14   M&A premiums paid for global public targets, 1990–2005, based on the price of the target company four weeks prior to the deal announcement

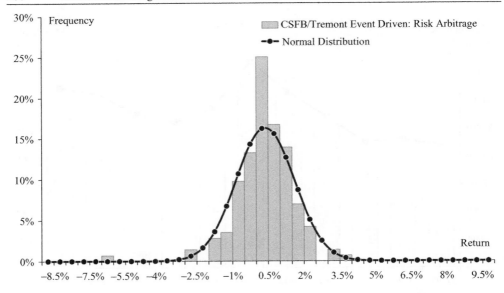

Figure 11.15   Return distribution of the CS/Tremont Event Driven:Risk Arbitrage Index, 1994–2005

The distribution of monthly returns of the CS/Tremont Event-Driven: Risk Arbitrage Index is not normally distributed, primarily because of an excess kurtosis that is far too high (Figure 11.15). This is essentially due to the losses experienced in August 1998 (−6.15%) – Table 11.2.

The drawdowns of the strategy are limited, but coincide with equity drawdowns (Figures 11.16 and 11.17). It must not be forgotten that the number of deals is closely linked

Table 11.2   Monthly returns of the CS/Tremont Event Driven: Risk Arbitrage Index, 1994–2005

	1994	1995	1996	1997	1998	1999	2000	2001	2002	2003	2004	2005
Jan	0.57	1.61	1.02	1.28	−0.54	−1.51	0.15	1.91	0.29	−0.39	0.83	−0.09
Feb	−0.44	1.88	1.57	0.22	3.81	−1.37	3.52	1.49	−1.22	−0.71	0.50	0.46
Mar	1.86	0.63	0.63	−0.42	2.38	2.56	0.05	0.33	1.00	−0.27	0.73	0.09
Apr	−0.96	−0.45	2.00	−1.67	1.64	3.39	1.81	0.50	0.88	1.52	−0.58	−0.54
May	0.25	0.61	1.09	1.31	0.23	2.47	0.68	1.31	0.03	2.56	0.44	0.32
Jun	0.18	2.07	0.28	2.39	−0.53	1.22	1.43	−0.43	0.75	0.25	0.79	
Jul	0.57	1.56	1.05	1.21	−0.37	0.16	1.58	0.68	−2.73	0.48	−1.52	0.46
Aug	1.69	0.60	1.23	0.57	−6.15	0.80	1.57	1.01	−1.23	1.16	0.18	0.60
Sep	0.38	1.14	2.15	1.48	−0.65	2.16	1.01	−2.65	−0.56	0.95	0.63	0.23
Oct	0.20	0.16	0.45	0.02	2.41	1.75	0.35	−0.01	0.52	1.21	0.92	−1.12
Nov	0.61	1.68	0.45	1.09	2.04	0.52	0.28	0.81	0.21	0.42	1.67	1.01
Dec	0.26	−0.16	1.12	2.01	1.55	0.47	1.39	0.67	0.53	1.00	1.32	0.85
Total	5.26	11.90	13.83	9.84	5.59	13.23	14.67	5.69	−3.46	8.99	5.46	3.08
S&P 500	−1.54	34.11	20.26	31.01	26.67	19.53	−10.14	−13.04	−23.37	26.38	8.99	3.00
WGBI	2.34	19.04	3.62	0.23	15.30	−4.27	1.59	−0.99	19.49	14.91	10.35	−6.88

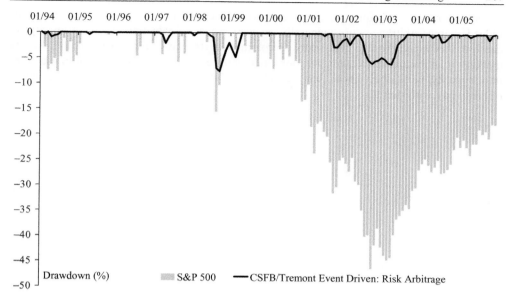

Figure 11.16 Drawdown diagram of the CS/Tremont Event Driven:Risk Arbitrage Index compared to the S&P 500, 1994–2005

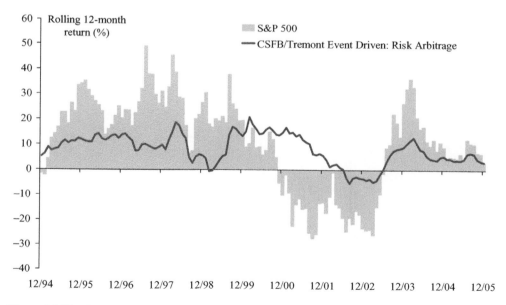

Figure 11.17 Comparision of the 11-month rolling performances of the CS/Tremont Event Driven: Risk Arbitrage Index with the S&P 500, 1994–2005

to the performance of equity markets and, more generally, to the growth of the economy. Indeed, merger arbitrage returns generally lag corporate activity by one-quarter, primarily because the average arbitrage deal takes approximately 100 days to complete. Falling equity markets or an uncertain economic outlook can therefore throw a large number of transactions into jeopardy, particularly those that are linked to a stock merger, that is, where the bidder offers to pay with shares.

12

Convertible Arbitrage

Insomnia becomes a real problem when you cannot sleep during office hours.

At first glance, corporations wishing to raise capital seem to have an almost infinite variety of instruments at their disposal – most of them springing from the fertile imagination of investment banks. But in reality, most if not all of these esoteric instruments can be seen as a dynamic combination of two basic types of securities, namely debt and equity. In a nutshell, corporations just have to choose between issuing debt and issuing equity. Issuing debt is not dilutive but sets stringent requirements in terms of mandatory coupon payments. Issuing equity dilutes existing equity holders but has no imposed cost, as dividends are not mandatory.

Convertible securities are a perfect example of such a combination. Basically, convertible securities are bond-like instruments that can be converted into equity at the discretion of their owner. For several reasons that are discussed below, convertible securities are often issued below their fair value. This creates an opportunity for arbitrage that attracts hedge funds like a magnet. Initially, the funds' favourite strategy consisted in purchasing undervalued convertibles and selling short the stock of the issuer to hedge the associated equity risk. Over the years, the strategy has evolved to include directional bets on credit risk, volatility, convexity, etc. But before going into these more complex variations, let us start by reviewing the essential features of an ordinary convertible bond and examining how the basic arbitrage strategy works.

12.1 THE TERMINOLOGY OF CONVERTIBLE BONDS

Convertible bonds are relatively complex securities, because they blend the characteristics of equity, debt and option securities. In addition, convertible arbitrageurs and traders often use a jargon which is somewhat opaque for the profane. For the sake of simplicity, let us assume that the date is now 1 January 2006 and that we have in mind a fictive convertible bond denoted XYZ convertible 2% 2010. First we shall describe the various parameters that characterize this convertible bond – see Table 12.1.

The fixed income features of the convertible bond are as follows:

- The *issuer* is the XYZ Company Inc., a company with a BBB *rating*.
- The convertible bond has a five-year *time to maturity*.
- The convertible bond pays a 2% *annual coupon*, with the first coupon paid in exactly one year.
- There are no *accrued interests* – the bond has just been issued.
- The *nominal value* or *par value* of each bond is $1000. It is the amount for which each bond can be redeemed at maturity.[1]

---

[1] The nominal value of convertible bonds is often 1000 units of the relevant currency in the euro-convertible bond market and ¥1 000 000 in the Japanese domestic and euro–yen markets.

Table 12.1   Summary of the terms offered by the XYZ convertible 2% 2010 bond

Fixed income features	
Issuer	XYZ Company Inc.
Rating	BBB
Coupon	2% (annual)
Issue date	1 January 2006 (today)
First coupon date	31 December 2006 (in one year)
Accrued interest	0
Maturity	1 January 2010 (in 5 years)
Nominal value	$1000
Yield to maturity	2% p.a.
Equity features	
Issuer	XYZ Company Inc
Stock price	$80 per share
Stock volatility	20% p.a.
Stock dividend	None
Conversion features	
Conversion ratio	10
Conversion price	$100
Call protection	None
Market valuation	
Convertible price	100 (i.e. 100% of face value)
Parity	80 (i.e. 80% of face value)
Conversion premium	25%

- The *yield to maturity* is the total rate of return expected on the convertible bond if it is bought today and held until maturity, assuming that market conditions remain identical and that no conversion occurs.

The convertible bond can be converted into shares of stock of the issuer. These shares have the following characteristics:

- The *issuer* is the XYZ Company Inc., i.e. the same issuer as the convertible bond.
- The stock price is currently $80 per share
- The volatility of the stock is 20% p.a.
- The stock pays no dividend.

The terms of the conversion are fixed in the convertible bond's indenture as follows:

- The *conversion ratio* denotes the number of shares obtained if one converts $1000 of face value of the bond. In our example, each bond with a $1000 face value can be converted into 10 ordinary shares. The conversion ratio is therefore 10. This number usually remains fixed through the life of the instrument unless stock splits, special dividends or other dilutive events occur.
- The *conversion price* denotes the price at which shares are indirectly purchased via the convertible security. It is equal to the market price of the convertible security divided by the conversion ratio. If we assume that the XYZ convertible trades at par, then a $1000 face value of the XYZ convertible is needed to obtain 10 shares. The conversion price is

therefore $100 per share. At maturity, if the share price is higher than the conversion price, the bondholder will convert into shares. A convertible is said to be "in the money" if the underlying share price is higher than the conversion price.

- *Call protections* grant the issuer the right to call back the convertible bond before its stated maturity. This can either be a *hard call*, i.e. the issuer can call the bond at a pre-fixed price regardless of any other circumstances,[2] or a *soft call* where the issuer can only call the bond if the equity price has risen significantly above the strike price or some other hurdle rate. In our example, for the sake of simplicity, we have assumed that there was no call protection.

The market valuation parameters of the convertible bond are observable in the market:

- The *convertible price* denotes the quoted price of the convertible bond, which is usually expressed as a percentage of the nominal value (in line with the straight bond market). In our example, the convertible is quoted at par.
- The *parity* is the market value of the shares into which the bond can be converted at that time. In our example, it is calculated as 10 shares per bond × $80 per share = $800. The parity is normally quoted as a percentage of the par amount of the bond, i.e. $800/$1000 = 80%, or simply 80. Note that when a convertible bond is in the money, its parity is higher than 100.
- The *conversion premium* is the difference between parity and the convertible bond price, expressed as a percentage of parity. The premium expresses how much more an investor has to pay to control the same number of shares via a convertible. In our example, the parity is $(100 - 80)/80 = 25\%$. Another way to understand the conversion premium is to compare shares resulting from the conversion with shares purchased on the market. At this stage, investors buying the XYZ convertible and converting immediately would have paid $1000 to obtain 10 shares. Investors buying 10 shares directly in the market would pay only $800 (10 × $80). The extra $200 represents the convertible's conversion premium. This premium also gives an indication of how a convertible should perform in relation to the underlying shares. Convertibles with very low premiums will usually be much more sensitive to movements in the underlying share price (i.e. parity) than convertibles where the premium is higher (see Box 12.1).

Box 12.1 Convertible bond variations

In this chapter, we limit our analysis to simple convertible bonds. However, the reader needs to be aware that the development of the convertible market has extended to bonds with more complex structures than simple income-paying bonds. Let us mention some of them.

- Zero-coupon convertible bonds are typically issued at a deep discount to par value and are redeemable at par. The most famous examples of such bonds are the Liquid Yield Option Notes (LYONs), which are both callable (by the issuer) and putable (by investors).
- Mandatory conversion securities (MCS) are convertibles whose conversion is mandatory at some stage. They tend to trade and behave like shares, although some have specific additional features. For instance, a preferred equity redemption cumulative stock (PERC) is a mandatory preferred convertible with a pre-set cap level above which the conversion

---

[2] Most of the time, the issuer must give public notice of its intention to redeem a convertible bond early, and bondholders are usually given a limited period of time to decide if they want to convert their convertible bond into shares.

ratio is adjusted to keep the total return payoff constant (the PERC becomes convertible into fewer and fewer underlying shares).

- Convertible preferred shares are preferred stocks that include an option for their holder to convert into a fixed number of common shares, usually any time after a predetermined date.

As of January 2006, the $280 billion US convertible market was still dominated by standard income-paying bonds, followed by zero-coupon bonds.

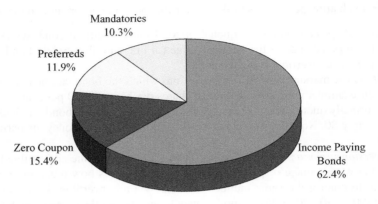

Figure 12.1   US Convertible type (as percentage of total index value)

12.2   VALUATION OF CONVERTIBLE BONDS

Let us now focus on the problem of calculating the "fair" value of a convertible bond. By fair value, we mean an unbiased estimate of what the price of a convertible bond should be in a deep, liquid and efficient market to preclude any arbitrage opportunity. This is clearly not a trivial problem, due to the simultaneous presence of three sources of risk, namely interest rate risk, credit risk, and equity risk, as well as the interaction between these risks. In addition, convertible bonds often have an array of specific features (call clauses, put clauses, etc.) which need to be modelled correctly in order to price them. As usual in such cases, academics and practitioners have taken two radically different approaches.

12.2.1   Valuation from an academic perspective

Academics have taken the intellectual challenge of convertible bond modelling as a playing-field and/or as a source of inspiration for publishing numerous research papers. These can essentially be grouped into three families, namely the structural approach, the reduced-form approach, and the simulation-based approach.

The structural approach was initiated by Merton (1974), who devised a simple model to relate credit risk to the capital structure of an issuing firm. Merton observed that the value of a firm's assets is essentially the sum of the firm's equity and debt. The firm goes into default if the value of its assets drops below the face value of its debt. With this approach, both equity and debt can be seen as contingent claims on the total assets of the firm, and their prices may be calculated using the Black and Scholes option pricing model or, equivalently, binomial trees.

Ingersoll (1977) extended this approach to convertible bonds, which he modelled as options on debt and equity, i.e. compound options. The result is a closed form solution for pricing basic convertible bonds. Later, Brennan and Schwartz (1977, 1980) extended Ingersoll's model to allow discrete dividends and stochastic interest rates, but lost the elegance of the closed form solution – the convertible bond price is the numerical solution of a partial differential equation.

Structural models are based on a powerful and compelling intuitive economic interpretation of firms' credit risk. Unfortunately, most of them usually assume only one debt issue with a unique maturity, while real life firms have complex capital structures with several liabilities. And any liability senior to convertible bonds needs to be modelled in order to price them. Second, the key variable to model in the structural approach is the value of the assets of a firm, which is not directly observable. This makes the implementation of structural models extremely difficult.[3]

The second family of convertible bond-pricing models follows the reduced form approach. This approach assumes that a firm's default time is exogenous and results from a single jump loss event that drives the stock price down to zero. The probability of default over the next short time interval is determined by a specified hazard rate that is a function of latent state variables. When default occurs, a certain portion of the bond's value is assumed to be recovered. Jarrow and Turnbull (1995), Duffie and Singleton (1999), Hull and White (2000), and Jarrow (2001) suggested several well-known credit models that can be calibrated to historical default and recovery rates, or even to a series of credit spreads. Their models have been extended to handle convertible bonds – see for instance Davis and Lischka (1999), Takahashi *et al.* (2001), Hung and Wang (2002), and Andersen and Buffum (2003).

The third family of convertible bond-pricing models is more pragmatic and relies on Monte Carlo simulations. That is, several thousands of possible scenarios for interest rates and equity prices are simulated on the basis of some prespecified statistical properties. Each scenario yields a possible value for the convertible bond. The convertible bond price is then calculated as the average of all these values. This approach is obviously more flexible than the structural and reduced form approaches, because it can capture any dynamics for the stock price or interest rates and it deals easily with complex contractual specifications of actually traded convertible bonds – see Ammann *et al.* (2005).

From the practitioner's viewpoint, all these academic approaches are founded on solid theoretical grounds, but the resulting pricing models are too complex, either mathematically or numerically. Most of them require – and are very sensitive to – the correct specification/ calibration of the stochastic behaviour of underlying state variables (stock price, interest rates, credit risk). This opens the door to model risk, i.e. misusing a model and/or obtaining misleading prices. This explains why most practitioners are still waiting for "the" convertible bond-pricing model. In the meantime, they seem to have adopted a much more pragmatic approach, which is sometimes called the "component approach".

12.2.2 Valuation from a practitioner perspective (the component approach)

Although theoretically questionable, the component approach is extremely intuitive. Simply stated, it considers a convertible bond as being a package made up of two components, a

---

[3] Several models attempt to solve this calibration problem by modelling convertible bonds as contingent claims on equity rather than on the value of the firm. However, the dilemma then becomes how to introduce credit risk. McConell and Schwartz (1986), Cheung and Nelken (1994) and Ho and Pfeffer (1996) suggest adding an ad hoc risk premium to the discount rate used in the model, but lack solid theoretical foundations for the suggestion.

straight bond and an option:

$$\text{Convertible bond} = \text{Straight bond} + \text{Option}$$

The straight bond component corresponds to the pure fixed income part of the convertible bond. It ignores the conversion possibility, so that its value is easily obtained by discounting all the future expected cash flows (coupons and final repayment) at an appropriate discount rate. The option component only considers the conversion features of the convertible bond. It is essentially an out-of-the-money American type option to exchange the straight bond against a certain quantity of shares of stocks. This option can easily be valued using the closed form solution for exchange options introduced by Margrabe (1978). Alternatively, one could also consider this option as being a call option on a certain quantity of shares of stock and value it using the Black and Scholes (1973) formula. However, unlike the case of usual options, the exercise price of this option is not constant – it is equal to the value of the bond to be delivered in exchange for the shares.[4]

As an illustration, let us take again our XYZ convertible bond. We can value the bond portion by discounting all cash flows at 5% (the yield to maturity) and summing the present values. This gives a total present value of $870.12 for the bond component.

Time (years)	0	1	2	3	4	5
Cash flows		20.00	20.00	20.00	20.00	1,020.00
PV(CF) @ 5%		19.05	18.14	17.28	16.45	799.20
Total PV	870.12					

Let us now consider the option component. Each option gives the right to exchange one bond for 10 shares. If we use the Black and Scholes model as a first approximation to value this option, given the five-year maturity and the volatility of 20% p.a., we obtain a price of $182.00. That is, the theoretical value of the convertible bond is $1052.12 (=$870.12+$182.00) – see Box 12.2.

Box 12.2 Put–call parity

Using the put–call parity, a convertible bond can also be analysed from a put option perspective. We obtain:

$$\text{Convertible bond} = \text{Parity} + \text{Put option} + \text{Value of income advantage}$$

The put option is interpreted as the right to sell a prespecified number of shares at the convertible bond redemption price, and the income advantage value is calculated as the present value of the stream of income provided by the convertible bond.

The component approach offers an intuitive interpretation of the convertible bond price behaviour as a function of the stock price. Let us first have a look at the two individual

---

[4] Note that from a theoretical perspective, both the Margrabe and the Black and Scholes models implicitly assume that the assets underlying the option follow a geometric Brownian motion (i.e. have a lognormal distribution of returns). This is generally not the case for bonds, which tend to come back towards their par value as they approach maturity. Also, both models refer to European-style options whereas almost all convertible bonds can be exercised prior to maturity and are American style. These models also need to be adjusted for the dilution that results from the conversion of convertible bonds into equity.

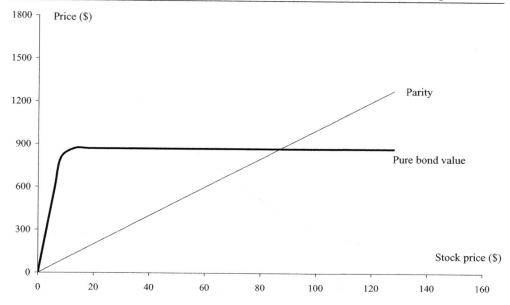

Figure 12.2   The pure bond value of the convertible bond

components. The pure bond price is, in a sense, the minimum value of our convertible bond, because it ignores its conversion features. It should be unaffected by stock price variations and stay at $870.12, unless the issuer's ability to face its debt obligations is called into question. This only happens for very low stock prices – at the extreme, the debt value could even fall to its liquidation value if the issuer becomes bankrupt. For the sake of simplicity, we have assumed in our illustration that concerns about a possible default only start when the stock price slides below a threshold price of $17 – see Figure 12.2.

As shown in Figure 12.3, the pure option value exhibits the typical payoff of a call option on the stock, with an exercise price of $81.012 (the current bond price divided by the conversion ratio) and a five-year maturity. Remember, however, that this exercise price could change as a result of changes in interest rates, so that the payoff could change as well.

The overall payoff of the convertible bond is obtained by summing the payoffs of its components. As can be seen from Figure 12.4, there are four possible states for a convertible bond:

- *Junk* or *distressed (area 1)*: The very low stock price reflects doubt about the issuer's ability to face its debt obligations. The call option is worth zero, the convertible faces some default risk and behaves as a distressed bond. The parity is typically between 0 and 30% of the face value.
- *Busted (area 2)*: The conversion is unlikely, because the stock price is too low. The value of the call option is negligible, and the convertible bond behaves essentially like a straight bond with no equity sensitivity. The parity is typically between 40 and 80% of the face value. Such convertibles are said to be "out of the money".
- *Hybrid (area 3)*: When stock prices are high enough, the option to convert gains value. The parity is typically between 80 and 120% of the face value, and the convertible is said to be "at the money". This is the area preferred by most convertible arbitrageurs, because it offers

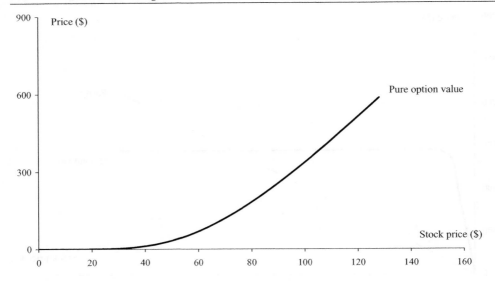

Figure 12.3   The pure option value of the convertible bond

the traditional convertible benefits with both fixed income and equity sensitivities and the features of the option.

- *Equity proxy (area 4)*: When stock prices are extremely high, conversion is likely and solely conversion value matters. The convertible is said to be "in the money", its equity sensitivity is high and its fixed income sensitivity is low. The parity is typically above 130% of the face value.

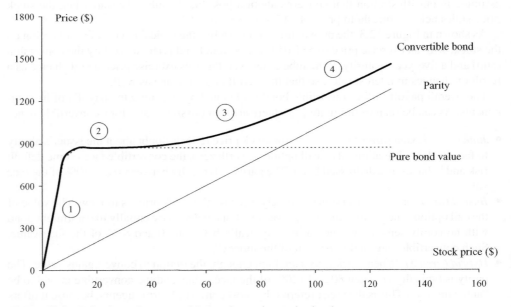

Figure 12.4   Behaviour of a convertible bond at various price levels

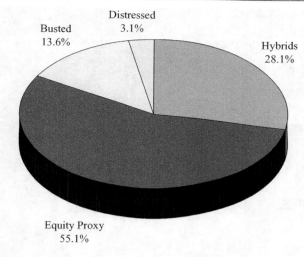

Figure 12.5   US convertible bond profile (as percentage of total index value)

As of January 2006, the US convertible bond market consisted mostly of bonds in an equity proxy profile (Figure 12.5). However, this was essentially the result of the robust performance of equity markets in 2003, 2004 and 2005. A few years previously, most of the bonds were rather busted or distressed due to the technology stock crash and three years of bear markets.

Arbitrageurs often use a graph similar to Figure 12.4 to determine the cheapness or expensiveness of the convertible bond. If a convertible bond plots significantly above its fair value, it is expensive, while if it plots significantly below its fair value, it is cheap – see Figure 12.6.

12.2.3   Risk measurement and the Greek alphabet

Finally, the component approach also allows us to understand the sources of risks embedded in a convertible bond – they are simply those of its two components. As expected, we find the usual suspects, i.e. interest rate risk and credit risk for the bond component, and equity risk, volatility risk and interest rate risk for the option component. But the beauty of the component approach is that, since we know how to quantify the risk exposure of a bond and the risk exposure of a call option, we also know how to quantify the risk exposures of the convertible bond.

The risk of the bond component is usually assessed using the duration, convexity and credit sensitivity:

- *Duration* (or, to be more precise, modified duration) measures the sensitivity of the bond component's price to changes in the level of interest rates. For instance, a modified duration of 3 means that the bond component will decline about 3% for each 1% increase in interest rates, or rise about 3% for each 1% decrease in interest rates – remember that bond prices and interest rates are inversely related!
- *Convexity* measures the change in duration for small shifts in the yield curve. In a sense, it is the second-order price sensitivity of the bond component to changes in interest rates.
- *Credit sensitivity* can easily be approximated by duration. Indeed, if interest rates increase by 1%, the impact on the bond component will be the same, regardless of whether the increase is due to rising government rates or to rising credit risk premium.

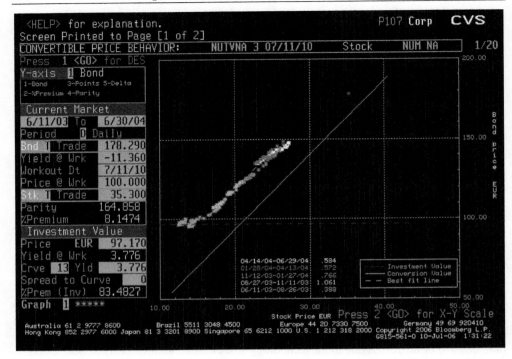

Figure 12.6 Example of the analysis of a convertible bond price over time on a Bloomberg. The bond analysed is the Numico 3% 2010

For the option component, the risk assessment relies on Southeast Europeans. The Greeks have given us feta cheese, philosophy, mathematics, and the Oedipus complex. They can also tell us how much risk our option component has. Indeed, option traders are familiar with the use of Greek letters to estimate the risk of their positions.

Delta measures the equity sensitivity of a convertible bond's theoretical value. Conventionally, delta is expressed as the change in convertible price for a one-point change in parity. Thus, a delta equal to 0.4 means that if parity rises by 1 point, the convertible price will rise by 0.4 points (0.4 times the one-point change in parity). Delta changes along the convertible price curve between 0 and 100% – intuitively, it is the slope of the convertible bond price curve, as illustrated in Figure 12.7. A steeper slope indicates a higher sensitivity to the underlying stock price. When a convertible bond gets very deep-in-the-money, it begins to trade like the stock, moving almost dollar for dollar with the stock price (delta = 1). Meanwhile, far-out-of-the-money options do not move much in absolute dollar terms (delta = 0), unless there are some serious bankruptcy concerns. Note that traders often calculate a convertible position's delta, which is the convertible's delta multiplied by the conversion ratio times the number of bonds.

Gamma measures the rate of change in the delta for movements in the underlying share price. Similarly to convexity for bonds, it is the second-order price sensitivity of the convertible price to changes in the stock price. Conventionally, it is expressed as the change in delta for a one-point change in parity. Figure 12.7 shows that gamma is larger for the at-the-money convertibles and gets progressively lower for both the in- and out-of-the-money convertibles.

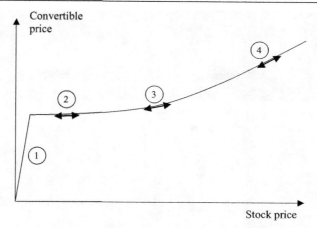

Figure 12.7   Delta as the slope of a tangent drawn on the convertible price line

Vega measures the sensitivity of the price of a convertible bond to changes in volatility of the underlying stock. An increase in volatility raises the prices of all the options on an asset, and a decrease in volatility causes all the options to decline in value. Conventionally, vega is expressed as the change in the fair value of the convertible for a one percentage point increase in the assumption for stock volatility.

Theta, also known as time decay, is the change of the convertible price due to the passage of time. Conventionally, theta is expressed as the percentage change in the convertible price for the passage of one day, other things being equal. Theta is used to estimate how much an option's extrinsic value is whittled away by the always-constant passage of time. For an at-the-money convertible, theta will be negative if the time decay of the option element outweighs any upward drift in the bond floor.

Rho is an estimate of the sensitivity of a convertible price to movements in interest rates.

Conventionally, it is expressed as the change in convertible price for a given one basis point move in interest rates (a parallel shift in the whole yield curve). Rho also evolves along the convertible curve – it increases when parity decreases, i.e. as the convertible starts trading more based on its fixed interest characteristics.

That makes a lot of Greek letters but they are useful in understanding the risks and potential rewards of a convertible position (Figure 12.8). Of course, it must be remembered that the numbers given for each of these sensitivities are calculated using mathematical models (e.g. Black and Scholes), so they are subject to assumptions and hypotheses.

12.3   CONVERTIBLE ARBITRAGE: THE BASIC DELTA HEDGE STRATEGY

The idea of convertible arbitrage started with the observation that most convertible bonds were often trading at a price that was below their fair value. Surprisingly, this undervaluation was well known and most market participants were used to it. They considered it normal, and in

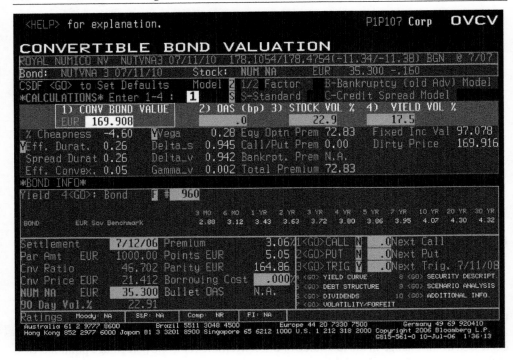

Figure 12.8 Example of a Bloomberg Screen showing all the sensitivities for the Numico convertible bond previously analysed

some cases even tried to justify it using a variety of qualitative arguments:

- A large number of convertible bond issuers were rated below investment grade, so the demand for their securities was limited. At that time, institutional investors and mutual funds did not want to venture into the non-investment grade area.
- Several convertible issues were small in size and analysts did not necessarily follow them closely. This argument was supported by the observation that the degree of undervaluation usually increased as the market capitalization of the issuer decreased.
- Convertibles arrived late on the scene as an asset class and were at the outset somewhat too small, illiquid and opaque. Markets for different types of securities such as stocks and bonds were not closely integrated, and investors preferred securities with a pure nature (stock or bond) rather than hybrid ones.
- Convertible bond issuers were so much in need of the cash that they were willing to give a discount on the issue price. This discount was appreciated and encouraged by investment banks because it facilitated the selling process.
- At issue, most convertible bonds contained a deeply out-of-the-money option, and these options were known to be underpriced by the market on average.
- The fair price of a convertible bond includes assumptions about future volatility and the credit risk of the issuer. As a result, buyers erred on the side of caution and priced them for the worst eventuality.

- Since new cheap convertible issues were regularly brought to the market, they continually refreshed the cheapness of the convertible universe, because the "old" issues were not able to become fairly valued.

In actual fact, none of these arguments was valid. Indeed, the fair price of the convertible bond should already take into account the impact of the above-mentioned arguments, so there is no reason for the market price to differ significantly from the fair value. Moreover, since convertible bonds are guaranteed to be fairly priced at some point in the future,[5] they *must* be fairly priced at any time relative to their fixed income and option components. If this is not the case then an arbitrage exists and should be *immediately* exploited. This was exactly the reasoning of the first convertible bond arbitrageurs.

By way of illustration, let us return to our XYZ convertible bond. Given current market conditions, the fair convertible bond price was determined to be $1052.11. But the market value of the bond was only $1000, according to Table 12.1. The question is, of course, how can one exploit such a mispricing? Buying the cheap convertible and waiting for market prices to adjust is not an arbitrage, because the long convertible position comes with a variety of risks that could easily wipe out the expected gains. To arbitrage, it is necessary to buy the cheap convertible and to hedge its risks until the mispricing has disappeared – a dynamic process that is very similar to what option traders do all day long. Here again, our component approach will be useful to illustrate how the process works.

The interest rate risk (long duration, long convexity) of the long convertible position can be hedged by selling interest rate futures contracts or using interest rate swaps – see for instance Hull (2005). Once this has been done, the next important risk comes from the potential variations of the underlying stock price. This equity risk can easily be eliminated by selling short an appropriate quantity of the underlying stock. This quantity corresponds to the position's delta, i.e. the delta of the option component times the number of shares into which the bond may be converted. If the stock price gains $1, the convertible bond will gain approximately *delta* dollars, and the short stock position will lose delta dollars, so that the overall variation will be nil. Conversely, if the stock price drops by $1, the convertible bond will lose approximately *delta* dollars, and the short stock position will gain delta dollars, so that the overall variation will again be nil. In both cases the overall position's value no longer depends upon variations of the stock price.

Consider for instance our XYZ convertible bond. We found that its delta was 6.85. That is, if the stock price drops by $1, the convertible bond is expected to lose $6.85. To hedge this risk, the arbitrageur can simply sell short 6.85 stocks per convertible bond that he bought. For a small change in the price of the stock, the arbitrageur's position will be hedged. However, once the stock price has changed, the delta of the convertible bond is no longer 6.85, so that the net delta of the position is no longer equal to zero. In order to keep the position delta-hedged, a rebalancing of the hedge (rehedging) is needed.

As the stock price increases and the option component moves more into the money, the convertible bond becomes more equity sensitive (see Figure 12.9). The delta of the convertible bond increases, so the arbitrageur must adjust his hedge by selling short more shares. Conversely, as the stock price declines and the option moves out of the money, the delta of the convertible bond declines and the arbitrageur must reduce his hedge by buying back some shares. In any case, the hedge needs to be rebalanced again and again as the stock price

---

[5] Convertible bonds have a finite maturity and they will therefore converge toward their fair value, either relative to the bond (final repayment) or relative to the stock (if there is conversion). Note that we say nothing about the correct valuation of the stock...

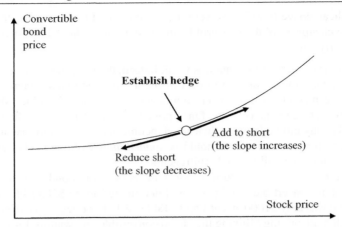

Figure 12.9   Delta hedging a convertible bond

moves. This investment approach, called dynamic "delta hedging" in options terminology, is the commonest way of extracting value from convertibles without taking directional views on the underlying stock.

A key question for most arbitrageurs is how often they should rebalance their hedge. Most theoretical approaches to delta hedging assume that re-hedging is done continuously, i.e. infinitesimally small stock transactions are done for every infinitesimally small stock price movement. This is not feasible in the real world: stock prices change in finite increments, fractional shares are normally not traded, and even if they were, transaction costs would skyrocket along with the number of transactions. In practice, therefore, arbitrageurs rehedge in discrete time, usually on a time-based or price-based basis. In the former case, rehedging takes place at prespecified time intervals, e.g. every day or every hour. In the latter case, rehedging takes place whenever the stock price reaches a certain level (e.g. every $1 move or every 1% move in the stock price) or when the size of the necessary adjustment reaches a certain threshold. If the selected rehedging interval is small enough, the risk of running a poorly hedged position is limited. Of course, mixes of the two approaches can also be implemented, but in practice the optimal choice of rehedging strategy often varies, not only from stock to stock but also over time and depending on market conditions (Figure 12.10).

An interesting issue is what arises for larger movements of the underlying stock price. Due to the non-linear nature of their payoff, most convertible bonds at the money exhibit a nice property known as "high convexity" or "high gamma": they appreciate at a greater rate than they depreciate with respect to change in the underlying stock. Consequently, the delta hedged position will actually benefit from *any* large movement of the underlying stock. Convertible securities that demonstrate this property should prove to be of value in a volatile market – other things being equal, the more volatile the stock price is, the greater the expected profit on the position and the more valuable the position.

Figure 12.11, which shows the expected profit and loss of the hedged position as a function of the stock price, may give the impression that there is a pure arbitrage. The worst outcome seems to be a zero profit in the case of an unchanged stock price while a positive profit occurs in any

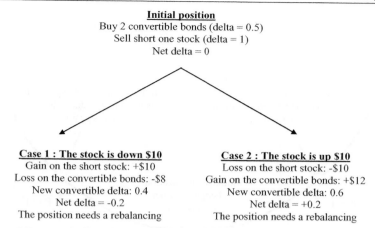

Initial position
Buy 2 convertible bonds (delta = 0.5)
Sell short one stock (delta = 1)
Net delta = 0

Case 1 : The stock is down $10
Gain on the short stock: +$10
Loss on the convertible bonds: -$8
New convertible delta: 0.4
Net delta = -0.2
The position needs a rebalancing

Case 2 : The stock is up $10
Loss on the short stock: -$10
Gain on the convertible bonds: +$12
New convertible delta: 0.6
Net delta = +0.2
The position needs a rebalancing

Figure 12.10   An illustration of a delta hedge situation. Note that the convertible bond price changes by more than its initial delta due to its convexity (the delta of the convertible bond changes as the stock price varies)

other case. Unfortunately, this is not strictly true. We have considered stock price variations, but ignored other aspects of the convertible position, and in particular the loss of time value of the option component.[6] This time decay offsets the convexity gains to such an extent that the expected return on the continuously delta-hedged position actually equals the risk-free rate. The curve in Figure 12.11 should therefore be shifted down to reflect the possibility of a loss around the current stock price.

Of course, the exact shape of the profit and loss curve will also depend on the *realized* volatility of the stock price versus its implied volatility. In particular, if the realized volatility is higher than the implied volatility, the delta-hedged position will make a profit in excess of the risk-free rate. This is exactly what convertible arbitrageurs expect. Indeed, saying that a convertible bond is cheap is equivalent to saying that its implied volatility is too low. Conversely, if the realized volatility is below the implied volatility, the loss on the time decay will outweigh the profit made from the realized volatility and the position will underperform a risk-free investment, perhaps even making a loss (see Figure 12.12).

Of course, all these elements must be carefully analysed and closely monitored. Strongly risk- adverse arbitrageurs even go one step further and implement hedging strategies to eliminate all the risk in their portfolio – they delta hedge, gamma hedge, vega hedge, etc. The reader may well wonder how such a position can ever be profitable once all the risk sources have been hedged. In fact, the major sources of profit are not in these risks. First, the convertible bond position pays a regular coupon, which is cashed in by the arbitrageur. Second, the short stock position generates interest income on the sales proceeds. And third, the mispricing of the call option embedded in the convertible relative to the hedging instruments is captured at some point, at the latest at the convertible's maturity date.

---

[6] This is understandable if one considers that a long-term American call option is always worth more than a shorter-term American option with the same exercise price. Other things being equal, as the maturity of the option draws closer, the option value decreases.

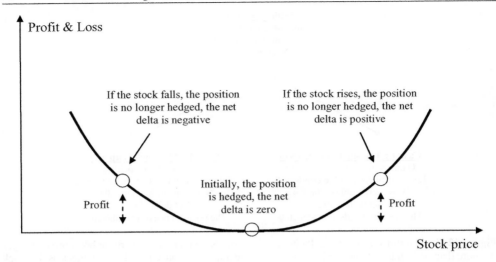

Figure 12.11   Profit on a delta hedged position (long convertible, short stock). The net delta is the slope of the curve

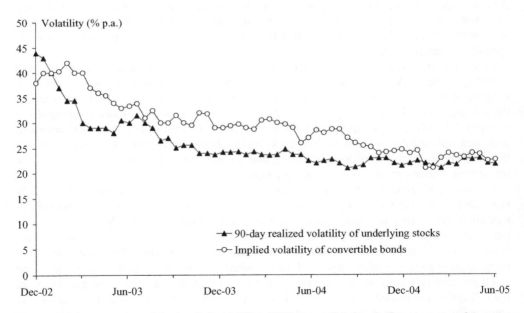

Figure 12.12   Evolution of the implied volatility of US convertible bonds (investment grade) versus realized 90-day volatility of underlying stocks

12.4 CONVERTIBLE ARBITRAGE IN PRACTICE: STRIPPING AND SWAPPING

Once interest rate and equity risks have been eliminated from the convertible position, our arbitrageur is left with credit risk, i.e. possible changes in credit spreads. This risk is important, because the majority of convertible issuers are below investment grade, at least in the US – see Figure 12.13. Moreover, many convertible bonds are unsecured, subordinated and issued by firms with high volatility of earnings, high leverage and/or intangible assets. They are particularly sensitive to the business cycle, so the arbitrageur cannot ignore credit risk and needs to hedge it.

To some extent, one could argue that the short stock position hedges a portion of the credit-spread risk because, as spreads widen, stock prices generally decline. But to eliminate entirely the credit-spread risk with a short stock position, the arbitrageur would need to short considerably more stock than the delta hedge calls for, placing the position at considerable risk should spreads not widen and stock prices appreciate. One alternative is to sell short a straight bond of the same issuer. This is usually an effective hedge against credit risk, but it is only feasible if other bonds from the same issuer are still actively traded and can be borrowed easily. This is clearly not the case for all issuers. Using credit default swaps might also be considered, but it exposes the arbitrageur to a serious call risk. Arbitrageurs who wish to unwind a default swap are reliant on finding a counterparty, but if the deliverable convertible bond has been called there is unlikely to be a market. Of course, a workaround is to buy credit default swaps that mature before the call date, but there is no guarantee that the arbitrage profit will be realized at this date.

Until recently, it was almost impossible to hedge properly the credit risk of a specific convertible bond issuer. Now one has to remember that real arbitrageurs are not really interested in the fixed income/credit portion of convertible bonds. They are just keen to purchase the associated cheap equity call options that they can offset against either the equity or other equity-linked securities. On the other hand, many investment banks and prime brokers have

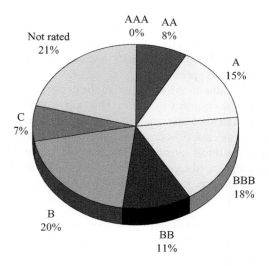

Figure 12.13   US convertible credit breakdown (as percentage of total Merrill Lynch Convertible Bond Index value)

Convertible Market

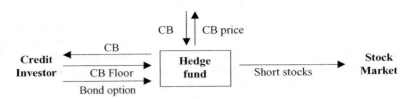

Figure 12.14   Typical flows in an asset swap

clients who are interested in the fixed income portion of convertible securities but have no real desire to hold the associated call option. Once again, financial intermediation has done miracles: a key development that has boosted the demand for convertible bonds in recent years has been the asset swap. This new instrument offers the ability to split a convertible bond into its two implicit components, the fixed income part and the equity call option. Most of the time, the asset swap involves a "credit seller" who will keep the equity option, and a "credit buyer" who will acquire the fixed income component. This unlocks the theoretical value of the convertible bond and greatly facilitates the implementation of arbitrage strategies.

Although asset swap arrangements can be technically complex, their basic construction is very simple. The process can be summarized in two steps (see Figure 12.14).

- *Step 1*: A hedge fund manager identifies an undervalued convertible bond. He verifies with his prime broker that the underlying stock can be borrowed. If such is the case, he purchases the convertible bond, which generally bears a fixed rate coupon and an option for its holder to convert into equity. In terms of risk, the manager is now exposed to rising interest rates, falling equity prices, and widening credit spreads.
- *Step 2*: The fund manager enters into an asset swap with a credit investor. This swap is usually made up of two transactions:
  - The fund manager sells the convertible bond to the credit investor at a large discount with respect to its market price. The selling price is typically set at the bond floor value, that is, the present value of the bond's future cash flow (coupons and repayment) discounted at LIBOR plus a fixed credit spread.
  - In exchange for the discount on the sale price of the convertible bond, the credit investor gives the fund an over-the-counter call option. This option allows the fund to purchase the convertible bond back at a fixed exercise price. The latter is also typically set at the present value of the bond's future cash flow (coupons and repayment) discounted at LIBOR plus a fixed recall spread. The recall spread is tighter than the one used for calculating the bond floor value to discourage rapid turnover of positions and to deliver a minimum return to the credit buyer. For instance, the swap terms could allow for a call at par value at the maturity of the bond.

Before going any further, we need to verify that after the asset swap, each party has only its desired exposures. The hedge fund, for its part, still has the equity upside exposure inherent in the convertible bond by virtue of owning the call option but is no longer exposed to the risk of widening credit spreads. This option is useless as long as the convertible bond is out of the money, but will allow participation in the upside potential of the stock. The good news is that, if the convertible bond was underpriced on the market, the floor value (at which the bond was sold to the credit investor) was correctly priced. This means that the hedge fund now holds an option whose final purchasing price was much less than its theoretical value. To capture the price difference, most hedge funds will simply delta hedge this option until it comes back to its fair value. Note that the hedge fund's loss is limited to the option premium, whose strike price depends on the credit spread initially agreed in the asset swap. On the other hand, the hedge fund can benefit if the credit trades to a tighter spread by calling the initial asset swap and simultaneously establishing a new one at a tighter spread.

After the asset swap, the credit investor holds a synthetic straight callable bond.[7] He is solely interested in betting that the credit quality of the issuer will improve in the future. He has no equity exposure, but faces credit risk and interest rate risk. Several credit investors will eliminate the interest rate risk by entering into another swap, in which they will pay a fixed rate equal to the convertible bond coupon and receive a floating rate, typically LIBOR plus a spread. This leaves them with only the credit exposure of the original convertible bond.

Now, let us consider what can happen at expiration. There are five basic cases to be considered:

- If the convertible bond matures out of the money, the hedge fund manager lets his option expire. The credit investor redeems the convertible bond and is repaid at par by its issuer.
- If the convertible bond matures in the money, the hedge fund manager calls back the convertible bond and pays the par value to the credit investor. The hedge fund manager then exercises the conversion option and receives the parity value, which is higher than his payment to the credit investor.
- If the convertible bond is called out of the money by the issuer, the hedge fund manager lets the option expire. The credit investor is then repaid at the call price by the issuer.
- If the convertible bond is called in the money by the issuer, the hedge fund manager calls back the convertible bond and pays the agreed call value to the credit investor. The hedge fund manager then exercises the convertible bond and receives the parity value, which is higher than his payment to the credit investor.
- Finally, if the issuer defaults, the hedge fund manager lets his option expire. The credit investor receives the recovery value of the convertible bond, if any, from the issuer.

In practice, asset swaps may take several forms, but their basic function remains the same, i.e. to split the convertible bond into its two core components. Convertible bond arbitrageurs will use them to gain equity exposure to a company while avoiding credit and interest rate risk exposures.

12.5 THE STRATEGY EVOLUTION

Initially set up as a niche business for dedicated proprietary trading desks in large investment banks, convertible arbitrage became a niche strategy within the alternative investments world in the early nineties. The initial strategy was remarkably simple: look for cheap convertible bonds, buy them and delta hedge them, and wait for the mispricing to disappear. A good proprietary pricing model, access to the deal flow and the ability to run serious credit analysis – there were no tools to properly hedge credit risk – were sufficient to generate attractive returns with a reasonable level of risk.

---

[7] The term "synthetic" is used because the position is not a straight callable bond but it behaves exactly as a straight callable bond.

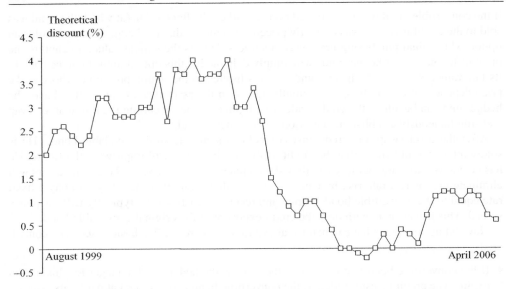

Figure 12.15   On average, US convertible bonds are underpriced with respect to their theoretical value. However, they became overpriced in the first quarter 2004

Over the years, the barriers to entry progressively crumbled and lots of money flooded into the convertible arbitrage strategy. The competitive advantage of advanced pricing models was eroded – a Bloomberg terminal already offers several pricing models of high quality. The excessive number of hedge funds in that space created intense competition and dramatically reduced the effectiveness of the strategy, to the point that some convertible bonds were actually sold at a premium to their fair value – see Figure 12.15. To remain profitable, most convertible arbitrage managers had to take some directional risks rather than neutralize them. The arbitrageurs became traders and started carrying some equity risk, some credit risk, some interest rate risk and/or some volatility risk. The quest for higher returns also spurred them to innovate in two directions: more leveraged and more illiquid, with all the associated dangers that these two trends implied. Today, hedge funds are ironically more important than ever as the primary liquidity providers to convertible buyers and sellers (see Box 12.3). According to some estimates, convertible bond arbitrage trades currently represent more than 70% of the secondary market trading in convertible securities at the institutional level, and US hedge funds are said to own around 50% of all convertible bond issues outstanding in the US. They have also expanded in other countries, e.g. in the Asia Pacific region and Europe.

Box 12.3 Privately placed convertibles

Convertible bonds can be sold as a public issue to investors at large or placed privately with a few investors. In the latter case, the issuer does not have to go through the SEC registration process and can raise funds faster with lower flotation and distribution costs.[8] A significant

---

[8] Flotation costs include the direct and indirect expenses of security issues. Direct expenses are the underwriter's spread, filing fees, legal fees, and taxes. Indirect expenses include management time on the new issue. Flotation costs can range from less than 5% to 20% of gross proceeds.

portion of these cost savings is usually passed on to the convertible bond buyers in the form of a lower issue price, which further strengthens the initial cheapness of convertible bonds. Several hedge funds have attempted to profit from this new opportunity. Rather than relying on investment banks to supply new convertible bonds, they have decided to go directly to issuers and purchase their convertible bonds in private placements.

The danger of this approach is that, by construction, private placements are less liquid than public issues. Indeed, investment banks have no incentive to create and maintain a secondary market for securities that they have not underwritten. This can create serious difficulties when a hedge fund manager wants to sell his position, particularly during a stressed market.

Today, it would be incorrect to see convertible arbitrage as a low-risk strategy. In truth, it is immersed in risks. Convertible arbitrageurs have to continuously determine which risks they want to isolate and exploit. Proper disclosure from a convertible arbitrage fund should therefore provide some clarity regarding the real risks that sustain the strategy, and investors should assess whether the manager has the necessary skills and capital to take these risks.

In addition, beyond equity, credit and interest rate risks, the major perils of convertible arbitrage are:

- Event risk, such as a sudden dividend payment or capital distribution. Even when they are properly delta hedged, convertible arbitrageurs may face abrupt variations in their hedge ratios that are costly to follow.
- Liquidity risk. The liquidity of convertible bonds is considerably lower than that of equivalent straight bonds, and bid–ask spreads can widen significantly. In addition, the short position is subject to recall risk.
- Specific clauses, which may dramatically impact the value of the convertible bond. For instance, "screw clauses" may state that bondholders converting into shares will not be paid the accrued interest on their bonds by the issuer, or "clean-up clauses" may state that the issuer may force conversion if a certain percentage of bonds has been converted into shares.
- Currency risk. When using convertible bonds from foreign countries, currency risk is always present. Arbitrageurs generally employ currency futures or forward contracts to hedge this risk.

Last but not least, convertible arbitrage is also subject to *hedge risk*. In a few situations, the convertible bond and its hedge portfolio can behave in an unexpected way, and result in heavy losses – see Box 12.4. Diversification across issuers, industries, countries, ratings and types of convertible is obviously a way to reduce the impact of such risks.

Box 12.4 When being hedged turns into a disaster

While in normal times convertible arbitrage can generate low risk and high returns, in rare situations it becomes very high risk and big trouble. This is what a large number of hedge funds realized in early 2005 when they were long General Motors (GM) convertible bonds and short GM shares. In theory, they were hedged. In practice, things went ... really wrong, and arbitrageurs got a double whammy (see Figure 12.16 and 12.17).

On 5 May 2005, while most hedge fund managers were celebrating Karl Marx's 187th birthday, some Standard and Poor's analysts decided to spoil the party and downgraded General Motors from investment grade to junk status. The downgrade sent the price of all

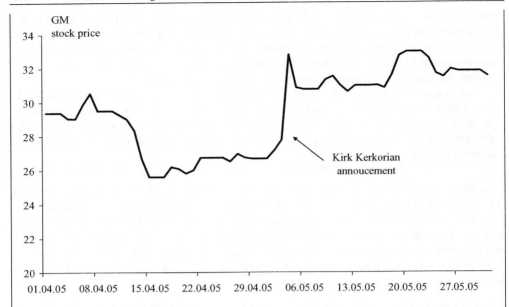

Figure 12.16   Evolution of GM stock

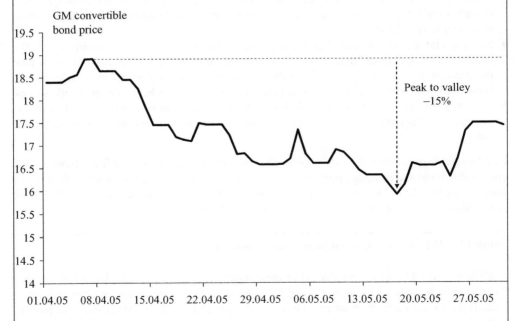

Figure 12.17   Evolution of GM convertible bond (5.25% GM Series B Convertible Senior Debentures maturing in 2032)

GM bonds tumbling, because all institutional investors became massive forced sellers and there was no buyer capable of absorbing the resulting flow. For hedge fund managers, it was not too much of a concern, because their short stock position would normally have provided some protection against this event. Unfortunately for them, billionaire Kirk Kerkorian announced the same day that he would bid $31 for a 28 million shares stake in the firm. This drove the price of the stock from roughly $28 to $32.

Hedge funds that were long the bond and short the stock lost in both directions – instead of being hedged they found themselves doubly exposed, most of the time with leveraged positions. The large losses at some hedge funds immediately sparked speculation and even dented equity markets amid concern that the troubles could spread to investment banks that provide trading and other services to the industry.

Note that this was not the first time such a situation had occurred. In the summer of 1998, the convertible arbitrageurs that were long convertible bonds and short Treasury futures to hedge their interest rate risk were severely hit as the flight to quality smashed convertible prices and pushed Treasury prices up. Allowance should always be made for the unexpected.

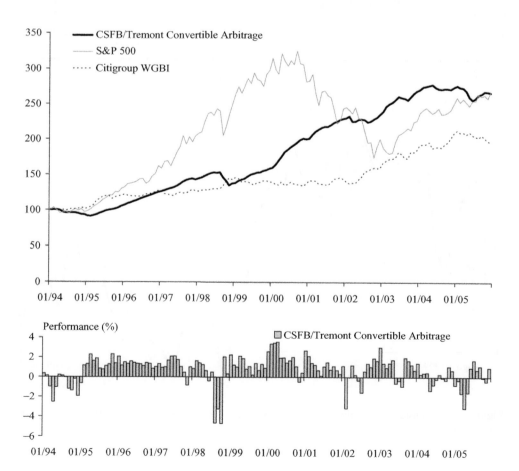

Figure 12.18   Evolution of the CS/Tremont Convertible Arbitrage Index, 1994–2005

Table 12.2   Performance comparison of the CS/Tremont Convertible Arbitrage Index, the S&P 500 and the Citigroup World Government Bond Index, 1994–2005

	CS/Tremont Convertible Arbitrage	S&P 500	Citigroup WGBI
Return (% p.a.)	8.61	8.55	5.87
Volatility (% p.a.)	4.89	16.00	6.74
Skewness	−1.32	−0.58	0.37
Kurtosis	3.01	0.61	0.37
Normally distributed?	No	No	Yes
Correlation with strategy		0.14	−0.08
Positive months frequency	76%	62%	58%
Best month performance (%)	3.57	9.67	5.94
Average positive month performance (%)	1.29	3.44	1.73
Upside participation		39%	122%
Negative months frequency	24%	38%	42%
Worst month performance (%)	−4.68	−14.58	−4.28
Average negative month performance (%)	−1.22	−3.53	−1.18
Downside participation		−216%	−395%
Max. drawdown (%)	−12.04	−46.28	−7.94
Value at Risk (1-month, 99%)	−4.03	−10.24	−3.36

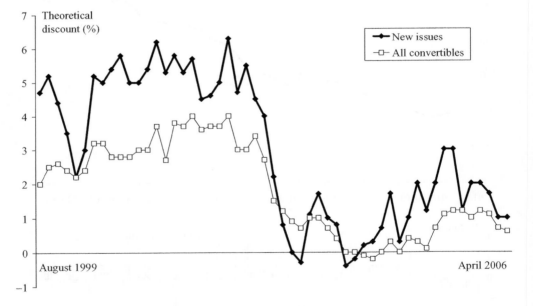

Figure 12.19   Discount/Premium of newly issued US convertible bonds compared to all other convertibles

Table 12.3   Monthly returns of the CS/Tremont Convertible Arbitrage Index, 1994–2005

	1994	1995	1996	1997	1998	1999	2000	2001	2002	2003	2004	2005
Jan	0.36	−0.62	2.07	1.03	0.84	2.27	2.59	2.68	1.12	3.02	1.42	−0.80
Feb	0.15	1.18	1.18	1.33	1.63	1.22	3.37	2.12	−3.15	1.39	0.29	−0.31
Mar	−0.97	1.32	1.50	0.94	1.42	1.04	3.46	1.42	−0.02	0.95	0.42	−1.63
Apr	−2.52	2.28	1.34	1.02	1.27	2.14	3.57	1.22	1.21	1.42	0.46	−3.13
May	−1.02	1.65	1.59	1.68	0.65	1.89	1.94	0.69	0.23	1.76	−1.33	−1.55
Jun	0.21	1.90	1.45	2.09	−0.37	0.81	1.97	0.13	−0.33	−0.62	−0.76	0.96
Jul	0.14	0.86	1.36	2.11	0.52	1.09	1.46	1.08	−1.55	−0.35	−0.20	1.71
Aug	−0.04	0.77	1.31	1.75	−4.64	0.23	1.69	1.50	0.60	−0.91	0.28	0.72
Sep	−1.19	1.12	1.12	1.03	−3.23	1.39	2.02	0.74	1.37	1.97	−0.07	1.10
Oct	−1.36	1.29	1.44	0.46	−4.68	0.70	1.09	1.11	1.03	1.67	−0.29	−0.07
Nov	−0.17	2.31	1.35	−0.82	2.06	1.30	−0.47	0.71	1.92	1.25	1.08	−0.43
Dec	−1.92	1.39	0.85	1.01	0.35	0.90	0.44	0.32	1.66	0.70	0.69	0.96
Total	−8.06	16.55	17.87	14.48	−4.42	16.03	25.65	14.58	4.04	12.88	1.98	−2.55
S&P 500	−1.54	34.11	20.26	31.01	26.67	19.53	−10.14	−13.04	−23.37	26.38	8.99	3.00
WGBI	2.34	19.04	3.62	0.23	15.30	−4.27	1.59	−0.99	19.49	14.91	10.35	−6.88

12.6   HISTORICAL PERFORMANCE

Convertible arbitrage managers in the aggregate have produced high absolute returns with a low level of volatility. Over the January 1994 to December 2005 period, convertible arbitrage hedge funds – as measured by the CS/Tremont Convertible Arbitrage Index – delivered an average return of 8.6% p.a. with a volatility of 4.9%. By contrast, over the same period, the S&P 500 delivered an average return of 8.6% p.a. with a volatility of 16.0%, and the Citigroup World Government Bond Index delivered an average return of 5.9% p.a. with a volatility of 6.7%. As shown in Figure 12.18 and Table 12.2, convertible arbitrage had its best years from

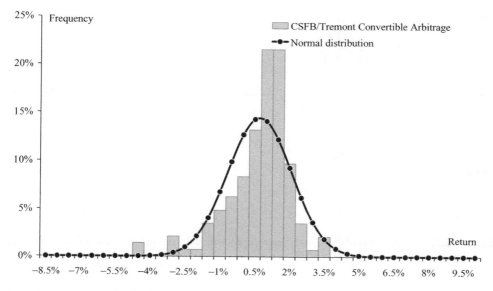

Figure 12.20   Return distribution of the CS/Tremont Convertible Arbitrage Index, 1994–2005

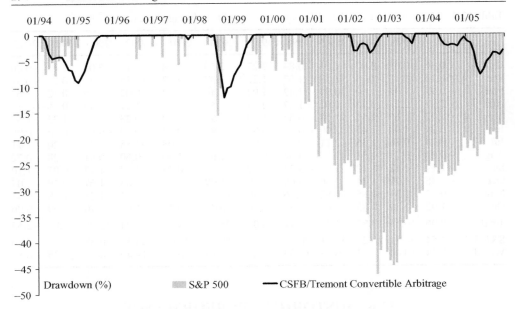

Figure 12.21 Drawdown diagram of the CS/Tremont Convertible Arbitrage Index compared to the S&P 500, 1994–2005

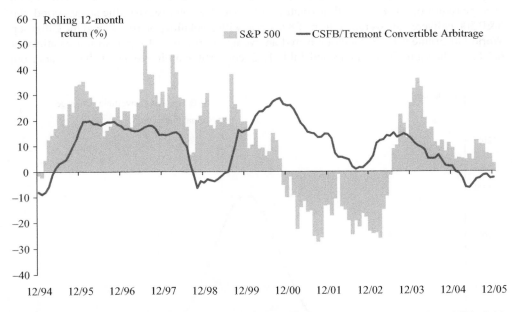

Figure 12.22 Comparison of the 12-month rolling performances of the CS/Tremont Convertible Arbitrage Index with the S&P 500, 1994–2005

1995 to 1997 and, to a lesser extent, from 1999 to 2003. The worst year was 1994 (primarily because of rising interest rates) followed by 1998 (the flight to quality following the LTCM crisis) and 2005 (the GM crisis). However, as already mentioned, the strategy has considerably evolved since 2000 and credit plays now seem to be again the dominant factor.

The average monthly profitability of convertible arbitrage has been decreasing over the recent years, due to the excessive number of hedge funds active of the strategy with respect to its limited capacity. The newly issued convertibles (less than six months) are over-monitored, and their cheapness is lower than for older issues – which are already held by existing arbitrageurs. At some points in 2003 and 2004, newly issued convertible bonds were even issued on average at a small premium compared to their fair value, due to excessive demand (see Figure 12.19 and Table 12.3). In addition, volatility has been going down, credit risk is poorly rewarded, so that the potential return sources are drying up one after the another.

The returns exhibit negative skewness and positive kurtosis (mostly due to three months during the summer 1998 as well as the GM crisis in April 2005), so that the return distribution cannot be considered as being normally distributed (Figure 12.20).

The drawdowns of the CS/Tremont Convertible Arbitrage Index compared to the S&P 500, 1994–2005, are shown in Figure 12.21.

Lastly, the rolling 12-month returns of Figure 12.22 illustrate the cyclical nature of the strategy.

13

Fixed Income Arbitrage

I am sorry. The convergence trade diverged...

A trader

Fixed income markets are a particularly fertile territory for hedge funds, due to: (i) the lack of agreement on a standard absolute pricing model; (ii) the existence of multiple *relative* pricing relationships between various fixed income instruments; (iii) the influence of irrational but predictable supply and demand on specific asset prices; and (iv) the complex nature of some fixed income securities. The combination of these four elements opens the door to a broad set of strategies intended to exploit valuation differences and pricing anomalies between various fixed income securities. In the following, we will refer to them as fixed income arbitrage, although most of these strategies are not arbitrage in the purest sense. Some of them carry some risk and may actually lose money. But their risks are fundamentally different from the traditional buy and hold fixed income strategies, and they often mix long and short positions, therefore the name "arbitrage".

In practice, one can distinguish three major investment styles in fixed income arbitrage strategies: relative value, "market" neutral and directional trading.

- Relative value strategies seek to construct a portfolio which takes advantage of a relative pricing anomaly between two or more fixed income securities while maintaining a diversified risk profile. Neutrality with regard to interest rate variations is not systematically targeted, as the main objective is usually to maximize the portfolio's return while controlling the risk.
- Market neutral strategies are similar to relative value trades, but they systematically hedge their exposure to interest rate variations. Most of the time, the long and short positions are regularly rebalanced in such a way as to maintain neutrality, i.e. ensure zero duration of the resulting portfolio.
- Directional trading strategies focus on absolute pricing anomalies, or equivalently, take directional bets in the fixed income area, primarily on spreads but also on interest rates. This trading style is at the frontier of global macro investing.

Fixed income arbitrage was traditionally the speciality of proprietary traders in large investment banks. However, the high level of leverage necessary to successfully implement the strategy, the costly equity capital requirements from regulators and the collapse of LTCM in 1998 have convinced most banks to shut down, or at least externalize, their fixed income trading activities. Today, most fixed income arbitrage hedge funds are run by these ex-proprietary traders.

13.1 THE BASIC TOOLS OF FIXED INCOME ARBITRAGE

For the sake of simplification, one could almost say that the fundamental tool in fixed income arbitrage is the *term structure of interest rates*, i.e. the pure "price of time". Simply stated, the term structure of interest rates is the relationship between pure interest rates and their maturity (see Figure 13.1).

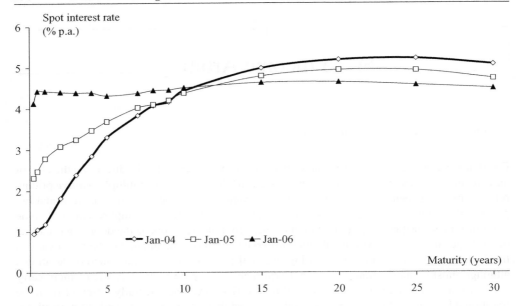

Figure 13.1 Examples of the US term structure of interest rates at different point in time, calculated from STRIPS (i.e. zero coupons bonds)

The term structure of interest rates can easily be obtained from zero coupon bonds. However, the majority of bonds pay a regular coupon. In practice, market participants therefore calculate the term structure of interest rates from coupon-paying bonds, and refer to it as the yield curve. In a sense, it is a snapshot of the current level of yields in the market – see Figure 13.2.

The shape of a yield curve may vary over time, but unless markets have specific expectations, it should be mostly upward sloping, because investors want to be compensated for going towards longer maturities. One exception is of course the very long end of the yield curve, due to supply and demand effects. For instance, the 30-year US Treasury bond is usually in a great demand from institutional investors (pension funds and insurance companies) to meet their long-term liabilities. As a result, the price of a long-term bond is forced upwards, and this moves the yield down to below what it should be.

There are as many yield curves as ways to split the universe. For instance, one can consider the US Treasury curve, the BBB-rated curve, the Euro government curve, the zero-coupon curve, etc. For a given maturity, one can therefore calculate the spread, which is the difference between two rates taken from different curves.

Yield curves are the building blocks of fixed income markets. They are used for:

- *Benchmarking*: Some yield curves serve as a benchmark to other debt instruments. For instance, corporate bonds or swaps should always offer a spread over the equivalent Treasury bond yield, because the latter is a "default-free" instrument backed by the full faith and credit of the US government.
- *Forecasting*: Yield curves implicitly contain market expectations about future yields. In particular, by comparing spot interest rates of different maturities, it is possible to extract forward interest rates.

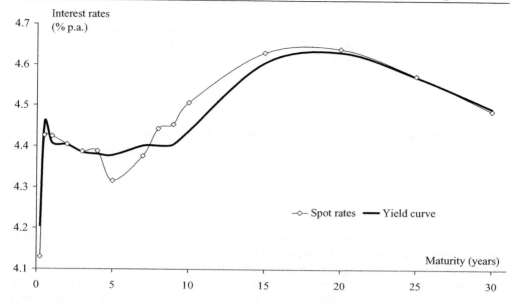

Figure 13.2 The US yield curve as of 1 January 2006, compared to the term structure of interest rates. The yield curve is calculated using coupon-paying bonds, while the spot rates are obtained from zero-coupon bonds

- *Comparison*: Yield curves indicate the returns that are available at different maturity points. Portfolio managers therefore use the yield curve to assess the relative value of investments across the maturity spectrum, as well as to assess which point of the curve offers the best returns relative to others.
- *Valuation*: A given yield curve can be analysed to indicate which bonds are cheap or expensive to the curve. Stated differently, if the yield of a bond is traded at a level below the yield curve, the bond is expensive.

13.2 EXAMPLES OF SUB-STRATEGIES

Fixed income arbitrage strategies rely heavily on mathematical and/or statistical valuation models. Interest-rate-sensitive securities fluctuate in accordance with yield curves, call covenants, expected cash flow, credit ratings, volatility curves, etc., and therefore often generate pricing anomalies that dynamic, sophisticated arbitrageurs can capture. Let us describe some of these. Rather than following on the details of the pricing of these trades, we will try to give the rationale behind the corresponding positions, as well as the associated risks.

13.2.1 Treasuries stripping

Treasuries stripping, at one time, was a profitable fixed income arbitrage strategy at investment banks in the early 1980s, due to an obvious mismatch between the demand and supply of high-quality zero coupon bonds. Pension funds, for instance, needed to match the cash flows of their assets with those of their liabilities to make benefit payments. They would have loved

Time :	1	2	3	4	5	
Cash flows :	55	55	55	55	1,055	
NPV :	52.38	49.89	47.51	45.25	826.62	
	↓	↓	↓	↓	↓	→ 1,021.65
Selling price :	52.90	50.39	47.99	45.70	834.89	
	↓	↓	↓	↓	↓	→ 1,031.87

Figure 13.3 Arbitraging a Treasury bond by stripping it into an equivalent portfolio of zero-coupon bonds

to purchase zero coupon bonds, but they were not available – Treasury bonds were all coupon-paying bonds. Fixed income arbitrageurs quickly imagined a solution. They bought large amounts of Treasuries, placed them in escrow and stripped them – that is, they separated the original coupon-bearing bond into its individual cash flows, which were then sold individually to investors. The result was a series of separate zero coupon instruments, each with its own maturity date and each tradable separately until its maturity date. Known as receipt products, these zero coupon bonds were recognized by feline names such as CATS, TIGRS, or LIONS.[1] Unlike regular bonds, they did not make regular payments of interest to their holders. Instead, investors bought them at a deep discount from their face value – the difference between the face value and the actual price of the zero coupon bond represented the interest earnings of the investment. The arbitrage was remarkably simple: the new zero coupon bonds were sold at a price that was higher than their fair value. The premium was justified because they were the only available default-free financial product for investors who did not want to deal with the problems of reinvesting coupon payments that accompanied US Treasury bonds. As the arbitrage operation was completely back to back, there was virtually no risk for the stripper.

As an illustration, consider a 5-year 5.5% annual coupon bond with a face value of €1000. This bond could easily be stripped into its principal (€1000) and its five annual interest payments (€50). The fair value of each zero-coupon bond is easy to determine. For the sake of simplicity, let us assume that interest rates are all equal to 5% p.a. whatever the maturity. Then, the fair value is the final payment of each bond discounted at 5% p.a. The first bond pays €55 in a year and is worth €52.38 today; the second bond pays €55 in two years and is worth €49.89 today; etc. The sum of the fair values of the five zero-coupon bonds equals the fair value of the original coupon-paying bond by construction. Now, if the arbitrageur is able to sell the zero coupons with a premium of, say, 1% above their fair value, he will make a total profit of €10.22 per €1000 face value, that is, 1% of the fair market value of the initial bonds. In fact, as soon as the selling price of some of the zero coupon bonds is sufficiently different from their fair value, stripping trades will be profitable (see Figure 13.3).

In 1986, the US Treasury introduced its own coupon-stripping programme called STRIPS (Separate Trading of Registered Interest and Principal Securities), which essentially allowed any brokerage firm to create zero coupons based on book-entry receipts for US Treasury

---

[1] CATS (Certificates of Accrual on Treasury Securities) were issued by Salomon Brothers, TIGRS (Treasury Investment Growth Receipts) by Merrill Lynch, and LIONS (Lehman Investment Opportunity Notes) by Shearson Lehman Brothers.

instruments of 10 years or more. The process involved wiring Treasury notes and bonds to the Federal Reserve Bank of New York and receiving separated components in return. This practice significantly reduced the legal and insurance costs customarily associated with the process of stripping a security, and marked the end of easy money for US Treasury strippers. However, they easily extended the concept to other types of bonds and their implied zero-coupon components, as well as to other countries. The strategy was essentially the same. If the coupon bond price is lower than the price of the stripped components, short the set of strips, use the proceeds to buy the coupon bond, and strip the coupon bond to close out the short position. If the coupon bond price is higher than the price of the stripped components, short the coupon bond, use part of the proceeds to buy strips, and repackage the strips into the coupon bond to close out the short position.

An efficient implementation of the stripping strategy requires that stripped components of the same type (same issuer, either coupon or residual) be fungible. That is, a given coupon payable at a given date and stripped from a given bond should be indistinguishable from another coupon with the same amount and the same payment date, but which was originally stripped from another bond from the same issuer. This allows for an easy reconstruction of the original bond (underlying bond) from the coupon strips and the principal strip – a prerequisite of arbitrage between the underlying bond and its components. Ideally, stripped components should also be allowed to be repackaged in different ways, and the package sold as a bond. For example, components stripped from high coupon bonds could be repackaged into low coupon bonds, or more generally into any bond different from the one from which they had been stripped. This extends the possible arbitrage to virtually any existing bond. Needless to say, arbitrageurs should also take into account transaction costs as well as the tax treatment of coupon bonds and strip bonds in their calculations.

13.2.2 Carry trades

Carry trades consist in taking a long position in a higher yield instrument and a short position in a lower yield instrument. For instance, if the yield curve is upward sloping, a hedge fund could borrow short term and invest long term, pocketing the spread between the two rates. In the early 2000s, by holding the nominal federal funds rate at a 40-year low of 1%, the Federal Reserve has aided and abetted a multiplicity of carry trades – from those in the Treasury market, to high-yield and emerging-market debt, to credit instruments and mortgage securities. The danger, of course, is that the high-yield instrument could suddenly see its price falling (for instance, because its yield has increased).

13.2.3 On-the-run versus off-the-run Treasuries

Treasury bonds, notes and bills are auctioned on a regular schedule by the US Treasury. Security dealers post bids in terms of yields, and bidders that submitted the lowest yields are awarded the securities, which they can subsequently market to their customers. While the process seems straightforward, it allows for some arbitrage, particularly on the most recently issued Treasury bonds.

The most recently issued treasuries of a particular maturity are referred to as "on-the-run" securities, while other bonds are "off-the-run". For example, a newly issued 30-year US Treasury bond is considered on the run, while a 29.5 year bond is a bond that was on the run six months ago, but is now off the run. On-the-run Treasury bonds are typically the

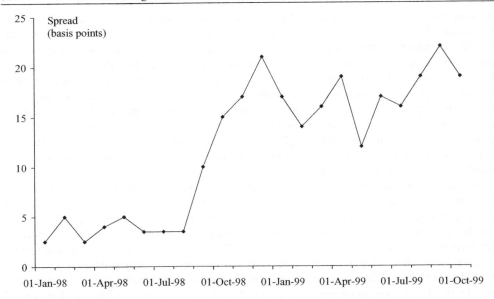

Figure 13.4   Monthly evolution of the spread between the yield on the on-the-run and the off-the-run 5-year US Treasury bonds

most liquid and most actively traded of Treasury securities and, therefore, are often referenced as pricing benchmarks. They frequently trade at higher prices (i.e. lower yields) than more seasoned Treasuries with similar cash flows, which are called "off-the-run" (see Figure 13.4). The rationale for this mispricing is hard to justify. Existing theoretical and empirical analyses have argued that these higher prices were due to the liquidity premium that investors were willing to pay to hold more liquid securities. However, this liquidity is only temporary, and a counter-argument is that the superior liquidity of on-the-run Treasuries makes them ideal securities for market intermediaries who wish to create short positions. They can easily be located, borrowed and sold when initiating a short position, and just as easily repurchased when closing one out. This short-selling pressure should push their price down rather than up.

Nevertheless, for hedge funds, on-the-run and off-the-run Treasuries with similar maturities are essentially the same instruments. The spread between on-the-run and off-the-run Treasuries is an irrational difference on which they can make a profit, because at some point, the prices of these bonds will have to converge. As long as one is not concerned with liquidity and does not have to liquidate its positions unexpectedly, arbitraging between on-the-run and off-the-run Treasuries is a low-risk strategy.[2] The arbitrage consists in buying the cheaper off-the-run bond while simultaneously selling the more expensive on-the-run bond. This locks in the spread between the two bonds while immunizing the position from interest rate movements.

The usual difficulty in these types of arbitrage is the size of the spread, which tends to be very small. For example, in August 1993, 30-year bonds yielded 7.24%, while $29\frac{1}{2}$ year bonds yielded 7.36%, i.e. a 12 basis points spread. To magnify this return, it is necessary to use leverage. On this particular trade, magnification is easy: the hedge fund receives cash when it

---

[2] Note that LTCM was an active player in the on-the-run/off-the-run arbitrage, but experienced problems when it had to liquidate its positions.

shorts the on-the-run bond and it can then use that cash to buy the off-the-run bond. Since both positions are very closely related, the request for collateral will be small. This explains why hedge funds often implement the on-the-run/off-the-run arbitrage with 30 or 40 times leverage.

13.2.4   Yield-curve arbitrage

Yield-curve arbitrage involves taking long and short positions at various points (maturities) on a yield curve, typically a Treasury bond curve. The goal is to profit from unusual patterns and/or expected future deformations of the yield curve. For instance, during the first half of the year 2000, there were several forecasts of a diminishing supply of long bonds as a consequence of the US Treasury's plans to use the growing budget surplus to buy back the national debt. This created an excess number of buyers for these very long bonds. Consequently, the price of US Treasury bonds was such that the yield on a 30-year issue was lower than the yield on a 10-year issue, resulting in a negative spread (see Figure 13.5).

This is clearly an abnormal pattern because longer maturing securities are usually considered more risky and therefore investors should demand a higher yield for a 30-year bond than for a 10-year bond. In addition, both 10-year and 30-year T-bonds are extremely liquid, so the liquidity argument seems hard to sustain. An arbitrageur would therefore typically buy the lower priced 10-year bonds and short sell the higher priced 30-year bonds. His bet is that the 10-year yield will go back below the 30-year yield. The outcome of the strategy does not depend on the absolute level of the interest rates, but just on the relative level of 10-year and 30-year rates.

If we look at what happened in this particular case, we can see that the markets did indeed end up by pushing the 30-year yield above the 10-year yield. However, the time it took to make

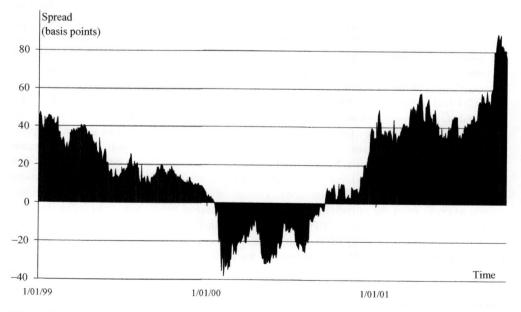

Figure 13.5   Evolution of the spread between the 30-year Treasury bond yield and the 10-year Treasury bond yield

the correction – about 8 months – is surprisingly long. This constitutes a hint that 'arbitrage' profits may take some time to materialize. As an illustration, there are other anomalies that have still not been rectified, such as the spread between the 30-year and the 20-year T-bond yield, which has been negative for more than six years.[3]

13.2.5 Swap-spread arbitrage

The interest rate swap market is one of the most important fixed income markets for the management of interest rate risk by both financial and non-financial firms. Interest rate swaps are riskier than Treasuries, and therefore trade at a spread which is closely monitored and used as a speculating support by hedge funds. The curve to monitor is called the swap curve, which represents the fixed rate at which companies can enter into interest rate swaps.

The interest swap spread is determined by fundamental economic and financial variables, but also by the "arbitrage" activity of convergence traders. Convergence traders form an expectation of the fundamental level of the spread and trade in an attempt to profit from that expectation.[4] For example, if the swap spread is above its estimated fundamental level, the trader who expects the spread to fall would take a long position in an interest rate swap[5] and an offsetting short position in a Treasury security. If the spread between the rates fell, with the swap rate falling relative to the Treasury rate, the long swap position would gain value relative to the short Treasury position and the trader would earn the difference by closing out the position. Conversely, if the swap spread is perceived to be above its fundamental level, in which a trader expects the spread to fall back to that level, the convergence trade is a long swap position and a short Treasury position.

Alternatively, carry traders may also step in the game and take offsetting long positions in a swap and short positions in Treasury bond. Since swap rates are higher than Treasury rates, this simple strategy generates a stream of positive cash flows equal to the spread provided that default of the swap counterparty does not occur. If there is a default, of course, then this strategy may suffer a large loss. In practice, however, the default risk is negligible because (i) swaps are usually fully collateralized under master swap agreements between major institutional investors and (ii) the actual default exposure in a swap is far less than for a corporate bond since notional amounts are not exchanged.

LTCM had a number of these swap trades on its books. For instance, in 1994, LTCM's principals felt that investors were irrationally bearish on a type of Italian Treasury bond known as a BTP. Specifically, they noticed that the Italian swaps curve was below the Italian yield curve, so that Italian Treasury bonds actually provided a higher yield than Italian corporate swaps of comparable duration. Stated differently, investors in the Italian bond market felt that there was a greater likelihood that the Italian government would default on its bonds than there was that Italian companies with high credit ratings would default. They therefore structured a trade to profit from the mispricing while being immunized from changes in Italian interest rates. In the first part of the trade, LTCM received Italian Treasury coupon payments from one bank in exchange for Lira LIBOR – economically this is equivalent to being long Treasuries, but without holding them. The second part of the trade was a short Italian swap position, in

---

[3] A possible explanation is that true 7-year and 20-year Treasuries are not issued, but instead the yields for these maturities are based upon 10- and 30-year Treasuries that were issued 3 and 10 years ago. Since 10-year and 30-year bonds are more popular, there may be a small liquidity premium embedded in the price of these bonds.

[4] Note that once again, this is not a pure arbitrage, but rather some directional trading based on the value of a spread.

[5] Being long a swap means to contract to receive the fixed rate in a new swap.

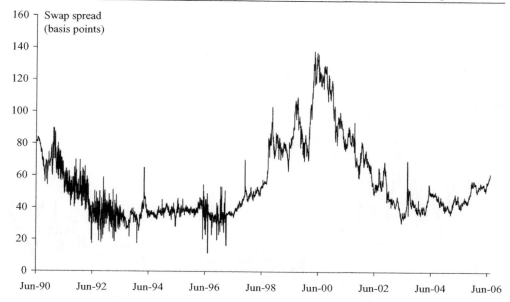

Figure 13.6 Swap rates versus Treasuries

which they received Lira LIBOR in exchange for the fixed swap rate from a different bank. The net effect of these two trades was that LTCM was receiving Italian Treasury coupon payments in exchange for paying the fixed swap rate. This allowed them to lock in the spread between the BTP and swap rates, while taking no view on the future direction of Italian interest rates. Risk-free trade? Not really. Lowenstein (2000) reports that LTCM lost $1.6 billion in their swap-spread positions before their collapse.

13.2.6 The Treasury–Eurodollar spread (TED)

Another common fixed income arbitrage strategy focuses on the Treasury–Eurodollar spread (TED spread). The TED spread (Figure 13.7) is defined as the difference between yields on US Treasury bills and those on Eurodollars with an identical maturity. US Treasury bills represent a loan to the US government while Eurodollars are certificates of deposit in US dollars in a non-US bank. The TED spread therefore reflects investors' views of the relative credit quality of the US Treasury and of the highest quality international banks. It typically widens during times of international banking stresses, such as a spike in the London Inter-Bank Offered Rate, the collapse of a major bank or a flight to quality.

Many hedge funds are actively trading the TED spread, with a *directional view* on how this spread will change. Hedge funds that trade the TED spread generally want to isolate the spread from the level of yields. Their typical positions are long TED Spread, i.e. long Treasury Bill futures and short Eurodollar futures, if they expect the TED spread to widen; they go short TED Spread, i.e. short Treasury Bill futures and long Eurodollar futures if they expect the TED spread to narrow. For example, assume that the rate of a 1-year US T-bill is 94.20 (implied

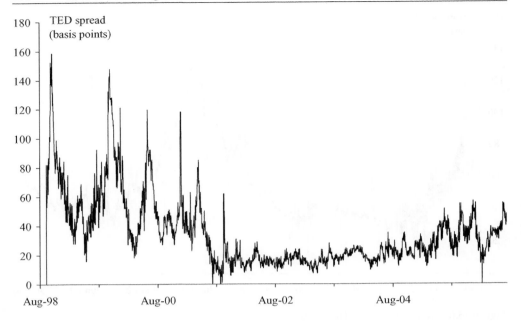

Figure 13.7   TED spread

discounted rate of 5.80%) and the Eurodollar future[6] is trading at 93.10 (implied Eurodollar deposit rate of 6.90%). In this case the TED spread would be $94.20 - 93.10 = 1.10$, and would be quoted at 110. An arbitrageur expecting the TED spread to widen from 110 to 125 would buy the TED spread, that is, he would buy, say, 10 T-bill futures and sell 10 Eurodollar futures. Say, for instance, that the spread widens to 126, with the T-bill contracts at 93.95 and the Eurodollar contracts at 92.70. The "arbitrageur" then sells 10 T-bill contracts and buys back 10 Eurodollar contracts. His profit would be 40 basis points $\times$ \$25 $\times$ 10 contracts = \$10 000, and his loss is 25 basis points $\times$ \$25 $\times$ 10 contracts = \$6250, leaving a net profit of \$3750.

13.3   HISTORICAL PERFORMANCE

The historical performance of fixed income arbitrage hedge funds has been relatively low in comparison to other strategies. Over the January 1994 to December 2005 period, fixed income arbitrage hedge funds – as measured by the CS/Tremont Fixed Income Arbitrage Index – delivered an average return of 6.28% p.a., with a volatility of 3.88%. By contrast, over the same period, the S&P 500 delivered an average return of 8.6% p.a., with a volatility of 16.0%, and the CS/Tremont Hedge Fund Index delivered an average return of 10.7% p.a., with a volatility of 8.1%. However, the strategy clearly outperformed bonds, as the Citigroup World Government Bond Index delivered a 5.87% return with 6.74% volatility (see Figure 13.8 and Table 13.1).

---

[6] The Eurodollar price is based on the three-month LIBOR for deposits of US\$1 million. The LIBOR is quoted as an annual interest rate. The futures price is quoted as 100 − (Interest rate, in percentage terms, of a 3-month Eurodollar deposit for forward delivery).

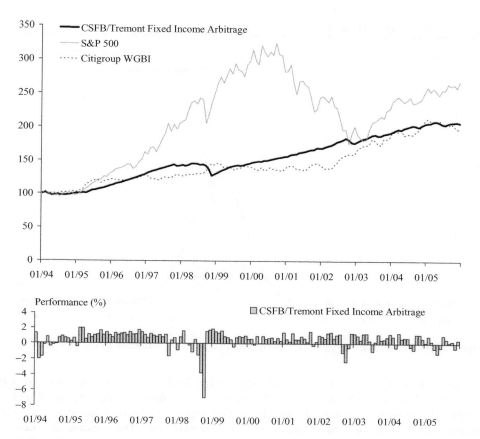

Figure 13.8 Evolution of the CS/Tremont Fixed Income Arbitrage Index, 1994–2005

Table 13.1 Performance comparison of the CS/Tremont Fixed Income Arbitrage Index, the S&P 500 and the Citigroup World Government Bond Index, 1994–2005

	CS/Tremont Fixed Income Arbitrage	S&P 500	Citigroup WGBI
Return (% p.a.)	6.28	8.55	5.87
Volatility (% p.a.)	3.88	16.00	6.74
Skewness	−3.10	−0.58	0.37
Kurtosis	16.41	0.61	0.37
Normally distributed?	No	No	Yes
Correlation with strategy		0.03	−0.10
Positive months frequency	80%	62%	58%
Best month performance (%)	2.02	9.67	5.94
Average positive month performance (%)	0.92	3.44	1.73
Upside participation		34%	119%
Negative months frequency	20%	38%	42%
Worst month performance (%)	−6.96	−14.58	−4.28
Average negative month performance (%)	−1.08	−3.53	−1.18
Downside participation		−9%	−215%
Max. drawdown (%)	−12.47	−46.28	−7.94
Value at Risk (1-month, 99%)	−3.11	−10.24	−3.36

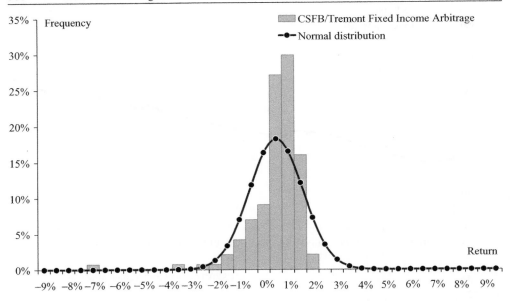

Figure 13.9 Return distribution of the CS/Tremont Fixed Income Arbitrage Index, 1994–2005

The track record of fixed income arbitrage hedge funds evidences large losses in 1998 (LTCM) and just after the summer 2002 (following the default of Adelphia and Worldcom combined with several accounting scandals, the Fed surprised markets by lowering rates 50 basis points calling the risks of inflation and recession balanced). The negative skewness and considerable positive kurtosis put the low volatility characteristics of this strategy into a new light. In exchange for lower risk in the second moment (the middle, i.e. "usual", part of the return distribution) investors incur higher tail risks on the negative side of the distribution (see Figure 13.9 and Table 13.2).

Table 13.2　Monthly returns of the CS/Tremont Fixed Income Arbitrage Index, 1994–2005

	1994	1995	1996	1997	1998	1999	2000	2001	2002	2003	2004	2005
Jan	1.30	0.27	1.43	1.48	−0.84	1.90	0.54	1.42	1.03	1.26	1.23	0.09
Feb	−2.00	0.65	1.06	1.10	0.81	1.52	0.57	0.53	0.87	0.99	0.87	0.91
Mar	−1.68	−0.44	0.77	0.72	1.61	1.34	−0.15	0.24	0.63	0.42	−0.49	0.27
Apr	−0.20	2.02	1.35	1.24	−0.01	1.63	0.93	1.32	1.35	1.25	1.34	−0.63
May	0.79	2.01	1.09	1.01	−0.21	0.88	0.02	0.52	1.44	1.28	0.63	−1.24
Jun	−0.40	0.52	1.25	0.87	−1.08	0.75	0.93	0.50	0.65	0.34	0.71	−0.52
Jul	−0.18	1.12	1.34	1.09	0.48	0.49	0.55	0.91	1.08	−0.98	0.70	1.00
Aug	−0.09	0.77	1.04	0.82	−1.46	−0.41	0.67	0.64	1.23	0.21	−0.41	0.51
Sep	0.70	1.04	1.47	1.15	−3.74	0.74	0.75	0.18	−1.14	1.16	−0.78	0.12
Oct	0.89	1.14	1.16	−1.58	−6.96	0.91	0.29	1.55	−2.27	0.46	1.14	0.27
Nov	0.69	1.68	1.17	0.40	1.55	0.78	0.70	−0.27	−0.53	0.52	1.12	−0.58
Dec	0.57	1.07	1.75	0.71	1.73	0.97	0.32	0.23	1.32	0.80	0.61	0.45
Total	0.33	12.48	15.93	9.35	−8.16	12.10	6.29	8.03	5.73	7.96	6.85	0.63
S&P 500	−1.54	34.11	20.26	31.01	26.67	19.53	−10.14	−13.04	−23.37	26.38	8.99	3.00
WGBI	2.34	19.04	3.62	0.23	15.30	−4.27	1.59	−0.99	19.49	14.91	10.35	−6.88

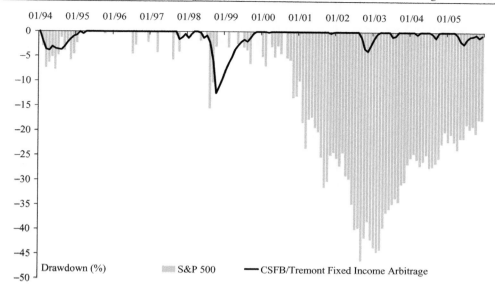

Figure 13.10   Drawdown diagram of the CS/Tremont Fixed Income Arbitrage Index compared to the S&P 500, 1994–2005

The maximum drawdown of the strategy is relatively large (−12.47%) compared to the returns, and it occurred precisely during the summer 1998, when LTCM experienced serious troubles (Figure 13.10). Lastly, the 12-month rolling return evidences the relative stability of the track record if we omit 1998 (Figure 13.11).

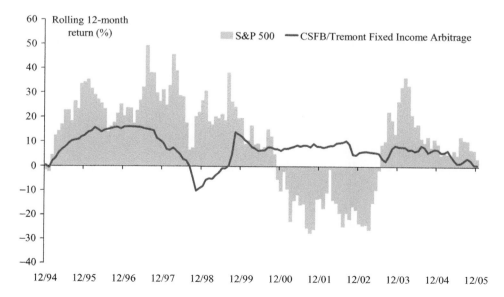

Figure 13.11   Comparison of the 12-month rolling performances of the CS/Tremont Fixed Income Arbitrage Index with the S&P 500, 1994–2005

14

Emerging Markets

Emerging market investing found its official roots in the mid-1980s when the International Finance Corporation (IFC), an arm of the World Bank, decided to set up the first mutual fund focusing on securities from emerging markets.[1] The Emerging Market Growth Fund initially started with a seed capital of $50 million, primarily provided by the IFC alongside a few pension funds and insurance companies that expressed interest. Its investment universe covered 32 countries with a market capitalization of $67 billion, i.e. approximately 2.5% of the world markets. Since then, interest for emerging markets has dramatically surged, thanks to the epic transformations that took place in these countries. Across the globe, democratically elected governments have replaced dictatorships, artificially pegged currencies have become freely floated, financial disclosure has replaced secrecy, and state-owned companies have been finally privatized. Many emerging countries have come a long way in establishing sound fiscal and monetary policies, opening their financial markets, addressing corporate governance, and improving their economic fundamentals. Despite several crises on the way, emerging markets as a group have proved they could sustain high growth and attract capital. As summarized by Mark Mobius, the manager of the Franklin-Templeton Group: "Emerging markets may be a euphemism, but it is also a declaration of hope and faith. Although some of the stock markets of developing nations may sometimes seem submerged; they are generally emerging into bigger and better things."

14.1 THE CASE FOR EMERGING MARKET HEDGE FUNDS

Today, emerging markets are approaching the $2 trillion mark for the first time in their history. They still only represent 7.15% of the world's float-adjusted capitalization, but they are growing fast. The MSCI Emerging Market Index now numbers 26 countries, but with large disparities in terms of weighting – see Table 14.1. Korea, for instance, has a higher weight than the 17 last emerging countries all together, and Korea, Taiwan, Brazil and South Africa represent more than 50% of the total emerging market capitalization.

Over the years, the definition of what constitutes an emerging market has also changed. Today, a country is characterized as "emerging" when it profits from a substantial economic growth based on significant productivity gains, technological change and/or a change in its economic philosophy. Emerging countries are also often characterized by political instability, strong currency turbulence and a high foreign debt, but many investors choose to turn a blind eye to these macroeconomic and geopolitical issues. They prefer to focus primarily on the growth potential of these markets.

On paper, emerging markets seem obviously very attractive – they represent over 85% of the world's population, 75% of the world's natural resources and account for nearly 25% of the world's GDP. Their economies are growing at two to three times that of the US, Europe

---

[1] The term "emerging market" was first coined by Antoine van Agtmael of the IFC in 1981 to represent an economy with low-to-middle per capita income which has embarked on capital market reforms.

Table 14.1   Emerged markets versus emerging markets, as a percentage of the MSCI All Country World Index

Country	%	Country	%
United States	46.35	Korea	1.26
Japan	10.99	Taiwan	0.96
United Kingdom	10.15	Brazil	0.79
France	4.23	South Africa	0.75
Canada	3.20	China	0.60
Germany	3.08	India	0.46
Switzerland	2.92	Russia	0.44
Australia	2.19	Mexico	0.44
Italy	1.64	Israel	0.22
Spain	1.63	Malaysia	0.20
Netherlands	1.50	Turkey	0.15
Sweden	1.05	Thailand	0.12
Hong Kong	0.70	Chile	0.12
Finland	0.66	Poland	0.12
Belgium	0.50	Indonesia	0.11
Singapore	0.36	Hungary	0.08
Ireland	0.35	Czech Republic	0.06
Norway	0.35	Egypt	0.06
Denmark	0.29	Argentina	0.06
Greece	0.28	Peru	0.03
Austria	0.22	Philippines	0.03
Portugal	0.14	Columbia	0.03
New Zealand	0.07	Pakistan	0.02
		Morocco	0.02
		Jordania	0.01
		Venezuela	0.01
Total	92.85	Total	7.15

or Japan, yet their stock valuations are still attractive, at sometimes half or even a third of their developed market competitors'. Moreover, their long-term fundamental positives include large rapidly industrializing populations, undervalued currencies, improving infrastructures, declining current account deficits, high savings rates and long-term propensity towards growth.

However, investing in emerging markets is certainly not for the faint of heart. Emerging markets form a risky asset class which often takes its investors on a wild ride, repeatedly doubling their money and then slashing it in half again. As an illustration, consider a $25 000 investment in the MSCI Emerging Markets Index[2] in May 1991. Ignoring dividends, this investment would have risen to $50 000 by July 1994, fallen to $25 000 in September 1997, risen again to $50 000 in March 2000, fallen to $25 000 in September 2001, and passed the $50 000 threshold in November 2004 before rallying to $80 000 in early 2006. Such a roller coaster ride would have been quite stressful, and many investors would have left the battlefield in the middle with large losses (see Figure 14.1).

---

[2] The MSCI Emerging Markets Index is a free float-adjusted market capitalization index that is designed to measure equity market performance in the global emerging markets. As of June 2006 the MSCI Emerging Markets Index consisted of the following 25 emerging market country indices: Argentina, Brazil, Chile, China, Colombia, Czech Republic, Egypt, Hungary, India, Indonesia, Israel, Jordan, Korea, Malaysia, Mexico, Morocco, Pakistan, Peru, Philippines, Poland, Russia, South Africa, Taiwan, Thailand and Turkey.

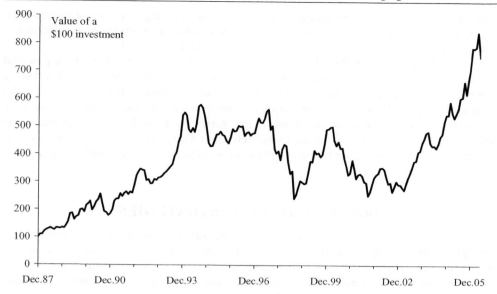

Figure 14.1   Evolution of the MSCI Emerging Market Index since December 1987

Even when investors are willing to accept such a level of volatility, indexing is not necessarily the best approach to emerging markets, for at least three reasons. First, indexing emphasizes diversification instead of picking winners and losers; but diversification does not function well in emerging markets, at least not when it is most needed. Certainly, emerging market correlations relative to each other are still quite low, but during crises, these markets tend to behave as a group and become suddenly highly correlated. If one of them catches a cold, the others catch the flu – a phenomenon known as "contagion". In addition, many emerging markets have their largest companies concentrated in a few sectors (e.g. energy, mining, etc.), so that an indexed portfolio will in fact be poorly diversified. Consequently, indexing will not necessarily reduce dramatically the overall risk of an emerging market portfolio.

Second, emerging markets often have specific characteristics that make systematic indexing difficult and sometimes even undesirable. Let us mention, for instance, the lack of liquidity of some securities, the high transaction costs (trading in Peru is over three times more costly than in Taiwan), the speed of execution (buying or selling securities can take weeks in Columbia), the operational risks (do you really want to settle your trades in Russia?), the event risks (civil war in Liberia), etc. Some countries or securities might be included in an index for statistical purposes, but they are highly unattractive from a portfolio management perspective, or are even simply forbidden to foreigners.

Third, emerging markets tend to be highly inefficient compared to traditional markets. Most companies are under-researched and their prices exhibit serial correlation, which is symptomatic of infrequent trading and slow adjustment to current information.[3] At the aggregate level, an important part of emerging markets' performance is driven by foreign asset flows, governments' tendency to meddle in the markets, and local investors' habit of trading in herds.

---

[3] See Harvey (1995) and Kawakatsu and Morey (1999).

And there is an important literature on stock selection in emerging markets that suggests that relatively simple combinations of fundamental characteristics can be used to develop portfolios that exhibit considerable excess returns with respect to their benchmark.[4]

Given what precedes, it should be clear that a portfolio maximizing the upside potential of emerging markets requires more than just some benchmark exposure. The high volatility and relative inefficiency provide a fertile climate for active strategies that aim at picking the right stocks, the right sectors and/or the right country. As usual, hedge funds are generally better suited than traditional mutual funds to implement these highly active strategies while still having the flexibility to withdraw completely from the market whenever necessary. It is therefore not surprising to see that emerging market hedge funds have proliferated in recent years.

14.2   EXAMPLES OF STRATEGIES

Although emerging market hedge funds are often considered as a monolithic category, their strategies differ widely. Some follow long/short equity strategies, others are global macro, some are active on the fixed income side, and some are purely event driven, to name a few. In this section, we will therefore simply illustrate some of the specific characteristics of these strategies when applied in emerging markets.

14.2.1   Equity strategies

Most emerging market equity hedge fund managers are fundamental bottom-up stock pickers. Contrarily to the rest of the world, they perceive the high volatility of emerging markets as an advantage, because high fluctuations in stock prices often result in short-term mispricing. Consequently, they continuously screen the universe of emerging market companies and look for opportunities to buy shares at a substantial discount and/or sell them at a premium. Not surprisingly, their portfolios tend to have a long bias, either because short selling is not permitted or not practised in the target countries, or because no viable futures markets exist to hedge on a large scale.[5] However, by comparison to mutual funds' portfolios, those of hedge funds are often more concentrated and their content differs significantly from any emerging market index.

The stock selection process of emerging market equity hedge fund managers is usually a mix of qualitative information gathering (travelling, conferences, third-party research, consultants, meetings with analysts, and management contacts) and quantitative analysis (valuation metrics, cash flow and dividend, growth, gearing and profitability metrics, size, etc.). Their primary focus is on the appraisal of intrinsic valuations and the strengths of potential target companies. Only the most compelling opportunities are selected to enter their portfolio, with a clear price target and stop loss level. The size of each position is usually based on its estimated upside potential, the conviction of the portfolio manager and/or the liquidity of the underlying company. Some funds remain primarily focused on an individual region, while others shift their weightings across countries based on their market perception.

---

[4] See, for instance, Achour *et al.* (1999), Fama and French (1998) and Rouwenhorst (1999).
[5] See Chapter 5.

Most emerging market equity hedge funds invest in local securities, although some of them also use American Depositary Receipts (ADRs). ADRs are certificates issued in the US, quoted in US dollars and traded on a US exchange that represent and are backed by shares of a foreign company held in custody. ADRs and assimilated securities offer several advantages over trading the original shares directly, e.g. better liquidity, lower transaction costs, familiar trading mechanisms, etc. However, in some cases, ADRs display significant price differences with their underlying shares, which open the door to arbitrage – see Box 14.1.

Box 14.1 The case of Gazprom

With a market capitalization of $270 billion as of April 2006, Gazprom (see Figure 14.2) is the world's largest listed energy company in terms of reserves and the biggest company in emerging markets by capitalization. Yet, for many years, foreign investors were prohibited from buying Gazprom shares traded on Russian exchanges – a restriction designed to prevent a foreign takeover of the company. The only possible access for foreigners was the Gazprom American Depositary Shares (ADS) traded in London, which accounted for just 3.5% of the company's equity. The resulting scarcity meant that ADSs were more expensive than the locally traded shares, at one time trading at a premium of almost 100%. Of course, a few grey schemes existed, the most popular one being Russian entities buying local Gazprom shares and then giving foreigners an opportunity to gain indirect access at a premium. Surprisingly, the company and the Kremlin were aware of this loophole, but showed a large degree of tolerance towards this odd arrangement.

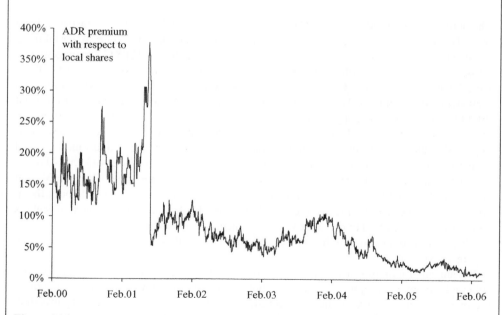

Figure 14.2   Evolution of Gazprom ADR premium with respect to local shares

Exploitation of anachronistic capital structures has always been a favoured technique of hedge fund managers. In early 2004, the Russian government started talking publicly about lifting the ring-fence on foreign investments in Gazprom, and several hedge funds rushed to buy local shares via grey schemes and sell short ADS.

On 23 December 2005, President Vladimir Putin signed into effect a law and the accompanying presidential decrees that fully liberalized the foreign ownership of Gazprom shares. The sudden increase in Gazprom's free float made it the heaviest-weighted stock in the MSCI Emerging Market Index. Gazprom's weighting in the MSCI Russia index also increased from 6.3% to 42.8%. Gazprom's stock soared with the removal of the restrictions, rising by 24% in the first three trading days. The daily volume of Gazprom share trading surged to 90 million shares per day, three times higher than a typical day's trading. Last, but not least, the discount between local shares and ADSs vanished, as they became interchangeable.

More recently, some emerging market equity hedge funds have also adopted the activist approach of their long/short equity cousins. Their targets are usually large emerging market corporations, because the high profile of these companies guarantees a level of international visibility that a campaign against a smaller, local company would not receive. The KT&G saga, for instance, was the first public battle in Asia waged by activist hedge funds (Box 14.2).

Box 14.2 Carl Icahn in Korea

The activist hedge fund operators Carl Icahn and Warren Lichtenstein, for instance, have recently focused on KT&G, the largest Korean tobacco and ginseng group. After taking a stake in the company, they sent two representatives to Seoul to give KT&G's management a message: slim down, spin off your ginseng arm, sell your real estate assets, and install three Americans on your board. On 25 January, Chief Executive Kwak Young Kyoon rejected their demands. Icahn and Lichtenstein then showed its teeth and announced an informal offer to purchase the company, valuing it at about US$10 billion. The offer was also rejected but, in the meantime, they had amassed 6.72% of the stock and become the firm's second-largest shareholders. At the 17 March annual general meeting, the hedge funds secured a board seat for Lichtenstein, and threatened to launch a formal tender offer if KT&G's management did not sell non-core assets and improve shareholder value. Franklin Mutual Advisers LLC – KT&G's largest shareholder with a 9.37% stake – said it would back them. At the time of the writing, the dispute is still going on. KT&G has rejected most of Icahn's demands, but has agreed to exit a local convenience store chain and said it was considering the disposal of some non-core businesses, ranging from real estate to pharmaceuticals (see Figure 14.3).

If Icahn and Lichtenstein's attempt to acquire KT&G succeeds, it would mark the first unsolicited buyout of a major South Korean company by overseas investors. In the meantime, the operation created a xenophobic backlash in Korea, fuelling concern among investors that the country may be going backwards in terms of corporate governance.

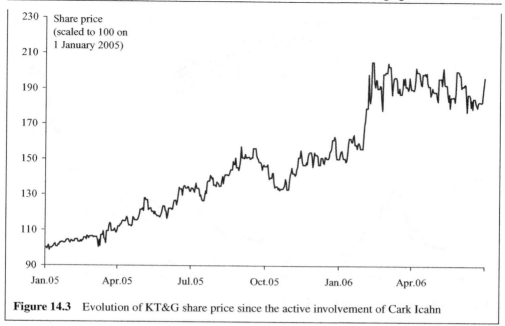

Figure 14.3 Evolution of KT&G share price since the active involvement of Cark Icahn

Activist hedge funds are becoming increasingly visible in emerging markets where they compete aggressively with traditional investors, including trade buyers and private equity funds. In Japan, for instance, their primary targets were companies sitting on a pile of unused cash and whose market capitalizations were lower than the cash break-up value. For example, Warren Lichtenstein's Tokyo affiliate, Steel Partners Japan Strategic Fund, targeted the textile-dyeing firm Sotoh in 2003, which responded by inviting a rival bid from a fund affiliated with Daiwa Securities. Steel Partners raised its bid and Sotoh increased its dividend payout, boosting the share price. Yushiro Chemical Industry was another such firm. When Steel Partners Japan launched a tender offer for Yushiro, the latter countered by raising its dividend more than 10-fold.

The reaction to such activism is mixed. On the one hand, many analysts and reform-minded regulators believe that emerging markets need such external pressure to push reforms. On the other hand, the appearance of these foreign barbarians at the gate has caused some market participants to demand more effective defences. The dazzling success of a few activists may have created the impression that emerging markets have fully embraced the basic rules of capitalism. But this impression is misleading, and some fund managers have realized it at their expense, particularly when they targeted a local oligarch – see Box 14.3.

Box 14.3 Welcome back to Russia, Mr Browder!

The Hermitage Fund (see Figure 14.4) is often quoted as an example of a real success story in emerging markets. With more than $4 billion of assets, it is Russia's largest foreign equity fund. It is technically a hedge fund (winner of the EuroHedge award for Best

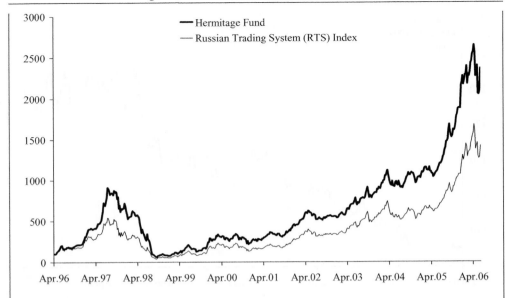

Figure 14.4 Evolution of the Hermitage Fund (base 100 in April 1986)

Emerging Market Fund in 2005), Hermitage's current investment strategy is long-only and unhedged – but this could change if needed. Hermitages's founder and CEO, William Browder, is a prominent activist shareholder that has crusaded against several corporate governance abuses, most notably at partly state-owned Russian companies. Despite holding only minority stakes in these firms, he has obtained changes in company charters, seats on boards, and even changes in Russian legislation. The large size of his fund and his focus on relatively few positions (he usually had at most investment in about a dozen firms) made it both possible and worth while for him to fight.

In 2000, Browder won a campaign to make the restructuring of electricity monopoly Unified Energy Systems more accountable to minority shareholders. In 2003, he sued the savings bank Sberbank and its majority owner, the Russian central bank, over corporate waste and lack of transparency. Browder also attacked corporate waste and the misappropriation of billions of dollars in assets at the giant Gazprom. He initiated a bid to raise corporate transparency and win a seat on the board. He also launched lawsuits against PricewaterhouseCoopers, Gazprom's auditor, asking the government to withdraw its licence. More recently, Browder crossed swords with the large oil company Surgutneftegaz for using a complicated system of Treasury shares that allowed the management of the company to retain control – the company stopped producing international financial accounting reports in 2002, however, so investors can't tell for sure who owns the Surgut Treasury shares.

Browder's public condemnations of management corruption, corporate malfeasance and alleged governance abuses were featured in the *Financial Times*, *The Wall Street Journal*, the *Economist*, *Fortune* and *Business Week*. This large media coverage and the systematic use of litigation are part of his overall strategy. In addition, Hermitage's research reports and analysis were regularly distributed at the annual meetings of its target companies, which then triggered questions from other shareholders and forced managers to react. Needless to say, this was moderately appreciated by corrupted bureaucrats and their businessmen accomplices.

On 13 November 2005, border officials refused Browder entry as he arrived at Shereme-tyevo Airport from London, despite a visa valid until March 2006. The decision was initially believed to be a mistake. But a letter from the Foreign Ministry to Hermitage deputy CEO Vadim Kleiner explained that Browder had been denied entry in accordance with the Russian Federal Immigration Law's Article 27, which bars entry to foreigners considered to be a threat to "the security of the state, public order or public health". Of course, there were no legal proceedings to understand the decision or even appeal it.

In June 2006, William Browder was still fighting to get the decision overturned. In the meantime, he had to run his fund from London, with his team of analysts travelling back and forth. In theory, this should not be a major problem: of the 15 largest funds in Russia, 12 are located outside the country. But Browder himself declared in an interview with the *Financial Times:* "There is no substitution for being on the ground in Russia." However, this was not the first time a member of Browder's family has had a falling out with the Kremlin. Josef Stalin had Earl Browder, William's grandfather, cast out of the party in 1946, at the dawn of the Cold War after he declared that communism and capitalism could peacefully coexist.

14.2.2   Fixed income strategies

Historically, sovereign emerging market debt has always been associated with the classic feast famine syndrome. Periods of spectacular out-performance were followed by the inevitable liquidity crisis, volatility spikes, market meltdowns and ultimately defaults. Most of the time, these defaults resulted in protracted, frustrating and – most importantly – costly salvage operations, and the whole cycle could start again. Despite the financial trauma, investors always came back to the asset class because of its high promised yield, with the argument that "this time, it will be different".

Today, emerging market fixed income securities consist essentially of three types of instruments.

- *Brady bonds* are dollar-denominated bonds backed by the US Treasury. They were first issued in 1989, when Mexico persuaded its bank creditors to accept a reduction in the principal they were owed in return for long-dated bonds with US Treasury collateral. Other sovereigns followed suit. Their risks can partially be hedged using US Treasury futures and currency forwards (if the investor's currency is not the US dollar).
- *Eurobonds* are issued in the Eurobond market and denominated in any major hard currency. They are more liquid and can be hedged using several instruments, such as interest rate futures and emerged markets government bonds for the interest rate risk, asset swaps or credit derivatives for the default risk, and currency forwards for the exchange rate risk.
- *Local currency bonds* offer the highest yields, but also the greatest credit and currency risk exposures. Their liquidity and the potential to hedge them are usually extremely limited, but they now represent the majority of emerging market debt.

Most of these instruments are below investment grade and offer a yield that is higher than US Treasuries with an equivalent maturity. However, this extra yield is simply a reward for a mix of (i) interest rate risk, (ii) sovereign risk and (iii) eventually currency risk. These three risks tend to be highly correlated, so that, at the end of the day, a long position in an emerging

Table 14.2   Examples of a few S&P ratings (as of June 2006)

Rating	Countries
AAA	Australia, Singapore
AA	Hong Kong (AA−), Iceland (AA−)
A	China (A−), Chile, Cyprus, Greece Latvia (A−), Lithuania, Malaysia (A−), South Korea (A)
BBB	Bulgaria, Croatia, Hungary (BBB+), Kazakhstan (BBB−), Poland (BBB+), Romania (BBB−), Russia
BB	Brazil (BB), Columbia (BB), India (BB+), Philippines (BB−), Serbia (BB−), Turkey (BB−), Ukraine (BB−), Peru (BB)
B	Argentina (B), Bolivia (B−), Mongolia, Pakistan (B+), Uruguay
CCC	Belize (CCC−), Ecuador (CCC+)

market debt is essentially a bet on the evolution of sovereign risk. Hedge fund managers active on emerging market fixed income therefore tend to build their investment process around three pillars, namely country selection, security selection and risk management. Country selection is essentially a top-down macroeconomic process which examines the fundamental economic and fiscal data, political conditions and market characteristics of various emerging markets. Its goal is to evaluate the countries that offer the best risk/return characteristics. Security selection compares the various securities available, their relative pricing, liquidity and collateral value, if any. Investments in each country are then selected based on yield-curve analytics and technical considerations. Risk management relies primarily on market risk diversification, although the concept could be easily be challenged in emerging market debt, and on adequate credit analysis and eventually protection via credit default swap contracts or index or put options (see Table 14.2).

Note that emerging market fixed income securities may be approached from various angles. Some funds have a short term approach and focus primarily on forecasting the evolution of emerging market spreads, with the goal of realizing short-term capital gains. Other funds attempt to capture the risk premium and associated income offered by emerging market debt, which implies a medium-term holding horizon. Finally, a few funds are taking a more activist and long-term angle, particularly when they specialize in defaulted debt securities (Box 14.4).

Box 14.4 The *active* approach to sovereign debt restructuring

In the olden days, creditors were quite tough with their defaulted debtors. For instance, in 1881, after the Ottoman empire defaulted on its obligations, European powers simply seized Ottoman customs houses and helped themselves to their due. In 1902, when Venezuela defaulted on its sovereign debt, German, British and Italian gunboats immediately blockaded the country's ports until the government paid up in 1903. Today, the techniques used by hedge funds are sometimes as tough as in the good old days. For instance, when Peru defaulted in 1996, the hedge fund Elliott Associates paid $11.8 million on the secondary debt market to buy $20 million face value of Peru's sovereign debt. In 1997, Elliott Associates rejected the debt restructuring agreement and sued the country for full repayment plus capitalized interest. A Federal Court of Appeals, overturning a state court, ruled in the firm's favour.

Elliott Associates then took legal action in Canada, Belgium, Luxembourg, the Netherlands, Germany and the UK, serving restraining orders on any payment on Peru's Brady bonds. Because of the legal decision in New York, they were able to argue that they had preferred creditor status, so that no payment should be made on any Brady bond until they had been *fully* repaid. In theory, Peru had to make two payments each year of about $80 million to its Brady bond holders, but a freeze on payments would have forced the country to default on its Brady bonds. The Peruvian government therefore agreed to settle for almost $58 million in October 2001. Elliott's partner Paul Singer, adviser Jay Newman and attorney Michael Straus have since carried out similar practices with debts from Panama, Ecuador, Poland, Cote d'Ivoire, Turkmenistan and the Democratic Republic of Congo.

Although capital markets appear to have a remarkably short memory and prefer to focus on recent good performance, one should remember that default risk is the largest risk in emerging market fixed income securities. As an illustration, Argentina has defaulted on its foreign debts five times in the past 175 years, Brazil seven times and Venezuela nine times. Each of these situations provided great investment opportunities *after* the default, but may dramatically hurt funds that were holding securities *prior* to their default. Remember that some countries are now experts in debt restructuring – see Box 14.5.

Box 14.5 Argentina's default

In December 2001, after four years of deepening recession and mounting social unrest, Argentina defaulted on over $80 billion worth of foreign bonds (Figure 14.5). This hardly came as a surprise to most creditors, as they had anticipated it for many months. However, the restructuring case turned out to be much more complex than initially expected. Argentina's foreign debt represented 152 different bonds denominated in seven currencies, governed by eight jurisdictions and held by more than 500 000 creditors, therefore opening the door to numerous inconsistencies. For instance, debt falling under British and Japanese law operated under collective-action clauses, which makes for relatively easier resolution by allowing a majority of bondholders to make binding decisions for all. But collective-action clauses did not apply to debt governed by US, German or Italian law, so that multiple class-action and individual law suits had to be filed. This prevented a coordinated or decisive fashion to apply sanctions on the Argentinean state.

Argentina only started negotiating with private bondholders March 2003, i.e. 15 months after its default. In September 2003, it offered to pay 25 cents on the dollar of the principal value of its debt, with no recognition of past due interest, an unprecedented stand in emerging markets. This represented a 90% reduction in the total value of the bonds and interests. The creditor groups, their governments, and the IMF rejected the offer. Bond prices immediately fell to less than 20 cents on the dollar, but several hedge funds were net buyers. They knew that Argentina had to settle with foreign bondholders at some point if it ever wanted to return to the sovereign debt market, which was necessary for financing its long-term growth.

In December 2004, creditors were offered a swap of their old bonds, no matter their original maturity date, coupon, or currency denomination, into new bonds worth roughly 35 cents on the dollar. The new bonds offered a coupon of 2 to 5% in the first 10 years, compared to 10% in Brazil, and a maturity of . . . 42 years.[6] Argentina's demand for such

---

[6] Note that no Latin American government has ever fully repaid a 30-year bond. . .

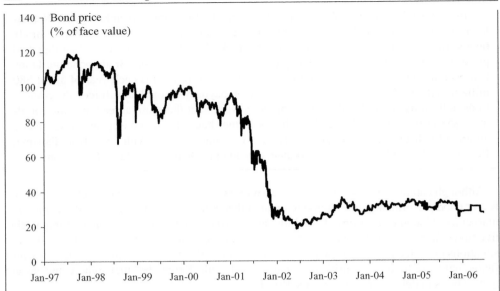

Figure 14.5 Evolution of Argentina's bond price (maturity: January 2011, coupon of 113/8%, in US$)

massive debt relief was without precedent. It can only be compared with the relief obtained by much poorer countries (for example, Albania in 1995, Bolivia in 1992, Guyana in 1999, Niger in 1991 and Yemen in 2001), but in these cases the sums involved were far smaller and the creditors were commercial bank lenders rather than bondholders. In other restructurings, creditors had to accept either a cut in principal, a lengthening of maturity or a reduction in interest payments (Table 14.3). Argentina was basically requesting all three... and it obtained them all.

Despite the unattractive terms, the majority of creditors, tired with the endless negotiations, accepted the offer. This led Néstor Kirchner, Argentina's president, to declare the restructuring a triumph. While long-term bondholders were crying, hedge funds, in the meantime, had almost doubled the value of their investment.

Table 14-3 Comparison of sovereign debt restructurings

	Argentina 2005	Ecuador 2000	Pakistan 1999	Russia 1998	Ukraine 1998	Uruguay 2003
Scope (US$ billion)	81.8	6.8	0.6	31.8	3.3	5.4
Number of bonds	152	5	3	3	5	65
Number of jurisdictions	8	2	1	1	3	6
Months in default	38	10	2	18	3	–
Recognition of interest arrears	Partial	Yes	Yes	Yes	Yes	–
Haircut on discount bonds	66.3	40	0	37.5	0	0
Lowered coupons	Yes		Yes		Yes	
Extended maturities	Yes	Yes	Yes	Yes	Yes	Yes

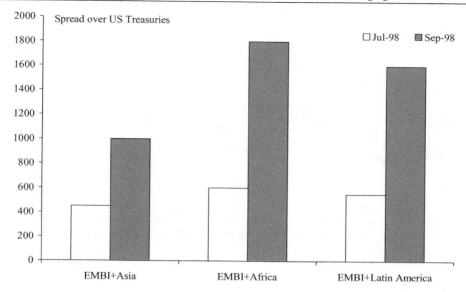

Figure 14.6   Examples of contagion among emerging markets. The graph shows the evolution of the spread over Treasuries offered by the Emerging Markets Bond Index Plus for various regions just before and just after the default of Russia in August 1998

As already mentioned, a key problem with emerging markets is contagion – particularly for fixed income securities. Emerging market debt as an asset class responds to its own idiosyncratic shocks, but also to developments in other emerging markets and to inflows of foreign capital. The latter are primarily driven by changes in the fundamental macroeconomic indicators, including in other countries. Consequently, emerging market countries do not need to be linked directly by macroeconomic fundamentals in order to transmit shocks. A crisis in one country accompanied by a liquidity shock to the investors' capital can act as a sunspot for another country and drive resources out of it. This explains how contagion has occurred between weakly linked markets such as those of Latin America, Africa and Asia (see Figure 14.6). For hedge funds, this also implies that (i) crises may be difficult to predict and (ii) diversification across emerging markets will usually not be effective in a real crisis period.

14.3   HISTORICAL PERFORMANCE

Emerging market hedge fund managers in the aggregate have produced average returns with a very high level of volatility. Over the January 1994 to December 2005 period, emerging market hedge funds – as measured by the CS/Tremont Emerging Market Index – delivered an average return of 8.4% p.a. with a volatility of 18.2%. By contrast, over the same period, the S&P 500 delivered an average return of 8.6% p.a. with a volatility of 16.0%, and the MSCI Emerging Market Index (long only) delivered an average return of 2.3% p.a. with a volatility of 26.7%. It therefore seems that emerging market hedge funds performed better than emerging market long-only indices, but worse than traditional US equities (see Figure 14.7 and Table 14.4).

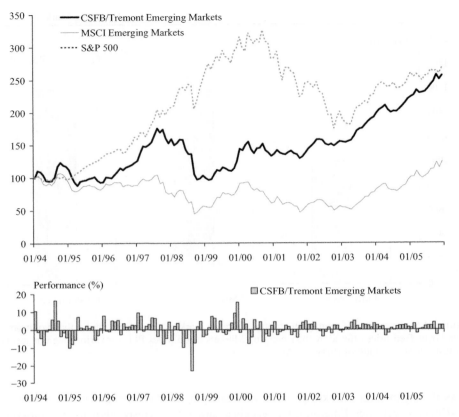

Figure 14.7 Evolution of the CS/Tremont Emerging Market Index, 1994–2005

Table 14.4 Performance comparison of the CS/Tremont Emerging Market Index, the MSCI Emerging Market Index and the S&P 500, 1994–2005

	CS/Tremont Emerging Markets	MSCI Emerging Markets	S&P 500
Return (% p.a.)	8.36	2.28	8.55
Volatility (% p.a.)	18.16	26.74	16.00
Skewness	−0.66	−0.82	−0.58
Kurtosis	4.64	2.12	0.61
Normally distributed?	No	No	No
Correlation with strategy		0.78	0.48
Positive months frequency	63%	60%	62%
Best month performance (%)	16.42	13.55	9.67
Average positive month performance (%)	3.47	4.56	3.44
Upside participation		200%	125%
Negative months frequency	38%	40%	38%
Worst month performance (%)	−23.03	−29.29	−14.58
Average negative month performance (%)	−3.69	−5.73	−3.53
Downside participation		21%	−298%
Max. drawdown (%)	−45.15	−58.37	−46.28
Value at Risk (1-month, 99%)	−9.89	−16.14	−10.24

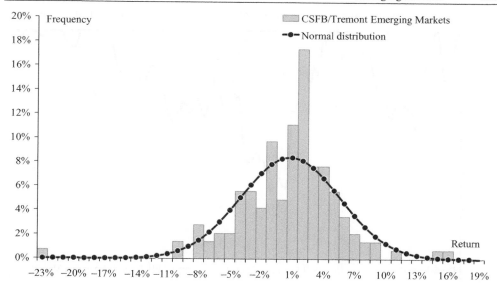

Figure 14.8   Return distribution of the CS/Tremont Emerging Market Index, 1994–2005

As shown in Figure 14.8 and Table 14.5, the performance of emerging market hedge funds has been characterized by surges abruptly terminated by major economic or financial crises, such as the Mexican crisis at the end of 1994, the Asian crisis in 1997–1998, followed by the Russian and Brazilian crises in 1998–1999. Consequently, the returns exhibit negative skewness and very large positive kurtosis, so that the return distribution cannot be considered as being normally distributed.

The drawdowns of the CS/Tremont Emerging Market Index seem closely related with those of the long-only MSCI Emerging Market Index, both in terms of timing and magnitude

Table 14.5   Monthly returns of the CS/Tremont Emerging Market Index, 1994–2005

	1994	1995	1996	1997	1998	1999	2000	2001	2002	2003	2004	2005
Jan	10.54	−9.98	7.86	9.46	−5.90	−2.92	−1.52	4.35	2.76	−0.45	2.53	1.13
Feb	−1.14	−7.88	−0.57	7.69	2.00	1.17	6.04	−2.89	2.89	1.02	1.39	3.35
Mar	−4.61	−5.51	−0.93	−0.78	3.63	7.43	3.10	−1.29	3.95	1.00	1.83	−1.88
Apr	−8.36	7.25	5.06	1.97	−0.18	6.49	−7.76	−0.52	0.12	3.89	−3.31	0.28
May	−0.73	1.34	4.51	2.97	−9.78	−1.23	−4.13	2.39	−0.73	5.01	−1.81	0.67
Jun	0.47	0.78	5.36	6.81	−4.68	4.90	5.53	1.63	−3.75	2.02	0.87	2.01
Jul	5.81	2.22	−2.68	6.46	0.08	−1.55	0.58	−2.95	−1.19	0.56	−0.14	2.30
Aug	16.42	0.98	3.56	−3.65	−23.03	−2.66	4.32	−1.08	1.26	2.98	1.83	2.29
Sep	5.20	1.88	1.57	2.78	−7.40	−0.65	−6.79	−4.38	−1.98	2.65	2.33	4.12
Oct	−3.51	−5.66	1.70	−7.86	1.68	3.66	−2.47	2.19	2.38	2.25	2.40	−2.78
Nov	−1.42	−3.13	2.60	−4.76	4.68	9.29	−3.64	3.96	2.24	1.17	2.69	2.43
Dec	−4.21	0.74	2.43	4.30	−3.84	15.34	2.32	4.82	−0.53	3.56	1.39	2.44
Total	12.50	−16.90	34.48	26.57	−37.66	44.83	−5.51	5.85	7.36	28.74	12.47	17.38
MSCI EMG	−8.67	−6.94	3.92	−13.40	−27.52	63.70	−31.80	−4.91	−7.97	51.59	22.45	30.31
S&P 500	−1.54	34.11	20.26	31.01	26.67	19.53	−10.14	−13.04	−23.37	26.38	8.99	3.00

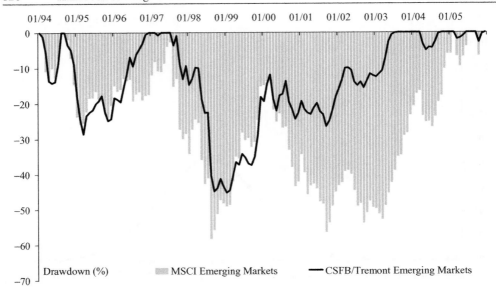

Figure 14.9   Drawdown diagram of the CS/Tremont Emerging Market Index compared to the S&P 500, 1994–2005

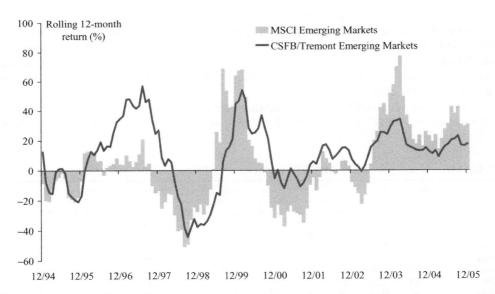

Figure 14.10   Comparison of the 12-month rolling performances of the CS/Tremont Emerging Market Index with the MSCI Emerging Market Index, 1994–2005

(Figure 14.9). It is only during the 2000–2002 bear market that emerging market hedge funds have somehow limited their losses relative to long-only markets, which allowed them to recover faster.

Lastly, the rolling 12-month returns of Figure 14.10 confirm the highly cyclical nature of emerging market hedge funds, as well as their correlation with their long-only cousins.

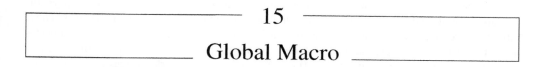

15
Global Macro

Investors should keep their eye upon the doughnut and upon the hole.

Global macro investing finds its roots in the early 1980s, as a result of the style drift of a few opportunistic hedge fund managers coming primarily from long/short equity and managed futures. The long/short equity people were typically bottom-up managers who had been very successful in taking long and short positions in under-researched small cap stocks. As the size of their portfolios increased, they needed to move to more liquid markets where larger bets could be placed. This was the case of George Soros (Quantum Fund) and Julian Robertson (Tiger Fund). The managed futures people, on the other hand, came from the derivatives and managed futures industry, which was already global and macroeconomic in nature. This was the case of Louis Moore Bacon (Moore Global) and Paul Tudor Jones (Tudor Investments). Despite their different origins, both groups of managers converged towards the same investment approach, i.e. investing globally and dynamically allocating capital and attention to the asset class, sector or region where the best opportunities lay.

Global macro funds have long been the most successful and largest category of hedge funds. Their reputation was essentially due to the phenomenal success of a few star managers, such as George Soros, Julian Robertson, Lewis Bacon and Bruce Kovner. Despite their popularity (or unpopularity!), it is important to realize that today they represent only a very small percentage of the hedge fund managers' universe, although they still manage a sizeable proportion of the corresponding assets.

15.1 GLOBAL MACRO INVESTMENT APPROACHES

Global macro investing is relatively difficult to characterize precisely. The way global macro managers approach markets and trade them is not homogeneous, but rather discretionary and opportunistic. It should therefore not come as a surprise that, within the global macro category, managers can be very different from one another. Nevertheless, most global macro funds have two typical features:

- The global nature of their strategies, which involves taking leveraged bets across a variety of liquid markets to profit from anticipated trends, market biases, or expectations regarding future cyclical or structural changes in specific countries or regions.
- Their primary focus on structural macroeconomic imbalances and the detection of macroeconomic trends. Most global macro funds only invest once markets have swung furthest from equilibrium and get out once the imbalance has been corrected, usually with generous profits. George Soros once put it in a nutshell by saying, "I don't play the game by a particular set of rules; I look for changes in the rules of the game."

The approaches used by global macro managers to detect macroeconomic trends can generally be classified into three major categories, namely, the feedback-based approach, the model-based approach and the information-based trading approach.

Feedback-based global macro managers focus primarily on understanding market psychology and exploiting the few situations where market participants deviate from rationality. These situations are rare; most of the time, market participants are rational, or at least, market prices are set as if investors were rational and there are no investment opportunities. But in a few circumstances, market participants may become irrational and market prices are affected by behavioural biases. Typical examples of such cases include periods where investors have made money too easily and become complacent, or situations where they have lost money very quickly and rush to sell. Feedback-based global macro managers often act as counterparties to these irrational investors. In a sense, they try to smell out fear, greed, hysteria and mania in order to be "smart" trend followers – they usually step in just as the first signs of a post-crash recovery appear, and step out when a bubble seems likely to burst.

Model-based global macro managers use sophisticated macroeconomic models to understand the way the world behaves, to extract implied market expectations from observable data and to compare them to sensible estimates. Large differences between implied market expectations and sensible estimates are often good indicators of disequilibria in financial markets, i.e. a signal to invest.[1] However, macroeconomic models are by definition short-lived – once they become public knowledge, their ability to detect investment opportunities diminishes. Global macro managers must therefore continuously update their models and test the new theories, models and frameworks developed by academic researchers in order to maintain their competitive edge.

Information-based global macro managers are essentially systematic data crunchers. They typically collect, aggregate and analyse piles of information on the micro level (e.g. central bank publications, survey data, confidence indicators, liquidity measures, forecasting agencies, political commentators and of course personal contacts' opinions[2]) to form their view on the macro picture. The rationale behind their approach is that micro-level information is normally available much faster than official macro-level statistics, which are often released with significant lags. However, micro-level information is usually scattered and needs to be collected and aggregated in an adequate way. Since most market participants are not willing to undertake this arduous task, the result is an information asymmetry that is worth exploiting.

Although there are a few systematic managers who employ trend-following, non-traditional and currency-focused models, the majority of global macro managers use a discretionary approach to form their portfolios. Should their analysis point at a relatively high-probability scenario, then the corresponding trading positions are taken. The right entry and exit moments are usually again discretionary and result from a combination of fundamental analysis, traditional technical price analysis and experience.

15.2   EXAMPLES OF GLOBAL MACRO TRADES

The simplest way to fathom the actions of global macro managers is to review some of their trades and understand the rationale behind them. Below, we present a picture of various past

---

[1] There are several books that describe global macro fund managers' models. The most famous one is undoubtedly *The Alchemy of Finance* by George Soros himself. Soros does not accept the theory prevalent among economics and finance professors that markets are rational and efficient. He claims, rather, that there are some systemic conditions of macroeconomic disequilibrium that are worth looking for and betting on. For instance, the combination of a huge government deficit, an expansionary fiscal policy (higher government spending and taxation) and a tight monetary policy (higher interest rates to stem borrowing) should result in the appreciation of a currency. Soros is prominently interested in such discontinuities and in deploying the best assortment of financial instruments to profit from them.

[2] It is now well known that some large global macro funds employed private investigators to follow the presidents of central banks around important meeting dates so as to know exactly who they were seeing and when.

trades, including crisis situations, periods of economic convergence or divergence, and carry trades. For each trade, we review the associated macroeconomic scenario as well as the risks that were associated with the trade.

15.2.1 The ERM crisis (1992)

The first – and maybe most famous – example of a global macro trade relates to the ERM crisis that occurred in September 1992. The European Monetary System (EMS) that existed in Europe at that time aimed at creating some sort of monetary stability. For that purpose, it introduced an artificial unit of account named the European currency unit (ECU) and a fixed exchange rate system known as the Exchange Rate Mechanism (ERM). The ECU was constructed merely as a fixed basket of European currencies. The ERM was essentially a managed-float exchange rate system where the currencies of participating countries were allowed to fluctuate within prespecified bands. Initially, central exchange rates for each currency against the ECU were established, and each currency was allowed to fluctuate ± 2.25% against this central rate (± 6% for Spain, the UK and Portugal, which joined later). Each central bank had to intervene to make sure that its currency remained within the prescribed band. Such intervention took the form of purchases of the currency in question in the event of a fall *vis-à-vis* the central rate, or of sales in the event of a rise.

Although the ERM was theoretically appealing, its construction suffered from two major weaknesses. First, because the ECU was a fictitious accounting unit and not a real currency used as a medium of exchange, the ERM effectively turned into a system where fluctuation bands were maintained with respect to the most stable currency of the group, the German mark. As a side effect, most countries with the exception of Germany had only reduced control over their own monetary policy – they had to hold reserves and intervene when the exchange rate was getting too close to the edge of the band. Second, one could argue that exchange rate uncertainty was in fact accentuated rather than reduced by the ERM. Consider, for example, the case of the Italian lira, which was allowed to fluctuate in a band of ± 2.25%. If the Bank of Italy ever decided to expand its money supply, Italian inflation would start rising, interest rates would fall and the lira would depreciate against the German mark and other European currencies. However, as soon as the lira hit the lower bound of its ERM fluctuation band, the Italian central bank would start buying lire and selling marks to keep the exchange rate fixed. If that situation were to continue, the Italian central bank could run out of mark reserves. Then, it would either have to get more marks from Germany, which would only temporarily delay the problem, or devalue the currency, i.e. set a new central value for the lira and adjust the ERM exchange rate band accordingly. The ERM mechanism therefore ended up substituting frequent, small movements for infrequent, large movements in the currency. And whenever these fluctuation band realignments became likely, speculative activity heightened because there was easy money to be made.

The source of the 1992 ERM crisis can be traced back to the reunification of West and East Germany, which started in 1990. To support the assimilation process, the German government spent an enormous amount of money and made large fiscal transfers to its eastern region. In particular, it converted the old East German marks into marks at a rate of roughly 1.8:1, which far exceeded their former value. However, East German consumers spent most of the transferred money on consumption, which fuelled domestic demand and created inflationary pressures. As a result, the Bundesbank, sticking to its traditional tight monetary policy, had to raise interest rates sharply at a time when other countries were seeking to lower their rates in order to get out of recession. This triggered large inflows of foreign funds into the German economy, particularly from ERM currencies like the Italian lira, the Spanish peseta and the British pound, but also from the US as the interest-rate differential surpassed 600 basis points. These large capital inflows brought about an appreciation of the mark, which reached a historical high to the dollar during the summer of 1992. It also affected countries like Sweden and Finland that had remained outside the EMS but had chosen to fix their exchange rates to the German mark.

In theory, the German mark appreciation should have provoked either some currency devaluation or further deflation-oriented policies in other EMS member countries, in order to regain competitiveness. However, policy makers in Italy, the UK, Ireland, Spain and Portugal were confronted with substantial inflationary pressures accompanied by high unemployment. They therefore decided to maintain the peg, mainly for fear of the domestic inflation cost of any realignment, while they refused to increase sharply their already high interest rates. However, after the rejection of the Maastricht treaty in the first Danish referendum and serious uncertainties about the French vote on the same topic, speculative pressures on the Italian lira and the British pound increased during the summer of 1992. Speculators sold short these two currencies in exchange for US dollars and German marks, hoping to profit from the difference between the exchange rate before and after a possible devaluation.

It is important to understand that the risk associated with such positions was relatively low. Take, for instance, the case of the UK. At that time, the British pound was universally deemed to be overvalued and all fundamentals pointed towards its devaluation. The UK was experiencing its worst recession since the end of World War II and had an unemployment rate well in excess of 10%. Had it been acting in isolation, the UK would likely have resorted to an expansionary monetary policy to get out of the slump, but it was handcuffed by the ERM mechanism – the British pound was already at the lower level of its fluctuation band, and an expansionary monetary policy would have pushed it further down. If speculators were to break the ERM, being short the pound could turn out to be an extremely profitable position. Even if the devaluation did not occur, the chances of seeing the pound strengthen were small – it was more likely to stay at the bottom of its fluctuation band. The only downside for speculators was their transaction costs, the interest rate differential between their long and short currencies, and the risk that the UK authorities might impose capital controls or otherwise penalize speculators for taking large short positions. Clearly, the trade-off was appealing.

The Bank of England initially attempted to support its currency by selling US dollars and German marks and buying pounds, but its foreign currency reserves, which had amounted to $40 billion at the beginning of 1992, dried up rapidly. This put further pressure on the pound and encouraged more speculators to play the devaluation theme. George Soros and his Quantum Fund were among the most aggressive speculators, with a position of more than 10 billion short pounds, but most global macro funds were engaged in the same trade. The Chancellor of the Exchequer, Norman Lamont, tried to borrow $15 billion to defend the pound, but the aggregate speculators' net short position was still growing. On 16 September 1992, additional massive short selling of the pound forced the Bank of England to raise rates to 12% then to 15%. During the day, the Chancellor repeated his insistence that he was prepared to do whatever was necessary to defend the pound, but rumours of an impending devaluation gained ground as the day wore on. In the evening, the British government finally decided to let the pound float and suspended Britain's membership of the ERM. This decision represented a humiliating retreat for the Chancellor and the Prime Minister, who had staked enormous credibility on being able to resist devaluation. As expected, the Italian lira followed suit and the Spanish peseta had to be devalued by 6% (Figure 15.1).

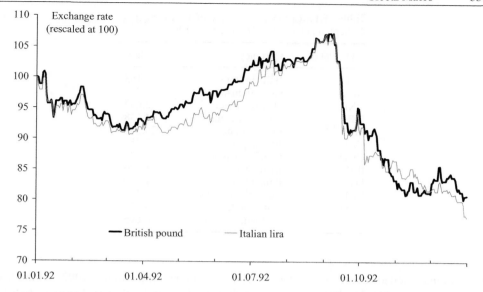

Figure 15.1 Evolution of the British pound and the Italian lira at the time of the 1992 crisis. Both exchange rates have been rescaled at 100 on 1 January 1992

Call it fame, call it infamy, call it what you will. One thing at least is certain: George Soros was happy as he pocketed a profit of $1 billion on that operation (Figure 15.2). The media coverage that followed was enormous and the public at large suddenly became aware of global macro trading. The initial admiration for Soros' achievement was soon followed by disapproval from the investment community and various governments, who associated global macro hedge funds with highly leveraged trading by powerful and ruthless managers. Nevertheless, global

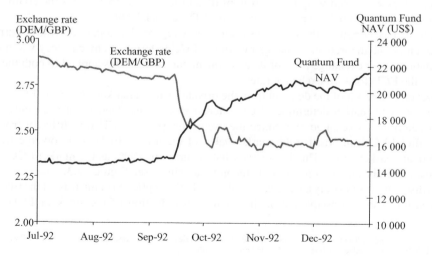

Figure 15.2 The Quantum Fund net asset value and the British pound in 1992

Table 15.1   Composition of the ECU basket,
21 September 1989 to 31 December 1999

ISO symbol	Currency	Weight (%)
BEF	Belgian franc	8.183
DEM	German mark	31.915
DKK	Danish kroner	2.653
ESP	Spanish peseta	4.138
FRF	French franc	20.306
GBP	British pound	12.452
GRD	Greek drachma	0.437
IEP	Irish punt	1.086
ITL	Italian lira	7.840
LUF	Luxembourg franc	0.322
NLG	Dutch guilder	9.87
PTE	Portuguese escudo	0.695

macro funds fuelled several other attacks, against the French franc in late 1992 and the Irish punt in January 1993. The latter had to be devalued by 10% on 1 February. Germany reduced interest rates in February, March and April to reduce tensions, but on 14 May the peseta and the escudo were devalued by 8% and 6.5% respectively. Finally, on 2 August 1993, the currency bands in the EMS were widened from 4.5% to 30%, putting an end therefore to the previous ERM system.

15.2.2   The ECU arbitrage

As mentioned above, the European currency unit (ECU) was conceived on 13 March 1979 by the European Economic Community (EEC) as an internal accounting unit. Later, it was replaced by the euro. Technically, the ECU was a theoretical basket of the currencies of the EEC member States with fixed weights. By way of illustration, Table 15.1 shows the composition of the ECU basket from 21 September 1989 to 31 December 1999.[3]

Due to its basket nature, the ECU was traditionally regarded as a pure derivative currency. Consequently, the theoretical exchange rate of the ECU in terms of any currency was a linear combination of the exchange rates of its component currencies. This applied to both the ECU spot and the ECU forward exchange rates.

However, as a result of the demand from the private sector, a market for private ECU started developing, with market-determined ECU interest rates, bank deposits or securities, and a market-determined exchange rate. Since the use of this private ECU was different from that of the official ECU, in practice the market value of the private ECU could diverge from its "theoretical" basket value. This is exactly what occurred in 1996, as the market ECU traded at almost a 3% discount compared to its theoretical value – see Figure 15.3.

This discount was not only an indicator of the market's scepticism or mistrust of the European currency, but also a consequence of the significant reduction of the stock of ECU bonds

---

[3] These weights and the list of currencies were rebalanced as new countries joined the Community. Note that the GBP was included in the ECU before Black Wednesday (October 1992), but not afterwards.

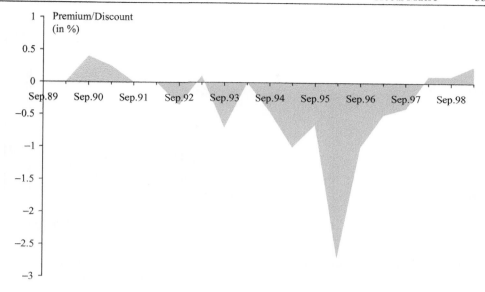

Figure 15.3 Premium/discount of the market ECU to its theoretical value, calculated semi-annually using noon spot rates in New York and the currency composition of the ECU basket as of 21 September 1989

outstanding. Only on the eve of the introduction of the euro at the start of 1999 did ECU bond issuance recover and the ECU traded at a premium compared to its theoretical value. In the meantime, global macro hedge funds had largely profited from the mispricing (Figure 15.4).

15.2.3 The Asian crisis (1997)

The Asian crisis of 1997 is another example of a troubled period often attributed to hedge funds. For some mystifying reason, it was a crisis that almost all academics, financial analysts and debt-rating agencies had failed to predict. The feeling that the Asian Tigers would replace the Bull of Wall Street as the symbol of financial strength in the world had led investors to believe that there was little risk involved. Even the Asian Development Bank's Asian Development Outlook 1997 and 1998 noted that "over the near term, prospects for growth look good", and the World Bank had coined the term "East Asian miracle" to describe the economies of that region. Indeed, on paper, most of them looked great. They had low public deficits or even budget surpluses, limited public debts, moderate inflation (except in the Philippines and Indonesia), high savings and investment rates, high GDP growth, high and apparently sustainable net capital inflows and low unemployment rates. However, several weaknesses were hidden beneath the surface. Current account deficits were primarily financed by short-term foreign debt, and the maintenance of pegged exchange rates encouraged external borrowing and led to excessive exposure to foreign exchange risk in both the financial and corporate sectors. In particular, it was common practice to obtain capital from abroad (at low interest rates on a short-term basis) and to lend in the domestic market (at high interest rates on a long-term basis) Excessive lending inflated a bubble in real estate prices and stock markets

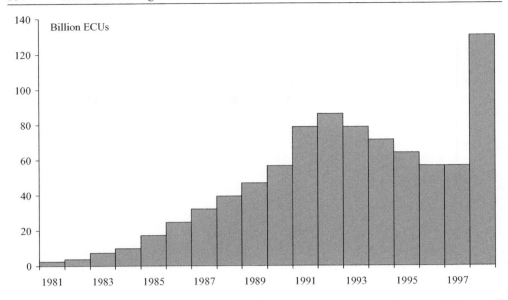

Figure 15.4 Evolution of the outstanding ECU international bonds and notes (in billion ECUs, data from national authorities)

and contributed to overinvestment by private manufacturing firms, which, as a result, faced a decline in capital efficiency. More importantly, limited disclosure requirements and inadequate asset classification systems disguised the extent of problems related to non-performing loans – (see Table 15.2.)

In the first half of 1997, exports felt the pressure of cyclical overproduction in semiconductors, stagnation of the Japanese economy, and the emergence of low-cost producers such as China. Foreign and domestic investor sentiment deteriorated as a result of increasing current account deficits and several notable bankruptcies in South Korea. Tremendous capital outflows put severe downward pressure on local currencies, thereby raising the cost of repaying foreign loans. Many banks, already undercapitalized and carrying an abundance of non-performing loans, went bankrupt.

Table 15.2 Net private capital flows to Indonesia, Malaysia, the Philippines, South Korea and Thailand (expressed in US$ billion)

	1995	1996	1997	1998	1999
Equity	15.3	18.6	4.4	13.7	18.5
–Foreign Direct Investments	4.2	4.7	5.9	9.5	12.5
–Private Investments	11.0	13.9	−1.5	4.3	6.0
Private Creditors	65.1	83.7	−4.2	−41.3	−18.2
–Commercial Banks	53.2	62.7	−21.2	−36.1	−16.0
–Non-bank Private Creditors	12.0	21.0	17.1	−5.3	−2.3
Total	80.4	102.3	0.2	−27.6	0.3

Given this shaky macroeconomic environment, many speculators interpreted the first signs of political instability – a reshuffling of the Thai government – as a presage of weakness. On 14 and 15 May 1997, the Thai baht, which was pegged at 25 to the dollar, was hit by massive speculative attacks. On 30 June, Prime Minister Chavalit Yongchaiyudh, said that he would not devalue the baht but would use foreign reserves to maintain the peg with the US dollar. However, he could not fight the reversal of capital inflow, which led to an unexpected liquidity crunch in Thai banks and several bankruptcies. The government initially announced its intention to bail out troubled institutions, but it soon realized that it did not have the resources to sustain both the currency and sagging companies, as the majority of its available funds were already tied up in forward contracts to support the baht. On 2 July 1997, when the peg was finally abandoned, the baht plunged immediately and lost half of its value (Figure 15.5). The Thai stock market dropped by 75% in 1997. Finance One, the largest Thai finance company collapsed. On 11 August, the IMF unveiled a rescue package of more than $16 billion for Thailand, and on 20 August another bailout package of $3.9 billion. But in the meantime, the infernal spiral had come into play. The outflow of capital by foreigners was followed by an outflow by local people. Companies holding baht receivables used forward contracts to sell them and hedge. Local businesses and even private citizens exchanged their volatile baht for more stable yen and dollars. As the baht continued to fall, repayment costs of foreign loans rose, leading to more corporate bankruptcies. And since the economic structure of Thailand was similar to that of many countries of Southeast Asia, the crisis spread rapidly from Thailand to Malaysia, to Indonesia, to the Philippines, then to South Korea, as investors discerned similar problems in these countries – see Figures 15.6 and 15.7.

What was the role of hedge funds during the crisis? Most agree that they were not much involved during the build-up of the very one-sided market in Asia during 1995–1996, but were active during the crisis. A report in *Business Week* in August 1997 revealed that several global macro hedge funds had made big profits in July 1997, when the Thai baht slumped by 23%. The Quantum Fund, for instance, gained 11.4% in July, and confirmed on 5 September in

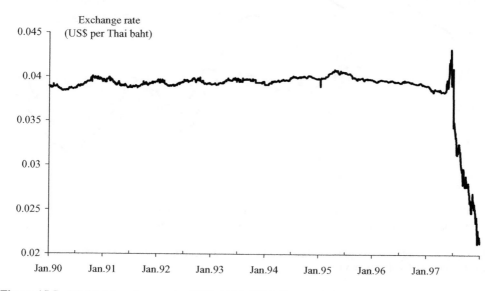

Figure 15.5 Thai baht exchange rate, 1990–1997 (US dollars per baht)

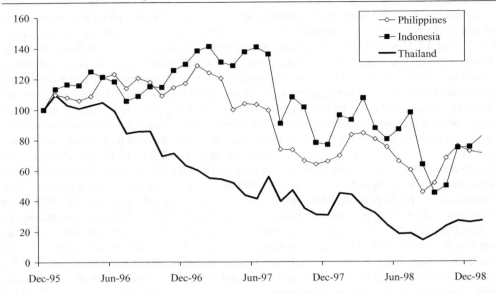

Figure 15.6 Evolution of equity markets of selected Asian economies during the 1997 crisis (based on MSCI indices in local currency)

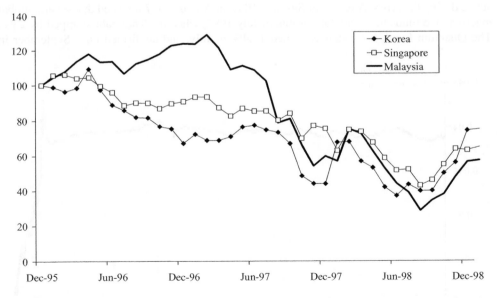

Figure 15.7 Evolution of equity markets of selected Asian economies during the 1997 crisis (based on MSCI indices in local currency)

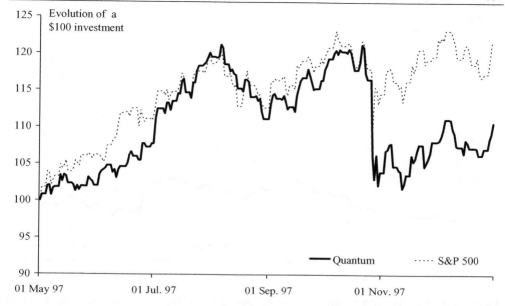

Figure 15.8   Evolution of $100 investment in the Quantum Fund (net asset value) and in the S&P 500 during the Asian crisis period. The correlation is 0.64

The *Wall Street Journal* that it was short the Thai baht and the Malaysian ringgit. But the burning question is whether global macro funds sparked the mass selling or simply profited from the herd behaviour. The Malaysian Prime Minister, Mohamad Mahatir, attributed the crash to hedge funds, which he termed the "highwaymen of the global economy". However, Brown et al. (1998) used sophisticated regression techniques to analyse the impact of hedge funds on some Asian currency values, but found no evidence that hedge funds had caused any depreciation. And even a naïve comparison of the Quantum Fund with the S&P 500 seems more promising (see Figures 15.8 and 15.9).

15.2.4   The euro convergence (1995–1997)

Although global macro funds seem to love macroeconomic crises, they also find profitable opportunities in regulatory changes and monetary unions together with their associated convergences. As an illustration, let us examine the creation of the European Monetary Union in January 1999, and more specifically the launch of the euro.

The European Monetary Union as we know it today was born out of the Maastricht Treaty in 1993, which set forth the three steps required for its creation: by the end of 1993, capital flows were to be completely freed within the EU; by 1999, member States preparing to adopt the euro currency upon its launch had to satisfy a set of convergence criteria by which major economic policies were coordinated across nations[4]; and effective at the beginning of 1999,

---

[4] The Maastricht Treaty convergence criteria were as follows: (i) the ratio of general government deficit to GDP must not exceed 3%; (ii) the ratio of gross general government debt to GDP must not exceed 60%; (iii) the average inflation rate over the year before assessment must not exceed by more than 1.5 percentage points the average of the three best performing member States in terms of price stability; (iv) the long-term nominal interest rate must not exceed by more than 2 percentage points the average of the three best performing member States in terms of price stability; and (v) the Exchange Rate Mechanism must be respected without severe tensions for at least the last two years before assessment.

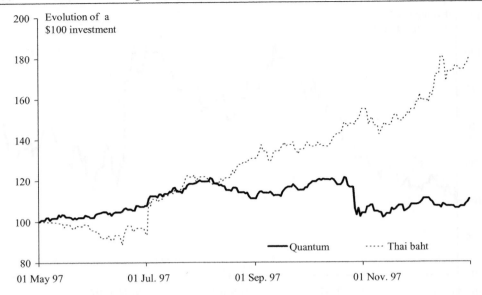

Figure 15.9 Evolution of $100 investment in the Quantum Fund (net asset value) and in the Thai baht (baht per US$) during the Asian crisis period. The correlation is 0.15

the European Central Bank would be established along with the official euro currency, for which member-country conversion rates were irrevocably set. In 1995, three new members were admitted to the EU (Austria, Finland and Sweden), bringing the total number of member States to 15. Among these member States, Austria, Belgium, Finland, France, Germany, Ireland, Italy, Luxembourg, Netherlands, Spain and Portugal were fighting to meet the convergence criteria, Denmark, the UK and Sweden could voluntarily opt not to participate, and Greece was disqualified (Figure 15.10).

Before the creation of the euro, investors on European fixed income markets had to deal with exchange rate risk. Bonds in different currencies were considered as distinct assets, even though foreign exchange risk between these currencies was low historically. As a result, the dominant factor governing European government bond yields was not really the credit risk of the issuing country, but more its likelihood of being accepted in the final set of euro-countries and the expected strength of its currency. In particular, Germany was considered as the benchmark European country, and all countries had to pay an annual spread above German rates.

With the creation of the euro, these spreads were expected to narrow. Indeed, since the signing of the Single European Act in February of 1986, long-term government bond yields had already started to converge as a result of the harmonization of monetary and fiscal policies – and several global macro funds had already participated in the convergence phenomenon and pocketed significant gains (Figure 15.11). However, in early 1995, as a result of the flight-to-quality associated with the global bond market correction in 1994 and the Mexican crisis in 1994/95, the spreads peaked at 1.18% for France, 5.46% for Italy, 4.38% for Spain, 3.19% for the United Kingdom and 1.32% for European currency unit (ECU) bonds (Figure 15.12). From a pure credit risk perspective, this was far too much.

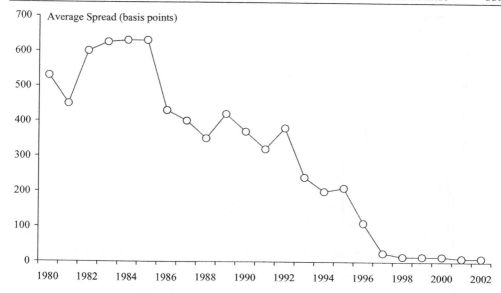

Figure 15.10   Average spread observed on long-term government bond yields over German government bonds. The countries considered in the average include Austria, Belgium, Finland, France, Italy, the Netherlands, Portugal and Spain

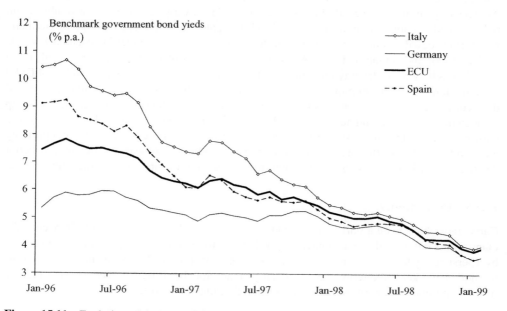

Figure 15.11   Evolution of the bond yields offered by government bonds in Europe

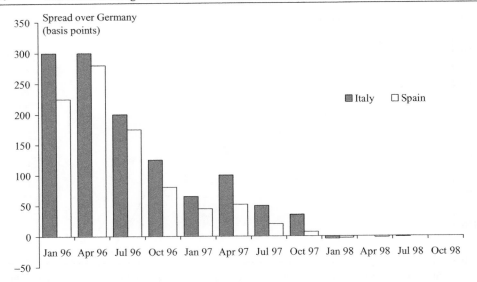

Figure 15.12   Evolution of five-year, five-year forward swap spreads over Germany

Convinced that the euro would come into being, several global macro funds entered the game and played the convergence. The more conservative among them bought French or Euro-denominated bonds and shorted German bonds, while the more aggressive ones ventured into long positions in Italian and Spanish bonds and shorted German bonds. All of them were right. As monetary union approached, there was a noticeable convergence in yields, as doubts about political and economic commitments to EMU dissipated, and monetary policy in Germany was further eased. French and Dutch long-term yields even fell below Deutschmark yields by late 1996, and Italian and Spanish yields also declined markedly – although with more volatility as they were strongly influenced by fluctuations in the perceived probability of EMU participation. The gains for global macro funds were large, because most of them implemented their convergence trades via interbank currency swaps[5] rather than cash markets. Using swap avoided much of the capital outlay required to establish positions in cash markets and therefore allowed for more leverage. By late 1997, most of these convergence positions were reportedly unwound with the further narrowing of spreads. For once, European politicians felt better disposed towards hedge funds because their trades were rather supportive of the convergence.

15.2.5   Carry trades

Carry trades have been a fairly widespread strategy in the global macro world. They can take many forms but have the same underlying principle: to exploit profit opportunities presented by a persistently low cost of funds in one market segment combined with sustained high returns in another market – the term "carry" actually stands for the difference between the income from the purchased securities and the corresponding financing cost.

---

[5] A simple example is a cross-currency interest rate swap in which the hedge fund makes a stream of interest payments denominated in Deutschmarks in exchange for a stream of interest payments denominated in the higher yielding currency. If the interest rate spread narrows before the contract maturity date, the investor effectively books a profit equal to the change in the spread times the number of months to maturity.

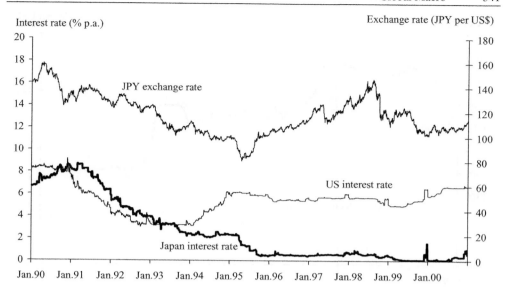

Figure 15.13   Differential between US dollar and yen interest rates (one month LIBOR) in the 1990s

In the early 1990s, global macro funds made handsome profits on carry trades along the US yield curve. For instance, between 1991 and 1993, the spread between the yield on the 10-year Treasury bond and the 3-month Treasury bill averaged a comfortable and stable 300 basis points. To capture it, global macro funds sold short 3-month Treasury bills and used the proceeds to purchase 10-year Treasury bonds. In addition to the carry, they benefited from the Federal Reserve's decision to keep policy rates at very low levels and the rising prices of long-term Treasury bonds.

However, the most famous carry trade is likely to be the yen carry trade that persisted from 1995 to 1998 (Figure 15.13). During this period, many hedge funds used to borrow cheaply in the Japanese money market and invest the proceeds in a wide array of assets ranging from US Treasuries to high-yielding emerging market securities. To understand the attraction of such a position, it is worth recalling market conditions at the time. First, the yen was on a declining trend, as it went from 80 yen per US dollar in April 1995 to 147 yen per US dollar in July 1998 – a loss of 66% purchasing power. Second, interest rates were extremely low in Japan, as the Bank of Japan had lowered the official discount rate from 6% (August 1990) to 0.5% (September 1995). Third, US Treasuries as well as emerging market securities were offering a much higher return than Japanese money market yields. And finally, East Asian currencies were firmly pegged to the US dollar.

Although highly profitable, the yen carry trade was not a real arbitrage. Global macro funds that implemented it had to face duration risk (short-term liabilities versus long-term assets) as well as exchange rate risk (dollar or emerging assets versus yen liabilities). They made a profit as long as the yen did not appreciate, US interest rates stayed high and the peg to the US dollar was maintained. Needless to say, the US Treasury loved carry traders as they were net buyers of US debt instruments and helped to maintain US interest rates lower than they would otherwise have been. However, in the summer of 1998, the Russian default and LTCM difficulties suddenly heightened market participants' risk aversion, depressed prices and fuelled

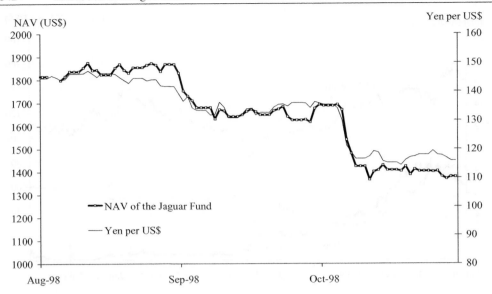

Figure 15.14   Net asset value of the Jaguar Fund and yen/ US dollar movements

a flight to safety. As liquidity dried up, many speculators were obliged to reduce their leverage and, by unwinding their carry trades, created an increased demand for yen. Consequently, the dollar fell by about 9% against the yen in the period between 31 August and 7 September, and then by a further 12% on 7 and 8 October. This induced even the most sanguine hedge funds to take their losses and unwind a sizeable part of their carry trades, further strengthening the Japanese currency. As an illustration, Figure 15.14 shows the daily share value of the Jaguar Fund, the flagship macro hedge fund of the Tiger Management Company, alongside the yen/dollar exchange rate. It is quite evident that the fund had substantial short yen positions and suffered losses of about 12% in the course of a couple of days. The financial press reported that losses were as high as $2 billion during that period.[6]

In the early 2000s, other currencies became big beneficiaries of the carry trade where hedge funds used to borrow in cheap US dollars, euros, and yens to chase better returns in countries with higher interest rates such as Iceland or New Zealand. The currencies of these smaller countries were propped up by the sudden demand for foreign investors. For example, the Japanese yen had a short-term interest rate of 0%. Consequently, many Japanese investors parked their money in New Zealand dollars which had a short-term interest rate of 7.25%. A similar trade was executed by European investors who parked their money in Iceland's krona which offered a short-term interest rate of around 10% versus 2.50% for the euro. Unfortunately for these investors, rates started tightening on the US and in the Euro-zone, with the risk that Japan may follow suit later, and rating agencies started focusing on the large current account deficits in Iceland.

---

[6] According to the financial press, the Jaguar Fund had a $35 billion long dollar/yen position, which it started reducing in early September. However, this number should be taken with a pinch of salt, because the associated transactions can take a variety of forms and use different instruments.

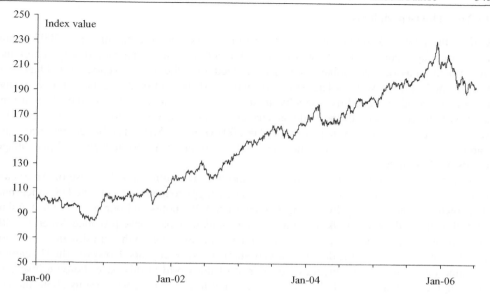

Figure 15.15   Evolution of the carry trade index that involves being long the New Zealand dollar and short the yen. The index starts at 100 on 1 January 2000

The downgrading of Icelandic debt by Fitch ratings agency triggered foreign investor retreat and resulted in the rapid unwinding of the carry trade in Iceland, with the nation trying to stave off a financial meltdown. In the first quarter of 2005, the Icelandic krona felt more than 12% against the US dollar, despite increases in Iceland's central bank's lending rate to 11.5%, and the Icelandic stock market tumbled nearly 20%. The krona's meltdown set off a chain reaction that hit New Zealand, Poland, Hungary and Brazil. The New Zealand dollar, for instance, lost 10.7% as carry trades suddenly unwound. Although the crisis did not turn into a debacle, it was highly reminiscent of the 1997 Asian currency crisis.

Figure 15.15 illustrates the evolution of the value of the carry trade index that involves being long the New Zealand dollar and being short the yen. Over a given period, the value of the carry trade index is calculated by combining the pure currency return (percentage change in the cross exchange rate between the high-yield and low-yield currencies involved in the trade) with the interest rate differential (cumulative return from the difference in interest rates earned on the long high-yield/short low-yield currency position). The carry trade index is what really matters for investors.[7]

The most amusing thing is that the US today has many of the same problems as Iceland, including record trade deficits, massive debts, heavy reliance on foreign nations to buy their securities, and lending booms that have fostered soaring property values. These problems were also those of emerging countries in 1997, just prior to the crisis. But hush! This is another question ...

---

[7] Note that some hedge funds, in particular managed futures funds, use carry trade indices to implement trend-following strategies. They enter in the carry trade whenever the trend is positive, and exit as soon as they perceive some mean reversion.

15.2.6   The twin deficits

One of the new focal points of global macro managers since the beginning of 2005 seems to be the magnitude of the US twin deficits (budget and current balance of payments) and their potential associated global imbalances. Indeed, over the past 20 years, the US has been transformed into the world's largest debtor nation. At the end of 2004, its total debt to the rest of the world exceeded its assets by about $2.5 trillion, i.e. 21% of its GDP. The current account balance-the sum of the trade balance and what the US earns from its assets abroad – was negative 5.7 percentage points of GDP in 2004 (Figure 15.16). The budget balance – the gap between government tax revenues and total spending – was also negative 4.7 percentage points of GDP in 2004.

So far, the twin deficit has been largely ignored by US politicians. Because of America's reserve currency status, foreign investors have been happy to lend dollars to the US rather than their own currency, mostly by buying US Treasury bills, notes and bonds. And most Asian central banks, led by the Bank of China and the Bank of Japan, have provided America with cheap finance to prevent their currencies from rising and export growth from slowing. This kept US interest rates low and the dollar relatively stable for several years. However, the US cannot continue increasing its indebtedness to the rest of the world at this pace. Foreign investors hold unprecedented financial claims on the US and have grown a bit nervous about the US economy, particularly when they realize that the easiest solution for the US government would be to decrease the dollar's value relative to other currencies, which would improve the competitiveness of American goods in world markets, increase exports and slow imports. Even the International Monetary Fund's *World Economic Outlook* of April 2004 noted that "the prospect of continuing large US fiscal and external deficits and the implied external borrowing adds to concerns about international imbalances, increasing the chances of a disorderly resolution, including a rapid fall of the dollar and a rise in US long-term interest rates".

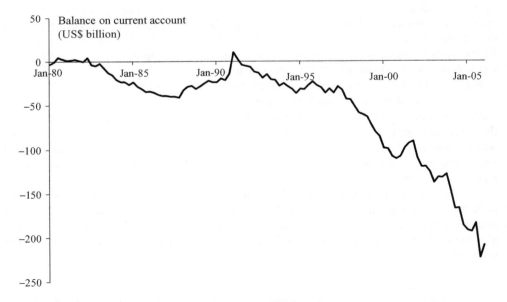

Figure 15.16   US current account balance evolution, 1980 onwards

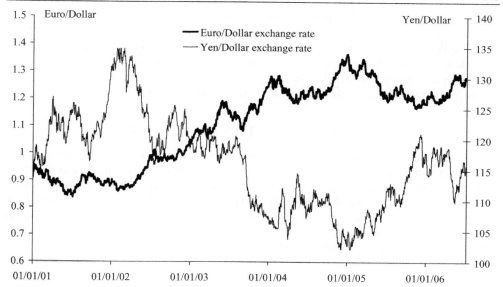

Figure 15.17   The euro and the yen versus the US dollar

Interestingly, most global macro managers agree that the twin deficits are unsustainable and that some dollar devaluation, as happened in the 1980s, is likely. However, they simply do not know *when* the journey might commence, *how quickly* we might get there, or *how rough* the road might be. Several global macro funds profited handsomely from their short dollar positions in 2003 and 2004, but they were hit by the rising dollar at the beginning of 2005 and exited their positions. Some of them temporarily changed their mind and started trading around the upward trend. Others profited from the dramatic increase in the price of gold, which has virtually replaced the US dollar as a safe-haven "currency". But they are all attentively monitoring the evolution of the US dollar, as it is likely to be the next El Dorado – see Figure 15.17.

15.2.7   Risk management and portfolio construction

In their youth, global macro funds were primarily one-man shops placing directional bets with a lot of leverage and very few risk controls. Their volatility was extremely high, but large losses were also frequent – the Quantum Fund gained one billion against the British pound in 1992, but lost two billion in Russia in 1998. This old-style school of global macro has gradually disappeared. Today's global macro managers still enjoy a high degree of flexibility, but risk management and a disciplined investment approach are essential components of their activity, as well as the ability to react quickly to changes in macroeconomic conditions.

Most global macro managers use a combination of Value at Risk and stop losses. The former measures the anticipated loss at different levels of probability and time horizons; it has the advantage of being applicable across all asset classes and instruments, as well as at the portfolio level. The latter is intended to impose rational and disciplined behaviour under pressure, allowing the manager to exit from losing trades rather than sticking to erroneous convictions. As summarized by Bruce Kovner, the manager of Caxton Corporation, stop losses should be set "at a point that, if reached, will reasonably indicate that the trade is wrong, not at a point determined primarily by the maximum dollar amount you are willing to lose". Note also that leverage is still employed today, but the focus is more on consistency of returns. The risk management culture has definitely changed and global macro managers aim at optimally diversifying their portfolio holdings in order to reduce and control risk.

15.3 HISTORICAL PERFORMANCE

For investors, the historical performance of global macro hedge funds has been relatively good. Global macro managers in the aggregate have produced high absolute returns, and they have also outperformed traditional asset classes with far less volatility. Over the January 1994 to December 2005 period, global macro hedge funds – as measured by the CS/Tremont Global Macro Index – delivered an average return of 13.54% p.a. with a volatility of 11.66%. By contrast, over the same period, the S&P 500 delivered an average return of 8.6% p.a. with a volatility of 16.0%, and the Citigroup World Government Bond Index an average return of 5.9% p.a. with a volatility of 6.7% – see Figure 15.18.

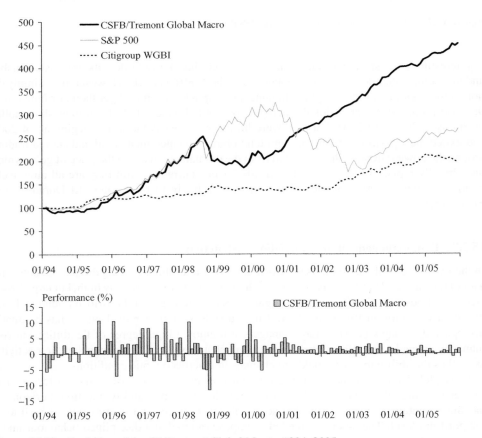

Figure 15.18 Evolution of the CS/Tremont Global Macro, 1994–2005

Table 15.3 Performance comparison of the CS/Tremont Global Macro, the S&P 500 and the Citigroup World Government Bond Index, 1994–2005

	CS/Tremont Global Macro	S&P 500	Citigroup WGBI
Return (% p.a.)	13.54	8.55	5.87
Volatility (% p.a.)	11.66	16.00	6.74
Skewness	0.03	−0.58	0.37
Kurtosis	2.79	0.61	0.37
Normally distributed?	No	No	Yes
Correlation with strategy		0.23	−0.13
Positive months frequency	73%	62%	58%
Best month Performance (%)	10.60	9.67	5.94
Average positive month Performance (%)	2.44	3.44	1.73
Upside participation		83%	241%
Negative months frequency	27%	38%	42%
Worst month Performance (%)	−11.55	−14.58	−4.28
Average negative month Performance (%)	−2.45	−3.53	−1.18
Downside participation		−714%	−352%
Max. drawdown (%)	−26.78	−46.28	−7.94
Value at Risk (1−month, 99%)	−7.03	−10.24	−3.36

Global macro funds had their best years from 1995 to 1997 and from 2001 to 2003. In 1994, they had a negative performance (−5.70%) as the Federal Reserve started to change the direction of interest rates upwards by aggressively raising rates. This caused bond markets to crash worldwide while global macro hedge funds had large long positions in European bonds. In 1998, the performance was again negative (−3.63%) due to the LTCM crisis and the associated sudden lack of liquidity.

Note that the year 1999 was also relatively disappointing in terms of performance (5.81%), as most global macro funds stayed away from the dot-com bubble and the irrational exuberance of equity markets. Consequently, their performance slipped and investors flocked to outsized returns from technology stocks (Table 15.3). No less a person than Julian Robertson (Box 15.1) brought down the curtain on the Tiger funds and retired after a series of wrong bets. A few months later, Stanley Druckenmiller, portfolio manager of the Quantum Fund, and Nick Roditi, portfolio manager of the Quota Fund, decided to retire from asset management and left the Soros Fund Management group. In his April 2000 letter to shareholders, George Soros himself wrote: "My own needs are for a more reliable stream of income to fund my charitable activities. To meet those needs, we shall convert the Quantum Fund into a lower risk/lower reward operation". This marked the end of the "old-style" global macro world.

Box 15.1 Tiger Asset Management

Julian Robertson is undoubtedly one of the most legendary asset managers in the hedge fund industry. Born in 1933 in Salisbury, North Carolina, he graduated from Episcopal High School in 1951 and the University of North Carolina at Chapel Hill in 1955 with a degree in business administration. He then served as an officer in the US Navy before joining Kidder

Peabody, where he stayed for 20 years and ended up heading Webster Management, the asset management unit.

In 1980, Robertson left Webster Management to create Tiger Asset Management. The initial capital of Tiger was $8 million, including $2 million of Julian Robertson's. His strategy focused purely on global stock selection based on fundamentals, i.e. buying stocks at low prices and with good earnings prospects. To hedge his bets, Roberson used short selling and index put options, and diversified his portfolio widely. As the fund grew in size, it started moving away from pure stock selection and implemented several global macro plays. For instance, Tiger made money shorting copper futures contracts in 1995 as Sumitomo Corporation was under investigation for fraudulent efforts to manipulate prices.

The turnaround came in 1998. At the time, Tiger had approximately 180 employees, including 12 senior analysts, 10 industry teams a currency and bond team and a commodity team. Its assets reached $22.8 billion, making it the largest-ever hedge fund. The group counted several funds, all named after felines: Tiger (for qualified US investors), Jaguar (for non-US investors plus tax-exempt US foundations and institutions), Ocelot (a one-off fund created with Donaldson, Lufkin & Jenrette, with a 4% upfront fee, a five-year lock-up, and a $1 million minimum investment), Lion (a clone of Tiger), Panther (dissolved in 1997), and Puma. Robertson decided to hire Philip Duff, a former Morgan Stanley chief financial officer, as a chief operating officer with the mandate to map out a succession plan and give the firm more structure. But the same year, Tiger lost $600 million when Russia defaulted on its debt, and lost an additional $2 billion on a bad bet against the Japanese yen. Robertson immediately turned his focus from the global macro mode to the strategy he did best, i.e. stock picking. Unfortunately, he was highly sceptical about the "new economy" valuations. He decided to go long old economy stocks[8] and started shorting some of the new high-flying technology companies. Needless to say, the performance of his fund disappointed (−19% in 1999) and investors started redeeming their shares.[9] Tiger was forced to prune its leverage severely from 2.8 to 1.4 and liquidate some of its assets, which depressed the prices of its holdings even further. The death spiral had started.

In March 2000, a first quarter performance of −14% was announced. Tiger's assets had dwindled to $6 billion, of which $1.5 billion was Robertson's own money. Robertson, then aged 67, decided to retire and wrote a letter to his investors, explaining that "There is no point in subjecting our investors to risk in a market which I frankly do not understand. . . . After thorough consideration, I have decided to return all capital to our investors, effectively bringing down the curtain on the Tiger funds." Investors received about 75% of their money in cash and 5% in shares still held by Tiger. The remaining 20% came in cash as Robertson gradually sold his five largest holdings – US Airways, United Asset Management, Xtra Corp., Normandy Mining Management, and Gtech Holdings. Less than a month later, the technology bubble burst. Had Tiger still been around, it would have made a killing.

The return distribution of the CS/Tremont Global Macro Index has almost no skewness, but it displays positive kurtosis, due to a few very good months (July 1997 and March 1998)

---

[8] According to SEC filings, at the end of 1999 Tiger owned a 24.8% stake in US Airways, 14.8% of United Asset Management, 7.2% of Sealed Air, and 3.7% of Bear Stearns.

[9] Between August 1998 and April 2000, $7.65 billion was withdrawn from the Tiger funds. Note that in October 1999, Tiger changed its quarterly redemption policy to six-monthly.

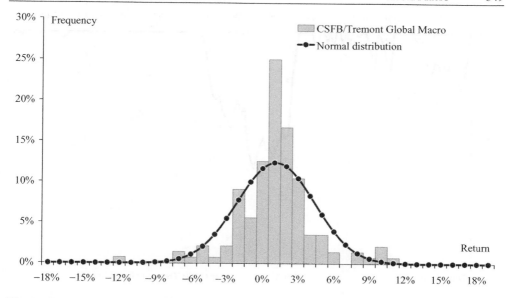

Figure 15.19   Return distribution of the CS/Tremont Global Macro, 1994–2005

and the LTCM crisis (October 1998). Consequently, it should not be considered as normally distributed see – Figure 15.19 and Table 15.4.

The drawdown diagram reveals the change in the nature of the strategy. Prior to 1998, global macro was a rather aggressive strategy, and its drawdowns could be large. But the LTCM crash forced them to reduce their leverage and focus on risk management. It took them almost three years to recover from the summer 1998, but their performance has been remarkably stable since, particularly during the bear markets of the early 2000s – see Figures 15.20 and 15.21.

Table 15.4   Monthly returns of the CS/Tremont Global Macro, 1994–2005

	1994	1995	1996	1997	1998	1999	2000	2001	2002	2003	2004	2005
Jan	0.17	−2.47	10.46	8.21	−2.18	−2.88	−2.42	3.32	2.64	2.03	1.45	0.69
Feb	−5.65	0.07	−7.07	1.82	0.21	−1.60	4.43	0.99	0.52	1.87	1.19	1.40
Mar	−4.27	5.96	1.22	−2.17	10.16	−2.00	−2.45	2.74	−0.19	−0.66	0.97	0.51
Apr	−1.59	0.91	3.00	5.95	1.57	1.79	−5.35	0.69	1.70	2.16	0.14	−0.25
May	3.80	0.99	1.99	−2.02	3.37	−0.05	2.32	2.14	0.78	2.96	0.05	0.07
Jun	−0.92	−0.68	3.23	2.10	3.28	3.02	1.32	1.03	1.42	1.63	0.48	0.52
Jul	−0.35	2.24	−6.97	10.13	1.80	−1.91	1.81	0.69	2.15	−0.11	0.82	1.04
Aug	2.75	10.60	2.93	−2.41	−4.84	−2.85	2.92	1.00	1.22	1.30	−0.75	0.71
Sep	0.25	0.20	3.01	4.63	−5.12	−3.18	−0.87	1.17	0.76	3.04	−0.49	2.43
Oct	−2.22	1.00	5.31	−1.89	−11.55	2.44	1.26	1.18	0.72	0.09	1.22	−0.86
Nov	2.09	4.87	8.13	3.46	−1.08	4.40	3.63	−0.37	1.23	0.55	2.42	1.08
Dec	0.50	4.05	−0.76	5.14	2.34	9.24	5.05	2.47	0.85	1.86	0.72	1.58
Total	−5.70	30.70	25.60	37.11	−3.63	5.81	11.69	18.38	14.67	17.97	8.49	9.25
S&P 500	−1.54	34.11	20.26	31.01	26.67	19.53	−10.14	−13.04	−23.37	26.38	8.99	3.00
WGBI	2.34	19.04	3.62	0.23	15.30	−4.27	1.59	−0.99	19.49	14.91	10.35	−6.88

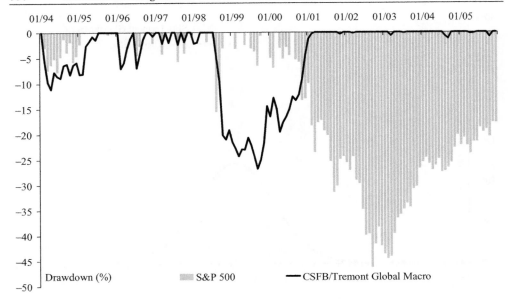

Figure 15.20   Drawdown diagram of the CS/Tremont Global Macro compared to the S&P 500, 1994–2005

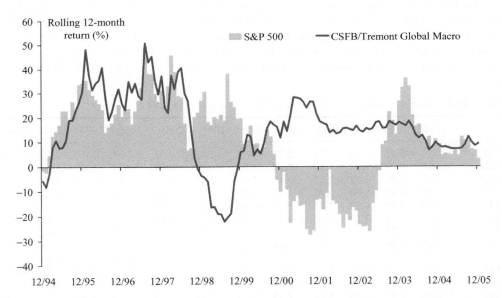

Figure 15.21   Comparison of the 12-month rolling performances of the CS/Tremont Global Macro with the S&P 500, 1994–2005

16
Managed Futures and Commodity Trading Advisors (CTAs)

Is it better to make little money most of the time, or to make a lot of money once in a lifetime?

Futures contracts and markets have been in existence for several centuries in one form or another – their origins can be supposedly traced to Ancient Greek or Phoenician times. However, futures trading on a formal futures exchange only originated in the US with the formation of the Chicago Board of Trade (CBOT) in the middle of the nineteenth century. The CBOT primarily attracted two categories of futures participants: hedgers and speculators. The former used futures contracts to hedge against future price variations in the underlying cash commodities, while the latter had the sole intention of making money and realizing capital gains by correctly forecasting future price variations.

In the early 1970s, as a result of the regulatory separation between the brokerage and investment management functions of the futures business, a third category emerged. It regrouped a few professional money managers that were using futures contracts as investment vehicles on behalf of their clients. At that time, futures contracts existed only for a few commodities. Hence, these new money managers were often referred to as *Commodity Trading Advisors* (CTAs), and their funds took the name of *managed futures*. Their success in raising assets was rather limited, primarily due to the fact that most investors were not yet familiar with the opportunities and risks of futures trading, nor did they really understand commodities investing.

The acceptance of managed futures only started in the late 1970s. As uncertainty rose in most financial markets, several exchanges introduced futures contracts on other assets than commodities, e.g. interest rates, bonds, currencies, and later on, stock indices. Most individuals or companies willing to participate in these new futures markets lacked the time and knowledge to trade them successfully. Consequently, they searched for experienced portfolio managers – typically former traders – to trade on their behalf on segregated accounts. Managed futures rapidly emerged as an interesting solution. In December 1979, Managed Account Reports (MAR) began publishing the *Managed Account Reports Trading Advisor Qualified Universe Index*, a US$ 300 million dollar-weighted index of CTAs having a minimum of $500 000 of assets under management and at least 12 months of track record.

Since then, managed futures have grown significantly (Figure 16.1). Today, they represent a disciplined and mature industry, running approximately $130 billion of assets according to Barclays Trading Group. The terms *managed futures*, *Commodity Trading Advisors* (CTAs) or *trading funds* are now used interchangeably to describe the group of professional money managers that use futures contracts as an investment medium or give advice on trading futures contracts or commodity options.[1] However, the term CTA has become a misnomer. In the 1980s, agricultural futures trading approximated 64% of market activity, metals trading comprised

---

[1] Legally, a CTA is defined as "any person registered or required to be registered with the CFTC as a commodity trading adviser under the Commodity Exchange Act (CEA) and that directs client commodity futures or options accounts".

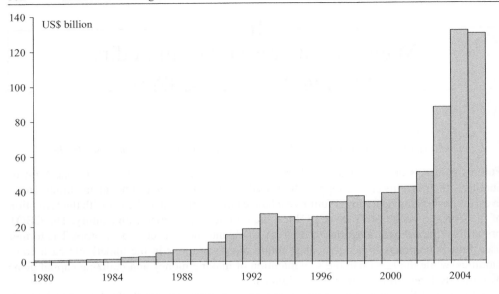

Figure 16.1   Growth of managed futures (based on data from Barclays Trading Group)

16%, and currency and interest rate futures accounted for the remaining 20%. Today, global futures markets are dominated by financial futures for currencies, interest rates and stock indices. The portfolios of CTAs have followed the same evolution, and the majority of their portfolios are now invested in non-commodity related futures contracts, despite their name.

16.1   THE VARIOUS STYLES OF MANAGED FUTURES

All managed futures fund managers are convinced, either explicitly or implicitly, that market prices do not move randomly and that they can capture some of the price variations. Most of them claim to have developed their own investment style and trading approach that makes them unique. Nevertheless, it is in reality relatively easy to partition the managed futures universe into a few homogeneous groups based on characteristics such as the trading approach, the type of analysis used, the source of returns and the target time frame of their trades (Figure 16.2).

16.1.1   Trading approach: discretionary versus systematic

The first managed futures funds were primarily run by discretionary traders, who used their judgement and knowledge of commodity markets to give buy and sell orders. In a sense, their investment approach was similar to global macro investing, as they attempted to anticipate price changes in commodities and position their portfolios accordingly using futures contracts. As the range of futures contracts expanded, managed futures funds extended their investment universe to other asset classes than commodities. However, their discretionary and judgemental approach rapidly became a limit to their expansion.

The increased availability of computing power in the last few years provided investment professionals and amateurs with the capability to access and analyse tremendous amounts of

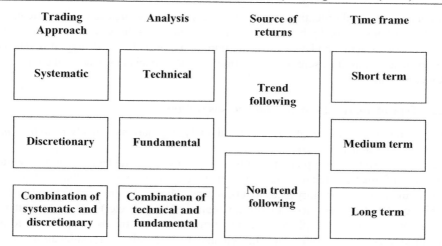

Trading Approach	Analysis	Source of returns	Time frame
Systematic	Technical	Trend following	Short term
Discretionary	Fundamental		Medium term
Combination of systematic and discretionary	Combination of technical and fundamental	Non trend following	Long term

Figure 16.2   A simple partition of the managed futures universe according to four criteria – adapted from Lungarella (2002)

financial data. Consequently, a large number of managed futures fund managers progressively removed the human judgement or intervention in their decision-making process. They adopted a systematic trading approach (also called algorithmic trading), i.e. they rely exclusively on computer models to manage their portfolio. These models, which are often called "systems", range from simple formulas on a spreadsheet to complicated proprietary software. They analyse market data such as prices and trading volume information and attempt to identify specific price patterns such as market trends or market reversals. Regularly, these models generate buy and sell signals that traders should follow to the letter.

Today, approximately 80% of the universe of managed futures trading advisers is composed of CTAs who rely on systematic, computerized approaches to generate market-trading decisions. While US and Japan investors are in love with the more systematic approach, Europeans still prefer CTAs who take their trading decisions based on an informed subjective opinion rather than the one utilizing a computerized black box. However, the debate about the superiority of the systematic trader over the discretionary trader is still – and will most likely continue to be – hotly debated by both factions. On one hand, systematic traders argue that few people have the mental discipline required to keep the decision-making process unfettered by the stresses and potential emotionalism of adverse price movement. By eliminating human emotion, failure of judgement and the other attendant fallibilities therein, they trade more consistently in terms of entry and exit points. They can also better diversify their portfolio by extending the number of markets that they can effectively trade. This increases the predictability of their performance – their profit expectancy and risk can be calculated and anticipated with a reasonable degree of confidence. On the other hand, discretionary traders criticize systematic trading due to its lack of economic support and excessive reliance on data mining. They suspect that the rules used by systems will fit the data of the past, but will not necessarily have any predictive value in the future or when applied to other markets. For them, being a truly systematic trader requires a phlegmatic character and a nonchalance about making trades that are sometimes the exact opposite of what one feels is the right thing to do.

Of course, we should mention that there exist managed futures funds that attempt to get the best from both worlds by being both systematic and discretionary at the same time. That is, they rely on systems to identify possible trading opportunities and suggest trades, but the portfolio manager has the discretion to override the system decisions or adapt them to changing market conditions.

16.1.2   Type of analysis: fundamental versus technical

Managed futures have essentially two ways of analysing markets, namely *technical analysis* and *fundamental analysis*.

Technical analysis aims at predicting future price movements and market trends by studying past market information. Technicians believe that there are systematic statistical dependencies in asset returns – i.e. that history tends to repeat itself. They make price predictions on the basis of published data (such as price variations, volumes of trading, etc.) looking for patterns and possible correlations, and applying systematic rules to assess trends, support and resistance levels. From these, they develop buy and sell signals. Interestingly, technicians are not much concerned with the underlying economics or the fair value of a given market. Their assumption is that markets are driven more by psychological factors than fundamental values, and that the emotional make-up of investors does not change. In a certain set of circumstances, investors will therefore react in a similar manner to how they did in the past, so that the resultant price moves are likely to be the same.

By contrast, fundamental analysis aims at determining the fair value (also known as intrinsic value) of markets and instruments based on economic, political, environmental and other relevant fundamental factors. This fair value is then used to ascertain future price movement, with the implicit wisdom that the price of an instrument currently trading for less than its fair value should increase while the price of an instrument currently trading for more than its fair value should fall. Fundamental analysis therefore tells us what ought to be the direction in which prices will move.

Fundamentalists and technicians have been at odds with each other since the advent of investing, but it is not clear why fundamental analysis should be considered superior to its technical alternative, or vice versa. After all, if markets were efficient, prices would incorporate all the information known and reflect it, and predicting future prices would be impossible regardless of the method employed. Conversely, if prices do not reflect all the information available, then surely investor psychology is as important a factor as the more fundamental indicators. It is therefore not surprising to see that while some managed futures funds only rely on technical analysis, others only use fundamental analysis, and some attempt to combine both to determine their positions.

16.1.3   Source of returns: trend followers and non-trend followers

The source of returns of managed futures is usually divided into two categories: *trend followers* and *non-trend followers*.

Trend followers represent the majority of managed futures funds. Their trading strategy is intimately connected with the idea of momentum, i.e. if a market moves in one direction in one period, then it is likely to continue in that direction in the next period.[2] Therefore, trend

---

[2] On some markets, such as currencies, momentum is known to occur because of long-term trends, which are in turn caused by long-term macroeconomic trends, such as interest rate tightening or easing cycles. On other markets, the psychology of investors and their behaviour may result in herding phenomena that support the creation and persistence of trends, at least in the short to medium term.

followers generally rely on quantitative models to perform technical analysis, with the goal of finding trends in the price movements of markets. Once a trend has been identified, they jump on the bandwagon, until their models indicate that the trend has ended.

Non-trend followers regroup all managed futures that do not attempt to follow trends. This includes, for instance, contrarian traders looking for sharp trend reversals that tend to occur when momentum reaches unsustainable levels. They establish their positions against the current trend of the marketplace – they look for market rallies to establish short sell positions and market dips to go long with buy positions. Timing and risk management are essential with this approach to avoid being carried away by the persistence of momentum – as John Maynard Keynes once wrote, "the market can stay irrational longer than you can stay solvent". Other managers may also engage in active and fast systematic trading approaches such as pattern recognition with the aim of capturing short-term profit opportunities that are not linked to market trends.

16.1.4 Timeframe for trades

The timeframe of managed futures varies greatly across their universe, depending upon their trading approach, the type of analysis they use and their source of returns. For instance, trend followers have time horizons that range from short term (several hours to several days) to medium term (up to 30 days) to long term (2–3 months). Non-trend followers tend to be rather short term and spend a significant amount of time out of the market, entering only when a trading opportunity arises and exiting shortly afterwards.

The timeframe selected influences the types of assets that can be traded. A short-term horizon strategy generally requires low transaction costs, highly liquid positions and automated trading. As an illustration, Man Investments AHL Group, a trend-following manager and currently the largest managed futures manager, re-analyses various futures markets with their computer models more than 2000 times per day. Trades are spread over a 24-hour period, since they operate in a global market. By contrast, a long-term horizon allows trades to be implemented over time in less liquid asset classes.

16.2 EXAMPLES OF SYSTEMATIC TRADING RULES

Since systematic traders represent the majority of managed futures fund managers, we are going to investigate further how their models typically operate. Most of the time, a systematic trading model is a collection of remarkably simple mathematical rules. These rules find their origin in *technical analysis rules* – what stocks analysts used to call Chartism in the old days of charts, tables and graphs. Today, computers have replaced charts, but the rules have remained. Let us now illustrate some of them.

16.2.1 Moving Average Convergence/Divergence (MACD)

Lagging indicators such as moving average rules are one of the most popular tools to detect the beginning or the end of a trend. In its simplest form, a moving average is an average of past prices calculated over a given period of time. Any time span can be considered from minutes to years. For example, a 10-day moving average takes the last 10 closing prices, adds them up, and divides the result by 10. On the next day, the oldest price is dropped, the newest price is

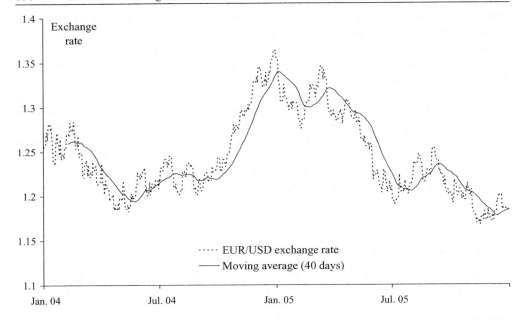

Figure 16.3 Evolution of the US dollar (dotted line) and its 40-day moving average (plain line). It is clear that strength is associated with a rising moving average and that weakness is denoted by a declining moving average

added, and the new sum of 10 prices is divided by 10 to obtain the new average. In this manner, the average "moves" each day.

By construction, moving averages work as a smoothing device, as they take the "noise" out of price movements and reduce the effects of short-term volatility. For instance, if an upward-trending market suddenly has one day of lower prices, a moving average would factor that day's price in with several other days, thus lessening the impact of one single trading day on the moving average and facilitating the recognition of underlying trends.[3]

At this stage, it is essential to understand that moving averages do not *predict* market trends, but rather systematically *lag* the current market price – see Figure 16.3. In a rising market, because of the lag, the moving average is below the current price line, whereas in a falling market it is above it. This should immediately suggest an interesting signal: whenever the current price changes direction, from rising to falling or vice versa, the moving average and the price lines will cross, as the moving average, by nature of the lag, will still reflect the preceding trend. The direction of the crossing provides the basic rules by which all moving average systems operate. These are: (i) buy when the current price crosses the moving average from below; and (ii) sell when the current price crosses the moving average from above. This basic approach provides opportunities for the CTA to enter and exit the market on a systematic basis – see Figure 16.4.

---

[3] Note that there also exist more complex weighting schemes. For instance, Linear Weighted Moving Average (LWMA) and Exponentially Weighted Moving Average (EWMA) weight each observation according to its relative position in the average, with generally more weight given to recent observations.

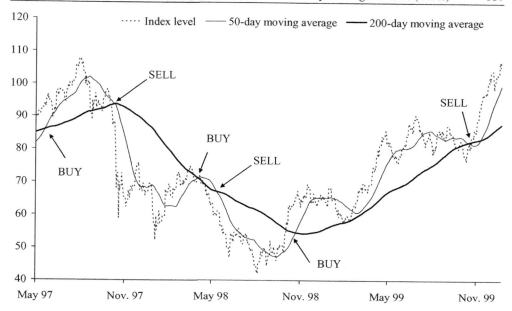

Figure 16.4 Example of trading signals based on moving average rules for a stock index. Trend reversals are indicated my moving average crossovers. When the 50-day moving average crosses the 200-day moving average going down, we sell (short). When the 50-day moving average crosses the 200-day moving average going up, we buy (long)

Of course, the number of days used to calculate the moving average window will dramatically impact its behaviour. Shorter-length moving averages tend to follow changes in underlying asset prices more closely. They are very sensitive to trends, but are also prone to "whipsaw" losses, as small erratic price movements generate false trading signals. Using them can result in excessive transaction costs and poor performance in ranging markets, as short-term rules always buy late (after a rise in value) and sell late (after a fall in value). By contrast, longer-length moving averages alternatively de-sensitize asset price movements and highlight only major trends. Their drawback is that they generate fewer signals than a shorter-length average and may therefore miss some opportunities (see Figures 16.5 and 16.6).

Most major primary trends can usually be monitored with a 40-week (200-day) moving average, intermediate term trends with a 40-day moving average and short-term trends by a 20-day (or less) moving average. However, the "optimal" length of a moving average should be determined on a case-by-case basis, as it depends on the market considered and its cyclicality. Besides the length of the moving average, one must also decide upon the types of prices used (closing, open, high, low, averages, etc.), as well as the threshold levels to signal a buy or a sell. Most of the time, the models used by managed futures are the result of hundreds of hours of development, testing and fine-tuning. The basic rules that constitute them are remarkably simple, but the calibration of these rules to specific markets is not. Remember that once set up, a systematic trading system should operate alone and undisturbed, until or unless it no longer works properly. It is therefore crucial to be confident in the system quality.

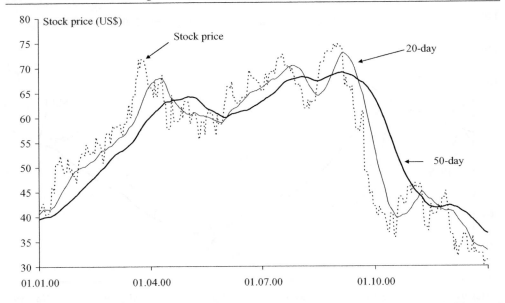

Figure 16.5 Comparing the evolution of short-term moving averages with different length. The trend reversals are indicated by moving average crossovers

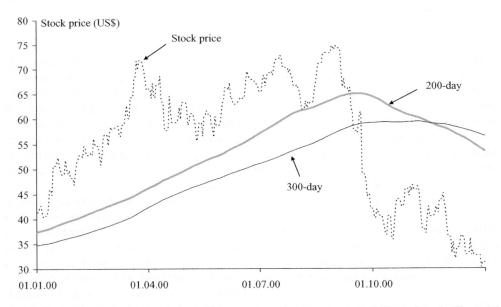

Figure 16.6 Comparing the evolution of long-term moving averages with different length. The trend reversals indicated by the moving averages crossover comes late, because we are only using long term averages

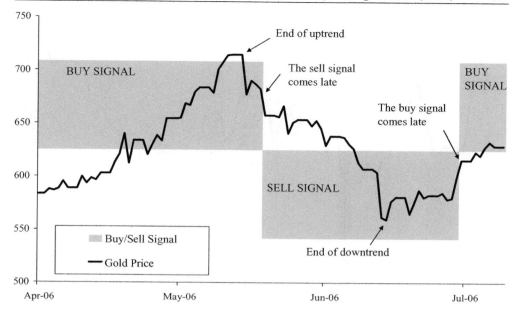

Figure 16.7   Illustration of a basic 30-day crossover rule for gold. The end of a trend usually coincides with losses because the trading signal arrives late

Even when properly calibrated, most moving average rules suffer from two drawbacks. First, because of the inherent lag of the moving average compared to market prices, trend-following systems tend to enter late in a trend and exit late, i.e. after the trend has reversed and losses have occurred (Figure 16.7). Second, moving averages tend to generate too many useless buy and sell signals in markets that evolve in a narrow range without any real trend (Figure 16.8).

Of course, CTAs are continuously working on finding more sophisticated moving average rules in order to solve these problems (Box 16.1). Let us mention a few of them:

- *Variable length moving averages* (VMAs) rules are based on the comparison of at least two moving averages. A buy signal is generated when the short-term average crosses over the long-term average from below. Conversely, a sell signal is generated when the short-term average crosses the long-term average from above. Following a buy (sell) signal, the long (short) position is maintained until the opposite signal is received.
- *Fixed length moving averages* (FMAs) rules are similar to VMA rules except that the position established following a signal is only maintained for a fixed holding period. The goal is to capture the beginning of a trend, but avoids the trend reversal.
- *Adaptive moving averages* (AMAs) are based on the premise that a short-length moving average will respond more quickly when market prices are trending, yet a long-length moving average will be preferred when markets are ranging. Consequently, adaptive moving averages seek to identify the current changing market conditions in order to adapt the length of the moving average that they use, as well as the minimum price movement that is required beyond crossing before a trade (buy or sell) is initiated.
- *High low moving averages* (HLMAs) run two moving averages, one of high prices and another of the low prices, effectively creating a channel of prices.
- *Triple moving averages* (TMVs) rules use three moving averages at the same time.

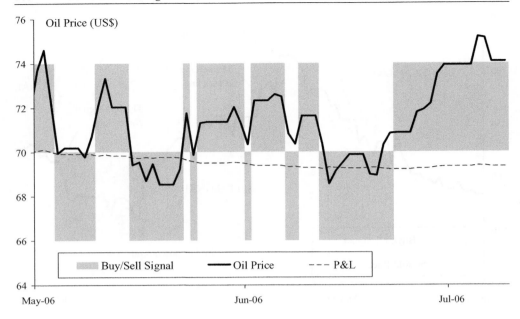

Figure 16.8 Illustration of a basic 30-day moving average crossover rule for oil. When there is a narrow trading range with several reversals, moving average strategies suffer because they cannot react fast enough, as illustrated by the negative P&L

Box 16.1 The Mount Lucas Management Index (MLM)

Mount Lucas Management (MLM) was founded in 1986 to provide alternative asset investments to institutional investors and high net worth individuals. In 1988, it created the MLM Index™ (Figure 16.9) with the goal of emulating an investment in managed futures and teaching institutional investors the value of adding managed futures to their portfolios. The MLM Index™ reflects the results of a purely mechanical, 12-month moving average based trading rule in 25 different commodity and financial futures markets.

The MLM Index™ rapidly became a widely recognized benchmark for evaluating managed futures performance, and turned into an investment vehicle. In 1993, Federal Express became the first institutional client to invest in the MLM Index™. Mount Lucas currently replicates more than $1 billion of this Index for a wide variety of investors, including more than 20 tax-exempt institutional investors.

However, caution should be exercised in using the MLM Index™ as a benchmark for CTA trend-followers, because trend-following techniques have evolved significantly since the 1980s while the MLM Index™ is still based on the same naive rule. In our view, CTA indices are preferable, because they represent the results of investing *in* CTAs, not the results of investing *like* CTAs. Nevertheless, for those that still want to replicate passively what CTAs are doing, Fung and Hsieh (2001) have suggested complementing the MLM Index™ with what they call Primitive Trend Following Strategies (PTFSs) – these are essentially an option-based replication of trend-following strategies.

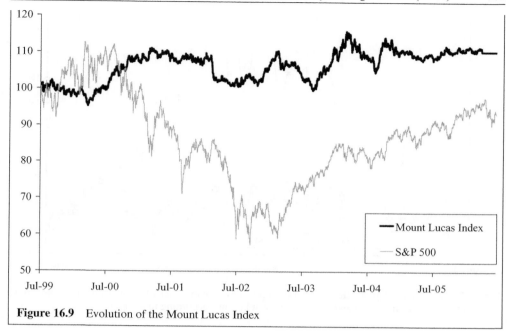

Figure 16.9 Evolution of the Mount Lucas Index

16.2.2   Examples of trading ranges signals

Since moving averages do not work very well in non-trending markets, managed futures'
systems also rely on rules that are directly inherited from technical analysis and Chartism.
Most of these rules aim at capturing opportunities during trading range markets. To illustrate
how these rules operate, let us mention two of them, namely the *relative strength index* and
the *stochastic oscillator*.

The *relative strength index* (RSI) is a counter-trend indicator which measures the ratio of the
upward trends (gains) in a market compared to its downward trends (losses) and standardizes
the calculation so that the index is expressed by a figure between 1 and 100. The RSI is
calculated as follows:

$$RSI = 100 - \left(\frac{100}{1 + RS} \right)$$

where RS is the ratio of total number of days with a higher close over the past N days over the
total number of days with a lower close over the past N days, and N days is the number of days
that one wants to consider.[4] RSI levels of 70% and 30% (sometimes 80% and 20%) are known
as overbought/oversold levels. A buy signal is generated when the market is oversold, and a
sell signal is generated when the market is overbought. In practical terms, a N-day criterion
means that a sustained move in one direction that exceeds N days will retain a very high RSI
value and may result in losses if a short position was entered (see Figure 16.10).

As many other signals, the RSI usually works well inside range-trading phases, but produces
losses during trend phase.

---

[4] Traders often use $N = 14$ days, because it represents one half of a natural cycle, but N can in fact be chosen arbitrarily.

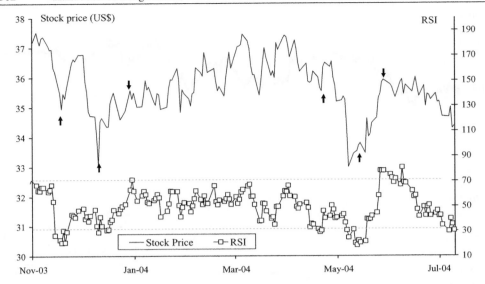

Figure 16.10 RSI implementation ($N = 14$ calendar days) on the stock of Home Depot Inc. The arrows correspond to entry (up arrow) and exit (down arrow) points, according to the RSI

The *stochastic oscillator* indicates the conditions of overbought/oversold on a scale from 0 to 100% by comparing a closing price for a market to its price range over a given time period. It is based on the observation that when a market is going to turn, say from up to down, its highs are higher, but the closing price often settles within the previous range.

The original stochastic oscillator, developed by George Lane, is plotted as two lines called %K, a fast line and %D, a slow line. The formula for %K is:

$$\%K = 100 \times \left(\frac{\text{Closing price} - \text{Lowest low}_N}{\text{Highest low}_N - \text{Lowest Low}_N} \right)$$

where Lowest low$_N$ represents the lowest low level reached over the past N periods, and Highest low$_N$ represents the highest low level reached over the past N periods. The formula for %D is a simple moving average of %K over some period of time, which needs to be specified.

Although this sounds complex, it is similar to the plotting of moving averages – simply think of %K as a fast-moving average and %D as a slow-moving average. Then, a stochastic oscillator generates signals in three main ways:

- Extreme values: The first rule is usually to buy when the stochastic (%D or %K) falls below 20% and then rises above that level. The second rule is usually to sell when the stochastic rises above 80% and then falls below that level.[5]
- Crossovers between the %D and %K lines: This is very similar to moving averages rules, i.e. buy when the %K line rises above the %D line and sell when the %K line falls below the %D line.

---

[5] Some systems also use more complex rules that analyse the pattern of the stochastic. For instance, when it stays below 40–50% for a period and then swings above, the market is shifting from overbought and offering a buy signal. And vice versa when it stays above 50–60% for a period of time.

- Divergences between the stochastic and the underlying price: for example, if prices are making a series of new highs and the stochastic is trending lower, this is usually a warning signal of weakness in the market.

Stochastic oscillators are very effective in trading ranges, but not during trending markets. In a trading range, as the price moves back and forth in a narrow range, the oscillator should indicate an oversold condition at the lower side of the range and an overbought situation at the upper side of the range. In contrast, during an upward or a downward trend, the stochastic oscillator will prematurely indicate an extreme in price, positioning the trader against the prevailing trend.

16.2.3 Portfolio construction

It is important to understand that the majority of managed futures managers run their portfolios using *several trading rules* applied *simultaneously* on a *large number* of futures markets. These rules may use different types of analysis, or cover different sources of returns (trends or non-trends) and different timeframes. This allows capturing returns from different origins and diversifying away the risks inherent to each individual futures position. In particular, the losses that usually occur at the end of a trend on a given market may easily be compensated by the gains linked to a starting or ongoing trend in another market.

An essential point when analysing managed futures is the portfolio construction rules used by the fund manager. One of the key advantages of trading futures contracts rather than their underlying assets is that they require a relatively small amount of margin. Consequently, managers have a lot of flexibility in designing their investment programmes, based on the return, risk, and correlation expectations of their client base.

The simplest approach is to systematically place identical size orders in terms of notional amounts invested (long or short) or in terms of margins. Its danger is that the risk of each position is not really taken into consideration. A better solution is to think in terms of capital at risk and allocate the same risk capital to each position in the portfolio, for instance using stop losses to limit the downside risk. Consider for instance a managed futures fund with $200 000 of equity capital. Say we have a buy signal on gold with a futures price at $400 per oz., and the manager wants to risk an initial 1% of its capital to each trade. Buying one future and setting a stop-loss at $390 results in a $1000 risk per contract (($400 - 390$) × $100/point). If the manager agrees to risk 1% of its capital on each trade, i.e. $2000 currently, he should buy two contracts. Note that the position needs to be continuously reassessed as prices are changing. For instance, if gold price increases, the manager has the choice between maintaining the position and adjusting the stop loss upward, or maintaining the stop loss at $390 but reducing the number of contracts – as the spread between the futures price and the stop loss price widens, the capital at risk increases. Some managers go even one step further and take into account the diversification benefits of their various positions when calculating the capital at risk.

16.2.4 Transparency or regulated black boxes?

Most managed futures managers tend to be very secretive about their models and the set of rules that they use. In a world that demands transparency, secrecy is a red flag for fear and suspicion. As a result, managed futures have often been nicknamed "black boxes" by investors. However, the seeming opacity of the trading systems usually hides a high level of transparency on the underlying positions. Most managed futures managers are willing to openly discuss their current positions with investors, and even to open managed accounts if the initial capital investment is large enough. These managed accounts can easily be customized to the needs of specific investors, e.g. volatility targets, minimum diversification, inclusion or exclusion of specific underlying markets, maximum leverage, etc. They are also more liquid than other investment vehicles – the contract terms usually include specific termination clauses and language.

The existence of several accounts running in parallel should immediately raise the question of the validity of the track record used by a manager, particularly when it is a composite return aggregating the performances of several accounts. Fortunately, the Commodity Futures Trading Commission (CFTC) has established very strict guidelines on this topic.[6] All CTAs have to publish a twice-yearly disclosure document in which *all* past trading of firm's principals (the firm, its owners and key staff) must be disclosed. This prevents the inflation of composite returns through the elimination of loss-making managed accounts or funds. The CFTC also mandates extensive disclosure of the nature of the trading style and strategy, and thus legally limits the opportunity for managers to bait and switch, i.e. generate good returns from one, perhaps capacity limited investment style and then apply the money raised to a different strategy.

The National Futures Association has also very stringent rules on CTAs' promotional material and communications with the public. For instance:

- Statements made in promotional material must be factually true and you the manager must be able to document them.
- Statements concerning profits must be accompanied by a statement about losses or potential losses, equally prominently.
- Simulated results in the past should be indicated as being "hypothetical" – in CAPITAL LETTERS.
- Statements regarding past results must say that past results are not indicative of future results.
- Rates of return must be calculated consistent with CFTC Regulation – see Box 16.2.
- Statements concerning past performance must be representative for *all* accounts over the same period of time.
- Statements of opinion must be identified as such and have a reasonable basis in fact.
- Members must have written procedures for reviewing and approving promotional material used by all associates and employees.
- Copies of promotional material and their approval must be readily accessible for three years after the date of last use.
- Copies of promotional material must be on file with the NFA immediately after use if required by the Director of Compliance.

In addition, CTAs must also provide "performance capsules" that summarize the performance history of any accounts or pools they operate. The performance capsules are required to include information on both open and closed accounts during the past five years and year-to-date with lifetime profits and lifetime losses. Hedge funds are far less transparent than CTAs with that respect, as a hedge fund manager can still close his fund and start a new one without having to disclose his past performance.

---

[6] In contrast to hedge funds managers, which did not need to register with the SEC prior to February 2006, CTAs always had to register with the Commodity Futures Trading Commission (CFTC) through membership in the National Futures Association. And as the US remains the largest market for CTAs, this regulation encompasses the majority of managed futures managers world wide on a *de facto* basis.

Box 16.2 Rate-of-return calculation

The usual approach for calculating returns consists of dividing the net dollar performance by the dollar amount of funds under management, usually over a one-month horizon. Unfortunately, most CTAs cannot blindly follow it, because (i) many of their accounts are facing daily additions and withdrawals of cash, and (ii) several accounts may open or close during the observation period. Additions and withdrawals of cash affect the denominator of the ratio and, accordingly, can distort the return.

Fortunately, the CFTC has advised as to the appropriate method to calculate returns, and its final rules allow two methods of accounting for additions and withdrawals, namely the daily compounding and the time-weighting of additions and withdrawals. In the former method, performance is calculated every day, as if books were closed on a daily basis, and daily performances are compounded to obtain the result over the desired period. In the latter method, additions, withdrawals and beginning equity are weighted over the number of days in the month. This gives an approximation of the true performance, because it assumes that the monthly performance was earned pro rata over the entire period. Other methods were initially allowed, such as the "Only Accounts Traded", which was considering the rate of return only for accounts that were open during the entire period and that had no additions or withdrawals. They were discarded in 2003.

16.2.5   Investment vehicles

From a practical perspective, there are three primary investment vehicles to access managed futures.

- *Managed accounts* are usually dedicated to institutional investors or high net worth individuals, because they require a substantial initial capital investment. Using a managed account offers the advantage of having full transparency on the underlying positions and being able to customize the account as needed, e.g. volatility targets, minimum diversification, inclusion or exclusion of specific underlying markets, maximum leverage, etc. Managed accounts are also more liquid than other investment vehicles – the contract terms usually include specific termination clauses and language.
- *Managed futures funds* commingle the commitments from several investors, usually into a limited partnership. Most of these pools have minimum investments ranging from approximately $25 000 to $250 000. These futures partnerships usually allow for admission/redemption on a monthly or quarterly basis.
- *Funds of managed futures funds*: For diversification reasons, some investors prefer to spread their risk across several managed futures funds. This allows for instance the simultaneous use of long-term and short-term traders, the coverage of specific markets, etc.

16.2.6   Back-testing and calibration

Before putting a new trading rule into action, managed futures managers have to test how well this strategy would have performed in the past using historical data. The rationale for back-testing is if a trading rule did not do well in the past, the chance that it will work in the future is slim. As we all know, reality is that past performance is not necessarily a forecast of future performance, but most people will nevertheless want to see the successful back-testing of a trading rule before accepting it.

As a result, trading rules often appear to work remarkably well once they have been back-tested. But this may hide several biases.

- *Pre-test bias*: Trading rules typically derive from personal experience or the observation of past market movements. In either case, the formulation of the trading rule is heavily influenced by history, so that the back-test of its performance using the very same historical period is likely to be attractive.
- *Data mining*: In the most extreme form, one could start with thousands of possible trading rules and test them all over some historical period. Some would appear to work simply because of chance.
- *Trading cost bias*: Many back-tests ignore the implicit and explicit trading costs that one has to pay to execute a trade, e.g. bid/ask spreads, commissions, margin deposits, etc. Failure to account for these trading costs will overstate the performance of a trading rule, especially for one that requires frequent trading and involves less liquid or more volatile markets.
- *Slippage control:* Many back-tests assume that they can buy and sell at the closing prices. In reality, there are slippage effects, i.e. differences between the price that triggers a buy or a sell order and the price at which the order has been executed. For CTAs, slippage may be a significant cost of doing business and is therefore more important than saving a few cents on commissions. To ensure best execution and limit slippage, most CTAs analyse the types of orders they place, when they place them, how they place them and the people they place them with. But this is rarely analysed in back-tests.
- *Look ahead bias*: During their back-testing, some trading rules use information that would not yet be available at the time of the trade, e.g. information which is published only a few hours or a few days after the closing of the market. Failure to exclude this future information in the back-testing period tends to significantly overstate the historical performance of a trading rule.

All these biases can cause spurious profits in the back-testing period and as a result past performance does not always foretell future performance. It is therefore essential to assess the robustness of the performance of any trading rule over different sub-periods and different market conditions before validating it.

16.3   HISTORICAL PERFORMANCE

Investors who are not familiar with managed futures tend to be disappointed by their track record. Managed futures in the aggregate have produced low absolute returns and have under-performed traditional asset classes with far more volatility. Over the January 1994 to December 2005 period, managed futures – as measured by the CS/Tremont Managed Futures Index – delivered an average return of 6.4% p.a. with a volatility of 12.8% . By contrast, over the same period, the S&P 500 delivered an average return of 8.6% p.a. with a volatility of 16.0%, and the Citigroup World Government Bond Index an average return of 5.9% p.a. with a volatility of 6.7% (see Figure 16.11 and Table 16.1).

However, when analysed more closely, the track record of managed futures is in reality much more attractive than initially perceived. When times are good, managed futures strategies perform modestly, but during difficult markets, they tend to produce sound relative returns. As an illustration, Figure 16.12 shows the behaviour of managed futures over the months when

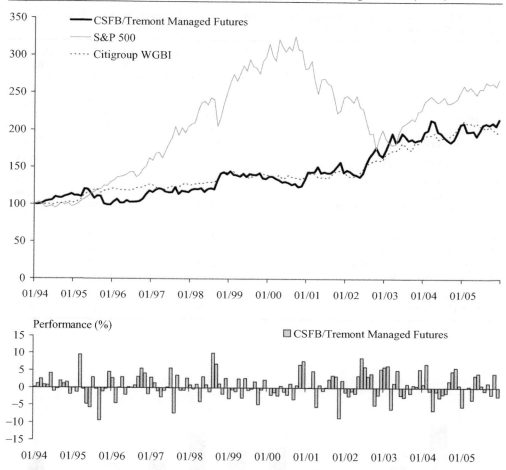

Figure 16.11 Evolution of the CS/Tremont Managed Futures, 1994–2005

the S&P 500 was down. Clearly, managed futures as a group seem to perform well during these periods. During the summer 1998, for instance, the managed futures industry had one of its best performances while all other asset classes (including hedge funds) were in difficulty. In addition, managed futures also tend to perform well during extended periods of market declines in equity markets, as illustrated in Table 16.2. As a consequence, managed futures may play an interesting role as a hedge for traditional portfolios. From a pure return perspective, the cost of this hedge may be the forgone opportunity of greater performance in alternative strategies, but the gains are there in terms of downside risk reduction.[7]

---

[7] The diversification properties of managed futures are well established in the academic literature. In one of the earliest studies, John Lintner (1983) found that the returns of managed futures showed a low and sometimes negative correlation to the returns of stock and bond portfolios. Lintner concluded that investment portfolios which incorporate an allocation to managed futures have historically offered a superior distribution of returns when compared to portfolios composed exclusively of stocks and bonds. Inspired by Lintner, subsequent and more extensive research has concluded that managed futures investments do indeed provide unique diversification benefits for traditional stock/bond portfolios, as well as for portfolios of stocks, bonds and hedge funds – see, for instance, Kat (2004).

Table 16.1   Performance comparison of the CS/Tremont Managed Futures, the S&P 500 and the Citigroup World Government Bond Index, 1994–2005

	CS/Tremont Managed Futures	S&P 500	Citigroup WGBI
Return (% p.a.)	6.37	8.55	5.87
Volatility (% p.a.)	12.75	16.00	6.74
Skewness	0.04	−0.58	0.37
Kurtosis	0.40	0.61	0.37
Normally distributed?	Yes	No	Yes
Correlation with strategy		−0.16	0.35
Positive months frequency	56%	62%	58%
Best month performance (%)	9.95	9.67	5.94
Average positive month performance (%)	2.92	3.44	1.73
Upside participation		39%	−13%
Negative months frequency	44%	38%	42%
Worst month performance (%)	−9.35	−14.58	−4.28
Average negative month performance (%)	−2.36	−3.53	−1.18
Downside participation		−469%	261%
Max. drawdown (%)	−17.74	−46.28	−7.94
Value at Risk (1-month, 99%)	−8.04	−10.24	−3.36

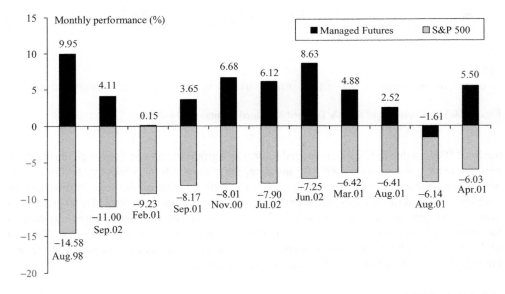

Figure 16.12   Performance of the CS/Tremont Managed Futures Index during the worst months of the S&P 500 since 1994

Table 16.2   Monthly returns of the CS/Tremont Managed Futures, 1994–2005

	1994	1995	1996	1997	1998	1999	2000	2001	2002	2003	2004	2005
Jan	0.22	−0.08	2.82	3.00	0.87	−3.14	0.01	−0.03	−1.27	6.07	1.09	−5.39
Feb	1.20	−1.27	−4.50	1.43	−0.28	−0.54	−2.10	0.15	−2.40	6.43	6.89	0.08
Mar	2.60	9.46	0.11	−0.95	1.06	−1.07	−1.31	4.88	−0.91	−6.10	−0.86	0.37
Apr	0.86	−0.33	3.12	−2.69	−4.03	2.67	−2.28	−5.49	−1.61	1.39	−6.46	−3.45
May	0.76	−4.70	−1.99	−0.76	3.25	−2.93	0.58	0.83	3.51	5.14	−1.05	3.62
Jun	4.15	−5.74	0.20	0.21	0.91	2.76	−1.12	−0.84	8.63	−2.21	−2.84	4.22
Jul	−1.01	3.05	0.10	5.69	−1.12	−0.72	−2.05	0.15	6.12	−2.75	−1.95	0.78
Aug	−0.27	−0.32	0.78	−7.27	9.95	−0.32	1.23	2.52	3.36	1.06	−1.53	−0.87
Sep	2.03	−9.35	3.22	3.63	6.87	1.81	−3.34	3.65	4.11	−1.60	1.96	1.38
Oct	1.18	−1.06	5.59	−0.73	1.21	−4.82	0.76	3.40	−5.03	0.78	4.82	−1.97
Nov	1.65	−0.27	4.21	−0.68	−1.80	−0.52	6.68	−8.62	−2.09	0.54	5.83	4.17
Dec	−1.89	4.59	−1.83	2.82	2.80	2.35	7.76	2.15	5.50	5.42	0.72	−2.53
Total	11.95	−7.09	11.98	3.11	20.66	−4.70	4.25	1.92	18.34	14.15	5.96	−0.11
S&P 500	−1.54	34.11	20.26	31.01	26.67	19.53	−10.14	−13.04	−23.37	26.38	8.99	3.00
WGBI	2.34	19.04	3.62	0.23	15.30	−4.27	1.59	−0.99	19.49	14.91	10.35	−6.88

One of the most persistent criticisms of managed futures is that they are "too volatile" or "too risky" an investment (see Box 16.3). In a general sense, this perception is rooted in the risk warnings associated with investing in derivatives. However, this claim needs to be moderated, as a key feature of managed future is their asymmetric returns. Managed futures may produce extreme returns, yet these extreme returns tend to be positive rather than negative. The reason is that most managed futures systems use stop-losses to exit bad trades before large drawdowns occur. Consequently, their volatility is high, but it is primary an upside volatility.[8] In addition, as futures are margined investments, the volatility of returns depends heavily on the level of leverage used. But the decision about what percentage of the assets under management to use

---

Box 16.3 Managed futures versus global macro

Global macro and managed futures often participate in the same market trends, but with different entry and exit points. Most of the time, global macro traders can get in and out earlier because they can be anticipatory, whereas managed futures are only reactive. Remember that macro managers primarily rely on fundamentals to analyse markets. They may enter the market during a consolidation period, building their position even before the trend begins. Similarly, they might identify a change in fundamentals that forewarns of a trend reversal and exit early from their positions, sometimes missing the final leg of the trend. By contrasts, managed futures are much more price-based in their analysis and do not necessarily look at the big picture. They generally will wait for confirmation that a trend has started before entering in a position, and they will wait for a clear signal that this trend is over before exiting. They are therefore always late compared to global macro, but will suffer accordingly when a trend ends abruptly.

---

[8] Volatility does not capture return asymmetry, which is extremely valuable for investors.

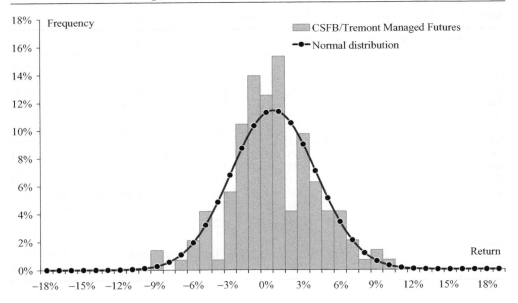

Figure 16.13   Return distribution of the CS/Tremont Managed Futures, 1994–2005

as margin (the margin/equity ratio), and therefore how much risk to take, is a business decision, not one determined by investment strategy. The very same trading strategy can be pursued at a higher or lower leverage (or gearing), by targeting the desired level of risk and setting the margin/equity ratio accordingly. And many managed futures funds offer different levels of leverage on the same underlying strategy. When comparing different managed futures track records to one another on the basis of some risk statistics, one must also bear in mind its direct relationship to leverage.

The returns of CS/Tremont Managed Futures Index have almost no skewness and kurtosis, and they can therefore be considered as normally distributed. In addition, their drawdowns seem uncorrelated with those of equity markets. However, the rolling 12-month performance evidences the high cyclicality of the strategy – when there are no trends, do not expect much (see Figures 16.13–16.15).

16.4   THE FUTURE OF MANAGED FUTURES

It is important to remember that excluding costs, futures markets are, by construction, a zero sum game – for every person who gains on a contract, there are some counterparties who lose. An interesting question is therefore why managed futures should keep earning a positive return over time, even after fees, as this implies indirectly that other futures market participants will actually be losing money. Even more puzzling is the fact that this positive return can be achieved by adopting a strategy as simple as monitoring a moving average. So far, we confess that we have not seen a real convincing answer to that question.

A frequently encountered argument is that trend-following strategies – which constitute the majority of managed futures – are successful because markets trend on the long run. But if this is true, then why are so many counterparties of the managed futures funds still willing to play

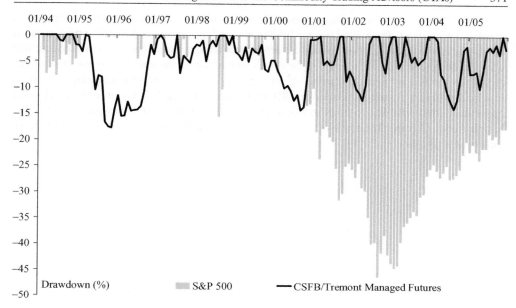

Figure 16.14   Drawdown diagram of the CS/Tremont Managed Futures compared to the S&P 500, 1994–2005

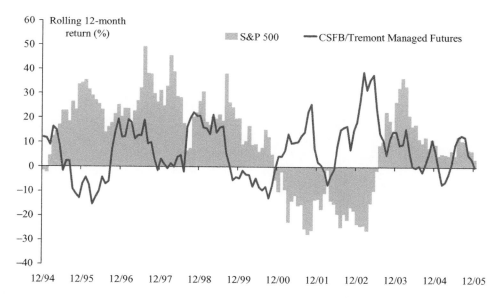

Figure 16.15   Comparison of the 12-month rolling performances of the CS/Tremont Global Macro with the S&P 500, 1994–2005

the game? Of course, these counterparties change over time and each of them trades for specific reasons. By contrast, a managed futures fund manager does not care whether the person on the other side of the trade is a floor trader, an arbitrage trader, a retail speculator, a producer that wants to hedge, or even another CTA. Nor does he care about the underlying asset or market, as long as there is a trend. And trending price action is an inherent characteristic of markets in which different participants act over different time horizons. It is not strictly an arbitrage opportunity that will disappear as markets become more efficient or more participants enter in that trade. This might be one of the reasons to explain the success and survival of trend-following strategies.

17
A Smorgasbord of Other Strategies

It is tough to make predictions, especially about the future.

The search for new profitable investment avenues seems inexorable in the hedge fund kingdom. New players typically populate existing strategies, who progressively become victims of their own success – their returns decline and the associated arbitrage opportunities shrink. Talented hedge fund managers must therefore constantly search for new investment opportunities and devise new strategies to exploit them, while simultaneously trying to anticipate and exit from crowded trades. Not surprisingly, these new hedge fund strategies closely parallel the development of financial markets and the availability of new financial instruments. In this chapter, we will simply illustrate and briefly discuss a few of these new strategies.

17.1 CAPITAL STRUCTURE ARBITRAGE AND CREDIT STRATEGIES

Capital structure arbitrage is a relative value strategy that has become popular within hedge funds over the recent years. Its goal is to invest long and short in different parts of the capital structure of the same firm in order to take advantage of pricing inefficiencies between related instruments which are traded simultaneously but on non-integrated markets.

Today, the liabilities of most companies consist of several types of securities (e.g. bank debt, senior bonds, subordinated bonds, preferred stock, common stock, convertible bonds, etc.), which investment banks then use as underlying assets for derivative products (e.g. warrants, equity and bond options, credit default swaps, etc.). This gives a plethora of unambiguously linked instruments that should all be fairly priced at least *relative to each other*. However, in practice, these instruments are often traded on different non-integrated markets and by different types of investors. Consequently, pricing inconsistencies sometimes occur, and this is precisely what capital structure arbitrageurs are waiting for. The least sophisticated arbitrageurs simply compare one claim to another and if there is a perceived mispricing, they buy the cheapest one and sell the expensive one. The most sophisticated arbitrageurs elaborate complex models of the capital structure of a company to determine the relative values of all its claims – in particular, stock, bonds, convertible bonds, and credit default swaps.

The simplest capital structure arbitrage trades are relative plays between different categories of debt, e.g. senior debt versus junior debt, secured debt versus unsecured, bank loans versus bonds, etc. One often observes discrepancies in the relative prices of debt instruments issued by the same company, particularly during periods of stress or financial distress for the issuer. Arbitrageurs are used to stepping in when there are such imbalances and their actions serve to repair them.

A second type of capital structure arbitrage trades involves debt versus equity. Convertible arbitrage, that we have seen in Chapter 12, can in a sense be considered as a capital structure arbitrage trade – one buys an undervalued convertible bond and hedges out the underlying equity risk by selling short an appropriate amount of common shares of the issuer. But arbitrage

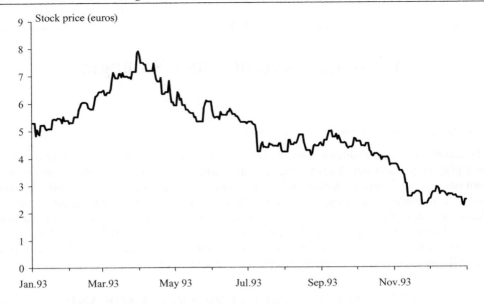

Figure 17.1   Evolution of the Euro-Disney stock price in 1993

between debt and equity is also frequent within stressed and distressed companies. Consider, for instance, Euro-Disney in 1993 (Figure 17.1). The company had a relatively simple capital structure made of senior secured bonds and equity. The bonds were trading at 60 cents on the dollar while common equity boasted a total market value of over one billion dollars. This situation was clearly inconsistent, because bonds ranked senior to common equity. Either the common equity was really worth one billion and the bonds should have been trading closer to par value; or the bonds were fairly priced at their distressed level but the common equity should have been worth almost nothing. Several hedge fund managers capitalized on this situation by purchasing the relatively cheap bonds and short selling the relatively expensive common shares.

More recently, the rapid development of credit derivatives has allowed hedge funds to extend significantly their playfield in the credit risk space. In particular, hedge fund managers have become specialists in arbitraging the differences in credit risk assessment by credit default swaps (CDS) and cash bond markets. In principle, the CDS spread plus the fixed rate on an interest rate swap corresponding to the maturity of the CDS should equal the yield on a same-maturity bond issued by the same issuer.[1] In practice, however, this is not always the case, and the theoretical relationship between the cash bonds and default swap spreads can dislocate for various fundamental or technical reasons – see Table 17.1. Credit-oriented hedge funds are therefore actively trading the basis, i.e. the CDS spread minus the bond spread. Two cases may be considered, namely the negative basis and the positive basis cases.

When bonds trade wider than swaps, the basis is negative, i.e. the bond market considers the default risk to be greater than the CDS market does. Consequently, both bonds and credit

---

[1] Market participants normally use swap rates rather than Treasury rates as the proxy for risk-free rates when analyzing spreads, essentially because of tax biases – in the US, yields from Treasury notes are exempt from state income taxes, while yields from corporate bonds are not.

Table 17.1 Possible reasons for a dislocation between the CDS and the bond market

Fundamental reasons	Impact on the basis
Funding levels: The average funding level of some CDS market participants is in excess of Libor.	Tighten
Delivery options: Protection buyers have the right to deliver the "cheapest to deliver" asset upon default.	Widen
Leveraged position: Unfunded transaction produces leveraged position.	Tighten
Par vs premium or discount: Bonds trading at a premium/discount expose the investor to greater/less credit risk than a CDS.	Tighten for bonds at a discount; widen for bonds at a premium
Counterparty risk: Protection buyers tend to require additional compensation for counterparty credit exposure.	Tighten

Technical reasons	Impact on the basis
Dealer hedging requirements: Dealers need to buy protection to hedge their exposure to primary market deals, and sell protection to support CDO transactions.	Widen when buying, tighten when selling
Repo market: Inability to source on repo markets to borrow cash bonds and sell them short forces participants to buy credit protection in more liquid CDS market.	Widen

protection (CDS) are cheap relative to each other – the former is cheap because bonds offer an excessive yield with respect to their default risk, and the latter is cheap because the CDS market underestimates default risk compared to the bond market. In this case, the arbitrageur will start by going long the bond. If it is a fixed rate bond, he immediately swaps it to earn a base floating rate of interest (LIBOR) plus a fixed spread. The asset swap allows the investor to gain exposure to the bond's credit risk while minimizing any interest rate risk (Figure 17.2).

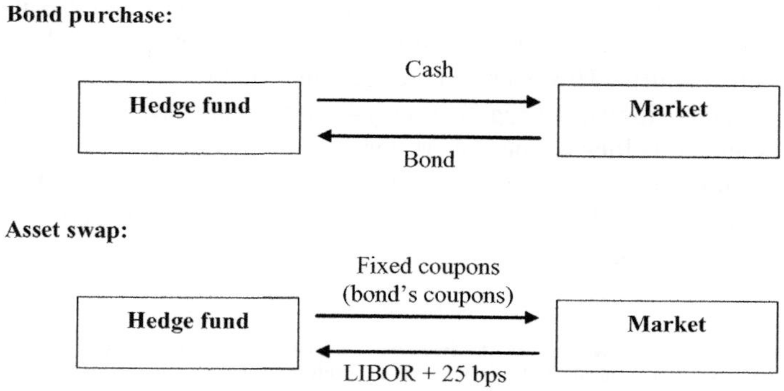

Bond purchase:

Cash

Hedge fund → **Market**

Bond

Asset swap:

Fixed coupons
(bond's coupons)

Hedge fund → **Market**

LIBOR + 25 bps

Figure 17.2 Initial purchase of the bond and swap of the fixed coupons to receive floating coupons. We have assumed a 25 bps premium over LIBOR in this example

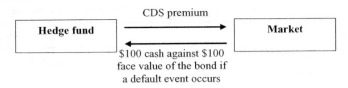

Figure 17.3   Eliminating the credit risk of the bond

In parallel, the arbitrageur will purchase credit protection via a CDS to hedge the credit risk of the bond issuer. If the bond issuer experiences a credit event (e.g. bankruptcy, failure to pay, restructuring, etc.) during the life of the credit default swap, the investor can deliver the bond to the CDS counterparty for payment at par. As long as the cost of credit protection is lower than the fixed spread over LIBOR previously gained, the strategy is profitable (Figure 17.3).

The net return to the arbitrageur will be the asset-swapped floating rate earned on the bond minus the cost of buying the CDS. In this example the net rate equates to 3-month LIBOR plus 25 basis points, after hedging both their interest rate risk and credit risk[2] (Figure 17.4). Of course, one may argue that 25 basis points is not worth setting the trade, but remember that leverage can be used to magnify returns.[3]

Negative basis trade opportunities arise from time to time, but tend not to last very long and tend to be quite small – hedge funds who are able to act quickly are the big beneficiaries. Examples of such trades in early 2005 included auto companies whose bond spreads were trading significantly wider than the associated CDS cost of protection.

In reality, many arbitrageurs argue that a non-zero basis should not in itself give rise to any particular trading opportunities, because there is no guarantee that the basis would disappear. For instance, Goldman Sachs, like several other major US investment banks, usually trades with a significant negative basis because the CDS market views the risk of Goldman defaulting as much lower than bondholders who demand more compensation for default risk in the form of a higher asset swap spread – see Figure 17.5. In such cases, it is preferable to compare the current basis to the *historical basis* and set the arbitrage position only when there is a significant deviation.

The positive basis case occurs when CDS trade wider than bonds, i.e. protection sellers demand a higher premium through the credit market while bond market participants are willing to buy bonds at a rather high price. Consequently, both bonds and credit protection are expensive. Arbitrageurs should then normally sell short the bond and sell protection, i.e. a CDS with the same maturity. However, in practice, this situation is more difficult to arbitrage, because a short bond position has a negative carry – arbitrageurs have to pay the bond's coupon to the securities lender as long as their short bond positions are open. This explains why the "arbitrage" is often limited to selling some expensive protection via the CDS market, or will only take place when *extremely large* or *unusual* basis are observed compare to historical levels (see Figures 17.6 and 17.7).

---

[2] Note that the arbitrageur has effectively replaced his credit exposure to the bond issuer with counterparty risk to the CDS issuer. Generally, the counterparty institution providing CDS protection is less likely to default than the CDS reference credit – but this doesn't mean that the CDS counterparty cannot default!

[3] CDS contracts are traded on an unfunded basis, which allows a manager to leverage the exposure to a specific credit or index of issuers. It also allows him to quickly and efficiently add or reduce credit exposure to a single issuer or an index without having to buy or sell large amounts of bonds in the secondary cash market.

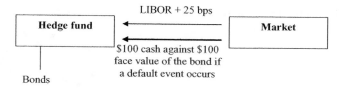

Figure 17.4 Economic summary of the overall transation. We have assumed a 25 bps premium over LIBOR in this example

Accordingly, arbitrageurs may also tilt the strategy to become more credit directional, i.e. enter negative basis trades (buy bonds, buy protection) on names on which they foresee a negative credit evolution, and positive basis trades (sell bonds sell protection) on names on which they are more positive.

Note that the arbitrage between CDS and bond markets is not limited to corporate bonds, but can also be extended to sovereign debt, particularly in emerging markets. During periods of financial or political crisis, the CDS market clearly leads the bond market. Bond liquidity dries up, while demand for insurance against default risk increases. Therefore, prices (and thus spreads, along with implicit default probabilities) derived from the CDS market, tend to be more reliable during sovereign debt crises. As an illustration, consider Figure 17.8 which shows the evolution of the 5-year CDS spread for Ukraine versus the 5-year bond spread during the Orange Revolution. Clearly, the CDS market reacts faster than the bond market.

Over recent years, hedge funds have become important actors in the CDS market. They are active on both sides of the market, i.e. both as protection buyers and as protection sellers. For

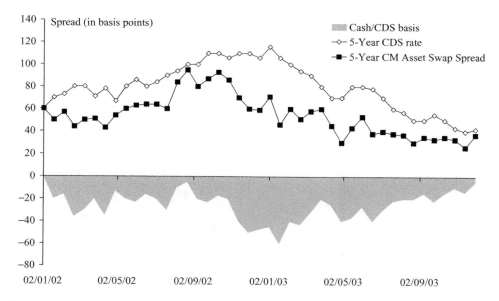

Figure 17.5   Comparing Goldman Sachs bonds and credit default swaps (data from Reuters)

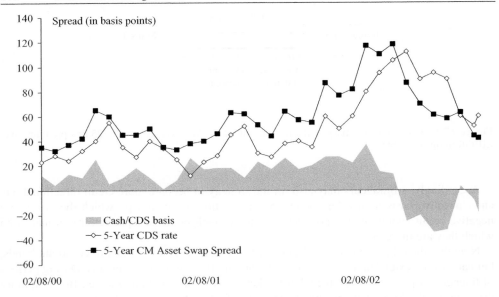

Figure 17.6   Comparing Merrill Lynch bonds and credit default swaps (data from Reuters)

instance, many hedge funds now use CDS as a tool to directional trade credit risk or to express their views on the expected default time of distressed companies – see Box 17.2. Only the CDS markets provide them with a level of customization, sophistication and liquidity that they require to manage their credit exposures.

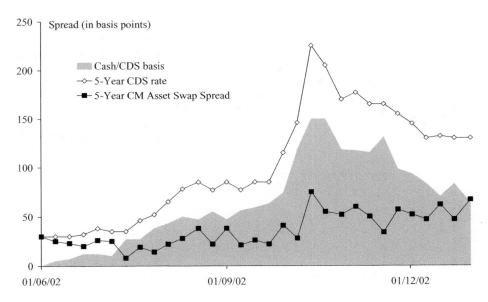

Figure 17.7   Comparing Commerzbank bonds and credit default swaps (data from Reuters)

Box 17.1 Trading the basis: an academic perspective

Given the short history of the credit derivatives market and limited data availability, there has so far been little empirical work on capital structure arbitrage and basis trades. Nevertheless, the existing papers seem to agree on the following: (i) on the long run, the determinants of CDS premium are quite similar to those of bond spreads, including ratings, yield curves, stock prices and leverage ratios; and (ii) CDS contracts isolate credit risk from other factors such as market risk, and therefore provide more accurate measurement and pricing of credit risk than other traditional credit-related instruments such as bonds. In particular, in the short run, the CDS market seems to lead the bond market in anticipating rating events and in price adjustment.

Lastly, another popular group of trades is the arbitrage between credit and equity markets (Box 17.3). Here again, the rational for the arbitrage is that the two markets respond differently to new information, giving rise to discrepancies in valuation and thus opportunities. Most of the time, the arbitrage consists in calculate an equity-implied CDS theoretical spread from a company's observable stock price, and comparing it with the level effectively quoted in the CDS market. In practice, the assessment about the relative richness and cheapness of the market CDS spread is often based on a structural model, typically a variant of the pricing model introduced by Merton (1974). This explains why most hedge funds focusing on pricing inefficiencies between credit-sensitive instruments and equity-sensitive instruments are active in equity derivatives – credit spreads can explicitly be shown to be related to the volatility skew.

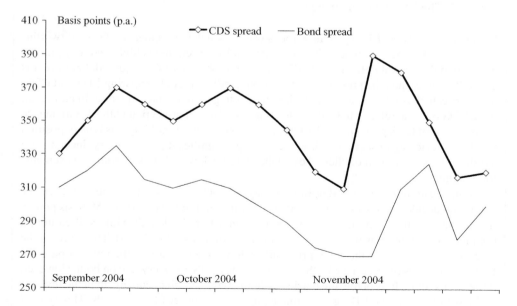

Figure 17.8 Comparison between the CDS spread and the bond spread for Ukrainian bonds (5-year). During the November 2004 crisis, the CDS market reacted faster than the bond market

---

Box 17.2 Default timing

Consider a distressed company which is expected to default in the next five years with a 50% recovery rate for its bondholders after liquidation. For the sake of simplicity, let us assume that the liquidation period will be very short. The company's CDSs trade at 2000 basis points, meaning a $10 million position requires $2 million a year in premiums for a $5 million payout at the end. Neglecting the time value of money, this implicitly shows that the market expects a default in 2.5 years, as $2.5 \times \$2$ million $= \$5$ million. If a hedge fund manager foresees a default occurring only *after* 2.5 years, he should sell some CDS protection, or equivalently, acquire exposure. If he is right, in 2.5 years, the company will still be solvent and he will keep collecting premiums over and above the $5 million he would have to deliver if the firm ultimately defaults. Of course, this is a highly dynamic strategy and the fund manager must continuously monitor the associated credit risk exposure in terms of timing and recovery rate.

In a few years, hedge funds have had a big impact on the popularity of CDS. They have a natural affinity with this kind of instrument because of its flexibility: it can be shorted, it does not need a lot of collateral upfront, it has built in leverage, and is very liquid. As a result, estimates by the International Swaps and Derivatives Association (ISDA) now put the CDS market at some $14 000 billion in notional amount with average daily volume in CDS indices in the client to multi-dealer space running between $20 and $30 billion. However, the market

---

Box 17.3 The EDS/CDS arbitrage

Equity default swaps (EDS) give investors a way in which to speculate on the creditworthiness of a stock in periods where the credit and equity correlation is high, and they pay out more often than credit default swaps (CDS) as the probability of an equity default event is generally higher than the probability of a formal credit default. Comparing EDS and CDS, investors can chose the most attractive instrument to get credit-like exposure. In particular, if the CDS is cheap relative to CDS, hedge funds tend to sell protection with EDS to finance the purchase of CDS protection. Most of the time, hedge funds holding this type of position will be protected against credit risk while earning a significant positive carry. Indeed, with the short EDS position, the seller takes on the extreme downside risk of equity in exchange for a premium.

As an illustration, say a hedge fund manager anticipates a credit default on Siemens bonds and decides to buy two CDS at 35 basis points and sell one EDS at 450 basis points. In a sense, this trade provides overprotection against credit default while still earning a running carry of 380 bps p.a. on the combined position ($=440 - 2\times35$). Therefore, in the case of a credit event, if the stock price falls below the EDS barrier, the investor pays the EDS, but receives twice via the CDS – if we assume a 50% recovery rate on both. However, if the equity value falls below the barrier without credit default occurring, then the investor will have to pay on the EDS and continue pay to running fees for the CDS. This type of strategy is well suited for highly leveraged companies, because it usually results in a high correlation between credit risk and equity risk.

remains young and its infrastructures are not always adequate. As an illustration, in September 2005, 55% of the CDS transactions were still captured on paper. This led to a huge backlog of unconfirmed trades – Alan Greenspan himself summoned dealers and regulators in September 2005, stating that the 150 000 outstanding confirmations represented "an unmistakable signal of the inadequacy of market practice". This lack of trade settlement infrastructure has been further compounded by the propensity of hedge funds and other investors to exit CDS trades without informing the original bank that they have a new counterparty. Fortunately, under pressure to get the backlog under control, the dealers committed themselves to developing and implementing a set of industry-wide guidelines by 31 October 2006.

17.2 WEATHER DERIVATIVES, WEATHER INSURANCE AND CATASTROPHE BONDS

Weather risk – the potential adverse impact of weather on corporate costs, revenues and cash flow – is obviously one of the largest variables impacting economic activity. It is also a new liquid and fast growing market for hedge funds seeking out the lesser-used niches to make money. Weather derivatives, weather insurance, as well as catastrophe bonds (Cat bonds) are now increasingly attracting their attention. Simply stated, they are tools designed to both provide protection and to mitigate the adverse financial effects of weather or disasters, but at different levels.

- Weather derivatives such as temperature-based index futures and options protect against lower risk, higher probability events, such as cooler summers or warmer winters. They quantify weather in terms of degrees above or below monthly or seasonal average temperatures and attach a dollar amount to the number of degrees the temperature deviates from the average values. The OTC market for weather derivatives started unofficially as a response to the deregulation of the power industry in the US, as utility companies had to rethink themselves as market participants rather than monopoles. The first deal was a heating degree day (HDD[4]) swap for the winter of year 1996 in Milwaukee between Koch Energy and Enron. Enron became rapidly a driven force of the weather derivatives market due to its aggressive trading strategy and willingness to make a market where others feared to trade. After its collapse, the Chicago Mercantile Exchange took the lead and introduced weather futures and options on futures – with a guarantee that trades will be honoured in the event of a counterparty default.
- Weather insurance is designed to cover high-risk, low-probability events such as hurricanes, heavy snowfall, hailstorms, and rainouts causing cancellation of outdoor events. It typically pays based on actual damages sustained by the insured, while the weather derivatives paid an amount based on a triggering event regardless of whether the derivative holder suffered a loss or not.
- Cat bonds are financial instruments that turn reinsurance contracts into securities and derivatives structures. They offer an alternative to traditional reinsurance, and are typically structured as bonds whose coupon payment and/or the return of the principal of the bond is linked to the occurrence of a specific catastrophic event (earthquakes, hurricanes, typhoons, winter storms). The coupon is defined as a spread over LIBOR, which is the premium investors are paid for taking on the natural catastrophe risk.

---

[4] Degree days (Heating Degree Days and Cooling Degree Days) are a measure of how much a day's average temperature deviates from a standard 65°F mean, on a midnight to midnight basis. The level of 65°F was chosen because this was the temperature at which the utility industry in the US switched its furnaces on.

Over the past years, these three markets have grown and reached a size of more than $20 billion in notional value for each category. While weather-dependent businesses, farmers and reinsurance companies were traditional users of weather derivatives, hedge funds are now the biggest drivers of growth. Their interest is fuelled primarily by three reasons. First, weather volatility and catastrophes have a direct impact on commodity prices, so that hedge funds may use these tools in conjunction with their trades in commodities to generate additional alpha or as a hedge. Second, it is one thing to be able to predict the temperature, but it is another to say how much it varies. Hedge funds are actively looking at weather volatility and how accurately futures markets predict it. At this early stage, serious inefficiencies seem to exist in the markets' predictive capabilities. In particular, markets often overestimate weather volatility, which means that some instruments will be overpriced, and the price of weather contracts fluctuates more slowly than commodity contracts, which opens the door to arbitrage opportunities. Having developed successful instruments and strategies to hedge, or reduce, the risk of price movements on illiquid assets, hedge funds are happy to apply them to this new asset class. As the icing on the cake, weather derivatives and Cat bonds are loosely correlated with other asset classes and offer an alternative source of diversification for hedge fund portfolios.

As a consequence, weather derivatives, weather insurance and Cat bonds are growing steadily and are solidifying their place in financial markets, not only from a hedging perspective, but also from a trading perspective. Specialized hedge funds have been set up to trade climate related instruments. Weather futures volumes at the Chicago Mercantile Exchange (CME) almost doubled between 2003/04 and 2004/05, and brokers say that volumes are at their highest for year in the more opaque over-the-counter market. Clearly, weather as an investment is here to stay.

17.3   MUTUAL FUND ARBITRAGE

Mutual fund arbitrage (also known as mutual fund timing) is an interesting example of a relatively old but highly controversial strategy. In its simplest form, mutual fund arbitrage denotes the rapid trading of mutual fund shares to capitalize on discrepancies between their official net asset values (NAVs) and the real value of their underlying holdings. As we will see shortly, these discrepancies exist because of the way some mutual funds calculate their NAV. In particular, funds investing in overseas markets provide fertile ground for mutual fund arbitrage – they use prices coming from already closed markets and therefore provide the highly desirable opportunity to trade at stale prices.

The profits made by mutual fund arbitrageurs are obviously realized at the expense of long-term shareholders. This explains why some cynically consider the strategy as unethical but profitable, while others view it as a pure robbery that should be prohibited. Surprisingly, most regulators tolerated the strategy until 2003, when a series of major abuses and frauds were reported and prosecuted. Since then, mutual fund arbitrage has almost disappeared from the US scene but still persists legally in Europe and Asia. Nevertheless, it remains a great illustration of how simple some arbitrage strategies can be, and also of how wrong things can go when greedy intermediaries bypass regulation. To understand the mechanics of mutual fund arbitrage, we must first examine mutual funds and how they calculate their net asset value. In the following, we will discuss primarily the situation in the US, but our observations and conclusions can easily be extended to other countries.

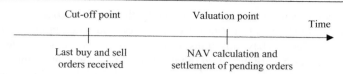

Figure 17.9   Cut-off point and valuation point

17.3.1   The forward pricing mechanism

The most common type of mutual fund is the *open-end* type. The term refers to how investors contribute to or withdraw from the fund. An open-end fund issues new shares when an investor buys; it redeems and cancels existing shares when an investor makes a withdrawal. In both cases, Rule 22c-1 of the Investment Company Act requires mutual funds to sell and redeem mutual fund shares at a price based on the NAV[5] next computed *after* receipt of an order to buy or redeem.

The NAV of a mutual fund scheme is basically the per unit market value of all the assets of the scheme. Most mutual funds buy and sell their shares on a continuous basis, but they determine their NAV only once a day. To limit the administrative burden, fund managers have defined two important points during the day (see Figure 17.9): (i) the *cut-off* point, which is the deadline given to investors for sending a subscription or redemption order to the fund; and (ii) the *valuation point*, which is when the NAV per share is calculated and all pending subscription and redemption orders are executed.

The cut-off point may coincide with the valuation point, but it should not be after it. Any order arrived before the cut-off point will be executed at the current day's NAV, which will be calculated *later in the day* at the valuation point. Any order arrived after the cut-off point must wait one more day to be executed *at the next day*'s NAV. This mechanism, called *forward pricing*, represents one of the fundamental principles of the Investment Company Act. It ensures that all investors are able to use the same market information that is available up to the deal cut-off time in order to make their decisions to invest or redeem, and prevents investors who might have access to the NAV of the portfolio from trading on that information. Its disadvantage is that buyers do not know how many units they will get for their money, and sellers do not know how much money they will get for their units, until after the next valuation point. To an extent, they are buying and selling blind. Fund managers like it, of course, because there is no risk of insider trading – well, at least in theory.

The cut-off and the valuation points must be specified in the fund's prospectus. Nearly all US-based funds have fixed them at 4:00 p.m. Eastern Time (ET), as it corresponds to the normal close of regular trading on the New York Stock Exchange. Consequently, orders placed any time up to 4:00 p.m. are therefore executed at the same day's NAV, while orders placed after 4:00 p.m. will be executed at the next day's NAV. In practice, however, investors can also purchase or sell mutual fund shares through various authorized intermediaries such as broker – dealers, banks, insurance companies, fund supermarkets, etc. It is common practice for these intermediaries to accumulate their clients' fund transactions received until 4:00 p.m. and then transmit them to the fund for processing *shortly* after 4:00 p.m. but still at that day's NAV. This tolerance allows investors who use intermediaries to be on equal footing with

---

[5] To simplify our presentation, and since they are not at the centre of the mutual fund timing controversy, we ignore the existence of sale charges on new investments as well as redemption charges or deferred sales charges on redemptions.

investors who deal directly with the fund. Also note that some licensed intermediaries, such as broker–dealers, are allowed to net or match purchase and redemption orders for the same funds among their clients. They only transmit the *net result* of the aggregate transactions to mutual fund companies, where they hold omnibus accounts representing the collective shares of their clients. Mutual fund companies generally do not have information about the identities and specific transactions of the individual investors in intermediaries' omnibus accounts.

17.3.2   The loopholes in forward pricing

Although the forward pricing mechanism seems arbitrage proof, it is not in reality. Indeed, at a fund's valuation point, the most recent transaction prices for some securities may not fully reflect all available market information because some of the corresponding markets have been closed for several hours. In that situation, the fund is being valued on the basis of stale prices for its underlying securities. As an illustration, consider a US-based mutual fund holding Japanese stocks. The normal closing in Tokyo is at 3:00 p.m. (i.e. 1:00 a.m. ET). Consequently, the closing prices used for Japanese shares are 15 hours old when the US fund calculates its daily NAV at 4:00 p.m. (Figure 17.10).

This opens the door to *time zone* arbitrage (see Box 17.4). Indirectly, US investors can buy Japanese shares at prices determined 15 hours earlier. It also provides possibilities for speculative trading. If significant world events occur or market information becomes available after the Japanese markets closed, it is possible to predict the direction of future NAV changes. For instance, say there have been strong positive market moves during the New York trading day. This is a reliable indicator that the Japanese market will go up when it later opens due to the positive correlation across global financial markets. However, the fund's NAV will not reflect this expected price change – it still uses the old prices, and thus will remain artificially low. Arbitrageurs could therefore purchase mutual fund shares and redeem them the next day for a quick, but legal, profit.

The stale pricing problem is even higher when Japan's national holidays differ from the US. Say, for instance, that Tuesday is a holiday in Japan. Then, our US fund calculating its Tuesday's 4:00 p.m. NAV would have to use the closing prices of 1:00 a.m. Monday (3:00 p.m. in Japan). Similarly, stales prices would occur when a foreign market is closed due to significant events, such as an earthquake or a tsunami.

Note that although it is often discussed in the context of US funds investing overseas, mutual fund arbitrage is also applicable to funds domiciled in *any* other countries and/or investing in *any* other asset classes. Indeed, the key element to allow the arbitrage is the existence of stale prices. As an illustration, consider a European fund that would calculate its NAV at 15:00

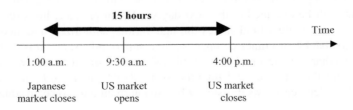

Figure 17.10   The non-synchronicity of market closes provides US investors in Japanese funds with 15 hours to gather and process information and make profit-motivated trade decision

Box 17.4 The mini-crash of October 1997

Time zone arbitrage is particularly successful during periods of very high volatility, such as market crashes followed by sharp rebounds. As an illustration, consider the Black Monday crash, where a basically bullish market started to be rattled by mounting worries over emerging markets, especially debt-laden Asia. On 27 October 1997, the Hang Seng Index plummeted 5.8% on rumours that the Hong Kong dollar could be de-linked from the US dollar. Losses then spread to Europe and the US, where securities markets fell by a record absolute amount on then-record trading volume. The S&P 500 lost 6.9%, the NASDAQ posted its biggest-ever one-day point loss, and trading was halted by the circuit-breaker system put in place after 1987. On 28 October, Asian markets fell even more than they did on the previous day – the Hang Seng Index declined a staggering 13.7%. As expected, at the opening, US stocks opened lower and continued their drop, but they started to recover later in the morning. At the close of trading at 4:00 p.m., the S&P 500 has recover most of its previous day losses with a gain of 5.12%.

For mutual fund timers, this was clear that Asian markets would follow suit when they opened for trading. But mutual funds invested in Asian securities calculated their NAV as usual, i.e. using 13 hours stale closing prices. Many arbitrageurs, anticipating a mechanical rise in the funds' next-day NAV, stood ready to exploit this pricing discrepancy. They poured money into Asia/Pacific funds and sold them the next day, as the Hang Seng Index gained 18.82%.

Central European Time (CET) using the last available closing prices. If the fund holds Far East and Pacific Rim securities, they will be valued at the same day close – the corresponding markets close between 8:00 CET and 11:00 CET. But if the fund holds US securities, the last closing price dates from the previous day – the US market closes at 22:00 CET, which implies using 17 hours stale prices (Figure 17.11).

The stale price effect is also present with thinly traded securities. In small-caps, micro-caps, high-yield convertible or municipal bonds, the most recent transaction price used at the

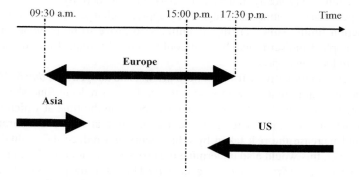

Figure 17.11 Overlap of international equity market trading for a European fund with a 15:00 CET valuation point. At this time, only European markets are active. Asia is closed, and US markets are no yet open

valuation point for the NAV calculation may be several hours or days old and significantly different from the price that would prevail in a liquid market. Moreover, thinly traded securities often have large spreads between their bid and ask prices, and this may influence upward or downward the published NAV. In either cases, arbitrageurs can step in and subscribe fund shares at a value lower than the market worth of the underlying assets, or redeem shares at a higher price than their intrinsic value.

17.3.3   Unethical, but persistent

Contrarily to the common perception, it is important to understand that mutual fund arbitrage is not illegal per se – it simply profits from a structural pricing inefficiency. Nevertheless, the practice is questionable ethically, because returns are made not from the market but at the expense of long-term fund shareholders. An arbitrageur subscribing at a NAV that is understated or redeeming at a NAV that is overstated will, in effect, dilute the interests of the fund's remaining shareholders. This occurs directly as a result of the arbitrageur's activity, but also indirectly through the increased trading and administrative costs, as well as the non-desired tax implications incurred by the fund. Moreover, mutual fund arbitrage can be disruptive to portfolio managers. For instance, managers confronted to arbitrageurs may experience difficulty with their cash management – too little cash to meet unexpected redemptions from arbitrageurs will require selling core holdings at short notice, while maintaining excess cash will result in a drag on performance.

Mutual fund advisers and regulators are fully aware of the damaging effect that such arbitrageurs can have on their funds. For instance, in 2001, the SEC published an industry letter providing guidance to investment managers on how to combat, prevent and neutralize the impact of market timing.

- Fund managers can select an optimal valuation point. If a fund is heavily exposed to Europe and the US, it makes sense to move the valuation point to a time after the US opening (i.e. after 15:30 CET) but while the European exchanges were also still open (i.e. somewhere between 15:30 CET and 18:00 CET).
- Fund managers can identify arbitrageurs by monitoring subscription and redemption activity, and then refuse their orders. Large monthly cash inflows and outflows of a similar size on the same account are typically indicative of market timing activity.
- Fund managers can discourage arbitrageurs by applying charges on short-term redemptions and transaction limits. However, this is unlikely to prove to be popular with long-term investors if applied indiscriminately, as it could eventually impact the investors that fund promoters are looking to protect.
- Fund managers can move away from forward pricing and adopt a *next day NAV* policy. With next-day pricing, an individual who wishes to purchase or redeem fund shares today does so tomorrow at tomorrow's NAV. A one-day gap between the time at which the investors' decision to transact in fund shares is made and the time at which those transactions are priced would increase the risk taken by arbitrageurs and reduce the profitability of their trades. However, this would also undermine the provision of liquidity by mutual funds.
- Fund managers can use *fair value pricing*, i.e. *adjust* the value the prices of the fund's underlying securities for staleness. The Investment Company Act of 1940 allows such adjustments when a significant event affects the market or when there is no reliable market quotation

for a security or if the underlying stock market is closed. However, few funds appear to use fair value pricing, mostly because they do not want to take the risk of losing investors' confidence or facing lawsuits.[6]

In practice, however, most US funds have been unable to effectively enforce their anti-arbitrage policies or impose redemption fees on the accounts of investors who trade fund shares through intermediaries rather than directly at the fund. The reason is that these share holdings are identified in the books of the fund in the name of the intermediary (in an omnibus accounts) rather than in the name of the fund shareholder. Mutual fund timing has therefore continued and was even widely documented in academia.[7] And while its average effects on individual shareholders were small, the aggregate impact was not – according to Zitzewitz (2002), mutual funds' losses due to arbitrageurs amounted to $4 billion per year and diluted mutual funds' returns by 2% p.a.

17.3.4 A brutal ending

Mutual fund timing was brutally halted in the fall of 2003, with the revelation that certain of the US most venerable mutual fund companies had been engaged in unlawful conduct. The scandal started on 3 September, when New York State Attorney General Elliot Spitzer filed a complaint against a hedge fund named Canary Capital Partners, its managers, and four mutual fund companies with which it had formal trading agreements: Bank of America, Janus Capital, Bank One, and Strong Capital Management. The complaint involved two separate forms of abuse: late trading and market timing.

- *Late trading* refers to the practice of placing orders to buy or sell mutual fund shares *after* 4:00 p.m., but receiving the price based on the already determined 4:00 p.m. NAV.[8] Spitzer compared it to "betting on a horse race after the horses have crossed the finish line". Late traders have a significant advantage since their buy/sell decisions are made with the hindsight gained from market information that is made available *after* the cut-off time – in addition to the stale prices effect. For example, in the event of an unexpected positive or negative corporate earnings announcement relating to securities in the fund's portfolio received after the deal cut-off, the old NAV – at which late traders can deal – will not reflect the information that will undoubtedly influence the next day's NAV. Late trading is a clear violation of Rule 22c-1 and can only be accomplished by nefarious means. Technically, it requires collusion with a mutual fund company or its brokerage intermediaries to be implemented. But this was apparently too difficult to obtain for some hedge funds.
- *Market timing* involves rapid buying and selling of fund shares to take advantage of short-term swings in their net asset value. As already stated, it is not illegal. However, if a fund states in its prospectus and other written materials that it discourages market timing, then it must adhere to that policy for all investors, large and small. Letting market timers operate while simultaneously claiming to fight them in a fund prospectus can be construed as a

---

[6] According to Sahoo (2001), one-third of US mutual funds do not monitor for significant events that may lead to adjustments. And for those that use fair value adjustments, more than half of them do not follow up to see how accurate their adjustments were.

[7] See, for instance, Bhargava *et al.* (1998), Chalmers *et al.* (2001), Goetzmann *et al.* (2001), Greene and Hodges (2002), Boudoukh *et al.* (2002), or Zitzewitz (2003).

[8] Late trading also includes the placement of conditional trades prior to 4:00 p.m. with the option of withdrawing or confirming them after 4:00 p.m.

Box 17.5 Canary Capital

The case of Canary Capital Partners is particularly illustrative. The $730 million hedge fund managed by Edward Stern was active in mutual fund timing. It posted returns of 110% in 1999, 50% in 2000, 29% in 2001 and 15% in 2002. How did Canary managed to post such returns, despite a strong bear market? The complaint filed by Spitzer mentions late trades (as late as 9:00 p.m.) with dozens of mutual funds on a daily basis from March 2000 until July 2003. Some of these trades were unbeknown by the traded funds, but a few unscrupulous firms were aware of them and even encouraged them as Spitzer was also a substantial investor in various funds they were managing. Bank of America (BOA), for instance, provided Canary with late trading capacity in its own Nations line of mutual funds. In exchange, Canary parked its cash in financial instruments controlled by BOA and its affiliates. BOA even installed its proprietary trading system in Canary's offices to enable the hedge fund to more effectively enter its late trades. As if that was not enough, Canary leveraged these activities by trading *on margin* borrowed from BOA. In effect, BOA actually loaned Canary the capital necessary to make illegal trades in its own funds...

---

violation of the fiduciary responsibilities of the fund to its shareholders. The major issue raised by Spitzer's complaint was precisely that several funds allowed large investors and in some cases fund employees, to engage in market timing while it was denied to other investors.

Unfortunately, Canary's activities (Box 17.5) were only the tip of the iceberg, and the scope and magnitude of the scandal turned out to be more far-reaching than originally believed (see Table 17.2). The investigations revealed what Attorney General Spitzer described as "egregious" conduct by "very senior people" in the mutual fund industry to the detriment of long-term investors. They resulted in criminal investigations, several civil lawsuits, multiple high-level firings, criminal and civil charges and a government imposed shutdown of several mutual fund intermediaries.

As of 31 December 2004, the SEC and several state attorneys general had formally indicted or investigated at least 25 mutual fund families. Settlements stemming from these charges totalled more than $3.1 billion in fines and restitution, and more than 80 executives lost their jobs, including Putnam's former chief executive, Lawrence Lasser. More importantly, investors' confidence was seriously upset – in 1993 they pulled $29 billion out of the funds of Putnam Investment Management, one of the miscreants, and added $36 billion to Vanguard, none of whose 75 funds was tainted. It will probably take years to regain their confidence.

17.4 ARBITRAGING BETWEEN NAVs AND QUOTED PRICE: ALTIN AG

In a few cases, hedge funds are setup as investment companies whose shares are traded on an exchange, generally at a discount to their fair value. If the discount becomes too large, there is an incentive to buy the undervalued shares to profit from the mispricing.

As an illustration, Figure 17.12 shows the performance of Altin AG's shares over the January 1998 to December 2001 period. Altin AG is a Swiss investment company comparable to a

Table 17.2 Mutual fund investigations and settlements

Fund Family	Initial date	Formal charges	Settlement ($ millions)	Parent firm
Janus	9/3/03	Y	$226.0	Janus Capital Group
Nations	9/3/03	Y	$455.0	Bank of America
One Group	9/3/03	Y	$90.0	Bank One
Strong	9/3/03	Y	$175.0	Private
Franklin Templeton	9/3/03	Y	$73.0	Franklin Resources
Gabelli Funds	9/3/03	N		Gabelli Asset Mgmt.
Putnam	9/19/03	Y	$110.0	Marsh & McLennan
Alliance Bernstein	9/30/03	Y	$600.0	Alliance Capital
Alger	10/3/03	Y	$0.4	Private
Federated	10/22/03	N		Federated Investors
PBHG Funds	11/13/03	Y	$260.0	Old Mutual PLC
Loomis Sayles	11/13/03	N		CDC Asset Mgmt.
Excelsior/US Trust	11/14/03	N		Charles Schwab
Fremont	11/24/03	Y	$4.2	Private
AIM/Invesco	12/2/03	Y	$451.5	Amvescap PLC
MFS	12/9/03	Y	$350.0	Sun Life Financial
Heartland Advisors	12/11/03	Y		Private
Seligman	1/7/04	N		Private
Columbia	1/15/04	Y	$220.0	FleetBoston Financial
Scudder	1/23/04	N		Deutsche Bank AG
PIMCO	2/13/04	Y	$68.0	Allianz Group
RS Investments	3/3/04	Y	$30.0	Private
ING Investments	3/11/04	N		ING Groep NV
Evergreen	8/4/04	N		Wachovia
Sentinel Group	10/7/04	Y	$0.7	Private
Total			$3113.8	

Source: Morningstar.com, *The Wall Street Journal*, the SEC, and the NYAG office.

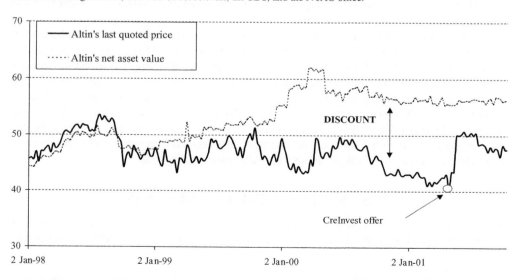

Figure 17.12 The discount observed on Altin was large enough for CreInvest to attempt the takeover

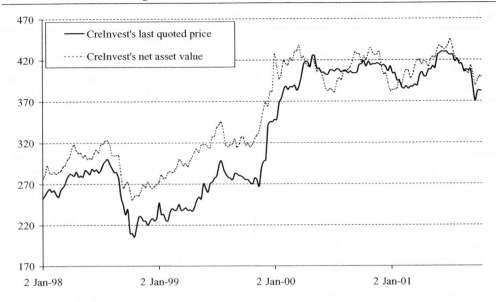

Figure 17.13   The discount observed on CreInvest was relatively small compared to Altin

closed-end fund investing in other hedge funds. It pursues simultaneously several investment strategies such as merger arbitrage and global macro, combined with investments in various commodity trading advisers. Clearly, the share price shows a significant and persistent discount with respect to the net asset value.

By way of comparison, Figure 17.13 shows the same information for CreInvest AG, one of Altin's competitors. Here too we observe a difference between the net asset value and the last quoted price for CreInvest. However, the difference is small and tends to disappear over the years, whereas it seems persistent in the case of Altin.

The persistence of the above-mentioned situation eventually resulted in an unsolicited bid for Altin by its competitor. On 14 May 2001, CreInvest AG offered to pay 90% of the value of Altin's holdings, that is, 15% more than Altin's share price at that time. CreInvest's intentions were to merge with Altin, therefore gaining access to a larger and more diversified hedge fund portfolio at a cheap price.[9] In the case of a merger failure, CreInvest announced that it would solicit Altin shares on the open market at 87% of the net asset value. Following the recommendation of Altin's board, Altin's shareholders rejected the merger offer and accepted a reduction in the nominal value of the shares. It also decided to return cash to shareholders and to appoint Deutsche Bank as an adviser to decrease the discount.

17.5   SPLIT STRIKE CONVERSION

What a complex serious name for a remarkably simple trade. "Split strike conversion" sounds much more appealing than "collar", but it is essentially the same strategy. Widely practiced by

---

[9] In addition, half of Altin's portfolio was made up of stakes in top tier hedge funds closed to new subscriptions. The merger would have given CreInvest a cheap means of entering into these funds.

proprietary traders in investment banks, it involves the following steps:

1. Select an equity index.
2. Purchase a basket of stocks which together account for the greatest weight of the index and therefore, when combined, present a high degree of correlation with the general market. The weights in this basket are typically optimised to obtain a low tracking error.
3. Sell out-of-the-money call index options representing a dollar amount of the underlying index equivalent to the dollar amount of the basket of shares purchased.
4. Purchase at-the-money or slightly out-of-the-money put options in the same dollar amount.

The primary purpose of the long put options is to limit the market risk of the stock basket at the strike price of the long puts. The primary purpose of the short call options is to largely finance the cost of the put hedge and to increase the stand-still rate of return. The overall payoff of the strategy can easily be determined by summing the payoffs of the individual components. Figure 17.14 shows the payoff obtained by buying the stock, buying a put option at $50 and selling a call at $60, and combining these positions with the long basket.

The overall position is essentially a bull spread, which sets a floor value below which further declines in the value of the stock basket are offset by gains in the put options, and sets a ceiling value beyond which further gains in the stock basket are offset by increasing liability of the short calls. Between these two values, there is a range of potential market gain or loss, depending on how tightly the options collar is struck. Some traders consider this trade as a "vacation trade", because you can establish the position and not worry about what happens until options expiration approaches.

In addition to its attractive payoff, the strategy has two possible sources of profitability: (i) the selection of stocks to be purchased and (ii) the choice of the options to be bought and sold. Many split strike conversion strategies rely on fundamental stock selection and/or

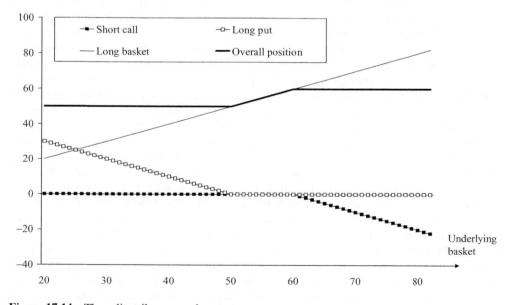

Figure 17.14   The split strike conversion strategy

market timing to add value over the index, but use quantitative premium/risk analysis to select their options. In particular, the net premium to be paid or received to establish the position is paramount to the success of the strategy and requires some cost and skew analysis (particularly the difference between upside and downside skew).

17.6   EVENT-DRIVEN SPECIAL SITUATIONS

Another type of situation which is fertile in arbitrage opportunities is the case of equity carve-outs in technology stocks. Also known as a partial public offering, an equity carve-out is defined as an IPO for shares (typically a minority stake) in a subsidiary company. The most prominent example of mispricing in the study is the case of Palm and 3Com (see Box 17.6),

---

Box 17.6   The negative stub value

Palm, which makes personal digital assistants (PalmPilot), was owned by 3Com, a profitable company selling computer network systems and services. On 2 March 2000, 3Com sold 5% of its stake in Palm to the public through an IPO for Palm, but still owned 532 million shares, or 95% of the venture – a stash of stock worth $50.6 billion at the day's closing price of $95.06.

Pending IRS approval, 3Com planned to spin off its remaining shares of Palm to 3Com's shareholders before the end of the year. 3Com shareholders would receive about 1.5 shares of Palm for every share of 3Com they owned. Investors could therefore buy shares of Palm directly or buy shares embedded within shares of 3Com. Thus, the price of 3Com should have been at least 1.5 times that of Palm, plus the value of the rest of 3Com activities.

The day before the Palm IPO, the price of 3Com closed at $104.13 per share. After the first day of trading, Palm closed at $95.06 per share, implying that the price of 3Com should have jumped to at least $145. Instead, 3Com fell to $81.81 per share, which implied that . . . the rest of 3Com was worth negative $62.27 per share (a total of negative $22 billion). The mispricing was so obvious that it was noted by *The Wall Street Journal* and *The New York Times*. Arbitrageurs referred to it as a "negative stub value", a not uncommon phenomenon in corporate spin-offs. To profit from it, one would have to buy the parent and sell short the subsidiary. In reality, the arbitrage of such a situation was not risk free. First, 3Com had announced its intention to distribute its Palm shares to 3Com stockholders, but the final date of the distribution was not yet determined. Second, the IRS might step in and make the spin-off prohibitively expensive for 3Com's shareholders by declaring it a taxable event. Third, only 5% of Palm's shares were publicly traded, and it was hard to borrow these shares and even riskier to sell them short – at the time of the Internet bubble.

Nevertheless, at the peak level of short interest, short sales of Palm were 147.6%, indicating that more than all floating shares had been sold short. Given that the typical stock has very little short interest, it is extremely unusual that more than 100% of the float was shorted. In addition, several arbitrageurs traded via the option market – the options on Palm display unusually large violations of put/call parity, with puts about twice as expensive as calls. This confirms that shorting Palm was either incredibly expensive or that there was a large excess demand for borrowing Palm shares that could not be met by the market.

but similar situations occurred for other carve-outs of technology stocks such as UBID, Retek, PFSWeb, Xpedior and Stratos Lightwave.

17.7 CROSS-LISTING AND DUAL-LISTING ARBITRAGE

Public companies have many good reasons for willing to list their securities on more than one exchange. A new listing widens the pool of potential investors, strengthens the company's visibility, enlarges the trading market for the company's securities, which is good for liquidity purposes and increases the amount of analyst coverage that the company receives. Given these advantages, it is not surprising that the number of companies listed on more than one exchange has accelerated over the past decade.

Being listed on more than one exchange provides a good framework to test the "law of one price", this economic rule which states that in an efficient market, a security should have a single price wherever it is. If this is not the case, buying the security in one market and selling it in another allows an arbitrageur to profit from unjustifiable price differences. In practice, as we will see, the law of one price is often violated in the case of multiple listings, due to segmented markets, time-zone differences, or trading practices. Hedge funds have naturally become specialists in profiting from such situations when they arise. As a matter of illustration, let us now consider the cases of (i) cross-listed companies with a particular focus on American depositary Receipts (ADRs), and (ii) dual listed companies.

17.7.1 Cross-listed companies and ADRs

A growing number of foreign issuers are voluntarily cross-listing their stocks on American capital markets, despite that, US securities laws are principally more demanding. This is usually done through American Depository Receipts (ADRs). In an ADR, the foreign issuer deposits a certain number of its common shares with a US holder, typically a US-based bank, in its home country. The US bank subsequently issues depository receipts to US investors. These receipts are securities within the meaning of the US securities regulations and provide investors with various benefits, such as, the capability to trade in non-domestic securities on US stock exchanges[10] in US dollars without worrying about currency exchange rates, foreign stock exchange rules, foreign languages and/or confiscatory central banks actions such as currency trading restrictions.[11]

However, from a functional perspective, an ADR remains an investment in shares of a non-US corporation. Its price should therefore be close to its "fair value", i.e. the price of the underlying stocks adjusted for the spot exchange rate. If an ADR price diverges sufficiently from its fair value, then there are essentially two methods to arbitrage.

- The first method consists of buying the cheap security and converting it into the expensive one. However, this requires fully fungible securities, no legal restrictions on taking securities

---

[10] Issuer can register ADRs on four different levels, some of which can only be traded in the over-the-counter markets (Level I ADRs) or between Qualified Institutional Buyers (Level IV ADRs). Level II and Level III ADRs can be traded on NYSE, NASDAQ or OTC-BB.

[11] Examples include Malaysia in 1997 and, more recently, Venezuela in 2002 where the Central Banks imposed extreme limitations on the conversion of the local currency in hope of preventing a further devaluation. Asset managers holding domestic shares might have been able to execute a sell, admittedly at a highly discounted price, but they were prevented from repatriating the currency proceeds from that transaction back to the relative safety of US dollars. Conversely, a holder of the ADR listing, who would have also had to sell at a steeply discounted price, at least was able to receive proceeds in the form of US dollars.

across borders, paying miscellaneous custodial and brokerage fees, paying a conversion fee to switch between the two securities, and fighting bureaucracy ... with the risk of seeing price adjustments wiping out the difference in the meantime.
- The second method consists of going long the cheap security and shorting the expensive one. The result is essentially a long/short portfolio that is market neutral by construction, since the two underlying securities represent exactly the same underlying asset. However, such an arbitrage might be impossible to implement due to a series of reasons, such as (i) cross border ownership rules, e.g. domestic investors are not allowed to own US ADRs, or US investors are not allowed to own home-market shares, or both; (ii) short selling restrictions in the home market; (iii) the non-fungibility of the two securities[12]; (iv) direct and indirect investment barriers, e.g. limits on the repatriation of capital, foreign exchange controls, withholding taxes, etc.; and (v) the number of time zones that separate the US and home trading market, as trading sessions need to overlap to have simultaneous prices.

In practice, ADRs sometimes diverge from the value of their underlying shares, essentially because of the segmentation between US markets and local markets, as well as the relatively low liquidity of the underlying shares – see Chapter 14 with Gazprom.

17.7.2   Dual-listed companies

A case closely related to ADRs arbitrage is the arbitrage of dual-listed (or "Siamese twin") companies. Dual listed companies (see Table 17.3) are the result of a merger between two firms, in which they agree to combine their operations and cash flows and make similar dividend payments to shareholders in both companies while retaining separate shareholder registries and identities. Most of the time, this structure is preferred over a simple merger for a series of reasons.

- Tax reasons: capital gains tax could be owed if an outright merger took place, while it is avoided with a dual-listed deal.
- Political reasons: by maintaining separate firms, there is no takeover of an important local company by a foreign firm, and the (national) identity of each of the twins is preserved.
- Regulatory reasons: the transaction does not require regulatory (anti-trust) consent and is not constrained by foreign investment approvals.
- Feedback reasons: in a normal transaction, some investors would have to sell the shares (limits on foreign shares, exit from domestic indices, etc.) and this could depress the stock price.

The two eldest twin companies are the Anglo-Dutch combinations Royal Dutch/Shell and Unilever, but several other companies are in the same situation. The mispricing of dual-listed companies is frequently cited as representing an anomaly to the efficient market hypothesis – see, for instance, Mullainathan and Thaler (2000) or Barberis and Thaler (2002).

---

[12] For instance, a number of Chinese companies had A-shares (local currency, domestic investors only) and B-shares (US dollar- or Hong Kong dollar-denominated, both domestic and foreign investors since February 2001) on Shanghai and Shenzhen exchanges; however, their ADRs traded on the basis of separate tranches of H-shares in Hong Kong or N-shares, which did not trade anywhere else.

Table 17.3   List of the major companies having a dual listing of their shares

Company	Country	Period of dual listing
Shell Transport & Trading Co PLC Royal Dutch Petroleum	UK Netherlands	Since 1907
Unilever PLC Unilever NV	UK Netherlands	Since 1930
ABB AB ABB AG	Sweden Switzerland	January 1988–July 1999
Eurotunnel Eurotunnel	France UK	Since 1989
SmithKline Beecham PLC SmithKline Beecham	UK US	July 1989–April 1996
Fortis (B) Fortis (NL)	Belgium Netherlands	June 1990–December 2001
Reed Elsevier PLC Reed Elsevier NV	UK Netherlands	Since January 1993
Rio Tinto Limited Rio Tinto PLC	Australia UK	Since December 1995
Dexia Belgium Dexia France	Belgium France	November 1996–February 2000
Nordbanken Merita	Sweden Finland	December 1997–March 2000
Allied Zurich PLC Zurich Allied	UK Switzerland	September 1998–October 2000
BHP Billiton Limited BHP Billiton PLC	Australia UK	Since June 2001
Brambles Industries Limited Brambles Industries PLC	Australia UK	Since August 2001
Investec Limited Investec PLC	South Africa UK	Since July 2002
P&O Princess Cruises PLC Carnival Corporation	UK US	Since April 2003

17.8   FROM PUBLIC TO PRIVATE EQUITY

Historically, hedge funds and private equity funds have occupied two distinct realms of the alternative investments space. Hedge funds were focused on short-term trading in public markets, while private equity funds made illiquid investments in non-listed companies. With rare exceptions, there was virtually no overlap between the two. However, as the hedge fund industry expanded, some managers have ventured beyond the traditional arena of public securities to invest in private companies, or to buy publicly traded companies and take them private – a domain that was traditionally that of private equity firms. In some cases, these less liquid investments are limited to a small portion of a fund's portfolio. In other cases, they comprise the fund's core strategy.

This convergence between private equity and hedge funds initially took place in the US, when the hedge fund ESL Investments took private Kmart, successfully restructured it and finally merged it with Sears Roebuck. Other high profile examples include Cerberus Capital Management leading a consortium of hedge funds in the auction for Texas Genco, and Cerberus's $5.5 billion offer for Toys 'R' Us, both bids losing out to a consortium of private equity funds. In Europe, Fortress Investment Group bought out the German housing group Gagfah for $3.5 billion and Perry Capital offered to acquire Drax Group, the owner of Europe's largest coal-fired power station. Duquesne Capital and a few banks bought British Energy's debt, converted it into equity, helped in the restructuring, and ultimately relisted the company on the London Stock Exchange, after a long battle first with the company's private shareholders and with the activist hedge fund Polygon, which tried to force a rewrite to obtain more shares in the new company. We have also seen the acquisition of WestLB's interests in TV rental company Boxclever by Cerberus and Fortress, the bid for Peacock by Perry Capital and Och Ziff, and the involvement of hedge funds in the bid for Manchester United, just to mention a few.

The convergence between private equity and hedge funds has been obviously facilitated by the increasing use of auctions in takeovers and buyouts, which now form a real alternative to the "proprietary" deal flow that long made the pride of private equity firms. Via auctions, hedge funds can gain access to transparent private equity deals and compete with private equity firms. Hedge funds, after all, have a number of advantages over them:

- They have lower return expectations (mid-teens) compared to private equity firms (mid-20s), which allows them to consider more deals.
- They can invest across all layers of the capital structure, including public debt and equity, but also be active providers of subordinated debt such as second lien and mezzanine debt and PIK securities.[13]
- They leverage at the fund level rather than having to finance each buyout separately. Moreover, hedge funds have speedier access to financing via their prime brokers' credit lines.
- Their annual performance fee payouts enable them to compensate employees in some cases more favourably than private equity houses – no carried interest, no clawback clause in the case of subsequent losses, but an immediate annual compensation.
- They can freely invest in hostile transactions, while private equity firms may be reluctant to do so because of the pressure of their institutional limited partners.

Nonetheless, hedge funds also suffer from some disadvantages in comparison with private equity firms.

- They are often too liquid. Monthly or quarterly redemption are only feasible if the fund's assets are readily realizable at their market price, but not when those assets are illiquid shares in unquoted companies. To avoid cheating its investors, a hedge fund engaging in such transactions should have a compatible redemption policy, and investors could hardly blame the manager for imposing specific terms, e.g. a lock-up of several years.
- They need to be marked to market on a monthly basis when they produce their NAV. However private equity investments are hard to value and their valuation is often subjective, given the absence of market comparables.

---

[13] Payment in Kind (PIK) debt are bonds that may pay bondholders compensation in a form other than cash, typically other bonds or stocks.

- Hedge funds are value finders while private equity funds are value creators. Private equity investments require specific skills, e.g. the expertise to enhance value and drive growth at an operational level, which are not necessarily what characterize hedge fund managers.
- Shares of private companies cannot be sold short, and hedging private equity investments is therefore extremely difficult.

It is therefore essential for investors to validate whether a hedge fund has the infrastructure to source deals, complete rigorous due diligence, and work with companies to create long-term value, before engaging in these mixed hedge fund/private equity transactions. Nevertheless, in the short term, the convergence between private equity and hedge funds is likely to continue. We are likely to see the emergence of more *hybrid funds*, which will combine the features of both private equity and hedge funds. These may hold a mix of liquid and illiquid assets, offer greater liquidity than classic private equity funds and hedge fund-style marked-to-market fees. Interestingly, we should also mention that the convergence is taking place in both directions, as several private equity firms are also entering the hedge fund universe. Firms like Blackstone or Bain Capital have created pure hedge funds, Hamilton Lane has acquired the fund of hedge funds group Richcourt, Texas Pacific Group has entered a partnership with former Goldman Sachs trader Dinakar Singh, and Hellman & Friedman has acquired Gartmore, which includes a significant hedge fund group.

17.9 REGULATION D AND PIPES FUNDS

Hedge funds are now a key participant of the private investments in the public equities (PIPEs) market (Figure 17.15), alongside venture capitalists. PIPEs allow publicly listed companies to issue new *restricted* shares and sell them directly against cash to a small number of investors

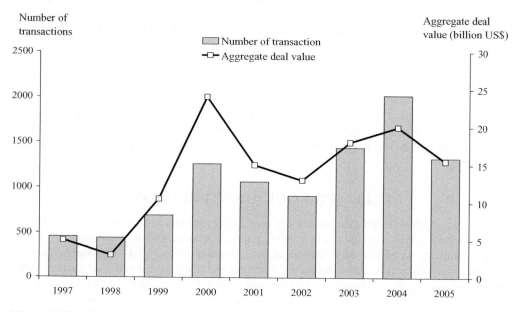

Figure 17.15 More public equities turn to private investments. The year 2005 only covers the period until the beginning of September

in a private transaction. The issuing process is much simpler and faster than for a traditional seasoned equity offering, and there is no need to distribute a prospectus. However, the price of these new restricted shares is usually set at a discount compared to the market price of the unrestricted shares. Therefore, PIPEs seem to be the favourite approach of younger and smaller firms with a high rate of growth. According to Dresner and Kim (2003), 63% of the US PIPEs would be issued by companies from the technology and healthcare fields.

As we have seen already, Regulation D is a part of the Securities Act (1933) that allows securities sold exclusively through private placements to avoid the rigorous filing requirements of the Securities and Exchange Commission. Most domestic US hedge funds rely on Regulation D to place their securities directly to a selected set of individuals. But Regulation D is also widely used by small public companies experiencing difficulties in raising additional equity in the US essentially through private deals, in particular, private investments in public equities (PIPEs). This type of transaction has been popular in the US since January 2000, when *Janus*, the $240 billion Denver-based mutual fund giant, announced that it had just bought $930 million worth of securities issued by Healtheon/WebMD, the first end-to-end Internet healthcare company connecting physicians and consumers to the entire healthcare industry. Since, Regulation D securities have spawned a new hedge fund category.

More generally, the issue of Regulation D securities takes essentially two forms:

- In the case of equity issues, investors purchase the company stock at a discount with respect to the market price. As an illustration, the above-mentioned Healtheon/WebMD issue was discounted by about 6%, but smaller offerings are often forced to issue at much larger discounts. A SimPlayer.com issue in February 2000 was even discounted by 34%!
- In the case of convertible issues, investors purchase a convertible bond that converts into a specific dollar value of the underlying stock, whatever happens to the stock price during the holding period. This means that the number of shares received when converting is not known, but the value of these shares is known. In a sense, the investment is "market neutral". The convertible security is usually sold at a discount with respect to the value of the shares.

The profit from Regulation D securities comes from the discount between the purchase price and the market value at the issue. In exchange for this price concession, investors – who must be accredited – are taking a risk, because (i) the underlying shares are not registered on an exchange, (ii) the issuer may default and (iii) there is virtually no liquidity. Legally, the required holding period before public sale of privately placed securities is two years. However, the issuer usually files the necessary registration statements with the Securities and Exchange Commission within 180 days. In between, the shares can only be traded among accredited investors.

17.10   IPO LOCK-UP EXPIRATIONS

Another example of an event-driven strategy is related to the expiration of initial public offering (IPO) lock-ups. Typically, upon a firm going public, the owners tend to sell only 15 to 20% of the company. As part of the IPO process, the remaining 80 to 85% of the shareholders are almost always subject to a lock-up period, during which they cannot sell their shares. At the end of the lock-up period (typically 180 days after the IPO completion), they become free to sell their existing shares and there is usually a permanent and large shift in the supply of shares, as well as a significant drop in the stock price. For instance, Field and Hanka (2001) analyzed nearly 2000 IPO share lock-up agreements and found negative returns of 1.5% from Day −1 to Day +1 and 1.9% from Day −5 to Day +1, where Day 0 is the IPO lock-up expiration date. They also found that IPO issues of companies with venture capital backers declined more than IPO issues which were held solely by company executives and employees, and conjecture that venture capitalists are much more aggressive in selling after the IPO lock-up expiration date because they want to recoup their initial investment. Nevertheless, these small variations are difficult to arbitrage because of the associated transaction costs and the limited supply of shares.

More recently, Said Haidar (2004) from Haidar Capital Management published a study focusing on longer observation windows, but also on more recent IPOs. According to him, from Day −3 to Day +2 there is a significant negative total return of 6.1%; from Day −9 to Day +1, there is a −11.1% drop; and from Day −19 to Day +20, the average stock falls 21.24%. The magnitude of these losses, which are all statistically significant, clearly opens door to arbitrage, as a 21.34% decline over 2 months or an 11.1% drop over 11 days are not easily wiped out by dealing costs, whatever they are. In addition, borrow the shares to short the IPO issue might be considerably easier 2 weeks in advance of the lock-up expiration date as opposed to a few days before.

Part III
Measuring Returns, Risks and Performance

18

Measuring Net Asset Values and Returns

Remember that a stock that fell by 90% is a stock that felt by 80% and then halved.

The two basic factors to be weighted in investing, risk and return, are obviously the opposite sides of the same coin. Each must be measured to assess and understand past performance, and convince investors that their money is in the right hands. Both must also be predicted in order to make intelligent investment decisions for the future. Of course, we all know that the future is uncertain and that history may not repeat itself, but understanding what happened in the past is likely to be a guide in formulating expectations about what may happen in the future.

Measuring the *ex-post* return and risk of an investment may sound somewhat trivial. However, the number of hedge fund managers claiming that their fund has superior risk-adjusted returns and belongs to the top quartile often amazes me, particularly when we simultaneously hear the dissatisfaction of investors and the tentative explanations of consultants. The reason for this discordance is simply the lack of standards on how to measure risk and return, the multidimensionality of hedge fund returns in terms of descriptive statistics, and the lack of agreement on what constitutes an appropriate benchmark. Today, the hedge fund industry is so diverse that it is impossible to define a small number of sectors that are homogeneous enough to ensure apples-with-apples comparisons.

In the traditional investment world, formal standards of performance measurement were drawn up and adopted in the early 1990s, under the influence of the Association of Investment Management and Research (AIMR). Compliance with the AIMR Portfolio Presentation Standards (AIMR-PPS) and the more recent Global Investment Performance Standards (GIPS) ensures full and fair disclosure of investment results to clients and prospective clients, and guarantees that all managers act on the same level playing field. Unfortunately, we do not have the equivalent yet for hedge funds and alternative investments.

As long as clearly defined standards are lacking, performance measurement will have much in common with religion: it means something different to everyone, it results in veneration by some, and it is often the source of disputes and conflict. To make matters worse, smart swindlers take advantage of the lack of consensus by propagating hedge fund statistics that claim to be of value to investors, but which are in reality based on misconceptions, misinterpretations and flawed assumptions.

This situation is of some concern, particularly when we recall that risk and return – the two keys of performance – play an essential role in comparing different funds as well as in evaluating the compensation of hedge fund managers. It also raises serious doubts about the possibility of evaluating hedge funds from an *ex-ante* perspective. If we cannot agree about what happened in the past, how can we attach any value to our forecasts for the future?

In order to interpret correctly the statistics of hedge fund performance and separate the wheat from the chaff, the reader must first understand the basic quantitative concepts and know what is hidden behind the notions of "risk" and "return". In this chapter, we attempt to demystify both the statistical analysis of hedge fund returns and result interpretation, in an effort to enhance our future decision-making process. Although we have made every effort to offer a clear and intuitive explanation of the associated issues, we could not avoid a few equations, some of them probably intimidating. But do not worry: the material is primarily covered in the text and in examples.

You may be tempted at this point to skip this chapter and go straight to the next one. This would not be a judicious move, however, because the rest of the book builds upon what is learned in this chapter. When the wind blows, a house with no foundations will not resist for long. The same applies to the hedge fund investor without a clear understanding of the material that follows. Without a thorough understanding of risk and return, it would be an uphill task to carry out the necessary quantitative analysis.

18.1   THE DIFFICULTIES OF OBTAINING INFORMATION

Investors accustomed to high levels of control and transparency in traditional investments often find the variations in what hedge funds disclose discouraging. In some cases, even the phone number of the hedge fund manager seems to be proprietary information.

Transparency is obviously a touchy subject for hedge fund managers. After Alfred Winslow Jones had formed the first hedge fund in 1949, he managed to operate his fund in complete secrecy for 17 years. Almost 50 years later, the hedge fund Long Term Capital Management (LTCM) was considered as being the very paragon of modern financial engineering, with two Nobel prize winners among its partners and Wall Street's most celebrated trader as its CEO. It shrouded its operations in secrecy, denying lenders and their regulators any data about its positions or its liabilities to other lenders. "Do you want us to refund your money?" was the usual question to LTCM partners that were too inquisitive about the fund's activities.

These two examples, although not recent, are quite representative of the reputation of operating under a cloak of secrecy that most hedge fund managers have today. They still tend to avoid disclosing the securities they hold, their views on the market, the extent to which they are leveraged, or even in some cases their past performance figures. This attitude has often been perceived as hubris and arrogance. The true picture is somewhat different. In reality, there are at least three reasons that may help to justify the relative secrecy surrounding hedge fund operations.

First, one should remember that, unlike mutual funds, onshore hedge funds are privately organized investment vehicles subject to minimal oversight from regulatory bodies. The numerous funds incorporated offshore for tax purposes are even less regulated. As long as smaller, unsophisticated investors do not join the band, regulators do not bother with the situation. Consequently, hedge funds are not required to disclose holdings, returns or even their existence beyond what is spelled out in the contract with their investors. And many hedge fund managers are very happy to remain boutiques catering primarily to high net worth individuals. They do not really care about attracting new investors. Hence, the lack of transparency to non-investors is not surprising!

Second, most regulators do not allow hedge funds to advertise or solicit money from the general public. Onshore hedge funds are only allowed to target limited groups of accredited investors, and offshore hedge funds are legally debarred from making domestic public offerings. Releazing information about past performance could easily be regarded as advertising, particularly if the figures are good and attract the attention of potential investors. Hedge fund managers will not take that risk and prefer to remain in the shade.

Third, many hedge fund managers shy away from disclosure, particularly those active in illiquid markets (e.g. distressed securities or merger arbitrage) or who frequently engage in heavy short selling or highly leveraged positions (e.g. fixed income arbitrage or global macro, for example). These managers believe that allowing competitors to see their trades is tantamount to revealing the underpinnings of their strategies and exposing them to disastrous short squeezes and numerous competitive risks. Arbitrage is often based on being the first to find rare market inefficiencies before anyone else has the chance to squeeze profit out of the trade, which effectively irons out the inefficiency. The more secretive you stay, the higher the profit. Furthermore, the market could easily trade against a hedge fund manager once its positions are revealed.[1]

For these reasons, among others, it is common practice for hedge fund managers to structure their funds so as not to trigger reporting requirements imposed by regulators[2] and to supply minimal information to their existing investors. This typically includes an estimate of the monthly return, a few statistics such as volatility and correlation, and possibly a quarterly letter from the manager himself. In a sense, the situation could be described as relatively opaque.

It was only after 1998 and the bail-out of Long Term Capital Management that regulators, investors and prime brokers started requiring greater disclosure, particularly in relation to the risk side. The demand for more transparency strengthened with the interest of institutional investors such as pension funds and insurance companies, which had, and still have, limited exposure in this market, but constitute a large potential source of demand for hedge fund products in the future. Under pressure from these new investors and fearing regulatory controls, the hedge fund industry is progressively institutionalizing itself. Many hedge funds have evolved from the start-up structure of a one-man trading company to a global financial institution, with written policies and procedures, separation of front, middle and back office, succession planning, disaster recovery, independent risk management, etc. This seems to be the new pattern of evolution for hedge funds.

In parallel, transparency has swept across markets, and while some hedge fund managers may not like it, they will have to live with it. An increasing number of managers are now willing to discuss portfolio information openly and directly with investors, at least on a monthly basis. Many investors are quite satisfied with this approach, as they have confidence in the manager. But some request more information, ranging from the dollar exposure by trader or portfolio manager, asset class, sector/industry, currency, strategy or style, to the leverage, the performance attribution and the complete Value at Risk analysis. In a few cases, the request concerns the individual position details on a weekly or even daily basis. For the time being, the majority of experienced hedge fund managers are still unwilling to offer this level of transparency, but things could change very rapidly, as the demand for increased transparency is still around.

The question of determining the level of detail beyond net asset values that constitutes adequate or appropriate portfolio transparency still fuels an ongoing debate.[3] A few hedge funds have agreed to provide full transparency by allowing investors to gather position data

---

[1] The case of Long Term Capital Management in 1998 is a prime example of the market trading against a manager once the company was in distress and positions were revealed to the market.

[2] The only exception occurs if a hedge fund holds large public equity positions. In this case, the manager, like any other large institutional manager, must disclose these positions to the local market supervisor, e.g. the SEC in the United States.

[3] It is interesting to note that investors and fund managers have very different perceptions of the transparency situation. As an illustration, consider the results of a recent survey conducted by Capital Market Risk Advisors Inc. (CMRA) at the request of the Alternative Investment Management Association (AIMA). On the one hand, only 7% of funds of funds and 4% of individual hedge funds reported cases of potential investors declining to invest because of the lack of transparency. On the other hand, 64% of investors claimed they had declined to invest in a fund for the same motive. And 86% of investors indicated that transparency is an issue when selecting hedge funds and funds of funds.

from prime brokers. But most investors lack the skills and resources to interpret position-level information, so that complete transparency actually makes the job of analysing risk and return more complicated. The emergence of risk transparency rather than position transparency seems to offers a good compromise, at least for the time being, and provides investors with a meaningful snapshot of a hedge fund's risks. It addresses investor concerns while avoiding position detail that may be difficult to obtain and overwhelming to receive.

The next step of risk transparency is the standardization of risk factors, so that the risk exposures can be aggregated across an investor's portfolio of hedge funds. Riskmetrics™ and other market leaders in the field of risk management are now offering solutions in order to fulfil this task. Value at risk (VaR) in particular has been used by both investors and managers in analysing their portfolios and provided a common language for risk communication. But this is another topic that we will come to later.

18.2 EQUALIZATION, CRYSTALLIZATION AND MULTIPLE SHARE CLASSES

Obtaining a time series of historical net asset values for a given hedge fund may be difficult. Unfortunately, it is only the first part of the story. Unlike traditional mutual funds that have a clean way of calculating their net asset values, the world of hedge funds is a real jungle with its particularities and conventions. Hence, several adjustments must usually be made to historical data before performance can be measured. Among these, the most frequent are equalization calculations and crystallizations.

Equalization calculations are a series of accounting methods used to ensure that incentive fees are charged in a fair and equitable way to all investors in a hedge fund. Conceptually, determining the incentive fee at the fund level should be a fairly straightforward exercise. Incentive fees are typically calculated as a percentage of the annual or semi-annual increase in the gross asset value of the fund, either as a straight percentage of the appreciation or as a percentage of the increase over a certain threshold (hurdle rate). However, computational complications arise when investors are allowed to buy into the fund at different times during the year and, therefore, at different net asset values per share. Indeed, purchases at different times result in differing percentages of appreciation relative to other investors at the end of each measurement period. This raises several potential problems.

18.3 THE INEQUITABLE ALLOCATION OF INCENTIVE FEES

In the absence of any adjustment, when the fund performance is positive, an investor who buys into the fund in the middle of the measurement period may be charged a full incentive fee, although he has only participated in a part of the performance. In a sense, he will be subsidizing another shareholder.

As an illustration, consider a hedge fund launched on 1 January at a share price of $100. To keep things simple, say the fund charges no management fee. Its incentive fee is equal to 20% of the performance, charged semi-annually without any hurdle rate. On 1 January, investor A subscribes for $1 000 000 to the fund, that is, 10 000 shares. The situation is as follows:

1 January
Gross asset value per share $100
Net asset value per share $100

At the end of the first quarter, say the fund displays a positive performance of $+10\%$. The gross asset value per share increases to $110. The hedge fund publishes a net asset value of $108, net of $2 incentive fee accrual. The $2 amount is still included in the gross asset value, but has not yet been paid to the fund manager. The situation is now as follows:

> *31 March*
> Gross asset value per share $110
> Incentive fee per share (accrual) $2   (20% of performance)
> Net asset value per share $108

Investor B then steps in and subscribes 10 000 shares at a price equal to the published net asset value of the fund ($108).

Three months later, the gross asset value per share of the fund is, say, $120. The semi-annual profit of $320 000 should be split between investor A ($20 per share) and investor B ($12 per share). However, if the fund charges its semi-annual incentive fee at the fund level based on the gross asset value, the corresponding fee would be 20% of $320 000, that is, $64 000 in total, or $3.2 per share. The final net asset value published by the fund would therefore be $116.8 per share ($120 − $3.2). The situation would be as follows:

> *30 June*
> Gross asset value per share $120
> Incentive fee per share (accrual) $3.20   (20% of performance)
> Net asset value per share $116.80

Consequently, investor A would have paid $3.2 for an effective profit of $20, which implies a performance fee equal to 16.4%. Investor B would have paid the same $3.2, but for an effective profit of $12, which represents a 26.66% performance fee. This allocation of incentive fees is clearly inequitable. The problem lies in the calculation of the fee using the gross asset value, which is the same for both investors and includes the incentive fee accrual, while investor B only benefited from a portion of the upside.

18.4   THE FREE-RIDE SYNDROME

Another type of problem may occur with incentive fees when a hedge fund has lost money and recoups its losses. In such a case, a shareholder who buys into the fund in the middle of the measurement period (at a price lower than the previous highest net asset value) may avoid part of the incentive fee until the fund has recovered, although in reality this investor enjoys an effective appreciation on his investment. This is called the free-ride syndrome.

As an illustration, consider again a hedge fund launched on 1 January at a share price of $100. As before, the fund charges no management fee, but a performance fee equal to 20% of its performance, charged semi-annually. A high-water mark clause in the offering memorandum states that the 20% incentive fee can be charged only if the fund manager makes money and has recovered from all previous losses. On 1 January, investor A subscribes for $1 000 000 to the fund, that is, 10 000 shares. The situation is as follows:

> *1 January*
> Gross asset value per share $100
> Net asset value per share $100

At the end of the first quarter, say the fund displays a negative performance of -10%. The gross asset value per share decreases to $90. The hedge fund publishes a net asset value of $90. There is no incentive fee accrual, because the fund manager did not perform well. The situation is now as follows:

> *31 March*
> Gross asset value per share $90
> Incentive fee per share (accrual) $0
> Net asset value per share $90

Investor B then steps in and subscribes 10 000 shares at a price equal to the published net asset value of the fund ($90).

Three months later, say the gross asset value per share of the fund is now back at $100. The total quarterly profit is $200 000. To be fair, it should be split equally between investors A and B ($10 per share). Only investor B who gained 11.11% should pay the incentive fee, because investor A just recovered his previous loss and simply broke even. However, if the fund charges its semi-annual incentive fee at the fund level based on the gross asset value evolution, there is no incentive fee because the performance is considered as being flat. The final net asset value published by the fund will therefore be $100 per share.

> *30 June*
> Gross asset value per share $100
> Incentive fee per share (accrual) $0
> Net asset value per share $100

Now, if investor B decides to realize his 11.11% return and redeem his shares, he will pay no performance fee, since the fund manager did not make any money according to the semi-annual high-water mark. This gives investor B a free ride on his profits. This once again implies an inequitable allocation of incentive fees, as the manager did not receive his incentive fee although some investors obtained gains since they entered the fund later than the others.

18.5   ONSHORE VERSUS OFFSHORE FUNDS

The inequitable allocation of incentive fees and the free ride syndrome do not occur with onshore hedge funds that are structured as limited partnerships. There are two reasons for this. First, most limited partnerships are closed structures, so that no new investor may come in after the fund has been launched. Second, the partnership agreement may allocate portions of gains and losses in an individual way, if this is stated in the bylaws.

However, the two problems are present in offshore funds, which are often "open ended". They allow investors to make capital contributions on a regular basis, therefore creating the potential for inequity between new investors and the original ones. The difficulty stems from the fact that all investors are usually offered a single class of shares, of which a fixed number has to be issued each time a new investor invests, and which is traditionally used also as a measure of the fund's performance. As soon as investors subscribe at different net asset value levels, calculating incentive fees may become quite complex. At the end of any measurement period, each investor may have a differing percentage appreciation or depreciation for his shares relative to other investors. Hence, the calculation of the incentive fee applicable to any appreciation in fund shares must be adjusted accordingly, in order to treat each investor equitably.

18.6   THE MULTIPLE SHARE APPROACH

A straightforward solution to avoid the above-mentioned problems consists in considering each shareholding individually and issuing multiple series of shares. The first series of shares at the fund's creation is called the "lead series", and another series is created each time there is a new subscription. Then, each group of investors entering the fund at the same date and at the same net asset value will hold the same series of shares and will pay the same incentive fee based on the performance effectively earned.

By way of example, consider the case of a new hedge fund that has just started operations. We assume that the fund has a monthly subscription policy and has adopted the multiple share approach. The fund manager charges a 20% incentive fee on a quarterly basis, conditional on a 1% quarterly high-water mark. Say the performance for the first three months is as follows: +7% in January, +5% in February, and −4% in March.

On 1 January, investor A buys 1000 Series I shares of the fund at $1000 per share. This series of shares will constitute the lead series. At the end of January, the gross NAV of the lead series of shares has increased to $1070 per share (+7%) and the published NAV is $1056, net of $14 incentive fee accrual (20% of the $70 increase). A new series of 1000 shares called Series II is created, with a net asset value per share of $1000. Investor B then buys all Series II shares for $1 million.

At the end of February, the gross NAV of the fund's shares is now $1123.50 for the lead series (+5%) and $1050 for Series II shares (+5%). The hedge fund publishes a net asset value of $1098.80 (net of $24.70 incentive fee accrual) for the lead series and a net asset value of $1040 (net of $10 incentive fee accrual) for Series II. A new series of 1000 shares called Series III is created, with a net asset value per share of $1000. Investor C then buys all Series III shares for $1 million.

At the end of March, the gross net asset value of the fund's shares is now $1078.56 for the lead series, $1008 for Series II shares and $960 for Series III shares. The lead series and Series II shares pay their incentive fee ($15.71 and $1.60 per share, respectively). Series III shares are not profitable and do not pay any incentive fee. Table 18.1 summarizes the overall process.

Table 18.1   Evolution of gross and published net asset values in the case of multiple series of shares

	1 Jan.	31 Jan.	28 Feb.	31 Mar.	1 Apr.
Performance		+7%	+5%	−4%	
Series I (lead series)					
Gross NAV	$1000	$1070	$1123.50	$1078.56	$1062.85
Net NAV (published)	$1000	$1056	$1098.80	$1062.85	$1062.85
Accrual of incentive fee	$0	$14	$24.70	$15.71	$0
Series II					
Gross NAV		$1000	$1050	$1008.00	$1006.40
Net NAV (published)		$1000	$1040	$1006.40	$1006.40
Accrual of incentive fee		$0	$10	$1.60	$0
Series III					
Gross NAV			$1000	$960	$960
Net NAV (published)			$1000	$960	$960
Accrual of incentive fee			$0	$0	$0

The major advantage of this procedure is its simplicity. Each series of shares is valued independently of the others and has its own incentive fee accrual. There is no longer a free rider syndrome and no problem of incentive fee allocation. The drawback is that things can easily become cumbersome as the number of series rises. The coexistence of multiple series of shares implies tracking and reporting multiple net asset values (one for each series), which is quite confusing for an investor holding shares in several series. Furthermore, the independence of each series implies that the listing requirements and fees (for instance, on the Irish Stock Exchange) must be applied to each series!

Funds that adopt multiple series regularly attempt to consolidate series of shares with the lead series in order to reduce the number of series outstanding. The necessary conditions to implement such a consolidation are (i) that the end of an accounting period for the lead series and another series coincide and (ii) that an incentive fee has been paid for both of them. In our previous example, Series II shares could be merged with the lead series on 1 April, just after the payment of the incentive fee. Investor B would have to exchange his 1000 shares, which are worth $1006.40 per share, against 946.89 shares of the lead series, which are worth $1062.85 per share. This reduces the number of outstanding series but introduces holdings of fractional shares, which is not necessarily much better. Moreover, an external observer monitoring only the net asset value of the shares held by B would conclude that the share appreciated from $1006.40 to $1062.85, which is wrong. It is precisely to avoid such situations that alternative methodologies have been suggested.

18.7   THE EQUALIZATION FACTOR/DEPRECIATION DEPOSIT APPROACH

If the fund manager wants to publish only one net asset value, another way to overcome the above-mentioned problems is to use the equalization factor approach. The latter is a correction mechanism that uses depreciation deposits and equalization factors as compensation for the inequitable allocation of incentive fees.

Consider, for instance, the case of a hedge fund that charges its incentive fee annually but allows monthly subscriptions and redemptions. Under the equalization factor approach, any subscription of shares that takes place within the year (that is, between the payment dates of the incentive fee) is made at the *net asset value* on the date of the purchase, plus an equalization factor if the net asset value has increased since the base net asset value.[4] Depending on the level of the net asset value at the end of the year, all or part of the equalization factor may be refunded to the investor, usually by granting him some "free" shares for the corresponding amount. Similarly, if the net asset value at the purchase date is lower than the base net asset value, the investor will receive a depreciation deposit. At the end of the year, all or part of the depreciation deposit is either paid to the investment manager by redeeming shares (if the fund's net asset value has gone up) or kept on deposit for the benefit of the investor and used in future years (if the fund's net asset value has gone down).

---

[4] The base net asset value refers to the highest net asset value the fund has reached at the end of any fiscal year. At the inception of the fund, the base net asset value equals the initial subscription amount. If the fund appreciates during its first year, the base net asset value becomes the net asset value at the end of its first year. If the fund depreciates, the base net asset value remains the initial net asset value. The base net asset value is essentially equal to the high-water mark of the shares issued upon initial subscription.

As an illustration, let us reconsider our previous example. Our first hedge fund started as follows:

1 January (inception)
Gross asset value per share $100
Net asset value per share $100

with investor A owning 10 000 shares. After a quarterly increase of 10%, the situation is as follows:

31 March (before subscriptions)
Gross asset value per share $110
Incentive fee per share (accrual) $2   (20% of performance)
Net asset value per share $108

Allocation to A   10 000 shares $1 080 000

We assume that the fund uses an equalization factor approach. When investor B steps in and subscribes 10 000 shares, the price is equal to the published net asset value of the fund ($108), plus the incentive fee ($2). Thus, investor B pays $1 100 000 and receives 10 000 shares, plus an equalization credit equal to the current performance fee (10 000 times $2 = $20 000). This equalization credit is accounted for as a liability of the fund. It is at risk in the fund and will therefore fluctuate with the performance of the fund subsequent to the investment. However, the value of the equalization credit will never increase above the performance fee at the time the investment was made ($20 000).

31 March (after subscriptions)
Allocation to A   10 000 shares $1 080 000
Allocation to B   10 000 shares $1 080 000
                        Equal. credit $20 000

Three months later, say the gross asset value per share of the fund is now down to $105. We have the following situation:

30 June
Gross asset value per share $105
Incentive fee per share (accrual) $1   (20% of performance)
Net asset value per share $104

Allocation to A   10 000 shares $1 040 000
Allocation to B   10 000 shares $1 040 000
                        Equal. credit $10 000

Note that the equalization credit of investor B has been reduced to $10 000, which corresponds to the 10 000 shares times the $1 incentive fee.

In the next quarter, say the gross asset value per share of the fund is down again to $95. The performance fee disappears, since it is calculated with respect to the base net asset value of $100 at the beginning of the year. The equalization credit of investor B is therefore marked at a value of zero.

30 September (before subscriptions)

Gross asset value per share		$95
Incentive fee per share (accrual)		$0
Net asset value per share		$95
Allocation to A	10 000 shares	$950 000
Allocation to B	10 000 shares	$950 000
	Equal. credit	$0

Investor C then steps in and subscribes 10 000 shares at a price equal to the published net asset value of the fund ($95). He pays $950 000 and receives 10 000 shares plus a depreciation deposit of −$10 000 on his account, which corresponds to the fee due on the performance of the 10 000 shares from $95 (the NAV at which he invested) to $100 (the previous high NAV per share). This depreciation deposit is at risk in the hedge fund and will therefore fluctuate with the performance of the fund subsequent to the investment. However, the value of the equalization debit (in absolute value) will never increase above $10 000.

30 September (after subscriptions)

Allocation to A	10 000 shares	$950 000
Allocation to B	10 000 shares	$950 000
	Equal. credit	$0
Allocation to C	10 000 shares	$950 000
	Equal. debit	−$10 000

For the sake of illustration, say the fund goes up during the next month, so that the gross asset value per share of the fund is $140 at the end of October.

31 October (before subscriptions)

Gross asset value per share	$140	
Incentive fee per share (accrual)	$8	(20% of performance)
Net asset value per share	$132	
Allocation to A	10 000 shares	$1 320 000
Allocation to B	10 000 shares	$1 320 000
	Equal. credit	$20 000
Allocation to C	10 000 shares	$1 320 000
	Equal. debit	−$10 000

Investor D then steps in and subscribes 10 000 shares at a price equal to the published net asset value of the fund ($132), plus the incentive fee ($8). He pays $1 400 000 and receives 10 000 shares, plus an equalization credit equal to the current performance fee (10 000 times $8 = $80 000). Similarly to B, this equalization credit is at risk in the hedge fund and will therefore fluctuate with the performance of the fund subsequent to the investment. However, the value of the equalization credit will never increase above the performance fee at the time the investment was made ($80 000).

31 October (before subscriptions)

Allocation to A	10 000 shares	$1 320 000
Allocation to B	10 000 shares	$1 320 000
	Equal. credit	$20 000
Allocation to C	10 000 shares	$1 320 000
	Equal. debit	−$10 000
Allocation to D	10 000 shares	$1 320 000
	Equal. credit	$80 000

Finally, at year-end, say the gross asset value per share of the fund is now down to $125. The situation is as follows:

31 December

Gross asset value per share	$125	
Incentive fee per share (accrual)	$5	(20% of performance)
Net asset value per share	$120	
Allocation to A	10 000 shares	$1 200 000
Allocation to B	10 000 shares	$1 200 000
	Equal. credit	$20 000
Allocation to C	10 000 shares	$1 200 000
	Equal. debit	−$10 000
Allocation to D	10 000 shares	$1 200 000
	Equal. credit	$80 000

As we are at the end of the year, the new net asset value becomes the new offering price and a new high-water mark needs to be determined for the next year. This operation is often referred to as *crystallization*. The investment manager is due his incentive fee and a new calculation is made of any remaining equalization factor attributable to shareholders.

- Investor A invested at a gross asset value equal to $100, so he has to pay the full performance fee from $100 to $125, that is, $5 per share. This corresponds to what the fund charges, so there is no particular need for adjustment. Investor A therefore starts the next year with 10 000 shares having a net asset value of $120 per share.
- Investor B invested at a gross asset value equal to $110, so he only has to pay the performance fee from $110 to $125, that is, $3 per share. As the fund charges a total incentive fee of $5 per share, investor B is owed back $2 – the incentive fee from the gross asset value of $100 to the gross asset value of $110. This amount corresponds to the $20 000 of equalization credit. Hence, 166.6667 new shares representing this value will be issued and granted to investor B. The equalization credit disappears, and investor B therefore starts the next year with 10 166.6667 shares having a net asset value of $120 per share.
- Investor C invested at a gross asset value equal to $95, so he has to pay the performance fee from $95 to $125, that is, $6 per share. As the fund charges a total incentive fee of $5 per share, investor B still has to pay $1, that is, the incentive fee from the gross asset value of $95 to the gross asset value of $100. This amount due corresponds to the −$10 000 of equalization debit. Hence, 83.3333 shares representing this value at the year-end net asset value will be redeemed from the account of investor C. The equalization debit disappears, and investor C therefore starts the next year with 9916.6667 shares having a net asset value of $120 per share.
- Investor D invested at a gross asset value equal to $140, so he should not be charged anything. He is the only investor below his high-water mark. As the fund charges a total incentive fee of $5 per share, investor D is owed back $50 000 – the incentive fee from the gross asset value of $100 to the gross asset value of $125. Hence, 416.6667 new shares representing this value will be issued and granted to investor D. The equalization credit is reduced by $50 000, and the remaining $30 000 equalization credit is carried over to the next year if the investor stays in the fund.[5] Investor D therefore starts the next year with

---

[5] Note that some funds will simply cancel out the remaining equalization factor if investor D leaves the fund in December. Their argument is that the fund has lost 37.5% of its year's gains (15 out of 40) since investor D subscribed, so that investor D loses a similar proportion of his equalization factor ($30 000 out of $80 000). As usual, the details are in the fine print.

10 416.6667 shares having a net asset value of $120 per share and an equalization credit of $30 000.

1 January (following year)

Gross asset value per share		$120
Incentive fee per share (accrual)		$0
Net asset value per share		$120
Allocation to A	10 000 shares	$1 200 000
Allocation to B	10 166.6667 shares	$1 220 000
Allocation to C	9916.6667 shares	$1 190 000
Allocation to D	10 416.6667 shares	$1 250 000
	Equal. credit	$30 000

The new high-water mark for all investors is $120 for the next year, except for investor D, who has a high-water mark of $140. The $30 000 equalization credit guarantees that investor D will be compensated for the fees taken at the fund level below the $140 threshold. In a sense, the equalization factor is only a memorandum account showing each shareholder's previous high-water mark.

18.8 SIMPLE EQUALIZATION

An alternative approach that is also sometimes implemented by hedge funds is "simple equalization". It consists in calculating the fair performance fee for each investor based on the latter's effective entry level and allocating it investor by investor. Investors who came into the fund at different levels will end up with different net asset values, similarly to the example of multiple series of shares. However, in order to arrive at a common net asset value for all shares in the fund, the lowest of all the net asset values calculated at the end of the year is selected to become the new net asset value of the fund for all investors. Shareholders with a higher individual net asset value per share will be exactly compensated by the distribution of a fractional number of new shares. The procedure is relatively simple, and there is only one net asset value for each fund. However, the historical net asset values no longer accurately reflect the fund's performance, and the distribution of free equalization shares to investors is rather confusing.

18.9 CONSEQUENCES FOR PERFORMANCE CALCULATION

Whatever the final choice, any equalization accounting methodology obviously imposes an additional burden on the administrator of the hedge fund and needs to be clearly explained to investors, who generally have great difficulty in understanding that nothing underhand is going on. Nevertheless, its application effectively ensures that all investors are fairly rewarded or penalized when buying into the fund at different times and different net asset values. Furthermore, it allows the net asset value to be uniform and common to all shareholders. This explains why it is often employed by offshore funds. However, it is worth noting that in such a case, the net asset values published by the fund – and obtained on a subscribing database system – no longer reflect the effective performance, unless the investor has been in the fund since its inception. Surprisingly, very few academic papers so far have taken into account accurately the potential biases that are likely to result from this.

While much of the early work on quantitative analysis involved the statistical behaviour of asset prices (e.g. the random walk of asset prices), much of the recent work in financial econometrics has involved time series of returns rather than net asset values or prices. The major reason for this paradigm shift is that returns standardize the evolution of a price by considering price *per unit of investment*. In addition, returns often have more attractive statistical properties than prices. In the following section, we will therefore convert our net asset values into return figures.

18.10   THE HOLDING PERIOD RETURN

Let us denote by NAV_t the net asset value at time t of a given hedge fund, with the index t representing any point in time. We assume that the net asset value has already been adjusted to take into account all realized and non-realized capital gains, accrued dividends and interest income, capital distributions, splits and all the impacts of equalization and crystallization. We therefore ignore these aspects henceforth.

The *simple net return* R_{T_1, T_2} on the fund between any time T_1 and $T_2 \geq T_1$ is defined as

$$R_{T_1, T_2} = \frac{NAV_{T_2} - NAV_{T_1}}{NAV_{T_1}} \tag{18.1}$$

It measures the relative change in the fund's net asset value over the considered time period and is sometimes called the *holding period return* or percent return. The simple net return can be used to express the future net asset value as a function of the present net asset value:

$$NAV_{T_2} = (1 + R_{T_1, T_2}) \times NAV_{T_1} \tag{18.2}$$

The term $(1 + R_{T_1, T_2})$ is often called the *simple gross return*.

As an illustration, Table 18.2 shows the calculation of several holding period returns over different holding horizons. The series of end-month net asset values provided in the second column and equation (18.1) are the only inputs needed to calculate these holding period returns.

Table 18.2   Calculation of a series of holding period returns from a series of end-month net asset values

Time	Date	End-month NAV ($)	Monthly return	Quarterly returns	Annual returns
0	Dec. 01	134.64			
1	Jan. 02	135.81	$R_{0,1} = 0.87\%$		
2	Feb. 02	135.95	$R_{1,2} = 0.10\%$		
3	Mar. 02	136.73	$R_{2,3} = 0.57\%$	$R_{0,3} = 1.55\%$	
4	Apr. 02	137.49	$R_{3,4} = 0.56\%$		
5	May 02	137.80	$R_{4,5} = 0.23\%$		
6	Jun. 02	135.15	$R_{5,6} = -1.92\%$	$R_{3,6} = -1.16\%$	
7	Jul. 02	132.47	$R_{6,7} = -1.98\%$		
8	Aug. 02	132.88	$R_{7,8} = 0.31\%$		
9	Sep. 02	133.03	$R_{8,9} = 0.11\%$	$R_{6,9} = -1.57\%$	
10	Oct. 02	133.24	$R_{9,10} = 0.16\%$		
11	Nov. 02	135.40	$R_{10,11} = 1.62\%$		
12	Dec. 02	137.04	$R_{11,12} = 1.21\%$	$R_{9,12} = 3.01\%$	$R_{0,12} = 1.78\%$

Although the net asset value is only measured at a monthly frequency, it is possible to calculate holding period returns over more than one month. To do so, one may use the standard definition provided by equation (18.1) and use the final and initial net asset values. Alternatively, the holding period return may also be calculated by compounding the impact of several consecutive returns. Obviously, the cost of carrying money from time T_1 to time $T_3 \geq T_1$ is the same as the cost of carrying money from T_1 to $T_2 \geq T_1$, and then from T_2 to $T_3 \geq T_2$, since

$$\text{NAV}_{T_3} = (1 + R_{T_1,T_3}) \times \text{NAV}_{T_1} = (1 + R_{T_1,T_2}) \times (1 + R_{T_2,T_3}) \times \text{NAV}_{T_1} \qquad (18.3)$$

More generally, we can have as many intermediary periods as we want, so that the simple gross return over N periods can be expressed as the product of the N simple gross returns of each shorter period[6]:

$$1 + R_{T_1,T_N} = (1 + R_{T_1,T_2}) \times (1 + R_{T_2,T_3}) \times \ldots \times (1 + R_{T_{N-1},T_N}) \qquad (18.4)$$

Algebraically, this is denoted as follows:

$$1 + R_{T_1,T_N} = \prod_{i=1}^{i=N-1} (1 + R_{T_i,T_{i+1}}) \qquad (18.5)$$

The process of multiplying several gross returns is called *compounding*.[7] As an illustration, the first quarterly return of Table 18.1 can be obtained by using equation (18.1), that is,

$$R_{0,3} = \frac{136.73 - 134.64}{134.64} = 1.55\%,$$

or by compounding the three monthly returns $R_{0,1} = 0.87\%$, $R_{1,2} = 0.10\%$ and $R_{2,3} = 0.57\%$. Both approaches yield exactly the same result. However, one should not compare any monthly return with the 1.55% figure, which is expressed on a quarterly basis.

An essential question with respect to holding period returns is whether they are calculated before the deduction of management fees and other expenses (gross returns) or after (net returns). Both figures are useful, since gross returns reflect a manager's raw investment performance, while net returns reflect actual investor results. Similarly, it is also important to know the net asset value calculation methodology used by administrators, in particular:

- The type of prices used to determine the net asset value. A recent survey by Capital Market Risk Advisors on valuation practices evidenced no consistent market practice across hedge funds when several quotes were available. About 50% of hedge fund respondents used an average quote, 36% made a subjective judgement, 7% used the median quote, and 7% dropped the high and low values and then averaged the remaining quotes. In addition, 60% of hedge funds indicated that they marked their long positions to the mid-point of the market versus the more conservative approach of using the bid side, and 75% of hedge funds marked their shorts to the mid-point rather than the more conservative approach of using the offered side. All these choices may be justified in specific situations, but in any case it is important to be aware of their existence.
- The adjustments made to the "market" prices received from the valuation sources. The above-mentioned survey also evidenced that about 22% of hedge fund respondents adjusted the prices used to calculate the net asset value of their fund, mostly for liquidity and time zone differences. Although the adjustments represented less than 2% of the final net asset

---

[6] Note that this property applies even if the N periods considered have different lengths.

[7] We will often loosely say that we compound simple returns. In reality, we will use the corresponding gross returns in the calculation.

value in the majority of cases, they represented up to 30% of the net asset value in a few cases.

- The valuation methodology and the source of information for infrequently traded or non-marketable assets, such as non-listed stocks, real estate, private placements and distressed securities. Those who believe that valuation does not matter should remember that several hedge funds (e.g. Granite Partners, Lipper Convertible Arbitrage) collapsed when investors evaluated their holdings at market value rather than at the manager's estimated value!
- The use of cash versus accrual accounting. In cash accounting, income is recorded only when received and expenses are recorded only when paid. Accrual accounting is based on the fundamental rule that all income earned for a period must be matched with the expenses that are assignable to that period. The industry recommended standard is accrual accounting, as required under Generally Accepted Accounting Principles (GAAP), but some hedge funds prefer the simplicity of cash accounting
- The use of trade date versus settlement date. Trade date is the day on which an order is executed, while settlement date is the date on which an executed order must be settled (e.g. for purchases, the cash for the purchase must be paid; for sales, the proceeds of the sale are placed in a cash account). The industry recommended standard is trade date. The current settlement period is usually two to three business days after the trade date for stocks and mutual funds and one business day after the trade date for options trades. It can be considerably longer in emerging markets.
- The manager's choice of return adjustment methodology for intermediate withdrawals and contributions, if any.

All these elements are likely to affect net asset values considerably and should be explicitly disclosed by managers in the prospectus of their funds.

18.11 ANNUALIZING

We mentioned earlier that a monthly return should not be compared with a quarterly figure, or more generally with a figure calculated over a different time horizon. Although holding period returns are scale-free (with respect to the size of the investment), they are not unitless, as they are calculated with respect to some holding period. A return per month is obviously not expressed in the same units as a return per year. As a consequence, stating the value of a holding period return without mentioning the time interval considered is not very informative.

Among practitioners and in the financial press, there seems to be an implicit convention, particularly for comparison purposes: all rates of return should be expressed on a yearly basis.[8] Hence, investors frequently need to transform a holding period return into an annual figure, which they call the compound annual growth rate, or CAGR. This process is called "annualizing". Most of the time, returns calculated on a period shorter than one year (e.g. year-to-date, last-month, first quarter) are not annualized, except for predictive purposes.

When the holding period is more than a year, annualizing means figuring out the constant annual return necessary to achieve the observed holding period return once compounding effects are taken into account. When the holding period is less than a year, annualizing means taking the return made over a short period and calculating what the annual return would have been if the investment had continued to gain at the same rate for a full year.

---

[8] There are some exceptions, such as the current monthly performance or year-to-date figures, which are usually not annualized.

A quick estimate of the annualized return is obtained by simply comparing the length of the holding period with one year, and adjusting linearly the holding period return. For instance, a six-month return of 5% would give a 10% annual return (as a six-month period represents one half, or 6/12 of a year), while an 18-month return of 15% would also result in a 10% annual return (12/18 of the original value). Although useful, this rough-and-ready approach is flawed because it does not take into account the compounding effects. The correct way of annualizing the holding period return (HPR) is:

$$\text{Annualized return} = (1 + \text{HPR})^x - 1 \tag{18.6}$$

where x, the number of holding periods in one year, must be expressed as a ratio with respect to one year. As an illustration, if a six-month holding period return is equal to 5%, the equivalent annualized return would be $(1 + 5\%)^{2/1} - 1 = (1.05)^{2/1} - 1 \approx 10.25\%$. Similarly, an 18-month return of 15% would result in an annual return of $(1 + 15\%)^{(12/18)} - 1 = (1.15)^{(12/18)} - 1 \approx 9.77\%$. We see from this that the number of holding periods in one year does not necessarily have to be a whole number.

18.12   MULTIPLE HEDGE FUND AGGREGATION

Frequently, we also need to calculate the performance of a portfolio of funds or the average performance of a sample of funds over a common time period. How should we proceed?

Let N be the number of funds. First, we need to compute the holding period return for each hedge fund over the common period. Let us denote the holding period return of fund number i by R_i, with $i = 1, \ldots, N$. Ideally, these returns should be measured over exactly the same period and according to the same calculation rules. In practice, they are often based on the monthly variation of the net asset value provided by each manager.

Next, we need to assign a weight w_i to each fund at the beginning of the considered period. Three major weighting schemes are used in the industry: the equal weighting approach, the asset weighting approach and the arbitrary weight approach.

- In the *equal-weighting* approach, each hedge fund return has an equal weight in the average. If there are N funds in a sample, each of these has a weight $w_i = 1/N$. The corresponding average can then be perceived as the "average fund behaviour", irrespective of the assets under management. If each fund in the sample has its dedicated manager, the equal-weighted average will then also capture the average manager behaviour.
- In the *asset-weighting* approach, each hedge fund return has a specific weight w_i in the average. This weight is based on the fund's assets under management in proportion to the total assets managed by all hedge funds considered. If fund number i has assets A_i (with $i = 1, \ldots, N$), the weight of fund i in the average is $w_i = A_i / \Sigma A_i$. The resulting average figure can therefore be perceived as the "average dollar invested" behaviour.
- In the *arbitrary weight* approach, each hedge fund return has a specific weight w_i in the average. This weight is arbitrarily chosen, and may change over time. The only requirement is that the sum of all the weights should equal 100%.

Once the return (R_i) and the weight (w_i) for each hedge fund have been determined, the performance index is simply computed as a weighted average of the individual returns:

$$R_{\text{Index}} = \sum_{i=1}^{N} w_i \cdot R_i \tag{18.7}$$

Table 18.3   Calculation of a monthly performance index

Fund name	Return in 2005	Assets in January 2005	Equal weights	Asset-based weights	Arbitrary chosen weights
Fund 1	2.61%	$4.5 billion	1/3	81.80%	20%
Fund 2	17.43%	$851 million	1/3	15.47%	20%
Fund 3	−10.42%	$150 million	1/3	2.73%	60%
		$5.501 billion			

As an illustration, consider the performance of the three funds listed in Table 18.3. All these funds were active in the same sector, namely, global long/short equity. With the equal-weighting approach, the performance of the group would be equal to 3.21%, while it would jump to 4.55% using the asset-weighting approach. Finally, with the arbitrarily chosen weights of Table 18.3, the performance would become negative at −2.24%. All these differences in final returns arise only because of the difference in weights used to calculate the average.

Note that in the case of multiple fund aggregation, several consultants prefer to report the median return rather than the average return. The *median fund return* can be defined by stating that half of the funds have a higher return than the median and half of the funds have a lower return. When the data set contains an odd number of funds, the middle value is the median value and corresponds to the median fund for the period considered. When the data set contains an even number of funds, the middle two numbers are added, the sum is divided by 2 and the resulting value is the median.[9] The fact that outliers are automatically excluded from the calculation makes the median more robust than the average.

18.13   CONTINUOUS COMPOUNDING

It is relatively easy to calculate simple net and simple gross returns over a single holding period return. However, it is tiresome to take into account compounding effects using multiplications and powers as soon as we have more than one period – see, for instance, equation (18.5). Things would be much simpler if we could just add and subtract simple returns rather than multiply and divide simple gross returns.

This has motivated an alternative approach to measuring returns, which produces *continuously compounded returns* or *log returns*. The continuously compounded return r_{T_1, T_2} on a fund between any time T_1 and $T_2 \geq T_1$ is defined as the natural logarithm of its simple gross return[10]:

$$r_{T_1, T_2} = \ln(1 + R_{T_1, T_2}) \qquad (18.8)$$

As an illustration, Table 18.4 shows the calculation of a series of continuously compounded returns from a series of monthly net asset values. We intentionally express the result with three decimals to show that simple returns and continuously compounded returns are in fact slightly different.

---

[9] In a sense, the median return is a very particular weighted average, where only one return (odd-size sample) or two returns (even-size sample) have a weight different from zero.

[10] Note the use of a lower case letter to emphasize the use of continuously compounded returns as opposed to the simple return.

Table 18.4 Calculation of a series of simple and continuously compounded holding period returns from a series of end-month net asset values

Month	End-month NAV	Simple compounding			Continuous compounding		
		Monthly return	Quarterly return	Annual return	Monthly return	Quarterly return	Annual return
Dec. 01	134.64						
Jan. 02	135.81	0.869%			0.865%		
Feb. 02	135.95	0.103%			0.103%		
Mar. 02	136.73	0.574%	1.552%		0.572%	1.540%	
Apr. 02	137.49	0.556%			0.554%		
May 02	137.80	0.225%			0.225%		
Jun. 02	135.15	−1.923%	−1.156%		−1.942%	−1.162%	
Jul. 02	132.47	−1.983%			−2.003%		
Aug. 02	132.88	0.310%			0.309%		
Sep. 02	133.03	0.113%	−1.569%		0.113%	−1.581%	
Oct. 02	133.24	0.158%			0.158%		
Nov. 02	135.40	1.621%			1.608%		
Dec. 02	137.04	1.211%	3.014%	1.783%	1.204%	2.970%	1.767%

The fact that continuous returns are close to simple returns is often confusing. Many people believe that continuously compounded returns are just an approximation of simple returns. This is not true. In a sense, simple returns and continuously compounded returns are parallel worlds, much like miles versus kilometres to measure distances. Do you feel more comfortable using miles or kilometres? The answer probably depends on which type of country you are from. Are miles more accurate than kilometres, or is it the opposite? Well, both measures are accurate as long as you do not mix elements from each world together in the same calculation. The same answers apply to simple returns and continuously compounded returns. Some people prefer continuously compounded returns (e.g. statisticians, or people dealing with option pricing in continuous time), while others stick to simple returns. In all cases, using simple returns would be correct; likewise using continuously compounded returns would also be correct.

The advantage of using continuously compounded returns is purely computational. Using logarithms converts a multiplication to an addition and a division to a subtraction, which simplifies some calculations greatly.

For instance, the one-period continuously compounded return is just the change in the log price.

$$r_{T_1,T_2} = \ln(1 + R_{T_1,T_2}) = \ln\left(\frac{\text{NAV}_{T_2}}{\text{NAV}_{T_1}}\right) = \ln(\text{NAV}_{T_2}) - \ln(\text{NAV}_{T_1}) \tag{18.9}$$

Also, multi-period log returns are simply the sum of the single period log returns over the period:

$$\begin{aligned} r_{T_1,T_3} &= \ln(\text{NAV}_{T_3}) - \ln(\text{NAV}_{T_1}) \\ &= \ln(\text{NAV}_{T_3}) - \ln(\text{NAV}_{T_2}) + \ln(\text{NAV}_{T_2}) - \ln(\text{NAV}_{T_1}) \\ &= r_{T_1,T_2} + r_{T_2,T_3} \end{aligned} \tag{18.10}$$

Hence, annualizing or compounding is a straightforward operation using continuously compounded returns. As an illustration, the annual continuously compounded return of 1.767% in Table 18.4 is simply obtained by summing the 12 monthly continuously compounded returns, or the four quarterly continuously compounded returns. Similarly, annualizing a monthly continuously compounded return is equivalent to multiplying it by 12.

In addition, as we will see shortly, continuously compounded returns offer the advantage of being easier to model. The reason is simply that it is much simpler to derive the properties of an additive process rather than the properties of a multiplicative process, particularly when using time series of returns. Thus, in the financial literature, it is common to see the use of continuously compounded returns when modelling the properties of time series of returns.[11]

Note, however, that the result of a calculation involving continuously compounded returns is itself a continuously compounded return. To obtain a simple return, it is therefore necessary to use an exponential, which is the inverse function of the logarithm. This gives:

$$R_{T_1,T_2} = \exp(r_{T_1,T_2}) - 1 \tag{18.11}$$

Hence, equations (18.8) and (18.11) define our conversion functions between the world of continuously compounded returns and that of simple returns. In the following discussion, to keep things simple, we will stick as much as possible to simple returns, unless otherwise explicitly stated.

---

[11] The disadvantage of using continuously compounded returns is, however, that the continuously compounded return of a portfolio is no longer a weighted average of the continuously compounded returns of its components. The reason is simply that the sum of a log is not equal to the log of a sum. In practice, this problem is usually minor, and most people use the weighted average of the continuously compounded returns as an approximation for the portfolio's log return.

19

Return Statistics and Risk

Surprisingly, it seems impossible to meet with a hedge fund manager that is not top quartile

Despite the deep-seated belief of many people that human beings are the most intelligent and complex animals on earth, we have to temper this belief about our intellectual superiority with a measure of humility. The average human brain fails miserably when dealing with more than 10 to 15 numbers. By comparison, the simplest computer is many times more powerful and more capable because it can perform calculations thousands of times faster, work out logical computations without error and store memory at incredible speeds with flawless accuracy.

19.1   CALCULATING RETURN STATISTICS

When the number of returns increases significantly beyond the threshold of 10 to 15, the human brain needs statistics to summarize and understand the information. As we will see, dimension reduction is a leitmotif of statistics.

As an illustration, consider Table 19.1, which shows the series of simple monthly returns for a hedge fund since its inception. In total, there are 233 numbers, far too many for our brain to be able to identify any pattern or trend. To be interpretable, this collection of returns must be organized in some sort of logical way.

One of the easiest ways to reorganize a return series and make it more intelligible is to plot it in some sort of graphical form. The graph preferred by marketers is the historical evolution of $100 invested in the fund in question – see Figure 19.1. While informative about the final value of the investment, this type of graph does not throw much light on progress since the inception. The reason is that the whole graph is conditioned on the terminal value, so that a large percentage loss at the beginning (e.g. −17.46% in November 1987, when the amount invested is small) will appear smaller than a small percentage loss towards the end (e.g. −6.53% in April 2000, when the amount invested is large).

We could partially solve this problem by using a logarithmic scale rather than a linear scale on the Y-axis. However, a better tool to visualize and summarize a large data set is the *relative frequency histogram*. It consists in grouping similar returns together and calculating their frequency. The advantage of grouping is that it hides some of the random noise that is not likely to be meaningful, while at the same time preserving the structure of the data.

To build it, we must proceed as follows:

- Define a set of mutually exclusive and exhaustive intervals, such that each observed return must fall into one and only one interval.
- Count the number of observed returns falling within each interval, and divide the result by the total number of all returns. This gives the relative frequency or percentage of observed returns in each interval.

Table 19.1 Monthly returns (in %) for a given hedge fund since its inception

	Jan.	Feb.	Mar.	Apr.	May	Jun.	Jul.	Aug.	Sep.	Oct.	Nov.	Dec.
1986								0.47	-5.84	1.04	-0.20	-0.17
1987	5.33	10.63	-2.81	-2.13	-1.37	5.81	2.37	3.27	-2.01	-9.56	-17.46	1.43
1988	1.20	4.34	2.35	3.17	-2.30	5.39	-0.88	-1.65	2.25	2.34	-2.65	3.51
1989	4.72	0.88	0.88	1.93	2.85	0.99	1.44	2.41	-0.34	-3.55	-0.01	0.39
1990	-3.53	-1.85	4.23	-3.35	4.85	0.93	-0.22	-7.97	1.36	2.33	1.34	1.45
1991	5.13	1.70	0.76	0.49	0.93	-0.69	2.10	5.02	2.65	2.35	-1.26	1.24
1992	3.12	1.24	-0.40	1.15	-0.03	-2.49	0.07	0.41	11.87	2.73	1.89	1.95
1993	1.07	2.43	0.34	4.13	1.97	4.61	4.53	1.11	-1.15	5.18	-0.26	8.49
1994	0.45	-6.87	-2.95	-5.45	0.08	-1.19	-1.44	0.51	2.09	-2.31	-2.24	-1.30
1995	-2.05	-0.88	3.43	0.44	0.34	1.25	1.24	3.40	1.74	-1.91	3.62	2.86
1996	4.24	0.86	-0.14	3.32	2.79	-1.70	-6.69	2.90	2.54	1.10	5.22	0.24
1997	4.38	1.63	-2.51	-0.20	4.53	1.95	5.58	0.76	3.76	-0.46	1.08	1.80
1998	0.02	3.80	5.23	-0.04	0.51	2.96	1.57	-7.67	-0.76	-2.73	1.29	2.90
1999	2.07	0.27	2.03	3.95	1.10	0.57	2.17	0.42	-1.02	1.17	7.02	7.24
2000	5.13	2.24	7.38	-6.53	-4.65	-0.86	3.69	2.60	2.00	-0.36	-1.84	3.57
2001	0.23	0.66	-1.43	0.97	0.63	0.55	-1.40	0.16	-0.60	-1.37	0.35	0.99
2002	-0.76	-0.64	-0.11	0.23	0.29	-1.05	-1.32	0.68	-0.38	-0.64	-0.85	1.76
2003	0.18	0.16	-0.72	0.03	1.84	-0.13	-1.05	0.50	1.21	1.34	0.46	2.01
2004	1.11	1.79	1.55	-2.27	-1.89	-0.08	-1.01	0.17	1.32	0.63	2.79	0.91
2005	-0.07	2.21	-0.56	-1.76	-0.12	1.95	2.23	1.34	2.61	-2.26	1.98	2.32

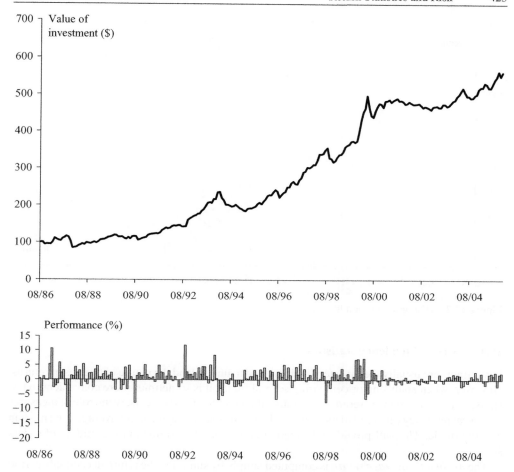

Figure 19.1   Evolution of $100 invested in the fund since its inception (top) and monthly returns (bottom)

- Finally, plot a bar chart, where each bar corresponds to a particular interval of the returns measured (plot horizontally) and the height of a bar represents the relative frequency of occurrence for a particular interval (plot vertically).

As an illustration, Figure 19.2 shows the histogram of monthly returns for our fund as well as a fitted normal distribution. We can observe that the data produce a nice mound or bell shape, with right and left tails that taper off roughly symmetrically, expect for one spike deep in the left tail. The minimum value is around −18%, the maximum value is around +12%, and the central peak lies at around 1%.

Clearly, the histogram is a useful device to provide an overall picture of the information present in the series of monthly returns and to explore the shape of the corresponding distribution. It gives us a picture of what the returns look like without having to deal in detail with the collection of raw returns of Table 19.1.

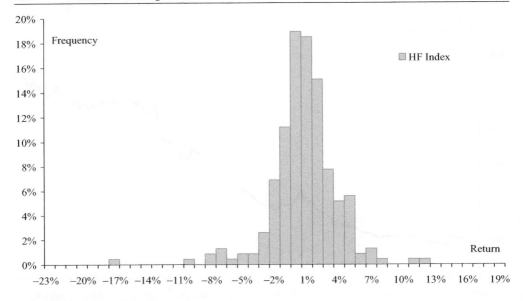

Figure 19.2   Histogram of monthly returns

19.1.1   Central tendency statistics

Histograms are usually the first step implemented to understand the nature of a series of returns. However, when analysing or comparing several funds, it is sometimes more convenient to use statistics to summarize the return series rather than graphs. This is precisely the role of measures of central tendency (also called measures of location) such as the mean (or average), the median and the mode. They all provide information about the observations in the middle of a data set.

The *arithmetic average return* is computed simply by summing the return in each sub-period $(R_{0,1}, R_{1,2}, \ldots, R_{T-1,T})$ and dividing the total by the number of sub-periods T. Each sub-period should have the same length (e.g. one day, one month). Mathematically:

$$\bar{R}^{(A)} = \frac{1}{T} \sum_{t=1}^{T} R_{t-1,t} \tag{19.1}$$

As an illustration, for the fund of Table 19.1, one would obtain an arithmetic mean return equal to:

$$\bar{R}^{(A)} = \frac{1}{233}(0.47\% - 5.84\% + \ldots + 2.32\%) = 0.80\% \text{ per month}$$

An alternative measure of the mean return is the *geometric mean return*, which represents the return that, once compounded, would produce the same holding period return for a given investment. Its formula is more complicated than the arithmetic average, because it accounts for the effect of compounding. It multiplies all the sub-period returns, expressed as $(1 + R_{t,t+1})$, where $R_{t,t+1}$ is the percentage return between time t and time $t + 1$, and takes

---

Box 19.1 Continuously compounded returns are easier to average

Due to their additive nature, continuously compounded returns are easier to average than simple returns. The geometric mean in the domain of simple returns becomes an arithmetic mean in the domain of continuously compounded returns. Hence, to average a series of continuously compounded returns, it is sufficient to add them up and divide the result by the number of values.

$$\bar{r}^{(A)} = \frac{1}{T} \sum_{t=1}^{T} r_{t-1,t} \tag{19.4}$$

The result is a continuously compounded return. Taking the exponential will bring us back to the domain of simple returns, and provides the geometric mean return.

$$\bar{R}^{(G)} = \exp\left(\bar{r}^{(A)}\right) - 1 \tag{19.5}$$

---

the root corresponding to the number of sub-periods T. Mathematically:

$$\bar{R}^{(G)} = \left[(1 + R_{0,1}) \cdot (1 + R_{1,2})...(1 + R_{T-1,T})\right]^{1/T} - 1 \tag{19.2}$$

or equivalently

$$\bar{R}^{(G)} = \left[\prod_{t=0}^{t=T-1} (1 + R_{t,t+1})\right]^{1/T} - 1 \tag{19.3}$$

Using the same data, the geometric mean return of our fund would be equal to:

$$\bar{R}^{(G)} = (1.0047 \times 0.9416 \times \cdots \times 1.0232)^{1/233} - 1 = 0.75\% \text{ per month}$$

Both the arithmetic mean and the geometric mean returns calculated above are monthly figures – they are calculated from monthly data. Annualizing them yields an annual arithmetic mean return of 10.03%, and an annual geometric mean return of 9.41%.

As this example shows, the arithmetic mean and the geometric mean yield different results. Which one should be preferred? Fund managers usually prefer using the arithmetic mean. It is easier to calculate than the geometric mean and results in higher values, which makes their fund look better.[1] However, in reality, the choice between the arithmetic mean and the geometric mean should depend on the context. The arithmetic mean return should be considered appropriate only if the objective is to measure a one-period mean return. On the other hand, if the goal is to obtain the mean return over several successive periods, then the geometric mean is a better measure because it takes compounding into account (see Box 19.1).

In most situations, the arithmetic mean return may be sufficient as a quick approximation to the geometric mean return for rough comparisons of performance. But in the case of applications requiring more precision, the approximation will break down and the geometric mean should be used. As an illustration, consider a hypothetical hedge fund that gained +50% every month for the first 11 months of its existence, and collapsed the next month (−100%). What

---

[1] The only situation where the two averages would be equal is if all monthly returns are identical.

can we say about this fund? The overall return was -100%, that is, the investors lost their entire initial investment. The geometric mean return is -100%. Yet the arithmetic average monthly return is still 37.5%, i.e. $[(11 \times 50\%) - 100\%]/12$.

Hence, the key point to remember is that it is improper to interpret the arithmetic mean return as a measure of the effective mean return over an evaluation period, because it does not account for compounding effects.[2]

The presence of outliers, that is, very high or very low returns, can significantly affect the value of the average. In this case, the *median return* is a better measure of central tendency. The median, as already stated, is simply the middle value in a data set. In the event that there is an even number of data points, the median is calculated by taking the average (mean) of the two middle points. Hence, in any case, unlike the average, the median is not affected by the presence of outliers: if we made the smallest value even smaller or the largest value even larger, it would not change the value of the median. As an illustration, if we take again our fund from Table 19.1, the median monthly return would be 0.88% per month, with 116 values below it and 116 values above it.

A median value that is different from the arithmetic mean signals an asymmetric return distribution. In general, the mean will be pulled in the direction of the skewness. That is, if the right tail is heavier than the left tail, the mean will be greater than the median. Likewise, if the left tail is heavier than the right tail, the mean will be less than the median. In our case, we have 0.80% for the arithmetic mean return and 0.88% for the median monthly return. This implies that the return distribution is skewed to the left. That is, below-average returns occur more frequently than above-average returns. We will see shortly other indicators of asymmetry.

Finally, the last average statistic we will mention in this chapter is called the *mode*. It represents the most frequently occurring observation. It is not widely used in practice for returns, which can take any value, but rather is used for variables that can only take a limited set of values, or that have been grouped in prespecified categories.

19.1.2 Gains versus losses

Several fund managers like to compare their *average gain* with their *average loss*. The average gain is the simple return average (arithmetic mean) of the periods with a gain. It is calculated by summing all observed positive returns and dividing the total by the number of gain periods. Similarly, the average loss is a simple average (arithmetic mean) of the periods with a loss. It is calculated by summing all observed negative returns and dividing the total by the number of loss periods. In our example, the average monthly gain would be equal to +2.28%, while the average loss would be –2.09%.

The *gain-to-loss ratio* is a simple ratio of the average gain divided by the average loss (in absolute value) over a given period. Fund managers often use it to compare winning period returns with losing period returns. Although it is a rather intuitive measure, its interpretation is subject to caution because (i) it hides the relative number of winning and losing periods, and (ii) it does not account for compounding. In our previous example, the gain-to-loss ratio would be 2.28/2.09 = 1.09, which means that, on average, the gains are slightly higher than the losses. However, when one looks at the time series, it is obvious that the manager of the

---

[2] The proper interpretation of the arithmetic mean rate of return is as follows: it is the average value of withdrawals, expressed as a fraction of the initial net asset value that can be made at the end of each sub-period while keeping the initial net asset value intact.

fund had mostly winning (positive) months. Whether this is luck or good management remains to be seen, but for sure it does not transpire from the gain-to-loss ratio.

19.2 MEASURING RISK

We are all familiar with the quip that if you put someone's feet in a bowl of ice and his head under the grill, his feet will be frozen and his head burned, but on average, his body temperature will remain "normal". This image is often used to convey the dangers of using averages to represent a large volume of information. The same principle applies to hedge funds.

Analysing funds solely on the basis of the average returns that they generated is certainly a straightforward way to make comparisons – see, for instance, the league tables showing fund managers ranked according to their returns over the last months or years. But returns alone do not tell the whole story. Central tendency statistics such as the mean return may provide a good indicator of the average behaviour of a sample of returns, but two funds with the same mean return may also have very different behaviours, depending on how representative the mean return is with respect to each individual return. Hence, we need some additional measure(s) to indicate the degree to which individual returns are clustered around, or deviate from, the mean return.

By way of illustration, consider Figure 19.3, which represents the monthly returns of two hedge funds over the period July 1996 to August 2001. The first fund is a market neutral fund active in utility stocks. The second is a long/short fund that focuses on the technology, healthcare and retail sectors.

These two funds have the same average annualized return over the period (about 19%). However, their behaviour differs greatly. In the case of the first fund, the average is quite representative of the individual monthly returns, while the second fund's returns fluctuate widely around their average. Most investors would probably agree that risk is essential and deem the second fund more risky than the first over the period in question. But what do they mean exactly by "more risky"?

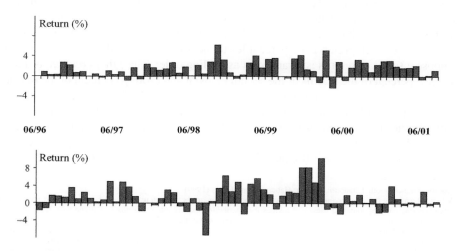

Figure 19.3 Same mean, but different risks!

19.2.1   What is risk?

It is difficult to reach a consensus on how to define risk. Indeed, different investors have different concerns, depending on the nature of their portfolio, the nature of the institution that employs them and their own risk aversion. They therefore perceive risk differently. A pension fund may see risk as the failure to meet its liabilities. An asset manager may perceive risk as a deviation from his benchmark. A statistician may define risk as a potential deviation from the average. And a private investor may consider risky any situation where he may lose money.

As a consequence, ways of measuring risk have proliferated to the point that they have become a matter of confusion for investors, essentially for two reasons. First, different risk measures will produce different rankings for the same set of funds. Second, there is little or no conceptual cohesion between the different approaches to measuring risk, which seem to have been developed completely independently of each other.[3] The reason for this muddle is that different risk measures basically answer different questions. Indeed, there is no fundamental reason for the answer to the question, "What is the fund that has the lowest probability of loss?" being the same as the answer to "What is the fund that has the smallest average deviation from its benchmark?" Nevertheless, all these definitions share common characteristics. They combine uncertainty with the possibility of a loss, disappointment or unsatisfactory outcome.

We attempt below to clarify the issue by discussing in turn the major risk measures that are applied in the hedge fund universe, starting with the simplest. We consider their goals and essential properties, compare their advantages and deficiencies, and illustrate their application. Once again, we attempt to favour intuition over mathematical developments, with the exception of providing a calculation formula for each risk measure.

19.2.2   Range, quartiles and percentiles

The simplest measure of risk is the dispersion of observed returns. The latter is measured by the *range*, which is the distance between the highest and the lowest observed returns. For example, the range of returns for the fund originally introduced in Table 19.1 is 29.33% (the minimum return is -17.46% and the maximum return is $+11.87\%$). This range is easy to measure using a histogram – see Figure 19.2. However, the range is extremely sensitive to the presence of outliers in the data. Furthermore, it only provides information about the maximum and minimum returns, but does not say anything about all the other returns in between. This is why economists often prefer using percentiles to measure the variability of a distribution.

Suppose a series of returns is arranged in ascending order. The *p*th *percentile* is a number such that p percent of the returns of the set fall below it and $(100-p)$ percent of the returns fall above it.[4] The median, by definition, is the 50th percentile. The 25th percentile, the median and the 75th percentile are called *quartiles*. They are often used to describe a data set because they divide the data set into four groups, with each group containing a quarter (25%) of the observations. Alternatively, we could also divide the returns into five equal-size sections and measure *quintiles*, or in 10 equal-size sections and measure *deciles*. Another quantity

---

[3] See for instance Booth, Chadburn, Cooper, Haberman and James (1999).

[4] When determining the *p*th percentiles, problems similar to those for the median usually occur, because most probably the set of observed returns will not contain a value that divides the distribution exactly into proportions of p and $1-p$, respectively. There are then two possibilities: (1) either that variable value can be taken as quartile that leads to proportions closest to the required ones (this is the only possible strategy on an ordinal level of scale; thus an error in the proportions has to be accepted but the quartile is an observed return) or (2) an interpolation rule can be applied to those two variable values leading to the two proportions closest to the required ones. Thus only a virtual value for the quartile is calculated but it has the advantage of diving the distribution exactly as it was required. The less data a set contains, the bigger these problems become.

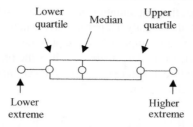

Figure 19.4   A box-and-whiskers plot

often reported is the inter-quartile range, which is equal to the 75th percentile minus the 25th percentile. It is useful because it is less influenced by extreme values, as it limits the range to the middle 50% of the values.

A graphical way to represent the median, the quartile distribution, and extremes of data is the box plot, also known as the box-and-whiskers plot. This is especially helpful in determining visually whether or not there are significant differences between several sets of returns. As an illustration, Figure 19.4 shows the box plot for the fund originally described in Table 19.1. The first quartile is −0.60%, the median is 0.88%, and the third quartile is 2.32%.

19.2.3   Variance and volatility (standard deviation)

Intuitively, over a single period, the risk of an investment should be associated with the possible dispersion of returns around their arithmetic mean, which is denoted $\bar{R}$. The larger the dispersion, the greater the potential risk. While the concept is attractive, its implementation is not. Indeed, the formula for calculating the 'average' dispersion around the mean return is not simple.

At first glance, if we have a series of T returns and we want to measure the dispersion of returns around the mean return, an appealing measure would be the average deviation (AD), calculated algebraically as the expected (E) deviation of the fund's returns from their mean:

$$AD = E(R - \bar{R}) = \frac{1}{T} \sum_{t=1}^{T} (R_{t-1,t} - \bar{R}) \tag{19.6}$$

The problem with this definition is that, whatever the observed returns, this formula will always return a zero value. The reason is simply that the average is by definition at the middle of all observations, so that negative deviations exactly offset positive deviations. This will not get us very far.

To avoid this problem, we may use the *mean absolute deviation*, which is calculated as the expected absolute deviation from the mean:

$$MAD = E|R - \bar{R}| = \frac{1}{T} \sum_{t=1}^{T} |R_{t-1,t} - \bar{R}| \tag{19.7}$$

The term "absolute", represented by vertical dashes in the formula, means that even the negative differences occurring for the data smaller than the average are counted as positive (e.g. a +3% difference stays +3%, but a −3% difference becomes +3%). The average deviation is not very difficult to calculate, and it is intuitively appealing. Some statisticians also use the median instead of the mean. However, the mathematics of absolute values do not have very attractive properties in subsequent statistical analysis, particularly when optimizing portfolios. Hence, we had better look for an alternative approach to the problem

A well-known statistical measure, the *variance*, solves the problem of the deviations averaging to zero. Denoted by the Greek letter sigma (σ), the variance is calculated as the average squared deviation from the mean return:

$$\sigma^2 = E\left(R - \bar{R}\right)^2 = \frac{1}{T-1}\sum_{t=1}^{T}(R_{t-1,t} - \bar{R})^2 \tag{19.8}$$

Squaring the deviations has several advantages. First, squaring makes each term positive so that values above the mean return do not cancel out values below the mean return. Second, squaring adds more weighting to the larger differences, and in many cases this extra weighting is appropriate since points further from the mean return may be more significant in terms of risk.[5] Furthermore, the mathematics of variance are relatively manageable in subsequent statistical calculations (e.g. portfolio optimization). It is therefore not surprising that the first papers in finance adopted variance as a risk measure.

However, the return differences are squared, so that the units of variance are not the same as the units of return. Hence, it is necessary to take the square root of the variance to come back to the same units as the returns. The corresponding quantity is called the *standard deviation* and is denoted by the Greek letter σ:

$$\sigma = \sqrt{\frac{1}{T-1}\sum_{t=1}^{T}(R_{t-1,t} - \bar{R})^2} \tag{19.9}$$

In finance, the standard deviation is referred to as the *volatility* (see Box 19.2).

If we apply equation (19.9) to the return series of Table 19.1, we obtain a volatility figure equal to 3.06%. This corresponds to the volatility of monthly returns. Like returns, volatility figures are generally annualized. To annualize, one needs to multiply the volatility estimated using equation (19.9) by the square root of the observation frequency ($\sqrt{12}$ for monthly observations, $\sqrt{360}$ for daily, etc.). In our case, the annual volatility of the fund would be 10.59% (3.06 times $\sqrt{12}$).

Box 19.2 Some technical remarks on measuring historical volatility

At this point, it is worth making a few technical remarks on the calculation of the volatility. These remarks are not fundamental for the remainder of the chapter, but they provide some answers to questions that are usually left unanswered.

Why ($T - 1$) rather than T?

First, it may be wondered why we divide by ($T - 1$) rather than T when computing the variance in equation (19.8). The reason is purely technical, and lies in the difference that exists between a sample and a population.

---

[5] As a side effect, the variance and standard deviation are very sensitive to extreme returns.

We are working with a sample of T historical returns of a given fund. From this sample, we are trying to infer the variance of the population, that is, the variance of all possible returns (past and future) of the fund in question. The population is not observable, so its variance is not measurable. Hence, we need to estimate it using a statistic that we can produce with our sample.

We could measure the variance of the sample using the more natural formula:

$$\tilde{\sigma}^2 = \frac{1}{T} \sum_{t=1}^{T} (R_{t-1,t} - \bar{R})^2 \tag{19.10}$$

where we divide by T rather than $(T-1)$. The value $\tilde{\sigma}^2$ effectively represents the variance of the series of returns that we have. The problem is that we can show that $\tilde{\sigma}^2$ is a biased estimator of the variance of the population. That is, if you consider all possible samples of size T and average all of the resulting variances, this average will not be the population variance.

The reason is that when we calculate the sample variance, we have already calculated the sample mean return. Hence, in reality, we do not have T different returns free to vary, but only $(T-1)$ if the mean return is to stay constant. In a sense, the Tth return is already specified by the $(T-1)$ other returns and the mean return. Hence, since there are only $(T-1)$ choices ("degrees of freedom"), we need to divide by $(T-1)$ rather than T when estimating the population variance.

Which average, geometric or arithmetic, should we use?

The second remark concerns the type of average return to use in the calculation of the variance. Should we use the arithmetic or the geometric average? So far, we have used the arithmetic average because we were only considering single-period applications. However, from a theoretical point of view, the real answer is rather surprising: neither of them. Because of the compounding property of simple returns, it does not make any sense to add up simple return differences. We should compound these differences, not add them up. And the use of an arithmetic average or geometric average does not change the question in any way.

The correct calculation of volatility is actually much easier using continuously compounded returns, due to their additive property. First, calculate the standard deviation of continuously compounded returns (σ_{cc})

$$\sigma_{cc} = \sqrt{\frac{1}{T-1} \sum_{t=1}^{T} \left(r_{t-1,t} - \bar{r}^{(A)}\right)^2} \tag{19.11}$$

where $\bar{r}^{(A)}$ is the arithmetic average of continuously compounded returns. Note that we do not need to compound returns, because they are continuously compounded.

Then, go back to the simple return universe by taking the exponential of the log-return standard deviation.

$$\sigma = \exp(\sigma_{cc}) - 1 \tag{19.12}$$

This will provide a return volatility estimate that accounts for all compounding effects. As an illustration, the volatility we would obtain for the fund of Table 19.1 is 3.16% per month or 11.31% per year, versus 3.06% per month using the simple returns and equation (19.8).

In practice, the difference between the correctly calculated volatility and the one given by equation (19.8) is usually negligible, so that most people prefer to ignore it and stick to the simpler formula. This is acceptable as long as all volatilities are wrongly calculated in the same way. Hence, all volatilities will be biased the same way, so apples will be compared with apples in a sense, even though they may be bruised.

How about the annualization procedure?

You guessed it. The method commonly used – multiplying the monthly standard deviation by the square root of 12 – is also only an approximation, which becomes inaccurate when the compounding effect is marked. The problem with this procedure is that the annualized return used in the calculation is itself a non-compounded return, determined from a series of returns that are in reality compounding.

As an illustration of the problem, consider a fictive investment strategy that has an average return of 100% per month with a monthly volatility of 100%. If the return distribution is normal, one can show that there is a 15% probability of negative monthly returns. When proceeds are reinvested every month, the expected value for the annual return is $(1 + 100\%)^{12} - 1 = 4.095\%$. Applying the $\sqrt{T}$ rule to find the annual volatility gives $\sqrt{12} \times 100\% \approx 346\%$. The distribution for the annual return is narrow, and the probability of having negative returns has become negligible. Clearly, there is something wrong with the $\sqrt{12}$ rule. Whatever the accumulated capital is at the end of the 11th month, for the 12th month, we should expect again about a 15% probability of losing all of it since all the capital is reinvested for the 12th month. Interested readers can find the derivation of the correct formula for annualizing the volatility in Janssen (2000).

How many data points?

Finally, another important question in assessing volatility is the choice of an observation period and the frequency of the observed data. Depending on the choices made, a variety of estimates for the volatility figure can be obtained. The difficulty when using historical volatility is the implicit trade-off between the number of observations chosen (T) and the window of data used. If volatility is stationary over time, then the choice of T is irrelevant, and T should be chosen as large as possible to maximize accuracy in the estimation process, since more information will enhance estimation. If volatility is not stationary, a compromise has to be found between using long measurement intervals that will give stable figures, but are very slow to reflect structural changes, and using short measurement intervals that reflect changing circumstances rapidly, but are very noisy. In a sense, the choice is between accurately estimating a biased quantity and inaccurately estimating the real value. The issue is particularly important with hedge funds, whose returns are only observable on a monthly basis. As a rule of thumb, a volatility figure calculated with less than 24 data points makes no sense and should be considered as irrelevant.

19.2.4   Back to histograms, return distributions and z-scores

Interpreting an average return or a volatility figure using a histogram is relatively easy, particularly if the histogram is similar to a bell-shaped curve. In this case, it is tempting to approximate the histogram to a normal return distribution – see Figure 19.5.

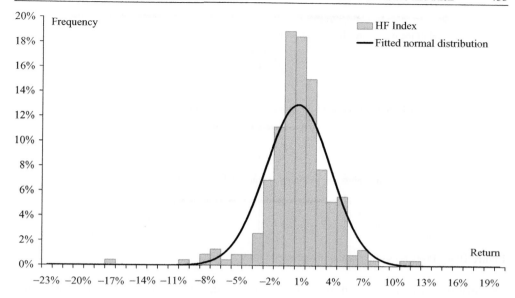

Figure 19.5   Histogram of returns and the corresponding normal distribution

The normal distribution, also known as the Gaussian distribution, is the most widely used general-purpose distribution, because it has several very attractive statistical properties.

- All normal distributions have the same general shape, the "bell-shaped curve". Each normal distribution is characterized by only two parameters: the mean and the standard deviation. Once these parameters are known, the distribution is completely specified.
- In a normal distribution, the mean (average), median and mode are equal, so that the distribution is symmetrical around the mean. That is, if we draw a vertical line through the mean, one side of the distribution is a mirror image of the other. Furthermore, half of the observations are above the average return and half below the average return.
- A theorem called the central limit theorem tells us that sums of random variables are approximately normally distributed if the number of observations is large. Thus, even when the distribution is not exactly normal, it may still be convenient to assume that a normal distribution is a good approximation. In this case, all the statistical procedures developed for the normal distribution can still be used.

When an empirical distribution is approximated to a normal distribution, the density curve of the normal distribution acts as a smoothed-out histogram or an idealized picture of the original distribution. In particular, the area under the normal density curve gives the proportion of observations that fall within a particular range of values. The proportions obtained from the density curve will not equal the observed proportions exactly, but if the normal is a good approximation, the proportions should be close enough to the originals.

This is particularly useful, because the area under any normal density curve is perfectly determined: 68.26% of the total number of observations fall within one standard deviation of the mean, 95.44% within two standard deviations of the mean, and 99.73% within three standard deviations of the mean. These percentages (as well as those for other multiples of

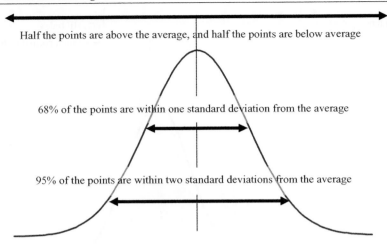

Half the points are above the average, and half the points are below average

68% of the points are within one standard deviation from the average

95% of the points are within two standard deviations from the average

Figure 19.6   Properties of a normal distribution

the volatility) are easily found in a standard normal distribution table. With their help, it is relatively easy to estimate the probability of any range of returns.

Say, for instance, that our target return is 5%, and the distribution of returns has a mean of 8% and a volatility of 12%. A quick calculation shows us that 5% is 0.25 standard deviations below the mean of 8%, as $(5\% - 8\%)/12\% = -0.25$. This value is called a z-score, or standard score. It is often used to compare values from different data sets (e.g. different mean and volatility) or to compare values within the same data set. Basically, it is the number of standard deviations by which a given value is above or below the mean.

Looking in a statistical table for the standard normal distribution, we can observe that 40.15% of the area under a normal distribution is to the left of the mean minus 0.25 standard deviations. Hence, assuming normally distributed returns, there is a 40.15% chance of experiencing a return that is less than 5%.

Assuming normally distributed returns is extremely appealing to researchers and practitioners alike because normal distributions have well-known mathematical properties that make them easy to process and understand (Figure 19.6). However, in practice, it is worth considering how good such an approximation is. Empirical observation of financial markets has often revealed that large movements occur more frequently than would be expected if returns were normally distributed. For instance, the 1987 equity crash recorded negative returns that were over 20 standard deviations from the mean (relative to the conventional measures of volatility just prior to the crash). In addition, most return distributions are also skewed, meaning that there is a greater likelihood of the portfolio yielding either higher or lower returns than would be expected under normal distribution conditions.

A histogram is again an effective graphical tool for visualizing such deviations from normality in a data set. In addition, two statistics, known as skewness and kurtosis, may be used to quantify these effects.

Skewness is the third central moment of a distribution.[6] It measures the symmetry of a return distribution around its mean. Zero skewness indicates a symmetrical distribution. A positively skewed distribution is the outcome of rather small losses but larger gains, so it has a long tail

---

[6] The mean is the first central moment and the variance, which equals standard deviation squared, is the second moment.

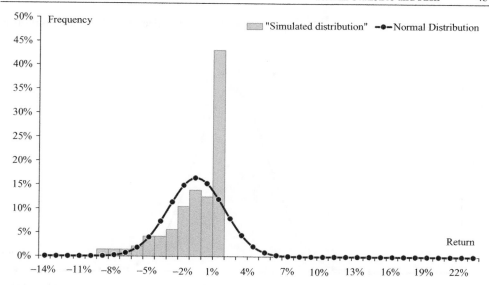

Figure 19.7   An example of a skewed return distribution

on the right-hand side of the distribution, which is usually desirable (Figure 19.7). Conversely, a negatively skewed distribution is the outcome of many small gains but larger losses, so it has a long tail on the left-hand side of the distribution, which is usually not desirable.

Mathematically, the skewness is calculated as:

$$\text{Skewness} = \frac{T}{(T-1)(T-2)} \sum_{t=1}^{T} \left(\frac{R_{t-1,t} - \bar{R}}{\sigma} \right)^3 \tag{19.13}$$

where T is the number of observations. The measure is free of units but preserves the sign of the deviation of the observation from the mean. As a reference, the standard normal distribution is perfectly symmetrical and has a skewness coefficient equal to zero.

Kurtosis is the fourth central moment of a distribution. It measures the degree of peakedness and heaviness of the tails of a distribution (Figure 19.8). On the one hand, distributions where a large proportion of the observed values lie towards the extremes are said to be "platykurtic" or display positive kurtosis. Graphically, they display a distinct peak near the mean, decline rather rapidly, and have heavy tails. If, on the other hand, the observed values are clustered near the mean, the distribution is said to be "leptokurtic" or display negative kurtosis. Graphically, they display a flat top near the mean rather than a sharp peak – a uniform distribution would be the extreme case. In contrast, a normal distribution is said to be "mesokurtic" and has a kurtosis value equal to zero.

Formally, the kurtosis is defined as:

$$\text{Kurtosis} = \frac{T(T+1)}{(T-1)(T-2)(T-3)} \sum_{t=1}^{T} \left(\frac{R_{t-1,t} - \bar{R}}{\sigma} \right)^4 - \frac{3(T-1)^2}{(T-2)(T-3)} \tag{19.16}$$

where T is the number of observations.[7] The measure is free of units but is always positive regardless of sign of the deviation of the observation from the mean.

---

[7] Note that some analysts do not subtract the second term from the kurtosis. As a result, when T is large, the threshold value for the normal distribution becomes 3 rather than 0.

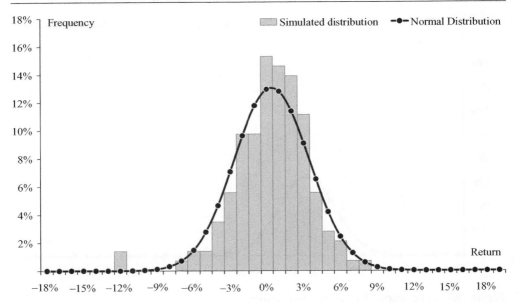

Figure 19.8   An example of a return distribution with kurtosis (the left tail of the distribution is too thick due to several crashes)

The normal distribution has skewness and kurtosis values equal to zero. Thus, it is fully described by its first two central moments, the mean and standard deviation. Distributions that exhibit skewness and kurtosis need more than the mean and standard deviation to be characterized (Box 19.3).

Box 19.3 Another technical question

Once again, one may wonder why we are dividing by $(T - 1)$, $(T - 2)$, etc. in equations (19.13) and (19.14). The reason is similar to the $(T - 1)$ argument for the variance. We are working with a sample of returns, and we are trying to estimate the skewness and kurtosis of the population. One can show that the more intuitive estimators

$$\tilde{S} = \frac{1}{T} \sum_{t=1}^{T} \left(\frac{R_{t-1,t} - \bar{R}}{\sigma} \right)^3 \tag{19.14}$$

and

$$\tilde{K} = \frac{1}{T} \sum_{t=1}^{T} \left(\frac{R_{t-1,t} - \bar{R}}{\sigma} \right)^4 - 3 \tag{19.15}$$

work perfectly in the sample, but are biased estimators of the skewness and kurtosis of the population.

Box 19.4 The Bera-Jarque test

The Bera-Jarque test evaluates the hypothesis that a series of returns has a normal distribution with unspecified mean and variance, against the alternative hypothesis that the series of returns does not have a normal distribution. Intuitively, for a normal distribution, the sample skewness should be near 0 and the sample kurtosis should be near 3. The Bera-Jarque combines skewness and kurtosis into a single statistic and determines whether the latter is unusually different from its expected value.

The Bera-Jarque statistic is defined as

$$BJ = \frac{T}{6}\left[\text{Skewness}^2 + \frac{\text{Kurtosis}^2}{4}\right] \tag{19.17}$$

The Bera-Jarque statistic follows a chi-square distribution with two degrees of freedom. If the value of BJ calculated from a sample is greater than a critical value, the null hypothesis of asymptotic normality is rejected. The relevant critical value depends on the level of significance desired. For instance, for a level of significance of 5%, the critical value is 5.99; for a level of significance of 1%, the critical value is 9.21. Note that the Bera-Jarque test is an asymptotic test, and should not be used with very small samples.

Armed with the estimated skewness and kurtosis of a distribution, it is possible to run a battery of statistical tests to verify if the assumption of normality is plausible. Among these, the Bera-Jarque (1987) test is one of the most popular – see Box 19.4.

19.3 DOWNSIDE RISK MEASURES

19.3.1 From volatility to downside risk

Intuitively, volatility seems an appealing measure of risk. It is easily calculated, based on well-known statistical concepts and is easily interpretable: it measures how consistently a series of returns was delivered in the past. Naturally, the implicit theory is that the more consistently returns occurred in the past, the more likely it is that the investor will receive similar returns in the future. However, volatility also has some drawbacks as a measure of risk.

First, volatility measures only the dispersion of returns around their historical average. Since positive and negative deviations from the average are penalized equally in the calculation process, the concept only makes sense for symmetrical distributions. Most investors will feel comfortable with this symmetry assumption, because they recall normal distribution from their introduction to statistics. However, in practice, most return distributions are neither normal nor even symmetrically distributed. This creates problems, because even though two investments may have the same mean and volatility, they may significantly differ in terms of their higher moments such as skewness and kurtosis. This is particularly the case for: (i) dynamic trading strategies, such as portfolio insurance and stop losses; (ii) strategies involving buying or selling options; and (iii) strategies that actively manage their leverage. All these strategies are likely to be used by hedge funds and they create asymmetries and "fat tails" in return distributions that render the volatility less meaningful and require asymmetric risk considerations.

Second, it is questionable how relevant the dispersion of returns around an average is from an investor's standpoint. Indeed, this runs contrary to the way most investors feel about returns. Few investors fret about their portfolios doubling. Most only perceive risk as a failure to achieve a specific goal, such as the risk-free rate or a benchmark rate. The level of this rate may vary from one investor to another, but the failure carries certain consequences. For instance, a pension fund that fails to achieve a minimum return may have to raise contributions. It would only consider "risk" as the downside of the return distribution, the upside being "success", "talent" or just "luck". Volatility clearly does not capture this distinction.

Finally, the third argument against volatility is that investors are often more adverse to negative deviations than they are pleased with positive ones of the same magnitude.[8] This calls for a heavier weight on negative returns, whereas in calculating volatility, deviations above and below the mean return are given weights equal to their probability of occurring. Therefore, even when the distribution is symmetrical, volatility will not be in line with investors' perceptions.

As a result of these limitations, misleading conclusions may easily be drawn when analysing an investment using standard deviation alone. Just as an illustration, consider the case of a position combining a long stock protected by an at-the-money put option. Even though we assume a normally distributed stock return distribution, the protected stock distribution is not normal any more, but is positively skewed. Its downside risk is limited, while its upside potential is still virtually unlimited. The problem when using the volatility of such a position is simply that it no longer measures the risk! Since the downside is limited, an increase in the volatility can simply arise from outliers on the right side of the distribution, that is, from an increased probability of higher returns. Uncertainty is therefore greater, but risk clearly remains the same.

These major drawbacks of volatility as a measure of risk explain why investors and researchers have developed several alternative risk measures.

Unlike standard deviation, downside risk measures attempt to define risk more in accordance with the investor's perception. That is, they consider that returns above a prespecified target represent an opportunity rather than a financial risk, while variability of returns below this target is precisely what we should call risk – see Figure 19.9.

Hence, investors should be interested in minimizing downside risk rather than volatility for at least two reasons: (i) only downside risk or safety first is relevant to an investor and (ii) security distributions may not be normally distributed, so that variance does not perform well as a risk measure. Therefore a downside risk measure would help investors make proper decisions when faced with non-normal security return distributions.[9]

19.3.2   Semi-variance and semi-deviation

The calculation of a downside risk measure parallels that of variance and standard deviation. Starting from a sample of T returns $(R_{0,1}, R_{1,2}, \ldots, R_{T-1,T})$, the difference between each return $R_{t-1,t}$ and the prespecified target rate of return R^* is computed. These differences are then squared and averaged. This gives a form of downside variance. Taking the square root yields the downside risk.

---

[8] This is called "prospect theory", and was originally conceptualized by Kahneman and Tversky (1979).

[9] When distributions are normally distributed and, more generally, when distributions are symmetrical, both the downside risk measure and the variance provide the same measure of risk. In a sense, the downside risk will be equal to the upside potential.

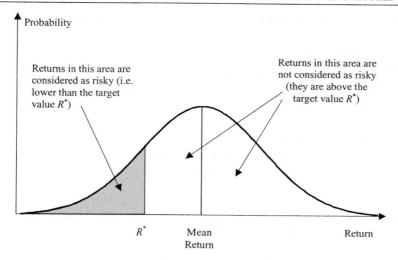

Figure 19.9   Measuring downside risk on the return distribution

Mathematically:

$$\text{Downside risk}_P = \frac{1}{T}\sqrt{\sum_{t=1}^{T} d_{t-1,t}^2} \qquad (19.18)$$

where

$$d_{t-1,t} = \begin{cases} R^* - R_{t-1,t} & \text{if } R_{t-1,t} < R^* \\ 0 & \text{otherwise} \end{cases} \qquad (19.19)$$

Unlike standard deviation, downside risk accommodates different subjective views of risk by changing the target rate R^*. However, it is obvious that the choice of a specific target rate will have a large influence on the downside risk measure, and therefore on its accuracy and stability.[10] In practice, investors often set R^* equal to the average (historical) return, zero, or a given moving target such as the risk-free rate or any benchmark rate.

• When R^* is set equal to the average return, the corresponding downside risk measure is called the below-mean semi-deviation, or *semi-deviation*; its square is called the below-mean semi-variance or *semi-variance*. Markowitz (1959) already considered it as a valuable alternative to volatility for those who are concerned about below-average performance, but he did not apply it in his ground-breaking analysis. The reasons were essentially that (i) computing power in the 1950s was insufficient to deal with the corresponding calculations; and (ii) with normally distributed returns, semi-deviation is proportional to volatility and provides no greater insight into the relative risk of different assets or portfolios. Subsequently, the improvement in computing power and the gradual realization that returns were not normal

---

[10] Stability implies that, whatever the target rate chosen, the value of the downside risk will change by only an infinitesimal amount as we vary the target rate. Graphically, this means that the graph of the downside risk as a function of the target rate is approximately horizontal around the chosen point (or "locally stable", as some would say).

led to the development of semi-deviation-based portfolio theories. However, semi-deviation has the major drawback that it is only observable *ex-post*, i.e. once things have happened, because it requires the average return.

- When the target rate R^* is set at zero, the corresponding measure captures the variability of negative returns (i.e. losses). This measure is often used in the case of risk-averse private clients who are particularly worried about the risk of losing money.
- Finally, when the target rate R^* is set equal to a moving target such as the risk-free rate or a market index, the corresponding measure captures the variability of returns below a benchmark. It is called the below-target semi-deviation and its square is called the below-target semi-variance. This measure of risk is of particular interest to institutional investors, who typically have minimum return requirements and are benchmarked against reference indices.

After proposing the semi-variance measures, Markowitz (1959) stayed with the variance measure because it was computationally simpler. In addition, all the modern portfolio theories developed in the 1960s assumed normally distributed returns, that is, a particular case in which the below-mean semi-variance should be one-half of the variance.[11] Nevertheless, research on semi-variance did continue, both by practitioners and by academics. Other more intuitive downside risk statistics were developed to provide investors with more information than simply a downside deviation number. They also offer insight into the causes of the risk. These include:

- The *downside frequency*, which tells investors how often returns fall below the minimum target return. It helps investors to assess accurately the likelihood of a bad outcome.
- The *gain standard deviation*, which is similar to standard deviation except that it calculates an average (mean) return only for the periods with a *gain* and then measures the variation of only the *gaining* periods around this gain mean. In a sense, the gain standard deviation measures the volatility of upside performance.
- The *loss standard deviation*, which measures the volatility of downside performance. It calculates an average (mean) return only for the periods with a *loss* and then measures the variation of only the *losing* periods around this loss mean.

Although downside risk measures can provide additional insight into the risk profile of potential investments, downside risk is only slowly gaining acceptance in the financial community. There are essentially two reasons for this. First, as we mentioned earlier, in the context of normal distributions, downside risk measures are simply proportional to volatility and do not add much information. Most investors feel comfortable assuming normal distributions, even though this is not very realistic in practice. Second, many practitioners have just adopted standard deviation as a risk measure and they are reluctant to embrace another measurement tool that could yield conflicting results. This is accentuated by the fact that there are a number of ways to calculate downside risk, each of which can potentially yield different results. It is therefore essential that individuals interpreting downside risk statistics understand the calculation methodology because downside risk statistics calculated using different assumptions are not comparable.

---

[11] In fact, taking the variance and dividing it by the below-mean semi-variance yields an alternative measure of skewness. If the ratio is not equal to 2, then there is evidence that the distribution is skewed or asymmetric.

19.3.3   The shortfall risk measures

The starting point of *shortfall risk measures* is a target return denoted R^* and predefined by the investor. Risk is then to be considered to be the possibility of not attaining this target return. Special cases of shortfall risk measures are the shortfall probability, the shortfall expectation and the shortfall variance.

The shortfall probability is the probability of a fund's returns dipping below the target R^*. Mathematically:

$$\text{Risk} = \text{Probability}\,(R_{t,t+1} < R^*) \tag{19.20}$$

The target rate R^* may be static (e.g. equal to zero) or stochastic (e.g. equal to an inflation rate, the risk-free rate or a market index return). The concept is therefore relative rather than absolute. Investment strategies that minimize the shortfall probability are referred to as "probability maximizing strategies", in that they maximize the probability of reaching the investment goal.

Note that the shortfall probability only evaluates the probability of a shortfall with respect to the target but does not evaluate the potential extent of this shortfall. Hence, to assess how severe an undesirable event might be, shortfall probabilities are often accompanied by an indication of the maximum loss or the average shortfall (that is, the expected value of the underperformance, conditional on being below the benchmark rate), as well as by the shortfall variance (that is, the variance of the underperformance, conditional on being below the benchmark rate).

19.3.4   Value at risk

Value at risk (VaR) is a relatively recent risk measure in finance, but its equivalent has been used for several years in statistics. Simply stated, the value at risk of a position is the maximum amount of capital that the position can expect to lose within a specified holding period (e.g. 10 days or one month) and with a specified confidence level (e.g. 95% or 99%). In terms of probability theory, VaR at the p percent confidence level is the $(1 - p)\%$ quantile of the profit and loss distribution. Note that VaR is often expressed as a percentage loss rather than as in absolute dollar loss to facilitate comparisons.

An example will make this clearer – see Figure 19.10. Say we want to compute the one-month 99% value at risk of the Morgan Stanley Capital Index USA, from December 1969 to October 2000, using monthly non-annualized data. All that needs to be done is to observe the series of one-month returns for the stock, build up the corresponding return distribution, and exclude 1% of the cases as being "abnormal" market conditions. The worst-case remaining return (-9.6%) is the value at risk of the index, expressed in percentage terms. It corresponds to the 1% percentile of the return distribution, i.e. 1% of the observed values are lower than the VaR and 99% are higher than the VaR.

When the distribution of returns is a normal distribution,[12] VaR is simply equal to the average return minus a multiple of the volatility (e.g. for a confidence level of 99%, VaR is equal to the average return minus 2.33 times the standard deviation). In this case, the concept of VaR does not generate any new information; it is just a different, less technical form of risk reporting, in which the term "volatility" is replaced by the perhaps easier to understand term "value

---

[12] More generally, this holds for all elliptic probability distributions.

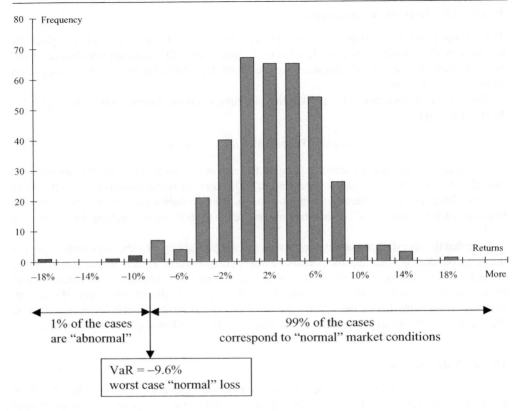

Figure 19.10 Graphical interpretation of value at risk

at risk" (Box 19.5). However, it is well known that in practice, the assumption of a normal distribution is questionable for most assets, and particularly for hedge funds. It is therefore not surprising that VaR has become the standard tool in risk management for banks and other financial institutions.

However, without the assumption of a normal distribution, VaR is a very problematic risk measure. In particular, VaR may violate second-order stochastic dominance and therefore does not always describe risk aversion in the traditional sense – see Guthoff *et al.* (1998). But more importantly, VaR is not sub-additive – see Artzner *et al.* (1997, 1999). That is, the sum of the risks of two separate funds (X and Y) may be lower than the risk of the pooled portfolio ($X + Y$). Mathematically,

$$\text{VaR}(X + Y) \geq \text{VaR}(X) + \text{VaR}(Y). \tag{19.21}$$

Consider as an illustration two funds F_1 and F_2 and 10 possible scenarios. Table 19.2 shows the losses of funds F_1 and F_2 in each scenario. Clearly, the value at risk at an 85% confidence level violates the sub-additivity property. This creates an incentive to divide the two-fund portfolio into single-fund sub-portfolios to lower the apparent level of risk. This lack of sub-additivity makes VaR a problematic criterion for portfolio optimization, the internal allocation of capital, and for the design of VaR-type risk-adjusted compensation schemes.

Box 19.5 Calculating VaR in practice

To calculate the VaR of a portfolio, one needs to specify the duration of the holding period and the desired probability level – say one month and 99%. Then, the estimation of the VaR is generally a three-step process: (i) evaluate the portfolio returns; (ii) estimate the distribution of gains and losses over the given holding period; and (iii) calculate the VaR from this distribution.

There exist several methods to estimate the return distribution of a portfolio, and most of them imply a trade-off between simple assumptions and accurate modelling. The most frequent methods are:

- *Closed form VaR* or *parametric VaR* assumes that all returns on all assets are normally distributed, so that the portfolio returns are also normally distributed. Consequently, the VaR can easily be calculated from the volatilities and correlations of the underlying assets.
- *Historical VaR* assumes that history will repeat itself in the future. It therefore calculates the VaR by looking at how the portfolio would have behaved in the past.
- *Monte-Carlo VaR* relies on the simulation of portfolio returns to obtain the return distribution, and therefore the VaR. It usually involves the specification of stochastic processes and their parameters.

Last, but not least, VaR provides no information about the expected size of the loss beyond the considered "normal market conditions". This is why VaR is often complemented by the *expected shortfall* (or conditional VaR), which measures the expected loss of a portfolio conditional on the portfolio loss exceeding the VaR. An interesting discussion of expected shortfall is Rockafellar and Uryasev (2002). Note that one can easily show that the expected shortfall is sub-additive.

Table 19.2 The VaR is not necessarily sub-additive. In this example, the VaR of the combined investments is larger than the sum of individual VaRs

Scenario	Loss F_1	Loss F_2	Loss $(F_1 + F_2)$
1	0	0	0
2	0	0	0
3	0	0	0
4	0	0	0
5	0	0	0
6	0	0	0
7	0	0	0
8	0	0	0
9	0	-1	-1
10	-1	0	-1
VaR$_{85\%}$	0	0	-1

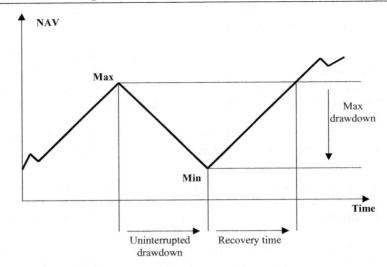

Figure 19.11   The drawdown concept

19.3.5   Drawdown statistics

Another key measure of track record quality and/or strategy risk is the notion of drawdown, which is defined as the decline in net asset value from the highest historical point. Often expressed as a percentage loss, it can be interpreted as the "regret" an investor would have for not selling at the highest price (see Figure 19.11).

There are in fact several ways of calculating drawdown statistics. An individual *drawdown* is basically any losing period during an investment record. The *maximum drawdown* or "*peak to valley*" is therefore the maximum loss (in percentage terms) that an investor could have experienced within a specific time period. The *uninterrupted drawdown* calculates the length and severity of an uninterrupted drop. The *recovery time* or *drawdown duration* is the time taken to recover from a drawdown and come back to the original level. By looking at the size and duration of past drawdowns (expressed as a percentage of portfolio value), an investor can realistically assess the pain he would feel with that fund manager, were the situation to recur.

Drawdowns have one major advantage over volatility: they refer to a physical reality, and as such they are less abstract. In the US, the Commodity Futures Trading Commission requires managed futures advisers to disclose their maximum drawdown. However, a large number of hedge fund managers also voluntarily disclose this statistic to evidence the quality of their track record. As an illustration, Table 19.3 shows the list of drawdowns larger than 1% experienced on the CSFB/Tremont Hedge Fund Index since its inception in 1994.

Despite their intuitive nature, maximum drawdown statistics should be used with caution, for at least two reasons.

- Other things being equal, maximum drawdowns will be greater as the frequency of the measurement interval becomes smaller. Inter-month drawdowns are lower than daily drawdowns, and quarterly drawdowns are even lower, because the NAV curve is smoothed out the greater the measurement interval. Thus, investments that are marked to market daily, such as managed futures or traditional assets, may thus appear at a disadvantage to less

Table 19.3 List of drawdowns larger than 1% experienced by the CSFB/Tremont since its inception in January 1994

Peak date	Trough date	Decline (%)	Recovery date	Decline duration (months)	Recovery duration (months)
Jul-98	Oct-98	−13.81	Nov-99	3	13
Jan-94	Apr-94	−9.13	Jul-95	3	15
Feb-00	May-00	−7.74	May-01	3	12
Jun-96	Jul-96	−4.13	Sep-96	1	2
Jan-96	Feb-96	−3.59	Apr-96	1	2
May-02	Jul-02	−2.18	Dec-02	2	5
Sep-97	Oct-97	−1.64	Dec-97	1	2
Sep-05	Oct-05	−1.46	Nov-5	1	1
Feb-97	Mar-97	−1.41	Apr-97	1	1
Jul-97	Aug-97	−1.26	Sep-97	1	1
Dec-97	Jan-98	−1.21	Feb-98	1	1

frequently valued investments (e.g. hedge funds). Hence, it is never appropriate to compare maximum drawdowns between time series with different reporting intervals without making an appropriate correction.

- Other things being equal, maximum drawdowns will be greater for a longer time series, so that managers with longer track records will tend to have deeper maximum drawdown figures. Hence, it is never appropriate to compare maximum drawdowns between time series with different time lengths.

In addition, one should remember that the maximum drawdown is a single number derived from a single string of data without any sort of averaging process. Because of the uniqueness of that observation, the result is highly error-prone and thus not necessarily very useful in building statistical inferences for the future. From a statistical perspective, a better risk measure would be the average of a series of largest drawdowns. Last, but not least, one should remember that the maximum drawdown cannot identify the current risk in a portfolio until after losses occur.

19.4   BENCHMARK-RELATED STATISTICS

Although they are sold as absolute performers, hedge funds often produce ratios that compare their performance with that of a selected market index or benchmark. Some of these ratios do not rely on any statistical or financial theory, but are just intuitive by nature. Others find their roots in the origins of financial theory. In the following, we will only list the essential ones.

19.4.1   Intuitive benchmark-related statistics

Among the popular ratios on the investor side are the following:

- The *capture indicator*, which is the average of the captured performance (that is, the average ratio between the fund's returns and the benchmark's returns). It is somewhat hard to interpret, because conclusions depend upon the sign of the benchmark's returns.
- The *up capture indicator*, which is calculated as the fund's average return divided by the benchmark average return, considering only periods when the benchmark was up. The greater the value the better.

- The *down capture indicator*, which is the fund's average return divided by the benchmark average return, considering only periods when the benchmark was down. The smaller the ratio the better.
- The *up number ratio*, which measures the number of periods in which the fund was up when the benchmark was up, divided by the number of periods in which the benchmark was up. The larger the ratio the better.
- The *down number ratio*, which measures the number of periods in which the fund was down when the benchmark was down, divided by the number of periods in which the benchmark was down. The smaller the ratio the better.
- The *up percentage ratio*, which measures the number of periods in which the fund outperformed the benchmark when the benchmark was up, divided by the number of periods when the benchmark was up. The larger the ratio the better.
- The *down percentage ratio*, which is a measure of the number of periods in which the fund outperformed the benchmark when the benchmark was down, divided by the number of periods when the benchmark was down. The larger the ratio the better.
- The *percent gain ratio*, which is a measure of the number of periods in which the fund was up divided by the number of periods in which the benchmark was up. The larger the ratio the better.
- The *ratio of negative months over total months*, which is also a good indicator of the downside risk of a fund, although it neglects the absolute size of returns in positive and negative months.

As an illustration, Table 19.4 shows the values obtained for the fund considered in Table 19.1. The "benchmark" used for the calculations is the S&P 500.

19.4.2   Beta and market risk

Another interesting relative risk measure is called beta (see Figure 19.12) and is denoted by the Greek symbol β. Simply stated, beta measures how risky a fund may be as compared to the overall stock market, typically approximated to the Standard and Poor's 500 or the MSCI World. A fund that moves in harmony with the market is said to have a beta of 1.0. Other things being equal, if the market goes up 10%, the fund is expected to go up 10%. If the market goes down 10%, the fund is expected to go down 10%. When a fund has a beta that is less than 1, it is supposed to move less in price than the market in general. Conversely, a fund with a beta higher than 1 is supposed to move more in price than the market in general. Hence,

Table 19.4   Intuitive benchmark-related statistics for the fund of Table 19.1

Capture indicator	0.98
• Up capture	0.51
• Down capture	0.22
Up number ratio	0.79
Down number ratio	0.56
Up percentage ratio	0.29
Down percentage ratio	0.82
Percent gain ratio	0.91
Negative months over total	34%

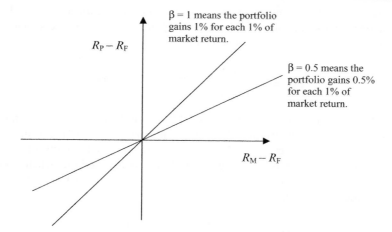

Figure 19.12   Interpreting beta as the slope of a regression line when plotting the excess returns of a portfolio $(R_P - R_F)$ against the excess returns of the market $(R_M - R_F)$

beta measures the risk of a fund by telling us how much its market price changes compared to changes in the overall stock market. A fund with a beta of more than 1 tends to be riskier than the market, while a fund with a beta of less than 1 is less risky.

As an illustration, the beta of the fund we considered in Table 19.1 was 0.36 against the S&P 500, which is rather low. This is not really surprising, because most hedge funds claim to deliver absolute performance, that is, returns that are independent of market conditions. Hence, they should display low levels of beta in general.

It is essential at this stage to understand that beta focuses only on the impact of the overall stock market, and ignores all other influences, which are considered as specific risk. In a sense, beta is an incomplete explanation of risk and returns. A low beta fund does not necessarily mean low risk. It simply means low exposure to the market, or more simply, low market risk. A fund that has a low beta and a high volatility is an indication that most of the risk carried by the fund is not coming from market movements, but is completely specific.

19.4.3   Tracking error

Tracking error (TE) is one of the most commonly used measures in traditional fund management, where performance is usually evaluated against a prespecified benchmark portfolio. Tracking error quantifies precisely the degree to which the performance of a fund differs from that of its benchmark. The lower the tracking error, the more the fund resembles its benchmark's risk and return characteristics. Although the concept is simple, readers should be aware that there are several definitions of the tracking error in financial literature.

Tracking error is sometimes defined as differences between the fund returns and the benchmark portfolio returns – see Hwang and Satchell (2001). For this definition, a positive tracking error is synonymous of outperforming the benchmark.

$$\mathrm{TE}_{\mathrm{Diff}} = \frac{1}{T} \sum_{t=1}^{T} \left(R_{t-1,t} - R_{t-1,t}^{\mathrm{benchmark}} \right) \tag{19.22}$$

Tracking error can be defined as the standard deviation of the returns difference between the fund and the benchmark portfolio. In this case, a high tracking error reflects a large deviation (either positive or negative) from the benchmark.

$$\text{TE}_{\text{SD}} = \sqrt{\frac{1}{T-1} \sum_{t=1}^{T} \left(R_{t-1,t} - R_{t-1,t}^{\text{benchmark}} \right)^2} \tag{19.23}$$

Rudolf *et al.* (1999) argue that the quadratic form of TE_{SD} is difficult to interpret, and that portfolio managers typically think in terms of linear and not quadratic deviation from a benchmark. Hence, they suggest a linear version of the tracking error expressed in terms of mean absolute deviations (MAD) of the differences between portfolio returns and the benchmark portfolio returns. In this case, a high tracking error also reflects a large deviation (either positive or negative) from the benchmark:

$$\text{TE}_{\text{MAD}} = \frac{1}{T-1} \sum_{t=1}^{T} \left| R_{t-1,t} - R_{t-1,t}^{\text{benchmark}} \right| \tag{19.24}$$

All of these definitions can be used for *ex-ante* tracking error (using forecast active and benchmark returns) as well as *ex-post* tracking error (using realized active and benchmark returns). In all cases, the benchmark is key as it is the *de facto* position of neutrality for the fund manager. If a manager were simply to follow the benchmark, the expectation would be that his performance should equal the performance of the benchmark, and his tracking error should be nil.

Note that, so far, the notion of tracking error has not yet entered the hedge fund world. But things are likely to change in the near future, as some institutional investors will certainly attempt to track some of the recently created investable hedge fund indices.

20

Risk-Adjusted Performance Measures

If you cannot measure it, then you cannot manage it.

Most comparisons of hedge funds concentrate exclusively on total return figures. They openly ignore risk measures and risk-adjusted performance and claim to care only about absolute returns. Even worse, they provide no means of establishing the extent to which good past performance has been due to chance as opposed to skill. Nevertheless, these comparisons are widely used by marketers to show that their funds are superior to the competition. A 50% return over one year sounds better than 10%. Needless to say, if the funds or indices in question exhibit different risk characteristics, naive comparisons of this nature become extremely misleading. Investors who rely solely on returns to pick a hedge fund may not be prepared for the wild ride that lies ahead. Investing is by nature a two-dimensional process based not only on returns, but also on the risks taken to achieve those returns. The two factors are, however, opposite sides of the same coin, and both should be taken into consideration in order to make sound investment decisions.[1]

Comparing funds that have the same risk characteristics or the same return characteristics is straightforward: at equal risk, more return is always better; at equal return, less risk is always preferable. Difficulties start when we have two or more funds with different expected returns and risks. In particular, given that a higher expected return is desirable but a higher risk is not, how should one compare a high-return, high-risk fund with another fund that has a lower return and a lower risk? The question, then, is this: on a relative scale, how much additional return is sufficient compensation for additional risk? This is precisely where risk-adjusted performance measures are helpful.[2]

Condensing return and risk into *one* useful risk-adjusted number is one of the key tasks of performance measurement. When correctly done, performance measurement reduces the rugged terrain of investment to a level playing field; it thus becomes possible to compare the performance of a given fund with other funds having *similar* risk characteristics, as well as with other funds having *different* risk characteristics. It also opens the door to the correct measurement of excess performance over a benchmark – the famous so-called "alpha". These aspects are of prime interest to both investors and money managers, as members of the former group typically select members of the latter group on the basis of their past performance statistics, and will reward them with incentive fees calculated on the basis of their future performance.

In practice, we have a number of performance measures at our disposal that will help us to choose between risky investments.[3] The list is so long that it almost seems as if each hedge fund

---

[1] Unfortunately, depending on the market conditions, investors tend to concentrate their attention more on either return or risk, but rarely on both at the same time. When markets rose as they did through much of the 1990s, many investors worried only about missing out on the market's huge gains felt comfortable just to be participating. After all, double-digit returns every year were good enough for anyone, right? However, with the end of the equity cult, as fear overtook greed, investors were somehow forced to rediscover risk.

[2] Note that, in the following, we tend to anthropomorphize hedge funds. We should keep in mind that when we evaluate their performance, we are in fact judging the performance of their manager, who takes the investment decisions for the portfolio.

[3] See, for instance, Amenc and Le Sourd (2003) for a survey.

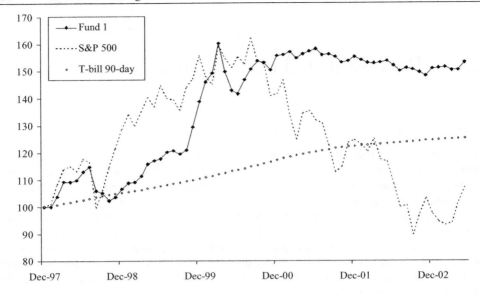

Figure 20.1   Evolution of $100 invested in Fund 1 since January 1998

manager can choose his own measure. How should we select just one to use in our evaluations? Or do we really need them all? Or, perhaps more importantly, can we identify which approach is best? Below we review various measures of risk-adjusted performance, describe their logic, strengths and weaknesses, and answer some key, but typically ignored, questions. As we will see, each performance measure answers a specific question; there is no all-round champion. There is, however, a performance measure for each specific goal.

We illustrate our review by looking at a sample of five hedge funds over the January 1998– May 2003 period, making no claim that the sample or the period is representative of anything in particular. The selection simply consists of funds that have very different qualitative and quantitative characteristics in different market conditions. As the names of the funds are not relevant to the exercise, they have been omitted. Instead, each is identified by a number.

Fund 1 (Figure 20.1) is a fund of hedge funds that aims at producing long-term risk-adjusted capital appreciation. It focuses on several strategies, e.g. long/short, global macro, arbitrage and managed futures. Its portfolio is diversified, with around 25 to 30 managers. The total fund size is $1 billion.

Fund 2 (Figure 20.2) invests and trades primarily in US equities, both long and short. Stock selections are opportunistic, bottom up, and are based on fundamental analysis. The portfolio is widely diversified, with 200 to 250 stocks and a maximum of 4% allocation per position, inclusive of both long and short positions. The portfolio is actively traded. The fund size is larger than $3 billion.

Fund 3 (Figure 20.3) invests primarily in US equities and bonds, both long and short. In selecting investments for the fund, the investment manager emphasizes both individual stock selection and general economic analysis. The portfolio is widely diversified, with a maximum of 2.5% allocation per position, and historically a long bias. The fund size is larger than $2 billion.

Fund 4 (Figure 20.4) is a relative value, fixed-income, arbitrage fund. The fund trades actively, with 15 to 25 different strategies (yield-curve arbitrage, options, OTC derivatives, short

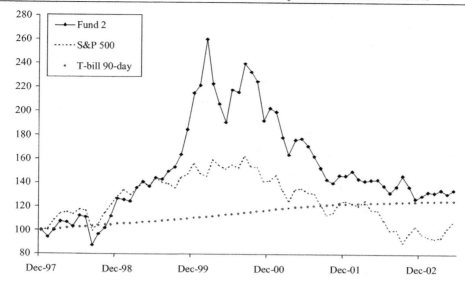

Figure 20.2 Evolution of $100 invested in Fund 2 since January 1998

swaps and long corporate credit, etc). Its portfolio typically contains 50 to 100 positions, mostly from G10 countries (in fact, 90% in the US fixed income market). The fund size is $1.8 billion and the maximum leverage 20 times.

Fund 5 (Figure 20.5) seeks maximum capital appreciation, mainly in the US, with the flexibility of investing internationally. Its primary asset class is equity, although it may use derivatives from time to time. The fund utilizes a bottom-up approach in security selection and

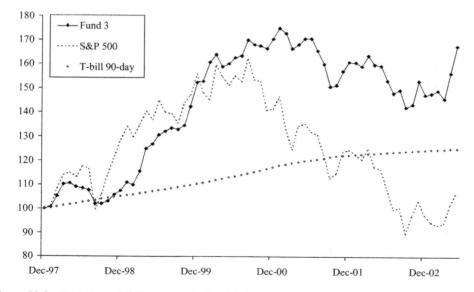

Figure 20.3 Evolution of $100 invested in Fund 3 since January 1998

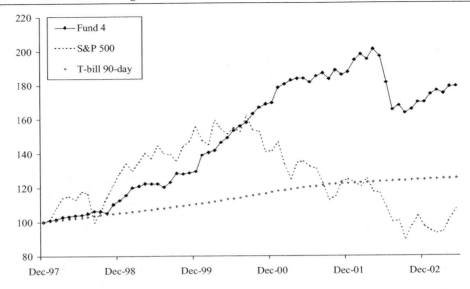

Figure 20.4   Evolution of $100 invested in Fund 4 since January 1998

does not place major bets on the direction of the market. It invests in a concentrated number of stocks, both long and short. The fund size is $120 million, the maximum leverage is two times, and the least we can say is that the manager is rather aggressive.

The risk and return figures differ widely between funds. For instance, it is relatively difficult to compare directly the return of Fund 5 (39.96% p.a.) with the return of Fund 1 (8.16% p.a.), because of their different volatility level (79.53% versus 9.55%). Thanks to the performance

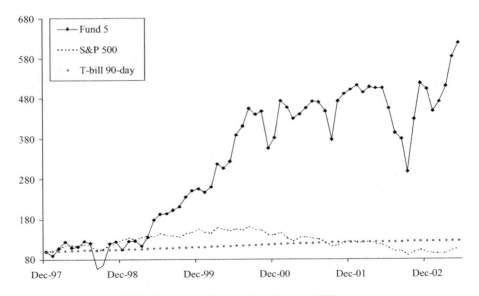

Figure 20.5   Evolution of $100 invested in Fund 5 since January 1998

Table 20.1   Average return and volatility calculation for our five different hedge funds. All data are annualized

	Fund 1	Fund 2	Fund 3	Fund 4	Fund 5
Mean return (%)	8.16	5.56	9.98	11.36	39.96
Volatility (%)	9.55	29.48	11.45	8.95	79.53
Best month (%)	7.38	17.44	8.10	7.49	80.90
Worst month (%)	−7.67	−21.17	−5.80	−8.81	−53.57
% of positive months	65%	49%	60%	78%	65%

measures we review below, we will be able to do an apples-to-apples comparison (see Table 20.1).

20.1   THE SHARPE RATIO

Devised by William Sharpe (1966), a Nobel-Prize-winning economics professor, the Sharpe ratio undoubtedly remains the most commonly used measure of risk-adjusted performance.

20.1.1   Definition and interpretation

The definition of the Sharpe ratio is remarkably simple. The Sharpe ratio measures the amount of "excess return per unit of volatility" provided by a fund. It is calculated by dividing the excess return[4] of the fund by its volatility. Algebraically, we have:

$$\text{Sharpe ratio}_P = \frac{R_P - R_F}{\sigma_P} \tag{20.1}$$

where R_P is the average return on portfolio P, R_F is the risk-free asset, and σ_P is the standard deviation of returns on portfolio P. All numbers are usually expressed on an annual basis, so the Sharpe ratio itself is expressed on an annual basis.[5]

As an illustration, Table 20.2 shows the Sharpe ratios calculated for our five hedge funds. The interpretation of the Sharpe ratio is straightforward: the higher the ratio the better. A high Sharpe ratio means that the fund in question delivered a high return for its level of volatility, which is always good. In contrast, a Sharpe ratio of 1.0 indicates a return on investment that is proportional to the risk taken in achieving that return, and a Sharpe ratio lower than 1 indicates a return on investment that is less than the risk taken. In our case, over the period in question, we can see that Fund 5 was in fact better than Fund 1 because it offered a reward of 0.45% p.a. per unit of volatility, while Fund 1 only offered 0.41% p.a. However, the best fund in the group appears to be Fund 4, with a reward of 0.80% p.a. per unit of volatility – which corresponds to a Sharpe ratio of 0.80.

How can one interpret this 0.80 figure? Consider, for instance, the case of an investor who holds the risk-free asset (4.23% return, no volatility). If this investor agrees to purchase Fund

[4] Excess return here means return above the risk-free rate. The risk-free asset is often specified as Treasury Bills, even though in his 1966 study, Sharpe used the yield on 10-year Treasury bonds as a risk-free proxy. Note that the use of a zero risk-free rate in calculating the Sharpe ratio is neither especially realistic nor the standard way in which this measure is commonly used. Nevertheless, it is sometimes encountered, because the benefits of the simplicity and comparability that it provides outweighs these two considerations.

[5] If this is not the case, some caution is necessary, as the Sharpe ratio is in fact time dependent. As a first order approximation, return increases proportionally with time, while volatility increases proportionally with the square root of time. Hence, the overall Sharpe ratio increases proportionally with the square root of time. An annual Sharpe ratio will therefore be $\sqrt{12}$ bigger than a monthly Sharpe ratio.

Table 20.2 Sharpe ratio calculation for five different hedge funds. All data are annualized. The T-bill rate has an average return of 4.23% p.a. over the period

	Fund 1	Fund 2	Fund 3	Fund 4	Fund 5
Mean return (%)	8.16	5.56	9.98	11.36	39.96
Volatility (%)	9.55	29.48	11.45	8.95	79.53
Sharpe ratio	0.41	0.05	0.50	0.80	0.45

4 shares (11.36% return, 8.95% volatility), the incremental return is 7.13% (11.36% minus 4.23%) and the incremental risk is 8.95% (8.95% minus 0%). Hence, the ratio of incremental return to incremental risk is 7.13%/8.95% ≈ 0.80. In other terms, the investor is willing to accept an increase in volatility of 1% as long as this increase is rewarded by 0.80% return. This is precisely what a Sharpe ratio equal to 0.80 says.

Now, if our investor decides to allocate 50% of his portfolio to Fund 4 and the rest to the risk-free asset, he would get a portfolio with a return of 7.80% and a volatility of 4.48%. Compared to the risk-free asset, the incremental return is 3.57%, the incremental risk is 4.48%, and the Sharpe ratio is still 0.80. And if our investor decides to allocate 150% of his portfolio to Fund 4 and finance the extra 50% position by borrowing at the risk-free rate, he would get a portfolio with a return of 14.93% and a volatility of 13.43%. Compared to the risk-free asset, the incremental return is 10.70%, the incremental risk is 13.43%, and the Sharpe ratio is again 0.80. This clearly shows that the Sharpe ratio of a fund is not influenced by its leverage. All leveraged and unleveraged versions of Fund 4, and more generally, all leveraged and unleveraged versions of any portfolio, will have the same Sharpe ratio.

Graphically, in a mean return/volatility space, the Sharpe ratio is the slope of the line joining the risk-free asset to the fund being examined – see Figure 20.6. The equation of this line can

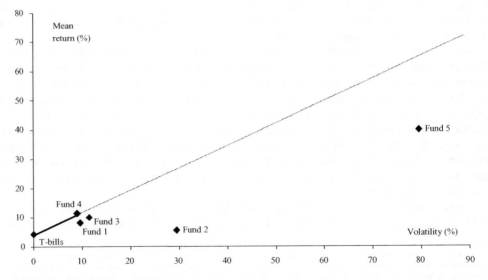

Figure 20.6 Risk/return trade-off achievable by leveraging (solid line) or deleveraging (dotted line) Fund 4. It shows that all combinations of Fund 4 and the risk-free asset generate higher returns at the same level of risk than any combination of another fund and the risk-free asset

be expressed as:

$$\text{Return} = \text{Risk-free rate} + (\text{Sharpe ratio} \times \text{Volatility})$$

That is, in the case of Fund 4,

$$\text{Return} = 4.23\% + (0.80 \times \text{Volatility}).$$

The financial literature often refers to this line as the *capital allocation line*.[6] Each point on this line corresponds to a particular allocation between the risk-free asset and Fund 4. Stated differently, any portfolio on this line can be created by leveraging or deleveraging Fund 4. It is clear from Figure 20.6 that any other fund combined with the T-bills will never reach the capital allocation line of Fund 4.

20.1.2   The Sharpe ratio as a long/short position

More recently, Sharpe (1994) revised the definition of the Sharpe ratio and suggested a new interpretation in terms of differential return with respect to a benchmark. Let R_P and R_B be the average returns on a fund P and on a benchmark portfolio B respectively. The differential return between the fund and its benchmark is defined as $(R_P - R_B)$. From a financial perspective, these differential returns correspond to a zero investment strategy that consists in going long on the fund in question and short on the benchmark. Alternatively, one could also swap the return on the benchmark for the return on the fund, and vice versa.

The revised Sharpe ratio – also called the information ratio – compares the average differential return with its volatility. The latter is nothing more than the tracking error of the fund P with respect to the benchmark B. Algebraically:

$$\text{Information ratio}_P = \frac{R_P - R_B}{\text{TE}_P} \tag{20.2}$$

When the benchmark equals the risk-free rate, the information ratio equals the traditional Sharpe ratio.

The beauty of this new definition is that it allows for a more general interpretation. Let us consider the benchmark as a hypothetical initial investment and let us try to select an asset that improves on the benchmark in risk-expected return terms. In this framework, a higher information ratio represents a better departure from the benchmark because it implies an expected return larger than the return for relatively little extra risk – see Figure 20.7. Hence, we should always pick the asset that has the highest information ratio.

20.1.3   The statistics of Sharpe ratios

Most of the time, Sharpe ratios are measured and reported without any information about their statistical significance. Once again, this is regrettable. The building blocks of the Sharpe ratio– expected/average excess returns and volatility/tracking error–are unknown quantities that must be estimated statistically from a sample of returns. They are therefore subject to estimation error, which implies that the Sharpe ratio itself is also subject to estimation error.[7] Thus, we

---

[6] When the fund considered is a proxy for the stock market, the capital allocation line is referred to as the *capital market line*. It represents the set of portfolios that are made up of only T-bills and of the market index.

[7] Sharpe himself (1994) pointed out that the Sharpe ratio can be interpreted as a *t*-statistic to test the hypothesis that the return on the portfolio is equal to the risk-free return.

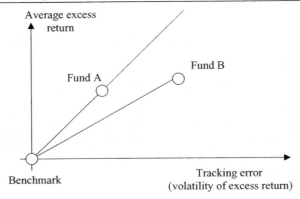

Figure 20.7   Illustration of the revised Sharpe ratio. Fund A provides a better departure from the benchmark than Fund B

should always verify the statistical significance of Sharpe ratio estimates before stating any conclusion about the performance of a fund.

The financial literature describes several approaches to dealing with the uncertainty surrounding Sharpe ratios.

- The first approach is the Jobson and Korkie (1981) test for the equality of the Sharpe ratios of any two portfolios (Box 20.1). It is the first formal test of the significance of performance, but it requires normality of asset returns, which is often not the case for individual hedge funds.
- The second approach is the Gibbons *et al.* (1989) test to verify *ex-ante* portfolio efficiency (Box 20.2). Although there is a substantial theoretical difference between the two concepts of portfolio performance and portfolio efficiency, there is a close relationship between them. In particular, the test shows whether the adjunction of new assets in a universe effectively results in a significant improvement of performance, by comparing the maximum Sharpe ratios obtained for the original universe with those for the augmented universe. This test has often been applied in the literature, for instance to examine the *ex-ante* efficiency of portfolios, to test the benefits of adding international investments to a domestic portfolio, or to compare equally weighted with optimized portfolios – see, for instance, Rubens *et al.* (1998) or Cheng and Liang (2000).
- Finally, the third approach is that described recently by Lo (2002). Although still at its early stages, this line of research is the most promising. It derives the statistical distribution of the Sharpe ratio using standard econometric methods. The derivation is made under several different sets of assumptions for the statistical behaviour of the return series on which the Sharpe ratio is based–e.g. mean reversion, momentum, and other forms of serial correlation. Lo finds that all these effects can have a non-trivial impact on the Sharpe ratio estimator itself. For instance, positive serial correlation can yield annualized Sharpe ratios that are overstated by more than 65%, therefore resulting in inconsistent rankings.

Whatever the approach, it is crucial that performance is investigated over a sufficiently long period of time. Without a minimum sample size, determining portfolio performance becomes a hazardous task, and it is difficult to really assess whether performance was due to luck or skill–or lack of it.

Box 20.1   The Jobson and Korkie test statistic

The Jobson and Korkie (1981) test statistic can be formulated as follows. Let μ_1 and μ_2 be the mean *excess* returns of the portfolios under investigation, σ_1 and σ_2 the return volatility of the two portfolios, and $\sigma_{1,2}$ the covariance of the two portfolio returns. The excess returns are assumed to be serially independent and normally and independently distributed.

   Jobson and Korkie use the following Z statistic:

$$Z = \frac{\sigma_1 \mu_2 - \sigma_2 \mu_1}{\sqrt{\theta}} \tag{20.3}$$

where θ is the asymptotic variance of the expression in the numerator, calculated as follows[8]:

$$\theta = \frac{1}{T}\left[2\sigma_1^2\sigma_2^2 - 2\sigma_1\sigma_2\sigma_{1,2} + \frac{1}{2}(\mu_1\sigma_2)^2 + \frac{1}{2}(\mu_2\sigma_1)^2 - \frac{\mu_1\mu_2}{\sigma_1\sigma_2}\sigma_{1,2}^2 \right] \tag{20.4}$$

Jobson and Korkie show that the Z statistic is approximately normally distributed, with a zero mean and a unit standard deviation for large samples under the null assumption that the two Sharpe ratios are equal.

   A significant Z statistic would reject the null hypothesis of equal risk-adjusted performance and would suggest that one of the investment portfolio strategies outperforms the other. However, Jobson and Korkie note that the statistical power of the test is low, especially for small sample sizes. As illustrated by Jorion (1985), at a 5% significance level, the test fails to reject a false null hypothesis up to 85% of the time. Thus, a statistically significant Z between two portfolios can be seen as strong evidence of a difference in risk-adjusted performance.

Box 20.2   The Gibbons, Ross and Shanken test

The Gibbons, *et al.* (1989) test compares the estimated maximum Sharpe ratio for the original universe (denoted Sharpe$_1$) with the estimated maximum Sharpe ratio for the augmented universe (denoted Sharpe$_2$). The authors show that the statistic

$$W = \left[\frac{\sqrt{1 + \text{Sharpe}_2^2}}{\sqrt{1 + \text{Sharpe}_1^2}} \right]^2 - 1 \tag{20.5}$$

follows a Wishart distribution, which is a generalization of the χ^2 distribution. Under the null hypothesis that the Sharpe ratio of the extended universe is not different from the Sharpe ratio of the original universe, the statistic W should not be statistically different from zero. Since increasing the number of assets in a universe can only improve the maximum Sharpe ratio, we are only concerned with positive values of W. Any large positive deviation from zero implies that the two Sharpe ratios are actually different.

---

[8] Note that the original Jobson and Korkie (1981) paper contains typographic errors in this expression, which led to an underestimation of the asymptotic variance, i.e. the null hypothesis is rejected too often.

Working with a Wishart distribution is not so convenient. Fortunately, a simple transformation suggested by Morrison (1976) shows that the statistic

$$F = \frac{T(T - N - 1)}{N(T - 2)} W \qquad (20.6)$$

has a central F-distribution with $(N, T - N - 1)$ degrees of freedom, where T is the number of returns observed and N is the number of assets in the original universe. As with any F-statistic, N must be low in relation to T for the test to have good discriminatory power.

20.2   THE TREYNOR RATIO AND JENSEN ALPHA

Two other widely used performance measures are the Treynor ratio and the Jensen alpha (frequently simply called "alpha"). Both find their roots in financial theory, more specifically in the Capital Asset Pricing Model (CAPM) developed by Sharpe (1964).

20.2.1   The CAPM

Centrepiece of modern financial economics, the CAPM was originally developed to (i) explain the rationale for diversification, (ii) provide a theoretical structure for the pricing of assets with uncertain returns in a competitive market and (iii) explain the differences in risk premiums across assets. A rigorous exposition of the CAPM principles and results is far beyond the scope of this book and may easily be found in the literature.[9] In the following paragraphs, therefore, we limit ourselves to recalling briefly the intuition behind the CAPM, listing its major conclusions, and then proceeding directly to their implications in terms of performance measurement.

The fundamental premise of the CAPM is that the volatility of an asset can be split into two parts: a systematic risk and a specific risk. The systematic risk part is the risk of being affected by general market movements. It represents the part of an asset's volatility that is perfectly positively or negatively correlated with the market. The specific risk, on the other hand, is specific to each asset. It represents the remaining part of an asset's volatility that is not correlated with the market.

When investors form portfolios, the systematic risk parts of individual assets are simply added up to give the systematic risk of the whole portfolio. This risk is non-diversifiable and will be present in all portfolios. The specific risk parts do not add up, however, but rather tend to compensate each other, particularly when the assets considered are negatively correlated. This is the impact of diversification. Hence, in a well-diversified portfolio, each asset's specific risk should be eliminated by diversification, so that the total portfolio's specific risk should be insignificant.

The second premise of the CAPM is that risk-averse and rational investors do not want to subject themselves to a risk that can be diversified away. Rather, they attempt to optimally construct their portfolios from uncorrelated assets in order to eliminate specific risk. As a consequence, investors should not care about the total volatility of individual assets, but only about the systematic risk component – the only risk that remains in the final portfolio.

---

[9] See for instance Newman *et al.* (1992), Bodie, Kane and Marcus (1999), Sharpe, Alexander and Bailey (1998), Elton and Gruber (1995), or Danthine and Donaldson (2001).

The logical consequence of the foregoing is that there should be no reward for non-systematic risk. Although measurable at the individual asset level, specific risk will disappear at the portfolio level. So why would the market ever reward something that does not exist any more in a well-diversified portfolio? At equilibrium, investors should only be rewarded for the systematic risk they take, not for the non-systematic risk they have eliminated. This is precisely what the CAPM says.

The CAPM asserts that the expected return on a given asset should be equal to the risk-free interest rate plus a risk premium. The latter depends linearly on the market risk exposure (i.e. the beta of the asset) and the market risk premium (i.e. what the market portfolio pays above the risk-free rate for taking market risk). Therefore, the expected return on a risky asset should be given by:

$$E^{CAPM}(R_P) = R_F + \beta_P\,[E(R_M) - R_F] \tag{20.7}$$

where R_P and R_M are respectively the percentage returns on the portfolio P and on the market portfolio M, R_F denotes the risk-free rate, β_P is the beta of portfolio P with respect to the market portfolio M, and E() denotes the unconditional expectation operator.

Equation (20.7) is the most important conclusion derived from the CAPM. It states that expected returns are linearly related to market risk (beta), but not, as often believed, to total risk (volatility). Other things being equal, a high beta asset should produce a higher expected return than the market and a low beta asset should produce a lower return. Similarly, increasing the market risk premium should increase the return of all assets with positive beta. In that respect, one could say that the CAPM philosophy is the exact opposite of traditional stock picking, as its attempts to understand the market as a whole rather than look at what makes each investment opportunity unique.

Note that equation (20.7) can easily be rewritten in terms of risk premiums by simply subtracting the risk-free rate from both sides of the security market line (SML) equation. This yields

$$E^{CAPM}(R_P) - R_F = \beta_P\,[E(R_M) - R_F] \tag{20.8}$$

Graphically, in a return-beta space, the CAPM implies that all fairly priced securities and portfolios should plot along a line. This line is the SML (Figure 20.8). Its intercept with the

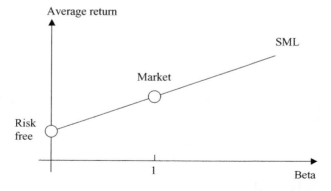

Figure 20.8   The security market line (SML)

vertical axis should be the risk-free rate, and its slope should be equal to the market risk premium. The more risk-averse investors are, the steeper the slope and the higher the expected return for a given level of systematic risk.

By construction, the risk-free asset and the market portfolio should fall exactly on the SML, with betas of 0 and 1 respectively. Consequently, any asset on the SML can be "replicated" by an appropriate mix of the risk-free asset and the market. This property – called the two-fund separation theorem – is particularly useful in creating a passive benchmark, when assessing the performance of an actively managed portfolio.

20.2.2 The market model

The CAPM and its graphical equivalent, the SML, give predictions about the expected relationship between risk and return. Theoretically, they should only be interpreted strictly as *ex-ante* predictive models. However, when doing performance analysis, the framework is different. Performance must be assessed *ex-post*, based on a sample of observed past data. What we need then is an explanatory model, and the *ex-ante* CAPM must be transformed into an *ex-post* testable relationship. The latter usually takes the form of a time series regression of excess returns of individual assets on the excess returns of some aggregate market index. It is called the *market model* (Figure 20.9), and can be written as:

$$R_i = \alpha_i + R_F + \beta_i [R_M - R_F] + \varepsilon_i \tag{20.9}$$

where R_i and R_M are the realized returns on security i and the market index, respectively, α_i is the expected firm-specific return and ε_i is the unexpected firm-specific return. If the CAPM holds and if markets are efficient, α_i should not be statistically different from zero, and ε_i should have a mean of zero. The coefficients α_i and β_i correspond to the slope and the intercept of the regression line.

Alternatively, equation (20.9) can also be rewritten in terms of risk premiums:

$$R_{i,t} - R_F = \alpha_i + \beta_i \lfloor R_{M,t} - R_F \rfloor + \varepsilon_{i,t} \tag{20.10}$$

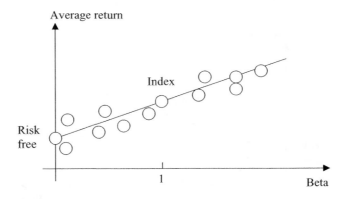

Figure 20.9   The market model

As we will see shortly, this equation constitutes the source of two major performance measures of financial portfolios, namely, Jensen's alpha (1968) and the Treynor ratio (1965).

Most practitioners tend to confuse the CAPM with time series regression. Although the two models look similar, they are fundamentally different. The market model is just an ad hoc, convenient, single-factor model fitted to observed data, while the CAPM is an economic equilibrium model. Furthermore, the market model uses a simple market index as a proxy for the entire (non-observable) market portfolio of the CAPM.

An interesting interpretation of the market model is given by rearranging the terms in equation (20.9) to obtain:

$$R_i = \alpha_i + (1 - \beta_i) R_F + (\beta_i) R_M + \varepsilon_i \tag{20.11}$$

The terms $(1 - \beta_i)$ and β_i can be interpreted as weights in a portfolio. Thus, equation (20.11) means that the return on a portfolio is made up of four components: (i) an asset-specific expected return α_i; (ii) an allocation to the risk-free asset; (iii) an allocation to the market portfolio; and (iv) an error term, which on average should be zero.

Several commercial firms provide estimates of beta but their data should be treated with caution. These firms often ignore the risk-free rate as well as dividends, and simply estimate betas by regressing the returns on stocks against the return on the market:

$$R_i = \alpha_i^* + \beta_i^* R_M + \varepsilon_i^* \tag{20.12}$$

This shortcut generally has no practical impact on the estimate of beta, but the corresponding alpha is useless for performance evaluation, as it differs significantly from the original alpha.

20.2.3   The Jensen alpha

According to the CAPM, it is impossible for an asset to remain located above or below the security market line (SML). If an asset produces a return that is higher than it should be for its beta, then investors will rush in to buy it and drive up its price, lowering the return and returning it to the SML. If the asset is located below the SML, then investors will hurry to sell it, driving down the price and hence increasing the return. Consequently, if all assets are fairly priced, deviations from the SML should not occur, or at least should not last very long.

Nevertheless, active fund managers are typically in search of assets that deviate from the SML. They attempt to identify them before the market reacts, so that they can profit from the mispricing. If they are successful, they will achieve a return that is above what could be expected, given the market risk taken. Hence, their portfolios will also be located above the SML. Conversely, unsuccessful managers will achieve a return that is lower than what could be expected, given the market risk taken. Hence, their portfolios will be located below the SML. This suggests a straightforward way of measuring performance, namely, the Jensen alpha, named after Harvard professor Michael Jensen (1968).

The Jensen alpha is defined as the difference between the realized return and the return predicted by the CAPM:

$$\alpha_P = R_P - E^{CAPM}(R_P) \tag{20.13}$$

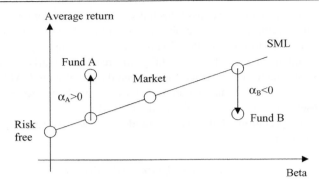

Figure 20.10   Undervalued and overvalued securities with the SML

That is,

$$\alpha_P = [R_P - R_F] - \beta_P [R_M - R_F] \tag{20.14}$$

Hence, the Jensen alpha is measured as the difference between the effectively realized risk premium and the expected risk premium. According to the CAPM, only market risk should be rewarded, so the alpha should be nil. If this is not the case, the alpha can be interpreted as an indicator of superior performance when it is positive or of poor performance when it is negative.

Graphically, a security with an alpha of zero will plot on the SML. A security with a positive alpha (e.g. Fund A in Figure 20.10) will plot above the SML. It generates more return than it should, given its systematic risk (measured by beta). A security with a negative alpha (e.g. Fund B in Figure 20.10) will plot below the SML. It generates less return than it should, given its systematic risk (measured by beta).

The Jensen measure can also be interpreted as the profitability of a net arbitrage position that goes long on the evaluated fund and goes short on both the risk-free asset and the market in proportions that neutralize market risk. For example, consider a fund with a beta of 0.6. Then Jensen's alpha measures the average profit of investing $1 in the fund, obtaining the funds from borrowing $0.40 (shorting the risk-free asset) and shorting $0.60 worth of the market portfolio. If the alpha is positive, that means that an investor who initially holds a portfolio made up of $0.60 worth of the market portfolio and $0.40 of the risk-free asset can improve his portfolio by diverting a small fraction of his wealth to the fund in question. If the alpha is negative, the investor should avoid the fund.[10]

When confronted with several funds, the alpha decision rule is of course to choose the investment that maximizes the value added-that is, the investment with the highest alpha. We will therefore prefer investment A over B if $\alpha_A > \alpha_B$. As an illustration, Table 20.3 shows the Jensen alpha calculations for our five hedge funds. Note that the alpha is calculated from

---

[10] If possible, he should even sell the fund short and invest the proceeds in the original portfolio. However, in practice, most funds cannot be sold short.

Table 20.3   Jensen alpha calculation for five different hedge funds

	Fund 1	Fund 2	Fund 3	Fund 4	Fund 5
Jensen alpha	0.36	0.44	0.54	0.59	4.09

monthly returns, so that it is itself a monthly figure. Clearly, according to the Jensen alpha, (Box 20.3), Fund 5 dominates the sample.

20.2.4 The Treynor (1965) ratio

In the market model, the value added (or withdrawn) by a manager is measured by the alpha, while the market risk exposure is measured by the beta. Jack L. Treynor, one of the fathers of modern portfolio theory and former editor of *The Financial Analysts Journal*, suggested comparing the two quantities:

$$\text{Treynor ratio}_P = \frac{\alpha_P}{\beta_P} \tag{20.16}$$

Replacing α_P by its definition and simplifying gives

$$\text{Treynor ratio}_P = \frac{R_P - R_F}{\beta_P} \tag{20.17}$$

All returns are usually expressed on an annual basis, so the Treynor ratio itself is expressed on an annual basis. The risk-free asset is often specified as Treasury bills, and beta is often measured against a diversified market index (e.g. S&P 500). Note that the derivations implicitly assume $\beta_P \neq 0$.

In a sense, the Treynor ratio is a reward-to-risk ratio similar to the Sharpe ratio. The key difference is that it looks at systematic risk only, not total risk. Higher values of the Treynor ratio are always desirable as they indicate greater return per unit of (market) risk. As an illustration,

---

Box 20.3 Jensen's alpha

It is possible to derive a precise interpretation of Jensen's alpha in terms of optimal portfolio choice by relating it to the Sharpe ratio. Suppose an investor initially holds a combination of an index portfolio tracking the market and the risk-free asset, in proportions w_M and $1 - w_M$). This investor considers whether he should add fund P to his portfolio. In other words, he considers whether he should take a small fraction w_P of his wealth and invest it in portfolio P, while reducing the fractions held in the risk-free asset and the index to $(1 - w_P)(1 - w_M)$ and $(1 - w_P)w_M$ respectively.

It can then be shown that the derivative (in the financial calculus sense) of the Sharpe ratio of the resulting portfolio with respect to ε, evaluated at $w_P = 0$ (no investment yet), is

$$\left. \frac{\partial \text{ Sharpe}}{\partial w_P} \right|_{w_P=0} = \frac{\alpha}{w_M \sigma_M^2} \tag{20.15}$$

Table 20.4   Treynor ratio calculation for five different hedge funds. The T-bill rate has an average return of 4.23% p.a. over the period

	Fund 1	Fund 2	Fund 3	Fund 4	Fund 5
Mean return (%)	8.16	5.56	9.98	11.36	39.96
Beta (S&P 500)	0.19	0.64	0.43	0.06	2.08
Treynor ratio	20.22	2.07	13.36	113.02	17.15

Table 20.4 displays the Treynor ratios obtained for our five hedge funds. We observe once again that Fund 4 seems to dominate the sample, with a Treynor ratio equal to 113.02, thanks to its relatively low beta (0.06).

20.2.5   Statistical significance

Once again, a crucial element in the Jensen alpha and Treynor ratio is the question of statistical significance. In particular, the quality of the regression used to obtain the beta coefficient should be scrutinized. First, are the coefficients statistically different from zero? Second, how high is the explanatory power of the regression? As an illustration, consider Figure 20.5, which displays a statistic called the R-square. Roughly stated, the R-square (R^2) measures the quality of the regression model used to calculate the Jensen alpha and the Treynor ratio.

We saw previously that Fund 4 seems to dominate the sample with a Treynor ratio equal to 113.02, thanks to its relatively low beta (0.06). However, we now see that the R^2 of the regression that provided this beta is only 0.02. This implies that the S&P 500 behaviour only explains 2% of the variance of Fund 4. Do we feel confident in basing our conclusions on a model that has such a low explanatory power? Not likely! Hence, we should be cautious and always assess the quality of our models before accepting their conclusions.

20.2.6   Comparing Sharpe, Treynor and Jensen

Investors frequently wonder why there are differences between the fund rankings provided by the Sharpe ratio, the Treynor ratio and the Jensen alpha. The three measures are indeed different. On the one hand, both the Treynor ratio and the Jensen alpha issue from the CAPM and measure risk the same way. However, the Treynor ratio provides more information than Jensen's alpha. In particular, two securities with different risk levels that provide the same excess returns over the same period will have the same alpha but will differ with respect to the Treynor ratio. The difference comes from the fact that the Treynor ratio provides the performance of the portfolio per unit of systematic risk. On the other hand, the Sharpe ratio focuses on a different type of risk – total risk, as opposed to systematic risk. It penalizes funds

Table 20.5   Statistical significance of the market model coefficients

	Fund 1	Fund 2	Fund 3	Fund 4	Fund 5
R^2 of regression	0.16	0.22	0.54	0.02	0.43

that have a high volatility and therefore funds that have non-systematic risk. Hence, in general, the ranking of Sharpe ratios will usually be different from that of Treynor ratios or Jensen alphas. Intuitively, it is only when applied to well-diversified traditional portfolios that the three measures will result in similar rankings because most of the risk will be systematic. In the case of hedge funds, the non-systematic component is usually large, so very different rankings may be obtained.

It is relatively easy to derive the exact conditions that must hold for the Sharpe ratio and the Treynor ratio to provide the same ranking. Consider two funds, A and B, such that fund A has a higher Treynor ratio than fund B. That is,

$$\frac{R_A - R_F}{\beta_A} > \frac{R_B - R_F}{\beta_B} \qquad (20.18)$$

Replacing the betas with their definitions and rearranging terms, we find that

$$\frac{1}{\rho_{A,M}} \frac{R_A - R_F}{\sigma_A} > \frac{1}{\rho_{B,M}} \frac{R_B - R_F}{\sigma_B} \qquad (20.19)$$

where $\rho_{i,M}$ denotes the correlation between fund i and the market. Therefore, the Treynor ratio will provide the same ranking as the Sharpe ratio only for assets that have identical correlations to the market.

Similarly, we can derive the conditions that must hold for the Sharpe ratio and the Jensen alpha to provide the same ranking. Consider two funds, A and B, such that fund A has a higher alpha than fund B. That is,

$$\alpha_A > \alpha_B \qquad (20.20)$$

Replacing the alphas with their definitions and rearranging terms yields

$$\sigma_A \left[\frac{R_A - R_F}{\sigma_A} - \rho_{A,M} \frac{R_M - R_F}{\sigma_M} \right] > \sigma_B \left[\frac{R_B - R_F}{\sigma_B} - \rho_{B,M} \frac{R_M - R_F}{\sigma_M} \right] \qquad (20.21)$$

Hence, the Treynor ratio will provide the same ranking as the Sharpe ratio only for assets that have identical correlations to the market **and** the same volatility. Most of the time, this condition will not be encountered so the rankings will be different.

Another frequent question from investors is: "Which measure should be used to evaluate portfolio performance?" The simple answer is: "It depends." To evaluate an entire portfolio, the Sharpe ratio is appropriate. It is simple to calculate, does not require a beta estimate and penalizes the portfolio for being non-diversified. To evaluate securities or funds for possible inclusion in a broader or master portfolio, either the Treynor ratio or Jensen's alpha is appropriate. However, they require a beta estimate and assume that the master portfolio is well diversified.

20.2.7   Generalizing the Jensen alpha and the Treynor ratio

As we will see, the market model is one of the simplest asset pricing models possible. It expresses everything in terms of a single factor, the market portfolio. However, one can easily extend the market model, for instance, by including additional factors or by postulating some non-linear relationships. In this case, alpha will be defined as the difference between the realized return and the new model-predicted return.

A particular and unfortunate case of what precedes is the tendency of some investment practitioners to use the term "alpha" to describe the extent to which a portfolio's returns have exceeded expectations, or simply to measure returns in excess of those over a benchmark index (e.g. S&P 500). In a CAPM framework, this implicitly assumes that the beta of the considered portfolio is in fact equal to 1, which is often not verified.

In the context of multi-factor models the Treynor ratio has also been generalized by Hübner (2003). Conceptually, the Generalized Treynor ratio is defined as the abnormal return of a portfolio per unit of weighted-average systematic risk. In a linear multi-index, these requirements are fulfilled by normalizing the risk premia using a benchmark portfolio and by rotating the factors to obtain an orthonormed hyperplane for risk dimensions. This performance measure is invariant to the specification of the asset pricing model, the number of factors or the scale of the measure.

20.3 M^2, M^3 AND GRAHAM–HARVEY

More recently, several researchers have provided new perspectives on measuring portfolio performance. Although not yet as popular as the Sharpe ratio or Jensen's alpha, these measures are gaining ground in the hedge fund industry.

20.3.1   The M^2 performance measure

Despite near universal acceptance among academics and institutional investors, the Sharpe ratio is too complicated for the average investor. The reason is that it expresses performance as an excess return per unit of volatility, while most investors are used to dealing with absolute returns. This motivated Leah Modigliani from Morgan Stanley and her grandfather, the Nobel Prize winner Franco Modigliani, to develop and suggest a replacement for the Sharpe ratio.[11] The new performance measure, called M^2 after the names of its founders, expresses performance directly as a return figure, which should ease its comprehension.

The key idea of the M^2 performance measure is to adjust all funds by leveraging or deleveraging them using the risk-free asset, so that they all have the same volatility – typically the market volatility. Say, for instance, that we want to compare the performance of a fund (named P) with the performance of the market (named M). In general, we observe that $\sigma_P \neq \sigma_M$, so that we cannot compare the two assets by just looking at their returns. According to M^2, we need to form a portfolio P^* composed of the original fund P and T-bills (with return R_F and no volatility) that has the same standard deviation as M. Then, one can simply compare the adjusted funds and the market solely on the basis of the return.

There are two possible situations. If the fund has a higher volatility than the market ($\sigma_P > \sigma_M$), then portfolio P^* will contain a mix of T-bills and the original fund P. This is the de-leveraging situation illustrated in Figure 20.11. In this case, we have:

$$\frac{\sigma_M}{\sigma_P} = \frac{R_{P^*} - R_F}{R_P - R_F} \tag{20.22}$$

Solving for R_{P^*} yields

$$M^2 = R_{P^*} = \frac{\sigma_M}{\sigma_P}(R_P - R_F) - R_F \tag{20.23}$$

---

[11] See Modigliani (1997) and Modigliani and Modigliani (1997).

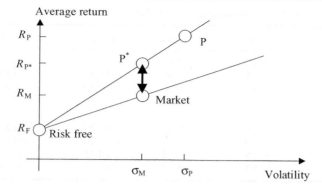

Figure 20.11 The M^2 performance measure when the fund has a higher volatility than the market ($\sigma_P > \sigma_M$). The adjusted portfolio P* is a mix of T-bills and P

If the fund has a lower volatility than the market ($\sigma_P < \sigma_M$), then portfolio P* will contain a short position in T-bills and a long position in the original fund P. This is the leveraging situation illustrated in Figure 20.12. In this case,

$$\frac{\sigma_M - \sigma_P}{\sigma_M} = \frac{R_{P*} - (R_P - R_F)}{R_{P*}} \tag{20.24}$$

Solving for R_{P*} yields

$$M^2 = R_{P*} = \frac{\sigma_M}{\sigma_P}(R_P - R_F) - R_F \tag{20.25}$$

In both cases, the resulting portfolio P* is compared with the market solely on the basis of return. In essence, for a fund P with a given risk and return, the M^2 measure is equivalent to

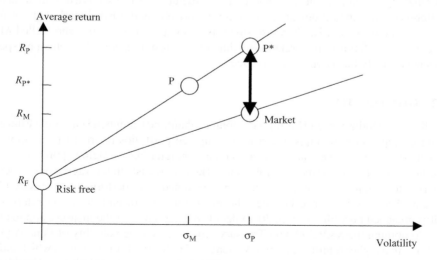

Figure 20.12 The M^2 performance measure when the fund has a lower volatility than the market ($\sigma_P < \sigma_M$). The adjusted portfolio P* is made up of portfolio P and a loan at the risk-free rate

Table 20.6   Calculating M^2 for our sample of hedge funds

	Fund 1	Fund 2	Fund 3	Fund 4	Fund 5
Mean return (%)	8.16	5.56	9.98	11.36	39.96
Volatility (%)	9.55	29.48	11.45	8.95	79.53
Sharpe ratio	0.41	0.05	0.50	0.80	0.45
Portfolio P*					
% of fund	217.3%	70.4%	181.2%	231.8%	26.1%
% of T-bills	−117.3%	29.6%	−81.2%	−131.8%	73.9%
σ_{P*}	20.75	20.75	20.75	20.75	20.75
$M^2 = R_{P*}$	12.77	5.17	14.65	20.76	13.55

the return the fund would have achieved if it had the same risk as the market. Thus, the fund with the highest M^2 will have the highest return for any level of risk – very much like the fund with the highest Sharpe ratio.

As an illustration, Table 20.6 shows the calculation of M^2 for our sample of five funds. The benchmark volatility level was set at 20.75%, which corresponds to the S&P 500 volatility over the period in question. The T-bill rate has an average return of 4.23% p.a. over the period. The ranking we obtain with M^2 is the same as the ranking of the Sharpe ratio. This confirms that the M^2 performance measure is essentially a new variant of the Sharpe ratio. It is just easier to interpret, because it is expressed directly in terms of return.

It is worth noting that any reference point other than the volatility of the market could equally well be chosen. With M^2, the market simply provides a standard risk level to which all portfolios are scaled so that they can be compared "apples to apples". The economic significance of the market, if any, is left aside.

Arun Muralidhar from J.P. Morgan Investment Management argues that M^2 is not a sufficient rule for making decisions on how to rank funds or structure portfolios. It is true that M^2 accounts for differences in standard deviations between a portfolio and a benchmark, but not for the differences in correlation. He therefore suggests a new performance measure called M^3 that corrects for the difference in correlations. Although interesting from a theoretical perspective, M^3 has never really been applied in practice.

20.3.2   GH1 and GH2

In parallel with Modigliani and Modigliani, John Graham and Campbell Harvey have developed two simple approaches to adjust the risk of compared portfolios in order to end up with the same volatility. Both of them are also based on a leveraging/deleveraging approach.

The first approach suggested by Graham and Harvey consists in leveraging or deleveraging the market to match the volatility of the fund examined. The performance measure GH1 is then defined as the difference between the mean fund return and the mean return on the volatility-matched portfolio. Figure 20.13 details the geometry of the measure applied to two funds. Combining the S&P 500 with Treasury bills to match the volatility of Fund A yields a portfolio with a higher return than Fund A. Hence, GH1 for fund A is negative, which indicates underperformance. In contrast, leveraging the S&P 500 to match the volatility of Fund B yields

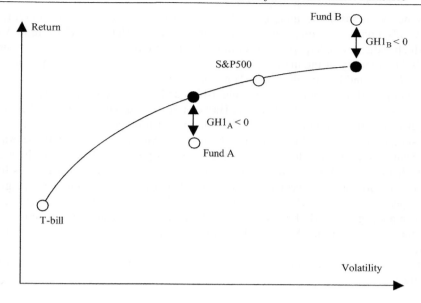

Figure 20.13   Interpreting GH1 by leveraging or unleveraging the S&P 500

a portfolio with a lower return than Fund B. Hence, GH1 for fund B is positive, which indicates outperformance.

The second approach suggested by Graham and Harvey consists in leveraging or de-leveraging the fund examined to match the volatility of the market. The performance measure GH2 is then defined as the difference between the mean return on the volatility-matched port-folio and the mean market return. Figure 20.14 details the geometry of the measure applied

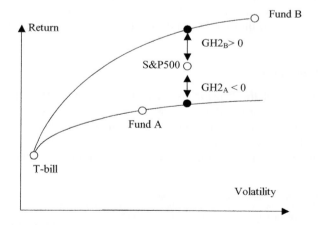

Figure 20.14   Interpreting GH2 by leveraging or unleveraging the analysed funds

to the same two funds. Leveraging Fund A with Treasury bills to match the volatility of the market yields a portfolio with a lower return than the market. Hence, GH2 for fund A is negative, which indicates underperformance. In contrast, combining Fund A with Treasury bills to match the volatility of the market yields a portfolio with a higher return than the market. Hence, GH2 for fund B is positive, indicating outperformance.

The sets of portfolios obtained by mixing T-bills and other assets form curves rather than straight lines. This is because Graham and Harvey reject the usual assumption that the T-bill return has zero variance and zero covariance with the portfolio being evaluated. In reality, the usual assumption does hold if the maturity of the T-bills coincides exactly with the evaluation period. That is, the cash is effectively a zero-coupon instrument maturing exactly at the end of the evaluation period. In practice, though, this is often not the case, and there is likely to be a non-zero correlation between the interest rate changes and asset returns, which gives the curve. Depending on the level of correlation, this could lead to misleading inferences about the performance, particularly for low volatility funds where substantial leverage is needed to achieve the market volatility. However, the impact is generally negligible for well-diversified portfolios.

The two Graham and Harvey measures look very similar but in fact they provide different perspectives.

- GH1 is similar to the Jensen alpha measure, except that, with Jensen, the benchmark portfolio (beta times the market index) has the same market exposure (beta) as the analysed portfolio, but not necessarily the same total volatility.[12]
- GH2 is similar to the M^2 measure, but does not rely on the assumption of zero risk for the cash proxy.

20.4   PERFORMANCE MEASURES BASED ON DOWNSIDE RISK

Dissatisfaction with the variance as a risk measure, coupled with other behavioural evidence, has led some researchers to propose alternative risk-adjusted performance measures. Several of these are based on the downside risk approach – see, for instance, Sortino and van der Meer (1991), Fishburn (1977), Sortino and Price (1994) Marmer and Ng (1993) or Merriken (1994).

20.4.1   The Sortino ratio

Frank Sortino, Director of the Pension Research Institute and a professor emeritus at San Francisco State University, reconsidered the issue of performance measurement from the perspective of downside risk. His contention was that the most important risk was not volatility, but rather the risk of not achieving the return in relation to an investment goal. Hence, he suggested replacing the Sharpe ratio by the Sortino ratio, which measures the incremental return

---

[12] To obtain a striking example of the advantage of the Graham and Harvey measures, consider the case of a fund that randomly selects between a 200% long in the market and 200% short in the market position, with an average zero exposure over a measurement period. If the alpha of this fund is positive (say 1%), then the strategy will be identified as superior. However, the volatility-matched portfolio is likely to be a leveraged version of the market portfolio with twice the variance of the market. Hence, the random strategy would appear as a clear underperformer according to the GH1 measure.

Table 20.7   Sortino ratio calculations for our five different hedge funds. All data are annualized

	Fund 1	Fund 2	Fund 3	Fund 4	Fund 5
Mean return (%)	8.16	5.56	9.98	11.36	39.96
Volatility (%)	9.55	29.48	11.45	8.95	79.53
Sharpe ratio	0.41	0.05	0.50	**0.80**	0.45
MAR = 0%					
Downside deviation	5.23	16.70	5.86	5.50	30.90
Sortino (MAR = 0)	0.75	0.08	0.98	**1.30**	1.16
MAR = Risk-free rate					
Downside deviation	15.09	25.55	15.69	14.13	37.54
Sortino (MAR = R_F)	0.26	0.05	0.37	0.50	**0.95**
MAR = Mean return					
Downside deviation	6.23	17.52	7.29	6.60	35.18
Sortino (MAR = mean)	**1.14**	0.41	0.98	1.08	0.20

over a minimum acceptable return (MAR) divided by the downside deviation (as opposed to standard deviation) below the MAR.

Algebraically, we have:

$$\text{Sortino ratio}_P = \frac{R_P - \text{MAR}}{\text{DD}_P} \qquad (20.26)$$

where R_P and MAR are respectively the average percentage returns on portfolio P and a minimum acceptable return, and DD_P is the downside deviation of returns of portfolio P below the MAR. All numbers are usually expressed on an annual basis, so the Sortino ratio is annualized.

As an illustration, Table 20.7 shows the Sortino ratios of our five funds calculated with respect to different minimum acceptable returns. If the goal of the investor is to avoid losing money, the MAR is set at zero and Fund 4 ranks as the best fund. If the goal of the investor is to achieve at least the risk-free rate, the MAR is set equal to the T-bill rate and Fund 5 comes out on top. Finally, if we use the mean return of each fund as the reference MAR, Fund 1 becomes the best performing fund.

Clearly, the Sortino ratio can accommodate different degrees of target returns. However, there are different downside deviations for different minimum acceptable rates and hence different Sortino ratios and different rankings of the funds under consideration. It is therefore essential to specify the minimum acceptable rate used to calculate any Sortino ratio, as well to use the same rate for different funds in order to be able to perform comparisons.

20.4.2   The upside potential ratio

Instead of searching for the manager who had the highest average return over some period of time, some, if not most, investors would prefer to find those managers who had the highest

Table 20.8 Upside potential ratio calculations for our five different hedge funds. All data are annualized

	Fund 1	Fund 2	Fund 3	Fund 4	Fund 5
Mean return (%)	8.16	5.56	9.98	11.36	39.96
Volatility (%)	9.55	29.48	11.45	8.95	79.53
Sharpe ratio	0.41	0.05	0.50	**0.80**	0.45
MAR = 0%					
Upside potential	1.97	6.52	2.77	1.80	12.13
Downside deviation	5.23	16.70	5.86	5.50	30.90
Upside potential ratio	0.38	0.39	**0.47**	0.33	0.39
MAR = Risk-free rate					
Upside potential	6.40	9.15	6.17	5.51	17.54
Downside deviation	15.09	25.55	15.69	14.13	37.54
Upside potential ratio	0.42	0.36	0.39	0.39	**0.47**
MAR = Mean return					
Upside potential	2.89	6.73	3.19	2.41	15.40
Downside deviation	6.23	17.52	7.29	6.60	35.18
Upside potential ratio	**0.46**	0.38	0.44	0.37	0.44

average returns above their MAR. Hence, Sortino, van der Meer and Plantinga (1999a, 1999b) suggested replacing the excess return used in the denominator of the Sortino ratio by the upside potential. The latter is defined as the expected return in excess of the MAR and can be thought of as the potential for success. The ratio of the upside potential to the downside risk is termed the "upside potential ratio".

An important advantage of using the upside potential ratio rather than the Sortino ratio is the consistency in the use of the reference rate for evaluating both profits and losses. An upside potential ratio of 1.6, for instance, means that the fund has 60% more upside potential than downside risk, where the term "risk" refers to the same concept.

As an illustration, Table 20.8 shows the upside potential ratios of our five funds calculated with respect to different minimum acceptable returns. If the goal of the investor is to avoid losing money, the MAR is set at zero and Fund 3 ranks as the best fund. If the goal of the investor is to achieve at least the risk-free rate, the MAR is set equal to the T-bill rate and Fund 5 comes out on top. Finally, if we use the mean return of each fund as the reference MAR, Fund 1 becomes the best performing fund.

20.4.3   The Sterling and Burke ratios

The Sterling and Burke ratios are widely advertised by commodity trading advisers, because those ratios illustrate what they believe they do best: namely, let their profits ride and stringently cap their losses.

The *Sterling ratio* goes one step further than the Sortino ratio by looking at the drawdowns to measure risk. It is defined as

$$\text{Sterling}_P = \frac{\bar{r}_P - r_F}{\overline{dwn}} \tag{20.27}$$

where $\overline{dwn}$ is the average of the most significant drawdowns during the observation period. What is meant by a "significant" drawdown remains to be defined. Some analysts use the maximum drawdown rather than the average drawdown.

Burke (1994) proposed using the square root of the sum of the squares of each drawdown, in order to penalize deep extended drawdowns as opposed to numerous mild ones. The Burke ratio is defined as

$$BU_P = \frac{R_P - R_F}{\sqrt{\sum_{i=1}^{N} \left(dwn_i^2 \right)}} \tag{20.28}$$

20.4.4   Return on VaR (RoVaR)

Another measure that is popular particularly among practitioners is the return on value at risk, or RoVaR (Box 20.4). This is defined simply as the return on the portfolio (RP) divided by the

---

Box 20.4   Return on Value at Risk (RoVaR)

In the case of normally distributed returns, it is relatively easy to express the RoVaR of a portfolio as a function of the Sharpe ratio, as the VaR typically depends on the mean return (R_P) and on the volatility of the portfolio (σ_P). More precisely,

$$VaR_P = -(R_P + k\sigma_P)$$

where $-k$ is the standard normal variable reflecting the confidence level on which the VaR is predicated (for example, $k = -1.645$ if we have a 95% confidence level). It follows that:

$$RoVaR_P = -\frac{R_P}{R_P + k\sigma_P}$$

Using equation (20.1) to replace R_P, we obtain

$$RoVaR_P = -\frac{R_F + \text{Sharpe}_P\sigma_P}{k\sigma_P + R_F + \text{Sharpe}_P\sigma_P}$$

This shows that there is a link between the RoVaR and the Sharpe ratio. It also evidences that we should not expect the same ranking of funds from both measures. As an illustration, if the risk-free rate R_F is zero, we have:

$$RoVaR_P = -\frac{\text{Sharpe}_P}{k + \text{Sharpe}_P}$$

As k can take any value, there is no reason for the RoVaR and the Sharpe ratio to provide equal rankings.

Table 20.9 RoVaR ratio calculations for our five different hedge funds. All data are annualized

	Fund 1	Fund 2	Fund 3	Fund 4	Fund 5
Mean return (%)	8.16	5.56	9.98	11.36	39.96
$\text{VaR}_{1M,99\%}$ (%)	−6.94	−16.97	−5.42	−8.17	−33.06
RoVaR ratio	1.18	0.33	**1.84**	1.39	1.21
$\text{VaR}_{1M,95\%}$ (%)	−2.55	−10.16	−3.80	−2.01	−16.27
RoVaR ratio	3.20	0.55	2.63	**5.65**	2.46

absolute[13] value at risk (VaR$_P$).

$$\text{RoVaR}_P = \frac{R_P}{|\text{VaR}_P|} \tag{20.29}$$

As in the case of the Sortino ratio, the RoVaR ratio can be customized to cater for different holding periods as well as different level of confidence for the VaR. As an illustration, Table 20.9 shows the RoVaR of our five funds using a one-month historical value at risk calculated at 99% and at 95% confidence. Once again, the ranking differs, because the risk definitions are different.

20.5 CONCLUSIONS

Over the last few decades, a number of sophisticated measures have been developed to monitor the risk-adjusted performance of hedge funds. These measures have much in common as regards their underlying framework and financial intuition, but they rely on different calculation techniques and parameters. Hence, when applied to a series of hedge funds, they often produce different rankings.

From the performance evaluator's point of view, this array of performance measures offers a rich choice but at the same time makes the selection of a method difficult – if at all possible. Not surprisingly, for some years, unscrupulous product marketers have taken advantage of this difficulty. They simply considered hedge fund performance measurement as a game, following one guiding principle: "Give me a fund and I will find the performance measure and the time period that makes it look attractive."

Today, hedge fund investing is no longer a game but a serious business. Each investor embarking on a hedge fund investment has his own strategic rationale and critical objectives, which will define his perception of risk. Hence, rather than waiting for all the pieces of the puzzle to fall into place, he should carefully assess his current situation in order to be proactive in his choice of a performance measure. Only by knowing what he is looking for can he identify the performance measure that best suits his requirements. Then, and only then, will the historical analysis of portfolio performance provide much more than just good marketing information (see Box 20.5).

---

[13] The VaR is usually expressed in absolute terms, so the RoVaR ratio is positive if the expected return is positive.

Box 20.5 The danger of using historical data to model uncertainty

At this point, we should stress that one needs to be cautious when analysing hedge funds for a future investment on the basis on their historical track record. Whatever the risk measure selected, history may sometimes be misleading, particularly for hedge funds that agree to be systematically exposed to a catastrophic risk and regularly pocket the associated risk premium. Until the Big Event materializes, such funds are likely to generate a low-volatility positive stream of returns, and any empirical measure will evidence them as being great investments. History looks great, but reality is that the underlying extreme risks are often excessively large and should deter most investors. As an illustration, consider a hedge fund that is guaranteed to make money 98% of the time with very limited average losses. Would you be interested? It is likely. Now, what if the fund's trading strategy turned out to be the following. Take a card in a 52 card deck. If the ace of spades comes up, you lose 52 million dollars; otherwise, you earn a million dollars. On average, you will lose $19,231 each time you play, but you will win 51 out of 52 hands. This is what is known as a negatively skewed trading strategy – although as long as losses did not occur, it is not really skewed.

To avoid such cases, the historical track record of hedge funds should always be analysed from a qualitative and quantitative perspective to understand the underlying risk factors, as well as the magnitude of the losses that could occur if an undesirable event-risk ever materialized.

21

Databases, Indices and Benchmarks

A long-term investment is a short-term investment that performed badly.

Due to the private nature of hedge funds, it is relatively difficult to obtain adequate information about the operations of individual funds or reliable summary statistics about the industry as a whole. Hence, for a long time, gaining insight into the performance characteristics of the hedge funds was no simple matter. Quantitative and qualitative information on hedge funds has only recently become more readily available, thanks to the creation of hedge fund databases and indices.

21.1   HEDGE FUND DATABASES

Since hedge funds cannot advertise, being included in a database and therefore on the radar screens of consultants is very important in terms of visibility. Thus, many hedge funds release monthly return information to specialized databases, such as Hedge Fund Research, TASS and Altvest. These databases collect information, and then sell it back to anyone interested in buying it – accredited investors, banks, funds of funds, consultants, and even lucky academics. Some of these data consumers may at some point become hedge fund investors, and this is the major motivation for managers to give out information on a consistent basis.

Most of the large data vendors provide additional services, ranging from fund selection and screening to asset allocation and product structuring. In addition, they use their databases to calculate a number of hedge fund indices that are widely used in the industry, particularly for strategic asset allocation and benchmarking and also for validating the superiority of hedge funds over traditional asset classes.

Unfortunately, as we will see, the existing hedge fund databases and their derived hedge fund indices are not necessarily representative of the entire (non-observable) hedge fund universe. Each database and/or index is built up from different funds according to different methods of construction, and is likely to be affected to a greater or lesser degree by several biases and inaccuracies. As a consequence, the performance of indices supposed to measure the same strategy will evolve at differing paces, which may seriously confuse investors. Some claim that properly accounting for these biases and inaccuracies may, in fact, change the perception of hedge funds. Without adopting this extreme viewpoint, it is important to be aware of the existence of biases and know their estimated extent, as well as some of the solutions that have been recently suggested in the financial literature (Tables 5.1 and 5.2).

21.2   THE VARIOUS BIASES IN HEDGE FUND DATABASES

The biases in hedge fund data come from two main sources. First, there are the biases in the way each database is constructed. Some of these biases are natural, in that they are inherent to the data-collecting process. They can be eliminated, usually at the cost of complicated calculations, but some will subsist as long as it remains impossible to observe the entire universe of hedge

Table 21.1   Major hedge fund and Commodity Trading Advisors (CTAs) databases

Database	Short description	Number of funds/CTAs
Altvest/InvestorForce	Originally developed by Altvest, this database was acquired by InvestorForce. It is now a commercial hedge fund website that provides information on alternative investments as well as integrated analytical and reporting tools	Over 2600
Barclays Hedge Fund and CTA Database	Barclays offers the newest, fastest growing, and most accurate and up-to-date hedge fund/CTA database available	Over 2200
CISDM/Zurich/MAR	Originally created by Managed Account Reports (MAR), this database was sold to Zurich Capital Markets in March 2001 and gifted to the University of Massachusetts Center for International Securities and Derivatives Markets (CISDM) in August 2002	Over 2500
Daniel B. Stark & Co.	Daniel B. Stark & Co.'s CTA & Futures Fund Manager Database contains 12 years of information on commodity trading advisers and futures funds	Over 420 CTAs Over 200 futures funds
EurekaHedge	EurekaHedge Advisors is an advisory firm registered with the Securities and Futures Commission of Hong Kong	Over 330 in Asia Over 500 in Europe 734 funds of funds
Eurohedge InvestHedge AsiaHedge	Managed by HedgeFund Intelligence – an independent publishing group – with the Bank of Bermuda, these online databases provide performance data and contact information on European funds, and funds of hedge funds	Over 650 in Europe 700 funds of funds
Financial Risk Management (FRM)	This proprietary database belongs to FRM, an independent investment management group dedicated to the construction and management of customized hedge fund portfolios. The database has been used in some academic research	About 8000
Hedge Fund Research (HFR)	HFR is an SEC-registered investment adviser specializing in structuring and managing fund of funds and multiple manager portfolios. It is a leading supplier of data on hedge funds	Over 2500

funds. Second, there is the problem of stale or, worse, "managed" hedge fund prices being reported by the managers directly. In extreme cases, these biases generate errors that make the data absolutely useless.

21.2.1   Self-selection bias

The self-selection bias is really innate to the private nature of the hedge fund industry. While mutual fund performance data must be disclosed to the public, hedge funds, as private investment pools, are not required to disclose performance or asset information to anyone other than their current investors. Plus, the hedge fund managers themselves decide what information is

Table 21.2   Major hedge fund and Commodity Trading Advisors (CTAs) databases

Database	Short description	Number of funds/CTAs
Hennessee	Hennessee is an SEC-registered investment adviser that provides only alternative investment advisory services	About 3000
Morgan Stanley Capital Indices (MSCI)	Introduced in 2002, the MSCI Hedge Fund Indices offer transparency in index construction and maintenance for qualified investors, a comprehensive hedge fund classification framework, and an extensive, growing and reliable database	More than 1300
TASS/Tremont	Founded in London in 1990, TASS Investment Research is the information and research subsidiary of Tremont, and one of leading providers of data, information and market intelligence to the hedge fund industry. The TASS database is one of the oldest and largest hedge fund databases in the industry	Over 3000
Tuna/Hedgefund.net	Hedgefund.net is a free hedge fund website that provides information on alternative investments to more than 35 000 accredited investors world wide	About 4000
US Offshore Funds Directory	An annual printed source of information on hedge funds	About 1000
Van Hedge Fund Advisors	A research and hedge fund advisory firm	Over 5000

to be provided in their prospectuses. Of course, some hedge fund managers may opt to report performance information to data providers, but this is only done on a voluntary basis. Hence, the sample of hedge funds observed will not constitute a true random sample of the general population.

This situation is likely to create a bias, because the characteristics and performance of reporting funds may differ from those of non-reporting funds. As an example, smaller funds with good track records have a strong incentive to report to databases, because this will increase their visibility and may attract new investors. Conversely, managers with sub-par performance will not report to databases because they do not want to compare badly with better-performing peers. Thus, at first glance, the conclusion would be that the reporting funds should have a better performance than the non-reporting funds. Consequently, databases where poorly performing hedge funds are likely to be missing should have a bias towards the best performing funds.

However, there are also a large number of very good, well-established hedge fund managers who do not report to databases because they do not need to or do not want to. Some have been successful in achieving the business desired, they already manage the assets they want, and they may have long lists of investors waiting to enter the fund. So, why take on the burden of reporting on a regular basis to a third party? Others are afraid that if they communicate their performance to a data vendor, they will be included in that data vendor's index and automatically raise the performance of that index, so their individual performance will appear less differentiated. The conclusion then would be that databases might have a bias towards only the average and below-average hedge funds.

In reality, the self-reporting bias may be positive or negative depending on the circumstances. As long as the non-reporting funds remain unobservable, it is not possible to quantify exactly the impact[1] of the bias. However, since investment talent combined with the ability to identify and take advantage of market opportunities is usually in short supply, it seems reasonable to assume that non-reporting managers with a poor performance outnumber those with a good performance.

21.2.2   Database/sample selection bias

Selecting a database or a sample of hedge funds to work with is also likely to be a major source of performance bias. Every existing database is incomplete. The reason is that most databases, samples and studies only cover funds that meet some specific criteria, such as a minimum asset base, an audited track record, or a few years of existence. Although rational and easily justifiable from an investment perspective, these criteria create a sample selection bias towards particular segments of funds. As an illustration:

- The worst hedge fund managers will never appear in databases simply because they do not survive long enough – most databases require at least two years of existence. The result is likely to be an upward bias in databases in comparison with the entire universe.
- Several data vendors (e.g. HFR) exclude particular investment styles such as managed futures funds from their database. The reason is that they consider them as being different from true hedge funds. However, this sentiment is not universally shared, and other databases (e.g. TASS, MAR) include them alongside hedge funds. The same problem applies to funds of hedge funds, which are sometimes excluded to avoid double counting the assets (once in the fund, and once in the fund of funds), and sometimes included.

In addition to these explicit selection biases, there are also implicit biases. For instance, managers may agree to report to one or two databases, but rarely to all the existing databases. Hence, the sample sets being different, there may be wide differentials in the statistics calculated by various databases. Differences in the data collection methods among databases may be the source of another bias. Some databases allow managers to directly input and revise their prices, while others collect data directly from the administrators. Needless to say, the latter source is far more reliable,[2] but more difficult to obtain.

21.2.3   Survivorship bias

Survivorship bias is probably one of the most discussed biases in the performance analysis literature. Simply stated, survivorship bias results from the tendency of some funds to be excluded from performance studies and databases due to the fact that they no longer exist. Most database vendors started collecting data in the middle of the 1990s, or even later in some cases. Historical returns from these databases are therefore conditioned by survival and may be overstated, while historical risk may be understated. This assumes, of course, (i) that funds

---

[1] Note that a similar bias has already been studied in economics. In fact, James Heckman, a Nobel Prize winner in 2000, developed a procedure for correcting this type of bias in linear regression models. The key insight in Heckman's work is that, if we can estimate the probability that a fund will be willing to report on a voluntary basis, we can use this probability estimate to correct the linear regression models.

[2] Liang (2000) made the noteworthy observations that (i) out of the 1162 funds in the HFR database and the 1627 funds in the TASS database, there were only 465 common funds, and that (ii) only 47% of the performances recorded for the common funds were strictly identical. For the other 53% of the funds, there were several significant differences in the net asset value, incentive fee, management fee and investment styles.

that disappeared did so for performance reasons, and (ii) that data on funds that disappear for performance or financial reasons are dropped from the database.

A good illustration of how survivor bias can skew inferences is the "marathon analogy". Say only 100 runners out of a field of 1000 contestants in a marathon actually finish. Bearing in mind that there were 1000 starters, if a person finished 100th out of these 100, what is his or her rank: last, or in the top 10%? The same question obviously applies to hedge funds. Indeed, it is important to realize that the hedge funds that contributed to the successful performance of the industry over the last 10 years are for the most part not the same funds that are still available today.[3]

Survivorship bias is not peculiar to funds and managed portfolios. It also exists in other asset classes, such as equity. As an illustration, Foster and Kaplan (2001) evidenced that only 74 stocks out of the 500 that made up the S&P 500 in 1950 survived until the year 2000, and only 18 companies of the Forbes 100 list published in 1917 were still present on the Forbes 100 list of 1987. But the phenomenon is magnified with mutual and hedge funds, because the annual attrition rate is much larger than for stocks. As an illustration, in 1986, the then existing 586 equity funds tracked by *Lipper Analytical Services* returned 13.4%. By 1996, the 1986 performance had magically improved to 14.7%, because 24% of the funds had disappeared or been merged into other funds. Of course, the poor returns investors had received from the defunct funds did not disappear; they just went unreported as if they had never existed. Brooks and Kat (2001) stated that around 30% of newly established funds do not survive the first three years, primarily due to poor performance.

Using four survival models, Gregoriou (2002) conducted survival analysis of hedge funds from the Zurich Capital Markets database from 1990 to 2001. He found that the median life of a hedge fund is 5.5 years and that most long-lived funds tend to be large in size, with high returns, low leverage and low minimum purchase requirements. Funds appear to fail more after the first year, and the conditional fail rate continues to be relatively high for several years before it eventually decreases. Not surprisingly, funds of hedge funds had the longest median survival time at 7.5 years.

Several data vendors now retain historical data about funds that have been liquidated or have stopped reporting for other reasons, so survivorship bias should gradually disappear. However, it still exists for historical data prior to the creation of the database and is influenced heavily by the decision to keep tracking funds that have disappeared. Other data vendors (e.g. HedgeFund.net) explicitly state that they do not care about survivorship bias and keep removing from their database the past performance of funds that have ceased operations.

Note that the motives for disappearing from a database are numerous and cover a variety of situations:

- The fund is liquidated, typically after a series of large and sudden losses.
- The fund is closed, typically after a long period of below-par performance that drives net asset values well below previous high-water marks for the payment of performance-based fees.
- The fund is merged with another hedge fund. This is typically the case of small non-performing funds that are absorbed into other funds.
- The fund stops reporting, but may still be active. In practice, people often refer to funds that exit from a database but still exist as "defunct funds", whereas a "dead fund" is one that has exited from the database and stopped operations.

---

[3] Brown *et al.* (2001) observed that 50% of hedge fund managers disappear within 30 months, and only 4% have been in business for 10 years.

Table 21.3   Estimates of the survivorship bias on average return

Study	Survivorship bias (% per annum)	Sample
Malkiel (1995)	0.5% or 1.5%	Mutual funds
Bares, Gibson and Gyger (2001)	1.3%	FRM (Incl FoF), 1996–1999
Ackerman, McNally and Ravencraft (1999)	0.16%	HFR and MAR databases, including funds of funds, 1989–1999
Brown, Goetzmann and Ibbotson (1999)	3%	Hand-collected data from the US Offshore Funds Directory, 1989–1995
Park, Brown and Goetzmann (1999)	2.6%	Offshore hedge funds
Fung and Hsieh (2000b, 2001)	3%	TASS database, 1994–1998
Fung and Hsieh (1997b)	3.4%	CTA funds from TASS database
Liang (2000, 2001)	2.2% to 2.4%	TASS database
Edwards and Caglayan (2001)	1.85%	MAR (incl. FOF), 1991–1998
Barry (2003)	1.4%	TASS database, 1994–2001

In theory, correcting for survivorship bias is fairly easy. We just need to obtain data for the entire set of funds that existed over the period under review and then calculate the annual performance of the average fund in the complete sample. The latter is then compared with the annual average performance of surviving funds (those that are still operating at the end of the sampling period). The return difference gives us the survivorship bias. This is the methodology that was adopted by Malkiel (1995) for mutual funds. With hedge funds, however, the entire sample of funds is not observable, as there are no disclosure or registration requirements. Hence, survivorship bias cannot be measured directly and needs to be estimated from samples of surviving funds and samples of dead funds.

The literature on hedge funds provides a series of estimates of the survivorship bias. They vary from 0.16% in Ackermann *et al.* (1999) to 3.0% in Fung and Hsieh (2000a, 2000b) – see Table 21.3. As demonstrated by Liang (2000), these differences are easy to explain if one considers the compositional differences in the databases (e.g. the proportion of dead funds retained), the inclusion of funds-of-funds (less susceptible to overall failure), and the starting date of the studies (leading databases only retain returns on dead funds that died after 1994).

The consensus in the industry appears to be that since 1994, the TASS and MAR databases better reflect the (unobservable) hedge fund universe than the HFR database. In addition, the attrition rate increased significantly in 1998, as well as during the bear market of 2000–2003. In these circumstances, one should imagine a potential survivorship bias of around 3 to 4% per annum. However, as illustrated by Brown and Goetzmann (1995) and Brown *et al.* (2001), survivorship is also likely to impact higher moments of the distribution of returns as well as the degree of serial correlation.

21.2.4   Backfill or instant history bias

Another important source of bias is the backfill bias (Table 21.4), also called the instant history bias. It occurs whenever funds joining a given database are allowed to backfill their historical

Table 21.4   Estimates of the backfill bias on average return

Study	Backfill bias (% p.a.)	Sample
Fung and Hsieh (2000b, 2001)	1.4%	TASS database, 1994–1998
Edwards and Caglayan (2001)	1.2%	MAR (incl. FOF), 1991–1998
Barry (2003)	1.4%	TASS database, 1994–2001

returns, therefore entering the database with "instant history", even though they were not part of the database in previous years.

This is equivalent to granting a free option to hedge fund managers, namely, the option to decide when to be included in the database with all or part of the fund's track record. Since it is in each fund's interest to display the most positive performance possible, most managers will go through an incubation period during which they will not report any performance figures. Then, if the mean performance displayed by a fund during its incubation period is better than that of funds that have belonged to the corresponding database for a long time, the manager will request its inclusion in the database with all its track record. Naturally, this is likely to bias the past performance upward. As an illustration, Barry (2003) studied the TASS database and observed that 80% of hedge funds backfill at least six months of data, 65% of all funds backfill at least 12 months and 50% backfill more than two years. More worrying is the observation by Liang (2000) that out of the 465 funds listed in common by the HFR and TASS databases, only 154 (or 33.1%) have the same starting date in both databases.

Different databases are not exposed to instant history bias in the same way. Both HFR and CSFB say they do not allow data to be backfilled, but some firms do let funds put the past few years of returns into the database, and this practice distorts the data.

The backfill bias may be estimated for a particular database by averaging the returns since inception and comparing them to the average returns since the fund's inclusion date. Academic research seems to suggest an estimate of 1.2% to 1.4% per annum using this methodology. However, correcting historical performance by removing the track record between the inception date and the database-inclusion date is not necessarily recommended, as it may create a new style bias of the truncated dataset *vis-à-vis* the original. For instance, over the period 1999–2000, it would remove a large proportion of returns to new funds, most of which were long-bias equity hedge funds that outperformed other funds during that period (Figure 21.1).

21.2.5   Infrequent pricing and illiquidity bias

Another serious problem with hedge fund data is the natural tendency for managers to "manage" optimally their monthly net asset value in order to smooth their returns. The problem is particularly acute for two categories of hedge funds:

- Hedge funds holding illiquid securities or securities that are difficult to price, such as very small cap stocks, emerging market bonds, over-the-counter securities and distressed assets. The marking to market of these assets is often difficult, due to the small trading volume and/or unavailability of effectively traded prices daily. Consequently, some fuzziness and subjectivity comes into play in the determination of fair net asset values. As an illustration, if a security does not trade on the first and last days of the month, the manager will often assign a price, which could be the price at which the security last traded (hence stale), or, worse, a price which the manager thinks is reasonable.

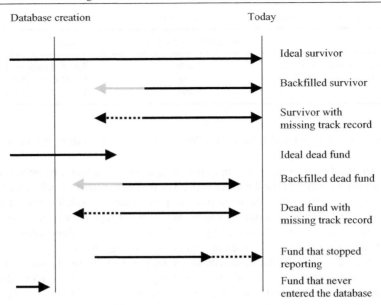

Figure 21.1   The different types of funds in a database

- US onshore limited partnerships, as the vast majority of these funds value their own portfolio. Only 30% use third-party administrators, and in most of the cases, they only use the so-called NAV-light service, which is simply an administrator rubber-stamping the prices supplied by the fund itself.

The Capital Market Risk Advisors (CMRA) survey on NAV/fair value practices, whose results are discussed in Rahl (2001), provides a good illustration of the potential magnitude of the valuation differences that different pricing approaches create. Overall, only 13% of respondents recognized that they were making adjustments of some kind to the "market" prices they received from their valuation sources. These adjustments were small in most cases, but could reach 30% of the net asset value in the largest cases. This is not so surprising when one learns that on 31 December 2000, the differences between the prices provided by five dealers of collateralized mortgage obligations (CMOs[4]) to a hedge fund ranged from 6% to 44%. With this type of price difference, the different methodologies for incorporating dealer quotes (using the average of the dealer quotes, the median, the worst, the best, etc.) can give rise to wide differences in valuation. The least honest managers will obviously use this opportunity to underestimate or overestimate the periodic changes in value of their portfolios in order to smooth their monthly returns, or even worse, to fraud.

More worrying are the results of the Investor Risk Committee of the International Association of Financial Engineers and CMRA survey of institutional investors, hedge funds, and funds of funds on hedge fund transparency and valuation practices. About 50% of investors and 20% of funds of funds do not know whether their funds are making any adjustments to NAV, and only

---

[4] Collateralized mortgage obligations are investment grade bonds that are backed by a pool of mortgage loans with a fixed maturity. The rules for the distribution of the principal payments and interest from the underlying collateral are specified in the CMO prospectus.

94% of funds of funds versus 50% of investors receive details on most or all of their hedge funds' valuation policies. If a manager, consciously or not, tends to smooth his returns (and systematically understates the volatility of his portfolio and its correlations with traditional indices), then there will be an associated systematic overstatement of risk-adjusted returns.[5] Consequently, when fed into an optimizer, these returns will look very attractive, and there will be an over-allocation to investment styles and managers that make use of less liquid securities. This phenomenon is referred to as the illiquidity bias.

Finally, a multi-period sampling bias may occur if the historical period analysed is too short. Ackermann et al. (1999) argue in favour of an estimation period of at least 24 monthly observations, whereas Fung and Hsieh (2000a, 2000b) require at least 36 historical returns for each fund in their analysis.

21.3 FROM DATABASES TO INDICES

Although hedge fund databases are marred by all the above-mentioned biases, they remain extremely useful tools. In the late 1980s and early 1990s, when hedge funds were identified with, for example, George Soros' Quantum Fund and Julian Robertson's Tiger Fund, there was no source of information other than the complacent self-reports of fund managers, which were generally not easily accessible for investors. The industry was hampered by a lack of information transparency, making an informed investment decision difficult. In those days, the appeal of hedge funds was their exclusivity: only those with the right contacts and sufficiently large amounts of money could buy a ticket on the hedge-fund train.

It is only in the last decade that hedge funds have matured from being cowboy investments for the rich to being a serious alternative to the traditional asset classes. The massive inflow of capital has brought an end to the relatively confidential nature of alternative investment strategies, which can no longer reasonably be regarded as a marginal activity within the asset management industry. Thanks to the creation of hedge fund databases, investors have progressively gained access to uniform, accurate and timely measures of valuation, return and risk at the fund level. But what about the industry level? There seems to be an index for just about anything these days, so why not an index for hedge funds? Boosted by the rising interest of institutional investors and the explosion in the number of managers and trading styles, a plethora of indices have sprung up to measure performance at the industry level.

21.3.1 Index construction

The least we can say is that hedge fund indices were initially regarded with scepticism. Indeed, there seems to be an inherent contradiction between the target of absolute performance generally shown by the alternative investment world and the fundamental idea of an index. But the contradiction is only perceived. In reality, the logic and potential benefits of a hedge fund index are essentially the same as for any other asset class:

- An index provides a broadly representative picture of the composition, valuation, performance and risks of the hedge fund industry over time, as well as its correlations with other asset classes. It is particularly useful in improving the soundness of the strategic allocation process, for instance in determining how much to allocate to hedge funds in a global

---

[5] Asness, Krail and Liew (2001) have focused on this problem and observe that once the data is adjusted, the effective risk (market exposure) of the corresponding hedge fund rises significantly.

diversified portfolio. It also helps people to better understand the performance profiles of different strategies, thus countering the negative publicity surrounding hedge funds.

- Not all hedge fund managers are equally skilled, and the evidence suggests that the dispersion in returns between good and bad managers is widening with time. An index provides a benchmark against which the performance of managers can be measured in a fair way.

- An index provides the basis for constructing a passive investment product, i.e. index funds, for investors seeking controlled exposure to the asset class through a single, efficient, convenient investment without carrying specific risks. Given the unique challenges of hedge fund investing, the potential benefits of an index-based, passive investment product are especially compelling. Moreover, its existence would open the possibility of creating hedge fund derivatives to participate in a particular investment style.

- An index provides the standardized data needed to measure the risk return profile of any fund compared with the index. In particular, it allows investors to take active bets in a conscious way by voluntarily diverging from the index.

However, the difficulties involved in the development of quality indices, which are already evident in the traditional universe, are exacerbated in the case of hedge funds. First, indices built from databases of individual hedge funds inherit all the database biases. Consequently, the performance of the index (based on the observed hedge funds in the database) will not necessarily match that of the unobservable hedge funds in the whole universe of funds. Second, the correct classification of observed funds based on their investment style is difficult. All existing classifications are ambiguous and arbitrary. Not only are the borders between the strategies and funds blurred, they are constantly changing.

Consequently, although the need for and value of a hedge fund index is clear, none of the indices constructed so far has gained universal acceptance in the marketplace. This is not surprising, given the diversity and complexity of the hedge fund industry. Consider just a few of the criteria that an index must meet, and the unique challenges that arise in trying to construct an index. To gain acceptance, a hedge fund index should be clearly positioned with respect to a series of key principles:

- *Transparency*: The list of funds included in an index and the weight assigned to each fund should be fully disclosed and readily obtainable. Guidelines for altering the index, its components or their weights should be specified in advance and be reasonable according to common sense. The prices or returns used to compute the indices should also be available – possibly for a fee – so that index returns can be independently verified and explained.

- *Index coverage and representativity*: Ideally, an index should represent the whole hedge fund universe accurately. However, this raises the question of being comprehensive versus being appropriate. A comprehensive index will include the as many funds as possible, ideally the whole universe. An appropriate index will exclude funds that a typical institutional investor would not hold, for instance because the track record is too short, the size too small or the reputation of the manager unsavory. It may also favour the purity of the investment style at the expense of covering a larger number of funds.

- *Weighting*: An important question with hedge fund indices is the weighting scheme. Should the index weight funds by market capitalization (i.e. assets under management) or assign an equal weight to all funds? In the traditional investment world, capitalization weighted indices have won the battle. They correspond more to the intuitive vision of investing, that is, (i) investors tend to allocate more to larger companies and (ii) in the absence of rebalancing, good performance results in an increase of the relative weight of a company in the index.

This corresponds to a momentum-type strategy, where more money is naturally allocated to winners. In contrast, equally weighted indices are rebalanced every month by removing money from well-performing funds and putting it into poorly performing ones ("selling winners and buying losers"). This corresponds to a contrarian strategy and is an artifact of equally weighted indices.

However, in the hedge fund world, there is only one index provider that systematically uses capitalization-weighted indices. This apparent success of equally weighted indices is founded on a series of reasons.

– Hedge fund indices are still in their infancy. It is worth recalling that the Dow Jones index at the beginning was a simple, equally weighted average of a few companies' share prices. This was justified by the lack of computing power at that time. More than a century later, the Dow Jones is still widely used, but it is completely unrepresentative of the US economy in general; investors prefer the Standard & Poor's 500. A similar evolution is likely to take place in the hedge fund universe.

– Standardizing for asset size is problematic in index construction. The assets under management of hedge funds are difficult to determine, since many managers combine managed accounts and onshore/offshore vehicles. Moreover, hedge funds may have different levels of leverage and those levels may vary over time, with the result that the real asset size may also vary significantly.

– Some claim that capitalization-weighted indices create a distorted picture, as "hot money" flows into a successful fund or strategy, which creates a temporary over-weighting. Although this is true, the same remark somehow applies to equally weighted indices, as the majority of new funds are usually created in the most successful strategies. Furthermore, equally weighted indices often double or triple the weight of individual funds by considering separately the different versions of the same fund (e.g. limited partnership, different series of shares for the offshore fund, managed accounts), which is not much better.

As you have probably guessed, our preference goes clearly to asset-weighted indices, which effectively measure the performance of the average dollar invested in the industry – just as the Standard & Poor's 500 measures the performance of the average dollar invested in the US stock market. Equally weighted indices are less useful, unless one wants to measure the performance of the average manager in the industry (Figure 21.2).

• *Investability*: The question of investability is a thornier one. Some claim that, to be useful to investors and advisers, a hedge fund index should represent the world of funds that are actually open to new investment – not the history of funds that are already closed – and that can provide adequate capacity to absorb new investment for the foreseeable future. While making perfect sense from an investment perspective, this goes against the idea of measuring the universe performance by encompassing the largest possible number of funds. It seems that there is no clear answer to the question. An index could adopt either attitude. It simply needs to be clearly situated in terms of its investability policy.

• *Timely reporting*: It is necessary to obtain the index performance in a reasonable amount of time after the end of the month in question.

• *Stability of performance over time*: Once published, the performance of an index should not be revised retroactively.

Despite the formidable task of getting information from hedge fund managers, a growing number of firms are now involved in the creation and publication of hedge fund indices, including leading traditional index providers such as Standard and Poor's and Morgan Stanley

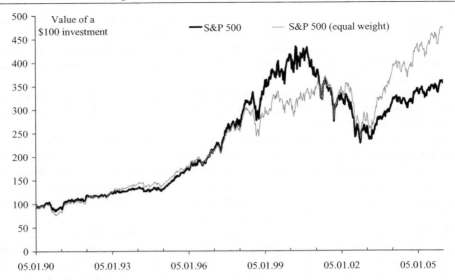

Figure 21.2   Comparison between the "usual" S&P 500 (thick line) and the equally weighted S&P 500 (thin line)

Capital Indices. Hence, the lack-of-index issue that once deterred many institutions from embracing hedge funds is now slowly being swept away. The proliferation of new hedge fund indices has even resulted in a new difficulty: that of choosing one.

21.3.2   The various indices available and their differences

For investors, selecting the right index is a real challenge, since the wrong choice may create disappointment resulting from unexpected risks and the lack of compliance with actual needs. The difficulty is that the strengths and weaknesses of competing indices are rarely evidenced, which makes the whole process that much more confusing. Rivalry has always been present in the clubby world of index design and maintenance, but it has always been subtle, even fraternal, in nature. Each index provider claims to have the best set of hedge fund indices, but none will criticize explicitly other indices. Thus there is not one index that can be considered definitive. Even worse, investors are increasingly concerned by the use of specific indices to enhance the marketing presentation of hedge fund products. Consequently they are losing trust in hedge fund indices and remain suspicious about which one to use. In order to step back from this vicious circle, we provide below a comparison of the major index providers as well as the structure and essential construction rules of their indices.

ABN Amro

ABN Amro, in conjunction with Eurekahedge Fund Advisors, publishes the EurekaHedge indices, which form a set of equally weighted indices tracking the performance of Asian hedge funds. There are currently three indices available: the ABN EH Index, the ABN EH Japan index and the ABN EH Asia ex-Japan index. The constituent funds all have minimum assets under management of $40 million. Rebalancing occurs "periodically", as material changes in assets under management become known.

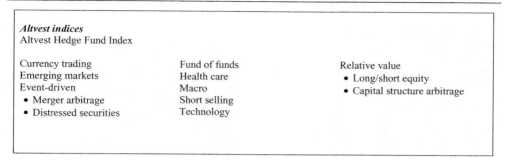

Altvest indices
Altvest Hedge Fund Index

Currency trading	Fund of funds	Relative value
Emerging markets	Health care	• Long/short equity
Event-driven	Macro	• Capital structure arbitrage
• Merger arbitrage	Short selling	
• Distressed securities	Technology	

Figure 21.3   The classification used by Altvest

Altvest

Altvest is a subsidiary of InvestorForce Inc., an information-providing company that targets institutional investors, consultants and money managers. Since the year 2000, Altvest has produced a family of 14 hedge fund indices from a database of about 2000 hedge funds, with data going back to 1993.

Altvest's indices consist of a master index, which is built from all funds in the database, and 13 sub-indices comprising funds that are included in the master index (see Figure 21.3). To map funds with categories, Altvest assigns each fund to the category in which the largest percentage of its assets is invested. If a fund changes category, its past performance remains with its previous sub-index and future performance is included in the new index. Note that a fund can be simultaneously included in several sub-indices. For example, a fund of funds specialized in technology stocks appears in both the "fund of funds" and the "technology" sub-indices. Additionally, the "event-driven" sub-index includes all funds from both the "merger arbitrage" and "distressed securities" sub-indices, and the "relative value" sub-index includes all funds from the "long/short equity" and "capital structure arbitrage" sub-indices.

Although only recently created, Altvest became popular when Calpers, the largest public pension plan in the United States, announced that it would be using Altvest's capabilities to manage its one billion dollar position in alternative investments. Since then, Altvest has also created an innovative technology platform that allows investors and consultants to search for information on alternative investments online. The information is updated online on a daily basis and provided through the web, which means it is available as soon as managers report their performance. Historical data are frozen after a month, so that it can never be modified by the addition or removal of new funds.

CISDM/Zurich/MAR

Founded in 1979, Managed Account Reports (MAR) is a subsidiary of Metal Bulletin plc, a London Stock Exchange listed publishing and information providing company. It has tracked managed futures investments since 1979 and hedge funds since 1994.

MAR used to publish a series of monthly hedge fund and managed futures indices that had the particularity of considering the median performance rather than the average (see Figure 21.4). With the acquisition of the company's alternative investment fund databases and related intellectual property by Zurich Capital Markets in March 2001, MAR's range of managed futures

CISDM hedge fund benchmarks

CISDM event-driven median
- Distressed securities sub-median
- Risk arbitrage sub-median

CISDM Global emerging median
CISDM Global international median
CISDM Global established median
- Global established growth sub-median
- Global established small-cap sub-median
- Global established value sub-median

CISDM global macro median
CISDM market neutral median
- Market neutral arbitrage sub-median
- Market neutral long/short sub-median
- Market neutral mortgage-backed sub-median

CISDM sector median
CISDM short-sellers median
CISDM fund of funds median
- Fund of funds diversified sub-median
- Fund of funds niche sub-median

CISDM trading adviser benchmarks

CISDM Trading Adviser Qualified Universe Index
CISDM Trading Adviser Qualified Universe Index (Equal-weighted)

Currency advisers sub-index
Diversified advisers sub-index
European advisers sub-index
Financial advisers sub-index

Stock index advisers sub-index
Discretionary advisers sub-index
Systematic advisers sub-index
Trend-follower advisers sub-index

CISDM futures fund benchmarks

CISDM Fund/Pool Qualified Universe Index

Guaranteed fund sub-index
Private pool sub-index
Public fund sub-index

Offshore fund sub-index
Multi-adviser fund sub-index
Single adviser fund sub-index

Figure 21.4   The classification used by CISDM

and hedge fund benchmarks was rebranded under the Zurich name. Zurich then announced its intention of boosting support for the MAR databases by "improving reported performance data, modernizing the technological platforms behind the databases and expanding the hedge fund categories, strategies and styles".

However, in August 2002, Zurich Capital Markets decided to donate its database to the Center for International Securities and Derivatives Markets (CISDM) at the University of Massachusetts, Amherst. This confirmed the CISDM's role as the premier university research centre for the study of alternative investments. The new database is called the CISDM Database and continues to be operated by MAR. It is listed monthly in MarHedge, a publication of Metal Bulletin plc.

CSFB/Tremont

CSFB/Tremont Index LLC is a joint venture between Credit Suisse First Boston and Tremont Advisors Inc. The former is one of the world's leading global investment banking firms and the latter is a diversified financial services company specializing in hedge fund consulting, information and research, and investment products.[6] The two companies joined forces to produce a series of hedge fund indices in 1998, with data going back to 1994.

The selection of funds for the CSFB/Tremont indices is done every quarter. The process starts by considering all 3000 United States and offshore hedge funds contained in the TASS database, with the exception of funds of funds and managed accounts. In order to qualify for inclusion in an index, a hedge fund must (i) have at least $10 million under management; (ii) provide audited financial statements[7]; and (iii) meet the CSFB/Tremont reporting requirements in terms of disclosure and transparency. In August 2003, only 448 funds met these three requirements. The qualifying funds are then divided into various categories based on their investment style, with the final constraint that the index in all cases should represent at least 85% of the assets under management in the corresponding universe. Funds are reselected on a quarterly basis as necessary and the indices are calculated and rebalanced monthly.

The weight of each fund in an index is given by the relative size of its assets under management. This makes the CSFB/Tremont indices the first asset-weighted indices for hedge funds and implies a more accurate depiction of the industry. The composition of the indices is public and available on the web.

In addition to the standard indices, in August 2003, CSFB/Tremont launched a series of investable indices, based on a sample of 60 funds. These 60 funds are selected from the funds included in the broader index. They are generally the six largest funds by assets under management in each of the 10 sectors comprising the CSFB/Tremont Hedge Fund Index. To be a member of the investable index, funds must fulfil the following criteria:

- Be a member of the CSFB/Tremont Hedge Fund Index.
- Be domiciled outside the United States (for access by non-US investors).
- Have no lock-up restriction.
- Be open to new investments and redemptions, with reasonable terms regarding the size of the investment as well as the time limits.[8]
- Be free of any investigation or review by a regulatory body or other authority for such reasons as wrongdoing or breach of any law, regulation or rule.

In August 2003, the aggregate assets under management by the 60 investable index constituents were equal to approximately $55 billion, making it the industry's largest investable hedge fund index (Figure 21.5).

EACM

Evaluation Associates Capital Markets (EACM) is an investment advisory firm based in Norwalk, Connecticut. It specializes in hedge funds and multi-manager investment programmes for institutional and high net worth clients. In January 1996, EACM launched a new benchmark for alternative investment strategies called the EACM100® Index, as well as indices for five broad strategies and 13 underlying sub-strategies, with data going back to 1990.

---

[6] Oppenheimer Funds, a US-based provider of traditional investment products managing assets of $127 billion, recently acquired Tremont Advisors Inc. for $140 million.

[7] Which implies that the fund has been in business for at least a year!

[8] The minimum amount, if any, for initial investment in a fund has to be less than or equal to the greater of (i) the product of $50 000 000 and its prospective weight in the index; and (ii) $100 000. The minimum amount, if any, for subsequent investments in the same fund, must be less than or equal to the lesser of (i) the product of $10 000 000 and its prospective weight in the index; and (ii) $200 000. Redemptions must be feasible no less frequently than monthly or, in the case of funds in the event-driven and convertible arbitrage sectors, no less frequently than quarterly.

CSFB/Tremont indices
Hedge Fund Index

Convertible arbitrage	Event driven	Long/short equity
Dedicated short bias	• Event driven: distressed	Managed futures
Emerging markets	• Event driven: multi-strategy	Multi-strategy
Equity market neutral	• Event driven: risk arbitrage	
Fixed-income arbitrage	Global macro	

CSFB/Tremont investable indices
Hedge Fund Index

Convertible arbitrage	Event-driven	Long/short Equity
Dedicated short bias	Fixed-income arbitrage	Managed futures
Emerging markets	Global macro	Multi-strategy
Equity market neutral		

Figure 21.5   The classification used by CSFB/Tremont

EACM's indices are computed from an equally weighted composite of non-audited performance information provided by a set of about 100 hedge funds. These funds are selected by EACM as being representative of their style, and the index may be rebalanced at the beginning of each calendar year. However, EACM does not disclose individual fund names or their weightings, which they consider proprietary (Figure 21.6).

Hedge Fund Research (HFR)

Hedge Fund Research (HFR) is a veteran of the hedge fund industry. The Chicago-based firm publishes a series of 37 equally weighted monthly performance HFRI indices based on both onshore and offshore funds from the HFR database. These indices are net of fees and free of

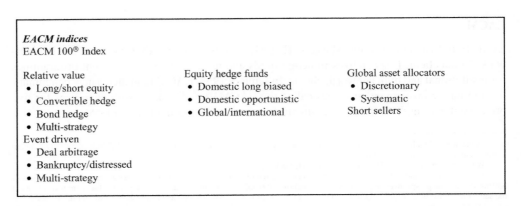

Figure 21.6   The classification used by EACM

HFRI
HFRI Fund Weighted Composite Index

Convertible arbitrage
Distressed securities
Emerging markets (total)
 • Emerging markets: Asia
 • Emerging markets: Eastern Europe/CIS
 • Emerging markets: global
 • Emerging markets: Latin America
Equity hedge
Equity market neutral
 • Equity market neutral: statistical arbitrage
Equity non-hedge
Event driven
Fixed income (total)
 • Fixed income: arbitrage
 • Fixed income: convertible bonds
 • Fixed income: diversified
 • Fixed income: high yield
 • Fixed income: mortgage-backed

Macro
Market timing
Merger arbitrage
Regulation D
Relative value arbitrage
Sector (total)
 • Sector: energy
 • Sector: financial
 • Sector: health care/biotech
 • Sector: miscellaneous
 • Sector: real estate
 • Sector: technology
Short selling
Fund of funds
 • Fund of funds: conservative
 • Fund of funds: diversified
 • Fund of funds: market-defensive
 • Fund of funds: strategic

Figure 21.7   The classification used by Hedge Fund Research

survivorship bias after 1994.[9] Funds are assigned to categories based on the descriptions in their offering memoranda. There is no minimum required asset-size, nor minimum length of track record for fund inclusion in the index. The weighting scheme is revised on a monthly basis to include new funds and to eliminate defunct ones. The indices are updated three times a month (flash estimate, mid and end month). The trailing four months are left as estimates and are subject to change. All performance prior to that is locked and is no longer subject to change (Figure 21.7).

Since March 2003, HFR has also published a series of HFRX indices (one composite index and eight primary investable indices). The styles covered are convertible arbitrage, distressed securities, event-driven, equity hedge, equity market neutral, macro, relative value and merger arbitrage. Rebalanced on a quarterly basis, the HFRX indices are designed to offer full transparency, investability, daily repricing and consistent fund selection.[10] All HFRX indices are composed of hedge funds that are open for investment and that passed extensive qualitative screening and due diligence (Figure 21.8).

HedgeFund.net/Channel Capital Group

Channel Capital Group Inc., based in New York City, owns and operates HedgeFund.net, one of the web's most popular sites for hedge fund information and performance data. HedgeFund.net produces a set of 32 hedge fund indices (called the Tuna indices) from a database of around 4000 onshore and offshore funds, with data going back to 1976. It also produces four aggregated indices using the same data (see Figure 21.9).

---

[9] Most HFR indices were created in 1994 and were backfilled until 1990.
[10] The fund selection uses a statistical technique called cluster analysis.

HFRX
HFRX Global Hedge Fund Index

Convertible arbitrage
Distressed securities
Equity hedge
Equity market neutral

Event driven
Macro merger arbitrage
Relative value arbitrage

Figure 21.8   The classification used by Hedge Fund Research (investable indices)

The Tuna indices are calculated as an equally weighted average of the performance of all funds within the corresponding category. Fund managers themselves select the category to which they want to be assigned. The funds that compose the indices are disclosed on the website of HedgeFund.net.

Hennessee

The Hennessee Group LLC is a New York-based research and consulting firm. It produces a set of 23 equally weighted indices and four composite indices, based on a sample of about 500 hedge funds selected from a database of about 3000 funds. Most of these indices were created in 1987 but became publicly available only in 1992.

To be included in the index, a fund should (i) have at least $100 million of assets, or at least $10 million of assets and a track record of more than 12 months; and (ii) satisfy the Hennessee Group LLC reporting requirements. Funds are assigned to categories based on "manager's core competency", and the performance of dead funds stays in the indices to reduce survivorship bias.

An interesting feature of the Hennessee indices is that they include several funds that are closed to new subscriptions, and that therefore do not report to other agencies. This is possible only because clients of the Hennessee Group are effectively investing in these funds (Figure 21.10).

HedgeFund.net (Tuna indices)
Hedge Fund Aggregate Index
Aggressive Aggregate Index
Equity Hedge Aggregate Index
Relative Value Aggregate Index

Aggressive growth	Fund of funds	Regulation D
Convertible arbitrage	Healthcare sector	Risk arbitrage
Country specific	Long only	Short bias
CTA	Long/short hedged	Short-term trading
Distressed	Macro market neutral	Small/micro cap
Emerging markets	Market timer	Special situations
Energy sector	Opportunistic	Statistical arbitrage
Event driven	Options arbitrage	Technology sector
Finance sector	Options strategies	Value
Fixed income	Other	Venture capital/private equity
Fixed income arbitrage	Other market neutral	

Figure 21.9   The classification used by HedgeFund.net

Hennessee Hedge Fund Indices
Hennessee Hedge Fund Index
Hennessee Correlated Index
Hennessee Non-Correlated Index
Hennessee Global/Macro Index

Convertible arbitrage	Healthcare/biotech	Pacific rim
Distressed	High yield	Regulation D
Emerging markets	International	Short biased
Europe	Latin America macro	Technology
Event driven	Market neutral	Telecom and media
Financial equities	Merger arbitrage	Value
Fixed income	Multiple arbitrage	
Growth	Opportunistic	

Figure 21.10   The classification used by HedgeFund.net

InvestHedge, Asiahedge and EuroHedge

HedgeFund Intelligence is an independent publishing group that focuses on providing information about the hedge fund industry, collecting performance data, and organizing hedge fund conferences. Its major characteristic is its independence, as it neither manages money nor advises investors, and the company is 100% owned by its directors and staff. HedgeFund Intelligence produces a series of European and global hedge fund indices with data going back to the year 2000, as well as a series of Asian hedge fund indices going back to 2001 (Figure 21.11).

InvestHedge indices
InvestHedge Composite

Global multi-strategy $		
Arbitrage $	US equity $	Asia Pacific funds of funds $
Global equity $	European equity Euro	Global-macro-currency-debt $
	Emerging markets hedge $	

Eurohedge indices

European long/short $	Fixed income and high yield	Combined arbitrage
European long/short £	Global equity	• Event-driven
European long/short Euro	Managed futures	• Mixed arbitrage
Macro		• Stat. & quant. arbitrage
		• Convertible & equity arbitrage

AsiaHedge indices
AsiaHedge Composite

Asia including Japan US$	Japan long/short US$	Australia long/short AUS $
Asia excluding Japan US$	Japan long/short Yen	Emerging markets

Figure 21.11   The classification used by InvestHedge, AsiaHedge and Eurohedge

LJH Global Investments
LJH Global Hedge Index

Asian hedge	Event driven	Risk arbitrage
Convertible arbitrage	Fixed income arbitrage	Risk arbitrage
Distressed securities	European hedge	Short only
Domestic hedge	Global macro	Technology
Emerging markets	Hedge index	
Emerging markets fixed income	Market neutral equity	

Figure 21.12   The classification used by LJH Global Investments

LJH Global Investments

LJH Global Investments is a consulting and advisory firm based in Naples, Florida. It has developed a set of 16 indices of various hedge fund styles (see Figure 21.12).

Each index is calculated as the performance of an equally weighted sample of 25 to 50 hedge funds. These funds are selected and mapped to a specific strategy by LJH Global Investments. They must provide audited statements and pass some due diligence tests. The composition of each index is revised on a regular basis but is not disclosed.

Morgan Stanley Capital Indices

Morgan Stanley Capital Indices (MSCI) is a leading provider of global equity and fixed income indices used by institutional investors world wide. Cashing in on its pre-eminent place in traditional asset class indices, MSCI teamed up with Financial Risk Management (FRM) to cover the hedge fund field in July 2002 with a new database of about 1500 hedge funds.

In parallel with its database, MSCI has created the industry's most comprehensive and detailed classification framework for hedge funds – the MSCI Hedge Fund Classification Standard. This standard uses multiple characteristics of funds to classify them, grouped together in several dimensions.

- The first dimension covers the investment process employed to generate returns, such as directional trading, relative value, security selection, credit specialist and multi-process. Each process group includes several sub-categories – see Table 21.5.
- The second dimension covers the asset class used to generate returns. This includes equities (split into equity and convertibles), fixed income (split into credit-sensitive, credit-insensitive and mortgage-backed securities), commodities, currencies (split into developed and emerging markets), real estate and options.
- The third dimension is the geographic location of the funds' investments. The categories announced are Europe, North America, Japan, Pacific ex-Japan, and emerging markets, as well as broader global developed and global categories.

Table 21.5 The MSCI Hedge Fund Classification Standard

Investment process		Asset class	Geography		Secondary characteristics	
Process group	Process		Area	Region		
Directional trading	Discretionary trading Tactical allocation Systematic trading Multi-process	Commodities Convertibles Currencies Equity Fixed Income Diversified	Developed markets	Europe Japan North America Pacific ex-Japan Diversified	GICS Sector	Consumer discretionary Consume staples Energy Financials Healthcare Industrials Information technology Materials Telecom services Utilities No industry focus
Relative value	Arbitrage Merger arb. Statistical arb. Multi-process		Emerging markets	EMEA Asia Pacific Latin America Diversified		
Security selection	Long bias No bias Short bias Variable bias		Global markets	Europe Asia ex-Japan Asia Diversified	Fixed income focus	Asset-backed Government sponsored High yield Investment grade Mortgage backed Sovereign No fixed income focus
Specialist credit	Long short credit Distressed securities Private placements Multi-process					
Multi-process group	Event driven Multi-process				Capitaliation size	Mid and large cap Small cap Small and mid cap No size focus

In addition, secondary classification characteristics are the Global Industry Classification Standard (GICS) and capitalization size for equity-oriented strategies, and fixed income focus for credit-oriented strategies. This gives a very large number of potential combinations, but it allows for a very precise definition of the strategy followed by a hedge fund, such as: "relative value – convergence arbitrage – fixed income – global – developed", or "directional trading – long bias – equity – Europe – financial sector – mid cap".

Equally weighted indices are calculated for any strategy where the number of funds is relevant. It is worth noting that MSCI is the first hedge fund index provider to make data on constituent hedge funds available and linked directly to the index, enabling clients subscribing to the indices and fund database to analyse index performance and risk characteristics fund by fund.

MSCI also provides three composite indices based on fund size. The Broad Hedge Fund Composite Index covers funds in excess of $15 million, the Core Fund Index considers only funds in excess of $100 million within a given strategy, and the Small Fund Index includes funds between $15 million and $100 million.

In total, this results in more than 160 MSCI hedge fund indices at the time of writing these lines. Given the prominence of the sponsor, these indices should become widely accepted.

More recently, MSCI also launched its Hedge Invest Index, which consists of a diverse sample of hedge funds that represent a broad range of hedge fund strategies and have weekly liquidity. Published every Friday, the index contains only open funds that have committed to liquidity and capacity terms with Lyxor Asset Management.[11] MSCI is responsible for designing and maintaining the index, classifying funds into strategies and publishing the index and constituent data. Lyxor is responsible for establishing each individual fund on their managed account platform, conducting initial due diligence, monitoring the investment mandate of each hedge fund manager and providing fund valuations independent of each fund's external adviser.

The MSCI Hedge Invest Index is clearly structured for use as the basis of index-linked financial products. As of July 2003, the index contained 64 funds in 11 investment processes. The number of funds in the index is expected to increase over time.

Standard and Poor's (S&P)

Standard and Poor's, the other global leader in index development, is a newcomer to the field of hedge fund indices but it has the ambition of becoming a major player. Since October 2002, it has published a main hedge fund index, as well as four sub-indices covering in total nine investment strategies (macro, equity long/short, managed futures, special situations, merger arbitrage, distressed, fixed income arbitrage, convertible arbitrage and equity market neutral).

The aim of the S&P index is to become the leading, transparent, investable index for hedge funds. Equally weighted, the index only contains 40 funds, which has prompted some skepticism from rivals who often consider it as a sort of fund of funds. The main index actually includes fewer than 1% of the known universe. But S&P insists that, according to its statistical research, 30 to 40 funds reliably reporting their performance data can accurately represent a much larger universe.

---

[11] Lyxor Asset Management (Lyxor) is a subsidiary of the Société Générale Group dedicated to structured funds activities, including management of alternative investment funds. As of June 2003, Lyxor managed a total of $26.7 billion, of which $9.8 billion were in alternative investments, and employed 93 professionals, 60 of whom were dedicated to alternative investment products.

Standard and Poor's Hedge Fund Index		
⇩	⇩	⇩
Arbitrage	**Event-Driven**	**Directional/Tactical**
Equity market neutral	Merger arbitrage	Long/short equity
Fixed income arbitrage	Distressed	Managed futures
Convert arbitrage	Special situations	Global macro

Figure 21.13 The S&P hedge fund classification approach

The S&P hedge fund index has been built from the beginning as an investable index. The funds included have to go through a very stringent quantitative and qualitative filtering process. The quantitative screening assesses each fund's representativity, while the qualitative screening addresses the quality and tenure of the funds, the risk and operating controls, and the capacity to accept new investments. A fund can be removed at any time from the index if it becomes closed to new investment, if it no longer represents its respective strategy, or if it fails to pass the due diligence reviews of Albourne Partners, a hedge fund consultant to S&P. The high level of transparency requested from the fund managers includes daily pricing, which enables S&P to calculate and publish the index on a daily basis. Derivatives Portfolio Management (DPM) is in charge of verifying the valuations.

For purposes of analysis, S&P constructed a pro forma version of the index that is based on the index constituents as of September 2002, using monthly performance data from January 1998 through September 2002 from the fund companies themselves. The pro forma version is rebalanced to its original equal weights annually in August.

Recently, Standard and Poor's granted PlusFunds, a developer of passive hedge fund investment products, an exclusive licence to develop investment products tracking the S&P hedge fund indices. Each manager of a hedge fund included in the index has agreed to manage a separate account identical to his or her private hedge fund (Figure 21.13).

Van Hedge Fund Advisors International

Van Hedge Fund Advisors International is a research and advisory services firm based in Nashville, Tennessee. It maintains a database of about 5000 funds (2650 US and 2350 offshore), primarily used to identify hedge funds for investors, and on request, to design custom hedge fund portfolios.

Van Hedge Fund indices were initially compiled in 1994 and published for the first time in 1995, with data going back to 1988. Van Hedge tracks the performance of 14 strategies, plus a global index, based on a sub-sample of about 750 offshore and onshore hedge funds (see Figure 21.14). Funds are assigned to categories based on their offering memorandums and interviews with their managers.

Zurich Capital Markets

Zurich Capital Markets (ZCM) was originally a wholly owned New York-based subsidiary of the Zurich Financial Services Group.[12] Over the years, ZCM has established itself as an

---

[12] Founded in 1872 and with its headquarters in Zurich, Switzerland, Zurich Financial Services is an insurance-based financial services provider with an international network. It has offices in approximately 60 countries and employs about 68 000 people.

Van Hedge Fund Advisors Van US Hedge Fund Index Van Offshore Hedge Fund Index Aggressive growth Distressed securities Emerging markets Fund of funds Income	Macro Market neutral – arbitrage Mkt neutral – securities hedging Market timing Opportunistic	Several strategies Short selling Special situations Value

Figure 21.14   The classification used by Van Hedge Fund Advisors

attractive niche provider of services to hedge fund investors and managers, and has made several attempts at creating series of investable hedge fund indices.

In October 1999, ZCM and Hedge Fund Research created a joint venture named ZCM/HFR Index Management for the purpose of offering hedge fund indices as well as funds of funds tracking these indices. The new company designed the methodology and started publishing indices tracking five strategies (merger arbitrage, convertible arbitrage, distressed securities, equity hedge and event driven). However, the concept never attracted more than $300 million from investors, mostly from Zurich Capital Markets. The major problem was that the methodology was rather opaque. To quote: "...each index is constructed as a diversified allocation to a collection of separately-managed accounts, weighted and rebalanced via a proprietary methodology developed by the joint-venture." The joint venture terminated in December 2000. ZCM bought back the investment platform of ZCM/HFR for an undisclosed sum and stopped calculating these indices.

In March 2001, following the acquisition of an alternative investment fund database and intellectual property from Managed Account Reports LLC, Zurich Capital Markets in partnership with Schneeweis Partners LLC again started offering five hedge fund indices. The five strategies selected were the same as those of the former ZCM/HFR hedge fund indices, that is, merger arbitrage, convertible arbitrage, distressed securities, equity hedge and event driven. Each index is built from an equally weighted portfolio of 10 to 15 hedge funds. These funds are carefully selected for the "purity" of their investment style, which manifests itself primarily in manager correlation with other pure style managers as well as specific style-related benchmarks. In addition, each selected fund must have had at least $25 million under management for at least two years, and must be likely to be considered for investment by institutional or sophisticated investors. The composition of the portfolio is public, and rebalancing is carried out on a quarterly basis, under the supervision of an independent committee.

In parallel, ZCM launched the Zurich Institutional Benchmark Series, a fund of hedge funds, with the goal of replicating the performance of the indices with modest tracking error and at relatively low cost. It collected $315 million in the first month, and had a target size of $2–$3 billion by the end of 2002. One of its particularities is that it invests with the managers represented in each index through managed accounts, in order to have a complete view of the assets (with Zurich acting as custodian).

In June 2003, however, Zurich Financial Services announced its intention to focus on its core insurance activities and decided to divest itself of the ZCM business line. In July, BNP Paribas and Zurich Financial Services signed an agreement for the transfer of certain structured products from ZCM to BNP Paribas, including structured products linked to alternative investment funds managed by ZCM. This transaction should enable BNP Paribas, already a European leader in structured fund-of-funds products, to become one of the top players in this business in the United States. At the time of writing, the future of the Zurich indices is not known yet, but it does not look so bright.

21.3.3 Different indices – different returns

The different hedge fund indices available on the market are built from different data sets, conform to diverse selection criteria and style classifications, and use different methods of construction. As a result, the observed performance varies considerably depending on the index used, and investors cannot rely on competing hedge fund indices to obtain a true and fair view of hedge fund performance (Table 21.6).

Table 21.6 Comparison between the major hedge fund index providers

	Altvest	CSFB	EACM	Hennessee	HFR	HF Net	MAR	S&P	Van Hedge	Zurich
Managed futures		X				X	X	X		
Global macro	X	X		X	X	X	X	X	X	
Long/short equity	X	X	X		X	X		X		X
Dedicated short	X	X	X	X	X	X	X		X	
Emerging markets	X	X		X	X	X	X		X	
Market neutral		X		X	X	X	X	X	X	
Fixed income arb.		X		X	X	X		X	X	
Convertible arb.		X	X	X	X	X		X		X
Merger arb.	X	X	X	X	X	X	X	X		X
Distressed	X	X	X	X	X	X	X	X	X	X
Funds of funds	X				X	X	X		X	X
Event driven	X	X	X	X	X	X	X			X
Relative value	X		X		X	X				
Special situations						X		X	X	
Regulation D				X	X	X				
Aggressive growth						X			X	
Value				X		X			X	
Energy					X	X				
Financial			X	X	X	X			X	X
Technology	X			X	X	X			X	
High yield				X		X				
Healthcare	X			X	X	X			X	
International				X				X		
Market timing					X	X			X	
Opportunity			X	X		X			X	
Statistical arb.					X	X				

Table 21.7 Performance comparison between the major hedge fund index providers (*source:* Amenc and Martellini, 2001b)

Strategy	Date	Worst index performance	Best index performance	Spread
Convertible arbitrage	Oct. 98	CSFB: −4.67	Henessee: 0.08	4.75%
Dedicated short	Feb. 00	Van Hedge: −24.3	EACM: −3.09	21.20%
Distressed	Aug. 98	HF Net: −12.08	Van Hedge: −4.70	7.38%
Emerging markets	Aug. 98	MAR: −26.65	Altvest: −7.2	19.45%
Event driven	Aug. 98	CSFB: −11.77	Altvest: −6.71	5.06%
Fixed income arbitrage	Oct. 98	HF Net: −10.78	Van Hedge: 0.2	10.98%
Funds of funds	Dec. 99	MAR: 2.41	Altvest: 10.42	8.01%
Global macro	May 00	Van Hedge: −5.80	HF Net: 12	17.80%
Long/short equity	Feb. 00	EACM: −1.56	Zurich: 20.48	22.04%
Market neutral	Dec. 99	Henessee: 0.2	Van Hedge: 5.2	5.00%
Merger arbitrage	Sep. 98	Altvest: −0.11	HFR: 1.74	1.85%
Relative value	Sep. 98	EACM −6.07	Van Hedge: 4.40	10.47%

Several papers have explicitly mentioned the measurement and interpretation problems that surround some hedge fund indices.[13] However, the first study that systematically documented the heterogeneity existing between **all** hedge fund indices is that of Amenc and Martellini (2001, 2003). Some of their results are spectacular. For instance, for the long/short equity strategies, Zurich Capital Markets reports a +20.48% return in February 2000 (non-annualized), while EACM reports a −1.56% return (non-annualized) for the same month and the same strategy. This represents a difference of 22.04% for indices that are supposed to be representative of the same strategy. Similar situations occur with other indices and other strategies, and using quarterly figures does not necessarily smooth out the differences. As an illustration, the maximum difference is 30.08% for long/short or 16.52% for relative value, as opposed to, respectively 22.04% or 10.47%, at the monthly level.

The average correlations between the indices that focus on the same strategy are usually acceptable – see Table 21.7 and Figure 21.15. However, the lowest correlations are extremely low, and even sometimes negative (case of Zurich and EACM long/short equity indices once again). These low correlations seem to occur more frequently in the case of "pure alpha" strategies, such as equity market neutral, long/short, global macro and fixed income arbitrage. In contrast, some strategies seem more homogeneous and consistent in their behaviour (e.g. merger arbitrage).

While not surprising, these results are bothersome because they clearly indicate that hedge fund indices fail to agree on what they measure. This is likely to result in significantly different portfolios, depending on what indices are used to model the asset class during the asset allocation process. Furthermore, the major inconsistencies between indices seem to occur precisely when reliable information is most needed, that is, during periods of market crisis (August/September 1998, February 2000, etc.).

In addition to the problems described above, Amenc and Martellini mention two other biases that affect hedge fund indices:

- The lack of representativeness, as (i) the existing databases only cover a relatively small fraction of the hedge fund population and (ii) some indices only cover a tiny portion of a

---

[13] See, for instance, Brooks and Kat (2001), Fung and Hsieh (2002), or Schneeweis, Kazemi and Martin (2001).

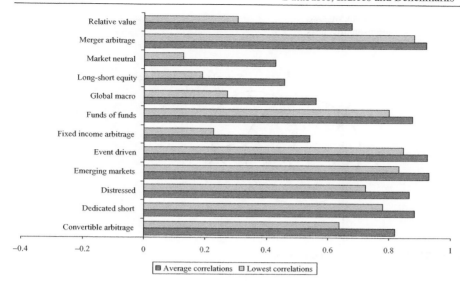

Figure 21.15 Measuring the average and lowest correlation between the indices for each hedge fund strategy (*source:* Amenc and Martellini, 2001)

database. For instance, Zurich Capital Markets and S&P use only 60 hedge funds to build their indices, that is, less than 1% of the total universe.

* The presence of a style bias: Most indices use the managers' self-proclaimed styles to classify funds. But in reality, nothing guarantees that a manager will follow a single investment style and avoid drifting away from it. As opportunities disappear in the original strategies, it is common practice for some hedge fund managers to start looking at other markets – see Lhabitant (2001). As a result, all competing indices for a given style are likely to encompass funds that should not be included.

These two biases can be represented as shown in Figure 21.16. As an illustration, Figure 21.17 shows what we obtain using the TASS, HFR and CISDM hedge fund databases.[14]

Such disturbing evidence poses serious problems. The heterogeneous picture provided by the set of existing hedge fund indices confuses investors and sheds suspicion on results based on a single hedge fund index. Today, it is probably still the major obstacle to the institutionalization of the alternative investment industry. It affects not only portfolio analysis involving hedge funds but also empirical tests of asset pricing theory.

21.3.4 Towards pure hedge fund indices

Rather than building a new index and claiming that the newcomer is better than all the existing ones, Amenc and Martellini (2003) and the EDHEC Risk and Asset Management Research Center recently suggested an original solution to the problem of hedge fund indices' heterogeneity and lack of representativeness. They use *all* the relevant information contained in *all* the competing indices available and compile them to produce a set of optimal alternative indices.

---

[14] We thank Drago Indjik from Fauchier Partners for providing these results.

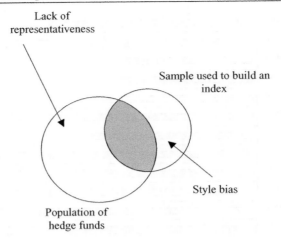

Figure 21.16   The biases in hedge fund indices

Optimal here means stable, more representative, easy to replicate, non-commercial and with fewer biases.

In a sense, each EDHEC index can be seen as a sort of "index of the existing indices". However, the methodology used to calculate the EDHEC index goes far beyond a simple average of the existing indices. It relies on a statistical technique called principal component analysis (PCA), which transforms a number of correlated variables (in our cases, the indices) into a smaller number of uncorrelated variables called *principal components*. The first principal component accounts for as much of the variability in the data as possible, and each succeeding component accounts for as much of the remaining variability as possible.

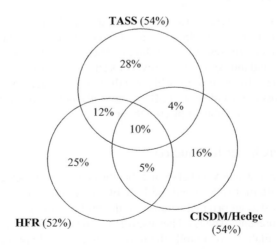

Figure 21.17   The universe according to TASS, HFR and CISDM/Hedge. (We thank Drago Indjik from Fauchier Partners for providing us these results)

Table 21.8   The performance of EDHEC indices (*source:* EDHEC Risk)

Strategy	May 2006 return	YTD 2006	Annual average return since inception	Annual volatility since inception	Sharpe ratio
Convertible arbitrage	0.91%	6.42%	6.89%	3.98%	0.73
CTA global	−1.46%	5.10%	7.45%	9.67%	0.36
Distressed securities	0.86%	7.93%	14.28%	3.93%	2.62
Emerging markets	−3.89%	7.85%	15.44%	8.11%	1.41
Equity market neutral	0.02%	3.67%	6.14%	1.44%	1.48
Event driven	0.08%	7.68%	9.85%	4.51%	1.30
Fixed income arbitrage	0.59%	3.75%	6.89%	1.72%	1.68
Funds of funds	−1.33%	5.31%	6.38%	3.45%	0.69
Global macro	−1.55%	4.37%	8.23%	4.09%	1.03
Long/short equity	−2.48%	5.60%	6.55%	6.18%	0.41
Merger arbitrage	0.09%	6.63%	4.84%	3.07%	0.28
Relative value	−0.25%	5.80%	7.23%	3.32%	0.97
Short selling	2.46%	−1.36%	2.39%	14.43%	−0.11

Without going into too much detail, the intuition behind the EDHEC methodology is as follows. In theory, there exists one true pure index that represents adequately what the hedge fund industry is doing. In practice, this index is not observable, because no one has yet gained access to the complete set of data that its calculation requires. Instead, there are several observable indices that are calculated by various index providers on a sub-set of the complete data set. Each of these indices can be represented as the true pure index, plus some noise capturing the existence of biases and lack of full representativeness. The idea of PCA is to combine optimally all indices in order to eliminate the noise as far as possible. That is, PCA will build a portfolio of the existing indices that best captures the common behaviour of the group of observed indices. Implicitly, the common behaviour identified by PCA should correspond to the true pure index.

In summarizing the group of observed indices into one single portfolio of indices, some information is lost, particularly where the heterogeneity of information provided by competing index providers is the most extreme. However, PCA ensures that the loss is minimal, in the sense that no other linear combination of competing indices implies a lower information loss. On average, Amenc and Martellini (2003) observe that pure style indices are able to capture about 80% of the behaviour of the time-series of competing indices.

How good is the resulting index? Amenc and Martellini prove two theorems that provide the answer to this question. First, a portfolio of competing indices encompasses more individual funds and is always less biased than the average of the set of indices it is extracted from. Second, a portfolio of indices is always more representative than any competing index. The empirical tests confirm the theory and suggest that PCA-based indices do achieve the improvement of representativeness for which they were designed (Table 21.8).[15]

EDHEC recently launched its new model (www.edhec-risk.com) and is now introducing the concepts to industry players and institutional investors. The least one can say is that the first reactions were extremely positive. In particular, passive strategies and products aimed at

---

[15] Amenc and Martellini suggest and test other methodologies to help build a pure style index or index of the indices for a given style, such as Kalman filtering and minimum bias with or without positivity constraints. More detail can be found in their original paper.

Table 21.9   Trackability of the EDHEC Alternative Indices (*source:* EDHEC Risk)

Strategy	EDHEC in sample	EDHEC out of sample	CSFB in sample	HFR in sample
Convertible arbitrage	0.73%	1.05%	2.23%	0.74%
Emerging markets	2.34%	3.39%	4.61%	3.19%
Event driven	0.95%	1.36%	2.40%	1.03%
Fixed income arbitrage	1.11%	1.25%	0.83%	2.70%
Global macro	0.12%	2.23%	0.17%	0.13%
Long/short equity	1.90%	3.25%	4.02%	2.07%
Market neutral	0.73%	0.86%	1.03%	2.28%

capturing the average return of a specific hedge fund universe could greatly benefit from the new set of indices.

To demonstrate the usefulness of their new pure indices, the EDHEC researchers constructed portfolios made up of single funds that replicate the EDHEC Alternative Indices. On average, there were 25 funds in each portfolio, drawn randomly (without replacement) from several database. The weights given to the funds were chosen in order to minimize the tracking error with respect to the EDHEC index. For the sake of comparison, the same procedure was applied with respect to the HFR and the CSFB/Tremont indices.

The tracking errors obtained are represented in Table 21.9. They confirm the superiority of the EDHEC indices in terms of ability to be replicated by a hedge fund portfolio. In particular, the low difference observed between the in-sample and out-of-sample tracking errors confirms that the tracking error is stable over time and remains at acceptable levels. These results, as well as others published on the EDHEC website, confirm that the new indices are ideal candidates to help investors to allocate a significant part of their portfolio to the alternative class. According to many researchers and investors, they even qualify as potential benchmarks – benchmarks that help to assess past performance on a risk-adjusted basis and help to identify the current risk characteristics of hedge fund strategies.

21.4   FROM INDICES TO BENCHMARKS

One of the most controversial topics on the hedge fund front these days is that of benchmarking returns. At first glance, the terms "hedge funds" and "benchmarks" would seem to be conflicting. Hedge fund managers are hired for their skills. They should be allowed to roam wherever their value-creating instincts take them, unfettered by benchmarks that discourage unconventional investment ideas. Their portfolios should aim to produce positive absolute returns rather than outperform a given benchmark. For many years, the perceived success of hedge funds nourished this anti-benchmark view, and as a consequence fostered the mystique, which the alternative investment industry had an enormous vested interest in maintaining. Not surprisingly, the most active opponents of benchmarks were often those who benefited the most from looser scrutiny.

However, with the continued growth of the alternative investment industry, the rising interest of institutional investors and the explosion in the number of managers and trading styles, the demand for benchmarks to measure performance has been rising. The term "benchmarks" should be understood here in the Association for Investment Management and Research (AIMR) sense, that is, as "an independent rate of return (or hurdle rate) forming an objective test of the effective implementation of an investment strategy". People want to be able to measure the performance of managers with whom they place their money but, without benchmarks, how can an investor really monitor a hedge fund's performance and formulate expectations on an ongoing basis? How can he assess whether a manager possesses sustainable skill in generating superior results, or if his performance just derives from the asset class or the particular market in which he has invested?

Performance benchmarks are important for three key reasons: they help to measure the investment performance of institutional fund managers, they provide clients and trustees with a reference point for monitoring that performance, and they can also have the effect of modifying the behaviour of portfolio managers. As investors have become more and more interested in this field, and as so many new hedge funds have come onto the market, it has become more important to maintain a clearer perspective by looking for an assessment of the average performance of the industry. Investing in a hedge fund is largely a matter of purchasing alpha, which is a manager's skill in identifying market inefficiency and exploiting it. Credible benchmarks, or at least references, are therefore necessary to assess alpha in a correct way. Benchmarks are also a good general tool to aid in the planning, implementation and review of investment policies. They provide a common language of communication between the investor and the investment manager, and provide an objective means with which to assess return and risk as well as to interpret and monitor a fund's behaviour.

21.4.1 Absolute benchmarks and peer groups

Originally, hedge fund managers avoided the benchmark question by establishing absolute return targets. These were loosely defined as a flat, stated rate of return which was theoretically achievable in any market environment (e.g. 15%). Hedge fund peer group universes were also used, but only as a supplemental form of comparative performance measurement.

In the year 2000, markets became increasingly challenging for hedge fund managers as well, and they started seriously underperforming relative to historical industry norms. In this new environment, benchmarking to an absolute return in its purest sense was almost impossible. Hence, several hedge fund managers started repositioning their targets in terms of an interest rate, plus a spread (e.g. LIBOR + 6%). However, this did not account for the huge fall in interest rates that the financial world was going to experience. Today, the new semi-absolute returns do not equate to the old calculations. Indeed, yesterday's 15% is far from today's LIBOR plus 5%, which effectively amounts to 6%.

Many managers also turned to a traditional index such as the Standard & Poor's 500 Index (S&P 500[16]) to benchmark the performance of their fund.[17] Although popular because of the recent performance of traditional assets, this type of index is a poor candidate for benchmarking hedge funds. There are three reasons for this:

- *Trading strategy*: Hedge funds normally adopt a dynamic trading strategy that can involve very short-term positions, sometimes buying and selling in the market on an intra-day basis. Hedge funds also change their market exposures significantly depending on market

---

[16] The S&P 500 is a widely recognized benchmark that comprises the 500 largest, publicly traded corporations in the United States.

[17] A point to remember is that, even with a hedge fund manager of superior caliber, it should be arithmetically impossible for the average invested dollar to consistently beat a correctly defined benchmark. By definition, without fees, about half of the managers should beat the benchmark and the other half should not. If all managers beat the benchmark, it is probably because the benchmark is not adequate.

conditions. Traditional indices, in contrast, correspond to a policy of buying and holding stocks for an extended period.

- *Leverage*: Hedge funds typically leverage their bets by margining their positions and by using short sales, whereas the use of leverage is not accounted for in traditional indices.
- *Non-benchmark assets*: Hedge funds typically invest in shares of companies that are not included in the S&P 500, but that make up the rest of the US or world stock and bond markets.

Consequently, the relationship between hedge fund returns and the returns on a traditional benchmark are complex and not linear, causing a loose observable correlation between hedge funds and traditional indices. To make matters worse, investors often set multiple benchmarks, which may conflict with each other (e.g. outperform cash in the short term and equity in the long term, while being correlated to neither of them). This leads to dissatisfaction on the part of both the client and the manager. In our opinion, a fund and its benchmark should exhibit similarities, and not be completely uncorrelated. Therefore, we tend to reject this type of comparison as being unfair.

On the investor side, many people started relying on relative peer group comparisons as their primary method of benchmarking. At first glance, peer groups offer several advantages: they look at the effective performance of other practitioners, they reflect the differences or similarities between managers in their trading decisions, and they take fully into account the transaction and trading costs. However, peer groups suffer from a strong arbitrary selection bias, given the lack of an established oversight process for determining universe participants in the peer group, and whether the universe accurately represents the entire asset class. They also suffer heavily from survivor bias, as disappearing managers are regularly deleted from the peer group. Last but not least, they are usually not considered as a viable passive investment strategy, so a portfolio manager will have no neutral position to take if he has no particular view on the market.

For these reasons, we believe that peer groups are useful as a means of comparing the results of similar managers within a given portfolio or the performance of funds within a narrow universe, but are inadequate to assess the performance of a manager in general. What is needed is a set of effective benchmarks.

21.4.2 The need for true benchmarks

Webster's New Collegiate Dictionary defines a benchmark as "a point of reference from which measurements may be made", or, "something that serves as a standard by which others may be measured". In the context of hedge fund performance, a benchmark should serve as a point of reference or standard to measure and evaluate the economic performance of a manager or a strategy. It should allow for better decision making in hiring, retaining and firing managers, as well as for a better understanding of a strategy in general. It is a crucial tool in determining asset allocation policy, implementing portfolio decisions and evaluating performance. The danger, of course, is that investors start focusing too much on short-term performance. Hence the importance of selecting an appropriate market benchmark.

Ideally, each hedge fund should be assigned a benchmark that takes into account all the details of its strategy, e.g. the markets and assets traded, the leverage, and the directional bias (net long vs net short), in order to get a real picture of which economic environments will favour or punish a given manager's actions. Jeffery Bailey's (1992a) essential elements of a manager benchmark represent a useful checklist. They are as follows:

- *Unambiguous*: The names and weights of securities constituting the benchmark should be clearly delineated.
- *Investable*: The option to forgo active management and simply hold the benchmark as an asset should be available.
- *Measurable*: The benchmark's return should be readily calculated on a reasonably frequent basis, typically at least monthly for hedge fund strategies.
- *Appropriate*: The benchmark should be consistent with the manager's investment style.
- *Reflective of current investment options*: The manager should have current investment knowledge of, and opinion about, the securities that make up the benchmark.
- *Specified in advance*: The benchmark should be constructed prior to the start of an evaluation period.

These properties look like common sense, but it is often the case in practice that benchmarks of individual hedge funds do not possess some of these properties, particularly the fourth and fifth ones.

In addition to dedicated fund benchmarks, it is also necessary to have benchmarks at the industry level. Credible benchmarks are useful as broad-based measures of what the industry is doing, and could help people to better understand funds' performance profiles and counter negative publicity about hedge funds. In line with Bailey, we suggest four properties that an ideal benchmark at the market level should have. These are:

- *Simplicity*: The industry benchmark should be easy to understand and easy to calculate. If the process is complicated or non-transparent, acceptance of the benchmark may be negatively impacted.
- *Replicability*: There should be a straightforward investment strategy that performs in line with the benchmark.
- *Comparability*: The industry benchmark should be calculated in a way that allows comparisons with individual managers (e.g. use of closing vs opening prices, fees, taxes, timing of reporting).
- *Representativity*: The benchmark should effectively represent the performance of the underlying market. In particular, a good benchmark should include all the "big names" to be credible.

Once again, most of these properties are common sense. But the latter unfortunately often goes by the board when it comes to investing, particularly in alternative assets.

Part IV
Investing in Hedge Funds

22

Introduction

I do not want a hedge fund manager to learn. At least, not with my money.

We now come to the fourth part of our book, which covers one of the most exciting and controversial topics of finance today: the analysis, selection and allocation to hedge fund investments. As of today, the primary form of individual and institutional investments is still composed of traditional assets such as stocks and bonds. However, during the past decade, interest in and financial commitments to alternative investments of all sorts have grown dramatically. Attracted by claims of superior risk-adjusted returns and low correlation to stock and bond markets, institutions and more recently affluent individuals have been allocating a small percentage of their portfolios to alternative investments, and more specifically to hedge funds. In parallel, the bulk of their assets remains invested in stocks, bonds, and other traditional securities. Both allocations are usually managed independently on a segregated basis. This gives rise to a number of interesting questions that we will examine in Chapter 23. First, what are the real benefits, if any, of including hedge funds in a traditional portfolio? Second, what is the optimal proportion of hedge funds in a portfolio? And third, how can one integrate traditional asset management with alternative investments? As we shall see, there are still lots of open questions, no single straightforward answer, and numerous common pitfalls that should be avoided.

Indeed, the existing literature shows widespread disagreement regarding the performance and benefits of hedge funds. This is not really surprising. Different observation periods combined with a wide variety of styles and types of hedge funds lead to different conclusions and make generalizations difficult. Moreover, traditional portfolio selection, portfolio management or performance measurement tools are badly placed to deal with the new risks and challenges posed by hedge funds. This is understandable when one remembers that for most practitioners, and also for many in academic circles, modern portfolio theory – which is now more than 50 years old – is still state of the art! Investors are therefore left naked, or even worse, often use inadequate tools when discovering the hedge fund kingdom.

If still convinced that investing in hedge funds may enhance the risk/return trade-off of their portfolios, investors have to identify the correct investment vehicle. Simply stated, there are currently four approaches to participation in hedge funds: investing directly, taking advantage of third-party services (e.g. consultants or hedge funds advisers), using funds of hedge funds, or following the safer road of capital guaranteed and other structured products.

Direct investments occur when an investor hires a single hedge fund manager or a combination of hedge fund managers on his own. As we shall see, there are significant barriers to this approach. In particular, it involves a complex evaluation process due to the diversity of existing hedge fund strategies as well as the lack of transparency with respect to their portfolios. It also requires a high level of net worth and liquidity. Moreover, the heterogeneity of hedge funds results in the best and the worst coexisting under the same roof, and even the best can fail – remember *Long Term Capital Management*! This explains why investors willing to venture along the road of direct investments often hire external advisers and consultants, who are supposed to be experts in the field. For a fee, these intermediaries act as financial matchmakers between investors and appropriate hedge fund managers. As an illustration, even Calpers, the California Public Employees' Retirement System, with more than $132 billion in assets and great investment experience, hired the New York-based investment firm Blackstone to screen potential managers' strategy and performance, help with due diligence and help monitoring the $1 billion hedge fund programme. However, whether implemented alone or with the help of external specialists, the task remains the same: to seek out from a very large universe the hedge fund(s) that best satisfies the precise requirements of an investor. The various steps of this process are detailed in Chapter 24.

Funds of hedge funds, for their part, are basically prepackaged portfolios of hedge funds usually diversified across many different managers and/or strategies. Their managers perform professional due diligence and have third-party asset allocation expertise. However, since the investor's assets are pooled with those of many other clients, managers of funds of hedge funds cannot offer any alteration to their product in order to accommodate individual needs. Nevertheless, funds of hedge funds are today the preferred hedge fund investment vehicle for many institutional investors. We examine their structure and their investment process in Chapter 25.

Chapter 26 focuses on the latest forms of access to hedge funds: principal-protected notes and structured products. Popular essentially in Europe and now gaining adherents in the United States, these new investment vehicles claim to offer hedge fund like returns with a guarantee that investors will get back at least the capital they started with if gains do not materialize over a set period. The reality is that they provide security, but at a price. More surprisingly, they rely on portfolio insurance principles that were implemented in the 1980s on traditional equity markets.

23
Revisiting the Benefits and Risks
of Hedge Fund Investing

For most people, applying intellect to investment is like trying to cut your grass with a vacuum cleaner

It may seem curious at this point to dwell on the benefits of hedge fund investing, as they are now well established and generally accepted by the vast majority of investors. Indeed, if you have managed to read up to this page, you are probably already convinced. But the important point with hedge funds is not simply to be convinced; it is to be convinced or unconvinced for the right reasons.

Hedge funds are entering the mainstream because they introduce a compelling new money management paradigm, which many investors are happy to embrace. Over the past few years, the difficult stock market conditions have made alternative assets in general and hedge funds in particular look like an El Dorado. Dazzled by the glitter of absolute performance, numerous investors have adopted hedge funds and included them in their portfolios, most of the time without really understanding what they were buying and with no clear understanding of the effective risk and return trade-off.[1]

There are anecdotes about extraordinary profits made by hedge funds as well as rumors about incredible failures due to fraud or excessive risk taking. On the one hand, the legendary manager, George Soros, is credited with having compounded annual returns in excess of 30% after fees from 1969 to 2001. On the other hand, the over-leveraged Long Term Capital Management collapsed and was rescued only by the intervention of the Federal Reserve. Although representative of press coverage, these two funds are anything but representative of a rather large universe. Unfortunately, these outliers contribute significantly to the lack of public understanding of what hedge funds are in reality. Investing in hedge funds or rejecting them needs to be motivated by well-founded facts, not just by rumors or press coverage.

Before proceeding any further, let us clarify what we mean by "investing in hedge funds". Critically, we mean exposure to a broad and well-diversified portfolio of hedge funds. In practice, this typically implies investing in a fund of hedge funds. Indeed, most people do not have the time or the staff to deal with the complexity of reviewing, selecting and monitoring a dedicated, diversified portfolio of hedge funds. Moreover, the extra fees of funds of funds are significantly lower than the costs of hiring and supporting in-house staff. The other option, hiring consultants, is a lower cost alternative, but very few consultants are able to provide dynamic, strategy allocation recommendations, high-quality and independent research, and access to the best fund managers.

---

[1] The situation is reminiscent of a classic Woody Allen joke at the end of the film, "Annie Hall". The character goes to a psychiatrist and says, "Doctor, my brother is crazy, he thinks he is a chicken." The doctor asks, "Well why don't you turn him in?" And the character answers, "I would, but I need the eggs." Needless to say, investors might end up being disappointed with their eggs!

Whatever the choice of investment vehicle, it is essential to have a sufficiently diversified portfolio. Investing in only one or two hedge funds is extremely risky and entirely inappropriate for the majority of investors. The best analogy is with equity portfolios. No rational investor would own only one or two stocks to gain equity exposure. The risk/reward trade-off is superior from holding a broad-based, diversified array of stocks. The same applies to hedge funds. Like equities, the specific risk associated with hedge funds is diversified away by holding a variety of investment styles. However, remember that hedge funds are not securities. Each hedge fund is a diversified and actively managed portfolio of securities.

So, assuming a well-diversified hedge fund investment, let us now highlight the benefits that hedge funds offer investors as part of an overall traditional portfolio.

23.1   THE BENEFITS OF HEDGE FUNDS

While past performance does not necessarily help in predicting future performance, it still provides valuable insight into past hedge fund performance relative to traditional investments. In the following section, therefore, we examine hedge funds from a historical perspective. For the sake of simplicity, we use the CS/Tremont Hedge Fund Index to represent hedge funds as a group, but all our discussions and conclusions are in fact independent of the choice of a particular index.[2]

23.1.1   Superior historical risk/reward trade-off

The first, and probably most important, reason for investing in hedge funds is simply superior performance. In sharp contrast to traditional buy-and-hold portfolios, hedge funds face few, if any, investment restrictions. Consequently, in the long run, hedge funds should be able to deliver returns that are better than those of bonds and equities. And historically, they did. Figure 23.1 shows the annualized rates of return produced by a buy-and-hold strategy in several asset classes from January 1994[3] to December 2005. The compound annual return of the CS/Tremont index was 10.69%, versus 8.55% for the S&P 500 and 5.87% for the Citigroup World Government Bond Index. Although we cannot say if this order will be maintained in the future, it highlights at least the fact that hedge funds have, if recent history is anything to go by, provided better returns than long-only equities and bonds. This is not surprising, as the most talented managers are attracted to set up or move into hedge funds. They can thus obtain greater investment freedom; they can use their talents in a less constrained fashion; and they are rewarded more directly for their good performance.

To many, the fact that hedge funds as a group have outperformed traditional asset classes would not be particularly surprising if these superior returns had been achieved at the expense of greater risk. However, this does not seem to be borne out in practice – see Figure 23.2. The flexibility enjoyed by hedge funds in their investment strategy, and notably their ability to combine long and short positions and diversify across various financial instruments, enabled them to mitigate risk significantly. Consequently, their annualized volatility (7.96%), represents about half of the S&P 500 volatility (16.16%) and roughly one fourth of the NASDAQ volatility

---

[2] Chapter 5 contains an extensive discussion of the discrepancies between the different indices available in the industry. The CS/Tremont Hedge Fund Index is capitalization-weighted, and uses only funds that have at least $10 million of assets and can provide audited performance figures. We believe these criteria make it relatively representative of a universe of funds in which an institutional investor may consider an investment.

[3] January 1994 corresponds to the starting date of the CS/Tremont index.

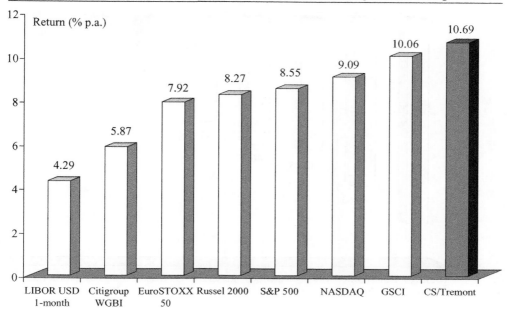

Figure 23.1   Annualized returns of several asset classes, January 1994 to December 2005

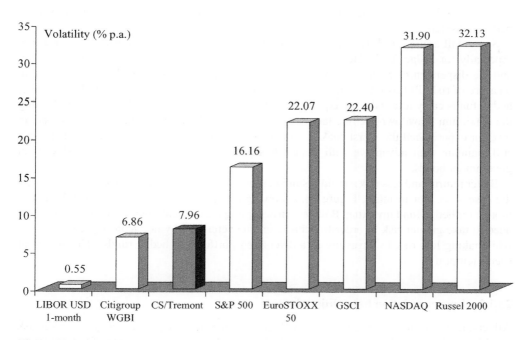

Figure 23.2   Annualized volatility of several asset classes, January 1994 to December 2005

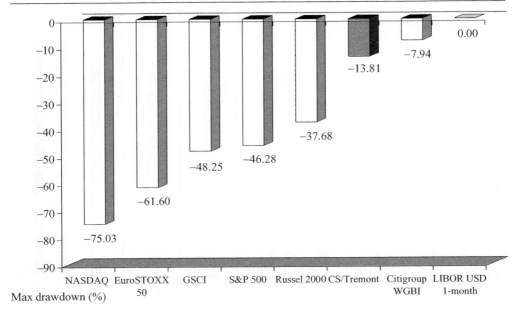

Figure 23.3   Maximum drawdown of several asset classes, January 1994 to December 2005

(31.90%). Only fixed-income-related indices had a lower volatility than hedge funds over the period considered.

Some will argue – rightly – that volatility is not necessarily an appropriate risk measure, especially for hedge funds. Hedge funds' return objectives are absolute rather than relative, and the dispersion of returns below a prespecified target level is probably a more accurate measure of risk. But using alternative risk measures in this case provides a similar message: hedge funds carry less risk than equities. As an illustration, Figure 23.3 measures risk using the maximum drawdown, i.e. the largest amount of capital that would have been lost had an investor experienced the worst peak-to-trough decline in value. We can see that hedge funds still maintain their advantage with respect to equities, and appear just slightly riskier than government bonds.

Better returns and less risk should result in higher risk-adjusted performance. This is indeed the case – see, for instance, Figure 23.4 showing Sharpe ratios – and constitutes the major motive for hedge fund investing. Rather than accepting the conventional wisdom that investors need to take greater risk in order to achieve greater returns, why not achieve greater returns while taking less risk by investing in a diversified portfolio of hedge funds? The argument seems tempting.

23.1.2   Low correlation to traditional assets

Allocating money to hedge funds because their managers achieve greater returns at lower risk would already seem like a sound investment decision. But the case for hedge funds becomes even more favourable when one considers correlation coefficients. Investors have historically taken comfort in the notion that a globally diversified portfolio of traditional assets (e.g. stocks and bonds) will provide good returns with only moderate risk, thanks to the important

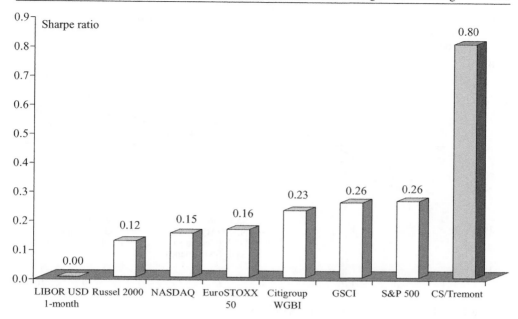

Figure 23.4   Sharpe ratios of several asset classes, January 1994 to December 2005

role that correlation between portfolio components plays in determining risk. The lower the correlation, the better, which was exactly what investors mixing stocks and bonds in their portfolios experienced. But the situation has changed dramatically in recent years.

On the equity side, the correlation between various markets now stands well above historical levels. For example, the correlation between the S&P 500 and the MSCI Europe, Australia and Far East (EAFE) Index spiked from just above 0.2 in the early 1990s to nearly 0.8 in the early 2000s, not far from the 1.0 mark that represents perfect unison. Several arguments have been proffered to explain this evolution. The primary support for the continuance of high correlation was the globalization of the world's economy, with companies making and selling products throughout the world and currencies unifying. An alternative explanation lies in some herd behaviour, with investors around the world pursuing Internet-related stocks and abruptly moving out of their positions as the bubble began to deflate. In any case, the result is there: correlation may change again in the future, but in the meantime the geographic and sector diversification benefits of the long-only market have shrunk, sometimes to the point that much of the difference in equities' return and risk stems from currency fluctuations.

Furthermore, the United States has come to dominate the global equity market, accounting for over half of the total market capitalization, and this naturally encourages investors to pay closer attention to what is happening there. When Wall Street sneezes, the world catches a cold. As an illustration, Figure 23.5 shows the average monthly performance of several equity indices ranked according to the S&P 500 performance. That is, first, S&P 500 monthly returns are placed into performance deciles based on univariate sorting. The lowest 10% S&P 500 returns are placed in the first decile, the second lowest 10% returns are placed in the second decile, and so on until the tenth decile, which contains the months with the highest S&P 500 returns. Next, for the first decile, we calculate the average return of another index (say the MSCI Europe) for the same months. The process is then repeated for each remaining decile

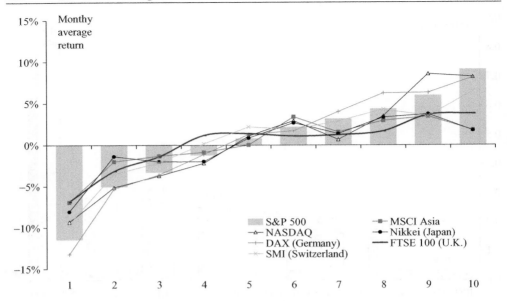

Figure 23.5   Ranked equity returns on the S&P 500

(i.e. each other index). The resulting series of averages is then plotted against the S&P averages. Clearly, we see that there is little evidence of diversification benefits across stock markets, at least over the period in question (1990 to 2005). Consequently, there is a need to find new diversification opportunities.

On the bond side, investors also observed an increase in correlation between various countries. In Europe in particular, adopting the euro eliminated currency risk and increased the degree of substitutability and the correlation between bonds of different governments. Consequently, investors started paying more attention to credit risk and liquidity issues as well as to doing some arbitrage along the yield curve. But the dominant driver across all types of bonds remains the overall level of interest rates, which is common to different bond markets and makes them move in unison. As an illustration, Figure 23.6 repeats our previous decile comparison, but this time with several fixed income indices. The index used as a reference for the construction of the deciles is the Merrill Lynch 10+ Years US Treasury bonds. Not surprisingly, the overall pattern seems to confirm the existence of a high correlation between the different bond markets considered, and therefore signals the lack of diversification opportunities within bonds.

Lastly, the question of the correlation between stock and bond markets is a trickier issue. Most investors are familiar with the idea that falling interest rates tend to go together with positive stock returns – the concept is usually encountered in introductory business textbooks. This should be statistically represented by a positive correlation coefficient between stock and bond returns, since bonds rise as interest rates fall. However, there are also times when the correlation becomes negative. As an illustration, the 1950 version of Benjamin Graham's *The Intelligent Investor* claimed that the correlation between stock and bond returns was negative, and advised a 50–50 split. But the 1970 edition dropped the argument, because the correlation structure had changed and become positive. More recently, following the peak of the equity

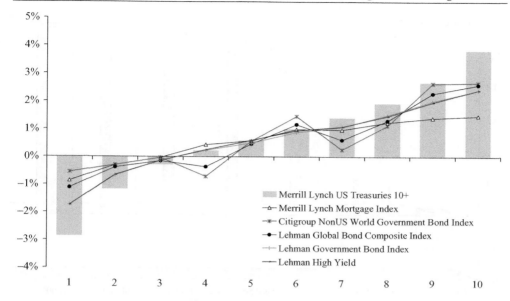

Figure 23.6   Ranked equity returns on the Merrill Lynch 10+ years US Treasury

markets, the correlation between stock and bond returns changed again to negative. It is likely to come back to its long-term average as soon as the global economic recovery is firmly established.

Overall, this lack of stability in the correlation coefficients makes it pretty clear that stocks and bonds are not always a good complement to one another in portfolios. Thus, we have to identify new directions if we want to diversify our traditional portfolios efficiently. This is precisely where hedge funds come into the picture. Driven by the skills of their portfolio managers, hedge funds aim at producing absolute returns, i.e. a positive return in both rising and falling markets. As a result, they tend to have a low to medium correlation with traditional asset class returns – see Figure 23.7. This is a clear sign that hedge funds can provide opportunities for diversification of traditional portfolios.

23.1.3   Negative vs positive market environments

All the statistics that we have presented so far capture essentially an average behaviour. In practice, the actual behaviour in up and down markets may diverge significantly. It is therefore worth while exploring separately the performance of hedge funds in negative versus positive market environments.

Figure 23.8 shows the average monthly return of our various asset classes when we consider separately the months when the S&P 500 displays a positive performance and the months when the S&P 500 shows a negative performance. It is clear that fixed income asset classes offer stable returns whatever the equity market is doing. Equity-based asset classes, on the other hand, seem to follow the behaviour of the S&P 500, and therefore do not offer much diversification potential when equity markets are falling. The hedge fund index also seems to be correlated with the movements of the S&P 500, but with much less variation. In particular,

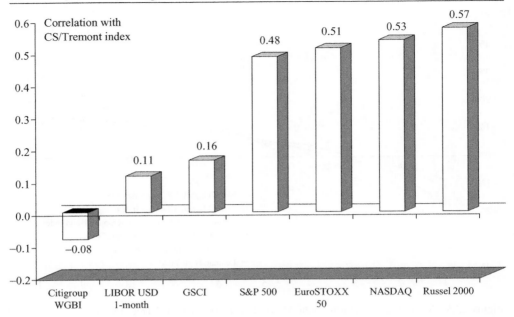

Figure 23.7 Correlation of various asset classes with hedge funds (CS/Tremont), January 1994 to December 2005

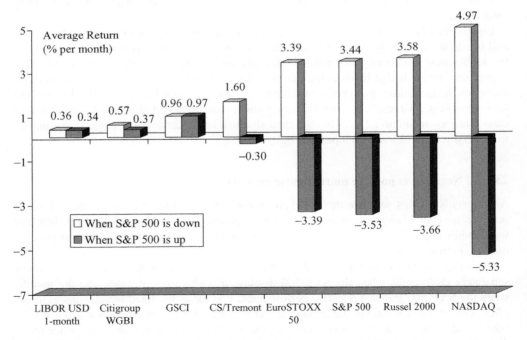

Figure 23.8 Average monthly performance of several asset classes in bearish and bullish months of the S&P 500, January 1994 to December 2005

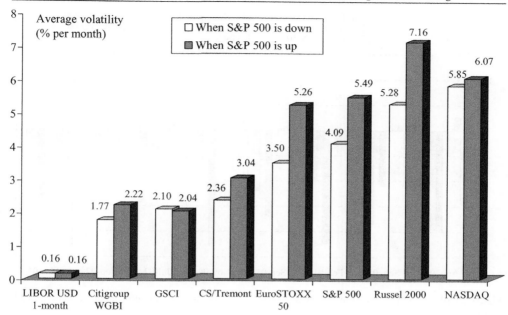

Figure 23.9   Average monthly volatility of several asset classes in bearish and bullish months of the S&P 500, January 1994 to December 2005

we see that its downside risk is much smaller than that of the S&P 500. It is precisely this better downside risk management that creates the better overall performance of hedge funds. Indeed, the first thing to do to make money is to avoid losses in difficult market conditions. Hedge funds are designed to offer downside protection in falling markets (that is the origin of the term "hedge") and the recent difficult environment for markets has allowed hedge funds to prove their value.

The volatility comparison of our asset classes during bearish and bullish months of the S&P 500 is also interesting – see Figure 23.9. First, we can see that all asset classes except commodities (GSCI) tend to have a higher volatility when equity markets display positive performance. Second, we also see that in both bearish and bullish S&P markets, hedge funds remain between equities and bonds in terms of volatility.

Figure 23.10 evidences that, in comparison with other asset classes, hedge funds were effective during the worst months of the equity markets, when capital preservation usually becomes a priority. Even in August 1998, at the time of the hedge fund crisis precipitated by the collapse of Long Term Capital Management, hedge funds as a group managed to display much better returns than equities (−7.55% for hedge funds versus −14.46% for the S&P 500).

With all these positive characteristics, it is not really surprising that the inclusion of hedge funds in traditional portfolios tends to have a favourable impact on both return and risk (see Figure 23.11). As an illustration, a portfolio made up of 50% equities (S&P 500) and 50% bonds (Citigroup World Government Bond Index) would have had a performance of 7.56% p.a. and a volatility of 8.33% p.a. over the January 1994 to December 2005 period. If we substitute 10% hedge funds (CS/Tremont) for 10% of the original equity allocation, we observe a modest

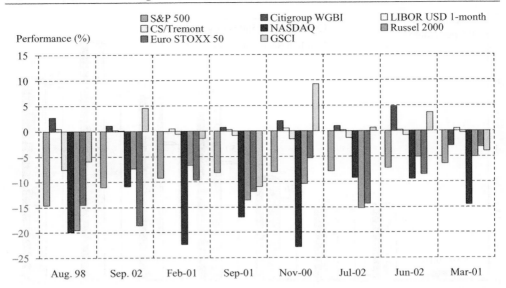

Figure 23.10   Monthly returns of several asset classes during the worst months of equity markets, 1994 onwards

increase in the return (7.76% p.a.), but a significant drop in volatility (7.28% versus 8.33% originally). If we substitute 20% hedge funds (CS/Tremont) for 20% of the original equity allocation, we still observe a modest increase in the return (7.95% p.a.), but a larger reduction of volatility (6.36% versus 8.86% originally). And the risk reduction keeps going as the hedge fund weight increases.

Starting from the same portfolio made up of 50% equities (S&P 500) and 50% bonds (Citigroup Government Bond Index), we may rather decide to substitute 10% hedge funds (CS/Tremont) for 10% of the original bond allocation. In this case, we observe an increase in risk as well as an increase in return. The goal is no longer to diversify, but rather to enhance the performance by taking additional risk. And the risk and return increases keeps going as the hedge fund weight increases and the bond weight decreases.

Starting once again from the same portfolio made up of 50% equities (S&P 500) and 50% bonds (Citigroup Government Bond Index), we may finally decide to substitute 10% hedge funds (CS/Tremont) for 5% of the original bond allocation and 5% of the original stock allocation. In this case, the risk decreases and the return increases! This lends weight to the idea that some allocation of hedge funds may be good for diversified traditional portfolios. The conclusion is generally valid, but with one important caveat. Comparisons of portfolio performance with and without hedge funds should take into account other features of their distribution of returns. For example, if the return distribution becomes more skewed in one direction (particularly in the negative direction), or it tends to bunch up at the extremes of the range of returns (i.e. have excessive kurtosis), the overall portfolio results may look improved in a mean-variance space, but it is not improved in reality. It is simply that the use of standard deviation as the sole measure of risk for distributions that exhibit a relatively high probability of gain/loss is misleading. This is exactly what happens here – note the systematic increase in kurtosis as the hedge fund allocation grows, as well as the initial decrease in skewness.

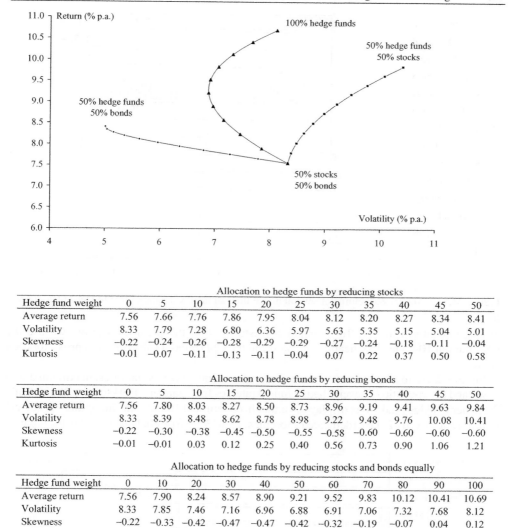

Figure 23.11 The impact of including hedge funds in a diversified portfolio (initially 50% US equities and 50% US bonds)

	Allocation to hedge funds by reducing stocks									
Hedge fund weight	0	5	10	15	20	25	30	35	40	45	50
Average return	7.56	7.66	7.76	7.86	7.95	8.04	8.12	8.20	8.27	8.34	8.41
Volatility	8.33	7.79	7.28	6.80	6.36	5.97	5.63	5.35	5.15	5.04	5.01
Skewness	−0.22	−0.24	−0.26	−0.28	−0.29	−0.29	−0.27	−0.24	−0.18	−0.11	−0.04
Kurtosis	−0.01	−0.07	−0.11	−0.13	−0.11	−0.04	0.07	0.22	0.37	0.50	0.58

	Allocation to hedge funds by reducing bonds									
Hedge fund weight	0	5	10	15	20	25	30	35	40	45	50
Average return	7.56	7.80	8.03	8.27	8.50	8.73	8.96	9.19	9.41	9.63	9.84
Volatility	8.33	8.39	8.48	8.62	8.78	8.98	9.22	9.48	9.76	10.08	10.41
Skewness	−0.22	−0.30	−0.38	−0.45	−0.50	−0.55	−0.58	−0.60	−0.60	−0.60	−0.60
Kurtosis	−0.01	−0.01	0.03	0.12	0.25	0.40	0.56	0.73	0.90	1.06	1.21

	Allocation to hedge funds by reducing stocks and bonds equally									
Hedge fund weight	0	10	20	30	40	50	60	70	80	90	100
Average return	7.56	7.90	8.24	8.57	8.90	9.21	9.52	9.83	10.12	10.41	10.69
Volatility	8.33	7.85	7.46	7.16	6.96	6.88	6.91	7.06	7.32	7.68	8.12
Skewness	−0.22	−0.33	−0.42	−0.47	−0.47	−0.42	−0.32	−0.19	−0.07	0.04	0.12
Kurtosis	−0.01	−0.05	0.02	0.23	0.54	0.91	1.29	1.62	1.90	2.11	2.29

23.2   THE BENEFITS OF INDIVIDUAL HEDGE FUND STRATEGIES

Although the conclusions of the previous section seem to be quite general, hedge funds are not an "asset class" according to the standard meaning of the term. In particular, they are not homogeneous but encompass a multitude of investment strategies whose return and risk characteristics differ widely. It is therefore interesting to analyse each of these strategies separately to verify whether they inherit the benefits of their ancestor, or whether their characteristics

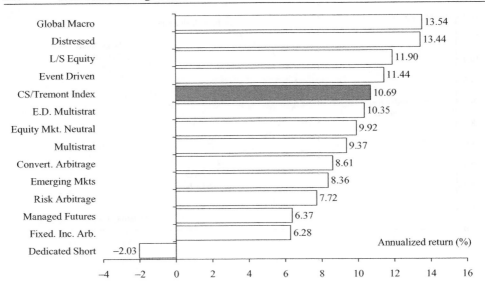

Figure 23.12   Annualized returns of several hedge fund strategies. January 1994 to December 2005

are significantly different. To maintain consistency with the previous section, we use the CS/Tremont 10-style classification standard and the CS/Tremont sub-index as a proxy for each strategy.

Figures 23.12 to 23.15 show the annualized returns, annualized volatilities, maximum drawdown and Sharpe ratio of several hedge fund strategies from January 1994 to June 2003. While the general hedge fund index displays an annualized return of 10.69%, the individual strategies' returns range from −2.03% (dedicated short bias) to +13.54% (global macro). The discrepancy

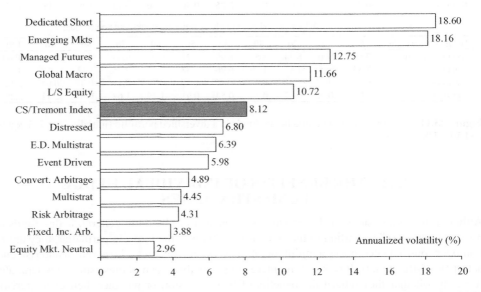

Figure 23.13   Annualized volatility of several hedge fund strategies. January 1994 to December 2005

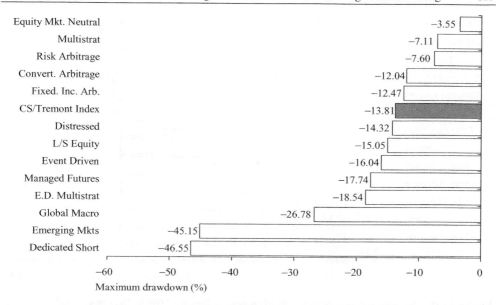

Figure 23.14   Maximum drawdown of several hedge fund strategies. January 1994 to December 2005

seems even larger on the risk side, with a volatility ranging from 2.96% (equity market neutral) to 18.60% (emerging markets), versus 8.12% for the hedge fund index. The so-called directional strategies (emerging markets, short bias, global macro and managed futures) as well as the long/short equity funds clearly have the highest volatility. Not surprisingly, equity market neutral funds and arbitrage strategies were the most consistent among the group.

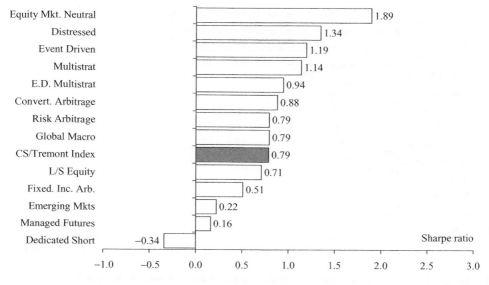

Figure 23.15   Sharpe ratio of several hedge fund strategies. January 1994 to December 2005

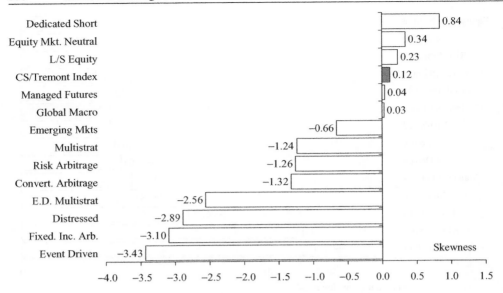

Figure 23.16 Skewness of several hedge fund strategies. January 1994 to December 2005

However, those making the case for hedge funds only based on their Sharpe ratio fail to consider that there are other measures of risk that should be of concern to investors. In particular, several hedge fund strategies tend to be exposed to an elevated probability of major loss, exhibiting significant negative skewness (a long left-hand tail) and excess kurtosis (a high probability of extreme outcomes). This is illustrated in Figures 23.16 for the skewness and 23.17 for the kurtosis. As a consequence, that standard deviation is an incomplete measure of

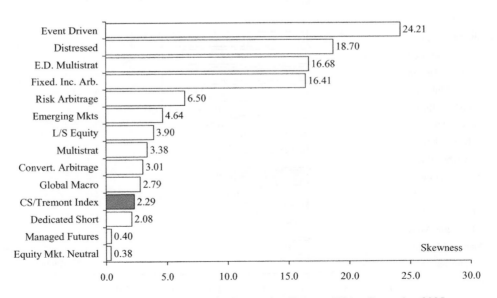

Figure 23.17 Kurtosis of several hedge fund strategies. January 1994 to December 2005

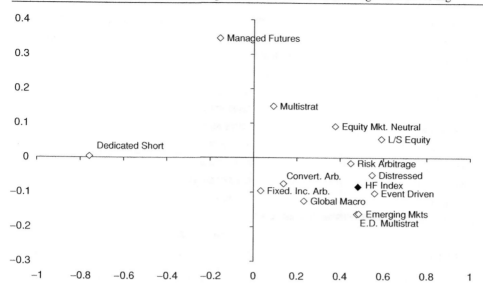

Figure 23.18 Correlation of various hedge fund strategies to US equities (horizontal axis) and bonds (vertical axis). January 1994 to December 2005

risk, and the Sharpe ratio an inadequate description of the risk/reward relationship for hedge fund substrategies.

Sources of skewness and kurtosis in the distribution of hedge fund vary over time, but one of them is persistent. A number of hedge fund strategies are directly or indirectly based on providing credit and liquidity to the market, often accompanied by high levels of leverage. These credit and liquidity risks subject hedge funds to occasional blow-ups when credit spreads widen or market liquidity dries up. Of course, the probability of blowing up is low, but its consequences when it occurs are extreme. This results in positive kurtosis and negative skewness.

Figure 23.18 shows the correlation of the various hedge fund strategies with equity markets (represented by the S&P 500, horizontal axis) and with bond markets (represented by the Citigroup World Government Bond Index, vertical axis). Clearly, individual hedge fund strategies have very different correlation characteristics. Long/short equity funds have the highest correlation to traditional equity markets, followed by distressed, emerging market and event-driven funds. These results are not really surprising as (i) most long/short equity managers have a net long investment style; (ii) distressed funds obviously come under pressure during periods of major financial stress, and most event-driven multi-strategy funds contain a substantial allocation of distressed securities; and (iii) most emerging market hedge fund managers are net long because of the inherent difficulties of borrowing stocks and selling short in emerging markets. However, even in these cases, the correlation remains between 0.46 and 0.59. In contrast, short sellers are consistently net short, and hence have a high negative correlation (−0.76) with equities. Managed futures also display a negative correlation (−0.16), while arbitrage strategies have generally low correlation figures with the S&P 500 returns, ranging from 0.03 for fixed income arbitrage to 0.44 for risk arbitrage. Finally, note the low level of correlation with the Citigroup World Government Bond index, which suggests that hedge funds could also be used to complement bond portfolios.

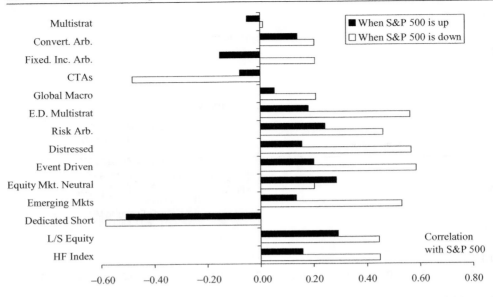

Figure 23.19 Conditional correlation of various hedge fund strategies to US equities (horizontal axis) and bonds (vertical axis). January 1994 to December 2005

Although the correlation figures seem quite low, we have to remember that in terms of diversification, low correlation with equity markets is not in itself enough. What investors really need is low downside correlation, that is, investments that will perform well when the equity markets are not performing well. Figure 23.19 shows the conditional correlation of our hedge fund strategies with the S&P 500, and reveals two interesting features. First, the correlation over the whole sample is not necessarily the average of the up-market and down-market correlation. As an illustration, consider the short bias funds. Their overall correlation with the S&P 500 is –0.76, while their upside correlation is –0.51 and their downside correlation is –0.51. Second, the majority of hedge fund strategies have a higher correlation with the S&P 500 when the latter is suffering from negative performance. This is not very good news, as it implies that many hedge fund strategies come under pressure during periods of major financial stress and partly lose their diversification properties precisely when we need them. However, the correlations remain at low levels for the majority of hedge funds, which also implies that there are still some diversification benefits to capture. But an investor wanting to achieve low overall correlation might have to draw on the whole menu of hedge fund strategies in order to construct an intelligently diversified portfolio.

Investors tend to use hedge funds for one of two portfolio design purposes. Most high net worth individuals view them as return enhancers – aggressive investment options that generate above market-level returns while taking greater-than-market levels of risk. Most institutional investors, however, view an allocation to absolute return strategies as a portfolio diversifier. If we divide the universe into four quadrants, with the CS/Tremont Hedge Fund Index at the centre, we can clearly identify four groups of strategies – see Figure 23.20.

- A first group of strategies is clearly positioned as a low-risk, low-return universe with respect to the overall hedge fund index. It encompasses all the relative value strategies, e.g. fixed

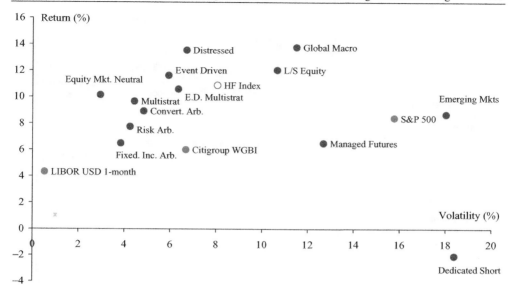

Figure 23.20   A return/volatility view of hedge fund strategies. January 1994 to December 2005

income arbitrage, convertible arbitrage, risk arbitrage, market neutral and multi-strategy. These strategies are relatively unaffected by the market factors that drive traditional equity markets and therefore are considered as risk-diversifiers for equity portfolios. However, while the volatility of these strategies is lower than that of government bonds, their return is higher, which suggests that they may also act as return enhancers when combined with bond portfolios.

- A second group of strategies, comprising the global macro and long/short equity investment styles, is clearly positioned as a high-risk, high-return universe with respect to the overall hedge fund index. The volatility of these strategies is lower than that of equities and their return is much higher, which suggests that they may act as return enhancers when combined with equity portfolios.

- A third group of strategies, composed of the managed futures, emerging markets and dedicated short investment styles, is clearly positioned as a high-risk, low-return universe with respect to the overall index. These strategies may possibly be used as risk diversifiers for equity portfolios.

- The last category contains only the distressed investment style, and it is positioned as a low-risk high-return strategy. However, we should be cautious in drawing conclusions on this strategy, as (i) its low volatility is in fact essentially due to the lack of regular market pricing and natural tendency of managers to smooth the return on their portfolios; and (ii) its assets are highly illiquid, so that realizing gains or limiting losses is likely to be a problem.

Figure 23.21 represents the same strategies, but from a return/maximum drawdown perspective. Interestingly, we reach exactly the same conclusions when using maximum drawdown as a risk measure.

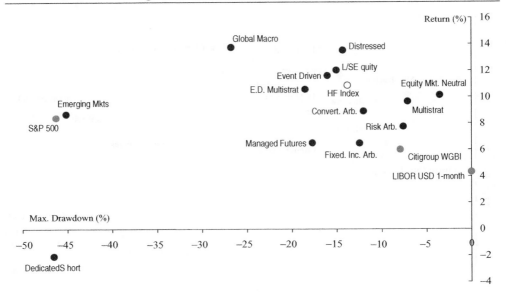

Figure 23.21 A return/maximum drawdown view of hedge fund strategies. January 1994 to December 2005

23.3 CAVEATS OF HEDGE FUND INVESTING

To better interpret our previous findings, some caveats should be stated. First of all, we should recall that a strong bull market prevailed during the first part of the period examined while there was only a short bear market in the second half. We recognize that a longer observation period would better represent strategy returns. Unfortunately, the hedge fund universe becomes very small for longer periods of analysis, as very few hedge funds have more than 10 years of existence.

Next, we should also recall that our results were historical figures based on the CS/Tremont hedge fund indices, i.e. *large diversified portfolios* of hedge funds. These indices are subject to biases that essentially result in overestimation of historical returns and underestimation of risk – see Chapter 21. Moreover, investors will generally hold a smaller portfolio of hedge funds than the hedge fund index. Hence, in practice, the superiority of hedge fund investments over traditional assets relies heavily on the ability of the investor or its adviser to select the right hedge fund managers. The difference between a first and fourth quartile manager can often be the difference between success and disaster – although all hedge fund managers now claim to be first quartile.

In addition to identifying the most talented managers, investors need to be able to invest in their funds. Unfortunately, the best managers tend to have enough capital and can do without additional investors. They close their funds to new investors, or at least they impose long lock-up periods of one to three years before investors can redeem. For this reason, it is often difficult for investors to gain exposure to certain hedge fund strategies without taking a chance on new managers who have no adequate track records. These neophytes may not produce the same result as their more experienced peers, and investors may be disappointed.

Table 23.1 Annual performance of hedge fund strategies and traditional asset classes (% p.a.)

	1994	1995	1996	1997	1998	1999	2000	2001	2002	2003	2004	2005
S&P 500	-1.5	34.1	20.3	31.0	26.7	19.5	-10.1	-13.0	-23.4	26.4	9.0	3.0
Citigroup WGBI	2.3	19.0	3.6	0.2	15.3	-4.3	1.6	-1.0	19.5	14.9	10.3	-6.9
CSF/Tremont	-4.4	21.7	22.2	25.9	-0.4	23.4	4.8	4.4	3.0	15.5	9.6	7.6
L/S Equity	-8.1	23.0	17.1	21.5	17.2	47.2	2.1	-3.7	-1.6	17.3	11.6	9.7
Dedicated Short	14.9	-7.4	-5.5	0.4	-6.0	-14.2	15.8	-3.6	18.2	-32.6	-7.7	17.0
Emerging Markets	12.5	-16.9	34.5	26.6	-37.7	44.8	-5.5	5.8	7.4	28.7	12.5	17.4
Equity Mkt. Neutral	-2.0	11.0	16.6	14.8	13.3	15.3	15.0	9.3	7.4	7.1	6.5	6.1
Event Driven	0.7	18.4	23.0	20.0	-4.9	22.3	7.2	11.5	0.2	20.0	14.5	8.9
– Distressed	0.7	26.1	25.5	20.7	-1.7	22.2	1.9	20.0	-0.7	25.1	15.6	11.7
– Risk Arbitrage	5.3	11.9	13.8	9.8	5.6	13.2	14.7	5.7	-3.5	9.0	5.5	3.1
– Multi-strategy	0.6	12.9	22.7	20.5	-9.0	23.0	11.8	6.8	1.2	17.2	14.0	7.2
Global Macro	-5.7	30.7	25.6	37.1	-3.6	5.8	11.7	18.4	14.7	18.0	8.5	9.2
Managed Futures	11.9	-7.1	12.0	3.1	20.7	-4.7	4.3	1.9	18.3	14.2	6.0	-0.1
Fixed. Income Arb.	0.3	12.5	15.9	9.4	-8.2	12.1	6.3	8.0	5.7	8.0	6.8	0.6
Convert. Arbitrage	-8.1	16.6	17.9	14.5	-4.4	16.0	25.6	14.6	4.0	12.9	2.0	-2.5
Multi-strategy	-2.9	11.9	14.0	18.3	7.7	9.4	11.2	5.5	6.3	15.0	7.5	7.5

Looking forward, the massive amount of capital pouring into the hedge fund business is also worrying. Some strategies are capacity constrained by nature, e.g. merger arbitrage or convertible bond arbitrage, because the supply of investment opportunities is limited. Large money flows into such strategies may therefore challenge their performance by arbitraging away profit opportunities. Some analysts have argued that the capacity argument was not applicable to long/short equity managers and fixed income arbitrage managers, because they are playing in markets whose size is measured in trillions of dollars – see, for instance, McFall, Lamm and Ghaleb-Harter (2001). However, all alpha-based strategies are inherently capacity constrained, either in terms of investment opportunities or in terms of talented managers. It is therefore not surprising that hedge fund returns appear to be in a long-term downward trend, with returns that fall far short of the stellar performance delivered in the early 1990s (Table 23.1).

In conclusion, we will therefore say that hedge fund investing offers several benefits, but it should not be considered as a "free lunch". It has its risks and its difficulties – the skewness and kurtosis evolution of Figure 23.11 should not be forgotten. Furthermore, most investors do not consider hedge funds as stand-alone assets but combine several different alternative strategies that, in the aggregate, produce a desired return pattern. As we will see in the following chapters, including hedge funds in a portfolio may sometimes be quite complicated, and constructing allocations to these products requires an extensive understanding of their investment strategies and risks.

24
Asset Allocation and Hedge Funds

Arbitraging is like making love to a gorilla. You do not stop when you are tired. You stop when the gorilla is tired.

Rule No.2

Finally convinced of the apparent advantages of hedge funds as risk diversifiers or as absolute return generators, many investers and advisers are now contemplating their inclusion in traditional portfolios. Indeed, if there are opportunities, hedge funds should provide a better means of exploiting them, due to their greater flexibility, ability to sell short, incentive structures, use of more esoteric instruments and more nimble management than on the long-only side. But the benefits of adding a fund of hedge funds to a traditional strategic portfolio are yesterday's news. The problem today is to reconcile the alternative and creative nature of hedge funds with the discipline required in an asset allocation process. This is a delicate task that raises several new questions. Should hedge funds be considered as a separate asset class or as a different way of managing traditional assets? What percentage should a rational investor allocate to them? How frequently should a hedge fund portfolio be rebalanced? All these issues should be clarified before any allocation is made. Unfortunately, as we will see, analysing hedge funds is not the same as analysing traditional fund managers. The option-like payoffs and unusual correlation profiles of hedge funds open new avenues in portfolio construction. Consequently, hedge funds do not fit easily into traditional asset allocation processes, so extra attention is needed to make the best use of their valuable characteristics.

In this chapter, we discuss the different techniques for incorporating hedge funds in an asset allocation. We begin with an allocation involving only a simple mix of traditional asset classes, and then we introduce hedge funds as a separate asset class. Although this is the standard approach to justify hedge fund allocations, we will see that it has several shortcomings, particularly when using a mean-variance framework. Hence, we will introduce other allocation techniques such as portable alpha construction, minimizing the correlation with the principal components of strategic portfolio risk, and risk budgeting. Although new in asset management, these quantitative techniques are borrowed from risk management, where optimizing risk by "spending" each unit of risk efficiently is a common objective.

24.1 DIVERSIFICATION AND PORTFOLIO CONSTRUCTION: AN OVERVIEW

Simply stated, diversification consists of spreading investments among different assets or asset classes in order to reduce the overall risk of a portfolio. To most investors, the logic of diversification is obvious and has been intuitively recognized for centuries in the adage: "Don't put all your eggs in one basket." However, it was only in the late 1950s that Harry Markowitz, a 25-year-old doctoral student at the University of Chicago, was able to analyse in detail how portfolio diversification worked. Using standard deviation (volatility) to quantify risk, Markowitz developed a new normative theory to demonstrate why and how portfolio diversification works to reduce risk for investors. His ideas were so innovative that at his doctoral dissertation defence, Milton Friedman, winner of the 1976 Nobel Prize for economic science, declared that it "was neither economics, mathematics, nor even business administration". Nevertheless, 38 years later, Markowitz shared a Nobel Prize with Merton Miller and William Sharpe for what is now regarded as one of the most important analytical tools in 20th-century finance.

24.1.1 Diversification

To understand the intuition behind diversification, let us simply start with a hypothetical economy where only two companies have listed their shares. The first is an umbrella-making firm and the second produces ice cream. Investors willing to invest in equities must allocate their assets between the stocks of these two companies and have no other choice. Which stock should be selected? There are several possible choices, each of which is supported by an investment theory. For instance, aggressive investors may take a bet on the weather and prefer the ice cream maker if they forecast a sunny summer or the umbrella maker if they forecast a rainy one. Chartists will look at the historical prices of both companies and apply some technical indicators to detect trends, support levels, etc., in order to reach their conclusion. Meanwhile, fundamentalists will analyse accounting data, priceearnings ratios or book-to-equity ratios. Momentum investors will prefer the company that has had the best recent historical performance, while contrarian investors will prefer the one that performed badly. Small-cap enthusiasts will invest in the smallest firm, while blue chip investors will favour the largest one. We could go on forever, but at the end of the day, who will be right? Hard to say!

Diversification provides a very natural answer to our security selection problem. Only a fool or a prophet would invest exclusively in one of the two stocks. Others – who are unable to forecast the weather accurately – should diversify risk by investing in both firms. The reasons are twofold. First, stocks have proven to be a superior way to preserve and create wealth for investors adhering to a conservative, long-term, buy-and-hold investment strategy. By investing in both companies, investors actually capture the higher long-term returns offered by equities as an asset class, but reduce the potential short-term variations. Second, both theory and practice suggest that taking on more company-specific risk does not imply greater potential returns in the long run (and this is actually the best reason for diversifying). In our case, betting on the weather is too much of a gamble. We have more or less one chance in two of being right, so that we should expect a zero sum game before fees on average. After costs, though, weather investing becomes a loser's game by definition. As summarized by John Bogle, CEO of the Vanguard Group, "the croupier rakes too much out".

By investing in both companies, investors therefore reduce the risk that is unique to a given security ("specific risk", such as weather risk in our case) and remain only with the risk that is common to all financial instruments ("market risk", or risk of the overall stock market). Graphically, the benefits of diversification are obvious, as illustrated in Figure 24.1. The expected return of the 50/50 allocation between the two stocks is exactly the average of the individual stock returns, while the standard deviation is less than the average of the standard deviations of the two stocks separately, thanks to diversification. This stretches the set of possible allocations to the left of the straight line joining the two securities. That is, for the same expected return, it is possible to incur a lower risk.

The exact shape of the curve of possible allocations between the two securities depends on a statistical coefficient called correlation. Correlation ranges from -1 to $+1$ and measures how

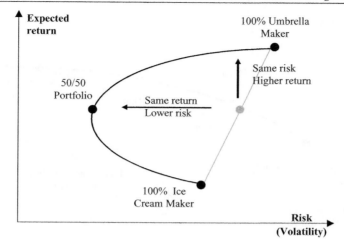

Figure 24.1   The benefits of diversification: creating an all-weather portfolio

frequently two securities' returns move in the same direction. For instance:

- Two securities having a correlation coefficient of +1 are perfectly correlated, i.e. they move systematically in the same direction, but not necessarily by the same magnitude.
- Two securities having a correlation coefficient of −1 are perfectly negatively correlated, i.e. they move systematically in opposite directions, but here again not necessarily by the same magnitude.
- Two securities having a correlation coefficient of 0 move independently of each other.
- Two securities having a correlation coefficient of say 0.60 are perfectly positively correlated 60% of the time and move independently of each other 40% of the time.[1] Similarly, two securities having a correlation coefficient of, say, −0.40 are perfectly negatively correlated 40% of the time and move independently of each other 60% of the time.

The smaller the correlation is between two securities, the smaller the volatility of a portfolio that combines them. The trick of portfolio construction is therefore to find assets that offer a worthwhile return while being less than perfectly correlated or even negatively correlated, so that most of their risk can be eliminated.

24.1.2   Portfolio construction

Once the risks and the benefits of diversification have been quantified,[2] the next logical step is to explain how, under conditions of risk, a risk-averse investor should build a portfolio in order to optimize market risk against expected returns. This is called mean-variance optimization, because the variance (or its square root, the volatility) is used to measure risk.

Markowitz showed that, starting from a limited set of securities, the set of portfolios that one could create by allocating assets among these securities is a region bounded by an

---

[1] Although this does not correspond to the statistical interpretation, it helps in understanding the overall concept.

[2] Markowitz's normative approach allows the calculation of the exact expected return and volatility of a portfolio composed of several securities based on four sets of inputs: the percentage of total funds invested in each security, the expected return and volatility associated with each security, and the correlation between these securities.

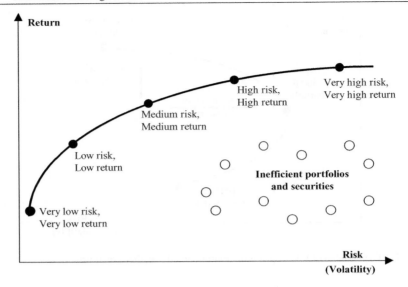

Figure 24.2 The efficient frontier and the trade-off between risk and return

upward-sloping curve that he called the "efficient frontier" (see Figure 24.2). Portfolios and securities below this frontier are not efficient in the sense that it is possible to find better risk/return combinations (e.g. a higher return for the same risk or lower risk for the same return). Portfolios and securities above this frontier do not exist – if they existed, the efficient frontier would be shifted accordingly to include them. The efficient frontier therefore represents the optimal trade-off between risk and expected return faced by an investor when forming his portfolio.

Note that:

- A key property of this efficient frontier is that it is curved, not straight. This is essentially due to the benefits of diversification. The curvature generally increases as (i) the number of assets available increases and (ii) more assets with low or negative correlation are introduced in the investment universe.
- To create an efficient portfolio, it is necessary to combine inefficient assets. As a consequence, the risk of an individual asset should be of little importance to the investor; what matters is its contribution to the portfolio's risk as a whole. This has brought about a revolution in the scrutiny given to portfolios. The entire portfolio should be considered when judging the suitability of investments rather than considering a single investment in isolation.
- It suddenly appears that one does not even need any fundamental information about firms. All necessary information is contained in expected returns, volatility and correlation statistics.[3]

The key result of mean-variance optimization is that one can reduce portfolio risk by diversifying, without necessarily lowering expected returns. In some cases, diversification combined with a regular portfolio rebalancing can even increase returns. As an illustration, consider the following example. Table 24.1 shows the annualized returns and standard deviations of four

---

[3] The new difficulty will be to forecast accurately these statistics, which is not necessarily an easier task!

Table 24.1   Diversification can reduce risk and increase returns

Asset class	Annualized return	Annualized volatility	Sharpe ratio
US stocks (S&P 500)	13.2%	16.8%	0.43
Intl. Stocks (MSCI EAFE index)	12.5%	21.9%	0.30
Real estate (NAREIT index)	12.5%	17.2%	0.38
Commodities (GS Commodities Index)	12.4%	24.9%	0.26
Intl. Stocks + Real estate + Commodities	13.9%	11%	0.72

Calculation period: 1972–2000. Risk -free rate for Sharpe ratio is assumed to be 6%.

asset classes over the period 1972–2000. Clearly, the S&P 500 dominates the three other in-dices, with a lower volatility and a higher return. But if we create an equally weighted portfolio of the three dominated indices and rebalance it on a monthly basis, it achieves a higher return and a lower standard deviation than the SBP 500. The reasons for this surprising result reside (i) in the relatively low correlation between the three corresponding asset classes for the risk part and (ii) in the rebalancing rule for the return part. The Sharpe ratio clearly evidences the better reward per unit of risk when investing equally in the three dominated asset classes.

24.1.3   Asset allocation

Asset allocation takes the diversification concept one step further. It does not simply mix several assets; it attempts to combine them optimally. Asset allocation consists in determining a capital allocation in each of the broad categories of assets to maximize overall risk-adjusted performance while ensuring consistency with the investor's goals, risk tolerance, constraints and time horizon.

Mathematically, asset allocation corresponds to a constrained optimization problem. Al-though the term appears complex, the concept is not. For instance, an investor looking for the optimal portfolio and targeting a 10% annual return would face the following constrained optimization problem:

Find: portfolio weights (i.e. asset allocation)
To minimize: risk (e.g. volatility)
Under the following constraints:
- no short sales
- fully invested
- target return is given (e.g. 10%).

Equivalently, if the investor now targets a maximum volatility of 7%, he would have to solve the following constrained optimization problem:

Find: portfolio weights (i.e. asset allocation)
To maximize: expected return
Under the following constraints:
- no short sales
- fully invested
- target risk is given (e.g. volatility of 7%).

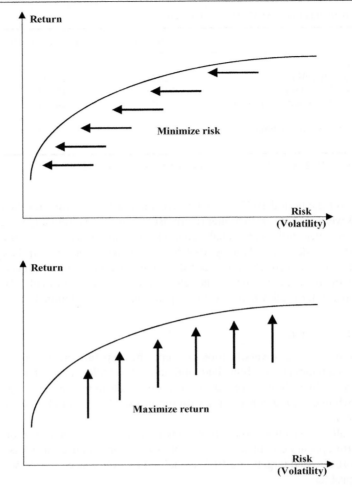

Figure 24.3   Two views on the same optimization problem

The two problems are equivalent and fortunately yield the same solution, i.e. the efficient frontier – see Figure 24.3.

Such optimization problems are usually solved at the asset class level rather than for individual securities. There are two reasons for this. First, several necessary parameters (expected returns, volatilities and correlations) are easier to estimate and more stable for asset classes than for individual securities. Second, the number of asset classes is usually much smaller than the number of securities, which reduces the complexity of the problem. Solving this optimization problem is not necessarily an easy task, but it is crucial for successful portfolio management.[4] If the asset allocation is too aggressive, the investor may risk more of his initial investment than he wants. If it is too conservative, he may not achieve the return he seeks. The idea is therefore to find a middle ground that is comfortable, sufficiently productive . . . and optimal.

---

[4] A Microsoft Excel spreadsheet with the Solver add-in is usually sufficient to solve most simple optimization problems within a reasonable amount of time.

24.2   STRATEGIC ASSET ALLOCATION WITHOUT HEDGE FUNDS

Strategic asset allocation consists of establishing a portfolio of asset classes that is consistent with an investor's long-term objectives and constraints and optimal in terms of risk/reward. It is known to be one of the most important decisions, if not the most important, in any investment process, as it is the key to achieving the investor's financial goals and is the primary determinant of long-term investment results.[5] Nevertheless, most investors hate spending time on their strategic asset allocation. They prefer to identify great investments on instinct or to read about how famous investors pick stocks rather than to challenge the steps involved in creating their portfolio. As a consequence, their strategic asset allocation often gets insufficient attention or simply exists at best on paper. The whole game often seems to turn into picking the best stocks individually, with no consideration whatsoever for portfolio construction rules. This is a pity, because strategic asset allocation is obviously the only key to long-term investment success.

In fact, one of the major differences between institutional investment strategies and the approaches employed by most individual investors is the influence of emotions. Institutional investors generally adopt a disciplined approach to asset management. They follow a transparent and systematic investment process that both explicitly recognizes and manages risks in a portfolio. Furthermore, they review and rebalance their holdings to ensure that the latter remain consistent with their asset allocation policies. Individual investors, on the other hand, often react emotionally, buy overvalued assets in bull markets and sell them when they have plummeted in bear markets. Clearly, most individual investors would benefit from employing some of the highly disciplined investment habits of institutional money managers, and particularly from establishing a clear asset allocation policy.

24.2.1   Identifying the investor's financial profile: the concept of utility functions

First, it is important to realize that one best overall portfolio does not exist. There is at most an optimal portfolio for each investor, or each group of similar investors. To determine this portfolio, it is necessary to take into account the investor's time horizon, his risk appetite, his overall objectives, his age, his available income and the rest of the assets of his portfolio (including, if relevant, his liabilities), as well as any constraints, tax status, etc. A thorough review of all these elements is required before choosing any asset – the only way to be successful is to know what we want to achieve and what we want to avoid.

Academia and practice seem to have taken different paths to modelling investors' portfolio decisions. Academics rely on microeconomic theory and use *utility functions* to explain investors' decisions. To keep things simple, we will say that utility is a measure of the happiness or satisfaction an investor obtains from his portfolio – the higher an investor's utility, the happier the investor.[6] Thus, most theoretical portfolio selection models rest on the assumption that rational investors maximize their *expected utility* (see Box 24.1) over a prespecified time horizon, and that they select their portfolios accordingly. Intuitively, expected utility should

---

[5] Brinson, Hood and Beebower (1986) found that strategic asset allocation explained nearly 93.6% of the variance in a sample of pension fund returns, versus only 6.4% for selectivity and timing. Brinson, Singer and Beebower (1991) reported similar results. Despite this, numerous investors spend sleepless nights worrying about which securities to buy or to sell, but still neglect their overall asset allocation!

[6] For the foundations of utility functions, see von Neumann and Morgenstern (1947).

Box 24.1 Expected utility and the St Petersburg Paradox

The notion of expected utility stems from Daniel Bernoulli's (1738) solution to the famous St Petersburg Paradox posed in 1713 by his cousin Nicholas Bernoulli. The Paradox challenges the idea that people value a random payoff according to its expected size. The Paradox posed the following situation: a coin is tossed until a head appears; if the first head appears on the toss, then the payoff is 2^n ducats. How much should one pay to play this game? The paradox, of course, is that the expected payoff is infinite, namely:

$$\text{Expected payoff} = (1/2)2 + (1/4)2^2 + (1/8)2^3 + \cdots = 1 + 1 + 1 + \cdots = \infty$$

Yet while the expected payoff is infinite, one would suppose, at least intuitively, that real-world people would not be willing to pay an infinite amount of money to play the game. Daniel Bernoulli's solution involved two ideas that have since revolutionized economics. First, a person's valuation of a risky venture is not the expected size of that venture, but rather the expected utility from that venture. Second, a person's utility from wealth, $U(W)$, is not linearly related to his wealth W, but rather increases at a decreasing rate – this is the famous idea of diminishing marginal utility. In the St Petersburg case, the expected utility of the game to an agent is finite because of the principle of diminishing marginal utility. Consequently, the agent would only be willing to pay a finite amount of money to play the game, even though its expected payoff is infinite.

---

be positively related to the return of a portfolio (investors are greedy and prefer more return) but negatively related to the risk taken (investors are risk-averse and prefer less risk to more risk for a given level of return).

In microeconomic theory, utility is usually derived from wealth. In our case, rather than modelling the wealth of an investor, we focus on the return of his portfolio. Thus, we will consider the utility derived from the portfolio return. In theory, the utility function $U(R_P)$ of an investor could take any functional form. As an illustration, Bernoulli originally used a logarithmic function,

$$U(R_P) = \ln(1 + R_P), \tag{24.1}$$

where R_P is the return achieved by the investor's portfolio, but we could also consider, for instance, a negative exponential utility function,

$$U(R_P) = 1 - \exp(-\lambda \times R_P), \tag{24.2}$$

where $\lambda \geq 0$ is a risk-aversion parameter that is investor-specific. Figure 24.4 shows the negative exponential utility function for different values of λ (0.1, 1.0 and 10). In all cases, when the return increases, there is a corresponding increase in utility or satisfaction. However, we also see that once the investor has reached a certain return, there is almost no increase in utility for each unit of additional return. In a sense, the investor becomes risk averse since he cares less about the additional return.

Other functions may also be used to model an investor's utility. However, maximizing a complex utility function is difficult from a mathematical perspective and generally does not yield nice analytical solutions. Therefore, many academics conveniently accept the idea that

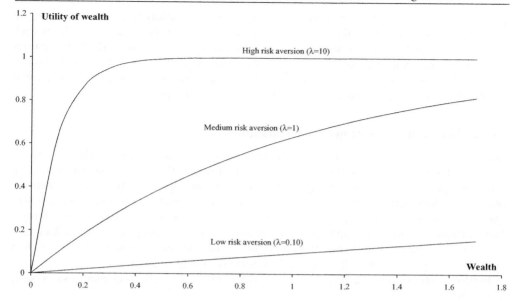

Figure 24.4 An illustration of negative exponential utility function for different risk aversion (λ) parameters.

utility functions should be simple trade-offs between risk and return, where risk is measured by variance. Mathematically, for a given investor owning a portfolio P with return R_P and variance σ_P^2, this type of utility function could easily be represented as

$$U(R_P) = R_P - \lambda \sigma_P^2 \qquad (24.3)$$

where $\lambda \geq 0$ is a risk-aversion parameter that is investor-specific.[7] Such a utility function is called a *quadratic utility function*, because it is a quadratic function of the portfolio returns. Maximizing such a function is extremely simple and forms the basis of mean-variance analysis. For a given level of return, it is equivalent to minimizing the variance σ_P^2, which draws the bridge between utility maximization and asset allocation.

Most of the time, practitioners understand well the concept of utility function, the idea of trading off risk against return, and they generally spend a considerable amount of time assessing the particular characteristics and needs of each of their clients, usually through questionnaires and face-to-face interviews. However, they do not use utility functions explicitly, but rely on *pre-optimized* standard investment profiles (conservative, balanced, aggressive, etc.). Hence, they aim at determining which one best suits an investor's long-term goals and personality, or if there is indeed a need to create a new dedicated profile. Although the practitioners' approach may appear unrelated to the academics' process, it is not. In fact, like Mr Jourdain[8] who wrote

---

[7] A high value of λ signals a highly risk averse investor, while a low value of λ signals a low level of risk aversion. As an illustration, consider an investor who has a λ coefficient equal to 2, and who is currently invested in an asset that offers 5% return with 6% volatility. The current utility level of this investor is $5\% - 2(6\%)^2 = 0.0428$. If the volatility of the asset increases to 20%, its return should increase to 12.28% to maintain the same level of utility. In contrast, an investor with a λ coefficient equal to 1 would simply require a new return of 8.64% to maintain his utility level.

[8] In Molière's *The Bourgeois Gentleman*, Act II, Scene 4, Mr Jourdain says, "For more than forty years I have been speaking prose without knowing anything about it, and I am much obliged to you for having taught me that."

prose without realizing it, practitioners are also assessing the utility function of investors. In fact, they are estimating the value of the above-mentioned risk-aversion parameter (λ) for each investor, even though they are sometimes not even aware of its existence. Then, they cluster investors in prespecified groups according to their risk aversion. The result of their work is some well-defined communities of investors, with similar utility functions. Then, they can start establishing the strategic asset allocation for each of these groups.

24.2.2   Establishing the strategic asset allocation

Strategic asset allocation is used to construct a portfolio of asset classes which meets an investor's long-term goals while matching his risk profile, rather than concentrating on the short-term performance of the varying asset classes. This strategic portfolio usually remains in place over a long period of time and is used as a reference to manage the effective portfolio.[9] Quantitative methods usually play an important role in strategic asset allocation. They bring a logical framework to the planning process, enhance discipline, transparency and risk control and allow the creation of scenarios. Most of the time, strategic asset allocation relies on modern portfolio theory (MPT) as well as on portfolio optimization techniques.[10]

Portfolio optimization usually proceeds in a well-structured way, the sequence of steps being as follows:

1. Select the set of asset classes to be considered for the portfolio, as well as the level of granularity required. In the following, we restrict our analysis to equities, bonds and cash.
2. For each asset class, forecast the necessary statistics (return, volatility of return, correlation with other asset classes, etc.). Note the word "forecast", which means some sort of prediction and not just historical averages. Unfortunately, in some respects, traditional asset allocation is now guided by hope: hope that equities will outperform other assets; hope that mainstream assets will return the same 10- to 25-year historical returns the industry has been showing clients for the last decade. But the key point for a forecast model used in an optimization procedure is to be forward looking.
3. Set appropriate constraints if necessary (e.g. minimum or maximum weights for some asset classes).
4. Run an optimizer, usually to create a portfolio of asset classes with the lowest possible risk for a target expected rate of return. That is, given N asset classes, the goal is to
   Choose the N asset class weights that
   Minimize the risk of the portfolio
   Subject to a target expected return for the portfolio.

Note that such a model will provide a portfolio having the smallest risk for a specified minimum level of return. However, a portfolio having a greater return and an equivalent level of risk may exist. In such a case, the portfolio returned by the optimizer would not be efficient. This is why optimizers are usually used to create a portfolio of asset classes with

---

[9] By contrast, tactical asset allocation focuses on moving the portfolio away from its long-term strategic benchmark to take advantage of short-term market opportunities.

[10] In recent years, portfolio optimizers have been increasingly applied to asset allocation, that is, at the asset class level rather than at the individual security level. This development is not really surprising. In many respects, asset allocation is a more suitable playing field for modern portfolio theory and its efficient frontiers than is portfolio selection. Whereas the stock selection problem usually involves a large universe of assets, an asset allocation problem typically involves a handful of asset classes and is therefore much easier to solve. Furthermore, the opportunity to reduce total portfolio risk comes from the lack of correlation across assets. Since stocks generally move together, the benefits of diversification within a stock portfolio are somewhat limited, while the correlation across asset classes is usually low and in some cases even negative.

the highest possible return for a target risk level. That is, given N asset classes, their goal is to

Choose the N asset class weights that
Maximize the return of the portfolio
Subject to a target risk for the portfolio.

5. Review the portfolios suggested by the optimizer, from both a quantitative and a qualitative perspective. It is important to take optimizers for what they are – powerful computing engines – rather than as producers of ideal solutions encompassing great quantities of wisdom and judgement.

6. Finally, perform sensitivity analysis by adjusting the assumptions on returns, volatilities and correlations, as well as constraints. If necessary, run multiple scenarios and compare the results.

These six steps should be part of any asset allocation using an optimizer. But the fundamental and as yet unresolved question is how "risk" should be measured. The majority of optimizers follow Markowitz's (1952) original conjecture, that is, investors have quadratic utility functions and/or returns are normally distributed. In this case, the portfolio optimization problems described above can be reformulated in terms of expected returns and covariance between the different asset classes.

24.3 INTRODUCING HEDGE FUNDS IN THE ASSET ALLOCATION

24.3.1 Hedge funds as a separate asset class

The majority of investors who include hedge funds in their investment process treat them as a distinct asset class, alongside cash, bonds and equities. However, the jury is still out on whether hedge funds – and more generally, alternative investments – constitute a distinct asset class or not. Hedge funds' returns are different from those of traditional assets, but this does not necessarily mean they are a separate asset class. The reason is twofold.

First, just as primary colours cannot be obtained by mixing other colours, primary asset classes are those whose returns cannot be obtained by mixing other asset classes together. The majority of hedge fund managers trade assets that already belong to an existing asset class, e.g. equity and fixed-income investments from the world's most liquid and highly regulated exchanges. In fact, most hedge funds involve all existing asset classes and are only alternative in the way they manage them. Rather than just holding assets and hoping that their price will go up, hedge fund managers use a variety of exposures (long, short, market neutral) and can therefore extract different returns at different times from familiar assets. But their returns are still functions of existing asset class returns.

Second, an asset class should normally comprise a set of assets that behave in some cohesive way. But hedge funds have no basic features that bind them together other than that they are different from traditional assets. In that sense, they would form an asset class made up of misfits unqualified for membership of any other club. This would be a rather bizarre asset class.

We therefore believe that, from a conceptual point of view, hedge funds are not really a new asset class and certainly not a cohesive asset class, but rather a collection of disparate and unconventional active management strategies. Nevertheless, for many investors, it is conceptually easier to consider hedge funds as a separate asset class, at least to begin with. This is particularly the case for institutional investors, both for regulatory and for reporting reasons.

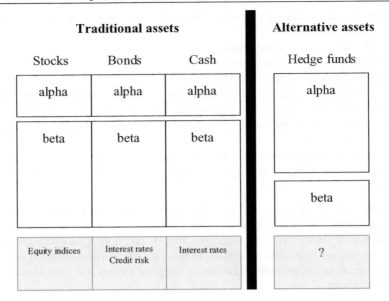

Figure 24.5   Hedge funds as a separate asset class

It is also convenient for investors who need to decide whether or not they want to capture an exposure to risks that are not correlated with the rest of their portfolio. In this case, the term "asset class" should be considered not in its original sense, but rather as one of the key components of a diversified portfolio. For this purpose each asset class needs to have a specific risk/return function, and hedge funds fulfil that function.

24.3.2   Hedge funds vs traditional asset classes

However, treating hedge funds as a separate asset class is likely to result in the situation illustrated in Figure 24.5. On the left-hand side, we find traditional asset classes, e.g. stocks, bonds and cash.[11] They are relatively well known and their risk drivers are clearly identified. Stocks move in keeping with the markets, which in turn are reflected in either general or specialized indices (countries, sectors, value vs growth, small caps vs large caps, etc.); bonds are essentially driven by interest rates, as well as by some credit spreads in the case of corporate bonds; finally, cash is almost exclusively influenced by short-term interest rates. All these risk drivers are "market based", and their influence is common to all traditional assets. Hence, by analogy with modern portfolio theory, we will say that most of the return of traditional asset classes is driven by "beta", that is, by exposure to these systematic market risks. The "alpha" part or value added, in contrast, is relatively small – if not negative after fees. There are two reasons. First, traditional money managers are so constrained by both regulations and benchmarks that it is difficult for them to generate a significant and consistent value added.

---

[11] To keep things simple, we deliberately omit currencies from our discussion.

Second, the benchmarks are clearly identified, so it is difficult to cheat and pretend that value has been added when it has not.[12]

On the right-hand side of Figure 24.5, we have hedge funds. In contrast to traditional assets, their managers emphasize their alpha advantage and claim to have very little beta embedded in their returns. Most investors blindly agree with this claim, which has been confirmed by numerous studies. Hedge funds in general are not strongly correlated with equity markets, and this is why we should include them in traditional portfolios.

However, this lack of correlation and low beta are precisely why most people feel uncomfortable with hedge funds. A low beta is a double-edged sword, because it also implies that we have not yet identified the return drivers of hedge funds. In this situation, how can we trust the alpha? Remember that a low beta often refers to equity and interest rate sensitivities, but there are numerous other types of risk that one can accept, e.g. liquidity risk, spread risk and commodity risk. The risk premiums associated with taking these risks would appear as alpha, while in fact they are just beta. Hence, the risk is high that many hedge funds are packaging some sort of beta and selling it at alpha prices.

Investors reluctant to go into complicated analyses are left with two extreme choices. The first is to consider hedge fund managers as people you would not want to associate with and to eschew hedge fund investments entirely. We disregard that option here. The second is to make a small fixed allocation (e.g. 5%) to hedge funds, while building a Great Wall between the universes of traditional and alternative investments. In a sense, what happens "behind the wall" is regarded as a lot of abracadabra. Needless to say, we wholly disagree with this approach to hedge fund allocation.[13] We believe that, while hedge funds can be considered as a separate asset class for reporting or regulatory purposes, this is probably not the best way to approach them from an investment point of view. Our understanding is that there should be no allocation in a portfolio – however small – if the risks, returns and interaction with other asset classes have not been carefully assessed.

24.3.3   Hedge funds as traditional asset class substitutes

An alternative way of looking at hedge funds is as substitutes (equivalent or superior in terms of risk and returns) for traditional asset classes, such as equities and bonds. Indeed, some hedge fund strategies are conceptually close to their long-only equivalent. For instance, sector-specialized long/short equity funds tend to be quite well correlated with their long-only peers, because they tend to maintain an inherent strong net-long investment bias. This bias has even strengthened over recent years with the migration of a series of talented long-only asset managers to the long/short industry. The possibility of going short allows these hedge funds to better control their downside risk, so that ultimately their returns compound at a higher rate or better than those of traditional funds. As an illustration, Figure 24.6 compares the performance of the long/short technology sector (HFR Index) with that of the NASDAQ. Although the

---

[12] For instance, systematically extending bond duration or over-weighting corporate bonds in fixed income portfolios is likely to provide higher returns in the long run. This additional reward is simply a compensation for taking more interest rate risk and more credit risk. In any good performance attribution model, the source of this additional performance will be identified as a beta, not an alpha, increase.

[13] I remember several conferences and meetings where I ironically challenged consultants and investors on their 2% allocation to hedge funds. "How did you arrive at this number?" The embarassed explanations in fact hid the reality. A 2% allocation is perceived as sufficient to boost returns. It makes you appear as hedge fund aware even though you do not necessarily understand what is happening behind the wall. And if the whole thing blows up, you can still bear the loss.

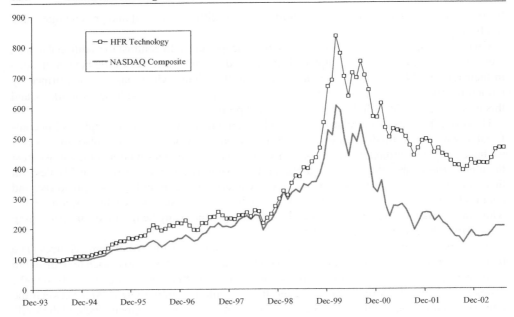

Figure 24.6 Comparison of the performance of the long/short technology strategy with that of the NASDAQ. The correlation between the two series is 0.90

two are obviously related, it is also clear that long/short managers managed their downside risk better. Hence, an idea might be to substitute some long/short technology hedge funds for traditional technology funds or even direct technology stock allocations. Naturally, the same argument is applicable to other equity sectors, e.g. biotech, energy, financials, etc.

During the downtrend in equity markets, several marketers have reacted by suggesting the replacement of traditional equity allocations by long/short equity portfolios. Important statistics to consider before following this suggestion are the correlation between hedge funds and the target sector, as well as the upside and downside capture.[14] Of course, investors should always prefer a high upside capture and a low downside capture relative to the target asset class.

More worrying is the fact that some marketers and even respected academics have also presented some hedge fund strategies as good substitutes for fixed income portfolios.[15] From a mean-variance point of view, this makes perfect sense. Many convertible arbitrage, fixed income arbitrage and market-neutral funds have indeed a volatility that is close to that of bonds, but with a higher average return (Figure 24.7). Hence, replacing bonds by hedge funds in a portfolio will substantially boost the expected return without increasing the standard deviation. On the cash side, there has also been an explosion of "dynamic Treasury" products, whose objective is to beat the short-term Treasury by doing low-volatility interest rate arbitrages on the term structure of interest rates.

---

[14] Upside capture refers to the percentage of upside performance attained by a manager relative to an index in periods of positive index performance. Downside capture refers to the percentage of downside performance recorded by a manager in periods of negative index performance.

[15] See, for instance, McFall (1999) or Cvitanic *et al.* (2003).

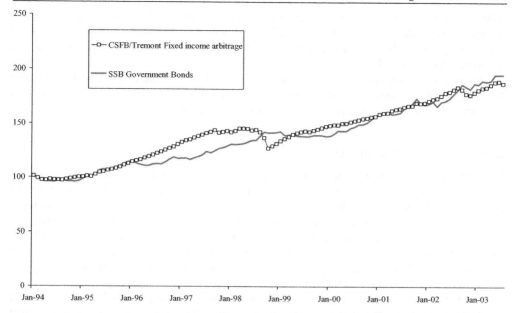

Figure 24.7   Comparison of the performance of the fixed income arbitrage strategy with that of the SSB Government Bond index. Despite the similarity, the correlation is between the two is less than 0.10

However, investors should be wary of considering hedge funds as enhanced bonds or cash equivalents. Low-volatility hedge funds are not exempt from risk, even if these risks did not materialize in the past. For instance, liquidity risk and credit risk are often present in low-volatility hedge fund strategies, and might exhibit non-trivial correlation with market returns precisely when diversification is needed. Furthermore, the skewness and kurtosis of hedge fund distributions are often very different from those of fixed income portfolios. Even if volatility is low, event risk is still present. Thus, the case for hedge funds as a replacement for fixed income products is less straightforward than is often suggested, obliging investors to make a trade-off between profit and loss potentials.

24.4   HOW MUCH SHOULD BE ALLOCATED TO HEDGE FUNDS?

"How much should we allocate to hedge funds?" Although investors ask us this question several times a day, we are still convinced that the problem itself is ill posed. As an illustration, consider the following two questions.

- What is the difference between having 10% of a portfolio in hedge funds with no leverage and 5% with a leverage of two (i.e. two dollars invested for one dollar of equity capital)?
- What is the difference between having 5% of a portfolio in hedge funds with a net long bias and 5% in hedge funds with a net short bias?

In the first case, the allocations in percentage terms are different, but the real exposures are identical. In the second case, the allocations in percentage terms are the same, but the real exposures are diametrically opposed. Clearly, by playing with the leverage and the direction of the net market exposure (long or short bias), it is possible to synthetically create *any* type of allocation, regardless of what the official allocation rule is. Moreover, a little bit of financial engineering can easily transform a hedge fund into a medium term note, which would then be accounted for as a bond.

This is why, in our opinion, the question of the exact percentage to be allocated to hedge funds as a separate asset class does not make much sense. Nevertheless, it is still on most investors' lips, so let us try to provide some elements of a solution.

24.4.1 An informal approach

Most of the time, strategic asset allocation is extremely informal as far as hedge funds are concerned. In fact, for many investors, reviewing their hedge funds' asset allocation is like going for an annual health check-up. They know it's the right thing to do, yet it is time-consuming and potentially disruptive; as long as there are no outward symptoms, it often gets put off. Some even do not care about it. As an illustration, a survey by Arthur Andersen (2002) on the risk approach adopted by the Swiss intermediaries investing in hedge funds evidenced that many hedge fund service suppliers do not have a hedge fund asset allocation strategy, or claim to apply a "qualitative approach" – see Figure 24.8.

These results are not really surprising. As we will see shortly, hedge funds do not fit traditional asset allocation approaches very well. This misfit, combined with the conventional and incorrect wisdom that hedge fund manager selection is the primary driver of returns at the portfolio level, is the reason for the scant attention paid to the portfolio construction process. Furthermore, falling equity markets and large capital inflows into hedge funds have done little to enforce any sort of investment discipline or to justify the extraction of greater value at the portfolio level. Rather, they have allowed hedge fund allocations to develop in a rather unsophisticated way,

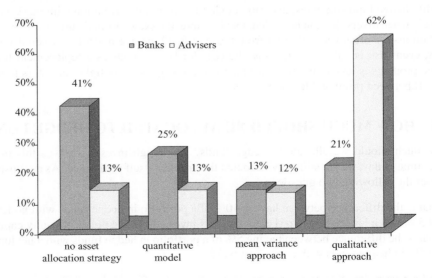

Figure 24.8 According to Andersen (2002), a large proportion of Swiss hedge fund service suppliers have no valid asset allocation strategy

compared with the risk management tools developed by investment banks and capital markets. In plain English, this is a shame. Hopefully, things are now changing. Cynics may argue that the sudden interest in quantitative asset allocation techniques is in large part a response to the marked underperformance of several funds of hedge funds since the NASDAQ crash in March 2000. Although that comment may not apply in all cases, there is probably some truth in it.

24.4.2   The optimizers' answer: 100% in hedge funds

Marketers commonly use mean-variance optimizers to justify and encourage hedge fund allocations. Figure 24.9 illustrates the impact of adding hedge funds to a universe of traditional assets. It is undoubtedly the most frequently displayed graph in any alternative investment conference, article or marketing brochure. With their historical equity-like returns, bond-like volatility and low correlation to bonds and equities, hedge funds can boast of ideal positioning. Consequently, their inclusion in traditional portfolios significantly improves the efficient frontier, which shifts to the northwest direction (i.e. less risk and more return). While past performance is no guarantee of future results, this chart seems to say that hedge funds may offer something that traditional investments may not. Some advisers even use the term "free lunch", i.e. more return and less risk. But is all this really a free lunch?

First, one needs to understand that the improvement of the efficient frontier is not specific to hedge funds. It is a technical feature: having a new asset in our allocation can only improve the efficient frontier, it will never deteriorate it. In a sense, adding stocks to a portfolio of hedge funds and bonds, or bonds to a portfolio of stocks and hedge funds, will also be beneficial.

Second, the problem with mean-variance optimizers is that, when used without any control, they tend to suggest inappropriate optimal portfolios. As an illustration, recall Figure 23.11. When starting from a portfolio made of 50% bonds and 50% equities, adding hedge funds was *always* beneficial from a mean-variance perspective. And when reducing both bonds and equities to allocate to hedge funds, the efficient frontier shrank to a single portfolio, which was simply 100% in hedge funds. This seems to strengthen the argument for high net worth individuals and institutions to include hedge funds as part of their overall asset allocation. But in fact, it strengthens it too much to be accepted by the majority of investors! Unfortunately,

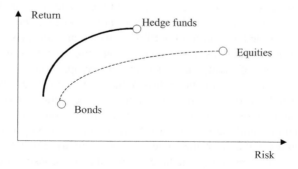

Figure 24.9   The traditional marketing vision of the efficient frontier without hedge funds (dotted line) and with hedge funds (plain line)

some financial advisers seem more interested in designing portfolios that are aesthetically appealing to clients than they are in building investment strategies that actually have a higher probability of achieving their client's objectives. Thus, they simply constrain the maximum weights for hedge funds in the optimization programme. Although this usually results in more appealing weights, we believe the approach is intrinsically flawed. First, establishing additional constraints on how much (or little) of any investment can be included in a portfolio is strictly subjective and not a scientific or objective approach to portfolio management. Second, it is contradictory to seek to maximize an objective function only partially. This suggests that the objective function – a function of mean and variance – was badly chosen. If the optimizer's answer is 100% in hedge funds, and we do not want 100% in hedge funds, it is simply because our objective function is incorrectly specified. The emphasis should therefore be on selecting the right objective function rather than on setting constraints to obtain the weights we want to have.

Third, we need to remember that when working with a mean–variance optimizer, we implicitly assume that investors are myopic and only care about the first two moments of the return distribution (expected return and volatility), but ignore features such as skewness and kurtosis. Reality is that investors are averse to negative skewnes and positive kurtosis. Hedge funds are peculiar animals because they offer relatively high means and low volatility, but they also tend to give investors negative skewness and high kurtosis. Thus, there is no free lunch – investors simply pay for the efficient frontier improvement by accepting more negative skewness and higher kurtosis.

24.4.3 Static versus dynamic allocations

Another problem with the majority of portfolio optimizers is that modern portfolio theory, which underlies the efficient frontier construction, assumes a single-period model of investment. That is, investors have to form a portfolio at time 0 and hold it until time T, which corresponds to their time horizon. During this period, each asset class generates a random rate of return so that at the end of the period (time T), the investor's wealth has changed by the weighted average of the returns. An optimizer will select the asset class weights at time 0 in order to maximize the expected return at time T for a given level of variance, or minimize variance for a given level of expected return from 0 to T. What happens in the middle of the period (between time 0 and time T) is irrelevant and does not influence the composition of optimal portfolios, because investors are not allowed to rebalance their portfolios.

The apparent superiority of hedge funds is therefore not surprising. The original asset classes, stocks and bonds, are static buy-and-hold portfolios, which are not revised during the period considered. An allocation that does not change through time is a myopic allocation, and in the microeconomic theory of saving and consumption, myopic solutions are rarely optimal. In contrast, hedge funds are dynamic portfolios. What we mean is that if we form a portfolio of hedge funds and hold it, our portfolio may appear to be static in terms of funds, but in reality, the underlying fund managers will react to new information or to the market conditions between time 0 and time T and adapt their portfolios accordingly. Comparing hedge funds with traditional asset classes is therefore the same thing as comparing a static investment policy with a dynamic one. Not surprisingly, the latter wins – it is less constrained.

Some may wonder what happens if we modify our framework to allow traditional asset managers to also trade in the middle of the period, while keeping the objective of creating the best portfolio at the end of the period. The answer, provided by Robert Merton in the early 1970s and recently implemented by Detemple, Garcia and Rindisbacher (2003), is quite complex. To summarize, the resulting optimal portfolio would contain three components: (i) an allocation to the "old" mean–variance portfolio; (ii) an allocation to a portfolio designed to hedge fluctuations in the risk-free rate of return by providing offsetting returns in environments when the risk-free rate of return is low; and (iii) an allocation to a portfolio designed to hedge against changes in the expected market price of risk (Sharpe ratios) across assets. Thus it is easy to understand why static mean–variance efficient portfolios are no longer efficient when multiple trading periods are considered: they are only a *part* of the optimal solution. Hedge funds, however, are allowed to trade dynamically and to invest in the two other hedge portfolios. Hence, comparing static mean–variance efficient portfolios with hedge funds is not very fair.

24.4.4 Dealing with "return management"

Another advantage that hedge funds may have over other asset classes lies in their valuation biases. Some strategies tend to invest in securities which are not actively traded, so that they are maintained at their acquisition cost until a new price is available. This is particularly true for the merger arbitrage, distressed securities, convertible arbitrage and emerging market strategies. On the long run, this does not affect average returns, but it seriously underestimates volatility and creates autocorrelation of returns – similar problems exist in real estate indices, due to smoothing in appraisals and infrequent valuation of properties. Fortunately, with an understanding of the causes of smoothing, a model can be developed to undo the lags in, or "unsmooth", the data – see Geltner (1991, 1993) and Box 24.2. As a result we can infer a "true" time series of returns offering a more accurate picture of what is happening in the market today and what happened in the past.

Box 24.2 Unsmoothing returns

To unsmooth returns, the observed (or smoothed) net asset value NAV_t^* of a hedge fund at time t is expressed as a weighted average of the true value at time t, NAV_t, and the smoothed value at time $t - 1$, NAV_{t-1}^*:

$$\text{NAV}_t^* = \alpha\text{NAV}_t + (1 - \alpha)\text{NAV}_{t-1}^* \qquad (24.5)$$

From there, it is possible to derive an unsmoothed series of returns with zero first-order autocorrelation:

$$R_t = \frac{R_t^* - \alpha R_{t-1}^*}{1 - \alpha} \qquad (24.6)$$

where R_t and R_t^* are the true underlying (unobservable) return and the observed return at time t respectively. In the case of hedge funds, Kat and Lu (2002) suggest setting α equal to the autocorrelation coefficient at lag 1 to ensure that the newly constructed series R_t has the same (arithmetic) mean as R_t^* and no first-order autocorrelation.

Table 24.2 Statistics for original and unsmoothed returns of various CSFB/Tremont indices (1994–2003)

Original returns	Volatility	Skewness	Kurtosis	Autocorrelation
Convertible Arbitrage	4.94	−1.67	4.39	0.56
Emerging Markets	20.16	−0.96	5.00	0.30
Event Driven	6.50	−3.70	25.07	0.35
Event Driven: Distressed	7.53	−3.00	18.16	0.29
Event Driven: Multi-Strategy	6.83	−2.92	18.59	0.35
Event Driven: Risk Arbitrage	4.66	−1.42	6.50	0.27

Unsmoothed returns	Volatility	Skewness	Kurtosis	Autocorrelation
Convertible Arbitrage	9.52	−1.32	6.49	−0.09
Emerging Markets	29.06	−1.45	7.11	0.03
Event Driven	9.64	−4.30	32.13	−0.01
Event Driven: Distressed	10.40	−3.34	22.19	−0.01
Event Driven: Multi-Strategy	10.13	−3.27	23.04	−0.02
Event Driven: Risk Arbitrage	6.22	−1.35	6.83	0.03

As an illustration, Table 24.2 summarizes the results obtained using the CS/Tremont indices for the convertible arbitrage, emerging markets and event driven strategies. It is clear that the higher the first-order autocorrelation found in the raw data, the higher the rise of the standard deviation – and consequently, the less attractive the strategy from a risk-adjusted perspective. Of course, one may object that the notion of unsmoothing is far from rigorous. It serves nonetheless to illustrate the possible impact of infrequent trading on hedge fund and hedge fund index returns.

A side effect of the ability to create smooth prices is that fund managers have a tendency to save for the rainy days and create reserves rather than reflect the true prices of their underlying securities. These reserves are typically used during a poor month to smooth returns and lower volatility. In case some reserves remain unutilized by the end of the year, fund managers can always include them in December returns . . . just before the payment of their incentive fees. As an illustration, Agarwal *et al.* (2006) document that average December returns for hedge funds are two-and-half times the average monthly return during January to November (2.5% compared to 1.0%). They also evidence that funds with greater incentives (funds with near-the-money compensation contracts and with poor performance relative to their peers) engage in returns management to a greater extent.

24.4.5 Optimizer's inputs and the GIGO syndrome

In addition to the above-mentioned problems, optimizers need to be fed with a scarce hedge fund resource – data – to create successful portfolios. In the case of a mean–variance optimizer, the necessary risk and return parameters are primarily the variance–covariance matrix of future returns, as well as the expected value of these future returns for all the asset classes considered. But by definition, future returns cannot be directly observed, so the required parameters must be estimated. Although there is ample evidence that the risks and returns of major asset classes

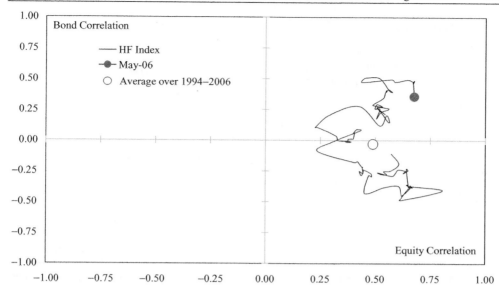

Figure 24.10 Evolution of the rolling 36-month correlation of the CSFB/Tremont Hedge Fund Index with stocks (S&P 500) and bonds (Citigroup World Government Bond Index). The most recent data point is indicated with a dark circle, the average over the whole sample with a white circle

are to some extent predictable,[16] perfect forecasting is not here yet, so some simplifying assumptions are required.

Taking the easy way out, many investors use the past to forecast the future. Unfortunately, this creates more problems than it solves. Implicitly, investors using long-term historical statistics are assuming (i) that returns in the different periods are independent and drawn from the same statistical distribution, and (ii) that the periods of available data provide a representative sample of this distribution. These hypotheses may simply be untrue, in which case the investment process will be comparable to driving a car forward while looking in the rear-view mirror. The result is that the optimizer provides the best *historical efficient frontier*, but not necessarily the best *future* one. This problem is particularly important with hedge funds, as their risk and return parameters change much more rapidly than those of traditional asset classes, so their behaviour cannot be modelled with the same level of confidence.

Consider, for example, Figure 24.10, which shows the 36-month rolling correlations of the CS/Tremont Hedeg Fund Index with equity and bond markets. It is clear that correlations are anything but stable over time. Their variations are in fact normal and even expected, as hedge fund managers are paid hefty fees to adjust their portfolios to market conditions. As a consequence, correlation should decrease when managers expect a bear market, and should increase when they foresee a bull market. Investors relying on historical data to build their asset allocation will therefore face what statisticians call estimation risk, i.e. divergences between historical estimates and the future reality. For some strategies such as Global Macro or Managed Futures, which are highly opportunistic, correlations are even more unstable and highly market dependent – see Figures 24.11 and 24.12.

---

[16] See, for instance, Irwin et al. (1994), Barberis (2000) or Amenc and Martellini (2002).

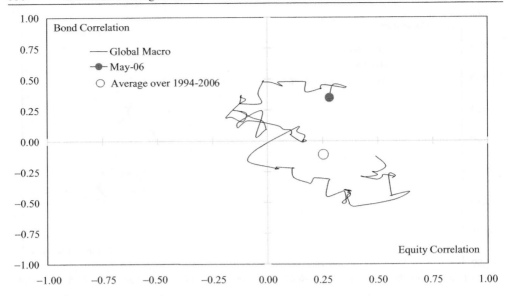

Figure 24.11 Evolution of the rolling 36-month correlation of the CSFB/Tremont Global Macro Index with stocks (S&P 500) and bonds (Citigroup World Government Bond Index). The most recent data point is indicated with a dark circle, the average over the whole sample with a white circle

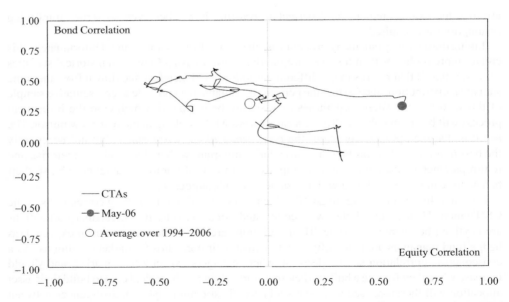

Figure 24.12 Evolution of the rolling 36-month correlation of the CSFB/Tremont Managed Futures/CTAs Index with stocks (S&P 500) and bonds (Citigroup World Government Bond Index). The most recent data point is indicated with a dark circle, the average over the whole sample with a white circle

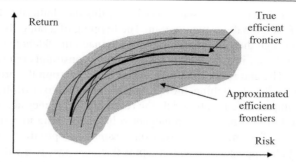

Figure 24.13   The impact of changing some inputs on the efficient frontier. The true efficient frontier is calculated using the "true" parameters (return, volatility, correlation), the approximated efficient frontiers are the result of using estimated parameters.

The literature provides several methods for reducing the impact of estimation risk, but the least we can say is that they are not very user-friendly for non-statisticians. Let us mention some of them:

- The Black–Litterman (1990, 1991) approach provides the flexibility to combine long-term market equilibrium values with additional market views of the investor about the expected returns of arbitrary portfolios. This approach seems to be best suited to long-only asset classes, but it is usually not an ideal way of taking allocation decisions with regard to alternative asset classes.
- The statistical shrinkage approach adjusts expected returns to reflect the fact that they are indeed estimates and therefore subject to estimation risk. The Stein approach and other Bayesian-based approaches can be used here to adjust these parameter estimates over time.
- The bootstrap approach simulates historical returns thousands of times using a bootstrap method in order to obtain a range of optimal mixes, which will provide a range for optimal weights of various investments. The bootstrap method can also be used to perform various stress tests as well as to create a return/risk surface rather than a single efficient frontier estimate (see Figure 24.13).

Alternatively, many investors forecast simply by adjusting historical statistics on mean rates of return, standard deviation and covariance coefficients according to their beliefs. While this approach is better than the non-adjusted one, it introduces some subjectivity into the process, which may result in estimation risk, i.e. uncertainty about the parameters of the return process. As evidenced by Lewellen and Shanken (2000), the observable properties of prices and returns can differ significantly from the properties perceived by rational investors.

In all cases, the key problem is that the answers provided by optimizers are very sensitive to small changes in the value of estimated parameters submitted by investors, whatever their source – see, for instance, Perret-Gentil and Victoria-Feser (2003). In particular, a small change in a parameter works its way through the optimization process and may result in a large change in the final allocations of efficient and near-efficient portfolios[17] – see, for instance, Kallberg

---

[17] Note that some loutish quantitative analysts have actually turned this feature to their advantage. As a judicious selection of inputs can justify almost any asset allocation policy, if at first the optimization model does not confirm the attractiveness of a favoured asset allocation, they simply tweak the inputs in the right direction (for instance, by changing the sampling period), or add a suitable constraint, and run the model again. *Et voilà* – the spectrum of efficient portfolios now includes the favoured asset allocation policy.

and Ziemba (1984) or Adler (1987). Some people call this the "butterfly effect", in reference to the complexity of the global weather system. The flapping of a butterfly's wings in Beijing may work its way through the system and result in a tornado in Oklahoma.

Faced with this problem, investors often include many constraints in order to stabilize the optimization results. The end result, however, is that they constrain the problem to what they want, and it is unclear what, if anything, the optimizer contributes to portfolio investment value. In order to limit the impact of estimation risk, the resampled efficiency algorithm invented and patented by Michaud (1989) provides an elegant solution to using uncertain information in portfolio optimization. The method is based on resampling optimization inputs, that is, it simulates a series of alternative optimization inputs that are consistent with the uncertainty in the investor's forecasts. For each series of inputs, it creates an efficient frontier. The "average" of all frontiers can then be used to select meaningful optimized portfolios.[18] Another interesting approach, suggested by Chopra and Ziemba (1993), consists in analysing the sensitivity of the final results to the optimization programme's parameters. For instance, Chopra and Ziemba establish that estimation errors have a lower impact when they concern covariance as opposed to variance. In any case, the main source of instability lies in errors concerning expected returns. This explains why some authors only attempt to determine the minimum variance portfolio rather than the whole efficient frontier – as the minimum variance portfolio does not require a forecast of expected returns.

24.4.6 Non-standard efficient frontiers

In recent years, a number of authors have suggested keeping the portfolio optimization framework, but replacing variance by a number of alternative measures of risk.[19] In particular, downside risk measures such as semi-variance, value at risk or expected shortfall clearly answer some of the critics of standard deviation by focusing only on the undesirable returns.

An important issue is whether, in practice, non-variance risk measures lead to significantly different efficient portfolios. Several studies have shown that using semi-variance rather than variance does not drastically change the optimal asset allocation when traditional asset classes are considered. However, when asset classes with non-symmetric return distributions (as is the case with hedge funds) are part of the asset allocation programme, the use of semi-variance or value at risk as risk measures may introduce significant changes in the optimal allocation. Therefore, these measures of risk may be more appropriate.

However, there are a number of problems with these new approaches. First and foremost, any measure of risk has to be predictable. It is one thing to use historical data to measure the past performance of a portfolio and it is another thing to forecast the risk of a portfolio. Statistical properties of semi-variance or value at risk are not well understood for non-normal distributions, and models for forecasting risk are not well developed yet. Second, the standard deviation of a portfolio is related to the standard deviations and correlations of the securities that comprise it, while the semi-variance or value at risk of a portfolio is not simply related to the semi-variances or value at risk and correlations of the underlying assets. And third, semi-variance and other measures of downside risk rely on about half the data points (i.e. only

---

[18] Because resampled efficiency is an averaging process, it is very stable. Small changes in the inputs are generally associated with only small changes in the optimized portfolios.

[19] See, for instance, Favre and Galleano (2000), Rockafellar and Uryasev (2002) or Acerbi and Tasche (2002).

negative returns are used); much longer series of returns are therefore needed to obtain accurate estimates. The problem is even more acute with value at risk. So the question becomes one of a trade-off between simplicity and tractability on the one hand and realism on the other.

Thus any thorough analysis shows that the alternatives often have their own serious shortcomings, and that none of them address the basic limitations of mean–variance optimization. This explains why mean–variance efficiency is sometimes far more robust than is appreciated.

24.4.7   How much should we allocate to hedge funds?

"Great, but how much should we allocate to hedge funds?" As the reader may have guessed, there is no standard answer regarding the weight that hedge funds should take in a portfolio. Most investors tend to forget it, and are convinced that they need hedge funds in their portfolios, even though they do not fully understand what they are. Not surprisingly, these investors face a high likelihood of disappointment, either because their expectations are too high, or because they are not fully aware of the new types of risk that hedge funds convey. Hedge funds are not the solution to all problems. When properly used, they are simply a solution to some problems.

Our recommendations are once again based on common sense. First, investors should understand what they are investing in. They should go beyond the usual marketing pitch and study until they feel confident with the asset class. Second, investors should fix their investment targets (in terms of risk, return, liquidity, maximum loss, etc.) and be as precise as possible on anything that may be relevant, particularly regarding the constraints they want to impose on their portfolios. Third, investors should be consistent in their objectives and beliefs. For instance, hedge funds are not necessarily appropriate for investors who do not believe in active management, or are not convinced that some of the best active managers can only be accessed via hedge funds. Nor are they in principle necessary for pension funds, because there is no evidence or argument that they match pension fund liabilities. It is only after agreeing that they must either produce superior returns and/or provide diversification benefits whenever needed that an allocation might be considered. Finally, investors should control their risks: not only volatility, but anything that they consider as a risk source.

24.5   HEDGE FUNDS AS PORTABLE ALPHA OVERLAYS

Another way of looking at hedge funds is as portable alpha overlays. This approach, initially suggested by Robert C. Merton when developing his functional perspective of financial institutions, is relatively simple and can be summarized as follows: with the growing availability of derivatives, it is possible to extract an alpha earned by an active manager and transport it into another market, sector, or even asset class with the same ease that "transporters" from the *Star Trek* science fiction series beamed individuals from one location to another. Consequently, there is no reason why an investor's choice of benchmark or asset class exposure needs to be tied to the source of alpha.[20]

---

[20] Note that Treynor and Black (1973) reached a similar conclusion and evidenced that the tools of risk management allowed asset allocation to be decoupled from active bets in the portfolio.

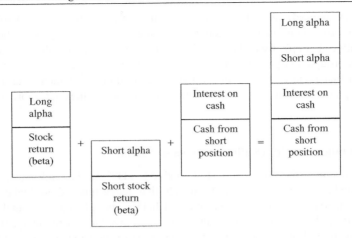

Figure 24.14 Creating a market neutral (beta neutral) portfolio from beta exposures

The concept of portable alpha is best illustrated with equity market neutral hedge funds.[21] These funds normally hold a large number of long equity positions and an equal or close-to-equal dollar amount of offsetting short positions. Their total net exposure is close to zero, and their performance is derived from two sources, regardless of the direction of the overall market: the return of the stocks held long versus the return of the stocks sold short (long alpha plus short alpha), and the interest on the proceeds from the short sales – see Figure 24.14.

The portable alpha approach goes one step beyond the market neutral approach. Simply stated, it suggests combining the market neutral portfolio with a separate overlay account that holds futures positions[22] in the desired weighted asset class mix with a value equivalent to the market neutral portfolio. For instance, mixing the market neutral portfolio with S&P 500 futures will create a new portfolio whose return should exceed the S&P returns by the long/short alpha while preserving its overall market exposure. Hence, investors can easily use the alpha produced by a market neutral fund to augment the returns of other portfolios, passive or active, in their overall investment programmes. The portable alpha portfolio can even be leveraged to match the risk and return preferences of the investor (Figure 24.15). The key to the process is of course to identify a fund that delivers true alpha – or more precisely, true portable excess returns.

The concept of portable alpha is also applicable to funds and strategies that are not necessarily market neutral. Consider for instance a hypothetical, non-market-neutral portfolio. In general, its return can be written as

$$\text{Total return} = \text{Benchmark return} + \text{Alpha}$$

where the benchmark is chosen by the fund manager (it is generally a market index) and may differ from the investor's target benchmark (say another market index). We may rewrite this

---

[21] By market-neutral hedge funds, we mean funds that are effectively beta-neutral with respect to equity markets. We have recently observed that a large number of self-called market neutral funds are in fact positively correlated to equity indices. Market neutrality is not a marketing argument, it has to be verified in performance.

[22] Alternatives to futures contracts are exchange traded funds, since (i) they can be bought and sold in much smaller amounts than futures and (ii) they exist for specific industry sectors, countries and risk factors (e.g. large caps vs small caps) that are not covered by futures contracts.

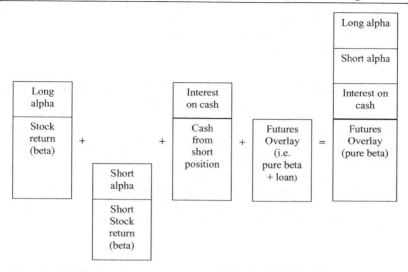

Figure 24.15   A market neutral portfolio can easily become a portable alpha overlay

equation as

$$\text{Total return} = (\text{Benchmark return} - \text{Cash return}) + (\text{Alpha} + \text{Cash return})$$

The first part of the equation represents the excess return of the manager's benchmark over a risk-free investment. In a sense, it is the beta component of the non-market neutral portfolio. Most of the time, this component can be hedged by selling futures on the benchmark itself, which transforms the non-market neutral fund into a market neutral one. The second part of the equation represents the risk-free rate of return plus the manager's skill, i.e. the alpha component. It is this part that we need to transport to another asset class, usually by buying futures on the investor's target asset class. Of course, we are assuming that alpha is positive (at least on average) and that it is uncorrelated with the target asset class.

For example, suppose we want to hold the S&P 500, but the only managers whose skills we truly respect manage (1) an Australian market neutral (long/short) electric utilities strategy, and (2) a Swiss bond portfolio. The former has no market exposure because the strategy is truly market neutral, but its fund has undesirable currency exposure. The latter has Swiss bond and Swiss franc exposure. If we hire both managers, we need to short the Australian dollar, Swiss franc and Swiss bond futures to an appropriate extent, and purchase S&P 500 stock index futures. Overall, the two superstar managers produce their alpha, which you have simply added on top of a passive S&P 500 return. The consequence is that in practical terms, the benchmarks chosen by portfolio managers should be more or less irrelevant to the investor as long as they can be hedged.

The concept of portable alpha – and the recognition that asset allocation and alpha generation are separable and independent decisions – is one of the most important developments of the 1990s. It applies also to traditional, actively managed portfolios, but hedge funds are a natural place to look for uncorrelated alpha. However, in practice, porting alpha is not without its costs and complications. In particular, it requires a fundamentally different mindset and structure for asset management. First, we need to find the managers that offer the most reliable prospective alphas, regardless of their strategy. Next, we combine these managers and port their overall alpha to the asset allocation that we want, and which is usually implemented using futures contracts and/or low-cost, indexed investment vehicles.

24.6   HEDGE FUNDS AS SOURCES OF ALTERNATIVE RISK EXPOSURE

Finally, the last way of considering hedge funds is as alternative risk sources, i.e. as investment vehicles that provide exposure to several types of risk – and therefore capture the associated risk premiums. Some of these risks are deemed traditional (equity markets, interest rates, credit), but the majority of them are still perceived as non-traditional (e.g. spreads, commodities, liquidity, volatility, correlation changes, market trends). This approach is conceptually very close to the multi-factor models we have been developing so far. It has the advantage of offering a consistent framework for both alternative assets and traditional assets, as illustrated by Figure 24.16.

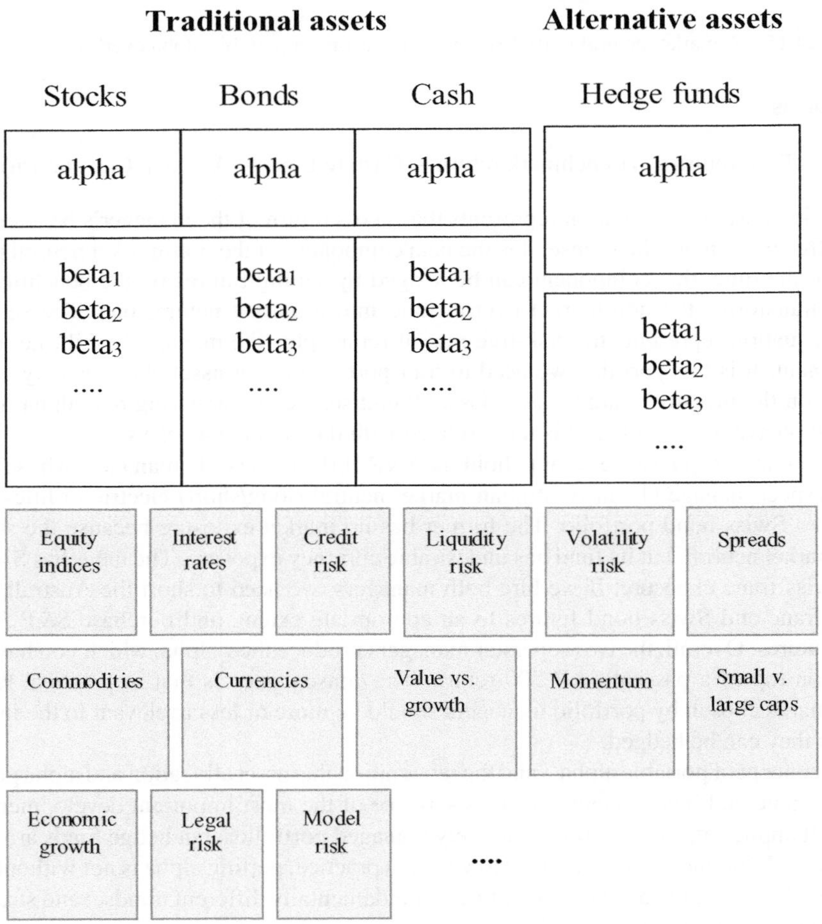

Figure 24.16   Hedge funds as risk exposure providers

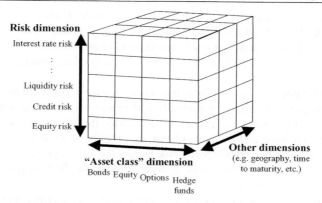

Figure 24.17   The risk cube provides a unified risk analysis framework for all "asset classes" and sources of risks

In this approach, the sources of risk are common to all assets, which can capture the associated risk premiums. For instance, buying a US T-bond will expose you to interest rate risk (measured by an interest rate beta) and grant you the associated risk premium. Buying a corporate bond will essentially expose you to interest rate risk (measured by an interest rate beta) and slightly to credit risk (measured by a credit risk beta), and grant you a mix of the two associated risk premia. Buying a junk bond or, to be politically correct, a high-yield bond, will expose you to the same risk sources, but will more heavily weight the credit. Finally, investing in a distressed securities hedge fund will expose you almost only to credit risk (measured by a credit risk beta), and perhaps slightly to interest rate risk, for instance if the hedge fund manager is using credit lines. What is important is that from the T-bond down to the distressed security, the risk sources are the same. It is only the exposures to these risks that change and, as a consequence, the quantity of risk premium that is collected. Hence, you should not manage the credit risk of a corporate bond differently from the credit risk of a distressed securities fund. And rather than thinking in terms of allocations, you should start thinking in terms of risk exposures and risk premia.

As an illustration, I must confess that I am often amused by the number of investors who adopt very conservative policies regarding the minimum rating and quality of the bonds in their traditional portfolios, but who are at the same time happy to enter funds of hedge funds where the distressed securities allocations represent up to 50%. Such behaviour is inconsistent. If you are negative on credit risk, you should reduce your overall credit risk allocation. If you are positive on credit risk, you should be willing to increase it. The same applies to any other source of risk.

An alternative way of representing risk exposures is by means of the "risk cube" – see Figure 24.17. This three-dimensional figure shows that asset classes, geography, and risk factors in fact all contribute to the risk and return of a given portfolio. It is therefore essential to have a unified framework for analysing and managing risk.

24.7   RISK BUDGETING AND THE SEPARATION OF ALPHA FROM BETA

Considering hedge funds as alternative risk sources opens the door to an increasingly popular activity in institutional asset management, which is termed "risk budgeting". Simply stated, risk budgeting recognizes that the isolation of risk management from the investment process is less than optimal. Therefore, it attempts to make risk management a more proactive part of the investment process by allocating capital to assets on the basis of their expected contributions to overall return and risk in order to achieve superior returns while maintaining a desired level of aggregate risk.

How does risk budgeting work? Risk budgeting is essentially nothing more than good risk management that is firmly, systematically and proactively embedded in the investment process. After agreeing on the risk exposures that hedge funds may provide, the question is then to determine the type and amounts of risk an investor is willing to accept. This is the establishment of the risk budget. Once the risk budget has been agreed on, the task is then to allocate capital in the most efficient way in order to generate the best possible return while remaining within the risk budget.[23]

Risk budgeting emerged in the late 1990s in response to concerns about the level of risk being accepted in portfolios and as a consequence of the development of risk measurement and management tools. However, what is new in the risk-budgeting formulation of asset allocation is the formalization of a risk lexicon and the application of new quantitative tools to improve portfolio performance. It is not the introduction of risk into the management process itself, as risk has long been an important element of portfolio management. In fact, most investment managers have engaged in some basic form of risk budgeting for many years, without really being aware that they were doing so. However, it is important to realize that risk budgeting is not just portfolio optimization, nor a guarantee against unforeseeable future mistakes. As stated by Rahl (2000), "Risk is not bad. What is bad is risk that is mispriced, mismanaged, misunderstood or unintended." Thus, the main aim of the risk-budgeting process is improved consistency of performance by more systematically targeting desired risk levels and avoiding unacceptable or unwanted risks. In a sense, we may also call it risk targeting or risk allocation. Used appropriately, it can be a valuable complement to investment judgement, but it is not a substitute for that judgement.

Risk budgeting and the quest for portable alpha can be pursued independently, but they are interconnected and best seen as two sides of the same coin. They are bound together by the simple fact that *strategic asset allocation and the quest for alpha are separable and should be separated.* If one can accept the notion that market returns (beta) on the one hand, and attempts to add value (alpha) on the other, are two different animals, which require their own set of skills, then there is no reason to keep them bundled the way they are in mutual funds (see Box 24.3). Indeed, investors can capture beta by using a core of low-cost indexation strategies and separately, seek to add value independently by selecting satellites of pure alpha strategies, such as hedge funds[24] and/or other absolute return vehicles focusing on the least efficient markets. Furthermore, the techniques used to manage the risk of "beta" or "alpha" portfolios are radically different: there is a compelling case for segregating these two sources of return in any portfolio.

Separating alphas from betas also means that the question of how much one should invest in hedge funds is no longer relevant. The important question now is how much active versus passive, where active means *really* active and passive means *really* passive. The result is that

---

[23] The term "risk budget" here should cover the galaxy of risks that a portfolio faces. This implies that risk needs to be more broadly defined than by VaR and/or traditional risk measures.

[24] Note that we are considering here "proper" hedge funds with no systematic or stable correlation with equity markets. The reality is that many hedge funds are nowadays mixing alpha and beta together and charge investors for both, blurring the picture.

Box 24.3 The real mutual fund costs

An interesting issue at this stage is that of costs. Unbundling alpha and beta allows investors to calculate the *real* fees charged by fund managers for their active exposure. As an illustration, consider the largest actively managed mutual fund, namely the Fidelity Magellan Fund. At the end of 2004, Morningstar reported that the R^2 of the regression of Magellan's returns on the S&P 500 was 0.99. Stated differently, 99% of the variance of Magellan is explained by the S&P 500. Nevertheless, Magellan still charges a 0.70% p.a. management fee. An investor could easily "replicate" what Magellan does by investing 90.9% of his assets in an S&P 500 tracker and the remaining 9.1% in an appropriately chosen market neutral hedge fund. If the tracker charged, for instance, 18 bps p.a., then 52 bps were overcharged to the investor. The 52 bps charge, compared to the 9.1% active portion of the portfolio, means that the investor is effectively paying a fee of 5.87% p.a. on the "real" active portion of his portfolio. Who said that hedge funds were expensive? Using the usual 2% management fee and 20% performance fee, a hedge fund would need to earn at least 19.35% p.a. to obtain such fees.

---

asset allocation becomes driven more by risk and return attributes and less by artifical or accounting asset categorizations. As an illustration, Figure 24.18 illustrates what we will call the economic asset allocation view. Hedge funds are no longer a separate asset class, but rather an active way to manage traditional asset classes. Equities, bonds and even real estate are split between pure low-cost trackers (in the most efficient markets) and pure high-fees alpha generators (in the least efficient markets). Even hedge funds indices can fit in this model. For instance, if one wants to do tactical asset allocation across hedge fund strategies, it is easy to split the portfolio into a pure "alternative beta" exposure (i.e. buying a hedge fund index) and a pure overweight/underweight overlay which measures the real value added of the active allocation decisions.

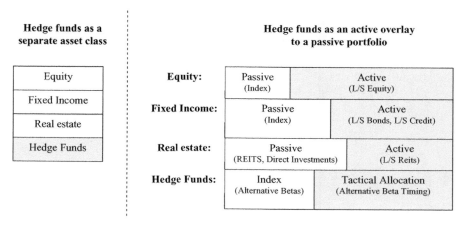

Figure 24.18   The shift from the regulatory/accounting view (left) to the economic view (right) of asset allocation

Of course, the economic view of hedge funds is not yet common practice – most private investors and intermediaries still perceive them as a separate asset class, and still allocate along asset class lines. However, sophisticated investors such as the large endowments and pension funds in the US are progressively adopting the economic view. They now separate their portfolios in cost-effective beta drivers that help to implement strategic asset allocations in an efficient manner, and high content alpha drivers designed to outperform their strategic benchmarks.

25

Hedge Fund Selection: A Route
Through the Maze

Markets can remain irrational longer than you can remain solvent.

John Maynard Keynes

Once the investor has decided the percentage of his portfolio to be allocated to hedge funds, the fund selection process can start (Figure 25.1). Simply stated, the role of the hedge fund selection process is to screen the industry for exceptional talents. Gaining access to one of the very few quality managers was for long the most difficult element of investing in hedge funds. Historically, hedge funds were only available through the "whisper network" of large institutional and very wealthy individual investors. There was no question of selection. The question was rather one of being invited to invest in a fund!

The strong economy and raging bull market of the 1990s have expanded the pool of vehicles, and the problem is now exactly the opposite: choosing a particular hedge fund in a universe of about 6000 funds can be one of the most daunting challenges an investor has to face, even though it need not be. The lack of publicly available information and the limited transparency of hedge funds do not facilitate the selection process. In addition, the consequences of being wrong are weighty. Even in a small peer group, the dispersion of risk and returns among hedge funds can be quite large, particularly on the downside, since no common benchmark or tracking error federates the asset allocation.

That being said, it is possible to avoid a large number of pitfalls by setting emotion aside and applying the appropriate analytical principles to the decision. In a sense, the process of selecting a particular hedge fund should be very similar to selecting a stock, that is, systematic, disciplined, well structured and rational. Research and common sense are keys to good decisions. If you are not an expert, hire one, but first ensure that he is a truly independent one! And remember that, in reality, most so-called experts who claim to use proprietary techniques to select hedge funds, based on their "personal relationships", "years of experience", or "quantitative models" simply follow the steps of the hedge fund selection process that we will now describe.

25.1 STATING OBJECTIVES

Before beginning the search for a hedge fund or a hedge fund manager, it is necessary to first state precisely what an investor wants to achieve. What type of hedge fund are we looking for? The answer should take the form of a coherent set of fund characteristics that are mandatory or desirable for this investor. Anything that may affect the final choice should be mentioned, such as:

- Should the fund be restricted and/or avoid a particular strategy or market or a specific investment style?
- For tax efficiency, should the fund have its domicile or be registered in a particular country?
- Should the fund have a minimum size of assets under management? A minimum length of identifiable track record? A minimum level of disclosure and/or reporting? These last two

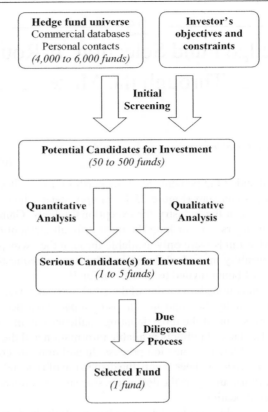

Figure 25.1   A typical hedge fund selection process

objectives are often conflicting: younger managers have less experience, but they are often more willing to open their funds to scrutiny.

- Should the fund have a specific redemption policy (e.g. monthly or quarterly)?
- Should the fund be willing to accept a given investment, whether large or small?
- Should the fund's returns be hedged against a specific currency?

Stating these objectives constitutes the foundation of the hedge fund selection process. Specifying them loosely will extract hedge funds that will not satisfy their investors. It is therefore essential to take the time needed to define one's needs precisely. Unfortunately, most investors who are new to alternative investments have only a vague idea of what their objectives are. How many requests have been made for funds that "add value" or hold "non-correlated assets"! These are neither clearly defined terms nor investment goals. And, by the way, non-correlated to what?

25.2 FILTERING THE UNIVERSE

Once the hedge fund's desired characteristics have been clearly stated, an efficient and effective elimination process can begin. It is usually implemented on a computerized database containing information on several thousand hedge funds. By applying the necessary filters to this database, one can effectively eliminate a large number of funds that do not fulfil the mandatory criteria, and grade the remaining funds according to their adequacy. The top funds – between 50 and 500, say, depending on how selective the search criteria were – will go forward to the next step.

The key element in implementing this filtering process is clearly gaining access to information. For several years, hedge fund databases were proprietary and investors looking to invest in hedge funds did not have access to performance data. Only those who were in the know and had committed capital for several years managed to obtain "behind the scene" information. Fortunately, since the mid-1990s, the situation has changed. A number of hedge funds databases have become publicly available – see Chapter 21. Some of them even now offer online access and search capabilities, with some analytics and portfolio risk monitoring. Investors can therefore leverage these powerful tools to make hedge fund investing easier and base their strategic decisions on comprehensive information.

However, no official database is complete. Since hedge fund managers are not required, and in many cases not allowed, to advertise or report performance data to any central authority, information is reported only on a voluntary basis. Consequently, many of the top hedge fund managers are not listed in commercially available databases. Therefore, hedge fund consultants and investment advisers often build their own database by subscribing to public databases, but also by adding in the managers they know through their network of professional contacts and with whom they feel comfortable investing. Funds closed to new money for the foreseeable future and funds where the management group refuses to disclose a sufficient amount of information should be systematically eliminated from these databases.

Keep in mind that very large databases are not necessary ideal. It is true that they increase the likelihood of finding suitable managers but they also include several funds that (i) are not truly hedge funds, (ii) are not suitable for investment or (iii) are totally unknown in the industry. As an illustration, I remember once visiting an asset manager who proudly exhibited a database of more than 60 000 funds. After a few checks, it transpired that (i) most of these funds were long-only, and (ii) the same fund appeared numerous times under different codes, once for each place where it was authorized for distribution, once for each class of shares, etc. This clearly demonstrates the advantage of working with a pre-filtered set of funds that fulfil minimum initial requirements.

Once the database is ready, it is subjected to a preliminary refinement based on quantitative criteria such as performance, volatility and correlation to traditional markets, assets under management, the experience of the fund manager, the track record length, the investment style, the selected financial instruments and leveraging. This first selection is made on the basis of marketing research, management meetings and short visits with the fund managers.

Once the filtering process is terminated, the investor is left with a short series of hedge funds (the "short list"). All meet the stated requirements and are therefore potential candidates for investing, at least from an external point of view. The next step is to look behind the screens, get a clearer picture of what these hedge funds are really doing and narrow the choice down from several hundred funds to a manageable pool of a few tens. The tools to perform this task are quantitative analysis and qualitative analysis.

25.3 QUANTITATIVE ANALYSIS

Hedge funds managers like to point to their long-term track record, if any, as evidence of their ability to weather different market conditions successfully. However, although desirable, a good track record is no guarantee of future performance, nor is it a reliable indicator of historical performance! One needs to look behind the numbers and extract the relevant information content from the time series. This is the role of quantitative analysis.

Quantitative analysis focuses on the statistical evaluation of the past performance of a hedge fund over different periods of time. It typically uses ratios and other statistical measures to compare absolute and relative performance, performance in rising and falling markets and risk-adjusted performance with that of managers and benchmarks with similar investment styles and risk levels. Ideally, it should focus on three aspects: manager's returns, strategy returns and portfolio contribution.

Knowing the effective primary drivers behind a manager's returns and a strategy's returns is particularly important to:

• Assess the consistency and validity of the track record, volatility patterns and correlations with major indices.
• Quantify the size and stability of the fund's exposures over time and compare them with the strategy's exposures.
• Understand the systematic and specific risks involved, at least on a historical basis.
• Analyse the risk premium received as well as the excess return ("alpha") over time.
• Validate a manager's specific implementation and/or trades.

If the selected fund needs to be incorporated in an existing portfolio (of other hedge funds, traditional assets, or a mix of these), it is also necessary to estimate the overall portfolio systematic and specific risk exposures as well as the fund's marginal contribution to risk.

Because it relies essentially on historical time series of net asset values, quantitative analysis has the advantage of low cost and easy access. However, it is often criticized as being a "backward looking" process. As we all should know, past performance is of questionable relevance when looking forward, because history may not repeat itself. It is therefore illusory to select hedge funds solely on the basis of their historical performance. However, the past may provide prudent guidance for the future. For instance, track records in stressful periods often tell something about how a manager behaves under pressure. Does the performance make sense, given the announced strategy and the underlying market conditions? Comparing managers to themselves at earlier periods can be quite revealing about their real-world style and risk appetite! Ideally, this type of quantitative analysis should be performed over a historical period of at least three to five years to allow a hedge fund to move through a full market cycle with both bull and bear markets. However, most hedge funds have a shorter time record, so shorter periods are not uncommon.

25.4   QUALITATIVE ANALYSIS

Qualitative analysis is the logical complement to quantitative analysis. Its primary aim should be to gain a clearer picture of the general strategy and investment philosophy followed by a given hedge fund, and in particular to understand where the performance (the "alpha") comes from and why the fund should be able to extract it. It also raises awareness of the returns and risks that are plausible. When correctly implemented, qualitative analysis provides a means of differentiating between two apparently identical statistical hedge fund profiles. It is often useful in eliminating an additional series of hedge funds that are not compatible with the investor's wishes.

The sources of qualitative analysis are usually to be found in the private placement memorandum, the marketing presentations and discussions with the fund manager.

25.5 DUE DILIGENCE: BETWEEN ART AND SCIENCE

Once the quantitative and qualitative analyses have yielded their conclusions, only a few funds should remain as suitable candidates for investment. Prior to committing any equity capital, it is necessary to analyse them in detail, not from an external perspective (past returns, offering memorandum, etc.), but from an internal viewpoint (investment process and philosophy, style, approach, risk controls, performance record against appropriate index, in various markets and against peers, depth and quality of internal organization, manager background, investment references, etc.). This is called "due diligence".

In a sense, due diligence is a form of more comprehensive and more thorough qualitative analysis. It is usually conducted by a team of experienced professionals through due diligence questionnaires combined with visits to the fund's offices and face-to-face interviews with each fund's senior management, chief operating officer and portfolio manager.[1] Each aspect investigated has usually a scoring system, which allows funds to be graded and compared on a similar basis.

Below we discuss five key areas that should be analysed in any due diligence process: the strategy, the fund itself, the management team, the infrastructure and the investment process.

25.5.1 The strategy

What is the hedge fund doing exactly? At this stage of the analysis, that may seem a silly question. With traditional investments, figuring out the strategy of a fund manager is easy. One just needs to look at the fund's benchmark, which is often very similar to the fund's asset allocation. However, with hedge funds and other absolute return performers, this is no longer the case. The idea of a benchmark is indeed the very antithesis of absolute performance. Most hedge funds do not use benchmarks, or just rely on some "increment to cash returns" approach.

Of course, most hedge funds disclose the general type of strategy that they intend to follow, and data providers often rely on this information to classify funds in a series of predefined categories. Unfortunately, managers' definitions are highly subjective, so that even within a particular investment strategy, one can find a mixture of four-star chefs and burger flippers. From my experience, the best way to understand a hedge fund strategy is to request the manager to provide examples of a few trades and then go over them in details. It is essential that these trades include not only successful ones, but also ones that failed. This will allow the investor to be aware of the risks associated with the strategy and what is done about them. And remember that a manager that claims to have no losing trades is untruthful or even worse, overconfident!

Once the current investment strategy is understood, the focus should turn to understanding historical changes with respect to this strategy, as well as the potential consequences in the future. For instance:

- Has the fund manager changed his strategy over time? Strategies are not carved in stone, and it is common for managers to change their initial positioning. If they have done so, it is important to know why.

---

[1] Hedge funds were long perceived as something of a black box, with managers unwilling to provide any significant information regarding their strategies or their portfolios. However, the situation has gradually changed with the competition resulting from the emergence of new managers and the increased interest of institutional investors. Most managers now employ some staff dedicated to answering due diligence questionnaires sent by serious potential investors.

- Is the current manager responsible for the fund's long-term performance or did he inherited it from another departed manager?
- Did the fund manager run the strategy prior to the inception of the fund? If so, were there any structural advantages or disadvantages?
- What are the prospects for the strategy? Are there limits to the amount the fund can manage effectively without sacrificing performance? If so, at what level will the fund's assets be capped?
- Are audited statements available? Are the returns consistent with the strategy?
- What is the average leverage? Is leverage necessary or just speculative?
- How concentrated are the positions? How liquid are they?

Finally, an important issue is that of competition. No one is better placed than the manager of the fund to describe its major competitors, their size, their differences, etc. This is extremely useful information to understand the value added by the manager and to be able to build a peer group to benchmark a fund.

25.5.2   The fund itself

Once a comfort level has been established with the strategy, the next step is the analysis of the fund itself. Well before committing to any investment, special attention should be paid to understanding the terms of the fund and its structures as well as the quality of the various parties involved. In particular, the following questions should be asked:

- Where is the fund's domicile? Why? What are the rights of investors under the jurisdiction of the country of domicile?
- What is the legal structure of the fund? What are the rights and duties involved?
- Is the management firm regulated? If so, by whom? If it is not regulated, what exemptions are relied upon?
- What is the subscription and redemption policy? Is it likely to change? Has it been changing already?
- What are the fees and expenses charged to the fund and to the investor?
- Who are the fund's service providers (custodian, administrator, etc.)? How were they selected? How is their performance monitored? Have there been any recent changes?
- Where are the assets of the fund held? Who can transfer the assets into the accounts of the fund and what process must be followed to do so? Are there liabilities or assets used as collateral?
- What is the process undertaken to value investments? Have there been any material problems in pricing, calculation of net asset values or remittance of proceeds?
- Is there an independent board of directors made up of people with the necessary background, experience and independence to fulfil their responsibilities?
- How many other investors are in the fund? How large is the largest investor or the five largest investors? How much of the equity capital was committed by the manager?
- Is there any other available means of investing in the same strategy with the same manager (e.g. onshore and offshore funds, managed accounts, different types of shares, etc.). What are their differences?
- Do any other investors in the fund have preferential terms (fees, liquidity, transparency)? It is often the case that closed funds reopen with worse terms for the new investors (longer initial lock-ups, higher fees, etc.).

The due diligence team may also require a review of the other agreements that are part of an offshore fund, i.e. investment advisory or administration agreements.

25.5.3   The management team

Once the above stages have been completed, the next step is to appraise the people involved in managing the fund. This is an important step, because a hedge fund's success is largely dependent on its manager's ability to navigate through different market conditions and business cycles.

In particular, it is essential to determine:

- The key individuals in the fund. Who are they? What are their backgrounds and reputation within the industry? How experienced are they? What does their experience give them? When and why did they leave their previous employer? Some investors may be reluctant to ask such personal questions, but (i) he or she should remember that a significant portion of their wealth would actually be at these people's discretion, and (ii) if desired, third parties can performed the necessary checks. The secretive nature of hedge funds makes them enticing vehicles for charlatans, but also for crooks.[2]
- Have the firm or any individuals been involved in or threatened with any legal action? Here again, the answers should be checked with different regulatory agencies that maintain sanctions and enforcement databases (the Securities and Futures Authority, the Commodity Futures Trading Commission, etc.).
- The nature and coherence of the management team. Does the senior manager really delegate, or is he more like a star surrounded by executants? How long have members of the team worked together? Do they share the same vision and strategy? Have there been any recent departures, or disciplinary or regulatory problems with any members of the staff or the firm as a whole? How vulnerable is the organization to the departure of a specific fund manager?
- The motivation of the management team. Is management sufficiently motivated? Did managers commit their own capital? If a hedge-fund manager is not willing to risk much of his own money, why should you? If he does, what is the sum involved? How many employees are also rewarded according to performance? How is staff paid?
- The potential conflicts of interest. Are there incentives for trades to be executed via any particular channel? Are managers dedicated to a single hedge fund, or do they manage several hedge funds simultaneously?

25.5.4   The infrastructure

Analysing the current and expected future infrastructure of a hedge fund in terms of software, hardware and office space is necessary but not easy. The reason is that there is no infrastructure that can be defined *a priori* as "right", but several valid competing ones that need to be in line with the fund's overall activity. It pays to build for success. Several funds end up being constrained in their business development opportunities because of inadequate infrastructures.

---

[2] For instance, Michael Smirlock, a former Goldman Sachs mortgage trader, raised $700 million to start three hedge funds just after the SEC had suspended him in 1993. Would you have followed him? Well, in 2000, the SEC sued him again for hiding $70 million in losses from his investors.

Key issues to monitor are:

- The software used in the front-office analytics, the mid-office risk systems and the back-office accounting and execution systems.
- How these systems communicate and are reconciled with one another.
- The automated backup processes and facilities for disaster recovery, as well as insurance policies, if any.
- The existence of a website and its usage to inform existing customers of developments at the fund.

25.5.5   The process

The last step of the due diligence should focus on understanding and validating the investment process of the hedge fund. Examples of critical questions are:

- What are the processes for taking investment decisions? Is there an investment committee, or are the final decisions taken by one single individual? How do new ideas enter the portfolio construction?
- Who is allowed to trade? What assets can be traded? How are trades executed, reported and entered into the systems? What are the safeguards to prevent any unauthorized trading, or to prevent tickets from being hidden?
- Is there an independent risk management unit? What are the risk management limits, at both the trade and the portfolio level? How are these limits imposed? Is there a risk committee? How is compliance with the risk limits monitored?
- How does the reconciliation process operate, both internally and with respect to the prime brokers and the administrator? Have there been any material issues, and how were they resolved?
- Who values the positions? How does the administrator get the fund positions and the associated prices? Is the process really independent?

Another important issue to be addressed here relates to the amount of cash balances held by the fund. Frequently, due diligence questionnaires request the average cash percentage of the fund over a year, as well as an explanation for any significant deviation from this average over the past five years or since the fund's inception.

25.6   ONGOING MONITORING

The final outcome of the selection process is a formal report that should fully document the "hire" or "do not hire" decision. It sometimes contains recommendations relative to the maximum size of the allocation, or if the fund is not retained, indications for the future. For instance, a fund may be temporarily excluded for a minor reason, but still monitored for future use.

However, once an investment has been made, things do not end there. Selected managers should be subject to a rigorous ongoing monitoring and oversight process to ensure that (i) they adhere to their stated investment strategy and (ii) their performance on a risk-adjusted basis compares favourably with that of their peers. Funds that fail to achieve their stated goals or that deviate from their stated philosophy should be subject to replacement.

This thoughtful and thorough monitoring programme should be structured as an ongoing analysis and due diligence. It focuses on the same issues (the people in the fund, the investment process, the nature of the portfolio and the resulting performance, etc.), is at least as time consuming, but reaches different conclusions. Once the investor has committed some capital to a hedge fund, there are three possible choices: leaving things unchanged (default), committing more capital, or redeeming assets in whole or in part. The role of monitoring should therefore be to support this type of decision making based on regular contacts with managers, on-site visits, conference calls, discussions with other industry participants, and internal quantitative and qualitative analysis.[3] Any information received as a shareholder in the fund (regular shareholder newsletters, non-audited monthly statements of positions and audited financial statements) should therefore be circulated for review within the due diligence team.

25.7 COMMON MISTAKES IN THE SELECTION PROCESS

Although there is no optimal hedge fund selection process, there are a series of common pitfalls that should be avoided.

Focus on immaterial issues

Attention should only focus on (the numerous) issues that are susceptible to affect the final selection decision. As used to say one of my former colleagues, "focus on coconuts, not on peanuts!"

Reliance on emotions

To be efficient, the selection process should eschew any emotional considerations. An excellent manager may be disagreeable, unfriendly or even arrogant, while a crook will often be extremely likeable and pleasant. What matters is not how one interacts emotionally with the manager, but the quality of the management process. However, in some cases, much like when hiring a manager or a doctor, the question of personal attitude may also weigh in the final decision. For instance, a manager who seems unfocused and disinterested or even unaware of his latest deals gives a strong signal that something is wrong in a hedge fund's organization.

Overreliance on qualitative aspects

This bias is unfortunately still too frequent. Several analysts do not feel very comfortable with quantitative measures, and tend to neglect them on the grounds that they rely solely on the past and are not good indicators of the future. They prefer to rely on qualitative analysis and due diligence, and solely use quantitative analysis to screen large databases of hedge funds, to rank them according to a particular choice of performance measures and to show the corresponding results with eye-catching graphics. As a result, they tend to produce thick quantitative reports, with several dozen pages filled with statistics, net asset values and other numbers, but without value added to these numbers, nor any real analysis. This is clearly a dangerous attitude, given

---

[3] An interesting question here is the availability of managers. Investors like to receive updates on performance, investment approach and/or outlook directly from the manager but on the other hand the role of the manager should be to focus on asset management, not on investor relations. It is therefore important to find a mutually acceptable communication arrangement.

the low transparency and loose regulation of hedge funds activities. We believe quantitative analysis has a useful role to play per se, but also as a complement of qualitative analysis. In particular, it is the only historical trace of what has effectively been done by a manager. Therefore, combining historical guideposts with current and ongoing personal knowledge of the hedge fund and its manager are the joint key to success.

Waste of information

It is important that any information collected during the selection process and, later, in the ongoing monitoring be recorded in a predetermined information management system. This helps to avoid oversights and throws light on the evolution of the fund manager and his strategy over time. It also provides for easy transfer of knowledge if someone else is designated to take care of the selection process in the future.

Tick the box syndrome

It is too often the case that due diligence is performed by young and inexperience analysts which have – and it is natural – a tendency to "check the boxes" from some preconceived form that outlines the questions to be asked. The result is a standardized due diligence process, but which fails to delve into issues that are manager specific, and that even managers might consider pertinent for the investor. As an illustration, in most of the recent hedge fund scandals (Moore Park, Bayou, Wood River, Refco, etc.), there were obvious signs that something was wrong. The standardized due diligence questionnaires were fine, but a few basic and intuitive questions would have pointed to the problems. Outsized performance numbers relative to the best funds in the same strategy space, self-dealing within a broker dealer for execution, self-administration, and in some cases and self-custody are obvious red flags that should at least justify additional questions.

26

Funds of Hedge Funds

And at the end of the day, they all report to me!

A famous central banker

As we saw in the previous chapter, although hedge funds may offer some specific benefits, it is quite difficult and time consuming for an investor to just go out and hire a single hedge fund manager on his own. Significant barriers, such as the complexity of the evaluation process and the experience that is necessary to perform effective ongoing monitoring of the selected fund(s), will discourage most investors. Furthermore, given the high minimum investment requirements of individual hedge funds, direct investments have every chance of turning into concentrated portfolios (i.e. one to three managers), which are inherently poorly diversified and often highly illiquid. This explains why investors with time constraints, little experience or limited capital often prefer to gain access to alternative investments through funds of hedge funds to reach a proper diversification.

26.1 WHAT ARE FUNDS OF HEDGE FUNDS?

Funds of hedge funds (hereafter: funds of funds) do exactly what their name suggests: they allocate capital to several hedge funds. Investors buying shares in a fund of funds are not investing in a specific hedge fund, but acquire a proportionate share of ownership in a collective portfolio of typically 30 to 60 hedge funds.

Although funds of funds may appear innovative for most investors, it is not really a new concept. Rothschild Capital Management started Leveraged Capital Holdings in November 1969, which was from the beginning a fund of funds. However, it is only recently that funds of funds have really begun to win significant business. In particular, they are now the preferred access path to hedge funds for many pension funds, endowments, insurance companies, private banks, high net-worth families and individuals. According to various surveys, funds of funds now represent between 30 and 50% of the whole hedge fund universe in terms of assets under management, and they will undoubtedly be an important catalyst in the evolution of the hedge fund industry. As an illustration, Europe's biggest pension plan – the Netherlands' Algemeen Burgerlijk Pensioenfonds – announced that it would invest up to 2 billion euros in funds of funds. That is nearly twice the amount that Calpers, the biggest US pension fund, has committed to hedge funds.

26.2 ADVANTAGES OF FUNDS OF FUNDS

In theory, well-designed and well-managed funds of funds can deliver a number of valuable benefits. Below we review and comment on the contributions that funds of funds commonly claim to offer, namely, risk diversification, affordability, accessibility, professional management, and built-in asset allocation.

26.2.1   Efficient risk diversification

Meaningful diversification benefits are the key argument advanced by promoters of funds of funds. Prudent investors would not sink all their money into a single stock, but rather lower the risk of loss by buying shares in a number of companies. They may not earn the stellar returns of the best performing stock, but they will not lose as much as they would if that single stock were to collapse in price. As with stocks, so with hedge funds! Investment returns, volatility and risk vary enormously among the different hedge fund strategies. By selecting managers rather than assets, funds of funds aim to provide investors with an extra level of diversification and allow them to smooth out the potential return inconsistencies of having all assets invested in a single hedge fund.

Risk diversification within a fund of funds can be achieved by two means. The generalist approach consists simply in using several hedge funds that cover a wide array of strategies, managers, markets and risk factors. It is often implemented by mixing hedge funds following different investment styles that historically have displayed low correlation. In practice, it yields to the biggest risk reduction, because the selected funds are likely to hold fewer stocks in common. By opposition, the specialist approach consists in investing in a large number of hedge funds following the same strategy. It aims at avoiding the risk of poor manager selection, while still remaining exposed to an investment style.

There are different opinions about the optimal number of hedge funds in a fund of funds, but the major danger is to consider hedge fund as individual securities and overdiversify. Indeed, there are several reasons to limit the number of hedge funds in a portfolio:

- Each hedge fund portfolio is already diversified, because it contains several securities including long and short positions. A portfolio of hedge funds is therefore a portfolio of diversified portfolios. There might be some diversification benefits, but they are rapidly captured.
- Each hedge fund manager charges fees on its portfolio. So, a portfolio made of a winning fund and a losing fund will end up paying performance fees to one of the managers, although the overall performance may be nil. This effect increases as the number of hedge funds increases – it is more likely to have poor performers.
- Monitoring hedge funds and doing a serious due diligence is a costly and time-consuming process. The more funds you have, the more costs you bear, or the lighter your selection criteria and controls.

Figure 26.1 illustrates the evolution of the volatility of a hedge fund portfolio when the number of hedge funds increases. The hedge funds are randomly selected from the Altvest database to span the universe of strategies, and are equally weighted in the portfolio – see Lhabitant and Learned (2004). The process is then repeated 5000 times for each portfolio size in order to have representative statistics. Clearly, diversification reduces volatility, but 10 to 15 hedge funds capture most of the diversification benefits. Looking at other risk statistics such as the worst monthly return provides similar results – see Figure 26.2. In reality, of course, it is likely that investors will do better than a random fund selection and and equal weighting, so that they will capture the diversification benefits with fewer hedge funds.

A side effect of overdiversification which is often ignored is its correlation with the S&P 500. Although individual hedge funds are not highly correlated with the S&P 500, a portfolio of hedge funds will tend to be more correlated than its components and this correlation increases with the number of components – see Figure 26.3. The reason is simply that diversification eliminates the specific risks of each manager, but retains the market risk, i.e. the portion that is

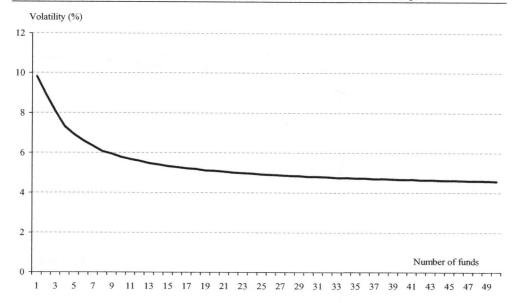

Figure 26.1   Impact of diversification on the volatility of a fund of funds portfolio

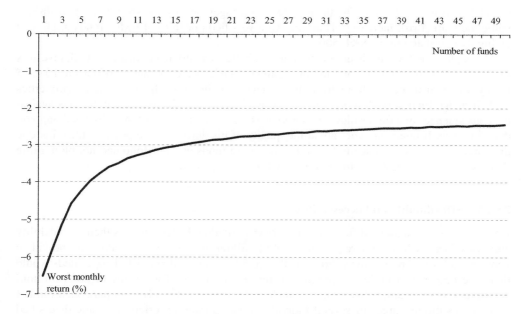

Figure 26.2   Impact of diversification on the worst monthly return of a fund of funds portfolio

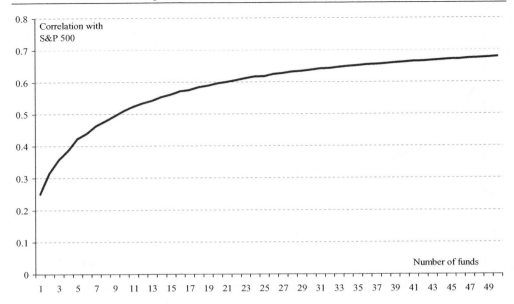

Figure 26.3   Impact of diversification on the correlation with the S&P 500 of a fund of funds portfolio

correlated with the S&P 500. As the number of managers grows, the specific portion shrinks while the market risk increases. Thus, an overdiversified portfolio of hedge funds might end up highly correlated to the S&P 500.

Although some level of diversification proves better than no diversification at all, investors should therefore be cautious and limit the number of hedge funds in their portfolios to 10 to 15 if they want to truly benefit from diversification while maintaining the decorrelation properties of their hedge fund portfolios. Of course, some often say that diversification protects against the consequences of a fund's blowup. Our view is that this is the task of the initial and ongoing due diligence. If one is not sure about the quality of his due diligence process, then that due diligence process is the place to focus. Having more funds in a portfolio and not monitoring them is actually the best way to ensure some blowup exposure.

26.2.2   Affordability and accessibility

Another major advantage of funds of funds over individual hedge funds is their affordability and ease of access. Minimum requirements of $1 million and above are the rule at the individual hedge fund level. An investor willing to allocate 5% of his total assets to hedge funds would therefore need a $15 million commitment, that is, a total portfolio value of $300 million! Anything less will subject his capital to inadequate diversification. By comparison, a fund of funds pools the resources of several individuals and commonly offers the same diversified portfolio with a minimum investment of around $20 000 or less. This makes hedge fund diversification affordable even for the smallest investors.

Furthermore, several European funds of funds are listed on an exchange (e.g. Dublin, Frakfurt, London or Zurich) and are member of a clearing system (e.g. Euroclear, Cedel). This facilitates investment and settlement procedures, because it is usually easier to invest in a listed share using familiar trading and settlement mechanisms than it is to purchase a basket of unregulated offshore funds domiciled in the Cayman Islands and Bermuda.

26.2.3   Professional management and built-in asset allocation

Through funds of funds, investors should be able to leverage the knowledge of professional managers, who have an extensive background in the investment or banking industry and/or experience in evaluating the very complex strategies employed by the funds that they select. In some occasions, they may be well connected to people who leave banks and brokerage houses to set up their own hedge funds. This gives them a competitive advantage to access a selection of tomorrow's hedge fund managers, sometimes even before the news becomes public.

These managers can also add value by optimizing the mix of hedge funds in the fund's portfolio to target specific goals. The two extreme choices are (i) to maximize the portfolio's expected return and (ii) to minimize some risk indicator, such as the portfolio volatility or value at risk, but there is also a whole range of intermediate targets. Value added can come from fund picking (selecting the best hedge funds), fund timing (identifying market cycles and investing in and out of hedge funds accordingly[1]), or simply strategic allocation (finding the best mix of funds to achieve a prespecified goal).

26.2.4   Access to closed funds

Several of the top-tier hedge funds are closed to small investors, but also to new money from any source. Their managers often have a capacity constraint and do not want to harm their existing investors by sharing some of their large but limited profits with newcomers. What funds of funds attempt to bring to the table is their ability to tap long-standing relationships with these prominent fund managers in order to provide access to their hedge funds, even though these are closed to new investments. If this were true, it would constitute a strong value proposition.

Unfortunately, reality is often somehow disappointing. It is true that hedge funds do not treat their clients equally: some funds are effectively closed to any new investors ("hard close"), while others may officially be closed but unofficially accept long-term investors with high commitments ("soft close"). However, there are so many funds of funds and the size of the requested commitment is so large that they cannot all have access to the "best of breed" hedge funds. How about successful fund picking? A manager of a fund of funds who claims to have some picking ability should *already* be invested in these highly desired closed funds. The reason is that he should have identified their talented managers when they needed money, not when they started closing their funds. Therefore, a fund of funds containing closed funds will be able to put a performance case deserving of scrutiny. In such a situation, any new investor in the fund of funds will indeed gain access to the desired single-manager hedge funds. But this will be at the expense of existing investors, who will see their initial allocation in these funds progressively diluted and replaced by cash.[2]

Moreover, open access at the fund of fund level is a good way to participate to closed funds, but it will also harm new investors once they are in. Of course, the process is reversed when investors redeem their fund of funds shares, but the number of redemptions will usually be small compared to the number of subscriptions, particularly if the performance is good. This

---

[1] This assumes, however, that the fund of funds manager is able to forecast (i) the next phase of the cycle and (ii) which funds will benefit during each phase.

[2] New shareholders solely bring cash but immediately gain access and enjoy the benefits of the so desired closed funds shares.

explains why several quality funds of funds have started closing their doors – they do not want to dilute their investors.

26.2.5 Better internal and external transparency

The hedge fund industry is known to be inefficient and opaque, at least in terms of information flow. This is the "black-box" syndrome. Retail investors often have no access or at best delayed access to information about individual hedge funds positions and strategies. In reality, information is available, but it is costly. Only long-term commitments and large investments will open the doors of hedge funds portfolios. As mentioned by Ineichen (2001): "We are all in a dark room; however, the one who has been in the room for some time has an advantage over someone who just entered." Fund of funds managers should therefore have an advantage over individual investors. In some cases, the size of their assets allows them to gain some additional transparency through confidentiality agreements with fund managers. This is precisely what institutional investors like in funds of funds: the ability to offload much of their fiduciary responsibilities to fund of funds managers.

In addition, fund of funds managers are often more transparent with respect to their portfolios than individual funds with respect to their positions. In particular, funds that are listed on an exchange must comply with some minimum regulatory requirements on reporting and documentation. Some even post on their web site a monthly listing of their underlying funds, as well as manager comments on their strategy and risk profile. This is often reassuring for the retail or less sophisticated investors.

26.3 THE DARK SIDE OF FUNDS OF FUNDS

26.3.1 Yet another layer of fees!

The major drawback of funds of funds structures is the cost of their services, which are not cheap. Indeed, funds of funds can charge several types of fees. The most visible ones are management fees, which are usually set at 1% of the total assets under management, and performance fees, which usually amount to 10% of the performance of the fund of funds. A few funds of funds also have a hurdle rate of some sort in place, varying from 0% (no loss) to the S&P 500 returns.

In addition to this, funds of funds also benefit from less rarely announced streams of income. These include retrocessions, which are fee-sharing agreements whereby a portion of the fees charged by the underlying hedge fund is returned to the fund of funds or its manager, and kickbacks, which are fees paid by a clearing broker to the fund of funds for forcing the underlying fund to use its clearing services. Some funds of funds also receive a trailing fee, which is a percentage of the assets that remain invested in a hedge fund after the lock-in period.

A few funds of funds credit these fees back to their clients, but most do not even mention them. Even if they do, the double fee structure remains and may significantly affect performance, at least from the investor's point of view. Consider, for example, a fund of funds charging 1% as a management fee plus 10% of any upside. This goes on top of the fees of the underlying fund managers, typically 2% of assets plus 20% of the upside. In total, this represents a potential of 3% p.a., plus 30% of the performance. If the underlying funds yield on average and before fees 20% p.a., the investor is left with a mere 11% annual return.

Even more dreadful: suppose the fund of funds simply diversifies by equally allocating assets between two managers. One makes 50% and the other loses 50%. Do you break even?

Not really. Before incentive fees (and not counting the management fees), you are breaking even. After incentive fees, you lose 10%. Thus, if the fund of funds manager has no skills, this is a terrible game for the investor.

Given the impact of this second level of charges, potential investors should naturally wonder whether the fund of funds concept really does provide added value, or whether it's just another device cleverly designed to extract fees from their credulity. Naturally, managers of funds of funds argue that the extra layer of skills justifies an extra layer of fees. They insist that they do provide a valuable service by monitoring the performance of hundreds or even thousands of funds in order to assemble the optimal selection of managers. Opponents, on the other hand, consider funds of funds as parasites, at best on the greatness of others and at worse on the artlessness of investors. They judiciously observe that several of these funds of funds profess a sophisticated quantitative process to identify and select managers, while they simply choose the top-performing managers from newspaper rankings.

Finally, another threat on the fees side is the increasing competition from hedge fund consultants. Overall, funds of funds are typically more expensive than appointing several managers directly through the traditional consulting model. For investors that do not face the minimum investment requirements, hiring consultants might be the least costly solution.

26.3.2 Extra liquidity

Liquidity is often a double-edged sword in the kingdom of hedge funds. By liquidity, we mean the conditions that must be fulfilled for an investor to be allowed to enter in the fund and/or redeem his shares. In theory, funds of funds should not offer greater liquidity than their components. In practice, they do. In particular, the redemption policies of funds of funds tend to be much more flexible than those of the underlying funds. About 80% of the funds of funds accept contributions and redemptions on a monthly or quarterly basis. At first glance, this may appear to be a positive feature. Unfortunately, it also has important repercussions on asset allocation, and therefore, on performance.

Fund of funds managers must ensure that their portfolios will not experience difficulties if investors start redeeming their assets. With that respect, their task is similar to asset liability management in a bank, where customers are allowed to come to the cashier and redeem their assets. However, it is unlikely that all customers would wish to redeem their shares at the same time.[3] By playing with expected redemptions and probabilities, most fund of funds managers are able to balance the liquidity desired by investors against the lengthy lock-up periods and infrequent redemption dates requested by individual fund managers.

However, to be able to cope with potential redemptions, fund of funds managers have four possibilities:

- They can rely on the cash from new contributions to pay for redemptions. This is quite hazardous: it may work well for a time, but in periods of poor performance, the fund will have to face important redemptions and will be short of new contributions. The only advantage is that new investors face lock-up periods, so that liquidity may not be a problem in the short run.
- They can hold a liquidity buffer. However: (i) the return on this buffer is usually extremely low compared to the expected return on the underlying hedge funds; and (ii) investors may not be willing to pay two layers of fees to end up not being fully invested.

---

[3] Except if there is a lack of liquidity and a flight to safe assets, as was the case in the summer of 1998, for example.

- They can invest in hedge funds with easier redemption policies. However, these funds are essentially directional players and their performance is more volatile. In addition, they are often correlated with each other because they are active on the same markets. Consequently, the fund of funds will not have access to star managers, who tend to focus on very profitable inefficiencies in smaller, less liquid and less efficient markets, but frequently impose long lock-up periods.
- They can get their shares traded on a regulated secondary marketplace – see Box 16.1.

Clearly, a balance has to be found. Liquidity is a desirable feature, but it comes at a cost.

Box 26.1 Regulated secondary marketplaces increase liquidity

The increased interest in hedge funds raised awareness that (i) most of the best performing non-US domiciled funds are closed or have restricted subscription and redemption clauses, and (ii) little independently verified valuation and risk information are available on hedge funds and their portfolios. Consequently, low liquidity can rapidly become a problem for sellers as well as access for buyers. A solution may go through the development of internet-based regulated secondary marketplaces dedicated to hedge funds. These offer several advantages: for example, increasing liquidity for investors, avoiding liquidations of assets to face redemptions for fund managers, and providing information on hedge funds exposures and risks.

Several of these marketplaces have been created very recently. For instance:

- HedgeTrust Exchange is an Electronic Communications Network (ECN) launched in February 2000. It offers accredited investors secure online trading facilities for existing non-US domiciled hedge funds that are closed or have restrictive subscription or redemption periods. It has a strategic partnership with the Bermuda Stock Exchange and offers integrated online access to the fund database TASS.
- Hedgebay.com is the latest in the list. Modelled after E-bay.com, the online auction site, it allows registered users to bid on and offer shares in well-known hedge funds. The clearing takes place through the Bermuda Stock Exchange or directly between buyers and sellers.

Some of them have already failed:

- PlusFunds.com was a New York based web platform founded by J.P. Morgan Chase, Credit Suisse First Boston, and Merrill Lynch. It published independently verified net asset values of 18 hedge fund shares on a real-time basis, as well as risk assessment reports containing value at risk, historical stress tests and risk concentration analysis on a daily basis. It also had a strategic partnership with the Bermuda Stock Exchange and managed a secondary market in their shares. It initially aimed at becoming a strong secondary trading market, but decided to migrate to become a managed account platform.

So far, the hedge fund industry reaction to these new trading platforms has been mixed. Some hedge fund managers perceive them as liquidity providers and like them, but others want to know who their investors are and will systematically redeem shares that are exchanged on such an exchange without their prior approval.

26.3.3   Lack of control, overdiversification and duplication

Another drawback of funds of funds from the investor's perspective is the lack of control. The investor does not have as much control over a fund of funds as he does over a portfolio of individual funds. For example, an investor who does not approve the presence of a certain type of strategy in a fund of funds is powerless to change that allocation, short of bailing out of the fund altogether. Moreover, fund of funds managers themselves have little control over what the underlying managers are doing. As an illustration, in a recent Capital Market Risk Advisors survey, several funds of funds disclaimed knowledge of what their underlying funds were doing regarding pricing issues and net asset values calculations. There are also anecdotal reports on managers allocating money in other "hot" funds without performing any serious due diligence, under threat of imminent fund closure.

Other typical problems include:

- The cancellation of trades. Fund A might sell short a share while fund B might buy it long. If both hedge funds are part of the same fund of funds portfolio, the two transactions will simply cancel each other in terms of risk exposure, but will generate ample commissions for brokers, as well as performance fees for one of the two funds.
- The duplication of positions within underlying hedge funds. This is particularly true when bubbles and hot sectors drive most of the allocation. In 1999, for example, most of the long/short equity funds were heavily invested in technology or internet-related stocks. They all collapsed when the bubble burst. So did the funds of funds that relied on them to diversify.
- The duplication of positions within funds of funds. Assuming that their popularity continues, the increasing number of funds of funds will eventually lead to a duplication of each other's holdings as a result of the sheer lack of available managers. Note that the same remark applies to risk management. Since individual hedge funds should primarily be concerned about risk control, the gathering of several hedge funds in a basket may only duplicate and not necessarily enhance the risk-control effort.

This strengthens our previous argument: beyond a certain number of managers, adding new ones is unlikely to result in major improvement on risk or on return. Although there is no consensus on the exact threshold value, common sense argues that portfolios of 10 to 20 hedge funds should be largely sufficient.

26.4   SELECTING A FUND OF FUNDS

It used to be hard to select stocks. It was harder to select traditional managers. As we have just seen, it is even harder to select hedge fund managers. How about selecting a fund of funds?

The major difficulty comes from the low barriers of entry to the fund of funds business. In this surreal world of investment advice anyone can claim to be an expert and get paid for it. Since the key talent is actually in the underlying hedge funds, funds of funds have proliferated, particularly in Europe, where almost every bank, insurance company and asset management firm has launched its own. Thanks to the marketing power of their founding group, these funds of funds have no problem attracting money, essentially from unsophisticated retail investors. However, the quality of some funds of funds' management teams approaches borderline incompetence.

Recognizing that talent still takes talent in its own right and being a good fund of funds manager requires several skills that are far beyond the simple analysis of past hedge fund performance. Among other things, we should mention an understanding of the hedge fund business, an experience of several market cycles, good connections in the industry and strong negotiation skills. In addition, a good fund of funds manager should be willing to identify hedge funds that develop mismatches between claimed strategy and effective actions, and replace them with new more promising funds. Even if the hedge fund that has to leave the portfolio is an in-house fund or pays a higher amount of retrocession . . .

Consequently, an investor selecting a fund of funds should, in a sense, act as if he was selecting an individual hedge fund. Initially, it is essential to (i) assess the manager's talent, search and identification capabilities, (ii) validate his due diligence process, (iii) understand his business model, including his asset allocation policy and investment goals and (iii) verify the quality and consistency of his track record, if any. Later on, it is necessary to ensure a rigorous ongoing monitoring of both the underlying managers and the fund of funds portfolio as a whole. Once again, there are numerous consultants that provide advice, but their independence and competence should be carefully verified. Some of them tend to favour managers who would rebate to the fund of funds part of their underlying manager's fee, others solely look at track record and past performance, and a minority of them . . . even manage funds of funds.

26.5 FUND ALLOCATION: A LOOK INSIDE THE "BLACK BOX"

The composition of a fund of funds portfolio is the result of two separate actions: the selection of a series of hedge funds as potential candidates for investment, and the effective allocation of assets among these funds. We regard the selection activity as a particular case of the approach that we presented in Chapter 24.[4] We will therefore not elaborate on the topic, but rather focus on the second aspect.

A fund of funds' allocation process is usually as opaque as the investment process of its underlying hedge funds. Most of the time, the manager only discloses marketing verbiage, e.g "experience", "proprietary database", "contacts", "privileged access" or "track record". In reality, what do things look like inside the black box? It all depends. Once again, qualitative approaches contrast with quantitative ones.

26.5.1 Qualitative approaches

Qualitative approaches usually rely on a balance between naive diversification and intuition to allocate assets. Managers relying on naive diversification simply invest in a number of different hedge funds and hope that the overall portfolio risk will be lowered. The most extreme version of this approach consists in allocating an equal amount of money to every manager in the portfolio and periodically rebalancing the latter to ensure that it remains well diversified. This is known as the $1/N$ rule, where N is the number of managers, and $1/N$ is the weight assigned to each of them. This rule has a long history in asset allocation: it had been recommended in the Talmud in the 4th century, when the Rabbi Isaac bar Aha used to say[5]: "A man should always place his money, a third into land, a third into merchandise, and keep a third at hand." Later on, even Harry Markowitz, the founder of modern portfolio theory and portfolio optimization, is reported to have used the rule for himself; see Zweig (1998).

---

[4] The only difference with respect to an individual investor is that a fund of funds manager usually has a clearer idea about the desired characteristics and properties of the hedge fund(s) he is seeking.

[5] See Talmud Bavli, Baba Metzia 42a.

The $1/N$ heuristics is not very sophisticated, but is it necessarily bad? The answer varies. When systematically applied, the $1/N$ rule conveys some risks. For instance, if one investment style predominates in the group of candidates resulting from the selection process, that style will also predominate in the fund of funds portfolio if the $1/N$ rule is applied. In addition, effective risk is not necessarily linearly related to asset allocation. For example, a 30% allocation to a truly market neutral fund may represent as much risk contribution as a 5% allocation to an emerging market hedge fund. It is therefore judicious to place ceilings on the amount of risk involved in each hedge fund allocation rather than on the weight itself.

Nevertheless, as we will see later, in practice the $1/N$ rule often gives good results, sometimes even better than several more sophisticated asset allocation models. But no fund of funds manager will ever admit to relying on it. There are two reasons for this. First, it is virtually impossible to charge a management fee for such a naive asset allocation service. Second, most managers are still persuaded – and so are their clients – that they can add value by relying on their "experience" and "feeling of the markets". They therefore tend to adjust the weights of their portfolio according to their own forecasts of future market and economic conditions. This approach does not aim at maintaining a constant allocation profile but rather at undertaking opportune short-term tilts in the hedge fund mix of a portfolio in response to the changing patterns of returns available in the capital markets. Typically, exposure periodically shifts away from hedge funds showing exceptional near-term vulnerability towards those showing the likelihood of an exceptional return.

26.5.2   Quantitative approaches

Quantitative approaches are just the opposite of qualitative ones. Rather than acting on subjective perceptions and intuition, they rely exclusively on predefined mathematical models. Their goal is usually quite ambitious: to find the best proportions to be invested among the set of hedge funds considered. Most quantitative managers take a two-stage approach when allocating money among hedge funds. First, expected returns and risk parameters for each hedge fund in question – often from some other sort of factor model[6] – and input into an optimizer. The money is allocated among them based on the optimizer's recommended allocation. We have already discussed the dangers of relying uniquely on such approaches, and will not repeat them here.

26.6   THE FUTURE OF FUNDS OF FUNDS

Funds of funds tie together many of the positive elements of building a hedge fund portfolio, while removing a number of the negatives. They offer an interesting investment vehicle for institutional and private investors who seek to access hedge funds without having to search for investment opportunities themselves. Fund of funds managers can help to add value as experienced pathfinders on this daunting unmapped terrain. In a sense, they are the panaceas for discerning investors.

However, there are valid fears that the proliferation of funds of funds may increase quantity at the expense of quality. In particular, due to capacity constraints, funds of funds should

---

[6] Simply stated, factor models assume that the return on any individual hedge fund can be expressed as a function of one or more factors, plus an error term that is independent of the factors and of the errors on all other investments. Rather than focusing on funds, analysts can therefore focus on factors' returns, risks and correlations.

soon – if they not already done so! – face a greater challenge in finding consistent performers among hedge funds. This could result in two possible consequences.

First, systemic risks that have the potential to hurt the entire industry are building up. The reason is that a definite talent shortage has developed among funds of funds. Consequently, a large number of less able and neophyte managers are entering the funds of funds business. This results in a lack of proper due diligence, poorly constructed portfolios, overconcentration in a few well-known hedge funds, and insufficient information disclosed to clients.

Second, there is likely to be a wave of consolidation in the fund of funds industry, with a few winners managing much larger amounts and closing their funds to new subscribers. These megafunds of funds would then find themselves in the position of gatekeepers to one of the world's fastest-growing and most dynamic marketplaces.

27

Structured Products on Hedge Funds

Investing is hard. Staying invested is even harder.

Many investors are attracted to hedge funds by the promise of diversification benefits and superior performance, but they feel nervous and uncomfortable once they actually have to commit capital. Several reasons justify this feeling. First, hedge funds are still perceived as being extremely risky and carrying a significant potential downside, particularly after the torrent of negative publicity that accompanied the debacle of Long Term Capital Management. Second, regulated entities such as pension funds and other institutional investors are often restricted by their supervisors from investing in loosely regulated and/or unlisted vehicles such as hedge funds without some kind of financial guarantee. Third, many individuals are still discouraged by the relatively high minimum amounts required to invest in hedge funds, or have tax, regulatory, accounting, foreign exposure or other concerns.

To bridge the gap between supply and demand, a growing number of financial intermediaries have solved the above-mentioned problems by proposing structured products tied to the performance of funds of funds (hencefourth: funds of funds) or hedge fund indices. These structured products now come in a variety of guises and engender much debate. Simply stated, they are packages that are structured with a preset formula for calculating returns and a preset formula for calculating risk relative to their underlying assets. These parameters are normally set at the beginning of the investment term and cannot be changed – if they do change, it is in a predictable way.

In this chapter, we review some of these structured products and discuss their pros and cons. We illustrate our analysis with several examples but would stress once again that these are chosen for illustrative purposes only and do not constitute a positive or negative investment recommendation.

27.1 TOTAL RETURN SWAPS LINKED TO HEDGE FUNDS

Total return swap (TRS) is the generic name used for any non-traditional swap where one party agrees to pay the other the "total return" of a defined underlying asset, usually in return for receiving a stream of LIBOR-based cash flows (Figure 27.1). Although TRSs are most commonly used with traditional market indices or defined portfolios of loans and mortgages, they also serve to gain exposure to the performance of a fund of funds or an individual hedge fund without having to actually purchase its shares.

Say, for example, that an investor wants to invest $100 million in XYZ fund of funds. Rather than investing directly in the shares of the XYZ Fund, the investor can enter into a $100 million total return swap with a dealer. The $100 million investment will be indexed to changes in the net asset value (NAV) of the XYZ Fund. Increases in the fund's NAV over a quarterly period will be paid by the dealer to the investor, while decreases in the fund's NAV will be paid by the investor to the dealer. Typically, the dealer will subscribe for $100 million interests in the underlying fund to hedge his exposure under the total return swap.

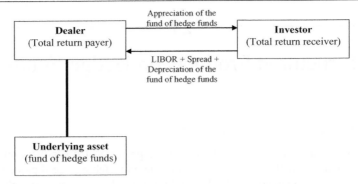

Figure 27.1   The typical flows in a total return swap on a fund of hedge funds

Such a TRS transaction offers several advantages over a direct investment:

- As mentioned above, it allows an investor to gain economic exposure to a hedge fund performance without having to purchase shares in the fund. In addition, a swap is an off-balance sheet instrument, while hedge fund shares would be on the balance sheet. These issues might be crucial for some investors that are not allowed to invest directly in hedge funds.
- The investor does not have to provide the initial cash needed to fund the hedge fund investment. In a sense, this amount is provided by the dealer, at a cost that equals LIBOR plus the spread (typically 20 to 50 basis points). Depending on the credit profile of the investor, intra-quarter exposure may be collateralized on a monthly basis, usually through posting cash or Treasuries, but this only represents a fraction of the purchase price of the hedge fund shares. As a consequence, leverage can easily be built in to any desirable level. In the above example, if the investor only has $50 million of equity capital but takes on a $100 million TRS, he is essentially using a leverage of two times.

Note that most dealers will reserve the right to terminate the TRS upon the occurrence of certain significant events, such as an amendment to the redemption procedures or investment strategies of the underlying fund, breaches of some of its financial or leverage ratios, or inability to receive periodic NAV statements.

Total return swaps are relatively easy to understand, but their creation requires a lot of legal documentation. Most TRSs are documented under standard International Swaps and Derivatives Association (ISDA) derivative documentation, but the actual swap confirmation is not standard and will vary from one dealer to another. The Credit Support Annex to the ISDA, which identifies the exact collateral and credit terms between the two parties, is also not standard and needs to be negotiated. In practice, therefore, TRSs must be of a minimum size to become economically viable, which restricts their use to large and sophisticated institutional and private investors.

27.2   CALL OPTIONS ON HEDGE FUNDS

Investors who do not have the financial resources to enter into a dedicated total return swap might decide to take the option path, i.e. purchase a long-term call option on interests in a fund of funds.

In its most basic form, the investor purchases from a dealer a cash-settled European call option on a fund of funds. This option is usually issued at the money and has a maturity of five to seven years. Long-term options are preferred because they allow investors to defer taxes on any unrealized gains in the underlying fund until the option is exercised. At the option expiration, if the fund's NAV is less than the strike price, then the option simply expires worthless, and the investor forfeits the premium he has paid. If the fund's NAV is higher than the strike price, the investor pockets the difference.

Several variants of this basic call option have been invented. For instance, the option can use an accreting exercise price. That is, the premium initially paid is equal to the exercise price and is usually financed in part by the dealer, thereby providing the investor with leveraged fund exposure. During the term of the trade, the exercise price increases (or "accretes") at LIBOR plus a spread. If the value of the fund investment relative to the accreting exercise price falls below negotiated thresholds, the dealer may terminate all or a portion of the call option, unless the investor decides to increase the exercise price by delivering additional margin. Upon settlement, the dealer liquidates his investment in the fund and pays to the investor the proceeds in excess of the amount financed by the investor.

27.3   BASIC NOTES AND CERTIFICATES

Indexed notes (also called "certificates") are the simplest form of structured product, particularly among retail investors. From a functional point of view, they are nothing more than a feeder into a fund of funds. Their issuer buys a hedge fund portfolio and issues some notes at par. These notes are backed by the hedge fund portfolio, and their final repayment is linked to the performance achieved by the hedge fund. Generally, there is no capital protection; if the hedge fund portfolio declines in value, the repayment of the note will be lowered accordingly and could even reach zero in the worst case.

Of course, one may wonder why an investor should pay for that extra structure – see Figure 27.2. The answer is essentially regulatory: some investors are barred from investing directly in hedge funds, or they are heavily taxed if they do so. Technically, the note repackages the hedge fund performance into a fixed income instrument that can easily be listed. This usually

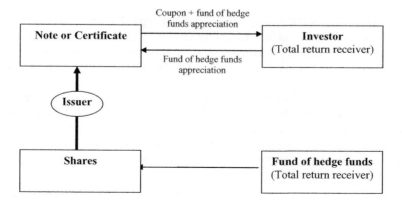

Figure 27.2   The typical flows in structuring a note on a basket of hedge funds

allows the regulation to be bypassed and avoids the burden of specific taxation while keeping the economic benefits of the hedge fund allocation.[1]

Of course, these basic notes can easily be structured to cater for the requirements of specific investors. For instance, they can pay a regular coupon – which makes them look even more like a fixed income instrument – or use some leverage to magnify the participation in the fund of funds performance. However, one of the most common requests from investors considering hedge funds for the first time is some sort of protection against the risk of loss of their principal. This has resulted in the creation of a large number of capital protected notes.

27.4   CAPITAL PROTECTED NOTES

Capital protected notes usually take the form of medium-term notes with a final repayment somehow linked to the performance of a fund of funds. They have five key elements, which can vary widely:

- The *term of the investment*. Most notes have a term in the three- to five-year range, but several longer term notes have also been issued.
- The level of *capital protection*. Notes with 100% capital protection are common, but some of them could offer a lower level of guarantee, depending upon the risk profile of targeted investors. The capital protection is applied irrespective of the performance of the underlying fund of funds.
- An *upside participation*, which is usually expressed as a percentage of the underlying hedge fund's positive performance.
- A *guaranteed minimum yield*, which may be capitalized into the investment and form part of the total terminal value paid out at maturity, or distributed at intervals during the investment term as coupon payments. This feature may be required, for instance, by investors who cannot invest in zero coupons.
- The *tax treatment* of the investment. Depending upon the jurisdiction, the returns can be taxed either as income or as capital gain.

In its plain-vanilla form, a typical capital guaranteed note has a redemption price calculated with a formula of the following form:

$$100\% + (\text{Participation rate} \times \text{Underlying fund's performance})$$

The participation rate is also called "gearing". Its level depends on the maturity of the note, the overall level of interest rates and the characteristics of the underlying hedge fund. The principal protection is usually bought at the expense of some of the fund of funds' profit potential. This explains why the participation rate is often not equal to 100%, or the maximum gain may be capped.

Capital guaranteed notes linked to a fund of funds offer several advantages. First, they allow risk-averse investors to learn the basics about hedge funds without exposing themselves to the downside risk. Second, they overcome the regulatory hurdles, because the capital guarantee meets the regulators' concerns for investor protection. Third, in most countries, the notes may be treated as an interest-rate security for tax, accounting and administration purposes. In

---

[1] Note that some countries disallow notes on hedge funds, but authorize notes and certificates on hedge fund indices. In this case, the note issuer first creates an index of hedge funds (which corresponds to the desired allocation), and then creates a vehicle to track the "index".

particular, this allows institutional investors to invest in hedge funds when they may otherwise be restricted, and offshore hedge funds to be indirectly distributed in several markets without needing to be registered with local authorities. However, these notes come at a cost, which is the remuneration taken by the financial intermediary offering them. In addition, investors need to understand that if they need to access the capital during the term of the note, they may not get back the full amount originally invested – the capital guarantee only applies at maturity.

27.4.1 The financial engineering process of capital protected notes

An interesting question for most investors is the functioning of the financial engineering process behind these capital protected products. In particular, many investors do not understand how financial intermediaries such as banks or insurance companies dare to provide guarantees on such unpredictable products as hedge funds. Some even believe that these intermediaries are taking large risks to provide them with these guarantees, or that they consent to share the risk with their clients.

Reality is completely different. First, most structured products are issued on funds of funds or a basket of hedge funds rather than individual hedge funds – the additional diversification reduces further the potential risk. Second, when a bank issues a capital guaranteed product linked to the performance of a hedge fund, it is in fact *selling* a guarantee to the investor, who pays for it. In a sense, the bank is short a put option on a fund of funds. As for any other derivatives position, the bank would immediately hedge the associated risks by dynamic trading or transfer them to another market participant.[2] Indeed, the goal of the issuing bank is not to profit from the variations in the underlying hedge fund's net asset value, or to take a directional view of the hedge fund's NAV, but rather to gain a series of commissions and fees while taking a minimum amount of risk. These include: (i) the various fees and commissions charged to issue and sell the notes; (ii) the bid/ask spread on the secondary market, where the issuing bank often acts as a market maker; (iii) the management and performance fees on the underlying fund of funds, which is often directly or indirectly related to the issuing bank; and (iv) the annual portfolio management and custody fees for managing the assets of the final client.

In practice, without using explicit put options, there are two hedging methodologies employed to provide capital protection: static hedging and dynamic hedging. Static hedging is simpler and performs relatively well in high interest rate scenarios while dynamic hedging is more complex, but less restrictive, as we will see shortly.

27.4.2 The first generation: the naive approach

The creation of capital guaranteed notes linked to a fund of funds dates back to the 1980s. The first generation of these notes relied on a very simple mechanism. The initial capital of the note was allocated partly to a high-quality zero-coupon bond maturing at the same time as the note and partly to shares of the underlying fund of funds. At the maturity of the note, the zero-coupon allocation provided the principal protection, while the fund of funds investment ensured some extra performance (see Figure 27.3).

---

[2] This explains why it is common to see capital protected notes linked to a fund of funds issued by a bank in association with an insurance company. The latter may agree to bear such a risk in exchange for the payment of a premium – that is its business after all!

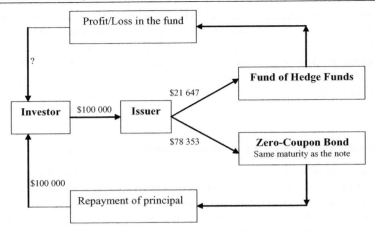

Figure 27.3   First generation of fund of hedge funds capital guaranteed notes

Consider, for example, the case of an investor purchasing $100 000 of a 5-year capital guaranteed note on a hedge fund. Let us assume that the 5-year interest rate is 5% per year, so that a 5-year zero-coupon with $1000 face value is worth approximately $783.53. The issuer of the note receives $100 000 from the investor and invests $78 353 in the zero coupon to provide the capital guarantee and the rest ($21 647) in the fund of funds.

Five years later, the zero-coupon bond matures and pays back $100 000. If, for instance, the fund of funds has delivered an average return of 10% p.a., the fund investment would be worth $34 863 and the total repayment to the investor would be $134 863 (i.e. a performance of 6.16% p.a.). If the fund of funds has lost 10% p.a. over the period, the fund investment would be worth only $12 783, and the total repayment to the investor would then be $112 783 (i.e. a performance of 2.44% p.a.).

Note that, given the initial level of interest rates and the expected fund of funds annual performance, we can easily calculate the terminal note value, and therefore obtain the note performance and/or the level of participation achieved by the investor – see Table 27.1 and Figure 27.4. Of course, the capital is always guaranteed, which means that the resulting note performance is always positive. However, one should remember that, over the long term, the "benchmark" should not be the initial capital, but rather the performance of a risk-free bond.

The main problem with this simple investment approach is that the fraction of the initial capital exposed to the fund of funds is relatively low, particularly in low interest rate environments. Consequently, the participation in the upside performance is rather limited. In our previous example, even when the underlying fund gained 10% p.a. over the period, the investor's total performance was only 6.16% p.a., that is, a mere 61.6% participation in the fund's upside progression. And this calculation was done in a perfect world, where the note issuer did not charge any fees.

Investors soon tumbled to the fact that these basic capital guaranteed products did not have any real added value and that they could, if necessary, be replicated directly without the costly help of investment banks. Creative issuers therefore started working on a means of increasing participation rates.

Table 27.1 Annual performance achieved by the investor in a first generation 5-year capital guaranteed note, assuming different interest rates and hedge fund performance scenarios

		Annual Hedge Fund Performance (p.a.)							
		−20%	−15%	−10%	−5%	0%	5%	10%	15%	20%
	1%	0.32%	0.43%	0.57%	0.74%	0.95%	1.21%	1.52%	1.88%	2.31%
	2%	0.61%	0.82%	1.09%	1.42%	1.82%	2.30%	2.87%	3.53%	4.30%
	3%	0.88%	1.19%	1.57%	2.04%	2.61%	3.28%	4.08%	5.00%	6.06%
Level of	4%	1.14%	1.53%	2.02%	2.62%	3.33%	4.18%	5.17%	6.31%	7.61%
Interest Rates	5%	1.38%	1.85%	2.44%	3.15%	4.00%	5.00%	6.16%	7.50%	9.00%
(p.a.)	6%	1.60%	2.15%	2.82%	3.64%	4.61%	5.75%	7.07%	8.57%	10.25%
	7%	1.81%	2.43%	3.18%	4.09%	5.18%	6.44%	7.90%	9.54%	11.38%
	8%	2.01%	2.69%	3.52%	4.52%	5.70%	7.08%	8.65%	10.43%	12.41%

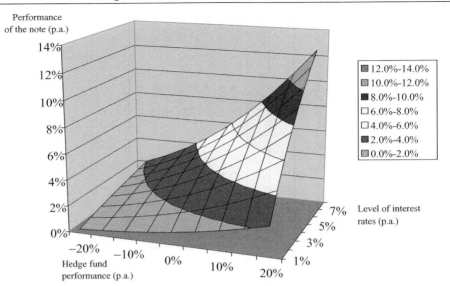

Figure 27.4   Annual performance achieved by the investor in a first generation 5-year capital guaranteed note, assuming different interest rates and hedge fund performance scenarios

27.5   THE SECOND GENERATION: THE OPTION-BASED APPROACH

The second generation of capital guaranteed notes linked to a fund of funds adopted a different approach, relying on option-based methodologies similar to those used in notes linked to equity indices or individual equities. They basically divided the initial capital between high-quality zero-coupon bonds and at-the-money call options on the underlying fund of funds.[3] Both instruments needed to mature at the same time as the note. The zero-coupon bonds provided the principal protection. The call options provided participation in the fund of funds' performance. The advantage of using options rather than direct investment in shares of the fund is their embedded leverage. Indeed, the option premium is small with respect to the underlying fund's investment, which means that one can obtain much better participation in the upside performance (see Figure 27.5).

As an illustration, consider again the example of our investor purchasing $100 000 of a 5-year capital guaranteed note on a fund of funds. Let us assume again that the 5-year interest rate is 5% per year, so that a 5-year zero coupon with $1000 face value is worth approximately $783.53. The issuer of the note receives $100 000 from the investor and invests $78 353 in the zero coupon to provide the capital guarantee and the rest ($21 647) in at-the-money 5-year call options on the fund of funds.

---

[3] An alternative to the "bond plus call" structure consists in investing directly in the fund of funds and protecting the investment by put options on the same fund. This gives exactly the same result in terms of participation rate because of the put-call parity. This relationship, which is well known to option traders, states that:

$$\text{Bond} + \text{Call} = \text{Underlying asset} + \text{Put}$$

where the call and the put options have the same maturity date, exercise price and underlying asset. It explains why the two strategies yield exactly the same results.

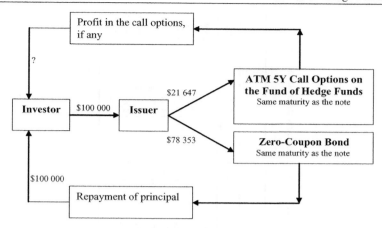

Figure 27.5   Second generation of fund of hedge funds capital guaranteed notes

For the sake of simplicity, let us use the Black and Scholes option pricing model to value the call options.[4] If the underlying fund of funds has a volatility of 5%, then a 5-year at-the-money call option costs approximately 22.16% of the net asset value. That is, to have the economic benefits of $100 000 invested in the hedge fund, the premium to be paid is $22 160. Since our issuer has $21 647 available, he can only purchase at-the-money call options on $97 672 worth of the fund of funds. His guaranteed upside participation rate will therefore be 97.672%.[5]

Now, let us look at what happens at maturity. 5 years later, the zero-coupon bond matures and pays back $100 000. This provides the capital guarantee. If, for instance, the fund of funds has gained 10% p.a. over the period, the call options would give a gain of $57 302. The total repayment to the investor in such a case would be $157 302 (i.e. a performance of 9.48% p.a.). If the fund of funds lost 10% p.a. over the period, the call options would expire unexercised and the total repayment to the investor would be $100 000 (i.e. no losses and no gains).

In order to compare the results of second generation capital guaranteed notes with those of the previous generation, we show in Table 27.2 the annual performance obtained on the note assuming different interest rates and hedge fund performance scenarios. By construction, second-generation notes only participate in the upside of the hedge fund, but offer no return if the hedge fund performance is negative. Consequently, second-generation notes surpass first-generation notes almost systematically as soon as the hedge fund performance is positive.

These second-generation structures offer the clear advantage of a constant and predetermined participation in the upside performance of the underlying fund of funds (see Figure 27.6). In addition, they can easily be customized to include a coupon, if required by some categories of investors or by their regulators. And investors who are willing to sacrifice some degree of principal protection can enjoy higher rates of participation, as lower protection levels mean more funds are available for the option portion of the investment (see Box 27.1). However,

---

[4] In practice, to value and/or hedge options on hedge funds, there are several more accurate option pricing models, whose mathematical complexity is far beyond the scope of this book. The interested reader can consult, for instance, Henderson (1999).

[5] Note that the participation rate can easily be calculated by dividing the relative amount left for the options ($21 647) by the option premium for a $100 000 investment ($22 160).

Table 27.2   Annual performance achieved by the investor in a second generation 5-year capital guaranteed note, assuming different interest rates and hedge fund performance scenarios, and a volatility of the underlying fund of hedge funds of 5% p.a.

		Annual Hedge Fund Performance (p.a.)								
		−20%	−15%	−10%	−5%	0%	5%	10%	15%	20%
	1%	0.00%	0.00%	0.00%	0.00%	0.00%	3.47%	7.12%	10.94%	14.88%
	2%	0.00%	0.00%	0.00%	0.00%	0.00%	4.49%	9.07%	13.70%	18.37%
Level of	3%	0.00%	0.00%	0.00%	0.00%	0.00%	4.80%	9.64%	14.50%	19.37%
Interest Rates	4%	0.00%	0.00%	0.00%	0.00%	0.00%	4.88%	9.79%	14.70%	19.63%
(p.a.)	5%	0.00%	0.00%	0.00%	0.00%	0.00%	4.89%	9.81%	14.73%	19.66%
	6%	0.00%	0.00%	0.00%	0.00%	0.00%	4.88%	9.79%	14.71%	19.64%
	7%	0.00%	0.00%	0.00%	0.00%	0.00%	4.87%	9.76%	14.67%	19.59%
	8%	0.00%	0.00%	0.00%	0.00%	0.00%	4.86%	9.74%	14.64%	19.55%

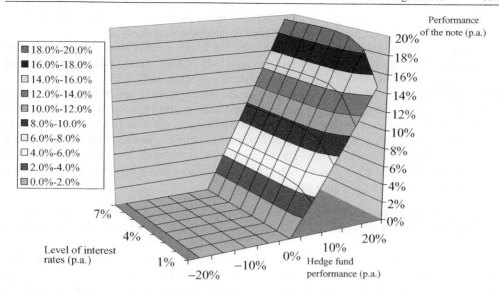

Figure 27.6 Annual performance achieved by the investor in a second generation 5-year capital guaranteed note, assuming different interest rates and hedge fund performance scenarios, and a volatility of the underlying fund of hedge funds of 5% p.a.

second-generation structures also suffer from several drawbacks:

- The note valuation is highly dependent on the future movement of interest rates. In particular, the zero-coupon component and its "deep discount" nature expose the strategy to interest rate volatility during the life of the investment. Of course, that risk is not an issue for investors who plan to hold the note – and therefore the underlying zero-coupon bond – until maturity, but it is for all other investors.

Box 27.1 An Asian tail to lower the option price

Capital guaranteed notes with an "Asian tail" are quite frequently encountered. The term refers to a pay-off at expiration that is based on the *average* of several successive net asset values (e.g. the average over the last 6 or 12 months) rather than on the net asset value at the time of expiration of the note. There is a twofold reason for using this Asian tail. First, using an average rather than a single value protects the investor against sudden downward movements in the underlying fund of funds' shares prior to maturity – but it also deprives him of any sudden appreciation. Second, the premiums of options on an average price are known to be less expensive than the premiums for a regular option on a single price at maturity. The reason is that the average smooths out the variations and reduces the volatility, which is a key determinant of the option premium. A lower option premium means that a larger number of options can be bought for the same price and therefore that the participation rate is higher – or that higher fees can be charged if the issuer pockets the difference.

- The participation level is highly dependent on the initial level of interest rates. Indeed, higher interest rates mean that less money is needed to purchase the zero coupon, or equivalently, that more capital is available for the options. But lower interest rates have the opposite effect and therefore reduce the participation level. This strong interest rate dependency was a serious concern in the low interest rate environment of the early 2000s.
- The participation level is highly dependent on the volatility of the underlying fund. A more volatile underlying fund of funds means that the call options are more expensive, i.e. that there will be a lower participation and therefore a lower performance. In addition, the pricing of the call options is generally based on an *expected* volatility level, which is often greater than the actual *historical* volatility for the underlying investment. Investment banks would argue that they need a margin of safety, but that translates into a higher cost for investors, as they "overpay" for their options.

An interesting problem with second-generation capital guaranteed notes is that of hedging. The note issuer, who has essentially sold a call option to the investor, needs to hedge his short position.

A first alternative is to pursue a dynamic trading strategy to delta hedge the option. This implies that the note issuer invests in and out of the underlying fund of funds as the value and therefore the delta of its call option changes. He must purchase shares of the fund of funds when its net asset value increases and sell shares of the fund of funds when its net asset value decreases. In theory, these adjustments should be made on a continuous time basis. In practice, the hedge is usually adjusted on a monthly basis – the note issuer normally has a special liquidity arrangement with the underlying fund of funds manager to trade in and out small quantities of his fund every month. However, even with specific liquidity conditions, there is still the risk of a sudden meltdown. If the market suddenly crashes, the readjustment at the end of the month will come too late.

A second possibility for the note issuer consists in delegating the hedging problem and purchasing the options on an over-the-counter market, essentially in the form of an insurance policy. Several reinsurance companies such as Swiss Re and Zurich Re have created dedicated subsidiaries that specialize in issuing these types of products. They pool the risk of the underlying alternative assets with the risks of their traditional insurance portfolios. In case of loss, they can draw on their premium income and accumulated reserves if necessary.

27.6   THE THIRD GENERATION: THE DYNAMIC TRADING APPROACH

The third generation of capital guaranteed products on hedge funds rely on dynamic trading principles. The basic mechanism is relatively simple. Initially, the proceeds of the note are invested in a portfolio composed of zero-coupon bonds and shares of the underlying fund of funds, as in first generation products. However, the difference is that the initial proportions may be much more aggressive, as we will see. Then, capital is shifted dynamically between the zero-coupon bonds and the underlying fund of funds according to prespecified asset allocation rules. The two most popular variants of these strategies are contingent immunization and constant proportion portfolio insurance.

Contingent immunization is similar to a stop loss rule (Figure 27.7). The note issuer starts with a full allocation to the hedge fund, and he constantly compares the value of his portfolio with the "floor", i.e. the amount of capital that would have to be invested in zero-coupon bonds

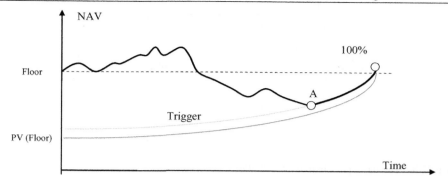

Figure 27.7   Contingent immunization with a stop loss rule. When the portfolio NAV reaches the trigger level (point A, slightly above the present value of the floor for safety reasons), the portfolio is entirely reallocated to zero-coupon bonds

to guarantee the capital at maturity. As long as the portfolio value is higher than the floor, then the entire capital remains invested in the hedge fund. But if the hedge fund does not perform well and the portfolio value drops close to the floor, the issuer withdraws entirely from the hedge fund to allocate all remaining capital to the zero-coupon bonds.

Contingent immunization strategies are remarkably simple to implement. They are also easy to adapt to investors' needs, such as using an initial leverage to ensure a higher participation in the upside, or paying a regular coupon. However, they suffer from two drawbacks.

- Once the capital is entirely invested in zero-coupon bonds, there is no possibility of switching back to the hedge fund portfolio. Participating in the recovery of the hedge fund, if it occurs, is therefore excluded. In such a case, investors must wait until the maturity of the structure to recover their initial capital.
- If there is a sharp drawdown in the fund's net asset value, the switch to zero-coupon bonds might occur too late, so that the capital will not be fully protected.

Constant proportion portfolio insurance (CPPI) is a more sophisticated dynamic asset allocation strategy that was first introduced by Black and Jones (1987) and later formalized by Black and Perold (1992). Although it was initially applied to equity markets, the technique recently reappeared in several hedge fund structured products. As opposed to passive buy-and-hold structures, the exposure to the underlying fund of funds is actively allocated with the CPPI technique, based on a very strict rule. If the value of the hedge fund shares rises, more capital is invested in the hedge fund. If the hedge fund performs poorly, more money is shifted into bonds. In a sense, CPPI is a form of feedback-driven investment strategy, where risky assets are sold in proportion to their price decline and bought in proportion to their price rise. The aim is to ensure that, at maturity, the product will be worth at least as much as the amount invested at inception.

Technically, a CPPI implementation (see Figure 27.8) just requires the definition of three parameters:

- The "floor", which is the amount of money that would have to be invested in zero-coupon bonds to guarantee the capital at maturity. Because of the time value of money, as maturity approaches the floor value should increase and converge towards the guaranteed amount.

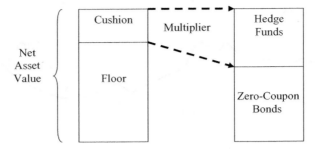

Figure 27.8   The basic principle of a CPPI allocation

- The "multiplier", which determines the aggressiveness of the strategy. A multiplier equal to 1 would be considered as non-aggressive, a multiplier higher than 1 may require the use of leverage.
- The rebalancing policy, e.g. at the end of every month or once the allocation is sufficiently different from what it should be.

The rules governing the allocation of a CPPI product can be summarized as follows. At each rebalancing date, one computes a quantity called the "cushion", which is defined as the difference between the value of the portfolio and the current value of the floor.

$$\text{Cushion} = \text{Portfolio value} - \text{Floor}$$

Then, an amount equal to the multiplier times the cushion is allocated to the fund of funds and the remainder of the portfolio is invested in zero-coupon bonds.

$$\text{Amount in hedge fund} = \text{Multiplier} \times \text{Cushion}$$

$$\text{Amount in zero coupon} = \text{Portfolio value} - \text{Amount in hedge fund}$$

This process is repeated at each rebalancing date. It provides a smooth deleveraging process to ensure that there is sufficient capital available to purchase the guarantee if need be, based on (i) the floor level, which rises with time because the zero-coupon bond increases in value until maturity, so it becomes more and more expensive to purchase the capital guarantee; and (ii) the evolution of the underlying fund of funds. If performance is poor, the cushion decreases and capital is progressively reallocated to the zero coupon. If performance is good and the strategy is run without any constraint, it might result in leverage, i.e. borrowing money to invest in the hedge fund. In practice, the level of leverage is often capped at 150 or 200%.

Let us now illustrate these rules with a practical example (Figure 27.9). Say a CPPI strategy is implemented on a $10 million portfolio with a multiplier of 3. The time horizon is one year and we want a 90% capital guarantee (floor of $9 million). Interest rates are at 5% p.a.

- At inception, the value of the floor is $8.57 million and that of the cushion $1.43 million. We therefore allocate $4.29 million (= 3 × $1.43) to the fund of funds and the rest ($5.71 million) to the zero-coupon bond.
- At the end of the first month, say the hedge fund has gained 2%, and the zero-coupon bond has gained 0.41% – to keep things simple, we assume constant interest rates in this example. The hedge fund allocation is now worth $4.37 million, and the bond allocation is worth $5.74 million. The total portfolio value is $10.11 million; the present value of the floor

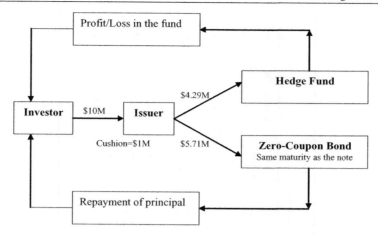

Figure 27.9   Third generation of hedge fund capital guaranteed notes: example of a CPPI strategy with a floor at $9 million and a multiplier equal to 3

is $8.61 million, so the new cushion is $1.50 million. We need to allocate $4.51 million (= 3 × $1.50) to the fund of funds and the rest ($5.60 million) to the zero-coupon bond. We therefore need to sell some bonds ($0.14 million) and invest the proceeds in the fund of funds.

- At the end of the second month, say the hedge fund has gained an additional 4.9%, and the zero-coupon bond has again gained 0.41%. The hedge fund allocation is now worth $4.73 million, and the bond allocation $5.62 million. The total portfolio value is $10.35 million; the present value of the floor is $8.64 million, so the new cushion is $1.71 million. We need to allocate $5.13 million (= 3 × $1.71) to the fund of funds and the rest ($5.22 million) to the zero-coupon bond. We therefore need to sell some bonds ($0.41 million) and invest the proceeds in the fund of funds.

This process is repeated mechanically every month until we reach the end of the year. If the fund of funds performs well, we will progressively allocate more and more money to it – see Table 27.3. However, if it performs badly, our mechanical rule will reduce its size in the portfolio and allocate more to the zero coupon to ensure that we stay above the floor at maturity – see Table 27.4.

The key advantage of CPPI products is that the cost of establishing the protection is not paid upfront, unlike the case of option-based strategies. Remember that the premium to pay for option-based capital protection is a direct function of the volatility of the underlying fund of funds. If the latter is high, the associated premium will also be high, which means that the upside participation will be limited. In such a case, CPPI may provide better participation rates. However, CPPI structures also have their drawbacks:

- There is a hidden cost, which comes from the fact that we always rebalance the portfolio *after* the fact. We reduce our exposure to the fund of funds *after* a decline of its NAV and we increase our exposure *after* a good performance. This hidden cost is only known retrospectively, but we know that it will be proportional to the volatility of the underlying fund of funds.

Table 27.3 Evolution of the CPPI portfolio in the case of good fund performance

Month	Fund NAV	Fund perf.	Bond price	Bond perf.	Before rebalancing		Portfolio value	PV(Floor)	Cushion	After rebalancing		Required change in the fund	Required change in bonds
					Amount in the fund	Amount in bonds				Amount in the fund	Amount in bonds		
0	100		95.24				10.00	8.57	1.43	4.29	5.71		
1	102	2.0%	95.63	0.41%	4.37	5.74	10.11	8.61	1.50	4.51	5.60	0.14	−0.14
2	107	4.9%	96.02	0.41%	4.73	5.62	10.35	8.64	1.71	5.13	5.22	0.41	−0.41
3	109	1.9%	96.41	0.41%	5.23	5.24	10.47	8.68	1.79	5.38	5.09	0.15	−0.15
4	110	0.9%	96.80	0.41%	5.43	5.11	10.54	8.71	1.83	5.48	5.06	0.05	−0.05
5	113	2.7%	97.19	0.41%	5.63	5.08	10.71	8.75	1.96	5.89	4.82	0.25	−0.25
6	115	1.8%	97.59	0.41%	5.99	4.84	10.83	8.78	2.05	6.15	4.68	0.16	−0.16
7	119	3.5%	97.99	0.41%	6.37	4.70	11.07	8.82	2.25	6.75	4.32	0.38	−0.38
8	121	1.7%	98.39	0.41%	6.86	4.34	11.20	8.85	2.34	7.03	4.17	0.17	−0.17
9	123	1.7%	98.79	0.41%	7.15	4.18	11.33	8.89	2.44	7.32	4.01	0.18	−0.18
10	124	0.8%	99.19	0.41%	7.38	4.03	11.41	8.93	2.48	7.44	3.97	0.06	−0.06
11	128	3.2%	99.59	0.41%	7.68	3.98	11.66	8.96	2.70	8.10	3.56	0.42	−0.42
12	130	1.6%	100.00	0.41%	8.23	3.58	11.80	9.00					

Table 27.4 Evolution of the CPPI portfolio in the case of poor fund performance

Month	Fund NAV	Fund perf.	Bond price	Bond perf.	Before rebalancing		Portfolio value	PV(Floor)	Cushion	After rebalancing		Required change in the fund	Required change in bonds
					Amount in the fund	Amount in bonds				Amount in the fund	Amount in bonds		
0	100		95.24				10.00	8.57	1.43	4.29	5.71		
1	98	−2.0%	95.63	0.41%	4.20	5.74	9.94	8.61	1.33	3.99	5.94	−0.21	0.21
2	95	−3.1%	96.02	0.41%	3.87	5.97	9.84	8.64	1.20	3.59	6.25	−0.28	0.28
3	92	−3.2%	96.41	0.41%	3.48	6.27	9.75	8.68	1.07	3.22	6.53	−0.26	0.26
4	90	−2.2%	96.80	0.41%	3.15	6.55	9.71	8.71	1.00	2.99	6.72	−0.17	0.17
5	89	−1.1%	97.19	0.41%	2.95	6.75	9.70	8.75	0.95	2.86	6.84	−0.09	0.09
6	90	1.1%	97.59	0.41%	2.90	6.87	9.76	8.78	0.98	2.94	6.82	0.04	−0.04
7	80	−11.1%	97.99	0.41%	2.61	6.85	9.46	8.82	0.64	1.93	7.53	−0.68	0.68
8	73	−8.8%	98.39	0.41%	1.76	7.56	9.33	8.85	0.47	1.41	7.91	−0.35	0.35
9	72	−1.4%	98.79	0.41%	1.39	7.95	9.34	8.89	0.45	1.34	8.00	−0.05	0.05
10	70	−2.8%	99.19	0.41%	1.30	8.03	9.33	8.93	0.41	1.22	8.11	−0.09	0.09
11	65	−7.1%	99.59	0.41%	1.13	8.15	9.28	8.96	0.32	0.95	8.33	−0.18	0.18
12	50	−23.1%	100.00	0.41%	0.73	8.37	9.09	9.00					

- CPPI structures are dependent on interest rates, although to a lesser extent than their option-based equivalent. Indeed, the floor level also varies with interest rates – higher rates mean a lower floor and a lower cushion, while lower rates raise the floor and reduce the cushion. Recently, the low interest rate environment was obviously a problem and forced issuers to lengthen the maturity of their CPPI-based notes in order to gain a few basis points of yield.
- CPPI structures suffer from a potential knock-out effect. If the value of the underlying investment falls below the cost of buying the guarantee (the floor), all the money is channelled towards the zero-coupon bond, leaving a participation of zero in the underlying investment. However, in a scenario where a steep decline in returns is followed by strong returns from the underlying fund of funds, the knocked-out investor completely misses out on all the gains. Since his cushion will always be small, he will not be able to participate again in the fund of funds until the term of the note. This is the price that has to be paid to benefit from the lock-in of gains in the opposite kind of scenario, i.e. initially bullish, but later turning bearish.
- A client investing in CPPI structures might lose money. The problem is particularly acute when the multiplier is high, the volatility of the underlying fund of funds is high or the shares cannot be sold in time to guarantee the minimum amount of cash.

27.7   THE FOURTH GENERATION: OPTIONS ON CPPI

The fourth generation of capital guaranteed notes uses an option on a CPPI structure, which can be seen as a mix between the second and third generation structures. Simply stated, these notes are structured as a zero-coupon bond investment, plus a call option on the performance of a feeder fund which implements the CPPI strategy.

In its common form, a typical capital guaranteed note based on an option on a CPPI will have a redemption price calculated by means of the following type of formula:

$$100\% + \text{Max} \, (0, \text{Performance of CPPI})$$

The key advantage is that it protects the capital of a CPPI investment in full, with non-zero minimum exposure to risky assets. In a structurally bullish market, this strategy will probably not generate more added value than a CPPI alone, with minimum exposure of 0%. However, it is highly likely that it will deliver a higher return in a volatile market.

27.8   THE FLIES IN THE OINTMENT

The concept of investing in hedge funds with a guaranteed return of principal after a certain number of years is quite appealing. However, we all know that there is no free lunch in finance, and before investing one should also consider some of the less publicized aspects of these products, which are:

- *Lack of liquidity*: Capital guaranteed notes linked to hedge funds are by definition not very liquid products. This is easy to understand if we recall that any change prior to maturity implies an adjustment of the note issuer's hedging portfolio. For instance, if an investor wishes to redeem his notes prior to maturity, the issuer will have to sell some zero-coupon bonds as well as some of the hedge fund shares that he owns as a hedge. Liquidity is therefore limited by the redemption policy of the underlying funds, but also by the willingness of the note issuer to engage in such transactions. To avoid having to implement these time-consuming monthly adjustments and redemptions, most issuers have created secondary markets where buyers and sellers can trade their notes on a regular basis. Some issuers even offer weekly liquidity, but solely on a best-effort basis. An important problem on such markets is the price at which transactions are executed, which may differ from the fair value on the note, depending on demand and supply. Another problem is the lag that may exist between the trading time and the official publication of the net asset value of the underlying hedge funds.[6] Some market participants might have better information and use it for their personal profit. As a result, the bid/ask spreads may be wide.

- *Guarantee at maturity*: Another important aspect is that the capital guarantee only applies to investors who remain invested for the *full term* of the bond. Investors should be aware that they might receive less than the guaranteed investment if they redeem midway through the term of a capital guaranteed structure. Early redemption values depend upon prevailing interest rates, market volatility and the time to maturity as well as the performance of the underlying fund and redemption flows. In particular, the note value may fall below the initial purchase price if interest rates rise, volatility decreases and/or the hedge fund's performance is poor. Investors redeeming their notes early in such conditions – if they can! – will usually suffer some loss on their initial investment.

- *Fees for what?* As already mentioned, most principal protected notes are linked to the performance of funds of funds rather than to individual hedge funds. The reason is simple: funds of funds already offer a form of risk reduction by spreading their assets among a variety of investment strategies. They are therefore less volatile on average than individual hedge funds. Since option premiums are an increasing function of the volatility of the option's underlying asset, a call option on a fund of funds will be less costly than a call option on an individual hedge fund. Since the cash available to purchase call options is limited, cheaper call options means the ability to buy more of them, i.e. a substantially higher participation rate for the investor. This extra participation is often perceived as good news by investors. However, a low volatility is also synonymous with less chance of outperforming, which is the only thing that should matter when capital is protected. The investor is therefore paying fees to participate in a fund of funds that is less likely to deliver high returns! In the same line of thought, several notes have specific clauses that force the underlying fund of funds to rebalance its portfolio if the volatility of its net asset value per share passes a threshold number. The rebalancing consists usually of reallocating assets into hedge funds that have exhibited a lower level of volatility, or even worse, of reallocating into cash and other short-term interest rate instruments. The investor then takes the risk of ending up with a long-term call option on a T-bills portfolio.

- *Hedge fund or what?* In low interest rate environments, the portion of the capital allocated to zero-coupon bonds is high, and the sensitivity of these bonds to interest rate variations is also high. This means that capital protected notes are highly exposed to interest rate hikes and may typically display a relatively high positive correlation with the short to medium term domestic bond market. In particular, the zero-coupon component and its "deep discount" nature expose the strategy to interest rate volatility during the life of the investment. Of course, that risk is not an issue for investors who plan to hold the note – and therefore the underlying zero-coupon bond – until maturity, but it is for all other investors. And it may reduce the diversification benefits of investors already owning fixed-income assets in their portfolios.

---

[6] This problem is particularly likely to occur with notes indexed on funds of funds, because it may take administrators several weeks to collect the net asset values of each hedge fund comprising the fund of funds.

- *Watch the fees!* The total fees that are levied on structured hedge fund products are usually hefty. This is particularly true if the underlying fund is a fund of funds. Annually, the individual hedge fund managers may charge 2% on the assets and take 20% of the profits. Next, the fund of funds manager may charge 1% of the assets and take 10% of the profits. On top of that, the note issuer usually charges a 1 to 2% fee at the note issuance, and guarantee fees can range from 0.5 to 3% annually depending on the size of the issue, the liquidity and volatility of the underlying investments, guarantee and participation levels, and the nature of the structure. In addition, structured hedge fund products may also charge a distribution fee. All these fees accumulate, gradually eroding the performance expected by the investor.

27.9   THE FUTURE OF CAPITAL GUARANTEED PRODUCTS

What does the future hold for guaranteed structured hedge fund products? There are currently two contradicting opinions. A few investors have rejected capital protection as an unnecessary expense. Their argument is twofold. First, they consider that, when the hedge fund underlying the capital guaranteed product is in fact a fund of funds, it is likely that most of the risk has already been diversified. Consequently, buying a capital guarantee means paying a lot of money to offset a very low level of risk. Second, given the superior returns and low volatility offered by hedge funds in the last few years, they consider that capital guarantees are superfluous. After all, you need to take risks to obtain some performance.

On the other hand, more conservative or risk-averse investors regard guaranteed structures as an excellent choice to gain exposure to hedge funds while enjoying some form of downside protection. They believe that, when the cost of the guarantee is set at a fair level, it does not necessarily lead to underperformance, particularly when markets are volatile. On the contrary, the guarantee provides them with an excellent means of avoiding anxious waits for the end-of-the-month net asset value.

In the current economic climate of low interest rates and uncertainty on global markets, our opinion is that the second school of thought will probably prevail in the near future. Today, capital guaranteed products on hedge funds are already extremely popular in Switzerland and Germany, where small and medium-sized banks package them and sell them to their private banking clients as well as to small institutions and retail investors. But they are also now gaining adherents in the United States, particularly in the retail market, as well as in other European countries with regulatory regimes that are not favourable to making direct investments in offshore fund structures.

Given the proliferation of these structured products, the problem is now to select the one that makes sense and that is fairly priced – if such a thing exists. Since capital guaranteed products were not all created equal and option pricing theory is not that easy to understand, consultants (once again!) may add substantial value by helping clients to evaluate the trade-offs adopted by the available products among initial participation levels, guaranteed coupon levels, and the characteristics of the underlying fund of funds portfolio.

27.10   COLLATERALIZED HEDGE FUND OBLIGATIONS

Among the more recent innovations in structuring technology is the collateralized hedge fund obligation (CFO), which may be seen as a new type of fund of funds leveraged with term debt. CFOs apply collateralized debt obligation (CDO) technology to fund of funds management.

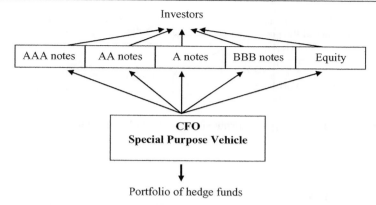

Figure 27.10   A typical CFO structure

In a CFO, a special purpose vehicle issues multiple tranches of rated notes and at least one class of equity securities, and uses the proceeds to purchase either (i) a portfolio of hedge fund interests or (ii) an investment in a single hedge fund or a managed account.

- Like other fixed income products, the debt of a CFO structure offers its holders a predictable stream of cash flows, which is backed by the performance of the underlying fund of funds.[7] The various debt tranches have different priorities in terms of cash flows – if some criteria such as par coverage.[8] and interest coverage are not met, cash flows are diverted from subordinated tranches to senior tranches. This allows the notes of a CFO to obtain credit ratings, making them suitable for an even larger audience than the typical investor base for direct fund of fund instruments. The most senior tranche is usually rated AAA and is credit enhanced due to the subordination of the lower tranches.
- The equity of a CFO structure enables holders to benefit from leverage on the underlying fund of funds portfolio and therefore from an enhanced performance. However, equity holders have the least priority on cash flows. Indeed, the equity tranche absorbs losses first, and once the equity tranche is exhausted, then the next lower tranche (i.e. the lowest rated debt) begins absorbing losses.

Figure 27.10 shows the typical structure of a CFO and its various tranches. The structural differences between a CFO and a fund of funds are (i) the limited life and the term leverage of the CFO, and (ii) the fact that CFO notes are rated and can be sold in capital markets.

Of course, a key question when creating such a CFO is the onshore versus offshore location of the special purpose vehicle (SPV). The answer will determine who can invest in the CFO as well as the type of hedge funds that will enter the CFO portfolio.

- Offshore CFOs are typically corporations established in a low-tax jurisdiction. They should only invest in offshore hedge funds to limit adverse tax repercussions. Their notes may be offered globally to US and non-US investors, but investors in the equity tranches are limited to non-US persons and in some transactions US tax-exempt entities (Figure 27.11).

---

[7] Interest payments to CFO note holders are generally expected to come from (i) redeeming some of the underlying hedge funds; (ii) cash reserve accounts which are a source of interest payments; and (iii) unused proceeds, if any.

[8] Par coverage is analysed by comparing the ratio of the market value of the CFO assets to the face value of the CFO liabilities.

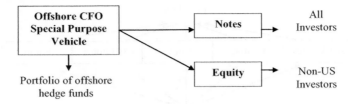

Figure 27.11   Illustration of a typical offshore (i.e. non-US) CFO structure

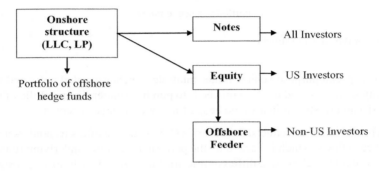

Figure 27.12   Illustration of a typical onshore (i.e. US) CFO structure

---

Box 27.2 The Phénix CFO

On 23 January 2006, IXIS Corporate & Investment Bank completed the Phénix CFO deal for AGF Alternative Asset Management. Phénix was the first CFO transaction on the French market. This structurally innovative deal involved the issuance by a dedicated special purpose vehicle of €300 million of tranches of equity and five-year debt underpinned by a portfolio of hedge funds, which in this case is the Phénix Alternative Holdings Fund managed by AGF Alternative AM. This fund of funds is by far the largest fund of its type in France and one of the largest in Europe, with almost €2 billion in more than 100 different hedge funds.

The five classes of notes were rated by Fitch and Moody's from Baa2/BBB to Aaa/AAA according to their level of protection in the deal. They were primarily placed in continental Europe. An original feature of the package was a variable debt tranche that allows the fund manager to vary the degree of leverage on the equity tranche based on the general market conditions for hedge funds, and therefore to enhance its performance.

- Onshore CFOs are typically organized as limited partnerships or limited liability companies. They should only invest in onshore hedge funds so as to minimize taxes. Their notes may be offered globally to US and non-US investors, and an offshore feeder fund may be organized to acquire the CFO equity on behalf of non-US investors (Figure 27.12).

Note that several regulations applicable to investment advisers, including the US Investment Advisers Act, are applicable to a manager advising a CFO offered to US investors or a CFO advised by a manager located in the US (Box 27.2). It is therefore essential for CFO issuers to ensure that they are not in breach of local regulations and that their payments will not be subject to withholding taxes.

28
Conclusions

It is not the strongest of the species that survive, nor the most intelligent, but the one most responsive to change.

Charles Darwin

Finally! You have made it, as we have now reached the end of our hedge fund journey. The trip was obviously long, but we hope it was also instructive and, to some extent, pleasant. Together we have explored and surveyed a large number of topics and dispelled some inaccurate perceptions. Some of these topics were relatively simple and probably well known. Others were less familiar or more complex. But all were aiming at the same goal, i.e. to increase the knowledge and understanding of what is really going on in the hedge fund industry.

Since the original concept created by Alfred W. Jones, hedge funds have indeed come a long shaky and shady way. After operating in almost complete secrecy for several decades, hedge funds only acquired public prominence in the 1992 when George Soros successfully assaulted the British pound. Later, the 1997 Asian crisis and the shocking bankruptcy of *Long Term Capital Management* threatened financial markets world wide, sparked talk of stricter regulation, and reinforced the view that hedge funds were taking on excessive risks. This put many investors off hedge funds for good, and at the end of 1998, in the opinion of most market participants the days of hedge funds were clearly counted. But this pessimistic view was obviously wrong. Almost 10 years later, hedge funds are still around, more numerous than ever and still springing up like mushrooms. The aggressive pioneers such as George Soros or Julian Robertson have left their seats, but thousands of new managers have replaced them. Attracted by the idea of charging performance fees, these newcomers come primarily from investment banks, asset management firms, or sometimes even from non-finance related fields. A few of them will succeed, many will just survive, and several will not make it until the end.

As hedge fund marketing intensifies, private and institutional investors are progressively considering the use of hedge funds and their vaunted benefits. The arguments supporting the investment are multifarious. "They increase returns." "They are non-correlated." "They reduce risk." "They profit in both bull and bear markets." "Their managers are tomorrow's stars." "We should invest today before they close." "At least, they protect capital." And so it goes. Some of these new investors will invest for better or for worse, but others will flee, still convinced that hedge fund managers are high rollers whose true place is in a casino. Indeed, depending on whom you ask, hedge funds will either be the next big thing in investment management, or a dangerous fad that has been grossly overcapitalized and all will end in ruin. In Europe, for instance, several retrograde political leaders denounced them as locusts, parasites and predators who contribute nothing, neglect larger social outcomes in favour of quick profits and disrupt the smooth workings of the economy. But economists and central bankers extolled their stabilizing role as liquidity providers, as well as acting as a balance against the flow, in contrast to index investors who blindly follow market trends. And even European regulators now talk about regulating hedge funds rather than prohibiting them.

Needless to say, investors are confused by this Capernaum. On one hand, they realize that equities with no downside protection are excessively risky in the short run, and that the associated returns may not be so exciting in the long run. Consequently, they are actively looking for true alternative investment opportunities, and hedge funds are one of them. But on the other hand, investing successfully in hedge funds is not an easy task. Reality is that the *average investor* does not always fully understand what hedge funds are doing.

This lack of understanding is primarily due to the use of technical jargon, the lack of good information sources and the plethora of bad or biased ones. As Don Quixote once said, "*...para sacar una verdad en limpio, menester son muchas pruebas y repruebas*", i.e. truth can only be found after profound and repeated verification. Similarly to Don Quixote's world, the kingdom of hedge funds is full of giants and windmills, of risks and returns, of mathematics and experience, of qualitative and quantitative analysis, of headline news and private reports. Investors willing to venture into hedge funds land should not blindly swallow the typical marketing pitch, nor consider the past performance as a guarantee of future success. Neither should they trust financial intermediaries who recommend managers while simultaneously pocketing distribution commissions or fees for servicing their funds. Rather, investors need to separate the wheat from the chaff. They should roll up their sleeves, do their homework, ask the right questions, take time to think things through, and repeat the whole process until they feel completely confident with their final decision and its implications. And more importantly, they should never lose common sense during that process. The "too good too be true" is often the first warning signal that should not be ignored.

As with many other financial intermediaries, hedge funds are in the business of turning risk into return. Their key advantage is that they are allowed to do what mutual funds and other traditional asset managers are barred from doing: hedging their bets against risk. This introduces additional complexity to their strategies, but also presents numerous traps for the unwary. This might put off many investors, but this is precisely where this book steps in. Throughout its pages, we have attempted to clarify the essential issues of what hedge funds are, what they do, how they make and lose money, but also of how one should include hedge funds in an asset allocation. This should make the road safer for most of our readers. Of course, a lot still remains to be put in place, but once one knows how to use a hammer, every problem looks like a nail . . .

In any case, understanding hedge funds is no longer an option, it is a requirement. Undeniably, hedge funds have become a permanent feature of the financial landscape. Could they become the mutual funds of tomorrow, a standard part of every investor's portfolio? Once again, it is not so sure. The barriers to entry in the hedge fund business are non-existent, but the barriers to succeed are high. The real alpha is rare, and the talent needed to extract it is not evenly distributed – credulous investors will learn it along the way. But there are still a few gems, and these are worth the alpha quest.

You may not be comfortable investing in hedge funds, but your children probably will be. At least in the surviving hedge funds, if any!

Bibliography

Acerbi C. and Tasche D. (2002), "On the coherence of expected shortfall", *Journal of Banking and Finance*, **26** (7), 1491–1507.

Achour D., Harvey C.R., Hopkins G. and Lang C. (1999), "Stock selection in emerging markets: portfolio strategies for Malaysia, Mexico and South Africa", *Emerging Markets Quarterly*, Winter, 38–91.

Ackermann C., McEnally R. and Ravenscraft D. (1999), "The performance of hedge funds: risk, return and incentives", *Journal of Finance*, **54** (3), 833–874.

Adler M. (1987), "Global asset allocation: some uneasy questions", *Investment Management Review*, September–October, 13–18.

Agarwal V., Daniel N.D. and Naik N.Y. (2006), "Why is Santa so kind to hedge funds? The December return puzzle!", Working Paper, London Business School.

Allen F. and Gale D. (1992), "Stock price manipulation", *Review of Financial Studies*, **5** (3), 503–529.

Amenc N. and Martellini L. (2001), "The brave new world of hedge fund indexes", Working Paper, EDHEC-MISYS Risk and Asset Management Research Center.

Amenc N. and Martellini L. (2002), "Portfolio optimization and hedge fund style allocation decisions", *Journal of Alternative Investments*, **5** (2), 7–20.

Amenc N. and Martellini L. (2003), "Desperately seeking pure style indices", Working Paper, EDHEC-MISYS Risk and Asset Management Research Center.

Amenc N. and Le Sourd V. (2003), *Portfolio Theory and Performance Analysis*. Chichester: John Wiley & Sons, Ltd.

Ammann M., Kind A. and Wilde Ch. (2003), "Are convertible bonds underpriced? An analysis of the French market", *Journal of Banking and Finance*, **27** (4), 87–105.

Andersen L. and Buffum D. (2003), "Calibration and implementation of convertible bonds models", Working Paper, Bank of America Securities.

Andrade S.C., di Pietro V. and Seasholes M.S. (2005), "Understanding the profitability of pairs trading", Working Paper, University of California, Berkeley.

Andersen A. (2002), *Hedge Fund Investing. Survey on the risk approach adopted by the Swiss marketplace*. Mimeo.

Artzner P., Delbaen F., Eber J.M. and Heath D. (1997), "Thinking coherently", *Risk*, **10** (11), 68–71.

Artzner P., Delbaen F., Eber J.M. and Heath D. (1999), "Coherent measures of risk", *Mathematical Finance*, **3** (9), 203–228.

Asness C., Krail R. and Liew J. (2001), "Do hedge funds hedge?", *Journal of Portfolio Management*, **28** (1), 6–19.

Bailey J.V. (1992a), "Are manager universes acceptable benchmarks?", *Journal of Portfolio Management*, **18**, 9–13.

Bailey J.V. (1992b) "Evaluating benchmark quality", *Financial Analysts Journal*, **48**, 33–39.

Barberis N. (2000), "Investing for the long run when returns are predictable", *Journal of Finance*, **55** (1), 225–264.

Barberis N. and Thaler R. (2002), "A survey of behavioural finance", NBER Working Paper.

Barry R. (2003), "Hedge funds: a walk through the graveyard", Working Paper, Ross Barry Macquarie Applied Finance Centre.

Bera A.K. and Jarque C.M. (1987), "A test for normality of observations and regression residuals", *International Statistical Review*, **55**, 163–172.

Bernheim A.L. and Schneider M.G. (eds) (1935), *The Security Markets*. New York: Twentieth Century Fund.

Betton S. and Eckbo B.E. (2000), "Toeholds, bid jumps, and expected payoff in takeovers", *Review of Financial Studies*, **13** (4), 841–882.

Bhargava R., Bose A. and Dubofsky D. (1998), "Exploiting international stock market correlations with open-end mutual funds", *Journal of Business, Finance, and Accounting*, 765–773.

Black F. and Jones R. (1987), "Simplifying portfolio insurance", *Journal of Portfolio Management*, **14** (1), 48–51.

Black F. and Litterman R. (1990), *Asset Allocation: Combining Investor Views with Market Equilibrium*. Goldman, Sachs & Co., Fixed Income Research.

Black F. and Litterman R. (1991), *Global Asset Allocation with Equities, Bonds, and Currencies*. Goldman, Sachs & Co., Fixed Income Research.

Black F. and Perold A. (1992) "Theory of constant proportion portfolio insurance." *Journal of Economic Dynamics and Control*, **16**, 403–26.

Black F. and Scholes M. (1973), "The pricing of options and corporate liabilities", *Journal of Political Economy*, **81**, 1–26.

Bodie Z., Kane A., and Markus A. (1999), *Investments*, Irwin-McGraw-Hill International Edition, 4th edition, Singapore.

Booth P.M., Chadburn R.G., Cooper D.R., Haberman S. and James D. (1999), *Modern Actuarial Theory and Practice*. CRC Press/Chapman and Hall.

Boudoukh J., Richardson M., Subrahmanyam M. and Whitelaw R. (2002), "Stale prices and strategies for trading mutual funds," *Financial Analysts Journal*, 53–71.

Branch T. and Yang B. (2003), "Merger arbitrage: evidence of profitability", University of Massachusetts, Working Paper.

Brennan M. and Schwartz E. (1977), "Convertible bonds: Valuation and optimal strategies for call and conversion", *Journal of Finance*, **32** (3), 1699–1715.

Brennan M. and Schwartz E. (1980), "Analyzing convertible bonds", *Journal of Financial and Quantitative Analysis*, **15** (4), 907–929.

Brinson G.P., Hood L.R. and Beebower G.P. (1986), "Determinants of portfolio performance", *Financial Analysts Journal*, July/August, 39–44.

Brinson G.P., Singer B. and Beebower G.P. (1991), "Determinants of portfolio preference II: An update," *Financial Analysts Journal*, May/June, 40–48.

Brooks C. and Kat H. (2001), "The statistical properties of hedge fund index returns and their implications for investors", Working Paper, The University of Reading, ISMA Centre.

Brown S., Goetzmann W. and Park J.M. (1998) "Hedge funds and the Asian currency crisis of 1997", NBER Working Paper.

Brown S., Goetzmann W. and Park J.M. (1999), "Conditions for survival: Changing risk and the performance of hedge fund managers and CTAs", Working paper, New York University.

Brown S., Goetzmann W. and Park J.M. (2001), "Careers and survival: Competition and risk in the hedge fund and CTA industry", *Journal of Finance*, **53** (5), 1869–1886.

Brown S. and Goetzmann W. (1995), "Performance persistence", *Journal of Finance*, **50** (3), 679–698.

Brouwer I., van der Put J. and Veld Ch. (1996), "Contrarian investment strategies in a European context", CentER Discussion Paper No. 9636.

Brunnermeier M. and Nagel S. (2004), "Arbitrage at its limits: Hedge funds and the technology bubble", *Journal of Finance*, **59** (5), 2013–2040.

Burch T.R. (2001), "Locking out rival bidders: The use of lockup options in corporate mergers", *Journal of Financial Economics*, **60** (1), 103–141.

Burke G. (1994), "A sharper Sharpe ratio", *The Computerized Trader*, March.

Chalmers J., Edelen R. and Kadlec G. (2001), "On the perils of security pricing by financial intermediaries: The wildcard option in transacting mutual-fund shares", *Journal of Finance*, **56** (6), 2209–36.

Chan L.K.C., Hamao Y. and Lakonishok J. (1991), "Fundamentals and stock returns in Japan", *Journal of Finance*, **46**, 1739–1764.

Chan L.K.C., Jegadeesh N. and Lakonishok J. (1996), "Momentum strategies", *Journal of Finance*, **51** (5), 1681–1713.

Chancellor E. (2000), *Devil Take the Hindmost: A History of Financial Speculation*. Farrar, Straus and Giroux.

Cheng P. and Liang, Y. (2000), "Optimal diversification: Is it really worthwhile?", *Journal of Real Estate Portfolio Management*, **6**, 7–16.

Cheung W. and Nelken I. (1994), "Costing the converts", *RISK*, July, 47–49.

Chopra V. and Ziemba W.T. (1993), "The effect of errors in mean and co-variance estimates on optimal portfolio choice", *Journal of Portfolio Management*, Winter, 6–11.

Conrad J.S., Johnson K.M. and Wahal S. (2001), "Institutional trading and soft dollars", *Journal of Finance*, **56** (1), 397–422.

Cornelli F. and Li D.L. (2001), "Risk arbitrage in takeovers", Working Paper, London Business School and CEPR.

Cvitanic J., Lazrak A., Martellini L. and Zapatero F. (2003), "Optimal allocation to hedge funds: an empirical analysis", *Quantitative Finance*, **3**, 28–39.

Danthine J.-P. and Donaldson J.B. (2001), *Intermediate Financial Theory*. Upper Saddle River, NJ: Prentice Hall.

D'Avolio G. (2002), "The market for borrowing stocks," *Journal of Financial Economics*, **66**, 271–306.

Davis M. and Lischka F.R. (1999), "Convertible bonds with market risk and credit risk", Working Paper, Tokyo-Mitsubishi International Plc.

de Brouwer G.J. (2001), *Hedge funds in emerging markets*. Cambridge University Press, Cambridge.

Detemple J.B., Garcia R. and Rindisbacher M. (2003), "A Monte-Carlo method for optimal portfolios", *Journal of Finance*, **58** (1), 401–446.

Diether K.B., Li K.H. and Werner I.M. (2005), "Can short-sellers predict returns? Daily evidence", Working Paper, Charles A. Dice Center for Research in Financial Economics.

Dresner S. and Kim K. (2003), *PIPE's: A Guide to Private Investment in Public Equity*. Bloomberg Press.

Duffie D. and Singleton K. (1999), "Modeling term structures of defaultable bonds", *Review of Financial Studies*, **12** (4), 687–720.

Eichengreen B., Mathieson D., Chadha B., Jansen A., Kodres L. and Sharma S. (1998), "Hedge funds and financial market dynamics", Occasional Paper, No. 166, International Monetary Fund, Washington, DC.

Elton E.J. and Gruber M.J. (1995), *Modern Portfolio Theory and Investment Analysis*, John Wiley & Sons, fifth edition.

Elliott R., van der Hoek, J. and Malcolm, W. (2005) "Pairs trading", *Quantitative Finance*, **5** (3), 271–276.

Engle R. and Granger C. (1987) "Co-integration and error correction: representation, estimation, and testing", *Econometrica*, **55** (2), 251–276.

Fama E.F. and French K.R. (1992), "The cross-section of expected stock returns", *Journal of Finance*, **47**, 427–465.

Fama E.F. and French K.R. (1998), "Value versus growth: International evidence", *Journal of Finance*, **53**, 1975–2000.

Favre L. and Galleano J.A. (2000) "Portfolio allocation with hedge funds: the case study of a Swiss institutional investor", Working Paper, HEC University of Lausanne.

Field L.C. and Hanka G. (2001), "The expiration of IPO share lockups", *Journal of Finance*, **56** (2), 471–500.

Fishburn P.C. (1977), "Mean-risk analysis with risk associated with below target returns", *American Economic Review*, **67**, 116–126.

Foster R. and Kaplan S. (2001), *Creative Destruction*. Doubleday/Currency.

Fung W. and Hsieh D.A. (1997), "Survivorship bias and investment style in the returns of CTAs", Working Paper, Duke University.

Fung W. and Hsieh D.A. (2000a), "Measuring the market impact of hedge funds", *Journal of Empirical Finance*, **7** (1), 1–36.

Fung W. and Hsieh D.A. (2000b), "Performance characteristics of hedge funds and commodity funds: natural versus spurious biases", *Journal of Financial and Quantitative Analysis*, **35**, 291–307.

Fung W. and Hsieh D.A. (2001), "The risk in hedge fund strategies: theory and evidence from trend followers", *Review of Financial Studies*, **14** (2), 313–341.

Fung W. and Hsieh D. (2002), "Benchmarks of hedge fund performance: information content and measurement biases", Working Paper.

Gatev, E.G., Goetzmann W.N. and Rouwenhorst K.G. (1999), "Pairs trading: performance of a relative value arbitrage rule", Working Paper, Yale School of Management.

Geltner D. (1991), "Smoothing in appraisal-based returns", *Journal of Real Estate Finance and Economics*, **4** (3), 327–345.

Geltner D. (1993), "Temporal aggregation in real estate return indices", *Journal of Real Estate Research*, **21** (2), 141–166.

Gibbons M., Ross S. and Shanken J. (1989), "A test of the efficiency of a given portfolio", *Econometrica*, **57**, 1121–1152.

Giraud J.R. (2005), "Mitigating hedge funds' operational risks: Benefits and limitations of managed account platforms", EDHEC Working Paper.

Gregoriou G. (2002), "Hedge fund survival lifetimes", *Journal of Asset Management*, **3** (3), 237–252.

Goetzmann W., Ivkovic Z. and Rouwenhorst G. (2001), "Day trading international mutual funds: evidence and policy solutions," *Journal of Financial and Quantitative Analysis*, 287–309.

Greene J. and Hodges Ch. (2002), "The dilution impact of daily fund flows on open-end mutual funds," *Journal of Financial Economics*, 131–158.

Grundy B.D. and Martin J.S. (2001), "Understanding the nature of the risks and the source of the rewards to momentum investing", *Review of Financial Studies*, **14** (1), 29–79.

Guthoff, A., Pfingsten, A. and Wolf J. (1998), "Der Einfluß einer Begrenzung des Value at Risk oder des Lower Partial Moment One auf die Risikoübernahme", in A. Oehler (Hrsg.), *Credit Risk und Value-at-Risk Alternativen*. Stuttgart, S. 111–153.

Haidar S. (2004), "IPO lock-up expirations", Working Paper, Haidar Capital Management.

Harvey C.R. (1995), "Predictable risk and returns in emerging markets", *Review of Financial Studies*, **8**, 773–816.

Haugen R.A. and Baker N.L. (1996), "Commonality in the determinants of expected stock returns", *Journal of Financial Economics*, **41**, 401–439.

Hübner (2003), "The generalized Treynor ratio: A note", Working Paper, University of Liège and Maastricht University.

Hull J. and White A. (2000), "Valuing credit default swaps I: No counterparty default risk", *Journal of Derivatives*, **8** (1), Fall.

Hull J. (2005), *Options, Futures, and Other Derivatives*. (6th edition). New York: Prentice Hall.

Hull J. and White A. (1990a), "Pricing interest rate derivative securities", *Review of Financial Studies*, **3** (4), 573–592.

Hull J. and White A. (1990b), "Valuing credit default swaps I: No counterparty default risk", *Journal of Derivatives*, **8** (1), 29–40.

Hung M.-W. and Wang J.-Y. (2002), "Pricing convertible bonds subject to default risk", *Journal of Derivatives*, **10**, 75–87.

Hwang S. and Satchell S.E. (2001), "Tracking error: Ex-ante versus Ex-post measures", Working Paper, City University Business School.

Ineichen A.M. (2001), "The search for alpha continues", Working Paper, Warburg Dillon Read.

Ingersoll J.E. (1977), "A contingent-claims valuation of convertible securities", *Journal of Financial Economics*, **4**, 289–321.

Irwin S., Zulauf C. and Ward B. (1994), "The predictability of managed futures returns", *Journal of Derivatives*, Winter, 20–27.

Janssen B. (2000), "Annualizing volatility", Working Paper, Gottex.

Jarrow R.A. (2001), "Default parameter estimation using market prices", *Financial Analysts Journal*, **57** (5), 75–92.

Jarrow R.A. and Turnbull S.M. (1995), "Pricing derivatives on financial securities subject to credit risk", *Journal of Finance*, **50** (1), 53–85.

Jayasankaran S. (1995), "Fear of flaying", *Far Eastern Economic Review*, **158**, 60.

Jegadeesh N. and Titman S. (1993), "Returns to buying winners and selling losers: Implications for stock market efficiency", *Journal of Finance*, **48** (1), 65–92.

Jensen M.C. (1968), "The performance of mutual funds in the period 1945–1964," *Journal of Finance*, **23**, 389–416.

Jobson J.D. and Korkie B. (1981), "Performance hypothesis testing with the Sharpe and Treynor measures", *Journal of Finance*, **36**, 888–908.

Jones A.W. (1949), "Fashion in forecasting", *Fortune*, **88**, March, 186.

Kahneman D. and Tversky A. (1979), "Prospect theory: An analysis of decision under risk", *Econometrica*, **47**, 263–291.

Kallberg J.G. and Ziemba W.T. (1984). "Mis-specification in portfolio selection problems". In G. Bamberg and A. Spremann (eds), *Risk and Capital*, Springer-Verlag, New York, pp. 74–87.

Kaplan S. (1989), "Management buyouts: Evidence on taxes as a source of value", *Journal of Finance*, **44**, 611–632.

Karl B. Diether, Kuan-Hui Lee and Ingrid M. Werner (2005), "Can short-sellers predict returns? Daily evidence", Working Paper, Fisher College of Business, The Ohio State University.

Kat H. and Lu S. (2002), "An excursion into the statistical properties of hedge fund returns", Working Paper, City University.

Kat H.M. (2004), "Managed futures and hedge funds: A match made in heaven", *Journal of Investment Management*, **2** (1), 1–9.

Kawakatsu H. and Morey M.R. (1999), "An empirical examination of financial liberalization and efficiency of emerging market stock prices", *Journal of Financial Research*, **22**, 385–411.

Lamont O.A. and Thaler R.H. (2003), "Can the market add and subtract? Mispricing in tech stock carve-outs", *Journal of Political Economy*, **111** (2), 227–268.

Lakonishok J., Shleifer A. and Vishny R.W. (1994), "Contrarian investment, extrapolation, and risk", *Journal of Finance*, **49**, 1541–1578.

Lewellen J. and Shanken J. (2000), "Estimation risk, market efficiency, and the predictability of returns", NBER Working Paper 7699.

Lhabitant F.S. (2001a), "Assessing market risk for hedge funds and hedge funds portfolios", *Journal of Risk Finance*, Spring, 1–17.

Lhabitant F.S. (2001b), "Hedge funds investing: A quantitative look inside the black box", *Journal of Financial Transformation*, **1** (1), 82–90.

Lhabitant F.S. and Learned M. (2004), "Finding the sweet spot of hedge fund diversification", *Journal of Financial Transformation*, **10**, 31–39.

Liang B. (2000), "Hedge funds: the living and the dead", *Journal of Financial and Quantitative Analysis*, **35**, 309–336.

Lintner J. (1983), "The potential role of managed commodity futures accounts and/or funds in portfolios of stocks and bonds", Working Paper, presented at the Annual Conference of Financial Analysts Federation, May, Toronto, Canada.

Lo A. (2002), "The statistics of Sharpe ratios", *Financial Analysts Journal*, **58**, 36–52.

Lo A. W. and MacKinlay A. C. (1988), "Stock market prices do not follow random walks: Evidence from a simple specification test," *Review of Financial Studies*, **1**, 41–66.

Loomis C. (1966), "The Jones nobody keeps up with", *Fortune*, April, 237–247.

Lowenstein, R. (2000), *When genius failed: The Rise and Fall of Long Term Capital Management*. Random House.

Lungarella G. (2002), *Harcourt AG. Strategy Focus: Managed Futures* SwissHEDGE, 4th Quarter.

Malkiel B. (1995), "Returns from investing in equity mutual funds 1971 to 1991", *Journal of Finance*, **50** (2), 549–72.

Margrabe W. (1978), "The value of an option to exchange one asset for another", *Journal of Finance*, **33** (1), 177–86.

Markowitz H. (1952), "Portfolio selection", *Journal of Finance*, **7** (1), 77–91.

Markowitz H.M. (1959), *Portfolio Selection: Efficient Diversification of Investments*. New York: John Wiley & Sons.

Marmer H.S. and Ng F.K. (1993), "Mean-semi-variance analysis of option-based strategies: a total mix perspective", *Financial Analyst Journal*, May–June, 47–54.

McConnell J.J. and Schwartz E.S. (1986), "LYON taming", *Journal of Finance*, **41**, 561–576.

McFall L.R. (1999), "Portfolios of alternative assets: Why not 100% hedge funds?", *Journal of Investing*, **8** (4), 87–97.

McFall L. R. Jr and Ghaleb-Harter T.E. (2001), "*An Update on Hedge Fund* Performance: *Is a Bubble Developing*? Deutsche Asset Management research monograph.

Merriken H.E. (1994), "Analytical approaches to limit downside risk: Semi-variance and the need for liquidity", *Journal of Investing*, **3** (3), 65–72.

Merton, R.C. (1974), "On the pricing of corporate debt: The risk structure of interest rates", *Journal of Finance*, **29** (2), 449–470.

Michaud R.O. (1989). "The Markowitz optimization enigma: Is 'optimized' optimal?" *Financial Analysts Journal*, January–February, 31–42.

Mitchell M. and Pulvino T. (2001), "Characteristics of risk and return in risk arbitrage", *Journal of Finance*, **61** (6), 2135–2175.

Mitchell M., Pulvino T. and Stafford E. (2002), "Limited arbitrage in equity markets", *Journal of Finance*, **57** (2), 551–584.

Modigliani F. and Modigliani L. (1997), "Risk-adjusted performance", *Journal of Portfolio Management*, **23**, Winter, 45–54.

Modigliani L. (1997), *Are Hedge Funds Worth the Risk?*, U.S. Investment Perspectives, Morgan Stanley Dean Witter, December.

Moody's Investors Service (2001) *Default and Recovery Rates of Corporate Bond Issuers: 2000*. Mimeo, February.

Mullainathan S. and Thaler R.H. (2000), "Behavioural economics", NBER Working Paper.

Newman P., Milgate M., and Eatwell J. (1992), *The New Palgrave Dictionary of Money & Finance: Two Volume Set*, Palgrave Macmillan.

Ofek E. and Richardson M. (2003), "DotCom mania: The rise and fall of Internet stock prices", *Journal of Finance*, **58** (3), 1113–1137.

Perret-Gentil C. and Victoria-Feser M.P. (2003), "Robust mean-variance portfolio selection", Working Paper, University of Geneva.

President's Working Group on Financial Markets (1999), *Hedge Funds, Leverage, and the Lessons of Long-Term Capital Management*. Report, April 28.

Rahl L. (2000), *Risk Budgeting: A New Approach to Investing*. London: Risk Books.

Rahl L. (2001), "NAV/Fair value practices survey results", *Journal of Alternative Investments*, Winter, 55–58.

Rankin B. (1999), "The impact of hedge funds on financial markets: Lessons from the experience of Australia", in L. Gower and D. Gruen (eds), *Capital Flows and the International Financial System*. Sydney: Reserve Bank of Australia, pp.151–163.

Rockafellar R.T. and Uryasev S. (2002), "Optimization of conditional value at risk", *Journal of Risk*, **2**, 21–41.

Rohrer J. (1986), "The red hot world of Julian Robertson", *Institutional Investor*, May, 86–92.

Rosenberg B., Reid K. and Lanstein R. (1985), "Persuasive evidence of market inefficiency", *Journal of Portfolio Management*, **11**, 9–17.

Roth P.N. and Fortune B. (2001), "A hedge fund regulation in the aftermath of Long-Term Capital Management", in Iain Cullen and Helen Parry (eds), *Hedge Funds: Law and Regulation*. London: Sweet and Maxwell.

Rouwenhorst K.G. (1998), "International momentum strategies", *Journal of Finance*, **53** (1), 267–284.

Rouwenhorst K.G. (1999), "Local return factors and turnover in emerging stock markets", *Journal of Finance*, **54**, 1439–1464.

Rubens, J.H., Louton, D.A. and Yobaccio, E.J. (1998), "Measuring the significance of diversification gains", *Journal of Real Estate Research*, **16**, 73–86.

Rudolf, M., Wolter H.J., and Zimmermann H. (1999), "A linear model for tracking error minimization," *Journal of Banking and Finance*, **23** (1), 85–103.

Sahoo A. (2001), "Funds still not up to snuff on valuation", *Survey Says*, November 19, www.ignites.com.

Schneeweis T., Kazemi H. and Martin G. (2001), "Understanding hedge fund performance: Research results and rules of thumb for the institutional investor", Working Paper, Lehman Brothers.

Schwert G.W. (1989), "Why does stock market volatility change over time?", *Journal of Finance*, **44** (5), 1115–1153.

Schwert G.W. (2000), "Hostility in takeovers: In the eye of the beholder", *Journal of Finance*, **55** (6), 2599–2640.

Sharpe W., Alexander G.J., and Bailey J.W. (1998), *Investments*, Prentice Hall.

Sharpe W.F. (1966), "Mutual fund performance," *Journal of Business*, **39**, 119–138.

Sharpe W.F. (1994), "The Sharpe ratio", Journal of Portfolio Management, Fall, 49–58.

Sobel R. (1965), *The Big Board: A History of the New York Stock Exchange*. New York: Free Press.

Sortino F. and Price L. (1994), "Performance measurement in a downside risk-framework", *Journal of Investing*, 59–65.

Sortino F. and van der Meer R.A.H. (1991), "Downside risk", *Journal of Portfolio Management*, **17** (4), 27–31.

Sortino F., van der Meer R. and Plantinga A. (1999a), "The Dutch Triangle: A framework to measure upside potential relative to downside risk", *Journal of Portfolio Management*, Fall, 50–58.

Sortino F., van der Meer R. and Plantinga A. (1999b), "The upside potential ratio", *Journal of Performance Measurement*, **4** (1), 10–15.

Takahashi A., Kobayashi T. and Nakagawa N. (2001), "Pricing convertible bonds with default risk", *Journal of Fixed Income*, **11**, 20–29.

Treynor J.L. (1965), "How to rate management of investment funds", *Harvard Business Review*, **43**, January–February, 63–75.

Treynor J.L. and Black F. (1972), "Portfolio selection using special information, under the assumptions of the diagonal model, with mean-variance portfolio objectives, and without constraints", in G.P. Szego and K. Shell (eds), *Mathematical Methods in Investment and Finance* (North-Holland: Amsterdam), pp. 367–384.

Various (2000), "Sound practices for hedge fund managers", Working Paper jointly published on the Internet by a group of hedge fund managers and now available from the Managed Funds Assocation (www.mfainfo.org).

Vidyamurthy, G. (2004), *Pairs Trading, Quantitative Methods and Analysis*. John Wiley & Sons, Canada.

Wyckoff R.D. (1968), *Wall Street Ventures and Adventures*. New York: Greenwood.

Zitzewitz E. (2003), "Who cares about shareholders? Arbitrage-proofing mutual funds", *Journal of Law, Economics, and Organization*, **19** (2), 245–280.

Zweig J. (1998), "Five investing lessons from America's top pension fund", *Money*, January, 115–118.

Websites

Several papers and references mentioned in this book are available on the following websites:

- Edhec Risk and Asset Management Research Center
    http:// www.edhec-risk.com
- Center for International Securities and Derivatives Markets
    http://cisdm.som.umass.edu
- Centre for Hedge Fund Research and Education at London Business School
    http://www.london.edu/hedgefunds.html
- Alternative Investment Research Centre at the Cass Business School
    http://www.cass.city.ac.uk/airc/index.html
- Social Science Research Network
    http:// www.ssrn.com
- Journal of Alternative Investments
    http:// www.iijai.com

Index

TJI79407-9780470026632-14-12-18

UNIVERSITIES AT MEDWAY LIBRARY